W9-ATI-823

American History through Literature
1820–1870

Editorial Board

American History through Literature
1820–1870

VOLUME **3**

"THE RAVEN"
to
"YOUNG GOODMAN BROWN"

INDEX

JANET GABLER-HOVER & ROBERT SATTELMEYER
Editors in Chief

CHARLES SCRIBNER'S SONS
An imprint of Thomson Gale, a part of The Thomson Corporation

THOMSON
★
GALE

Detroit • New York • San Francisco • San Diego • New Haven, Conn. • Waterville, Maine • London • Munich

American History through Literature, 1820–1870

Janet Gabler-Hover and Robert Sattelmeyer, Editors in Chief

LIBRARY OF CONGRESS CATALOGING-IN-PUBLICATION DATA

American History through Literature, 1820–1870 / Janet Gabler-Hover and Robert Sattelmeyer, editors-in-chief.
    p. cm.
  Includes bibliographical references and index.
  ISBN 0-684-31460-6 (set hardcover : alk. paper) — ISBN 0-684-31461-4 (v. 1) — ISBN 0-684-31462-2 (v. 2) — ISBN 0-684-31463-0 (v. 3) — ISBN 0-684-31492-4 (e-book)
  1. American literature—19th century—Encyclopedias. 2. Literature and history—United States—History—19th century—Encyclopedias. 3. United States—History—19th century—Historiography—Encyclopedias. 4. History in literature—Encyclopedias. I. Gabler-Hover, Janet II. Sattelmeyer, Robert.
PS217 .H57A84 2005
810. 9'358'09034—dc22   2005023615

This title is also available as an e-book
ISBN 0-684-31492-4
And may be purchased with its companion set,
American History through Literature, 1870–1920
ISBN 0-684-31468-1 (6-vol. print set)
Contact your Thomson Gale sales representative for ordering information

Printed in the United States of America
10 9 8 7 6 5 4 3 2 1

Editorial and Production Staff

Senior Editor: Stephen Wasserstein

Project Editor: Alja Kooistra Collar

Assisting Editors: Joann Cerrito, Jennifer Wisinski

Editorial Assistants: Angela Doolin

Manuscript Editors: Susan Carol Barnett, Gretchen Gordon, Jeffrey J. Hill, Teresa Jesionowski, Robert E. Jones, Jean Fortune Kaplan, Eric Lagergren, Janet Patterson, Linda Sanders, Jane Marie Todd, Julie Van Pelt

Proofreader: Julie Van Pelt

Indexer: Cynthia Crippen

Senior Art Director: Pamela Galbreath

Image Acquisitions: Kelly Quin, Jillean McCommons

Imaging: Lezlie Light, Michael Logusz

Cartographer: XNR Productions

Manufacturing Buyer: Wendy Blurton

Assistant Composition Manager: Evi Seoud

Publisher: Frank Menchaca

Contents

Volume 3

"THE RAVEN"

Edgar Allan Poe's (1809–1849) "The Raven" (1845) is a repetitive poem about repetition. And as Poe's most famous poem, perhaps the most famous poem in American literature, it has been endlessly repeated—reprinted, rewritten, rehearsed, and recited, the image of the raven recycled as an emblem of gothic horror and Baltimorean civic pride. Even in Poe's lifetime the poem was widely parodied—in at least fifteen different published works between 1845 and 1849, the year of Poe's death (Poe, *Complete Poems*, p. 352)—and "The Raven" has come to more or less define Poe's image in popular culture, from *The Simpsons* to the lyrics of Lou Reed. Students often wonder what the raven (and therefore "The Raven") means, but any attempt to answer that question must also address the question of what all that repetition means.

Within the poem, the repetition means simply that the speaker is obsessed with "the lost Lenore." Once he realizes that the raven will reliably repeat "nevermore" in response to anything he says to it, he turns the encounter into a perverse game in which the word "nevermore" reminds him of the grief, what Poe called "Mournful and Never-ending Remembrance," that will occupy him forever. The narrator transforms the bird into both an instrument of self-torture and a symbol of his personal mourning. The poem performs those functions as well through repetition. It is impossible to escape the insistent rhymes—internal, external, they are everywhere—the thudding trochaic octameter (lines of eight stressed/unstressed "beats": ONCE uPON a MIDnight DREARy, WHILE i PONdered WEAK and WEARy), the simple verbal repetitions ("followed fast and followed faster" [l. 64]; "Is there—*is* there balm in Gilead?—tell me—tell me, I implore!" [l. 89]), or the alliteration ("this grim, ungainly, ghastly, gaunt, and ominous bird of yore" [l. 71]), all of which, like the ecstatic pain of grief, both excites and torments the reader.

MOURNING, REPETITION, AND IMITATION

While the fame of "The Raven" is largely a result of its uniqueness, an awareness of what makes the poem typical might help the reader better understand the poem's place in nineteenth-century American culture. Specifically the performance of grief as a repetition compulsion is firmly rooted in mid-nineteenth-century mourning ritual. As Ann Douglas and Karen Halttunen have shown, the rural cemetery movement, the appearance of mourning guidebooks, the unwritten codes involving dress and comportment, and an outpouring of sentimental poems about loss marked a new set of expectations for bereavement. Halttunen quotes one mourning manual that delivers its message in the form of a catechism: "Why is that mother robed in mourning? It is the outward token of a mourning which the heart alone can feel" (p. 136). Paradoxically the unique experience of grief had to be shown through formal devices such as special clothing, tokens such as wreaths woven from the hair of the deceased, and graveyard visits—repeated by individual mourners and imitated by other mourners. The repetitious raven, likewise, is an objective correlative—a symbol that perfectly evokes the emotion it represents—for grief and the poem, with its insistence on the speaker's

Illustration from "The Raven," 1845. GETTY IMAGES

sincerity and solitude, struck the right note within a culture of sincerity that insisted on stereotyped outward signs of "inner" experience.

Ralph Waldo Emerson once referred to Poe as "the jingle man," alluding to what many have regarded as the cheap musicality of Poe's poetry. But "The Raven's" theme is equally the stuff of pop music. The poet Dave Smith, analyzing the poem's appeal, makes a fundamental point: "We have loved and lost, felt heartbreak, felt ourselves abandoned. This is a basic country-western song and it sells more than we may want to think about" (p. 8). In fact thinking about it will only get the reader so far. The poem probably owed much of its popularity to the fact that most people who read and heard it knew they did not have to think about it in order to "get" it. Like any good pop song, the power of "The Raven" comes through its manipulation of—not its defiance of—conventions, both stylistic and thematic. Poe's later explanation that the death of a beautiful woman is "unquestionably, the most poetical topic in the world" (*Essays and Reviews*, p. 19) puts a sexist spin on a tenet that his contemporaries seem to have shared: that bereavement begets poetry and that writing and reading such poetry is itself a ritual of mourning. *The Poetical Works of Alice and Phoebe Cary* (1865), for instance, contains twenty poems by Alice (1820–1871) and nine by Phoebe (1824–1871) under the heading "Poems of Grief and Consolation," and many other poems in the

collection deal with death and loss as well. Mary Louise Kete identifies the "three signal concerns of the sentimental mode" as "*lost* homes, *lost* families, and *broken* bonds" (p. 17), an assertion supported by her reading of a mid-nineteenth-century manuscript book alongside the more celebrated poems of Lydia Sigourney and Henry Wadsworth Longfellow. One striking convention of nineteenth-century mourning poems is the focus on an image that, like the raven, triggers memories of the deceased or an awareness of the mourner's loss (a portrait in Alice Cary's "Lost Lilies"; a "cross of snow" in a Longfellow poem by that name). Poe's black bird, arriving like a mourner to the speaker's never-ending wake, does not merely trigger but participates in the scene of mourning with its uncanny "speaking" ability, pushing this convention to the limit (and for many later readers, beyond the limit) at which it can be taken seriously. Alice Cary's poem "Most Beloved," for instance, also catalogs natural images that she associates with an unnamed lost beloved, concluding:

> All things, my darling, all things seem
> In some strange way to speak of thee;
> Nothing is half so much a dream,
> Nothing so much reality.
>
> *(Ll. 37–40)*

The speaker of her poem "A Wintry Waste" expresses hope that her son will return:

> But fancy only half deceives
> . . . .
> boughs go over the window-pane
> And drag on the lonely eaves, in vain,—
> That waste is all I see.
>
> *(Ll. 20, 27–29)*

These poems reinforce the point that although Poe was ringing changes—effectively, to be sure—on a conventional theme, not even the fact that his poem ends in despair rather than consolation is particularly unusual.

In his variorum edition of Poe's poems, Thomas Ollive Mabbott noted direct sources for "The Raven," the most significant of which is Elizabeth Barrett's (1806–1861) "Lady Geraldine's Courtship" (1844), also written in trochaic octameter and featuring a refrain that includes the word "evermore." As Eliza Richards has argued, Poe's poetic voice in "The Raven" and elsewhere draws heavily and self-consciously from Barrett and other women poets he knew, read, and reviewed, even as he seeks to displace the woman author: "Rather than rejecting the feminine, Poe becomes an expert in the field, out-feminizing the feminine in a masculine rendition that inverts female poetic practice and thus exoticizes the banal performativity of the female poet" (p. 8). In fact when "The Raven" appeared in the *American Review* in February 1845, an introduction (possibly written by Poe) apologized for the poem's "deep quaint strain of the sentiment" before praising the technical skill of the author, identified as "Quarles." The same headnote points to "the curious introduction of some ludicrous touches amidst the serious and impressive, as was doubtless intended by the author" (Poe, *Complete Poems*, p. 360). Poe, then, is tweaking and (if the *American Review* is correct) deliberately exaggerating well-established conventions of sentimental verse, responding not only to Barrett, one of his favorite poets, but also to a set of expectations associated with popular women writers (but employed by both women and men). Poe had hinted in a review of Barrett that she had imitated Alfred, Lord Tennyson's "Locksley Hall" (1842) in writing "Lady Geraldine's Courtship." The resemblance between those two poems is no stronger than the resemblance between "Lady Geraldine's Courtship" and "The Raven," suggesting to Mabbott that Poe was "acknowledging his debt to Barrett" in calling attention to her poem's debt to Tennyson. Like his more extended discussions of plagiarism, though, this reference to the imitation by one of his favorite poets of another of his favorite poets conveys Poe's skepticism of claims to literary originality generally and his awareness of the value of emulation, a term that suggests admiring, as opposed to exploitative, imitation. "Of course," Poe would write the following year, "I pretend to no originality in either the rhythm or the metre of the 'Raven'" (*Essays and Reviews*, p. 21).

LITERARY PRODUCTION AND REPRODUCTION

For all its reliance on a culture of mourning generally and "Lady Geraldine's Courtship" specifically, "The Raven" is nonetheless a striking, memorable poem, and it enjoyed immediate popularity. A few days before it appeared in the *American Review*, to whom he had sold it, Poe arranged with his friend Nathaniel Parker Willis (1806–1867) to publish the poem, revealing the name of its author, in the *New York Evening Mirror* to boost its circulation and interest. In contrast with the academic tone of the *American Review*'s headnote, Willis's introduction promised a blockbuster, "the most effective single example of 'fugitive poetry' ever published in this country, and unsurpassed in English poetry for subtle conception, masterly ingenuity of versification, and consistent sustaining of imaginative lift and 'pokerishness.' [spookiness] . . . It will stick to the memory of everybody who reads it" (Poe, *Complete Poems*, p. 361). Willis not only correctly predicted the poem's popularity but also spurred it on, initiating, even before it had been printed once, the career of "The Raven" as one of the

---

"LADY GERALDINE'S COURTSHIP" AS AN INFLUENCE ON "THE RAVEN"

Thomas Dunn English may have been the first to point out Poe's debt to Barrett in a review of The Raven and Other Poems *in the* Aristidean *in November 1845; according to John H. Ingram, an early Poe biographer and editor, Poe himself privately acknowledged Barrett's poem as inspiration for his (pp. 12–13). When Poe reviewed Barrett's* The Drama of Exile and Other Poems *weeks before publishing "The Raven," he singled out "Lady Geraldine's Courtship" as "the only poem of its author which is not deficient, considered as an artistical whole" (Essays and Reviews, p. 129). In the variorum edition of Poe's poems, Thomas Ollive Mabbott quotes this stanza from Barrett's poem for comparison to "The Raven."*

"Eyes," he said, "now throbbing through me! are ye eyes that did undo me?
Shining eyes, like antique jewels set in Parian statue-stone!
Underneath that calm white forehead, are ye ever burning torrid,
O'er the desolate sand-desert of my heart and life undone?
With a rushing stir, uncertain, in the air, the purple curtain
Swelleth in and swelleth out around her motionless pale brows;
While the gliding of the river sends a rippling noise forever
Through the open casement whitened by the moonlight's slant repose.["]

Poe's third stanza borrows the "uncertain" movement associated with a purple curtain as well as the metrical form:

And the silken sad uncertain rustling of each purple curtain
Thrilled me—filled me with fantastic terrors never felt before;
So that now, to still the beating of my heart, I stood repeating
"'Tis some visiter entreating entrance at my chamber door—
Some late visiter entreating entrance at my chamber door;—
This it is and nothing more."

Poe, *Complete Poems*, ll. 381–384, 13–18.

---

most widely reprinted poems of its time. Mabbott lists twenty variant texts over which Poe had some control; these represent only a fraction of the reprintings, most unauthorized, in periodicals. Meredith McGill has termed the publishing environment in which "The Raven" flourished a "culture of reprinting," emphasizing the ways writers such as Poe used the lack of copyright protection to their benefit even as they rallied in print for legislation protecting intellectual property. Poe neither expected nor received direct payments for the "countless" (according to Mabbott) reprintings of "The Raven"; as a magazine editor, he was in the habit of reprinting other poets' works, as well as his own, freely.

Not so much despite but because of the unwritten rules of reprint culture, Poe enjoyed a huge (albeit unsustained) career boost from "The Raven": by the end of 1845 he had published his first collection of poetry in fourteen years as well as a new collection of tales and found himself a desirable guest at New York literary salons. Poe wanted the poem to be reprinted freely in order to spread his fame: "'The Raven' has had a great 'run,'" he boasted, "but I wrote it for the express purpose of running—just as I did 'The Gold-Bug.' . . . the bird beat the bug, though, all hollow" (*Letters* 2:287). The bird also drew audiences in parlors, literary salons and lecture halls, where Poe performed the poem—repeatedly, like a human jukebox—as he sought literary respectability, subscribers for his never-realized magazine project, and after Virgina Clemm Poe's death in 1847, a new wife.

While Poe could not possibly regulate the reproduction of "The Raven," its success held out the promise of control over his own career not only because it brought him fame but also because it demonstrated his writerly discipline. As his review of Nathaniel Hawthorne's *Twice-Told Tales* (1837) and his own analysis of "The Raven" in "The Philosophy of Composition" (1846) make clear, Poe's aesthetics are grounded in the principle of authorial control: the reason poems and tales should be brief and conceptually unified is to ensure that readers remain under the spell of the writer. "The Philosophy of Composition" particularly trades inspiration (which is unpredictable) for method and the control that comes with it. And Poe saw signs of the "control revolution" (James Beniger's term) all around him: publishing was central to the transformation of everyday life brought about by mass production and consumer culture. Machine-made paper, stereotyped plates, and steam presses made possible an explosion of print, which in turn disseminated the information and ideas that drove the new economy. The rapid increase in the importance of publishing is reflected in P. T. Barnum's statement that "there was only one liquid that a man could use in excessive quantities without being swallowed up by it, and that was printer's ink" (Harris, p. 195).

In stories and sketches, such as "The Man That Was Used Up" (1850), "The Business-Man" (1843), and "Some Words with a Mummy" (1845), Poe satirizes believers in "the rapid march of mechanical invention" (as the man who was used up refers to it) and other forms of progress (which, the mummy tells us, never progresses). At the same time, though, he wanted to show that he could play the modern literary-publishing game as well as—or better than—anyone, that he could produce a "Raven" or a "Gold-Bug" at will. Like train schedules, assembly line tasks, and advertising slogans, Poe's pseudo-aesthetic in "The Philosophy of Composition" depends—as does "The Raven"—on a kind of predictable, repeatable set of questions of answers. Although Poe never did repeat the success of "The Raven," he did apparently write the poem "for the purpose of running," which is to say reproducing itself in print. The repetition of the raven (and "The Raven") mirrors that strategy of never-ending republication, recitation, and parody.

See also Death; "The Fall of the House of Usher"; Gothic Fiction; Lyric Poetry; "The Philosophy of Composition"; Popular Poetry

BIBLIOGRAPHY

Primary Works

Cary, Alice, and Phoebe Cary. *The Poetical Works of Alice and Phoebe Cary.* 1865. Boston and New York: Houghton Mifflin, 1882.

Poe, Edgar Allan. *Complete Poems.* Edited by Thomas Ollive Mabbott. Urbana and Chicago: University of Illinois Press, 2000.

Poe, Edgar Allan. *Essays and Reviews.* Edited by G. R. Thompson. New York: Library of America, 1984.

Poe, Edgar Allan. *The Letters of Edgar Allan Poe.* 2 vols. Edited by John Ward Ostrom. Cambridge, Mass.: Harvard University Press, 1966.

Secondary Works

Beniger, James R. *The Control Revolution: Technological and Economic Origins of the Information Society.* Cambridge, Mass.: Harvard University Press, 1986.

Douglas, Ann. *The Feminization of American Culture.* New York: Knopf, 1977.

Eddings, Dennis W. "Theme and Parody in 'The Raven.'" In *Poe and His Times: The Artist and His Milieu,* edited by Benjamin F. Fisher IV, pp. 209–217. Baltimore: Edgar Allan Poe Society, 1990.

Halttunen, Karen. *Confidence Men and Painted Women: A Study of Middle-Class Culture in America, 1830–1870.* New Haven, Conn.: Yale University Press, 1982.

Harris, Neil. *Humbug: The Art of P. T. Barnum.* 1973. Chicago and London: University of Chicago Press, 1981.

Ingram, John H. *Literary and Historical Commentary on "The Raven," by Edgar Allan Poe.* 1885. New York: Haskell House, 1972.

Kennedy, J. Gerald. *Poe, Death, and the Life of Writing.* New Haven, Conn.: Yale University Press, 1987.

Kete, Mary Louise. *Sentimental Collaboration: Mourning and Middle-Class Identity in Nineteenth-Century America.* Durham, N.C.: Duke University Press, 2000.

McGill, Meredith L. *American Literature and the Culture of Reprinting, 1834–1853.* Philadelphia: University of Pennsylvania Press, 2003.

Person, Leland S., Jr. "Poe's Composition of Philosophy: Reading and Writing 'The Raven.'" *Arizona Quarterly* 46, no. 3 (1990): 1–15.

Richards, Eliza. "'The Poetess' and Poe's Performance of the Feminine." *Arizona Quarterly* 55, no. 2 (1999): 1–29.

Smith, Dave. "Edgar Allan Poe and the Nightmare Ode." *Southern Humanities Review* 29, no. 1 (1995): 1–10.

Whalen, Terence. *Edgar Allan Poe and the Masses: The Political Economy of Literature in Antebellum America.* Princeton, N.J.: Princeton University Press, 1999.

Scott Peeples

REFORM

Material and political changes transformed America at a dizzying pace in the 1820s and 1830s. The expansion of industrialization, the creation of roads and canals to connect manufacturers to new markets, westward migration, a prolonged period of economic depression following the panic of 1837, and the broadening of voting rights triggered vast social upheavals. Reform movements were often attempts to cope with the consequences of these changes. Some movements wanted reform of institutions like prisons, schools, and asylums. Others looked to individual regeneration to transform the whole society. Some reformers drew attention to a particular group's suffering: Richard Henry Dana's *Two Years before the Mast* (1840), for example, pressed for expanded legal rights for sailors. Others, like the founders of Brook Farm, sought "radical and universal reform."

EVANGELICAL REFORM

A powerful source of reform emerged from the Second Great Awakening, the religious revivals sweeping the nation from the 1790s through the 1820s.

Like the Great Awakening of the 1730s and 1740s, this series of revivals emphasized individual, often emotional religious experiences. Yet unlike the first period of revival, the Second Great Awakening had an even broader impact. The disestablishment of religion in the early national period and the deism associated with America's founding fathers (that is, their belief in the power of reason and the existence of a Supreme Creator and their skepticism about supernatural religious explanations) seemed to threaten the nation's Protestant moral foundation. Moreover, many Christians attributed certain social ills (drinking, dueling, disregard for the Sabbath, and the like) to Christianity's decline. Ministers such as Lyman Beecher (1775–1863) and Charles Grandison Finney (1792–1875) responded with messages about wickedness, conversion, and the imminent return of Christ. Moving away from the Calvinist doctrines (such as predestination) associated with the initial Great Awakening, they preached individual moral agency and personal salvation, moral improvement and perfection, and a responsibility to hasten the coming of God's Kingdom.

These religious ideas contributed to the desire for reform and creation of voluntary benevolent societies such as the American Education Society (1815), American Bible Society (1816), and American Tract Society (1825). These organizations distributed religious literatures, but their members also led efforts to stem Sabbath-breaking, drinking, and other forms of vice. Various female moral reform societies focused on ending prostitution, sexual exploitation, and the sexual double standard. The ostensibly moral concern with sexual vice also helped justify the not-so-pious demand for reform literature featuring fallen and wronged women in texts like Maria Monk's *Awful Disclosures* (1836) and George Foster's *New York by Gas-Light* (1850).

Evangelical reformers also played important roles in other reform movements. Theodore Dwight Weld (1803–1895), a disciple of Finney, began his career distributing tracts and preaching against strong drink. In 1829 Weld shifted his efforts to the campaign against slavery and authored two antislavery classics, *The Bible against Slavery* (1837), which dismantled biblical proslavery arguments, and *American Slavery As It Is* (1839), the text that inspired Harriet Beecher Stowe (1811–1896) to write *Uncle Tom's Cabin* (1851–1852).

Evangelical reform spread popular literature as tracts, sermons, Sunday school books, and temperance testimonies. The revivals also had an important influence on developments in literary style. Religious writings became more emotional and imaginative, formally less rigid, and theologically less rigorous. Antebellum religious texts began to rely on vivid narratives to illustrate, edify, and entertain. This "new religious style," as David S. Reynolds calls it in his study *Beneath the American Renaissance* (p. 15), reshaped not only evangelical writing but also the style of liberal reformers, popular writers, and transcendentalists.

TRANSCENDENTALISM

Like evangelical reformers, transcendentalists emphasized moral perfectionism, individual moral agency, and the possibilities for a new social order. The transcendentalists, however, developed a radically individualistic form of perfectionism that looked with suspicion on institutions like churches and reform organizations that would impede self-culture. In his 1841 essay "Self-Reliance," Ralph Waldo Emerson (1803–1882) urges the individual to "Trust thyself" (p. 260) and to see "Society . . . in conspiracy against the manhood of every one of it members" (p. 261). Faith in the personal nature of one's salvation and distrust in social institutions were not inconsistent with evangelical reform, but Emerson took these ideas in a fresh direction. Nonconformity becomes a requirement for selfhood: "Whoso would be a man must be a nonconformist" (p. 261). And conventional moral categories become subjective constructions: "Good and bad are but names very readily transferable to that or this" (p. 262). Such reliance on oneself poses a danger to reform because it means opposition to collective action that might sway one from his or her individual path. Thus, Emerson distrusts the "foolish philanthropist" and those clothed in the "bountiful cause of Abolition" (p. 262). Henry David Thoreau (1817–1862) was an even harsher critic, diagnosing reformers as "sick" (p. 181) in "Reform and the Reformers" (1844) and calling philanthropy "greatly overrated" (p. 52) in *Walden* (1854). To many reformers, these transcendentalists were pretty poor activists. Their idealist thinking lent itself to social critique but not social action, and their affirmation of individual integrity looked like a pointless self-absorption. In "The Transcendentalist" (1842), Emerson acknowledges such criticism: "The philanthropists inquire whether Transcendentalism does not mean sloth" (p. 203).

Despite their ambivalence about reform, transcendentalists were among the most significant reformers in American history. At times, Emerson embraced reform without hesitation. In "Man the Reformer" (1841), reformers become transcendentalist heroes: "What is a man born for but to be a Reformer, a Remaker of what man has made; a renouncer of lies; a restorer of truth and good?" (p. 146). On certain humanitarian issues, Emerson joined the public fray.

In a public letter to President Martin Van Buren (1838), he protests the government's removal of Cherokee Indians from their lands in Mississippi and Georgia. Native Americans were not the focus of a major antebellum reform movement, but the horrific history of white-Indian relations did provoke writers such as Emerson, Lydia Maria Child in *Hobomok* (1824), and Catharine Maria Sedgwick in *Hope Leslie* (1827) to draw attention to the unjust treatment of American Indians. Although he avoided public comments on slavery for several years, Emerson spoke in support of abolition in the 1840s and later threw himself into the increasingly fierce battles over slavery with addresses on the radical abolitionist John Brown (in 1859) and the Fugitive Slave Law (in 1854), the harsh federal law passed in 1850 requiring northern states to return runaway slaves.

Despite its sharp criticism of reformers, *Walden* has long been recognized as a reform classic because of its anti-authoritarian stands, its criticism of society's corrupting influence, and its insistence that reform begin with the individual. Instead of joining those who were "hacking at the branches of evil," Thoreau in *Walden* was "striking at the root" of social wrongs (p. 51). A committed abolitionist and ardent admirer of John Brown, Thoreau opposed the imperialistic Mexican-American War and refused to pay his poll tax in protest. This act of civil disobedience led to a night in jail and the most famous reform essay in American literature, "Resistance to Civil Government" (1849). In that work, Thoreau defends those who would disobey "unjust laws" (p. 233) and resist morally bankrupt governments. He seeks instead the development of democracy redefined in terms of "progress toward a true respect for the individual" (p. 245).

Other transcendentalists were typically less contrary about reform. In "The Laboring Classes" (1840), Orestes Augustus Brownson (1803–1876) examines the exploitation of the working classes and argues, "men are rewarded in an inverse ratio to the amount of actual service they perform" (p. 255). To correct problems created by class hierarchy, he advocates radical reform of the economy and state, one that includes the abolition of inherited wealth, by force if necessary. Although he would eventually abandon transcendentalism for Catholicism, Brownson's essay and his journal, the *Boston Quarterly Review* (which enthusiastically championed transcendentalism), defend the individual against the corrupting influences of a damaged civilization. Concern with workers, economics, and poverty inspired a number of nontranscendental authors as well. In *The Quaker City* (1844–1845), the reform-minded George Lippard (1822–1854) uses lurid images and sensationalistic plot lines to attack social injustice. The dramatist Dion Boucicault (1820 or 1822–1890) exposes the poverty of urban tenement life in his play *The Poor of New York* (1857), which takes place during the panics of 1837 and 1857.

Another radical transcendentalist of the 1840s, Margaret Fuller (1810–1850), championed the equality of the sexes. The editor of *The Dial* from 1840 to 1842, Fuller published her pioneering feminist essay "The Great Lawsuit" in 1843. A hopeful and learned tour de force, "The Great Lawsuit" provides an androgynous image of the soul: "There is no wholly masculine man, no purely feminine woman" (p. 418). Such a vision supports her contention that the social restriction of women because of their wrongly imagined difference from men should be removed: "We would have every arbitrary barrier thrown down. We would have every path laid open to woman as freely as to man" (p. 394). In 1845 she expanded the essay into the feminist classic, *Woman in the Nineteenth Century*. In 1844 Fuller left parochial New England to work as a book review editor for Horace Greeley's *New-York Daily Tribune*. In 1846 she became a foreign correspondent and saw Europe on the brink of and in the thrall of the Revolutions of 1848. In a series of thirty-seven dispatches, she shared these experiences and her reflections on them. During three whirlwind years in Europe—in which she had a son, married an Italian aristocrat named Giovanni Angelo Ossoli, and participated in the Italian revolution of 1848–1849—Fuller developed a perspective on reform more expansive and radical than her transcendentalist friends had ever imagined. In 1850, as she was returning to the United States with her manuscript on the history of the revolution in Italy, her ship wrecked off Fire Island, New York, claiming the lives of Fuller, Ossoli, and their son, Angelino.

COMMUNITARIANS

An important expression of reform fervor appeared in the utopian communities that flourished during the period. New communities had been established prior to the 1820s; the famously chaste Shakers, for example, founded their first settlement in 1787. After the war of 1812, many more groups created their own communities, perhaps more than a hundred before the Civil War. Many were religious, such as the Mormons, brought into existence by Joseph Smith (1805–1844) in 1830. Others were secular and socialist. Robert Owen (1771–1858), a Scottish industrialist and the author of *A New View of Society* (1813), started the egalitarian New Harmony settlement in rural Indiana in 1825. More than thirty communities across the United States were established using the elaborate and meticulously detailed ideas of the French utopian socialist thinker Charles Fourier (1772–1837). Other new communities blended unconventional religious ideas with worldly concerns. John Humphrey Noyes (1811–1886), committed to evangelical perfectionism and to a "communism in love," founded a utopian community in 1837 and moved it to Oneida, New York, in 1848.

Two utopian communities, Brook Farm (1841–1847) and Fruitlands (1843), had transcendentalist origins. Amos Bronson Alcott (1799–1888), with British disciples Charles Lane (1800–1870) and Henry Gardner Wright (b. 1814), established their community, Fruitlands, on a ninety-acre farm near Harvard, Massachusetts. Based on high principles and various forms of self-denial, Fruitlands lasted just eight months. According to "Transcendental Wild Oats" (1873), Louisa May Alcott's (1832–1888) memoir of life at Fruitlands, the men who led this utopia "said many wise things and did many foolish ones," including a nobly reasoned abandonment of farm work: "the rule was to do what the spirit moved, so they left their crops to Providence" (p. 548). For Louisa May Alcott, Fruitlands is a symbol of utopian idealism's practical failure, although she sees such failure with irony and sympathy: "The world was not ready for Utopia yet, and those who attempted to found it only got laughed at for their pains" (p. 549).

Longer-lived than Fruitlands, Brook Farm became a remarkable part of American literary history by attracting the interest of thinkers and writers. Emerson thought carefully about moving there before deciding against it, while Nathaniel Hawthorne (1804–1864) did join. George Ripley (1802–1880) and his supporters established Brook Farm in West Roxbury, Massachusetts, about eight miles from Boston. Convinced that their community could be an example for the rest of society, the Brook Farmers embarked on a seven-year experiment that blended communal life with respect for individual freedom, manual labor with intellectual pursuits, and utopian idealism with practical existence.

Hawthorne's letters show that he was dismayed by the endless labor and lack of writing time. Leaving after seven months, he transformed his experiences into one of the most important American novels about reform, *The Blithedale Romance* (1852). The narrator is the ambivalent, reclusive, but voyeuristic Miles Coverdale. Despite his initial hopes about "the blessed state of brotherhood and sisterhood" (p. 46) at Blithedale, he soon develops grave doubts: "we stood in a position of new hostility, rather than new brotherhood" (p. 52). Hawthorne's picture of reform, particularly in its attention to Hollingsworth, reveals the ways philanthropic zeal can transform a reformer into

Many reformers, including those who drafted the "Constitution" for Brook Farm in 1844, approached their efforts with radical goals and high ideals. Convinced that their projects were grounded in "universal principles," not mere perspectives or opinions, they imagined themselves at the vanguard of human progress.

All persons who are not familiar with the purposes of Association, will understand from this document that we propose a radical and universal reform, rather than to redress any particular wrong or to remove the sufferings of any single class of human beings. We do this in the light of universal principles, in which all differences, whether of religion, or politics, or philosophy, are reconciled, and the dearest and most private hope of every man has the promise of fulfillment. Herein, let it be understood, we would remove nothing that is truly beautiful or venerable; we reverence the religious sentiment in all its forms, the family, and whatever else has its foundation either in human nature or the Divine Providence. The work we are engaged in is not destruction, but true conservation: it is not a mere revolution, but, as we are assured, a necessary step in the course of social progress which no one can be blind enough to think has yet reached its limit. We believe that humanity, trained by these long centuries of suffering and struggle, led onward by so many saints and heroes and sages, is at length prepared to enter into that universal order, toward which it has perpetually moved. Thus we recognize the worth of the whole Past and of every doctrine and institution it has bequeathed us; thus also we perceive that the Present has its own high mission, and we shall only say what is beginning to be seen by all sincere thinkers, when we declare that the imperative duty of this time and this country, nay more, that its only salvation, and the salvation of all civilized countries, lies in the Reorganization of Society, according to the unchanging laws of human nature and of universal harmony.

Brook Farm Association for Industry and Education, "Constitution of the Brook Farm Association for Industry and Education," in Myerson, ed., *Transcendentalism: A Reader*, p. 465.

a "monster" (p. 88) and "godlike benevolence" into an "all-devouring egotism" (p. 89). Hawthorne's attitude toward reform, filtered through the consciousness of his unreliable and hesitant narrator, seems pessimistic. *The Blithedale Romance* is not, however, simply an antiphilanthropic warning but rather a complex meditation on gender, programs for change, and the motivations of reformers.

REFORMING THE BODY AND MIND

Linked to evangelical, transcendentalist, and communitarian reform ideals were a multitude of attempts to improve minds, bodies, and souls through education and healthy living. Despite his failure at Fruitlands, Bronson Alcott was one of the preeminent educational theorists of the era. Seeing children as inherently good and education as the cultivation of their innate morality and inner selves, he insisted that "Instruction must be an Inspiration" (p. 18). In 1834, with teaching assistance from Elizabeth Palmer Peabody (1804–1894), the sister of Nathaniel Hawthorne's wife, Sophia, Alcott opened a school in Boston's Masonic Temple and began to practice what he preached. In an era of rote memorization, his pedagogy emphasized conversation, art, storytelling, and journal writing in comfortable classrooms full of light and air. He criticized corporal punishment and advocated discipline in which students took an active role. He was also an advocate of active learning involving games, exercise, and hands-on lessons. Peabody's *Record of a School* (1835) and Alcott's *Conversations with Children on the Gospels* (1836–1837) document their pedagogical innovations, but they also generated a public outcry that led to the school's demise in 1838.

Other educational reformers experienced more sustained success. Massachusetts's Horace Mann led the fight to create a nonsectarian and free public education. He helped establish the first teacher-training school, campaigned for public financing of schools, and championed compulsory school attendance laws. Through his nonfiction—his biweekly *Common School Journal* (founded in 1838) and advice book for young men, *A Few Thoughts for a Young Man* (1850)—Mann's influence became national. Free public education and compulsory attendance laws soon became confirmed parts of American society.

Peabody, Alcott's colleague and Mann's sister-in-law, was another important educational reformer. Influenced by Alcott and Friedrich Froebel (1782–1852), the leader of the German kindergarten

At least one of the Brook Farmers, Nathaniel Hawthorne, abandoned such high ideals. Looking back at his own partici-
pation in utopian reforms in his semi-autobiographical novel, The Blithedale Romance *(1852), Hawthorne remem-*
bered the lack of agreement on universal principles, the comic appearance of the reformers, and the mind-numbing
effects of physical labor (despite the reformers' attempts to see spiritual growth and hard work as one).

Our bond, it seems to me, was not affirmative, but negative. We had individually found one thing or another to quarrel with in our past life, and were pretty well agreed as to the inexpediency of lumbering along with the old system any further. As to what should be substituted, there was much less unanimity. We did not greatly care—at least, I never did—for the written constitution under which our millennium had commenced. . . . Arcadians though we were, our costume bore no resemblance to the beribboned doublets, silk breeches and stockings, and slippers fastened with artificial roses, that distinguish the pastoral people of poetry and the stage. In outward show, I humbly conceive, we looked rather like a gang of beggars, or banditti, than either a company of honest laboring-men, or a conclave of philosophers. Whatever might be our points of difference, we all of us seemed to have come to Blithedale with the one thrifty and laudable idea of wearing out our old clothes. Such garments as had an airing, whenever we strode afield! Coats with high collars, and with no collars, broad-skirted or swallow-tailed, and with the waist at every point between the hip and arm-pit; pantaloons of a dozen successive epochs, and greatly defaced at the knees by the humiliations of the wearer before his lady-love;—in short, we were a living epitome of defunct fashions, and the very raggedest presentment of men who had seen better days. It was gentility in tatters. . . .

While our enterprise lay all in theory, we had pleased ourselves with delectable visions of the spiritualization of labor. It was to be our form of prayer, and ceremonial of worship. Each stroke of the hoe was to uncover some aromatic root of wisdom, heretofore hidden from the sun. Pausing in the field, to let the wind exhale the moisture from our foreheads, we were to look upward, and catch glimpses into the far-off soul of truth. In this point of view, matters did not turn out quite so well as we anticipated. . . . The clods of earth, which we so constantly belabored and turned over and over, were never etherealized into thought. Our thoughts, on the contrary, were fast becoming cloddish. Our labor symbolized nothing, and left us mentally sluggish in the dusk of the evening.

Hawthorne, *The Blithedale Romance*, pp. 83, 85.

---

movement, she promoted American kindergartens and an organic approach to early childhood education that emphasized the distinctiveness of each child and cultivation of children's inner natures. In 1862 she published "Kindergarten—What Is it?" and followed up with the *Moral Culture of Infancy and Kindergarten Guide* (1863), coauthored with her sister Mary Tyler Peabody Mann (1806–1887).

Like the progressive educators who promoted physical activity in schools, reformers also championed exercise, healthy living, and what historians have called "body reforms," linking them typically to moral and religious beliefs. Sylvester Graham (1794–1851)—most famous for the cracker named after him—promoted a system for clean living that included regular exercise, frequent bathing, sexual restraint, and a plain diet with no meat, spices, alcoholic beverages, or coffee. In his crusade against overstimulation, Graham delivered numerous lectures, including his anti-masturbation guide, *A Lecture to Young Men, on Chastity* (1834), and collected them in a two-volume *Lectures on the Science of Human Life* (1839). Water cures, or hydropathy—a method for curing physical and mental ills by cleansing the body, internally and externally, with generous amounts of pure water—became an important focus for health reformers in the mid-nineteenth century. In books such as *Water-Cure for Ladies* (1844), Marie Louise Shew (c. 1821 or 1822–1877) and Joel Shew (1816–1855) advocated Graham-like dieting and bathing practices. Mary Gove Nichols (1810–1884) also devoted herself to the campaign for hydropathy and later authored an autobiographical novel about her reform experiences, titled *Mary Lyndon; or, Revelations of a Life* (1855). William Andrus Alcott (1798–1859) urged not only cold baths and vegetarianism but also a host of other self-help practices from right reading and good manners to temperance and "purity" in a series of popular advice books.

Orson Squire Fowler (1809–1887) and Lorenzo Niles Fowler (1811–1896) made their contribution to physiological reform in America by popularizing phrenology—the study of human skulls to determine character and health. With its lessons and drawings illustrating how physiognomy revealed personality, their *Illustrated Self-Instructor in Phrenology and Physiology* (1849) became a widely read self-help book. Phrenology drew the attention of writers including Louisa May Alcott, Mark Twain, and Edgar Allan Poe. The very jargon of this pseudoscience made its way into Walt Whitman's (1819–1892) poems. With phrenological terms like "amativeness" (meaning sexual love between a husband and wife) and "adhesiveness" (friendship or sociability, but also, in Whitman's use, love between men), Whitman found a vocabulary to describe the kinds of love he celebrates in his *Calamus* and *Children of Adam* poems, first published in the third edition of *Leaves of Grass* (1860).

TEMPERANCE

Temperance was the leading nineteenth-century reform movement advocating healthy restraint. With origins in the eighteenth century, the temperance movement had gradually established thousands of antidrinking associations by the 1830s. As the movement grew, a large and varied popular literature opposed to heavy drinking emerged. Early temperance classics were often simple moral tales. In Lucius Manlius Sargent's *My Mother's Gold Ring* (1833), the ring of the protagonist's dead mother helps him conquer his desire for spirits. Lydia Sigourney encourages readers to "Drink deep, but *only water*" (p. 77) in her temperance poetry from *Water-Drops* (1848). Other temperance works conjure more sinister visions. George Barrell Cheever's notorious *Deacon Giles' Distillery* (1835) paints an imaginative image of cloven-hoofed demons producing liquor in a distillery owned by a Unitarian deacon. Author of *An Autobiography* (1845), John Bartholomew Gough, an alcoholic turned temperance lecturer, became known for his moving if gruesome stories of heavy drinking. Melodrama also played an important role. Temperance plays feature villains who tempt characters into drinking. The dramatic plots of these plays move from indulgence to disaster and despair to redemption. Sensationalistic scenes of alcoholism were often the highlight of such dramas. In William Henry Smith's *The Drunkard* (1844), for example, Edward,

"*On ground in delirium,*" struggles with imaginary snakes and cries, "how they coil round me" (p. 290).

The most famous temperance author was Timothy Shay Arthur (1809–1885), who began his career with a set of journalistic "Temperance Tales" titled *Six Nights with the Washingtonians* (1842). He published in 1854 the phenomenally successful *Ten Nights in a Bar-Room*, a novel that illustrates how drinking is both a domestic and social problem. *Ten Nights* narrates Cedarville's decline following the introduction of a tavern, but it is also a story of the Morgan family's tragedy and partial redemption. In one of her attempts to retrieve her father from the saloon, Mary Morgan is fatally struck by a flying glass tumbler. Before taking her final breath, however, she wins from her father his pledge, "Never to drink a drop of liquor as long as I live" (p. 75). William W. Pratt's 1858 adaptation of the novel became a stage hit.

Antebellum temperance also left its mark on authors not so immediately identified with the movement. Hawthorne authored a temperance tale, "A Rill from the Town Pump" (1835), although it throws an ironically critical glance on temperance zealots. *Franklin Evans* (1842), Whitman's contribution to temperance, tells the story of an orphan whose drinking leads to a series of calamitous events. In stories such as "The Black Cat" (1843) and "The Cask of Amontillado" (1846), Poe, a member of the Sons of Temperance, demonstrates his mastery of temperance themes and images but emphasizes the horror and despair of addiction over the possibility of recovery.

SENSATIONALISM AND REFORM

Reformers often turned to provocative, sensational images to emphasize what they saw as the urgent need for social change. In *Ten Nights in a Bar-Room* (1854), Timothy Shay Arthur depicts the startling, accidental killing of an innocent girl as his way of emphasizing how drinking had horrible consequences for all of society, not merely those who drank alcohol. When an angry and intoxicated Simon Slade tries to throw an empty glass at Joe Morgan, the tumbler misses its mark and strikes the young Mary Morgan, who has come to the tavern in an attempt to persuade her father to come home.

ANTISLAVERY

Like temperance, the antislavery movement had a major cultural influence on antebellum America. With the militant assault on slavery in David Walker's *Appeal to the Coloured Citizens of the World* (1829) and the inaugural issue (1 January 1831) of William Lloyd Garrison's (1805–1879) incendiary newspaper *The Liberator*, abolitionism entered a new, more radical phase. In fiery speeches denouncing slavery and a corrupt American government, white orators like Garrison and the eloquent Wendell Phillips (1811–1884) demand unconditional emancipation. Despite widespread antebellum wariness about women who took an active role in public life, women contributed substantially to the antislavery movement and its literature. As daring and emotional as Garrison's orations, if not as harsh, Lydia Maria Child's (1802–1880) *An Appeal in Favor of That Class of Americans Called Africans* (1833) uses a carefully reasoned argument and extensive research into slavery and its history in her call for emancipation. Angelina Emily Grimké's (1805–1879) *Appeal to the Christian Women of the South* (1836) argues that slavery is a sin and makes an evangelical appeal to southern women to support slavery's abolition as part of their Christian duty.

African American antislavery activists such as Frederick Douglass (1818–1895) were powerful critics not only of slavery but also of racism and the paternalism of white reformers. In *Narrative of the Life of Frederick Douglass* (1845), Douglass directs his sharp, often sarcastic criticism at slaveholders, Christianity, and the racism of white northerners. In his orations, he takes on equally controversial topics, condemning the Constitution, the hypocrisy of the flag, and the Fourth of July, to make his antislavery point. In "What to the Slave is the Fourth of July?" (1852), Douglass reminds his audience that the Fugitive Slave Law has made the entire United States complicit with slavery and declares unequivocally, "There is not a nation on earth guilty of practices, more shocking and bloody, than are the people of these United States" (p. 127). A number of former slaves stirred the movement with written accounts of their lives in and flights from slavery. In *Incidents in the Life of a Slave Girl* (1861), Harriet Jacobs (c. 1813–1897) combines antislavery rhetoric with elements of sentimentalism to illustrate the insidious sexual exploitation of enslaved women, while *Running a Thousand Miles for Freedom* (1860) tells the story of William and Ellen Craft's bold escape (Ellen disguises herself as a white man, while William plays her servant).

Fiction assumed an important place in the antislavery literature of the 1850s. Less radical than Douglass or Garrison, Stowe produced the most influential antislavery text, *Uncle Tom's Cabin* (1852), a sprawling and contradictory but deeply compelling novel that intertwines stories of slaves, escaped slaves, slaveholders, and abolitionists. Looking for a peaceful resolution of slavery, Stowe wants to show readers the humanity of African Americans (and slaveholders) and the wickedness of slavery. The novel's enormous popularity (the second-best-selling book of the century, behind only the Bible) only exacerbated tensions between the North and South, tensions that led to the bloody Civil War that did end slavery. Several antislavery novels followed Stowe's, including the first novel published by an African American author, William Wells Brown's (c. 1814–1884) *Clotel* (1853), a story about Thomas Jefferson, his African American mistress, and their two daughters.

THE WOMEN'S MOVEMENT

Women's participation in abolitionism led to a heightened realization that gendered structures of power were also in need of transformation. When their antislavery activism made them public figures, Angelina Emily Grimké and Sarah Moore Grimké (1792–1873) exposed themselves to criticism that they were acting outside women's proper sphere. In *Letters to Catherine E. Beecher* (1838), Angelina responded with a powerful feminist argument emphasizing women's moral agency and the evil in distinguishing, morally, between male and female. Sarah followed up with *Letters on the Equality of the Sexes* (1838), a theologically grounded defense of gender equality and women's agency. Although they are not the first feminist works in American literary history, the Grimkés's texts provided a rhetoric and an example that would prepare the way for the women's rights activists who organized the Seneca Falls Convention of 1848 and produced the landmark Declaration of Sentiments, which was authored primarily by the renowned Elizabeth Cady Stanton (1815–1902).

The increasing public awareness of women's oppression and the demand for change shaped antebellum American writing in direct and indirect ways. Writers like Stanton, Fuller, and the Grimkés were reformers engaged in the transformation of American society; they used their nonfiction to persuade hearts and convince minds. Conversely, Frances Sargent Osgood (1811–1850) was not politically progressive, but her poetry subverts conventional notions of femininity in ironic, amusing, and sensual ways. Like Osgood, Fanny Fern (Sarah Payson Willis Parton, 1811–1872) was not an organizer. Yet her writings—from her novels *Ruth Hall* (1855) and *Rose Clark* (1856) to her newspaper columns collected in a series of books from *Fern Leaves from Fanny's Port-Folio*

(1853) to *Caper-Sauce* (1872)—use humor and sentiment to document the mistreatment of women and to satirize the social and legal conditions that reinforced this oppression. Despite the mainstream expectation that women devote themselves to domestic, not public, affairs, American women writers like Fern, Stowe, Susan Warner, Maria Susanna Cummins, and others experienced extraordinary success in the 1850s, selling huge numbers of books and opening the literary marketplace for women.

The women's rights movement saw its most significant success in 1920 when women were finally given the right to vote with the passage of the Nineteenth Amendment. Temperance too carried on throughout the nineteenth century and experienced its greatest triumph in the next century with the 1919 passage of Prohibition. Yet the reform impulse that inspired so many movements was clearly in decline in the years leading up to the Civil War. As utopian communities failed, slavery persisted, and moral perfectionism seemed increasingly remote, reformers gradually abandoned the hope of a glorious moral reformation of the American people. During the war itself, humanitarians turned to large, bureaucratic institutions, like the United States Sanitary Commission, to relieve suffering. As new ideals such as centralization and efficiency replaced faith in moral suasion, postbellum reformers looked increasingly to electoral politics, legislation, and institutions to accomplish their social aims.

See also Abolitionist Writing; *The Blithedale Romance;* Declaration of Sentiments; Education; Evangelicals; Feminism; Health and Medicine; *Letters on the Equality of the Sexes;* Seneca Falls Convention; Sensational Fiction; Slave Narratives; Suffrage; Temperance; Transcendentalism; *Uncle Tom's Cabin;* Utopian Communities

BIBLIOGRAPHY
Primary Works

Alcott, Amos Bronson. *The Doctrine and Discipline of Human Culture.* Boston: J. Munroe, 1836.

Alcott, Louisa May. "Transcendental Wild Oats." 1873. In *The Portable Louisa May Alcott.* Edited by Elizabeth Lennox Keyser. New York: Penguin, 2000. Pp. 538–552.

Arthur, Timothy Shay. *Ten Nights in a Bar-Room, and What I Saw There.* 1854. Edited by Jon Miller. Acton, Mass.: Copley, 2002.

Brownson, Orestes A. "The Labouring Classes." 1840. In *Selected Writings of the American Transcendentalists,* edited by George Hochfield. New York: New American Public Library, 1966.

Douglass, Frederick. "What to the Slave Is the Fourth of July?" 1852. In *Narrative of the Life of Frederick Douglass, an American Slave, Written by Himself,* edited by William L. Andrews and William S. McFeely, pp. 116–127. New York: Norton, 1997.

Emerson, Ralph Waldo. *Essays and Poems.* Edited by Joel Porte, Harold Bloom, and Paul Kane. New York: Library of America, 1996.

Fuller, Margaret. "The Great Lawsuit." 1843. In *Transcendentalism: A Reader,* edited by Joel Myerson, pp. 383–427. Oxford: Oxford University Press, 2000.

Hawthorne, Nathaniel. *The Blithedale Romance.* 1852. Edited by William E. Cain. Boston: Bedford Books, St. Martin's Press, 1996.

Myerson, Joel, ed. *Transcendentalism: A Reader.* Oxford: Oxford University Press, 2000.

Sigourney, L. H. *Water-Drops.* New York: Robert Carter, 1848.

Smith, William Henry. *The Drunkard.* In *Early American Drama,* edited by Jeffrey H. Richards, pp. 243–303. New York: Penguin, 1997.

Thoreau, Henry D. "Reform and the Reformers." 1844. In *Reform Papers.* Edited by Wendell Glick. Princeton, N.J.: Princeton University Press, 1973.

Thoreau, Henry D. *Walden and Resistance to Civil Government.* Edited by William Rossi. 2nd ed. New York: Norton, 1992.

Secondary Works

Abzug, Robert H. *Cosmos Crumbling: American Reform and the Religious Imagination.* New York: Oxford University Press, 1994.

Eiselein, Gregory. *Literature and Humanitarian Reform in the Civil War Era.* Bloomington: Indiana University Press, 1996.

Ginzberg, Lori D. *Women and the Work of Benevolence: Morality, Politics, and Class in the Nineteenth-Century United States.* New Haven, Conn.: Yale University Press, 1990.

Griffin, Clifford Stephen. *Their Brothers' Keepers: Moral Stewardship in the United States, 1800–1865.* New Brunswick, N.J.: Rutgers University Press, 1960.

Nye, Russel Blaine. *William Lloyd Garrison and the Humanitarian Reformers.* Boston: Little, Brown, 1955.

Packer, Barbara L. "The Transcendentalists." In *The Cambridge History of American Literature,* vol. 2, edited by Sacvan Bercovitch, pp. 329–604. Cambridge, U.K.: Cambridge University Press, 1995.

Reynolds, David S. *Beneath the American Renaissance: The Subversive Imagination in the Age of Emerson and Melville.* 1988. Cambridge, Mass.: Harvard University Press, 1989.

Ryan, Susan M. *The Grammar of Good Intentions: Race and the Antebellum Culture of Benevolence.* Ithaca, N.Y.: Cornell University Press, 2003.

Sánchez-Eppler, Karen. *Touching Liberty: Abolition, Feminism, and the Politics of the Body.* Berkeley: University of California Press, 1993.

Sanford, Charles L. "Classics of American Reform Literature." *American Quarterly* 10, no. 3 (1958): 295–311.

Thomas, John L. "Romantic Reform in America, 1815–1865." *American Quarterly* 17, no. 4 (1965): 656–681.

Tyler, Alice Felt. *Freedom's Ferment: Phases of American Social History to 1860.* Minneapolis: University of Minnesota Press, 1944.

Walters, Ronald G. *American Reformers, 1815–1860.* New York: Hill and Wang, 1978.

Yellin, Jean Fagan. *Women and Sisters: The Antislavery Feminists in American Culture.* New Haven, Conn.: Yale University Press, 1989.

Gregory Eiselein

RELIGION

Antebellum literature and culture reflected the energy and diversity of American religious experience. The era began with religious forms largely inherited from Europe, but its events placed a uniquely American stamp on both mainstream denominations and new faiths. The dominant tone was triumphant Protestant evangelicalism, but the religious diversity that erupted eluded any comprehensive theological label. For most Americans from 1800 to 1865 spiritual reality permeated everyday life in conscious and unconscious ways. Powerful conservative and liberal religious movements jostled for influence, stirring deep debates about the nature of God and the divine-human relationship. Dramatic religious revivals inspired some and appalled others and the era produced an unprecedented outburst of religious experimentation and innovation. American history has not seen anything like it since.

THE AFTERLIFE OF PURITANISM

American Congregational and Presbyterian Puritanism provided a long foreground for antebellum American literature and culture. Although Puritanism's institutional relevance ended with the death of the revivalist Jonathan Edwards in 1758, its thought, already cultivated for more than a century in New England and elsewhere, lived on in the imaginations and intellectual habits of orthodox and unorthodox Christians as well as those who had come to doubt the existence of God.

Puritanism was survived by its capacity to connect the literal and the symbolic. Puritan typology fused literal objects in nature with spiritual concepts, and it influenced much of the writing of American Romantics, including Herman Melville's (1819–1891) symbolic vision, Nathaniel Hawthorne's (1804–1864) self-conscious use of types and allegories, Henry David Thoreau's (1817–1862) observations of nature, and Ralph Waldo Emerson's (1803–1882) linguistic theory.

Puritan views of human nature and theodicy, the problem of evil, emphasized the fallen condition of humans and their inability to achieve salvation through individual effort. Early-nineteenth-century writers responded vigorously, either through the elevation of a more hopeful view of human self-reliance, as articulated by Emerson, or in Hawthorne's grudging acknowledgment that only depravity, albeit without salvation, could explain the darkness he saw in the human soul. Puritans perceived God as an active agent in his creation, a preoccupation shared by Emerson and other transcendentalists, Emily Dickinson (1830–1886), and orthodox antebellum poets such as William Cullen Bryant (1794–1878).

One of the most enduring intellectual and aesthetic legacies of Puritanism was its jeremiad rhetoric. Spoken by the first Puritan immigrants and honed in the pulpits of second- and third-generation divines in the seventeenth century, the jeremiad vividly painted sublime terrors awaiting the unrepentant. Its underlying tenor, however, was optimistic, picturing the rewards available when the sinning stopped. This ability to criticize American culture harshly from within while alluding to the rewards awaiting clarified vision and reformed behavior pervaded works by leading nineteenth-century writers such as Thoreau, Hawthorne, and Melville.

Puritan orthodoxy, formed by an ethical rationalism inherited from Plato and a pietistic awareness of religious experience, underlay the mainstream Protestantism that Harriet Beecher Stowe (1811–1896) learned from her Presbyterian father, the Reverend Lyman Beecher (1775–1863). This worldview was reflected in novels such as *Uncle Tom's Cabin* (1852) and *The Minister's Wooing* (1859). The colonial religious heritage of New England also provided a broadly familiar context for works such as Henry Wadsworth Longfellow's (1807–1882) poem "The Courtship of Miles Standish" (1858).

While Puritanism cast a long shadow over early-nineteenth-century literature, competing beliefs left lingering effects as well. The rites and practices of freemasonry allowed rationalism to cohabit with occultism. The mid-eighteenth-century mystic Emanuel Swedenborg taught that the world of spirits posited by orthodox Christianity could be entered by living humans. Franz Mesmer, the Austrian father of hypnosis, insisted that "animal magnetism" and hypnotic suggestion could restore physical health and reveal the answers to cosmic mysteries. The "Rochester Rappings" described by Margaret and Catherine Fox in 1848 encouraged many Americans that the world of spirits was capable of talking back. The spiritualist writer Andrew Jackson Davis, who had studied Swedenborgianism and practiced mesmerism, published *The Principles of Nature, Her Divine Revelation and a Voice to Mankind* (1847). The practices of some spiritualists were related to Native American shamanism and some early mediums were of Indian descent. These preoccupations held particular appeal during the great age of sentimentalism in the 1840s and 1850s when families disrupted by disease and infant mortality sought comfort in spiritual reunion. Many believed that continued communication with the spirit world would lead to spiritual progress and even closer ties between heaven and earth.

THE AGE OF UNITARIANISM

The more liberal, rationalistic side of Puritanism embodied in the preaching of Charles Chauncy underlay the development of Unitarianism in America. Its confidence in the ability of human reason to unravel scriptural mysteries, its emphasis on the morality and ethics of God as exemplar rather than judge, and its reliance on Christ as a model for humans rather than as a substitutionary savior appealed to intellectuals who were uneasy about revivalism and religious enthusiasm.

Not long after Unitarianism acquired a defining articulation of beliefs (William Ellery Channing's 1819 sermon at Jared Sparks's ordination) and an organizational structure (the American Unitarian Association, founded in Boston in 1825), a group of Unitarians led by Emerson expressed dissatisfaction with its underlying empiricism and sought more reliance on intuition, founding the Transcendentalist Club in 1836. According to Perry Miller, transcendentalist literature is "a protest of the human spirit against emotional starvation" (p. 8). Emerson led the transcendentalists to embrace Swedenborg's ideas about the correspondence between spiritual ideas and natural facts, a pantheistic view of God's presence in nature, and familiarity with Eastern religions. While it never became a denomination, transcendentalism was emphatically religious. Its adherents were few, but its emphasis on nature and individualism resonated throughout the antebellum period and set the tone for American liberalism.

The transcendentalist heyday coincided with a broader movement that cultivated American Romanticism in religion. Inspired by the German theologian Friedrich Schleiermacher's assertion that religious faith was based on immediate experience of the presence of God, American theologians such as Horace Bushnell (1802–1876), the "American Schleiermacher," reinvigorated Congregationalism by providing an alternative to revivalism and asserting a Romantic theory of language emphasizing its symbolic, literary aspects. While disavowing Unitarian rationalism, Bushnell welcomed its emphasis on the moral influence of Jesus Christ rather than on the forensic function of the atonement. Although he rejected transcendentalist pantheism, Bushnell held that the natural world was infused with supernatural influences. Bushnell brought religious liberalism to conventional pulpits much as Emerson introduced philosophical liberalism to audiences in drawing rooms and lecture halls. To some extent, the religious world of Bushnell touched the lives of American writers such as John Greenleaf Whittier (1807–1892), Dickinson, Hawthorne, and Melville. Other Romantic writers, including Longfellow, James Russell Lowell (1819–1891), Oliver Wendell Holmes Sr. (1809–1894), and Bryant, were nurtured in Unitarianism but evolved a Romantic concept of nature.

REVIVALISM

Revivalism in the nineteenth century was another debtor to eighteenth century Puritanism, particularly as it was modeled by Jonathan Edwards during the Great Awakening. The Second Great Awakening, germinating in Connecticut, swept New England at the turn of the nineteenth century and encouraged a series of revivals in the frontier. Edwards's own grandson, Timothy Dwight (1752–1817), and Dwight's student, Nathaniel William Taylor (1786–1858), shaped the theology underlying the revival: humans were sinful because of their own acts, not because of an existing state they had inherited. Such departures from earlier Puritan understandings placed more emphasis on the power of the individual to choose freely and to accept accountability for his or her actions, creating an orthodox religious basis for individualism. Lyman Beecher took Taylor's theology west to the Lane Theological Seminary in Cincinnati.

Charles Grandison Finney (1792–1875) migrated westward from his Connecticut roots to absorb a rural version of Presbyterianism and become the prototype of modern revivalists. Revival focus moved away from attempts to discover the mysterious will of God and toward emphasis on the potential of human effort to reach out toward God. Finney and others also stressed the human potential to achieve holiness that had shaped Wesleyan faith in the eighteenth century. The human capacity of choosing to keep Christ dwelling in the human heart made possible the victory over sin. This availability of salvation to vast numbers of humble urban dwellers and frontier folk coincided with the broad new vistas of Jacksonian democracy. On the frontier, Kentucky led the vanguard of revivalism, with large camp meetings in 1800 and most notably at Cane Ridge in 1801, where 20,000 congregants experienced dramatic conversions. Movements sparked by these revivals made the antebellum period a triumphant era for Protestant evangelicals.

As the Second Great Awakening settled down, wave after wave of diverse religious revivals continued to spread over upstate New York, which became known as the "burned-over district." Millennialism, an emphasis on the Second Coming of Christ and a thousand-year reign of peace and prosperity, dominated many of these movements. Premillenialists saw a gloomy future dominated by accelerating evil behavior and cataclysmic events until Christ intervened at the Second Coming to rescue a righteous remnant, who would then enjoy the millennium. Postmillennialists, who tended toward a liberal outlook interested in social improvement, believed that humanity would better itself until it achieved the millennium, after which Christ would return.

Several new religious denominations emerged from this fertile period. Alexander Campbell (1788–1866) and his Christian restorationist, or Campbellite, followers held that their scrupulous adherence to New Testament Christianity would hasten the millennial age. The group, initially cool toward formal organization, eventually took the name Disciples and later, Disciples of Christ. Postmillennialist optimism helped to shape the American notion of Manifest Destiny, a vision of progress that encouraged Christian settlement of the entire North American continent in hopes of ushering in the millennium.

Into this environment around 1818 stepped a lay preacher, William Miller (1782–1849), whose prophetic biblical interpretations led him to establish a time for the second coming of Christ, finally determined to be 22 October 1844. After preaching to hundreds of thousands and converting thousands in the 1830s and 1840s, Miller and his followers endured the Great Disappointment of 1844. Many Millerites, although disillusioned with attempts to set an exact date for the return of Christ, maintained their premillennialist beliefs and eventually became Advent Christians, members of various branches of the Church of God, or Seventh-Day Adventists. The latter group, one of the most successful products of the burned-over district, enthusiastically embraced temperance and reform movements but maintained an ambivalent stance toward the United States and its role in biblical prophecy. Adventists feared that American freedoms and opportunities could be threatened by groups ranging from Catholics to labor unionists.

Another product of the burned-over district in New York was the Church of Jesus Christ of Latter-Day Saints. The most successful product of American religious innovation, Mormonism was intended to build on Christianity as Christianity had built on Judaism. Its founder, Joseph Smith (1805–1844), translated the Book of Mormon from "reformed Egyptian" in 1827–1829. The book provided an American context for the faith, describing how the Jaredites emigrated from the Tower of Babel, and later how the Lamanites (Native Americans) extinguished all of the virtuous Nephites except for Mormon and his son Moroni, who buried the scriptures Smith later translated. Smith's followers saw themselves as the spiritual progeny of the Nephites. When Smith's successor, Brigham Young (1801–1877), led the faithful to the Great Salt Lake basin and founded the colony of Deseret, a succession of new towns thrived, with Utah achieving statehood in 1896. Mormon beginnings reflect many currents of the innovations in American religion in the early nineteenth century: revivalism, communitarian experiments, alternative social structures (including, for a time, polygamy), millennial intensity, and the expectation of a special role during earth's final days.

REFORM

Postmillennialist expectation and the holiness aspects of revivalism also reflected hope for the perfectability of human behavior. The antebellum years were characterized by many reform movements tied to various religious groups and reflected in American literature and culture. The goals of the temperance movement, women's rights activists, and abolitionist groups often intersected, and underlying them all was a desire to achieve widespread moral reform. The ethical stance of the Quaker faith led to prominent action on behalf of temperance, labor rights, peace, and abolition.

Reform movements encouraged religious denominations to develop interdenominational voluntary associations in many fields: The American Bible Society (1816), the American Sunday-School Union (1824), and the American Tract Society (1825) sought to evangelize America and the rest of the world with a flood of publications emphasizing the belief that the United States and its religious culture were agents of the millennium.

Some reformers sought to express their idealism in new social combinations and new ways of life. The antebellum period teemed with communal experiments dedicated to a vision of social progress. The United Society of Believers, the Shakers, saw their industrious, celibate colonies as the vanguard of the millennium. Drawn by religious intensity and economic security, several thousand members populated eighteen colonies from Maine to Kentucky by 1826, and the group became the most sustained communal experiment in the United States.

Attempts to restructure society in a communal way drew criticism from established churches in the United States. Robert Owen (1771–1858), an advocate of communal living, bought a colony from a German group, the Rappites, at New Harmony, Indiana, and opened several additional colonies. Like the socialist colonies built by the followers of Charles Fourier (1772–1837), Owen's communities were basically secular, but the opposition they stirred up among American churches aided in their demise by 1830. A longer-lived experiment was the Oneida Community, founded in New York by John Humphrey Noyes (1811–1886) in 1848. Noyes's singular religious doctrine held that once perfection was attained, it could never be lost. He rejected conventional practices and incorporated socialism and complex marriage into his colony. The colony was jeopardized in 1879 when Noyes fled to Canada ahead of legal inquiries into his marriage practices, and it closed in 1881.

Transcendentalists also devised communal experiments. A disenchanted Unitarian minister, George Ripley (1802–1880), founded a transcendentalist commune, Brook Farm, in Roxbury, Massachusetts, in 1841. Hawthorne participated in its early, experimental phases, later fictionalized in his novel *The Blithedale Romance* (1852). By 1844 Hawthorne had moved on and Brook Farm was restructured as a Fourierist phalanx, but the experiment was abandoned in 1847. In the meantime, Amos Bronson Alcott (1799–1888) had attempted another transcendentalist commune, Fruitlands, in Harvard, Massachusetts, from 1843 to 1844.

Energies stirred by revivalism, reform, and doctrinal innovation perhaps inevitably led to vigorous reactions. Competing notions of a chosen people singled out by God also suggested that some would never be chosen. In such an environment, nativist groups flourished, and recent immigrants who were distinctly other than Anglo-Saxon (and Protestant) were singled out for exclusion. Secret societies such as the Masons came under suspicion both because of their rumored rites and their distance from orthodox Protestant Christianity; anti-Masons scoured the burned-over

district in the 1820s and 1830s. Protestant luminaries such as Lyman Beecher and Horace Bushnell, perhaps anticipating the moment at the end of the Civil War when Catholics outnumbered any other single denomination in the United States, led a fervent wave of anti-Catholicism. Beecher's well-known *Plea for the West* (1835) urged Protestants to exclude Catholics from western settlements. The Catholic Church's official silence on the subject of slavery (large Catholic populations lived in New Orleans and other areas of the deep South) also rankled many suspicious northern Protestants. Intolerance became more than an attitude on 11 August 1834, when a mob set fire to an Ursuline convent in Charlestown, Massachusetts.

Protestant reformers were also suspicious of much of American popular culture during the antebellum years. Melodramatic theatrical productions and countless suspenseful novels captivated a vast audience, and fiction authors were suspected of subversion or worse. In the preface to *The Scarlet Letter* (1850), Hawthorne half-seriously worried that his Puritan ancestors would not have approved of his vocation. Some authors, however, saw a serious purpose for plays and literature. William H. Smith's drama *The Drunkard; or, The Fallen Saved* (1844) was both popular and seriously moral. Harriet Beecher Stowe insisted that *Uncle Tom's Cabin* was a combination of divine inspiration and nonfictional journalism, not to be confused with ordinary novels. She thought long and hard before approving and attending the wildly popular dramatization of *Uncle Tom's Cabin* staged by George L. Aiken (1852). Millions of evangelical Protestants followed Stowe to that production, which became their introduction to the previously suspect practice of theatergoing.

Many women authors capitalized on the interest in moral reform and the hope that useful lessons could be taught in story form. Susan Warner's *The Wide, Wide World* (1851), Augusta Evans Wilson's *St. Elmo* (1867), and Elizabeth Payson Prentiss's *Stepping Heavenward* (1870) were successful best-sellers and achieved a degree of popularity that mystified and eluded Hawthorne, who as early as 1855 had grumbled about "scribbling women" (*Works* 17:304).

Attempts by American Protestants to improve and reform society through temperance and moral education, however, were dwarfed by the movement to end slavery. Religious groups impatient for the beginning of the millennium found no greater impediment to its advent than slaveholding. Theodore Dwight Weld (1803–1895), an acolyte of Charles Grandison Finney, was moved by his millennial expectations to fight the institution in 1830. Influenced by the impassioned antislavery preaching of Lyman Beecher, the journalist William Lloyd Garrison (1805–1879) delivered a Fourth of July philippic against slavery at Boston's Park Street Church in 1829. Within a few months Garrison repented of his momentary support for gradual emancipation and launched his abolitionist newspaper, *The Liberator* (1831–1865). In 1854, fed up with his inability to rouse a majority of Americans to abolitionism, he publicly burned a copy of the U.S. Constitution at an abolitionist meeting in Framingham, Massachusetts, on the Fourth of July.

Garrison allied for a time with Weld and the wealthy merchant Lewis Tappan (1788–1873) to found the American Anti-Slavery Society, an abolitionist organization, in 1833. For evangelicals like Tappan, belief in the sinfulness of slavery made immediate repentance and repudiation imperative. These notions sifted the uncompromising stance of abolitionism from the more gradual, flexible approach of earlier antislavery movements and provoked an equally intransigent response in the South.

The Quaker faith produced several eloquent women who led the fight against slavery and other social ills. Lucretia Mott (1793–1880), a northern Quaker schoolteacher and reformer, traveled to the World Anti-Slavery Convention in London in 1840. Refused recognition as a delegate because she was a woman, she worked with Elizabeth Cady Stanton (1815–1902) to organize the first convention on women's rights in the United States, at Seneca Falls, New York, in 1848. Charleston, South Carolina, produced two influential Quaker sisters who became abolitionists in 1835: Sarah Moore Grimké (1792–1873) and Angelina Emily Grimké (1805–1879). Angelina took a courageous public stand against slavery the following year in her book *An Appeal to the Christian Women of the South*. The two sisters relocated to New York City and began speaking publicly at abolitionist meetings. Angelina developed a reputation for eloquence and is remembered as one of the first American women to speak in public. Her marriage to Theodore Dwight Weld in 1838 created a powerful abolitionist alliance.

Abolitionism found its greatest cultural inspiration in the publication of *Uncle Tom's Cabin* in 1852. Although Stowe feared her story would be too timid to suit abolitionists, with its displaced northern villains Haley and Legree, its benign southern slave owners (except for Mrs. St. Clare), and its concluding solution of African colonization, the South erupted in rage and abolitionists embraced the book. Whittier, the Quaker abolitionist poet, realized that Stowe's story had done more to advance the cause against slavery than two decades of abolitionist rhetoric. Noting that no mainstream best-selling author since Stowe has written a book claimed to be dictated by God, the contemporary critic Alfred Kazin has observed that "*Uncle Tom's Cabin* was New England's last holiness" (p. 85).

THE CIVIL WAR AND ITS AFTERMATH

The Civil War era became a backdrop for religious conflicts. The slavery question, which split every major Protestant denomination into northern and southern versions before the war began, openly encouraged disputants to connect armed combat and religious belief. More subtly reflected in the conflict was the argument between orthodox Protestantism and more liberal views. Such disputes were described in Harriet Beecher Stowe's prewar novel *The Minister's Wooing* (1859) and Elizabeth Stuart Phelps's postwar novel *The Gates Ajar* (1868). Although the trauma of civil war sent many forward-leaning Protestants back to the familiar images of their Calvinist childhood, it also became a watershed for the debate about whether God intervened in human history. When it was all over, the skeptical, more liberal view was significantly more influential.

The war evoked strong responses from religious groups in both the Confederacy and the Union. Confederates identified many signs that they were God's chosen people, noting in particular their spectacular early successes. Defending what they asserted was a legitimate, scripturally ordained way of life, some Confederate theologians and politicians portrayed the North as a coercive, enslaving power tantamount to the Antichrist in the Apocalypse.

Early Union religious response to the war was more chastened than assertive, particularly after the debacle at the first battle of Manassas. The civil religion of the North tended to internalize guilt for Union military failures, ultimately explaining them as God's judgment for tolerating slavery. Optimists looked beyond the disastrous present toward a bright postmillennial future once the evil of slavery had been expunged. Unionists and Confederates alike sought divine reassurance in government-ordained days of fasting and prayer. Both, as Lincoln famously remarked in his second inaugural address, "read the same Bible, and pray to the same God; and each invokes His aid against the other."

If *Uncle Tom's Cabin* was New England's last holiness, the Civil War was the United States' last holy war—the last conflict imbued with the confidence that God was personally involved. Herman Melville perfectly captured that moment and its ebbing in his collection of war poems, *Battle-Pieces and Aspects of the*

In his second inaugural address Abraham Lincoln noted the pervasive reliance both the Union and the Confederacy placed on scripture, prayer, and the certainty of divine approval. He also described a view of God more comprehensive than the deity envisioned by either side.

If we shall suppose that American Slavery is one of those offences which, in the providence of God, must needs come, but which, having continued through His appointed time, He now wills to remove, and that He gives to both North and South, this terrible war, as the woe due to those by whom the offence came, shall we discern therein any departure from those divine attributes which the believers in a Living God always ascribe to Him? Fondly do we hope–fervently do we pray–that this mighty scourge of war may speedily pass away. Yet, if God wills that it continue, until all the wealth piled by the bond-man's two hundred and fifty years of unrequited toil shall be sunk, and until every drop of blood drawn with the lash, shall be paid by another drawn with the sword, as was said three thousand years ago, so still it must be said "the judgments of the Lord, are true and righteous altogether."

The Portable Abraham Lincoln (New York: Viking Penguin, 1992), p. 321.

War (1866). Other leading writers of the day also grasped the significance of the war in American civil and religious life, including Walt Whitman (1819–1892) and the lesser-known Henry Howard Brownell (1820–1872) in the North, and William Gilmore Simms (1806–1870) and Henry Timrod (1828–1867), the foremost Romantic writers in the South. The purest essences of the war's scope and meaning, however, were distilled by writers not regarded during their lifetimes as leading literary lights: Julia Ward Howe (1819–1910) in "The Battle Hymn of the Republic" (1861) and Abraham Lincoln (1809–1865) in his second inaugural address (1865).

The Civil War devastated Romanticism and religious expectations of God's involvement in human affairs. However, in the South a persistent strain of faith in underlying Confederate motives developed into the potent postwar civil religion of the Lost Cause. Reasons for taking up arms were valorized, and devout military leaders such as Robert E. Lee and Stonewall Jackson became the cause's patron saints. Reverence for the literal meaning of the biblical text, exercised so frequently in prewar arguments about the relationship between slavery and the Bible, was put to use again when fundamentalism sprouted throughout the country in the early twentieth century.

In the postwar North, conservative Christians found meaning in holiness movements such as the camp meetings in Vineland, New Jersey, in July 1867. In general, holiness practices kept alive the early Methodist tradition of religious leadership for women. Phoebe Palmer (1807–1874), for example, reminded her audience in *The Promise of the Father* (1859) that the Old Testament had predicted prophesying by both sons and daughters. Holiness expectations of engagement in good works led to expanded social gospel efforts.

Liberal religion in the North became increasingly diverse. In 1866 the Unitarians stated that they were indeed liberal Christians. Religious liberals who resided outside the realm of orthodox Christianity included members of the Free Religious Association, founded in 1867 by Octavius Brooks Frothingham (1822–1895), who melded transcendentalist ethics and social gospel concerns. Felix Adler (1851–1933), who had been a Reform Jewish rabbi, founded the Ethical Culture movement in 1876. These movements reflected the erosion of antebellum Christian religious expectations.

The wane of postmillennial theology brought into question earlier notions of conversion, and newly applied higher biblical criticism questioned biblical certainties about the Apocalypse, heaven, and hell. Theologians and literary writers grappled with the implications of Darwinian evolution. Another challenge was posed by secularism. Robert G. Ingersoll (1833–1899), a Republican politician, peerless orator, and the "great agnostic," publically skewered conventional religion in front of the largest audiences any American speaker achieved before the age of radio and television. Mark Twain (1835–1910) demolished platitudes about God and country that had seemed unassailable before the Civil War. Religious and literary culture in the United States emerged from the Civil War more diverse, at times more defensive, and always less capable of a consensus about the relevance of God than it had been in the antebellum years. The possibility of the universe harboring a God who watched over and participated in earthly affairs became more problematic and unlikely.

See also The Bible; Catholics; Jews; Methodists; Mormons; Protestantism; Reform; Transcendentalism; Unitarians; Utopian Communities

BIBLIOGRAPHY

Primary Works

Bushnell, Horace. *Sermons for the New Life*. New York: Scribners, 1858.

Hawthorne, Nathaniel. *Works of Nathaniel Hawthorne*. Centenary edition. 20 vols. Columbus: Ohio State University Press, 1962–1988.

Stowe, Harriet Beecher. *Uncle Tom's Cabin, or, Life among the Lowly*. Boston: J. P. Jewett, 1852.

Secondary Works

Ahlstrom, Sydney E. *A Religious History of the American People*. New Haven, Conn.: Yale University Press, 1972.

Bercovitch, Sacvan. *The American Jeremiad*. Madison: University of Wisconsin Press, 1978.

Brumm, Ursula. *American Thought and Religious Typology*. New Brunswick, N.J.: Rutgers University Press, 1970.

Conkin, Paul K. *The Uneasy Center: Reformed Christianity in Antebellum America*. Chapel Hill: University of North Carolina Press, 1995.

Franchot, Jenny. *Roads to Rome: The Antebellum Protestant Encounter with Catholicism*. Berkeley: University of California Press, 1994.

Hatch, Nathan O. *The Democratization of American Christianity*. New Haven, Conn.: Yale University Press, 1989.

Heyrman, Christine Leigh. *Southern Cross: The Beginnings of the Bible Belt*. New York: Knopf, 1997.

Kazin, Alfred. *God and the American Writer*. New York: Knopf, 1997.

Lippy, Charles H., and Peter W. Williams, eds. *Encyclopedia of the American Religious Experience: Studies of Traditions and Movements*. New York: Scribners, 1988.

Mathews, Donald G. *Religion in the Old South*. Chicago: University of Chicago Press, 1977.

Miller, Perry, ed. *The Transcendentalists: An Anthology*. Cambridge, Mass.: Harvard University Press, 1950.

Moorhead, James H. *American Apocalypse: Yankee Protestants and the Civil War, 1860–1869*. New Haven, Conn.: Yale University Press, 1978.

Morgan, David. *Protestants and Pictures: Religion, Visual Culture, and the Age of American Mass Production*. New York: Oxford University Press, 1999.

Noll, Mark A. *America's God: From Jonathan Edwards to Abraham Lincoln*. Oxford and New York: Oxford University Press, 2002.

Noll, Mark A. *The Old Religion in a New World: The History of North American Christianity*. Grand Rapids, Mich.: Eerdmans, 2002.

Reynolds, David S. *Beneath the American Renaissance: The Subversive Imagination in the Age of Emerson and Melville*. New York: Knopf, 1988.

Sandeen, Ernest R. *The Roots of Fundamentalism: British and American Millenarianism, 1800–1930*. Chicago: University of Chicago Press, 1970.

Smith, James Ward, A. Leland Jamison, and Nelson Rollin, eds. *Religion in American Life*. Princeton, N.J.: Princeton University Press, 1961.

Smith, Timothy Lawrence. *Revivalism and Social Reform in Mid-Nineteenth-Century America*. New York: Abingdon Press, 1957.

Stein, Stephen J. *The Shaker Experience in America*. New Haven, Conn.: Yale University Press, 1992.

Tuveson, Ernest Lee. *Redeemer Nation: The Idea of America's Millennial Role*. Chicago: University of Chicago Press, 1968.

Tyler, Alice Felt. *Freedom's Ferment: Phases of American Social History to 1860*. Minneapolis: University of Minnesota Press, 1944.

Wilson, Charles Reagan. *Baptized in Blood: The Religion of the Lost Cause, 1865–1920*. Athens: University of Georgia Press, 1980.

Terrie Dopp Aamodt

RELIGIOUS MAGAZINES

The period of renewed religious evangelical fervor known as the Second Great Awakening began in America during the 1820s, or roughly a century after the Puritan minister Jonathan Edwards was at the forefront of a first Great Awakening, beginning in the 1730s, which had imposed on mesmerized audiences the need for repentance of sins to avoid religious damnation. Both movements were preceded by periods of impressive secular cultural advancement that contributed to a perceptible and widespread drift away from organized religion. While dozens of short-lived and specialized publications reached the press in the last decades of the eighteenth century, many periodicals in the early nineteenth century began to extend their longevity and increase readership by appealing to a broader range of issues germane to a specific audience. As a result, cosmopolitan Christian women would read *Godey's Lady's Book* or the *Ladies' Repository* and discover articles on fashion, cooking, keeping house, and short stories. One religious periodical, the *Christian Parlor Magazine* (1844–1849), took a hint from such secular publications by interlacing its didacticism with popular poetry by Lydia

Sigourney, Anne C. Lynch, Richard Henry Stoddard, and others, as well as including pictorial "embellishments." Initial reception of the religiously focused Catholic *Pilot* in the 1830s was tepid, but editors soon focused on Irish American issues and by 1866 the paper had 100,000 subscribers.

Several significant causes help explain why religious publishing increased soon after the turn of the century. Both American academics and laypeople were forced to reassess their links with parent countries and more specifically, to consider how their new identities as Americans would change family and worship patterns. In a period the historian Nathan Hatch calls "the democratization of American Christianity," the lack of a single government-prescribed religion led to an explosion of Protestantism. Many small groups, often pulled together by a charismatic leader, frequently utilized publishing as an effective tool to promote their particular take on American Christianity and to bolster those already converted.

In the early nineteenth century the United States as a nation was also looking to form its own identity apart from British custom. Even more secular-leaning publications like the *North American Review* wrestled with the conflict between old and new as the editor struggled to reconcile a desire to feature American authors and literature in a period when English literature was superior. In its early years the *Review* used slightly more English literature but progressively focused more on American political, including religious, issues.

MANY VISIONS, MANY VOICES

Early religious publications like Elias Smith's (1764–1846) *Herald of Gospel Liberty,* which commenced printing in 1808, were created first and foremost to purvey their specific Christian vision. The *Herald,* like Barton W. Stone's (1772–1844) later *Christian Messenger,* represented a small group of people unassociated with a denomination who strove to reunite the greater Christian family through a New Testament, back-to-the-Bible, primitivist understanding. Like many publications of this period, these two periodicals essentially died with their charismatic editors. Other periodicals stopped publishing when their basic tenets were refuted, like the *Midnight Cry* and the *Prophetic Times,* which both predicted that the Second Advent of Christ would occur in the mid-1840s, in keeping with the teachings of the millenarian William Miller. Yet other small publications were more successful at establishing certain ideals for years to come, most notably Isaac Mayer Wise's *American Israelite,* which successfully amplified Wise's appeals for Reform

Judaism beginning in 1854. Like the Irish Catholic *Pilot,* Wise's paper would regularly bolster and encourage readers in their struggles adjusting to life in America and especially in the case of the *Pilot,* such papers helped readers stay informed about the old world while simultaneously unraveling the new.

A second, more resilient type of religious publication was associated with established denominations. While some denominations were created and grew stronger through the influence of their periodicals throughout the period, like the *American Israelite,* many existing denominations created publications to encourage commitment within a denomination and reiterate beliefs. The *Christian Advocate* (Methodist), the *Lutheran Observer,* and the *Christian Examiner* (Unitarian) all complemented an existing denomination and typically featured a mix of general informative articles and more specific denominational writings.

One clear disadvantage for Christians during the Second Great Awakening was the fragmented nature of denominations; because no single group was endorsed by the government, denominations struggled to work together to exert their social and moral influence on society. Unified groups for abolition were not uncommon, but perhaps the most notable example of cross-denominational cooperation was the American Bible Society and its periodical, the *American Bible Society Record,* which aimed to distribute Bibles free of denominational commentary starting in 1818. Another example of interdenominational collaboration was the Evangelical Tract Society, which produced religious literature for Confederate soldiers during the Civil War.

SLAVERY AND THE CIVIL WAR

Many periodicals in the mid- to late nineteenth century strongly resisted open discussion of slavery, despite the obvious pertinence, because it was such a polarizing and divisive subject. Larger publishers and denominational periodicals were acutely aware that their readership was split on slavery and that discussion of the issue would at best depress readership and at worst create additional divisions. Discussions of slavery and the Civil War were often detrimental even to smaller publications as both issues ultimately drew attention away from specific religious themes. The *Guide to Holiness,* the leading publication of the American Holiness movement, took a severe hit in circulation and profits during the war and never fully recovered.

The *Christian Advocate,* the popular Methodist paper, went from 120,000 subscribers in 1841 to 60,000 in 1845 after the church split over slavery fifteen years before the Civil War. *Godey's Lady's Book* fully avoided any discussion of slavery or the Civil War save the occasional mention of suffering, in the belief that women's magazines should be kept distant from general public issues. The Methodist equivalent of *Godey's*, the *Ladies' Repository*, also largely ignored slavery and the war, even though the Methodist church was rent in half over the issue of slavery. The *North American Review* never addressed the issue directly, but a review of Harriet Beecher Stowe's 1852 novel *Uncle Tom's Cabin* that appeared in the journal did reveal muted proslavery sentiment.

Some smaller publications with more local appeal were freer to speak out on slavery, such as the strongly proslavery Texas-based *United Methodist Reporter*. Many publications featured some regular commentary about the war. The *Christian Advocate* featured a weekly "Progress of the War" summary, and the African Methodist Episcopal Church's *Christian Recorder* offered a unique perspective during the Civil War by providing regular factual updates and commentary about the likelihood of emancipation. Stone's *Christian Messenger* took a bold stand for repatriation of slaves, despite its mostly mid-South readership. The *Recorder* applauded President Abraham Lincoln's Emancipation Proclamation and encouraged readers to assist blacks after the war. While many periodicals shut down during the war some, like the *Army and Navy Messenger*, were created exclusively for partisan coverage. The *Messenger* was one of six religious publications written for Confederate troops that predominately focused on war news, health advice, blunt appeals to repentance, and reassurances of God's support for the Confederates.

While the war itself garnered little mention, the Episcopalian church made extensive efforts to assist newly freed slaves in the aftermath of the conflict. *Spirit of Missions*, a national Episcopal Church publication, encouraged and documented the building of schools and the influx of funds and Episcopalian workers in the Reconstruction South, as a means of supporting freed slaves economically and morally.

PARTICULAR CONCERNS: WESTWARD EXPANSION, WOMEN AND CHILDREN

Of particular import later in this period was a growing consideration of westward expansion by religious magazines. Periodicals like the *Western Recorder*, started in 1834 by Southern Baptists; the *Western Christian Advocate* of the same year by the Methodists; and the *Pacific* in 1851 were created specifically as Christianizing influences in the rapidly expanding West, which was commonly seen as wild and morally listless. The *Western Christian Advocate* and *Pacific* in particular

were accompanied by concerted church-planting and missions efforts. The Episcopalian *Spirit of Missions* was launched in 1836 to demonstrate and promote a strong, domestically oriented Episcopalian mission effort.

One of the most interesting and acknowledged social considerations of this era is the changing role of women. *Godey's Lady's Book* and the *Ladies' Repository* were popular monthlies that provide primary insight into the mind of the nineteenth-century American woman. *Godey's* zesty editor Sarah Hale (1788–1879) believed that women were morally and spiritually superior to men and that they thus held the key to family life and childhood development. Hale stressed that women should be educated in this limited domestic sense; she believed that *Godey's* would help women hone their spirituality, taste, and virtue, which they could then pass on to their children. The *Ladies' Repository* championed a similar ideal for women, regularly featuring stories about morally supportive mothers or wives. Clearly women were gaining limited rights and respect but all under the authority of men who still created and owned the *Ladies' Repository* and *Godey's*. This understanding of women as moral leaders can also be seen as a response to the changing dynamic of the household, which was no longer the sole base for economic production. With the rise of industrialism men no longer worked closely with women in the house, and women's responsibilities were forced to change accordingly.

Following her understanding of women and their abilities, Hale made a concerted crusade to allow women to train as medical missionaries, and in 1869 her efforts helped send Clara Swain to India as the first trained female medical missionary. But ultimately the women's movement of the mid-nineteenth century was ambiguous: commenting on a cover image featuring several heroic women and an inside picture featuring a traditional domestic mother, Hale wrote in *Godey's* in January 1861, "We are constrained to say that these exceptional women are the exception, not the rule of life. In our second picture is embodied the real worth, the true sublimity of woman's destiny and duty" (p. 78).

During the nineteenth century, local newspapers were frequently published for religious motive and contained considerable material that today would be called religious news and comment. One notably short-lived but eminently important example was the Alton *Observer*, founded by the abolitionist Presbyterian minister Elijah Parish Lovejoy (1802–1837) in free-soil Illinois across the Mississippi from St. Louis, from which he had fled as beleaguered editor of the *Observer* there. Lovejoy became the first American journalist killed on account of editorial policy—an emphatically religious denial of the institution of slavery—in November 1837.

One additional noteworthy publication was the *Child's Paper,* a religious newspaper put out by the American Tract Society that aimed to teach children and their families about sinfulness through didactic stories. Most commonly distributed free of charge, the paper had a monthly circulation of 355,000 in 1854 and necessarily avoided controversial issues like slavery.

See also The Bible; Catholics; Evangelicals; *Godey's Lady's Book;* Literary Marketplace; Oratory; Periodicals; Proslavery Writing; Religion

BIBLIOGRAPHY

Primary Work

Hale, Sarah. "Editors' Table." *Godey's Lady's Book* 62 (January 1861).

Secondary Works

Fackler, P. Mark, and Charles H. Lippy, eds. *Popular Religious Magazines of the United States.* Westport, Conn.: Greenwood Press, 1995.

Hatch, Nathan. *The Democratization of American Christianity.* New Haven, Conn.: Yale University Press, 1989.

Mott, Frank Luther. *A History of American Magazines.* 5 vols. Cambridge, Mass.: Harvard University Press, 1938–1968.

Schultze, Quentin J. *Christianity and the Mass Media in America: Toward a Democratic Accomodation.* East Lansing: Michigan State University Press, 2003.

Mark Fackler
Eric Baker

"RESISTANCE TO CIVIL GOVERNMENT"

Next to *Walden* (1854), Henry David Thoreau's (1817–1862) essay "Resistance to Civil Government" (1849) is his most famous work. Its influence on later writers and reformers such as Mohandas Gandhi and Martin Luther King Jr. has ensured that Thoreau's views on social issues would be not only controversial but misunderstood. To some he is the patron saint of passive resistance, whereas to others he is an anarchist. The truth lies somewhere between those extremes.

Henry David Thoreau. Daguerreotype, June 1856, by Benjamin D. Maxham. GETTY IMAGES

"Resistance to Civil Government" (often titled "Civil Disobedience") was neither the first nor the last of Thoreau's writings on social and political reform. These concerns occur throughout his writings and are rooted in the same transcendentalist self-culture that he espouses in *Walden:* an individual's highest duty is to perfect the spiritual connection to God within. By striving for personal perfection, one leavens the whole loaf of humanity. To attempt to reform society without first perfecting oneself is to hack at the branches of evil while ignoring its roots. Paradoxically, Thoreau's ideal program of social action requires no direct action on society.

Thoreau was often impatient with reform movements and utopian communities. In *A Week on the Concord and Merrimack Rivers* (1849) he complains: "It is a great pleasure to escape sometimes from the restless class of Reformers. What if these grievances exist? So do you and I" (p. 126). In his last years even the Civil War could not convince him that the ideal of self-culture should give way to social action. As he wrote to his friend Parker Pillsbury (1809–1898) about the war, "I do not so much regret the present

THE TITLE OF "RESISTANCE TO CIVIL GOVERNMENT"

In its original publication in the 1849 *Aesthetic Papers,* Thoreau's essay is titled "Resistance to Civil Government," and that title is used in the standard Princeton edition of Thoreau's works. However, in "Another Look at the Text and Title of Thoreau's 'Civil Disobedience,'" Fritz Oehlschlaeger argues persuasively that the change from the original "Resistance to Civil Government" to "Civil Disobedience" was authorial, part of a pattern of revisions by Thoreau himself. The later title does affect the reader's expectations about the essay. "Disobedience" is a softer term than "Resistance," and the word "civil" becomes a pun that can suggest both "relating to the state" and "courteous and polite." The earlier title is thus more aggressive and direct; the later title is more subtle and ironic, tones very common in Thoreau's other writings.

condition of things in this country (provided I regret it at all) as I do that I ever heard of it" (*Letters,* p. 195). Despite his clinging to the ideal of self-culture, however, when such issues came closer to home, he was sometimes forced to conclude that effective reform might depend on numbers. A crucial event was the night he spent in the Concord jail.

THE NIGHT IN JAIL

In July 1846, during the second summer of his residence at Walden Pond, Thoreau walked in from the pond to go to the cobbler and was stopped by Sam Staples, Concord's amiable tax collector and jail keeper. Staples asked him to pay several years of overdue poll tax (not a true voting tax but a "head" tax on every adult male over twenty years old). Thoreau's refusal to pay the tax was intended as a direct protest against an unpopular tax and as an indirect protest against the government's condoning of slavery. He also linked slavery to the Mexican-American War because Mexico refused to cede ownership of Texas, which had nonetheless been admitted to the Union as a slave state. Staples had until then chosen to ignore Thoreau's tardiness as not being worth his trouble, but Thoreau probably hoped that his refusal would lead to imprisonment so that he could dramatize his protest. So when Staples reminded him that his refusal to pay might lead to jail, Thoreau embraced martyrdom and volunteered for immediate incarceration.

Thoreau was marched off to jail and ushered into a cell with a man accused of burning down a barn. After his cell mate went to sleep, Thoreau restlessly stood by the cell window looking out at his neighbors going about their normal business oblivious of his plight. He likely hoped that the town would rally to his support once they knew about his protest. Thoreau's mother, however, soon learned of her son's dilemma and scurried home to find a way of getting him out before he could further embarrass the family. That evening, while Staples was out, his daughter at home took delivery of Thoreau's tax money from an anonymous donor (probably one of his aunts). By the time the daughter informed Staples of the payment, he already had his boots off and was relaxing for the evening, so he decided to let Thoreau stay put for the night and free him the next morning.

Thoreau had no visitors that night, and he soon realized that the community really did not care about his protest. The next morning, when he was freed, he left the jail "mad as the devil" at not being allowed to continue his protest. He eventually calmed himself, however, picked up his shoe at the cobbler, and went picking huckleberries. What he had intended as a clarion call of independence to wake his neighbors up had turned out to be only an unheard whisper. Passive resistance was not enough; it needed some press.

Thoreau included only one paragraph on his night in jail in *Walden,* but his disillusionment with the government and with his neighbors led him to work the experience up as a lecture that he delivered as "The Relation of the Individual to the State" to the Concord Lyceum in January 1848. Elizabeth Palmer Peabody (1804–1894), a fellow transcendentalist, published this lecture in 1849 as "Resistance to Civil Government" in a collection of essays titled *Aesthetic Papers.*

THE MEANING OF "RESISTANCE TO CIVIL GOVERNMENT"

Misconceptions abound about Thoreau's position toward the government. One of the most common is that Thoreau was an anarchist (see Buranelli and Van Dusen). But there is a difference between transcendentalist self-culture and anarchy. Thoreau does say in the essay that "that government is best which governs not at all" (*Reform Papers,* p. 63), hence the accusation of anarchy. This comment, however, more accurately affirms the transcendentalist ideal that if everyone were to connect fully with the God within,

On hearing Thoreau's lyceum lecture "The Relation of the Individual to the Statem," Amos Bronson Alcott wrote the following entry in his journal on 26 January 1848.

Heard Thoreau's lecture before the lyceum on the relation of the individual to the State—an admirable statement of the rights of the individual to self-government and an attentive audience.

His allusions to the Mexican War, to Mr. Hoar's expulsion from Carolina, his own imprisonment in Concord Jail for refusal to pay his tax. Mr. Hoar's payment of mine when taken to prison for a similar refusal, were all pertinent, well considered, and reasoned. I took great pleasure in this deed of Thoreau's.

Amos Bronson Alcott, *The Journals of Bronson Alcott* (Boston: Little, Brown, 1938), p. 201.

all would live in harmony. Furthermore, Thoreau insists that he is not waiting for such an ideal future but rather wishes to speak "practically and as a citizen" who asks for "not at once no government, but *at once* a better government" (*Reform Papers,* p. 64).

Thoreau does not deny the benefit of having, or even of obeying, a government that enacts just laws. He is even willing to allow a government its imperfections, for, he says, "if the injustice is part of the necessary friction of the machine of government, let it go, let it go" (*Reform Papers,* p. 73). But when the government enslaved some and demanded that others condone such slavery with their votes and taxes, Thoreau believed that the injustice was too great to be overlooked and that he must withdraw his support. Like Socrates, however, Thoreau believed the individual was not exempt from the power of the state; a decision to disobey also meant a willingness to accept the consequences. Although compelled by conscience to disobey specific unjust laws, Thoreau was willing to submit to the larger principle of government as a human necessity.

Whether or not one agrees with Thoreau's argument for resisting unjust laws depends entirely on whether one accepts the premise that conscience is a God-given "higher law" that takes precedence over human laws. If one believes that individual conscience is a more reliable test of a truth than the number of people who support it, one readily follows Thoreau to

his logical conclusion that "any man more right than his neighbors, constitutes a majority of one already" (*Reform Papers,* p. 74). If, however, one mistrusts the reliability of the conscience because it might as easily be the tool of the devil as of God, then one must assert law and majority rule as the antidote to dangerous individualism. This split between those who trust conscience and those who trust law remains a basic division in American culture.

Fully aware of this split, Thoreau begins the essay by giving reasons why government cannot be trusted. First, "government is at best an expedient" (*Reform Papers,* p. 63)—that is, a convenient tool used by the multitude of individual consciences from which it derives its power. By itself it can do nothing: it "never of itself furthered any enterprise, but by the alacrity with which it got out of its way" (p. 64). Instead, "the character inherent in the American people has done all that has been accomplished" (p. 64). When it fails to respond to the people from whom it derives its power, government becomes inexpedient. The second reason to be wary of government is that it is unreliable: it is often merely a "tradition" more concerned with perpetuating itself than with enacting the will of the people. It is often motivated more by self-interest and popular opinion than by justice.

Thoreau admits that the American government does provide avenues for change for dissenters, but these are often too slow and unreliable. Voting, for instance, is not as effective as Americans like to think: it is only "a sort of gaming, like chequers or backgammon, with a slight moral tinge to it." "Voting *for the right*," he points out, "is *doing* nothing for it" (p. 68). A voter whose side is defeated submits readily to the majority, an equation of numbers with justice that is unacceptable to the transcendentalist belief in "some absolute goodness somewhere" (p. 69). Other methods of reform, such as legislation or petition, "take too much time, and a man's life will be gone" (p. 68), by which Thoreau means both the life of the reformer and the life of the victim (the slave, for instance). Nor does the government really desire to reform its own evils. It is more likely to "pronounce Washington and Franklin rebels" (p. 73) than to welcome them as reformers.

Given these impediments to reform, the final recourse should be a direct appeal to the people themselves. What discouraged Thoreau about his night in jail, however, was what it revealed about his neighbors' indifference. They seemed unwilling to acknowledge, much less to desire to reform, the government's injustice. Looking out at Concord by moonlight through the jail bars, Thoreau came sadly to realize that his neighbors neither knew about his protest nor would care about it if they did. He understood "to what extent the people among whom I lived could be trusted as good neighbors and friends; . . . that they did not greatly purpose to do right; that they were a distinct race from me" (p. 83).

His night in jail forces Thoreau to reconsider one individual's power to leaven the whole loaf of society. He continues to believe that one person can make a difference and that "action from principle . . . changes things and relations" (p. 72). But what if the individual leads and no one follows? Then one must at least refuse to condone the evil and must withhold one's vote or obedience: "If I devote myself to other pursuits and contemplations, I must first see, at least, that I do not pursue them sitting on another man's shoulders" (p. 71). Noncompliance was Thoreau's preferred approach to most social injustice.

Thoreau was not a pacifist. "Resistance to Civil Government" is viewed by many as the source for modern passive resistance, but even in this essay he acknowledges the need for violence in extreme cases. He points out the hypocrisy of praising the American Revolution, a violent rebellion, while refusing to acknowledge violence to remedy contemporary injustices such as slavery. "All men recognize the right of revolution," he says, "but almost all say that such is not the case now. But such was the case, they think, in the Revolution of '75" (p. 67). Resisting injustice includes not only the right "to refuse allegiance" but also to "resist the government," presumably by violence if necessary (p. 67).

Elsewhere in his life and writing, both before and after this essay, Thoreau is even more explicit about using violence to resist extreme injustice. As early as 27 January 1841, Thoreau and his brother John participated in a debate for the Concord Lyceum on the question "Is it ever proper to offer forcible resistance?" Amos Bronson Alcott (1799–1888), a Concord philosopher and the father of Louisa May Alcott (1832–1888), argued the negative; Henry and John argued the affirmative. In *A Week on the Concord and Merrimack Rivers,* published the same year as "Resistance to Civil Government," Thoreau protests the effects of a dam near Billerica on the fish and farmers along the Merrimack River. Siding with the fish and farmers, he issues this threat: "I for one am with thee, and who knows what may avail a crow-bar against that Billerica dam?" (p. 37).

It was against slavery, however, that violence seemed most necessary. Outraged by an incident in Boston in which a runaway slave, Anthony Burns (1834–1862), was seized and shipped back to his southern owner, Thoreau issued this call to violent action in his essay "Slavery in Massachusetts" (1854): "I need not say what match I would touch, what system endeavor to blow up,—but as I love my life, I would side with the light" (*Reform Papers,* p. 102). He was also an enthusiastic supporter of John Brown's (1800–1859) raid on Harpers Ferry. In "A Plea for Captain John Brown" (1860), Thoreau explicitly asserts that violence can be justified: "I do not wish to kill nor to be killed, but I can foresee circumstances in which both these things would be by me unavoidable" (*Reform Papers,* p. 133). Of Brown's men he says admiringly, "I think that for once the Sharps' rifles and the revolvers were employed in a righteous cause" (p. 133). Of Brown himself he says: "It was his peculiar doctrine that a man has a perfect right to interfere by force with the slaveholder, in order to rescue the slave. I agree with him" (p. 132).

THOREAU AND RESISTANCE MOVEMENTS

Thoreau's ideas about resistance to social injustice must be seen in the context of his time. One source of his attitude was transcendentalism and Ralph Waldo Emerson's suspicion of society as a "joint-stock company" requiring that every individual sacrifice part of himself or herself for the general good ("Self-Reliance") at the expense of conscience. Emerson's concern about the tyranny of the majority over the individual was one that Thoreau shared.

More specifically, Thoreau imbibed the spirit of the debate that was in the air over how best to respond to injustice. He was not the first Concordian to risk jail by nonpayment of taxes. There were local examples available to him. In January 1843 Thoreau's friend Amos Bronson Alcott had been arrested by Sam Staples for nonpayment of the poll tax. He was held only briefly and not jailed because "Squire" Samuel Hoar (1778–1856), a leading Concord citizen, quickly paid Alcott's tax to save the town's reputation. In December of the same year Alcott's fellow idealist, Charles Lane (1800–1870), was also arrested briefly for nonpayment. Thoreau intended to follow in their footsteps even more emphatically.

There were several theories about "resistance" and "nonresistance" known to Thoreau. The issue of how best to resist injustice was of particular interest to abolitionists, who were split into several groups. One group, led by Nathaniel P. Rogers, argued that an ideal society could be achieved only through self-reformation of each individual, not through collective action. "Resistance" in this context meant self-culture as opposed to conformity to the majority, a view consistent with transcendentalism. In an essay in *The Dial* in 1844 Thoreau explicitly endorsed Rogers's views.

Another group, the New England Non-Resistance Society led by William Lloyd Garrison (1805–1879), endorsed more systematic resistance through antislavery societies. As Lawrence Rosenwald points out, the term "nonresistance" for Garrison meant noncooperation with an unjust government by refusing to pay taxes to, vote for, or hold public office in the offending government. Garrison also advocated a pacifism that condemned both individual and state violence, even for self-defense. Although Thoreau was suspicious of organized societies, even those supporting worthy causes, he found some of Garrison's ideas pertinent to his own situation. He would try passive resistance first, but he would also serve as a conductor on the Underground Railroad.

Frederick Douglass (1818–1895), a former slave and an abolitionist, offered an even more aggressive form of resistance. In his autobiographical *Narrative* (1845), with which Thoreau was probably familiar, Douglass recounts how as a young slave he defied an overseer who was beating him and fought back effectively, after which the overseer no longer dared to beat him. "Resistance" for Douglass thus means individual resistance by returning injury with injury; Thoreau's use of the word in his title points toward this interpretation, but from its first paragraph the essay itself backs off from Douglass's more aggressive stance. It would surface again, however, in Thoreau's defense of John Brown.

Throughout his career Thoreau made use of all of these approaches to reform. If there is a trend, it is his shift from pure self-culture toward more active, even violent, resistance.

LASTING INFLUENCES

These nineteenth-century ideas of resistance to injustice find their way through Thoreau's essay to twentieth-century social reformers. Leo Tolstoy read Thoreau's essay and expressed admiration for Thoreau's idealistic refusal to pay the tax. Although Mohandas Gandhi denied that his strategy of "civil resistance" was derived from Thoreau's essay, he expressed admiration for "Civil Disobedience" and kept Thoreau's ideas about resistance in mind while implementing Garrison's concept of collective passive resistance.

In America, Martin Luther King Jr. listed Thoreau's "Essay on Civil Disobedience" as one of the books that most influenced his thinking. He viewed Thoreau's philosophy as a "spiritual strategy" of nonviolence that provided a valuable supplement to the NAACP's strategies of legal resistance. Thoreau's essay has also inspired environmental activists. The concept of "monkey wrenching" or "eco-sabotage"

proposed by Edward Abbey (1927–1989) in his novel *The Monkey Wrench Gang* (1975) and used by such activist groups as Earth First! borrows from the more aggressive side of Thoreau's ideas of resistance. Thoreau's threat in *A Week* to take a crowbar to the dam on the Merrimack River is one that these groups are quite willing to carry out. Thus Thoreau's essay continues to influence the world in the early twenty-first century. As Edward Abbey says in "Down the River with Henry Thoreau," "wherever there is liberty and danger . . . Henry Thoreau will find his eternal home" (p. 48).

See also Abolitionist Writing; Concord, Massachusetts; Harpers Ferry; Mexican-American War; *Walden*

BIBLIOGRAPHY
Primary Works
Thoreau, Henry David. *Letters to Various Persons.* Edited by Ralph Waldo Emerson. Boston: Ticknor and Fields, 1865.

Thoreau, Henry David. *Reform Papers.* Edited by Wendell Glick. Princeton, N.J.: Princeton University Press, 1973. Includes "Resistance to Civil Government," "Slavery in Massachusetts," and "A Plea for Captain John Brown."

Thoreau, Henry David. *"Walden" and "Resistance to Civil Government."* 1854, 1849. Edited by William Rossi. New York: Norton, 1992.

Thoreau, Henry David. *A Week on the Concord and Merrimac Rivers.* 1849. Princeton, N.J.: Princeton University Press, 1980.

Secondary Works
Abbey, Edward. *Down the River.* New York: E. P. Dutton, 1982.

Buranelli, Vincent. "The Case against Thoreau." *Ethics* 67 (1957): 257–268.

Harding, Walter. *The Days of Henry Thoreau.* 2nd ed. New York: Dover, 1982.

Herr, William. "A More Perfect State: Thoreau's Concept of Civil Government." *Massachusetts Review* 16 (1975): 470–487.

Kritzberg, Barry. "Thoreau, Slavery, and 'Resistance to Civil Government.'" *Massachusetts Review* 30 (1989): 535–565.

Meyer, Michael. "Thoreau, Abolitionists, and Reformers." In *Thoreau among Others: Essays in Honor of Walter Harding,* edited by Rita K. Gollin and James B. Scholes. Geneseo, N.Y.: State University College of Arts and Sciences, 1983.

Oehlschlaeger, Fritz. "Another Look at the Text and Title of Thoreau's 'Civil Disobedience.'" *ESQ: A Journal of the American Renaissance* 36, no. 3 (1990): 239–254.

Rosenwald, Lawrence A. "The Theory, Practice, and Influence of Thoreau's Civil Disobedience." In *A Historical Guide to Henry David Thoreau*, edited by William E. Cain, pp. 153–180. New York: Oxford University Press, 2000.

Van Dusen, Lewis H., Jr. "Civil Disobedience: Destroyer of Democracy." *American Bar Association Journal* 55 (February 1969): 123–126.

Richard J. Schneider

REVOLUTIONS OF 1848

In 1848–1849 European nations rose in revolt against the system of hereditary, anti-nationalist monarchies most closely identified with the Austrian statesman Prince Klemens von Metternich (1773–1859). Beginning in France in February 1848, nationalist-republican revolutions soon challenged regimes in Italy, Austria, and Germany. Although Britain suffered no revolution, it was hardly placid. Parliament had rejected the Chartists' petition in 1842, but the specter of the movement lingered. Chartists sought to eliminate some inequities left unaddressed by the Reform Act of 1832. They demanded universal manhood suffrage, the secret ballot, salaries for Members of Parliament, and other reforms. In 1848 this movement was rejuvenated by events on the Continent and enjoyed a brief, if equally unsuccessful, revival. In fact, every one of these movements failed.

Americans were deeply interested in these developments. Newspapers and magazines reported the latest news from overseas in brash, bold headlines. The rhetoric of nationalist exceptionalism notwithstanding, the United States possessed long-standing connections with the Old World, most closely to Great Britain but also to nations on the Continent. Thus, many Americans felt a personal investment in political and social upheaval overseas. In addition, Americans assumed that their own Revolution of 1776 inspired some of these events. The revolutionary upheavals also transfixed Americans because many of them expected them to fail. They wished for the best but, given the precedents of 1789 and 1830, anticipated that the forces of reaction would triumph. A significant minority of Americans expressed opposition or skepticism from the very beginning. Either because they doubted the ability of European peoples to sustain free governments or because they discerned the influence of socialism or communism, they were wary from the early stages. Responses to the Revolutions of 1848 reveal the existence of a powerful strain of conservatism in American cultural life.

Events of 1848 not only illuminated conservative tendencies in the United States but also deepened them. The reactionary resurgence strengthened mutually reinforcing perceptions of American exceptionalism and European corruption. Because many observers believed that conservative forces had triumphed not over republicans but over socialists or other radicals, these regimes and their methods acquired legitimacy in American eyes they had not heretofore possessed. These sentiments were not universal. In some circles, the events of 1848–1851 strengthened liberal and reformist elements in American society. Margaret Fuller (1810–1850), whose reports of the rise and demise of the 1849 Roman Revolution appeared in the *New-York Daily Tribune*, was radicalized by her experience. The so-called forty-eighters—German exiles who fled to the United States—became articulate advocates of American engagement in support of liberalism abroad. The impact of the Revolutions of 1848 on American culture was therefore complex. In the final analysis, the settlements boosted the credibility of conservative exceptionalists over liberal internationalists.

REVOLUTION AND REACTION: 1848

Since 1845 Europe had suffered an agricultural crisis that impoverished farmers and confronted urban workers with high food prices and unemployment. These conditions made French peasants and workers ripe for revolution, but economic distress did not bring down the July Monarchy. Rather, frustration with the glacial pace of parliamentary reform among liberals precipitated the crisis. Reformers took to holding banquets to protest stagnation and corruption. When François Guizot (1787–1874), the prime minister, abruptly banned a liberal banquet and march scheduled for 22 February in Paris, crowds began setting up barricades. Guizot and King Louis-Philippe (1773–1850) fled for England when units of the National Guard refused to fire on the rebels; on 24 February a provisional government assumed power.

This edifice was creaky from the beginning. It was dominated by moderate republicans led by the poet-statesman Alphonse de Lamartine (1790–1869). To placate radicals, the government set up national workshops to provide out-of-work laborers with employment or, failing that, direct financial support. These workshops became centers of dissent. In June Parisian radicals took once again to the barricades, where troops under General Eugene Cavaignac dispersed them; thousands of soldiers and radicals were killed. This street battle is known as the June Days. Conservative forces, promising order before liberty, were soon ascendant. The Second Republic came to a quick end when Louis-Napoleon Bonaparte, the conqueror's

TIMELINE: REVOLUTIONS OF 1848

1839, 1842: Charters rejected by Parliament.

August 1846: Margaret Fuller arrives in England.

March 1847: Fuller, in Italy, begins her "Things and Thoughts in Europe" series for the *New-York Daily Tribune.*

October 1847: Ralph Waldo Emerson arrives in England.

February 1848: Louis-Philippe abdicates after street demonstrations in Paris. Samuel Goodrich (Peter Parley) and other Americans congratulate the provisional government.

March 1848: Riots in Vienna and Berlin. Metternich falls. Hungary declares separation within Austrian Empire.

April 1848: Constituent Assembly elected in France. Caroline Matilda Kirkland, author of *Holidays Abroad; or, Europe from the West* (1849) sets sail for England.

May 1848: Frankfurt Assembly convenes. Emerson, Kirkland arrive in Paris.

June 1848: Pan-Slavic Assembly meets in Prague; dispersed by Austrian troops commanded by Windischgrätz. Emerson returns to England. Kirkland in Genoa.

24–26 June 1848: June Days: army puts down workers in Paris. Donald Mitchell (Ik Marvel) arrives in Paris to report for James Watson Webb's *New York Courier and Enquirer;* Charles A. Dana arrives to report for Horace Greeley's *New-York Daily Tribune.*

October 1848: Vienna falls to Windischgrätz.

November 1848: Pius IX flees Rome following the assassination of his prime minister, Pellegrino Rossi.

December 1848: Louis-Napoleon Bonaparte elected president of the Second Republic.

April 1849: Frankfurt Assembly offers crown of united Germany to Frederick William IV. He refuses. The Assembly dissolves.

June 1849: French troops storm Rome; republican forces defeated.

August 1849: Hungarians defeated; Lajos Kossuth flees.

October 1849: Herman Melville sails to Europe via England.

April 1850: Pius IX returns to Rome, now under French-Austrian occupation.

July 1850: The *Elizabeth* sinks off Fire Island; Margaret Fuller, her child, and husband drown; her manuscript on the history of the Roman Republic is lost.

December 1851: Louis-Napoleon Bonaparte dissolves Assembly and reinstates universal manhood suffrage. Elected president for ten-year term.

December 1852: Louis-Napoleon dissolves Second Republic; proclaims himself Napoleon III.

---

nephew, declared himself emperor in late 1852 after handily winning the presidency in 1848.

Inspired by news from Paris, revolutionists also challenged the Hapsburgs in Central Europe. Crowds gathered in Vienna's squares when word of Louis-Philippe's abdication reached the city at the end of February. Radical workers demanded a constitution, to which the emperor consented. He also abolished manorial obligations, including forced labor. Despite these moves, the Hapsburg monarchy seemed to be teetering in late March. Developments in the provinces added to this perception. Rebellions in Venice and Milan forced Austrian troops to withdraw from these cities in mid-March. Revolutionary sentiment spread to Rome, driving Pius IX out of the city. In Hungary, a Magyar revolt led by Lajos Kossuth (1802–1894) sought independence from Vienna. Bohemian Czechs pressed for autonomy within the empire. When it became clear that Vienna would not accept even limited reforms, Czech nationalists took control of Prague.

Most of these uprisings were snuffed out nearly as soon as they had begun. A week before Paris's June Days, Field Marshal Alfred Windischgrätz shelled Prague into submission. Three thousand Viennese died when the army cleared the streets, after which Austrian leaders moved swiftly to curb the revolutions in Hungary and Italy. Roman Republicans fought heroically but proved no match for Napoleon's troops. Only Kossuth's Hungarians resisted the Austrian counterrevolution successfully. They declared their independence in April 1849 after forcing Windischgrätz to abandon Budapest. But soon after Tsar Nicholas

(1796–1855), applying Metternich's principles, sent in Russian troops and put an end to Hungarian independence. The Hapsburgs were supreme again.

Germany also was warmed by revolutionary winds, albeit briefly and superficially. In mid-March troops violently dispersed a crowd of demonstrators in Berlin. Word of events in Vienna emboldened Prussian liberals. After violence threatened to break out more generally, Frederick William IV (1795–1861) promised a constitution and invited liberals to form a ministry. But it came to nothing. Frederick William was no constitutional monarch, and few Germans wanted a republic anyway. Their priorities were unification and moderate liberalization. The constituent assembly that soon gathered at Frankfurt offered Frederick William the crown of "smaller Germany" (an empire short of Austria). He refused, declining to limit himself to constitutional rules imposed from his subjects. The Frankfurt Assembly disintegrated in impotence. Germany's springtime, like its counterparts across Europe, was over.

INITIAL REACTION

As in 1789 and 1830 Americans in 1848 responded warmly to news of the demise of the French monarchy. Street celebrations broke out in cities across the country. Newspapers outdid one another in expressing satisfaction with the events in Paris. Diplomats hastened to offer the congratulations of France's twin republic across the sea. Richard Rush (1780–1859), the American minister in Paris, granted diplomatic recognition to the new government. The Senate unanimously passed a resolution introduced by the Ohio Democrat William Allen (1803–1879) offering France the official congratulations of the United States; on 10 April the House overwhelmingly concurred. Intellectuals also lined up to praise the French for their apparently bloodless republican revolution. On a speaking tour of Britain early in 1848, Ralph Waldo Emerson (1803–1882), initially assumed his hosts' skepticism toward the events in France. But the earnestness of Parisian socialists forced him to reconsider. "I have been exaggerating the English merits all winter, & disparaging the French," he wrote in his journal. "Now I am correcting my judgment of both, & the French have risen very fast" (*Journals* 10:312).

It was the same story with the revolutions that followed. Demonstrators lined the streets and squares of American cities, offering speeches and toasts in support of the insurgents in Italy, Austria, and Germany. The press, which had traditionally devoted far more newsprint to foreign than to domestic affairs, became even more engrossed with events across the Atlantic. Profiles of Giuseppe Mazzini (1805–1872), Kossuth,

and other revolutionary leaders appeared on front pages. Diplomats rushed to recognize republican governments, sometimes with more enthusiasm than discretion. A minor diplomatic row ensued when word leaked out that an American diplomat had been sent to Hungary in hopes of recognizing a new republic. Writers and intellectuals stood in awe of the revolutionary wave that had swept through Europe. They were delighted to witness the downfall of monarchies and the realization of national aspirations by hitherto oppressed minorities and rejoiced in the enhanced status of the United States, whose own revolution they assumed had inspired the events of 1848.

From the beginning, however, critical voices marred this apparent consensus. France was the most common target of these skeptics. History justified circumspection, critics explained; the precedents of 1789 and 1830 did not auger well for the prospects of French republicanism, or even for peaceful, orderly change of any kind. Some critics of democracy—Herman Melville (1819–1891) and his Knickerbocker friends were prominent among these—idealized the culture of monarchial France and were loath to see it toppled by the mob. Overall, conservatives had little faith in the prospects for change inaugurated by revolutionary violence, particularly when history seemed to indicate that events would inevitably spin out of the control of moderates. Whig organs, such as the *North American Review* and *National Intelligencer,* made this argument most forcefully. Congratulating France was premature, they maintained, until the revolution had run its course.

Some antislavery activists made much of the provisional French government's abolition of slavery in its colonies and pointed up the hypocrisy of the slaveholding United States congratulating Europeans for achieving freedom. A few southerners stressed the dangers for the South in praising revolutionary change against constituted authority. But sectionalism was not a strong determinant of support for or opposition to the European Revolutions of 1848. When Kossuth toured the United States in 1851–1852, he alienated both apologists for slavery and antislavery activists. The former objected to his association with dubious "isms," and the latter recoiled from his refusal to endorse abolition. Southern voices, including that of Jefferson Davis (1808–1889), the future president of the Confederate States of America, were prominent in support of the Allen resolution in early 1848. Many northerners, from George Ticknor (1789–1871) to Daniel Webster (1782–1852), expressed caution or skepticism toward the prospects for liberalization in Europe. Such views were far more strongly rooted in ideology than sectional identity.

Reception of General Louis Kossuth at New York City, December 6, 1851. Painting by E. Percel. Lajos (Louis) Kossuth, leader of a short-lived Hungarian rebellion in 1848, arrived in the United States in 1851 for a triumphal tour that would raise money for the cause of Hungarian independence. Here Kossuth is shown in a beaver hat and riding a white horse in the parade that followed his landing at the Battery. In addition to the parade depicted here, Kossuth was welcomed to New York with a monumental torchlight parade, a municipal dinner, banquets, and rounds of receptions.
© MUSEUM OF THE CITY OF NEW YORK/CORBIS

Prejudices against French national character fed American skepticism toward its mid-century revolution. The French were widely believed to be dissipated, undisciplined, perfidious, and volatile, all qualities that were inconsistent with republican institutions. Ticknor, John C. Calhoun (1782–1850), and George Kendall (1809–1867), the European correspondent of the *New Orleans Daily Picayune,* were just a few of the prominent voices who doubted whether the people of France were capable of governing themselves. By mid-century, these convictions were informed by emerging concepts of scientific racism. Group features that had been attributed to environment and history began to be seen as hereditary, innate, and unchangeable. These concepts influenced American perceptions of revolutions in Austria and on the Italian peninsula. Nathaniel Niles (1741–

1828), the American minister at Turin, felt that prospects for republicanism in Italy were doomed because the "Italian character is so thoroughly imbued with intolerance and sentiments of hatred personal and political . . . as to forbid the establishment of any form of government founded on mutual concession and a partial surrender of rights and interests for the common good" (quoted in Noether, p. 383).

CYNICISM

Throughout 1848 these notions were clearly in the minority. As republicanism in France gave way to socialism and dictatorship the tide of public opinion began to turn decisively. The reactionary resurgence of 1849–1852 lent credibility to early critics of the revolution. The June Days in Paris fed American disillusionment. In *Mardi* (1849) Melville articulated his conviction that France's mob violence and conservative reaction were attributable to a misplaced faith in popular government. An anonymous scroll admonishes the people of Vivenza (the United States), "Better be secure under one king, than exposed to violence from twenty millions of monarchs, though oneself be of the number" (p. 529). Donald Mitchell's reports for the *New York Courier and Enquirer* stressed the cruelty and socialist ideology of the rioters. His portrayal proved to be more influential than reports such as those submitted by Charles A. Dana (1819–1897), whose sympathies for the rioters clashed with deep cultural prejudices against French violence and socialism. Others who had given the revolution their support reconsidered. Mob violence horrified Emerson, who was more sympathetic to the idea of mankind than he was to flesh-and-blood men (particularly in groups). He soon took to denouncing "Red Revolution" in his public lectures.

Americans also reevaluated their support for republicanism outside France when the conservative resurgence waxed. When the Frankfurt Assembly failed to unite Germany under a constitutional monarchy, Americans blamed the German people for their unfitness for American-style democracy. Even the Hungarian Revolution, by far the most popular of the 1848 uprisings in American public opinion, lost its luster in time. Large, supportive crowds greeted Kossuth in the initial months of his American tour. However, not only did he fail to garner any kind of concrete support for the Hungarian cause, but the excitement turned to apathy. On 12 July 1852 the penniless freedom fighter and his wife crept aboard a Cunard liner under assumed names and sailed for England (Morrison, p. 131).

By that time, the lessons of the failed Revolutions of 1848 seemed clear. Although they continued to celebrate their own war of independence Americans began to doubt the propriety of revolutionary change. Abolitionism, fire-eating proslavery expansionism, women's rights, and other "reforms" all seemed to threaten the stability of the union and social order itself. Revolutions seemed more likely to end in reaction than progress, more prone to produce violent disruption than liberalization. Americans put the Revolutions of 1848 into the broader context of domestic "revolutions" that placed the republican experiment itself at risk. No wonder they found them wanting.

Although over the long term the Revolutions of 1848 strengthened the credibility of conservatives in the United States, there were countervailing trends. Some observers kept faith in the righteousness of the revolutions and in the future of republicanism in the Old World. Margaret Fuller's experience reporting on the revolution in Rome and its subsequent defeat at the hands of the French not only produced the most passionate writing of her career but also deepened her commitment to radical causes. Tragically, she drowned with her husband and infant child when their boat sank within sight of Fire Island, New York, in 1850. Theodore Dwight (1796–1866), a New York editor, carried on Fuller's advocacy of Italian republicanism in *The Roman Republic of 1849* (1851), which challenged American cynicism toward Italian liberalism. Italians were both devoted liberals and genuine Protestants, Dwight maintained. Jesuitical intrigues and cultural prejudices conspired to keep Americans ignorant of these facts. Although Dwight's portrayal was condescending in its own way—he rehabilitated Italians by turning them into Americans—his faith in the ultimate redemption of the peninsula was a refreshing counterpoint to the quasi-racist disparagement assumed by most observers after the French and Austrians emerged victorious.

Some German republicans and radicals escaping failed revolutions in Central Europe did reach American shores. They exercised a liberalizing influence on American politics and culture for much of the nineteenth century. Though only a small fraction of German migrants during the late 1840s and 1850s were truly forty-eighters—those who left to escape prison for their revolutionary activities—enough radicals did enter the United States to provide leadership in German communities. They were a heterogeneous group, containing a few genuine Marxists and many more moderate republicans. Many, for obvious reasons, declined to engage in activism in their new home. Others were particularly active in journalism and politics, where they used their influence to urge their adopted country to use its moral authority to advance liberal causes abroad. These activists gravitated to the new Republican Party in the late 1850s. Carl Schurz, Friedrich Hecker, Franz Sigel, and others attained influential positions. Some earned high rank in the Union Army. Although their influence was deep and lasting, it was not powerful enough to counteract the general impact of the European Revolutions of 1848, which enhanced the credibility of advocates for American exceptionalism, deepened mistrust of Europe, and undermined the forces of radical reform and engagement with the world beyond America's borders.

See also Immigration; Reform

BIBLIOGRAPHY

Primary Works

Dwight, Theodore. *The Roman Republic of 1849, with Accounts of the Inquisition, and the Siege of Rome.* New York: R. Van Dien, 1851.

Emerson, Ralph Waldo. *Journals and Miscellaneous Notebooks.* 12 vols. Edited by William H. Gilman et al. Cambridge, Mass.: Belknap Press of Harvard University Press, 1960–1982.

Fuller, Margaret. *At Home and Abroad, or Things and Thoughts in America and Europe.* Edited by Arthur B. Fuller. Boston: Crosby, Nichols, 1856.

Marvel, Ik [Donald Mitchell]. *The Battle Summer: Being Transcripts from Personal Observation in Paris, during the Year 1848.* New York: Baker and Scribner, 1850.

Melville, Herman. *Mardi, and a Voyage Thither.* 1849. Edited by Harrison Hayford, Hershel Parker, and G. Thomas Tanselle. Evanston, Ill.: Northwestern University Press, 1998.

Secondary Works

Curti, Merle. "The Impact of the Revolutions of 1848 on American Thought." *Proceedings of the American Philosophical Society* 93, no. 3 (1949): 209–215.

Curtis, Eugene N. "American Opinion of the French Nineteenth-Century Revolutions." *American Historical Review* 29, no. 2 (1924): 249–270.

Davis, David Brion. *Revolutions: Reflections on American Equality and Foreign Liberations.* Cambridge, Mass.: Harvard University Press, 1990.

Gemme, Paola. "Domesticating Foreign Struggles: American Narratives of Italian Revolutions and the Debate on Slavery in the Antebellum Era." *Prospects* 27 (2002): 77–101.

Horgan, John C. "The South and the European Revolutions of 1848." *Consortium on Revolutionary Europe 1750–1850: Proceedings* (1992): 604–625.

Morrison, Michael A. "American Reaction to European Revolutions, 1848–1852: Sectionalism, Memory, and the Revolutionary Heritage." *Civil War History* 49, no. 2 (2003): 111–132.

Noether, Emiliana P. "The American Response to the 1848 Revolutions in Rome and Budapest." *Consortium on Revolutionary Europe 1750–1850: Proceedings* 15 (1985): 379–397.

Reynolds, Larry J. *European Revolutions and the American Literary Renaissance.* New Haven, Conn.: Yale University Press, 1988.

Rohrs, Richard C. "American Critics of the French Revolution of 1848." *Journal of the Early Republic* 14, no. 3 (1994): 359–377.

Vance, William L. *America's Rome.* Vol. 2, *Catholic and Contemporary Rome.* New Haven, Conn.: Yale University Press, 1989.

Zucker, A. E., ed. *The Forty-Eighters: Political Refugees of the German Revolution of 1848.* New York: Russell and Russell, 1950.

Daniel Kilbride

RHETORIC

It is widely acknowledged that during the nineteenth century the academic discipline of rhetoric enjoyed undisputed preeminence in the curriculum of both secondary and college education in the United States. It is also widely acknowledged that this is the last time it exerted such influence. Subsumed by the development of writing instruction within English courses and the growth of speech departments in the early twentieth century, rhetoric lost its integrated status during the increasing departmentalization and professionalization of the academy.

One explanation for its abrupt reversal of fortune is that rhetoric, understood as a formal university discipline rather than a field of discursive practices, shifted its emphasis from the study of persuasion to the appreciation of literary taste and fine writing. This aesthetic departure from the speakerly orientation of Greek and Roman authorities such as Aristotle, Cicero, and Quintilian is sometimes called the "New Rhetoric." New Rhetoric is associated with the literary approach of the British clergymen Hugh Blair, George Campbell, and Richard Whately and their many American adherents, such as Edward T. Channing, Adams Sherman Hill, and John Franklin Genung. Despite the practical aspects of this modification, many later American rhetoricians feel that it augmented the most superficial aspects of the discipline—the study of the ornamentation of discourse, rather than the study of its sinews and bones. For example, questions of style (word choice, diction, organization) began to eclipse a classical emphasis on the choice of the best kind of argument to use in a given situation (whether to argue from causes, effects, or different types of appeals to human emotions). This transformation had its origins in the English rhetoric texts that dominated American classrooms during the early nineteenth century, but it grew in a specifically American climate of widespread literacy, class mobility, and professional expertise. Rhetoric, which once advertised itself as the art of persuasion, or, more grandly, the master discipline for the study of all discourse, became the utilitarian study of expressive protocols that make people appear educated.

HUGH BLAIR'S RHETORIC

By most accounts, one of the primary engineers of this transformation was Hugh Blair (1718–1800), whose 1783 *Lectures on Rhetoric and Belles Lettres* influenced American education for more than one hundred years.

Blair was a member of the Scottish common sense school of professors who developed an integrated worldview of the empirical and hermeneutic sciences, humanities, and theology (Charvat). Rather than its modern meaning of *practical*, the philosophical term "common sense" derives from Thomas Reid (1710–1796), who argued that there were impressions, such as a feeling of *reality*, or a sense of *time*, that were common to all human beings. This view tended to ground the principles of rhetorical appeal on assumptions about the shared elements of human experience. Blair was a celebrated Presbyterian minister to a wealthy congregation prior to his formal appointment at Edinburgh, and his rhetoric, theology, and political thought were united by a genteel aesthetics.

Blair's text seems fairly unremarkable today. That is a testament to how thoroughly his approach to rhetoric became assimilated by American culture. Whereas most studies of rhetoric had previously focused on persuasive oratory, Blair gave equal attention to the importance of fine writing. Almost a quarter of Blair's lectures focus on the arts of written composition. They include discussions of cultured British writers for emulation, such as Joseph Addison (1672–1719). Blair eschewed theorizing about the broader dimensions of epideictic (ceremonial) and deliberative (legal and political) oratory, showing a more professional concern for shaping the modern arenas of pulpit eloquence, addresses to public assemblies, and legal arguments. Blair had virtually no interest in *inventio* (the processes of choosing one's argument), suggesting that appropriate arguments occur automatically to most writers and speakers. Although the place of *inventio* in rhetoric had been under attack since the French logician Petrus Ramus's works of the mid-1500s—Ramus asserted that it was part of dialectic or logic, not rhetoric—Blair's orientation further contributed to its exile.

The cumulative effects of Blair's modest departures from the classical tradition were to normalize middle-class standards of taste. Gone was a concern for listing the various techniques with which the elite orator could mold the opinions of different kinds of audiences. In its stead grew advice about how a middle-class professional could influence a middle-class audience through written prose. Blair's text was taught at Williams and Yale as late as 1860, and the text itself went through many later printings (Guthrie 15:62–63). Beyond its direct use, however, it was greatly influential on a variety of later American texts, such as George Quackenbos's *Advanced Course of Composition and Rhetoric* (1855), M. B. Hope's *Princeton Text-Book in Rhetoric* (1859), John Hart's *Manual of Composition and Rhetoric* (1870), or John Genung's *Working Principles of Rhetoric* (1900). As many scholars of rhetoric and public address have noted, Blair's influence is apparent in most college composition texts to the current day.

GEORGE CAMPBELL'S RHETORIC

A second British text that exerted an astonishing long-term influence was George Campbell's (1719–1796) *Philosophy of Rhetoric* (1776). Widely republished during the nineteenth century and used as an upper-level course text at many American universities through 1860, Campbell's book was a landmark attempt to theorize the physiological appeal of successful rhetoric on the human mind. It was drawn from the theories of associational psychology initially proposed by John Locke, David Hume, and David Hartley. Agreeing with Locke that the events of the world somehow made impressions on the human mind, Hartley suggested that our feelings and thoughts were connected to vibrations in our nervous system. For example, the feeling evoked by the word "boom" becomes associated with the feeling produced by a thunderclap. Similarly, our sensations, ideas, and feelings about explosive themes are connected by their associations with each other, organized by such principles as resemblance, contiguity, and causation.

Campbell applied these physiological and philosophical hypotheses to the way rhetoric works. For example, he argued that concrete words generated more intense physiological sensations and associations than abstract words (memories, imagined ideas). At the heart of Campbell's project was a term he borrowed from Hume: "vivacity." Campbell asserts that the vivacity of ideas is the quality primarily responsible for attention and belief. If mental operations were a mixture of immediately powerful sensations, the fading impressions of memory, and the fleeting dreams of the imagination, a strong writer or speaker will connect abstract ideas with the vivacity of immediate sensations. The third part of Campbell's text offers very specific advice about how to achieve vivacity through the choice, number, and arrangement of words.

Although Campbell's rhetorical advice was based on psychology that has been long drawn into question, his study treated his subject at an interdisciplinary level rarely achieved in rhetoric texts. His lucid and practical discussions about how to achieve vivacity and perspicacity (clarity) were copied nearly verbatim by later British and American rhetoric manuals for a hundred years. Unfortunately, his compelling rehabilitation of the study of passions as a worthwhile—if not preeminent—concern of rhetoric was lost in the late nineteenth century's growing pedagogical agenda for technical correctness, standardized word usage, and belletrism. However, Campbell's subtle vision of the mind as feelings-in-movement had great effect on American thinkers ranging from Ralph Waldo Emerson (1803–1882) to William James (1842–1910) (Berlin, pp. 42–57). Campbell's powerful influence appears as late as 1890, when William James approvingly quoted Campbell's account of how words acquire associations in the famous "Stream of Thought" chapter of James's *Principles of Psychology*.

RICHARD WHATELY'S RHETORIC

The third major New Rhetoric text to shape American thought during the nineteenth century was the English theologian Richard Whately's (1787–1863) *Elements of Rhetoric* (1828). Even though Whately's text is primarily an ecclesiastical debater's manual, he imagines that many of these debates will be carried out in journals, pamphlets, and articles. He begins his text by recommending habits of daily composition on familiar topics to develop students' minds. Unlike Blair, Whately discusses *inventio* in depth, and he also gives concise and lively advice on debating tactics, the interrogation of witnesses, and defense and offense strategies. Even today, one of the great appeals of his text is its frank instruction on the proper use of underhanded rhetorical techniques, such as circumlocution and fallacy. Despite Whately's obvious enthusiasm for rhetorical combat, the overall tone of his text, like Blair's, focuses much more on developing techniques of conviction, rather than persuasion. He insists that proper management of one's *ethos* (basically, the *character* of a speaker or writer) is more effective than firing volleys of persuasive tricks. Like Blair, Whately repeatedly recommends a "natural" style, free of affectation and laxity.

THE BOYLSTON PROFESSORS AND THE SHIFT TO TASTE

The influence of these texts in American colleges prior to the Civil War is well illustrated by the changes in Harvard's chair, the Boylston Professorship of Rhetoric and Oratory. Over the course of the nineteenth century, the successive holders of the position demonstrate a clear shift from classical theory to New Rhetoric, culminating in an emphasis on word choice, style, and poetic diction in writing. The first two Boylston Professors were John Quincy Adams (1767–1848), whose term lasted from 1806 to 1809, and the Reverend Joseph McKean

(1776–1818), who served from 1809 to 1818. As his collected *Lectures* indicate, Adams's work in rhetoric was based primarily in Aristotle, Cicero, and Quintilian, with the public persuasion of men as their primary object. Although McKean did not publish his addresses to the students, Dorothy Anderson and Waldo Braden report that McKean followed very closely to the professorship's job description, giving lectures on the rise and progress of oratory; sketches of famous orators; analysis of the functions and departments of the five-part oration; and application of the theories of the ancients to pulpit oratory.

The first chair to move away from classical practices was Edward T. Channing (1790–1856), Boylston Professor from 1819 to 1851. Assessing Channing's general influence on New England letters, the Harvard historian Samuel Eliot Morison wrote that "Channing and Edward Everett may be said to have created the classic New England diction—the measured, dignified speech, careful enunciation, precise choice of words, and well modulated voice that (for men of my age at least) will ever be associated with President [Charles] Eliot" (p. 216). Channing taught Emerson, Henry David Thoreau, Richard Henry Dana Jr., Oliver Wendell Holmes, James Russell Lowell, and Thomas Wentworth Higginson, to name only a few luminaries of American letters. Channing's *Lectures* were published in 1856 but they reflect addresses he made as early as 1819. Channing was a Unitarian like his brother, William Ellery Channing, and his recommendations are characterized by sobriety, reasonableness, and faith in the perfectibility of humankind. He felt that stable government and the growing diffusion of education were tending to make public discourse more temperate and egalitarian. Discussing the difference between modern and ancient oratory, Channing declared: "A modern debate is not a contest between a few leading men for a triumph over each other and an ignorant multitude; the orator himself is but one of the multitude, deliberating with them upon common interests, which are well understood and valued by all" (p. 17). Channing was mildly progressive as an educator and refrained from giving students too many exact rules that might make them awkward. Like Blair and Whately, he preferred that they should develop their own natural language of expression and learn to be versatile and sensitive to changing contexts.

Channing was primarily interested in developing students' taste as writers. Every two weeks, students wrote on topics such as "some of the causes of false judgment as to merit in the works of Literature and the Arts," "the reasons why criticism of recent works is to be distrusted," or "the English poets as advocates of Liberty" (Anderson and Braden, pp. xlvii–xlviii).

Afterward, he would meet his students for discussion in his office alone and in groups. He could be very sarcastic in his comments. Studying some of Channing's student papers held in the Harvard archives, Anderson and Braden note that Channing's written comments show a preference for "precision" and "graceful ornamentation and amplification without superfluity" (p. xl). As the number of students rose after 1845, Channing was forced to reduce the number of compositions they wrote to one a month. This reduction portended greater problems to come. By the end of the century, as rhetoric became more and more associated with writing, acute increases in college enrollment and overcrowded classes prompted the hiring of large number of lower-level writing instructors.

Although Channing was charged with supervising student declamation (in 1828 freshmen declaimed seven times a year; juniors and seniors four times a year) he seemed to have little interest in coaching oratory. After complaints about the quality of student speech, the university hired the elocutionist Jonathan Barber (1784–1864) from 1829 to 1835. Greatly influenced by Gilbert Austin's *Chironomia* (1806), which taught body language with elaborate drawings, Barber made his students practice declamation in a bamboo cage to learn the proper limits of gesture. Predictably, the students rebelled bitterly against his methods. After Barber's departure, the new assistant teachers used Ebenezer Porter's *Analysis of the Principles of Rhetorical Delivery* (1827), but complaints about the quality of student declamation were perennial until the elocution requirement was dropped in the 1870s.

After thirty years of teaching Edward Channing was succeeded in 1851 by a former student, Francis James Child (1825–1896), who had even stronger literary interests. Previously, literary authors had been read strictly as an extracurricular activity. Upon taking the Boylston chair, Child changed the title of his lectures to seniors from "Rhetoric and Criticism" to "English Language and Literature." Child aggressively pursued these interests in his own research, writing on Spenser and Chaucer and gathering source materials for his monumental *English and Scottish Popular Ballads* (1882–1898).

Child's hiring also reflected a larger movement at Harvard away from the study of Latin and Greek authors. As Albert Kitzhaber reports, when Charles Eliot (1834–1926) was inaugurated president of Harvard in 1869, he announced his intention to make the study of English a central part of the curriculum. Eliot augmented the system of entrance examinations in English (instituted just prior to his presidency) so that by 1874 students had to write an entrance composition based on an analysis of a Shakespeare play or a novel by Goldsmith or Scott.

FROM TASTE TO COMPOSITION

Because Child was absorbed in his ballad research, in 1872 Eliot hired Adams Sherman Hill (1833–1910) as an assistant professor of rhetoric. By 1876 Hill was given the Boylston chair. Although Hill was known to be ruthless in his comments on student papers (which seems to have been a tradition at nineteenth-century Harvard), his great achievement was the institution of a freshman year required writing course in 1885. He wrote the *Principles of Rhetoric, and Their Application* in 1878, enlarged in 1895. These texts, and Hill's *The Foundations of Rhetoric* (1892), modernize the advice of the Scottish rhetoricians, but more important Hill's texts show how thoroughly *rhetoric* had become *composition*. Hill's *Foundations*, three hundred pages divided into equal sections on word use, sentence construction, and paragraphing, indicates an almost desperate hope that students' advanced writing skills might be improved if they could only master the most basic parts of speech.

Hill was also an advocate of a genre-based approach to composition instruction that stressed four or five "forms" of discourse: description, narration, exposition, argumentation, and (in some authors) persuasion. The widespread acceptance of these genres as the basic templates for student writing cannot be overstated—many rhetoric texts of the late nineteenth century devote half their pages to them. This influence has continued through the twenty-first century in texts like *The Macmillan Writer*, which teach them as "modes."

The last Boylston chair of the nineteenth century was Barrett Wendell (1855–1921). Wendell took his post at the end of the age of the "theme," which had embittered several generations of faculty before him. Kitzhaber notes with humor that faculty would assign compositions on abstract topics like "Honesty," "the Evanescence of Pleasure," or "the Dice of the Gods Are Loaded" and then find themselves discouraged that the students could muster little of sense on these themes (pp. 104–105). Predictably, many faculty became bad-tempered and developed a sarcastic wit that students rarely appreciated. Wendell was known to tell students they had written "disgusting slop" (p. 66). There were alternative voices in composition-rhetoric studies that argued that students should write from personal experience or research, such as Alphonso Newcomer's *Practical Course in English Composition* (1893), Fred Newton Scott and Joseph Villiers Denney's *Composition-Rhetoric* (1897), and

Abraham Henry Espenshade's *The Essentials of Composition and Rhetoric* (1904), but there was consensus that students could not somehow visualize the simple goal of making meaning.

Wendell's 1891 *English Composition* was an attempt to try something new. Convinced that the terminology of the New Rhetoric was too technical for a modern student, Wendell sought to simplify the business of writing by applying a three-part heuristic of "unity," "mass," and "coherence" to composition. In the introductory chapter of his textbook, Wendell asserted that "every composition should group itself about one central idea" (unity); "the chief parts of every composition should be so placed as to readily catch the eye" (mass); and "the relation of each part of a composition to its neighbors should be unmistakable" (coherence) (pp. i, 28–29). "Mass," a curious term, was later redefined by other composition writers as emphasis. The discourse of "unity" and "coherence" as terms for paragraph creation had significant precedent in Alexander Bain's (1818–1903) *English Composition and Rhetoric* (1866), but Wendell sought to apply it at every level of composition: sentence, paragraph, and essay. Wendell's scheme was an admirable attempt to simplify the dizzying scope of rhetorical instructions from earlier eras. Its minimalist philosophy, however, pointed in the direction of William Strunk Jr. and E. B. White's famous seventy-one–page *Elements of Style* (1918; 1959), which can hardly be called a "rhetoric" text in the old sense of the term.

Although the study of integrated theories of rhetoric had been all but abandoned in classrooms by the twentieth century, rhetoric's practical transformations did not bring the immediate end of civilized discourse. In fact, the stultifying protocols for composition that evolved out of rhetoric during the nineteenth century were a response to astonishing democratic upheaval and competing professional interests. For example, in his study of literature and legal discourse, Robert Ferguson notes that the authority of a unified moral principle in law began to give way to a plurality of technical rights over the course of the century. Similarly, Kenneth Cmiel has argued that the nineteenth century is significant for its proliferation of "middling" rhetorical styles and lack of a single persuasive mode. The diversity of social and professional contexts in which people make meaning brought with it a multiplication of different discourses and audiences, such as the rhetoric of the economist, the lawyer, the parent, the psychoanalyst, and the farmer. In some ways, the sense of crisis many rhetoric faculty experienced in the late nineteenth century was legitimate: students did not intuitively know what to write, or for whom, or what truly counted as authority. In a larger sense, however, their teachers may have begun to feel a similar anxiety.

See also Classical Literature; Colleges; Curricula; Education; English Literature; Literary Criticism; Oratory; Philosophy; Psychology

BIBLIOGRAPHY

Primary Works

Adams, John Quincy. *Lectures on Rhetoric and Oratory Delivered to the Classes of Senior and Junior Sophisters in Harvard University.* Cambridge, Mass.: Hilliard and Metcalf, 1810.

Austin, Gilbert. *Chironomia; or, A Treatise on Rhetorical Delivery.* 1806. Edited by Mary Margaret Robb and Lester Thonssen. Carbondale: Southern Illinois University Press, 1966.

Bain, Alexander. *English Composition and Rhetoric: A Manual.* New York: American Book Co., 1866.

Blair, Hugh. *Lectures on Rhetoric and Belles Lettres.* 1783. Edited by Harold F. Harding. Carbondale: Southern Illinois University Press, 1965.

Campbell, George. *The Philosophy of Rhetoric.* 1776. Edited by Lloyd F. Bitzer. Carbondale: Southern Illinois University Press, 1963.

Channing, Edward Tyrrel. *Lectures Read to the Seniors in Harvard College.* 1856. Edited by Dorothy I. Anderson and Waldo W. Braden. Carbondale: Southern Illinois University Press, 1968.

Espenshade, Abraham Howry. *The Essentials of Composition and Rhetoric.* Boston: D. C. Heath, 1904.

Genung, John. *The Working Principles of Rhetoric.* Boston: Ginn and Co., 1900.

Hart, John S. *A Manual of Composition and Rhetoric: A Text-Book for Schools and Colleges.* Philadelphia: Eldredge and Brother, 1870.

Hill, Adams Sherman. *The Foundations of Rhetoric.* New York: Harper & Brothers, 1892.

Hill, Adams Sherman. *The Principles of Rhetoric, and Their Application.* New York: Harper & Brothers, 1878.

Hope, M. B. *The Princeton Text-Book in Rhetoric.* Princeton, N.J.: John T. Robinson, 1859.

The MacMillan Writer: Rhetoric, Reader, Handbook. 5th ed. Edited by Judith Nadell, Linda McMeniman, and John Langan. New York: Macmillan, 1997.

Newcomer, Alphonso G. *A Practical Course in English Composition.* Boston: Ginn and Co., 1893.

Porter, Ebenezer. *Analysis of the Principles of Rhetorical Delivery As Applied in Reading and Speaking.* Andover, Mass., and New York: M. Newman, J. Levitt, 1827.

Quackenbos, George Payn. *Advanced Course of Composition and Rhetoric.* New York: D. Appleton, 1855.

Scott, Fred Newton, and Joseph Villiers Denney. *Composition-Rhetoric, Designed for Use in Secondary Schools*. Boston: Allyn and Bacon, 1897.

Strunk, William Jr. *The Elements of Style*. 1918. With revisions, an introduction, and a new chapter on writing by E. B. White. Ithaca, N.Y.: Thrift Press, 1958.

Wendell, Barrett. *English Composition*. New York: Scribners, 1891.

Whately, Richard. *Elements of Rhetoric*. 1828. Edited by Douglas Ehninger. Carbondale: Southern Illinois University Press, 1963.

Secondary Works

Anderson, Dorothy I., and Waldo W. Braden. Introduction to *Lectures Read to the Seniors in Harvard College* by Edward Tyrrel Channing, pp. i–lii. Carbondale: University of Southern Illinois University Press, 1968.

Berlin, James. *Writing Instruction in Nineteenth-Century Colleges*. Carbondale: Southern Illinois University Press, 1984.

Charvat, William. *The Origins of American Critical Thought, 1810–1835*. 1936. New York: Russell and Russell, 1961.

Clark, Gregory, and S. Michael Halloran, eds. *Oratorical Culture in Nineteenth-Century America: Transformations in the Theory and Practice of Rhetoric*. Carbondale: Southern Illinois University Press, 1993.

Cmiel, Kenneth. *Democratic Eloquence: The Fight over Popular Speech in Nineteenth-Century America*. New York: W. Morrow, 1990.

Dimock, Wai Chee. *Residues of Justice: Literature, Law, Philosophy*. Berkeley: University of California Press, 1996.

Ferguson, Robert. *Law and Letters in American Culture*. Cambridge, Mass.: Harvard University Press, 1984.

Guthrie, Warren. "The Development of Rhetorical Theory in America, 1635–1850." *Speech Monographs* 13 (1946): 14–22; 14 (1947): 38–54; 15 (1948): 61–71; 16 (1949): 98–113; 18 (1951): 17–30.

Johnson, Nan. *Nineteenth-Century Rhetoric in North America*. Carbondale: Southern Illinois University Press, 1991.

Kitzhaber, Albert R. *Rhetoric in American Colleges, 1850–1900*. 1953. Dallas, Tex.: Southern Methodist University Press, 1990.

Morison, Samuel Eliot. *Three Centuries of Harvard, 1636–1936*. Cambridge, Mass.: Harvard University Press, 1936.

Granville Ganter

"RIP VAN WINKLE"

Appearing in *The Sketch Book* (1819–1820), Washington Irving's "Rip Van Winkle" became an immediate American classic and retains that position in the American canon today. Indeed, the central character, Rip, has attained iconic status in both popular culture and with academic critics. One reason for the story's popularity is the sheer humor of Rip's predicament: henpecked by a shrewish wife, he sleeps for twenty years and awakens after the American Revolution has radically changed the sleepy Dutch village where he had previously lived. Generations of readers have enjoyed the ways in which Rip slyly escapes Dame Van Winkle's authority and have laughed at his confusion as he walks into the same village twenty years later and finds himself in the new republic, accused of being a Tory spy—a British sympathizer who had opposed America's independence. Critics have focused on the story's theme of change, in which the contrast between the peaceful pre-Revolutionary colony and the bustling post-Revolutionary America reinforces a simultaneous sense of nostalgia for a simpler time as well as a sense of the reality of our always-shifting American world. Almost everyone, however, recognizes that the American Revolution is somehow central to the story's meaning. Indeed, the secret subject of "Rip Van Winkle" is the significance of the American Revolution vis-à-vis the new democratic nation that came into being in its aftermath. The story records Irving's own ambivalence as both an admirer and a critic of the new republican government the Revolution had wrought.

TEXTS AND CONTEXTS

To understand this ambivalence and its significance in the story, it is necessary to recover a series of contexts that impinge on the story's meaning. First, there is the biographical context of Washington Irving, who had moved to Liverpool in 1815 to look after the interests of his brother's soon-to-be bankrupt firm and who subsequently achieved literary prominence with the publication of *The Sketch Book*. Here at last, English critics proclaimed, was the first American who seemed to be worthy of literary recognition, an American who wrote like a cultured Englishman. The American public, gratified to have one of its own acknowledged by English critics who usually sneered at anything American, also hailed Irving's accomplishment. But not all of his compatriots were pleased, for Irving was identified as a sympathizer of the Federalists—the conservative American party of John Adams and others opposed to the Democratic-Republican Party of Thomas Jefferson. With Jefferson's election, Republicans like the poet Philip Freneau despised Irving and accused him of preferring to live abroad among aristocrats in a country that had just attempted to deprive Americans of their freedom. Irving was self-conscious that some were accusing him of not being American enough, and the American stories in *The Sketch Book*, such as the "The Legend of Sleepy Hollow," were his attempt to highlight his American identity as a way of making his return to the United States easier.

This most American of stories, "Rip Van Winkle" derives from a foreign source, specifically a German folklore story, "Peter Klaus," which Irving borrowed and subsequently Americanized. But Irving makes many substantive changes, lengthening the tale and adding a variety of cultural and political themes that constitute the true source of its originality. In addition, Irving incorporated a variety of texts and contexts into the plot, including two previous works that he had published: *Salmagundi* (1807–1808) and *The History of New York* (1809). *Salmagundi* and the *History* reveal Irving's hostility to both popular democracy and the French Revolution, which in the American mind started in 1789 and continued into the Napoleonic invasions and aftermath (1799–1815), finally subsiding after convulsing Europe for over two decades. To many Americans, the French Revolution represented the forces of a chaotic and bloody mob democracy. The *History* additionally includes almost all the names appearing in "Rip Van Winkle" as well as Irving's well-known hostility to New England Yankees, who are characterized as aggressive Puritan usurpers and interlopers who "invade" peaceful Dutch New York and who prefigure the appropriation of the American Revolution and hence America by their descendants—a ruthless demagogic people that Irving believed were imposing a republican tyranny on the rest of the country.

THE POSITIVE AMERICAN REVOLUTION

Despite Irving's criticisms, he was a patriot and admirer of both the Revolution and his country, but he had serious questions about their democratic excesses. He was interested in the Revolution throughout his life and had collected many books on the subject. On its primary level, "Rip Van Winkle" is a public celebration of the American Revolution. The story opens with the prefigurative imagery of family breakups, specifically the Kaatskill (Catskill) Mountains that "are a dismembered

---

The first quotation, from the American poet Philip Freneau (1752–1832), illustrates the hostility toward Irving by American republicans; the second shows Irving's self-consciousness about having lived abroad in England as he was writing The Sketch Book (1819–1820); *and the third, from Irving's* The History of New York (1809), *demonstrates the nexus Irving established between the American and French Revolutions.*

"To a New England Poet"
See Irving gone to Britain's court
To people of another sort,
He will return, with wealth and fame,
While Yankees hardly know your name.
Lo! he has kissed a Monarch's—hand!
Before a prince I see him stand,
And with the glittering nobles mix,
Forgetting times of seventy-six [the American
    Revolution of 1776].

> *(Philip Freneau, "To a New England Poet"*
> *[1823], ll. 11–18, in* The Norton Anthology of
> American Literature 1620–1865, *5th ed., vol. 1,*
> *edited by Nina Baym et al. [New York:*
> *Norton, 1998], p. 813)*

**From Washington Irving's Letter
to an American Friend**
Do not I beseech you, compute my lingering in Europe to any indifference to my own country or my friends. My greatest desire is to make myself worthy of the goodwill of my country [and to] return to my friends . . . but I am determined not to return home until I have sent some writings before me that shall, if they have merit, make me to return to the smiles, rather than skulk back to the pity of my friends.

> *(Washington Irving, letter to an American*
> *friend, 3 March 1819, quoted in Stanley T.*
> *Williams,* The Life of Washington Irving, *2 vols.*
> *[New York: Oxford University Press, 1935]*
> *1:173)*

From *A History of New York*
The hitherto scattered [American] colonies . . . waxed great and powerful, and finally becoming too strong for the mother country, were enabled to shake off its bonds, and by a glorious revolution became an independent empire—But the chain of effects stopped not here; the successful revolution in America produced the sanguinary revolution in France, which produced the puissant Buonaparte who produced the French Despotism which has thrown the whole world in confusion.

> *(Irving,* A History of New York *[1809], in*
> History, Tales, and Sketches, *p. 722)*

---

branch of the great Appalachian family" (p. 769). In the story, Rip's colonial family is also dismembered as he escapes from his tyrannical wife, but he is finally rediscovered and reintegrated into his new American family at the end. The context of family breakups is significant since there were a flurry of newspaper articles and pamphlets on the eve of the Revolution dealing with the misery of bad marriages and "bad wives" who made the marriage union impossible and hence divorce an inevitable reality. There was hence a psychological dimension to the sudden discourse on divorce, as if the colonists were rehearsing reasons for their inevitable divorce from England.

In this context, Rip is dominated and henpecked by his wife, who is associated with "petticoat government," the "yoke of matrimony," and "the yoke of Old England" (p. 783). Dame Van Winkle accuses Rip of being lazy, of not maintaining the patrimonial estate—an argument that the British used in the context of the Americans following the French and Indian War (1754–1763). The Americans were hence accused of neglecting their domestic, economic duty in maintaining the British empire in America. Rip, in this context, engages in a kind of passive resistance à la the prerevolutionary colonies. There is a series of suggested family resemblances encoded in the story, and Rip's marital evasions constitute a metaphoric rebellion against the monarchic wife, the domestic, colonial, petticoat governor. Thus it is significant that Rip, in contrast, helps his neighbors with their labor and that his neighbors take his part against the "bad" wife. The tale includes recognizable familial commonplaces impinging on Rip's eventual independence and integration into the new American family—the national "patrimonial estate" and "union" under new management (p. 771). In other words, Irving is engaged, on various levels, in an allegory of the American Revolution, starting in colonial times when "the country was yet a province of Great Britain" (p. 770). But despite Rip's resistance to the domestic petticoat "governor," he still identifies with the British monarchy, specifically George III, the king the Americans will rebel against in the future. Rip enjoys sitting under the "rubicund portrait of his Majesty George the Third," in a colonial inn, exchanging gossip and stories with his cronies (p. 772). Rip, like the colonists of the time, has not made the ultimate break with Great Britain and has consequently not discovered his new American identity. The story is, among other things, about this discovery, and there is an allusive autobiographical link to the American writer also accused of identifying with the British before coming "home."

After Rip falls in with the ghostly crew of Hendrick Hudson, drinks too much, and sleeps for twenty years, he awakens to a new America. The reference to Hudson—who discovered the Hudson River in 1609 and returns with his ghostly gang every twenty years—suggests that Rip must have fallen asleep in the year 1769, on the eve of the Revolution, when America was still a colony of Great Britain, and that when he awakens twenty years later the year must be 1789, the year of the French Revolution and the first inauguration of George Washington. Thus the implicit, allusive date is significant and not coincidental. When he awakens, the first thing Rip sees is an eagle, a conspicuous symbol of the new American nation. But Rip is disoriented; he does not recognize anything, and when he walks into his former village everything seems changed. Allegorically Rip still clings to his old colonial identity, something that is underscored when the suspicious villagers ask him to identify himself and he exclaims that he is "a loyal subject of the King [i.e., George III]—God bless him!" The villagers, of course, accuse him of being a Tory and a spy—a sympathizer and collaborator with the British. A beleaguered and bewildered Rip exclaims that "every thing's changed—and I'm changed—and I can't tell what's my name, or who I am" (pp. 780–781). Rip thus suffers an identity crisis and, consequently, must soon choose between his allegiance to Great Britain and his allegiance to the new nation. He must find out who he is within the political parameters of the new nation and the new reality. When his daughter, at the end, finally recognizes Rip, he is accepted into the community and reintegrated into the new American family: the familial breakup at the beginning ends with a new domestic and national union.

Irving highlights the change from colonial America to independent America in the scene where the Union Hotel has replaced Nicholaus Vedder's colonial inn and the portrait of George Washington has replaced that of George III. That it is now the Union Hotel puns on the new national "union" that is under new management: the proprietor is Jonathan Doolittle (since the Revolution, Jonathan had been the American national name), his surname identifying him as a New England Yankee. In other words, since New England was the cradle of the Revolution, the new national union is managed by New Englanders, descendants of the Puritans. Indeed, the original Jonathan Doolittle appears in Irving's *History* as one of the New England Puritan "warriors." The fact that an American flag is waving over the Union Hotel reinforces the great revolutionary change that Rip experiences.

Rip quickly accepts the new changes and hence assumes his new American identity: after learning about the Revolution and the correspondent political changes, he prefers to associate with "the rising generation," the first post-Revolutionary generation, rather than "his former cronies," clearly preferring the liberating

Rip Van Winkle at the Village Tavern. Illustration by Felix Octavius Carr Darley from *Harper's Weekly,* 20 September 1873. © CORBIS

present to the oppressive, colonial past. Thus he is pleased that his domineering wife has died and that the "yoke of Old England" and the "the yoke of matrimony" have been dissolved. America and England have been divorced and the result is new national union and "family." Rip's role in the new national accord is that of local historian "of the old times 'before the war'" (p. 783). Since he attaches himself to the rising generation, it is understood that Rip does not nostalgically extol the "English" past—he is the historical witness to how bad it was. In the end Rip is happily integrated into the new family union, where he is comfortably at home with his new role and identity as an American.

DEMOCRACY AND THE REVOLUTION QUESTIONED

This is how the story operates on its primary level. But Irving simultaneously encodes his ambivalence about both the Revolution and the new democratic nation. When Rip returns to the village, for instance, he is asked

on what side he voted and whether he is a Federal or Democrat—that is, a Federalist or a Jeffersonian Democratic-Republican (the conservative Federalists were friendly to Great Britain and hostile to revolutionary France while the liberal Democrats were hostile to Great Britain and friendly to France). Irving is conscious of Jefferson's electoral win over the Federalist Party in what was characterized as the "revolution of 1800." He, in fact, conflates various revolutions anachronistically to covertly suggest his disapproval of the intimidating mob democracy he believed had come into being with the Revolution. Thus, despite the humor of Rip being interrogated by his suspicious, patriotic countrymen, there is an air of mob intimidation and intrusive political conformity in the new land. In the new America there are political parties, and Rip is threatened with punishment: Loyalists, or "Tories," were conventionally tarred and feathered or hung during the Revolution. There are also allusions to Jefferson's "democratic" administration, something clear in the intertextual links between the story and Irving's 1809 *History*. In other words, Rip awakens and walks into a recognizably Jeffersonian America, with its obtrusive democratic politics and its aggressive Anglophobia. Irving is hence pushing us to question just how threatening an old man could be in 1789: If the Revolution was fought for freedom and independence, just how much is there in an America where political intimidation still exists? Is there really that much difference between colonial and revolutionary America?

If we return to the patriotic scene of the Union Hotel, the symbol of the new democratic America, we can see how Irving implicitly questions and undercuts both the Revolution and the new democratic nation. The transformation of Nicholas Vedder's Anglo-Dutch inn into the Union Hotel suggests that America, and control of what the Revolution signifies, is under Yankee Puritan management. How the Puritans arrived in the New World, specifically New England, and their "invasion" into other parts of the country, especially New York, and how they came to manage the new "union" is part of the story's between-the-lines history. This history appears in Irving's *History of New York*, where his sarcastic critique of New England Yankees reappears in the phrases and imagery of "Rip Van Winkle." For instance, Doolittle's Union Hotel is a "large, rickety wooden building . . . with great gaping windows, some of them broken, and mended with old hats and petticoats." Now compare Irving's *History* and the archetypal Puritan house: "A huge palace of pine boards . . . but so *rickety* and flimsy withal. . . . The outside remaining unpainted, grows venerably black with time: the family wardrobe is laid under contribution for *old hats, petticoats,* and breaches to stuff into the *broken windows*" (p. 499, emphasis added). Scratch the Union Hotel and underneath you find its Puritan prototype in the *History*, suggesting the new American "union" is based upon old, "rickety" Puritan foundations. That the Puritans in the *History*, with all their zealous intolerance and petty persecution, resemble the oppressive, inquisitional villagers in "Rip Van Winkle" suggests that despite apparent changes, nothing has changed at all. Colonial Puritan and British oppression resembles the new repression of an intrusive, (un)democratic people. Thus Irving subversively suggests that New Englanders co-opted the Revolution in the new union, just as their ancestors had previously co-opted and appropriated colonial history. While the original Puritans engaged in religious persecution, with its pertinent political implications, Irving suggests that their secular descendents continued the oppressive politicization and "bewitching" of America. When Rip first walks into the republican village, he begins to wonder "whether both he and the world around him were not bewitched" (p. 778).

In addition, beside the stars and stripes floating above the Union Hotel is "a tall naked pole with something on top that looked like a red night cap" (p. 779)—a liberty pole, symbol of the struggle for independence during the Revolution, and a red liberty cap, associated with the French Revolution. Both were first used in the American Revolution and were subsequently appropriated by the French in theirs. Irving and the Federalists considered the French Revolution to be a terrorist, democratic revolution of guillotines and mob violence. Republicans in America represented both revolutions as struggles for world liberation and commonly combined the respective national symbols in public ceremonies. In the 1809 *History,* Irving had conflated the American and French Revolutions with their Puritan prototypes, so there are a variety of political contexts in the seemingly innocent union of symbols. There is also a variety of connections between Irving's critique of the French Revolution in *Salmagundi* and his covert representation in "Rip Van Winkle." That the supposedly glorious American Revolution is linked to and thematically resembles the bloody French Revolution suggests that the War of Independence might have ironically imploded. That the year is allusively 1789, the beginning of the French Revolution and the inauguration of Washington as the first president, also engenders ironic complications.

Likewise, the portrait of George III that has been replaced with George Washington makes another subversive point. Ostensibly the changes are meant to be superficial: George III's red coat changed to Washington's blue and buff (the colors of the American revolutionary uniform), the king's scepter changed to Washington's sword. Irving is ostensibly joking about Jonathan Doolittle's proverbial Yankee stinginess—only touching up the sign but not replacing it with a true portrait of Washington. But scratch the sign of George Washington and underneath is another George, suggesting again that nothing has changed and that George Washington is, mutatis mutandis, George III and vice versa. Indeed, there is an implicit family resemblance between the two Georges, the royal and the democratic "father." Integrated into the new American union, Rip falls back into the "regular track of gossip" (p. 783), just like at the beginning of the story, suggesting in the end that despite the changes, the great American Revolution embodies a series of violent democratic revolutions as well as the repressive "past" it has supposedly transcended.

Written in England for an Anglo-American audience, Irving in "Rip Van Winkle" allegorically addresses his countrymen and reveals his own anxiety and ambivalence about the Revolution and democracy. That these issues are disguised and displaced in a comedy underscores the psychological pressures that compelled Irving to camouflage his critique allusively in a public celebration of the Revolution. In doing this, Irving was not being disingenuous but was writing out the ambiguities of his own place and time: an American in England feeling guilty about lingering, a proud yet ambivalent admirer of his country and the democratic revolution that still seemed ongoing. In a profound sense, the two dialectic readings of the Revolution are both artistically true. Patriots and Puritans, founding fathers and family resemblances—the story is a palimpsest of texts and cultures, in which *Salmagundi* and the *History* are refigured into a complex American classic. Like the disoriented Rip, Irving finally comes "home," albeit ambivalently, in a story of hopeful anxiety. Through the mediation of Irving's great, conservative imagination, the texts and contexts, the traces and secret signatures coalesce into a significant meditation on the many meanings of nineteenth-century America.

See also Americans Abroad; Democracy; Foreigners; Literary Nationalism; Short Story

BIBLIOGRAPHY

Primary Work

Irving, Washington. *History, Tales, and Sketches.* Edited by James W. Tuttleton. New York: Library of America, 1983.

Secondary Works

Blakemore, Steven. "Family Resemblances: The Texts and Contexts of 'Rip Van Winkle.'" *Early American Literature* 35, no. 2 (2000): 187–212.

Dawson, Hugh. "Recovering 'Rip Van Winkle': A Corrective Reading." *ESQ* 40 (1994): 251–273.

Pearce, Colin D. "Changing Regimes: The Case of 'Rip Van Winkle.'" *Clio* 22 (winter 1993): 115–128.

Ringe, Donald A. "New York and New England: Irving's Criticism of American Society." *American Literature* 38 (January 1967): 455–467.

Roth, Martin. *Comedy and America: The Lost World of Washington Irving.* Chicago: University of Chicago Press, 1976.

Rubin-Dorski, Jeffrey. *Adrift in the Old World: The Psychological Pilgrimage of Washington Irving.* Chicago: University of Chicago Press, 1988.

Steven Blakemore

THE ROMANCE

The roots of the term "romance" lie in both the medieval romance (twelfth to sixteenth centuries) and European Romanticism (eighteenth and nineteenth centuries). Medieval romances appeared first in Old French literature in the twelfth century and typically were in verse, although prose romances appeared later. Originally, the term denoted a work in the vernacular Romance languages rather than in Latin. The former were the everyday languages spoken by persons in countries once part of the Roman Empire, including what are now France, Italy, Spain and Portugal. The subject matter of these romances was usually love (courtly love to be more specific) and heroic adventure (often both) with a significant supernatural and magical component. Romances were secular narratives as opposed to epic tales and myths but typically reaffirmed the western Christian mythos. The best examples in English are the Arthurian tales and *Sir Gawain and the Green Knight* (fourteenth century). "The romance" has thus historically been associated with narratives of adventure, romance, and myth as opposed to realistic stories or portrayals of history, politics, or everyday life. This is one reason why, as European art and literature began to move consciously away from rigid formal rules and distrust of artistic innovation characteristic of the neoclassicism of the late eighteenth century and early nineteenth century, critics and writers chose the term "Romantic" to describe any work that featured the experimental and imaginative exploration of the ideal rather than the conventional and realistic representation of the actual. Whereas neoclassicism had emphasized reason and rationality in intellectual and artistic life, the writers now closely associated with European Romanticism favored imagination over reason and experimentation over rigid adherence to formal rules.

By the late 1700s romance thus had come to refer broadly to any literary work that could be distinguished from works principally realistic in form and subject matter. The novel is considered a highly realistic form of fictional narrative that takes as its subject matter everyday reality—the parlor, the domestic scene, the country estate—and renders it in close detail, paying attention to both verisimilitude and probability in plot, characterization, and theme. Medieval romances such as *Sir Gawain* render courtly life in detail, painstakingly chronicling the minutiae of such familiar scenes from everyday life as the arming of the hero or the hunt. They concern themselves with grand themes such as the nature of love, the chivalric ideal, or proper Christian conduct in a fallen world. The novel is not concerned with such ideals and certainly not with demonstrating the power of the imagination to go beyond the everyday except insofar as it provides insight into such fundamental aspects of humanity as personal identity and ethical decision making. As Terry Eagleton puts it:

> Novels are romances—but romances which have to negotiate the prosaic world of modern civilization.

They retain their romantic heroes and villains, wish-fulfillments and fairy-tale endings, but now these things have to be worked out in terms of sex and property, money and marriage, social mobility and the nuclear family. (P. 2)

American Romanticism in general and the romance in particular, however, are difficult to trace directly back to their major antecedents. Indeed, to claim that American Romanticism is an object of knowledge in the same way as are European and British Romanticism is to gloss over much of the material and literary history of the antebellum period. For one thing, by the time the writers now associated with the Romantic impulse in the United States began writing, including such figures as James Fenimore Cooper (1789–1851), Edgar Allan Poe (1809– 1849), Herman Melville (1819–1891), and Nathaniel Hawthorne (1804–1864), European Romanticism was no longer a vibrant, growing cluster of parallel (but often isolated and unaffiliated) cultural movements. Many of the important European Romantic figures, such as Lord Byron (1788–1824), Percy Bysshe Shelley (1792–1822), and William Wordsworth (1770–1850) in England and Johann Wolfgang von Goethe (1749–1832) in Germany, were dead. Furthermore, American readers generally preferred domestic and sentimental novels, history, and even poetry to the romances of the country's principal writers of experimental fiction; sales of Harriet

Beecher Stowe's (1811–1896) *Uncle Tom's Cabin* (1852), for example, far outstripped those of all four of Hawthorne's major romances and Melville's *Moby-Dick* (1851) combined. What might now be called romances were thus not very popular and certainly did not comprise a major literary movement at the time, only in retrospect. Melville, for example, was virtually forgotten by the time he died, and his work was only resurrected in the 1920s. Finally, the very usefulness of the term "romance" to describe the form taken by a minority of American antebellum novels is under debate. Although the word "romance" was initially defined negatively and simply as being un-novel-like (which is to say, unrealistic), critics have now shown that writers and critics in the period used the term in a variety of ways, many of them contradictory. The historical appropriateness of the term most often used to describe the style of the most significant antebellum writers is thus in question.

Romanticism in the antebellum period may best be understood as a second- (or even third-) generation emulation of European Romanticism from within a distinctly American historical context rather than as a cohesive, self-aware artistic movement. The definition of romance used to describe the practices of those American writers most influenced by European Romanticism must be broad and flexible rather than narrowly descriptive.

THE ROMANCE IN HISTORY

American romance emerged during a period of rapid historical growth and change. The United States was coming of age politically and economically and experiencing occasional tumultuous political conflict as a result. The very landscape and character of the country were changing at a rate the average American found unsettling at best. For example, it became commonplace for Americans to move far and often, splitting up the traditional family structure. The opening of the Erie Canal and especially the advent of the railroad began to erode regional differences, allowing for the flowering of a truly national culture and character but bringing with it cultural and economic pressures that threatened to dismantle long-established local traditions and political and material structures.

Jacksonian democracy unleashed powerful political and cultural forces. Its extension of suffrage beyond landowners and the upper class allowed a wider swath of the American populace to gain access to power and influence. Emergent divisions included farmers, nascent industrial workers, factory owners, and immigrants—all of whom were often at odds culturally and politically. Rapid industrialization fueled the growth of cities,

American romance is a mode of long fictional narratives (with the exception of Hawthorne's short tales, which also are often examples of the mode), so the following list of representative romances are limited to long narratives rather than to the entire canon of American Romanticism.

Charles Brockden Brown, *Wieland* (1798)

Charles Brockden Brown, *Arthur Mervyn* (1799)

Charles Brockden Brown, *Edgar Huntly* (1799)

Charles Brockden Brown, *Ormond* (1799)

James Fenimore Cooper, *The Pioneers* (1823)

James Fenimore Cooper, *Last of the Mohicans* (1826)

Catherine Maria Sedgwick, *Hope Leslie* (1827)

William Gilmore Simms, *The Partisan: A Tale of the Revolution* (1835)

William Gilmore Simms, *The Yemassee: A Romance of Carolina* (1835)

Edgar Allan Poe, *The Narrative of Arthur Gordon Pym* (1838)

James Fenimore Cooper, *The Pathfinder* (1840)

James Fenimore Cooper, *The Deerslayer* (1841)

Herman Melville, *Mardi* (1849)

Herman Melville, *Moby-Dick; or, The Whale* (1850)

Nathaniel Hawthorne, *The House of the Seven Gables* (1851)

Nathaniel Hawthorne, *The Blithedale Romance* (1852)

Nathaniel Hawthorne, *The Marble Faun* (1860)

---

putting their inhabitants' needs in conflict with the interests of farmers. Immigrants, who in the two decades before the Civil War were largely Catholic Germans and Irish, threatened to eclipse the country's Anglo-Protestant majority. The country's economy grew exponentially and rapidly, creating unease and bringing with it fairly regular economic downturns, including the panics of 1837 and 1857. Tensions among slave and nonslave states grew steadily throughout the first half of the nineteenth century, culminating in the catastrophe of the American Civil War.

The massive territorial expansion and resulting displacement of the indigenous North Americans that occurred actually added to the pressures rather than relieved them; the question of whether the new territories were to be slave or free drove political discourse and political action in countless facets of American life. In the decades preceding the war Congress enacted a series of legislative compromises that left both sides dissatisfied and served only to escalate tensions. Finally,

not to be overlooked is the impact the Mexican-American War (1846–1848) had on the American psyche, especially for its writers. The transcendentalist writer Henry David Thoreau's (1817–1862) refusal to pay his taxes in protest of the war is the most famous example, but a majority of American artists and intellectuals were disillusioned by the country's first experience of empire. Slavery was a horrific injustice that had been with the country since the eighteenth century, but the Mexican-American War was a war of aggression initiated with little justification other than to seize land and secure the country's expansion south and west. In the midst of this period of uncertainty, Americans struggled to define what it meant to be "American" and whether and how the American experiment in democracy would turn out.

There are many easy parallels between U.S. history and American romance. One of the first important critics of the country's romancers, F. O. Matthiessen, argued that all writers of what he termed the American Renaissance were united by their commitment to the promise of democracy. It is not surprising that the freedom and tumult of a country whose cultural and political centers shifted regularly produced art that was both experimental and at times as idealistic as the country imagined itself to be. Melville's whalers epitomized the pluralism rampant in the country, and Walt Whitman's great American epic poem, "Song of Myself" (1855), elevated the prostitute, the cabin boy, and the blacksmith, among countless other figures from the American scene, to heroic and mythic status. But critics have also shown how American romance interrogated American democracy at least as often as it celebrated it.

Melville's Captain Ahab in *Moby-Dick* (1851) has been seen as both a tyrant and a heroic but dangerous fanatic, the sort of figure democracies produce only to have them turn on the people who bring them to power. Thoreau and Ralph Waldo Emerson (1803–1882) were deeply critical of capitalism and especially suspicious of its effect on individualism, something Romantics of all stripes valued above virtually everything else. And Hawthorne's recastings of early American history were some of the first attempts by an American writer to revisit and reevaluate the earliest and perhaps darkest glimmerings of the American experience. American romance was perhaps a natural result of a set of historical conditions that encouraged strident personal expression and skepticism of established authority, as long as these were tempered by respect for the ideal and by the promise of republicanism variously defined. American romancers struggled in various ways to explore this complex milieu. As Hawthorne describes it in "The Artist of the Beautiful":

The chase of butterflies was an apt emblem of the ideal pursuit in which he had spent so many golden hours; but would the beautiful idea ever be yielded to his hand like the butterfly that symbolized it? . . . Alas, that the artist, whether in poetry, or whatever other material, may not content himself with the inward enjoyment of the beautiful, but must chase the flitting mystery beyond the verge of his ethereal domain, and crush its frail being in seizing it with a material grasp! (Pp. 457–458)

BRIEF CRITICAL HISTORY

As a critical descriptor, the term "romance" was first authoritatively established by Richard Volney Chase in *The American Novel and Its Tradition* (1957):

> The main difference between the novel and the romance is in the way in which they view reality. The novel renders reality closely and in comprehensive detail [*sic*] the romance is free to render reality in less volume and detail. . . . Character itself becomes, then, somewhat abstract and ideal. . . . The plot we may expect to be highly colored. Astonishing events may occur, and these are likely to have a symbolic or ideological, rather than a realistic, plausibility. (Pp. 12–13)

Chase's work was largely a formalist attempt to establish a descriptive, genre theory of the American novel form, and he was following a well-accepted distinction that could be traced back some 150 years. New Historicists and others who have done much important work in recovering a historical rather than strictly formalist understanding of the period have demonstrated that "romance" was used variously and often conflictingly by writers and critics and that Chase's account is ahistorical at best. Nina Baym, for example, has documented how nineteenth-century critics used "romance" and "novel" virtually interchangeably. Equally important, antebellum critics rarely if ever discussed the novel-romance dichotomy in the terms established by Chase. In Baym's words:

> There were reviews and essays that did make an effort to distinguish the two terms, but definitions varied from review to review. . . . In many cases the distinction appears to be entirely ad hoc; the reviewer is developing an idiosyncratic scheme and calls on these two words to make a point in a classification not duplicated in other critical writings. (*Novels*, p. 228)

In the context of nineteenth-century literary theory, then "romance" meant nothing other than "fiction" as opposed to nonfiction—the essay or history—and the writers who used it simply intended to distinguish their work from works of fact.

Michael Davitt Bell goes so far as to argue that as it was used by critics, romance denoted little or nothing

vis-à-vis the realism-romance distinction so germane to discussions of European Romanticism:

> To describe romance in this way was not, finally, to distinguish it from realism or mimesis, for the general run of nineteenth-century comments on romance distinguish it not from realism but from reality. . . . What matters most, then, in discussions of romance is neither content nor form but psychological motive and effect. (P. xii)

But as any cursory perusal of the major critical studies of the antebellum novel makes clear, readers of pre–Civil War American fiction must decide for themselves what romance means, taking into consideration antebellum critical and writerly practices; historical studies of audience and reception; and most importantly, the novels themselves. For example, Charles Feidelson has argued that it is the romancer's use of the "symbolistic imagination" that gives the romance its essential character. R. W. B. Lewis focuses on the Adamic myth he believes manifests itself throughout the tradition, whereas Harry Levin has tried to show that the tradition is best understood in terms of the "power of blackness" (a phrase coined by Melville to describe Hawthorne's work) present in the best examples of the form. Evan Carton focuses on how the American romance takes the very distinction between fact and fiction as both form and content. It is thus a "self-consciously dialectical enactment of critical and philosophical concerns about the relation of words to things and the nature of the self" (Carton, p. 1). Finally, Emily Miller Budick notes that although all romances reject mimesis, they also "insist on the reality of history and society in order to cast doubt on the mind's autonomy and to force the imagination to consider something outside itself" (p. ix).

What is important in understanding American romance is that the term does not apply to all novels of the antebellum period but is rather an approach to writing novels characteristic of several of the writers from the antebellum period most associated with the Romantic impulse in the United States. Romance may be regarded as a diverse array of supremely imaginative and experimental narrative modes. Melville and Hawthorne are perhaps the two best examples: Melville for how he practiced romance, and Hawthorne for how comprehensively he attempted to define it.

THE ROMANCER'S CRAFT

American romance chooses to sacrifice mimetic realism in hopes of achieving a heightened sense of the "Romantic" as it has been traditionally defined (see above). It is characteristically self-conscious in its forms and themes, tending heavily toward the experimental.

As the romance moves away from the domain of the realistic novel, it approaches the poetic, the mythic, and the symbolic. Whereas realistic novels take as their subject matter the everyday, the romance strives to leap beyond the everyday to the universal and transcendent. For example, in *Moby-Dick*, Melville exhaustively chronicles the minutiae of life on a nineteenth-century American whale ship, but in so doing he strives to go beyond the everyday to the very underpinnings of philosophy, politics, history, and the problems of human existence. As he discusses the significance of the whiteness of the whale, the book's narrator, Ishmael, muses beyond the color white to the very depths of the human condition: What is it about whiteness that so provokes the imagination?

> Is it by its indefiniteness it shadows forth the heartless voids and immensities of the universe, and thus stabs us from behind with the thought of annihilation, when beholding the white depths of the milky way? Or is it, that as in essence whiteness is not so much a color as the visible absence of color, and at the same time the concrete of all colors; is it for these reasons that there is such a dumb blankness, full of meaning, in a wide landscape of snows—a colorless, all-color of atheism from which we shrink? . . . of all these things the Albino whale was the symbol. Wonder ye then at the fiery hunt? (P. 195)

Romance is also highly self-conscious. It typically takes fictionality as one of its themes and so tends to be highly experimental in form, something critics in the period typically viewed with skepticism. American writers of romance shared the view that an artist should explore the limits of established literary genres and conventions creating new ones as needed. Poe is credited with inventing both the mystery story and science fiction, for example. Charles Brockden Brown's (1771–1810) novels recast the familiar gothic novel form in an American mold, replacing the medieval castle with the American frontier while retaining the gothic's penchant for the irrational and the mysterious. Melville broke new ground with each successive novel, challenging readers and critics in the process, so much so that one New York paper greeted the appearance of his sixth novel, *Pierre; or, The Ambiguities* (1852), with a headline declaring its author insane.

Hawthorne also played with established conventions. In "The Custom-House," the preface to *The Scarlet Letter* (1850), the relation of the actual to the imaginary is taken under consideration in a characteristically Romantic manner: as both form and content. Although prefaces usually function as part of the proscenium or narrative frame, setting off what follows as

---

FROM *MOBY-DICK*

Ahab had cherished a wild vindictiveness against the whale, all the more fell for that in his frantic morbidness he at last came to identify with him, not only all his bodily woes, but all his intellectual and spiritual exasperations. The White Whale swam before him as the monomaniac incarnation of all those malicious agencies which some deep men feel eating in them, till they are left living on with half a heart and half a lung. . . . All that most maddens and torments; all that stirs up the lees of things; all truth with malice in it; all that cracks the sinews and cakes the brain; all the subtle demonisms of life and thought; all evil, to crazy Ahab, were visibly personified, and made practically assailable in Moby Dick. He piled upon the whale's white hump the sum of all the general rage and hate felt by his whole race from Adam down; and then, as if his chest had been a mortar, he burst his hot heart's shell upon it.

Melville, *Moby-Dick*, p. 184.

"just pretend," it is quickly apparent that Hawthorne's preface is a fiction all its own. Specifically, it is the story of how Hawthorne came to write the tale of Hester Prynne and her scarlet letter, but by the end the narrator of the preface has been transformed from Nathaniel Hawthorne, real-life custom surveyor victimized by his political enemies, to a purely fictive and highly creative imaginative voice. Instead of providing a factual ground for the fiction which follows, the facts of the sketch themselves thus become fictions, allowing Hawthorne to explore one of the fundamental components of the literary transaction: the relationships among authors and readers, fact and fiction. The preface makes clear that for Hawthorne, romance involves experimentation, play, metafictional allusion, and narrative gamesmanship.

Insofar as writers in the period attempted to define the romance explicitly, Hawthorne's prefaces form the most important primary sources. In the prefaces to all four of his major romances, he describes his craft in provocative if not entirely unambiguous detail. Taken as a whole, they advocate for the "sacrifice with relation" most critics agree romance takes as its first principle and expound on the benefits the romancer hopes to achieve. The payoff is that in so doing the writer creates a space somewhere between the fantastic and the everyday within which to explore the imaginative, formal, and thematic possibilities of the subject matter. In "The Custom-House," this effect is described as follows:

> Moonlight, in a familiar room, falling so white upon the carpet, and showing all its figures so distinctly,—making every object so minutely visible, yet so unlike a morning or noontide visibility,—is a medium the most suitable for a romance-writer to get acquainted with his illusive guests. . . . the floor of our familiar room has become a neutral territory, somewhere between the real world and fairyland, where the Actual and the Imaginary may meet, and each imbue itself with the nature of the other. (Pp. 35–36)

And as might be expected, critics have written volumes on Hawthorne's characteristic practice of the romance mode. For the purposes here it is sufficient to note that the prefaces form a manifesto of sorts for American romance, advocating the benefits of experimentation in form and theme and demonstrating in the romances themselves how shunning mimesis perhaps allows for a deeper penetration into the entire range of human desires and behaviors, including sin, shame, jealousy, envy, and murder, among countless others.

See also The Blithedale Romance; "The Custom-House"; Democracy; *The House of the Seven Gables;* Individualism and Community; Literary Criticism; *Moby-Dick;* Romanticism; *The Scarlet Letter*

BIBLIOGRAPHY

Primary Works

Hawthorne, Nathaniel. "The Artist of the Beautiful." In *Mosses from an Old Manse,* edited by William Charvat, Roy Harvey Pearce, and Claude M. Simpson, pp. 447–477. Columbus: Ohio State University Press, 1974.

Hawthorne, Nathaniel. "The Custom-House Sketch." 1850. In *The Scarlet Letter,* edited by William Charvat, Roy Harvey Pearce, and Claude M. Simpson, pp. 3–46. Columbus: Ohio State University Press, 1962.

Hawthorne, Nathaniel. *The House of the Seven Gables.* 1851. Edited and with an introduction and notes by Michael Davitt Bell. Oxford: Oxford University Press, 1998.

Melville, Herman. *Moby-Dick; or The Whale.* 1851. Vol. 6 of *Writings of Herman Melville,* edited by Harrison Hayford, Hershel Parker, and G. Thomas Tanselle. Evanston, Ill., and Chicago: Northwestern University Press and the Newberry Library, 2001.

Secondary Works

Auerbach, Jonathan. *The Romance of Failure: First-Person Fictions of Poe, Hawthorne, and James.* New York: Oxford University Press, 1989.

Baym, Nina. "Concepts of the Romance in Hawthorne's America." *Nineteenth Century Fiction* 38 (March 1984): 426–443.

Baym, Nina. *Novels, Readers, and Reviewers: Responses to Fiction in Antebellum America.* Ithaca, N.Y.: Cornell University Press, 1984.

Bell, Michael Davitt. *The Development of American Romance: The Sacrifice of Relation.* Chicago: University of Chicago Press, 1980.

Bier, Jesse. "Hawthorne on the Romance: His Prefaces Related and Examined." *Modern Philology* 53, no. 1 (1955): 17–24.

Budick, Emily Miller. *Fiction and Historical Consciousness: The American Romance Tradition.* New Haven, Conn.: Yale University Press, 1989.

Budick, Emily Miller. "Sacvan Bercovitch, Stanley Cavell and the Romance Theory of American Fiction." *PMLA* 106 (1992): 78–91.

Carton, Evan. *The Rhetoric of American Romance: Dialectic and Identity in Emerson, and Dickinson, Poe, and Hawthorne.* Baltimore: Johns Hopkins University Press, 1985.

Chai, Leon. *The Romantic Foundations of the American Renaissance.* Ithaca, N.Y.: Cornell University Press, 1987.

Chase, Richard Volney. *The American Novel and Its Tradition.* Garden City, N.Y.: Doubleday, 1957.

Coale, Samuel. *Mesmerism and Hawthorne: Mediums of American Romance.* Tuscaloosa: University of Alabama Press, 1998.

Dekker, George. *The American Historical Romance.* Cambridge, U.K., and New York: Cambridge University Press, 1987.

Dekker, George. "Once More: Hawthorne and the Genealogy of American Romance." *ESQ: A Journal of the American Renaissance* 35 (1989): 69–83.

Dryden, Edgar A. *The Form of American Romance.* Baltimore: Johns Hopkins University Press, 1988.

Eagleton, Terry. *The English Novel: An Introduction.* Malden, Mass.: Blackwell, 2005.

Ellis, William A. *The Theory of the American Romance: An Ideology in American Intellectual History.* Ann Arbor, Mich.: UMI Research Press, 1989.

Engell, John. "Hawthorne and Two Types of Early American Romance. *South Atlantic Review* 57 (1992): 33–51.

Feidelson, Charles. *Symbolism and American Literature.* Chicago: University of Chicago Press, 1953.

Fluck, Winfried. "'The American Romance' and the Changing Functions of the Imaginary." *New Literary*

History: A Journal of Theory and Interpretation 27, no. 3 (1996): 415–457.

Foster, Edward Halsey. *The Civilized Wilderness: Backgrounds to American Romantic Literature, 1817–1860.* New York: Free Press, 1975.

Gilmore, Michael T. *American Romanticism and the Marketplace.* Chicago: University of Chicago Press, 1985.

Greenwald, Elissa. *Realism and the Romance: Nathaniel Hawthorne, Henry James, and American Fiction.* Ann Arbor, Mich.: UMI Research Press, 1989.

Levin, Harry. *The Power of Blackness: Hawthorne, Poe, Melville.* New York: Knopf, 1958.

Levine, Robert S. *Conspiracy and Romance: Studies in Brockden Brown, Cooper, Hawthorne, and Melville.* Cambridge, U.K., and New York: Cambridge University Press, 1989.

Lewis, R. W. B. *The American Adam: Innocence, Tragedy, and Tradition in the Nineteenth Century.* Chicago: University of Chicago Press, 1955.

Matthiessen, F. O. *American Renaissance: Art and Expression in the Age of Emerson and Whitman.* London and New York: Oxford University Press, 1941.

Merrill, Robert. "Another Look at the American Romance." *Modern Philology* 78 (1981): 379–392.

Millington, Richard H. *Practicing Romance: Narrative Form and Cultural Engagement in Hawthorne's Fiction.* Princeton, N.J.: Princeton University Press, 1992.

Porte, Joel. *In Respect to Egotism: Studies in American Romantic Writing.* Cambridge, U.K., and New York: Cambridge University Press, 1991.

Porte, Joel. *The Romance in America: Studies in Cooper, Poe, Hawthorne, Melville, and James.* Middleton, Conn.: Wesleyan University Press, 1969.

Schirmeister, Pamela. *The Consolations of Space: The Place of Romance in Hawthorne, Melville, and James.* Stanford, Calif.: Stanford University Press, 1990.

Stubbs, John Caldwell. *The Pursuit of Form: A Study of Hawthorne and the Romance.* Urbana: University of Illinois Press, 1970.

Thompson, G. R., and Eric Carl Link. *Neutral Ground: New Traditionalism and the American Romance Controversy.* Baton Rouge: Louisiana State University Press, 1999.

Michael J. Davey

ROMANTICISM

The young and expanding United States was fertile ground for the currents of Romanticism, the intellectual, artistic, and cultural movement that had an enormous impact on European thinking and European politics in the late eighteenth century and early nineteenth century. Having thrown off a colonial government with a revolution grounded in the Enlightenment values of the rights of private judgment in religious matters and self-governance in political matters, the new American nation found consonance with the Romantic emphasis on self-knowledge and self-expression and the Romantic orientation against the imposition of authority by elite classes. The unique conditions of the western frontier and the socially divisive challenges of the antislavery movement and the women's rights movement generated further conditions that nourished assumptions and attitudes that were essentially Romantic in nature. Emerging from these conditions was an assertion of the value of the individual self, an intense concern with the inner workings of the perceiving mind, and an affirmation of emotion and instinct. Ralph Waldo Emerson (1803–1882), in the 1841 essay "Self-Reliance," captured the spirit of his time when he termed it "the age of the first person singular" (*Early Lectures* 3:188). The self-reliant individualist and the figure of the hero were two key embodiments of this ethos. Their representation in fiction and poetry marked a distinctive era in American authorship and reading.

ROMANTICISM AND RELIGIOUS CULTURE

The Romantic movement gained its first American foothold in religion, the field of thought and expression that had had the longest hold on the American imagination. Throughout the eighteenth century, pressures grew to reform the principal tenets of Calvinism, the orthodoxy of the New England Puritans and an essential element of the Presbyterian, Reformed, and other established Protestant denominations. One of the distinguishing doctrines of Calvinism was election to grace, the assumption that the redeemed were not able to choose their salvation but were instead chosen by God. Because of this doctrine, Calvinism generated controversy and resistance from two quite different sides. A growing evangelical movement employed with new energy and proficiency the tools of religious revivalism that emerged in the eighteenth century. The evangelicals accentuated the place of choice and individual will in the process of salvation, thus making men and women the agents of their own spiritual fates. On the opposite side of the theological spectrum, a movement of religious liberalism contested the key theological assumptions of both Calvinism and evangelicalism and emphasized deepened spiritual awareness and character building as essential elements of religion. They held that salvation was less an instantaneous turn than a long-developing process of the cultivation of the soul. Both of these shifts in religious belief and practice had important later implications for literature in the United States. The assumptions of evangelicalism shaped much of the popular fiction and poetry of the mid-nineteenth century, and the liberal conception of religion as a continuing process of spiritual cultivation led to the rise of transcendentalism, the most important early American literary movement.

Different as they were in many essential ways, evangelical revivalism and transcendentalism shared two important attributes. First, each centered on an individual man or woman undertaking an act of choice as the basis of religious experience and religious truth. Revivalist preachers urged their hearers to moments of decision, in which they seized their own fates and consciously altered them. The revivalists created an inner drama in their hearers, challenging them to make their lives over through a momentous exercise of a choice that was their own to make. In his *Lectures on the Revival of Religion* (1835), Charles G. Finney (1792–1875), an important revivalist preacher and later president of Oberlin College, noted an important shift in attitude in the early nineteenth century about the process of religious revivals. Ministers and congregations were coming to believe that revivals must be planned and promoted. The revival was not a miraculous event come down from heaven, Finney argued, but an event dependent on human choice and will. It was also dependent on preparation, planning, and persuasion on the part of the minister. "A revival is the work of God," Finney wrote, "and so is a crop of wheat" (p. 268). Neither comes without human resolve and labor. Finney was representative of a new attitude that made religion less a given than a made thing, one that assumed new powers for, and placed new responsibilities on, the individual.

In contrast to the rise of evangelical revivalism, the religious liberals of New England, who came to be known as Unitarians, began to describe religion as a lifelong process of spiritual development, minimizing the significance of an isolated moment of conversion. The Unitarians emphasized an ongoing work of self-examination and self-discipline in which the will was constantly engaged in a creative expansion of receptive understanding and disciplined action. The momentous choice for salvation emphasized by the evangelicals was transmuted by the liberals into an unending series of choices in a series of ever-new creations of the self.

Romantic religion, in either its evangelical or liberal versions, was thus a religion of the individual's self-transforming power, in which choice played an central and essential role. It was also a religion of feeling, in which the emotions were powerful agents of expression. The revivals of the Second Great Awakening of the 1820s and 1830s were marked by their emotional intensity. At their core were experiences of great catharsis, in which powerful, submerged emotions were released with a potent mixture of searing remorse, anguished fear, and profoundly joyful relief. Emotion also played a role in the liberal reinterpretation of religion. In the emotionally fervent preaching, Unitarianism was often accused of a cold intellectualism. But in the emotionally fervent preaching of such liberal ministers as William Ellery Channing and Henry Ware Jr., the heart was made central to the religious experience. It was to this emotionally moving preaching that the young Ralph Waldo Emerson responded, bringing it not only into his own sermons but also into the descriptions of rapture with the natural world that marked his first book, *Nature* (1836), the starting point for one important strand of American literature.

THE ROMANTIC HERO

The inward turn of Romanticism, with its concentration on the individual self and on the importance of the emotions, manifested itself in the figure of the hero, an exemplary or representative self who undertook great or memorable actions as a principal form of self-expression. Two important forms of the hero emerged in American literature of the nineteenth century. The first was an individual who embodied enlarged spiritual awareness and perception of the natural and social worlds and who promised a fuller experience of life and thought to ordinary men and women. The second, also a figure of unusually deep perception and feeling, was an agent of dissent and social defiance, whose powers of perception revealed a flawed or corrupt social world that must be challenged and reformed. Closely related in their roles as prophetic awakeners, these heroic figures addressed a culture that many American authors felt was marked by unfulfilled promise and an incomplete enactment of the ideals that it professed. The United States was a nation that had to be called forcefully to realize its greater potential.

In the closing pages of Emerson's *Nature,* the narrative voice changes to that of an "Orphic poet" who "chants" a hymn of promise to the reader. The poet proclaims that each reader has the potential to create a world in accord with his or her dreams; the key is to seize the innate power that connects one to nature, and thus to God, and to translate this power into acts that are self-transforming. Emerson would later articulate this message of self-empowerment into one of his most influential essays, "Self-Reliance" (published in his *Essays: First Series,* 1841), in which he encouraged his readers to reject the pressures for social conformity and "trust" themselves, recognizing that "self-trust" finally implies a trust in a transcendent "Self," or "Over-Soul," an all-encompassing source of power from which each man and woman originates. Emerson's depiction of a heroic remaking of the world had great appeal to men and women who were struggling with aspects of Calvinist or evangelical theology that seemed oppressive and authoritarian in nature (his exhortation to personal power has remained one of the key aspects of his appeal even into the twenty-first century). His message also had a clear appeal to a young society, still engaged with expansion into the frontier and still forming its communities, cities, and way of life. Americans were in many senses making a world at this period, and Emerson's message of self-trust and confident advance rang true.

The "Orphic poet" of Emerson's *Nature* was given a different embodiment in the poetic narrator of Walt Whitman's "Song of Myself" (untitled when it first appeared in *Leaves of Grass,* 1855), the work that revolutionized poetic form through its long and flowing lines and its adoption of direct address to the reader. Whitman (1819–1892) presented the ordinary individual as the vehicle of a new era of perception and of social relationships. The "I" who speaks directly to "you" the reader in Whitman's poem implies a conversational dialogue that subtly encourages the reader to respond. It is a poem based on the principle of interaction, and it assumes that reading is an engaged rather than a passive act. Whitman's speaker is both an ordinary man and a visionary prophet who holds forth a utopian vision of joyful self-realization, brotherhood, and spiritual fulfillment. Whitman thought of himself as the poet of the people, and he used his poems to portray with sympathy a wide range of ordinary men and women in their everyday lives; he attempted to show how ordinary experience was itself miraculous when seen from the right perspective and thus to give his readers a new sense of empowerment in their judgments and decisions.

In a similar vein, Emerson's close friend Henry David Thoreau (1817–1862) described the process through which he resorted to the natural world to reclaim control over his life in *Walden* (1854). A description of a two-year sojourn in a cabin by Walden

The Picnic, **1846.** Painting by Thomas Cole. The pastoral setting of this painting is meant to represent an idealized middle landscape falling between an increasingly complex, industrialized civilization and raw wilderness. © BROOKLYN MUSEUM OF ART, NEW YORK, USA/THE BRIDGEMAN ART LIBRARY

Pond, Thoreau's work is also a celebration of the richness of life in nature and a critique of the hurried waste of life caused by the pursuit of unnecessary material goods and luxuries. Finding wealth through his own voluntary poverty, Thoreau showed how the world opened to him anew at Walden, his distance from society and its pressures an important asset in reasserting his hold on his own life. His experiment was intended not only as a work of self-rescue but also a warning call to his readers, who needed to understand that a new freedom was available to them if they would recognize the impediments of conventional patterns. They had the power, Thoreau believed, to seize life anew.

The affirmative tone and positive energy of Emerson, Whitman, and Thoreau forms an important strand of American Romanticism, but it was countered by a more embattled and defiant attitude that made the hero a figure of courageous resistance. Emerson called his society a conformist one; resistance to that conformity was a necessary step in both self-development and building a more just society. The age was also marked by extreme political conflict over issues of social justice, such as economic oppression, rights for women, and especially the persistence of legalized slavery in the American South. By insisting on the value and capacity of the individual, Romantic writers added a fuel to the forces of democratic reform that were emerging at mid-century.

One of the most memorable depictions of heroic defiance was Nathaniel Hawthorne's (1804–1864) Hester Prynne, the central character in *The Scarlet Letter* (1850). Hester conceived a child out of wedlock and was thus faced with anger and ostracism from the members of her New England Puritan village and the figures of religious authority there. The scarlet "A" that she is forced to wear to signify her adultery takes on a different meaning, however, as Hawthorne unfolds the story. It comes to symbolize not Hester's guilt but her bravery, and it also implies the intolerance and exclusion of her narrow and oppressive culture. Over the years, through her steadfast refusal to reveal the identity of her child's father and through her committed acceptance of her role as mother, even as a social outcast, Hester turns her badge of shame into a badge of honor. Her story is tragic, but it is also ennobling; one sees her create something positive out of her isolation and ostracism. Her principled resistance to oppressive authority wins her a kind of intellectual and moral freedom that few achieve. That she struggles against an overwhelmingly male-dominated social structure is also significant. She is a proto-feminist heroine, asserting a quality of honor and an independence that set her apart from her contemporaries.

Another example of defiant heroism emerged from the antislavery movement with the publication of *Narrative of the Life of Frederick Douglass, an American Slave* (1845), Frederick Douglass's (1817–1895) moving autobiographical account of his escape from the power of his masters to become a free man. His movement toward freedom entails a deliberate and disciplined program of self-cultivation, in which Douglass recognizes and then acquires the power of reading and the capacity for self-directed work, eventually turning these and other skills into crucial elements of his escape into the free states. Finding himself in a free state was "a moment of the highest excitement I ever experienced," he wrote. "I felt like one who had escaped a den of hungry lions" (p. 107). Having made his own escape, Douglass connected himself with the efforts of William Lloyd Garrison's antislavery newspaper *The Liberator,* turning his own story and his passion for freedom into a tool against the continuance of slavery. *The Liberator,* Douglass wrote,

> became my meat and my drink. My soul was set all on fire. Its sympathy for my brethren in bonds—its scathing denunciations of slaveholders—its faithful exposures of slavery—and its powerful attacks upon the upholders of the institution—sent a thrill of joy through my soul, such as I had never felt before! (P. 117)

Douglass was able to make his own private struggle into one that had larger social implications, as Hawthorne suggested that Hester Prynne had likewise done in her steadfast defiance of her community. In each case heroism is both a personal achievement and an enactment of principle that has a much wider social bearing. The Romantic hero or heroine thus becomes representative of a collective humanity as well as an agent of social reform.

Perhaps the most familiar form of the Romantic hero in the popular imagination is the frontiersman, the prototype of the cowboy star of western books and movies—one of the most characteristic and enduring symbols, for better or worse, of American culture. Real-life adventurers such as David Crockett, whose autobiographical memoir *A Narrative of the Life of David Crockett* was published in 1834, form part of the basis for this figure, but he is also mythological, an embodiment of the aspirations as well as the experiences of Americans who both lived on the frontier and viewed it imaginatively from a safe distance. James Fenimore Cooper (1789–1851) best brought this figure to life in fiction in his series of five Leatherstocking novels: *The Pioneers* (1823), *The Last of the Mohicans* (1826), *The Prairie* (1827), *The Pathfinder* (1840), and *The Deerslayer* (1841). All these works center around the character of Leatherstocking, or Natty Bumppo, the quintessential noble frontiersman. A white man with the ways and skills of an Indian, Leatherstocking lived in two cultures simultaneously. Although his sympathies were always finally with his white compatriots and their "civilization," he understood and respected the power and dignity of the Indian and viewed the advance of European settlers into the West as in many ways a tragic business. A new world was being created, but an old and valuable one lost.

Between both cultures, Leatherstocking had become a man entirely of himself and of the natural world. His attachment to nature, and his keen knowledge of it, is an especially crucial part of his character. The reverence for nature and its close identification with America's national self-image have long been in conflict with the drive to expand and develop the lands that are "unoccupied" or "unused." While the later figure of the cowboy, which evolved from Leatherstocking and characters like him, was generally associated with a celebratory support of continental expansion and the "winning of the West," Cooper's frontier hero is more complex. He is in certain senses himself a victim of that expansion, and he enables Cooper to present a more nuanced version of the moral conflicts entailed in the westward march. Through Leatherstocking, Cooper is able to show both the grandeur of western nature and the tragedy of its gradual demise.

THE ROMANTIC ANTIHERO

Such powerful heroes as the Emersonian poet and Cooper's Leatherstocking generate their opposites; one of the most compelling aspects of American Romanticism is its negative pole, the countercurrent of angst, terror, and chaotic violence that answers the heroic affirmations that define the aspirations of the new nation. That vision was given its most powerful and enduring articulation in the work of Herman Melville (1819–1891), whose *Moby-Dick* (1851) stands as one of the great works of the Romantic imagination. In the crazed Captain Ahab, who defines his wound as the wound of all humanity and his attacker as the source of all evil, Melville defines the frightening excesses to which the Romantic ego could be taken. Observed through the eyes of Ishmael, a perceptive young sailor with an orientation to philosophy and metaphysics, Ahab seems to embody a courageous and single-minded quest for truth, a central motif of Romantic thought. He searches for the whale that maimed him but through that search hopes to get behind the surface of material things, to strike through the "mask" of appearances, to confront the deeper metaphysical elements that define existence. Ahab's quest is clearly the sign of a wounded and unbalanced mind, as Ishmael recognizes. But Ishmael is also able

to see a tragic nobility in Ahab's quest. Ahab embodies the relentless drive to know all, however dark it may be, and he exhibits a concomitant courage that allows him to shake his fist in defiance even at the most sacred of things because he has seen that the universe is flawed. A less dramatically defiant, but no less disturbing figure is Melville's Bartleby, the copyist clerk in "Bartleby, the Scrivener: A Story of Wall-Street" (1853), who gradually withdraws from life, puzzling those around him by turning to the wall and refusing all work with the repeated and haunting comment, "I would prefer not to." Ahab resists the world with rage, Bartleby with a quiet withdrawal, but each signals his recognition of a world askew, in which ideals and aspirations cannot thrive.

DARK ROMANTICISM AND THE GOTHIC

Melville exemplifies the turn in Romanticism that inverts the hero and disavows the quest for unity and understanding, replacing it with a growing recognition of chaos and darkness. The terror implicit in Melville's dark vision is highlighted in Edgar Allan Poe's (1809–1849) haunting narratives, in which madness, gothic horror, and violent death take center stage and in which the precarious balance of the human psyche is exposed and explored. While his contemporaries Hawthorne, Thoreau, and even Melville might be considered moralist in their orientation, Poe was a psychologist, concerned less with the questions of the nature of right and wrong and more with the workings of the mind under extreme stress. In "The Fall of the House of Usher" (1839), widely considered to be one of Poe's masterpieces, the tale's narrator tells the terrifying story of his friend Roderick Usher's premature burial of his twin sister, Madeline. The horror of the burial is compounded by the glimpse Poe gives us of Roderick's gradual mental decay, as he hears the voice of his sister call him from her coffin. Roderick's mental suffering seems as acute as Madeline's, augmented as it is by guilt and by his own fear for his sanity. Roderick's fear is mirrored in a different way in the narrator, who struggles with his rational mind against the seemingly inescapable fact of supernatural forces at work in the Usher mansion and in the family curse. Poe's gothic tale of premature burial thus becomes a study of the psychology of mental derangement and of the rational mind's confrontation with events that seem to transcend rational explanation.

In other works, such as "The Cask of Amontillado" (1846), "The Tell-Tale Heart" (1843), and "The Black Cat" (1843), Poe employs the device of an insane narrator, whose madness slowly dawns on the reader as the story's details unfold. The gradual recognition that one is seeing the world through the eyes of insanity has a powerful impact. Poe relies on a similar experience in what is perhaps his best-known work, "The Raven" (1845), a poem in which the narrator gives a hypnotic account of his crushing realization of the finality of his lover's death. He begins as a seemingly rational man, but as the poem develops, he is tortured by grief and descends into a shrieking hysteria of denial before he collapses at the poem's end. It is Poe's testament to the mind's inability to bear the anguish of loss.

ROMANTICISM, SENTIMENTALISM, AND AMERICAN FICTION

Nineteenth-century fiction and poetry offered a different kind of heroism, and a different conception of the inner life of the self, in what has come to be known as the "sentimental" or "domestic" literature of the era. Largely a literature that was written and read by women, its importance was largely overlooked until scholars in the late twentieth century recognized its value as an expression of women's culture and women's identity in the Romantic age. "Sentimentalism" is the broad category that has come to represent the fiction and poetry that represent and validate the strong emotional experiences of women and men and draw the reader into sympathetic bonds with the heroines or heroes of fictional narratives. Aligned closely with the emotion-centered evangelical religion of the nineteenth century and with the rise of both female authorship and female readership, "sentimental" novels constituted an enormous proportion of the most popular and widely discussed works of the day. Sentimentalism was criticized by "realist" writers later in the century for an excessive use of emotion and dismissed by "modernist" writers of the twentieth century for its lack of objectivity. But sentimentalism has nevertheless persisted to the early twenty-first century as an important element of popular fiction and film. Many of the elements of plot, character, and theme that gave sentimental novels of the nineteenth century their wide appeal were translated directly into the Hollywood films of the early and mid-twentieth century. The historical importance of sentimentalism in the shaping of American literature and culture was belatedly recognized in the late twentieth century through the historical reclamation of women's writing and in the growing recognition of the importance of popular taste in the construction of literary history.

Important studies by scholars such as Nina Baym, Jane Tompkins, and Mary Kelley have shown the formative power of sentimental culture in nineteenth-century American culture, especially in its ability to empower women in a society dominated by men. Novels by such authors as Lydia Maria Child, Maria Susanna Cummins, Catharine Maria Sedgwick, and Susan Warner portrayed the familial and social struggles of women and the enormous inner strength and communal support that they could summon to meet those challenges. The situations and conflicts faced by the key characters in these novels—poverty, lack of meaningful outlets for intellectual and creative expression, unreturned love and desire, psychological cruelty and mistreatment—were drawn from the real experiences of women, and they undermine the general assumption that "sentimental" novels were somehow "unrealistic." Women readers saw themselves mirrored in these heroines and were thus provided with an important means through which to assess their own lives and circumstances.

While these novels were not explicitly "feminist" in a modern sense, they did address the lives of women and did provide their readers with an important creative stimulus and an empowering representation of alternative lives that were closely related to their own. The characters and situations they portrayed spoke to a wide readership of middle-class women in an era in which women's rights and protections were an emerging social issue but hardly an achieved social goal. In one of the most influential novels of the era, *Uncle Tom's Cabin* (1852), Harriet Beecher Stowe (1811–1896) translated sentimental concerns and values into the growing discourse of antislavery, making the slave Tom a powerful exemplar of the spiritual resolve and inner strength that marked the domestic heroine of the sentimental novel. Stowe's novel had an enormous impact on American culture, making powerful use of both evangelical Christianity and the sentimental tradition in the cause of antislavery. In the aftermath of the Compromise of 1850, which upset many in the North with its emphasis on the return of runaway slaves, Stowe's moving portrayal of Tom gave both reality and urgency to the slavery question.

Scholars disagree about the political implications of sentimental literature. Was its tendency essentially conservative, in that it provided its readers with a way of coping with, but not directly challenging, the existing social power structures that supported and legitimized the oppression of women and the legalized slavery of African Americans? Or did it provide both identity and a measure of strength and capability to women, using the sentiments or emotions as a means of teaching lessons in ethics and social justice? The question could never be answered in such starkly binary terms, but the linkages between sentimentalism and nineteenth-century reform movements such as antislavery provide support for a view of an engaged and committed sentimentalism, whose authors were determined to speak to the conditions and consciences of their readers. Sentimental fiction embodied a critical idealism that assumed the intrinsic worth of each individual and recognized his or her right to self-development and self-expression. This was a fundamental tenet of Romanticism and helps to account for its democratic and anti-authoritarian qualities. In the context of the mid-nineteenth century, this affirmation of individual dignity and self-worth had decidedly political implications.

The Romantic era in the United States was eclipsed by the rise of "realism" in the later nineteenth century, a movement that in many ways defined itself against both the sentimentality and the idealism of Romantic fiction. But Romanticism and sentimentalism, as literary and cultural modes, have persisted in American culture. It may be argued in fact that the United States continues to be a Romantic culture whose fundamental values and symbols were shaped in the first half of the nineteenth century.

See also Art; Borders; Democracy; Leatherstocking Tales; *Moby-Dick;* Philosophy; Publishers; Religion; The Romance; *The Scarlet Letter;* Sentimentalism; Transcendentalism; *Uncle Tom's Cabin*

BIBLIOGRAPHY
Primary Works
Child, Lydia Maria. *Hobomok and Other Writings on Indians.* 1824. Edited by Carolyn Karcher. New Brunswick, N.J.: Rutgers University Press, 1986.

Cooper, James Fenimore. *The Leatherstocking Tales: Volume One* and *The Leatherstocking Tales: Volume Two.* Edited by Blake Nevius. New York: Library of America, 1985. Vol. 1 contains *The Pioneers* (1823), *The Last of the Mohicans* (1826), and *The Prairie* (1827). Vol. 2 contains *The Pathfinder* (1840) and *The Deerslayer* (1841).

Crockett, David. *Narrative of the Life of David Crockett of the State of Tennessee.* 1834. Facsimile edition. Edited by James A. Shackford and Stanley J. Folmsbee. Knoxville: University of Tennessee Press, 1973.

Cummins, Maria Susanna. *The Lamplighter.* 1854. Edited by Nina Baym. New Brunswick, N.J.: Rutgers University Press, 1988.

Douglass, Frederick. *Narrative of the Life of Frederick Douglass, an American Slave.* Boston: Anti-Slavery Office, 1845.

Emerson, Ralph Waldo. *Early Lectures of Ralph Waldo Emerson.* 3 vols. Edited by Robert E. Spiller and Wallace E. Williams. Cambridge, Mass.: Belknap Press of Harvard University Press, 1972.

Emerson, Ralph Waldo. *Essays: First Series.* 1841. In *Collected Works,* vol. 2, edited by Alfred R. Ferguson et al. Cambridge, Mass.: Belknap Press of Harvard University Press, 1971. Includes "Self-Reliance."

Emerson, Ralph Waldo. *Nature.* 1836. In *Collected Works,* vol. 1, edited by Alfred R. Ferguson et al. Cambridge, Mass.: Belknap Press of Harvard University Press, 1971.

Finney, Charles G. *Lectures on Revivals of Religion.* 1835. Edited by William G. McLoughlin. Cambridge, Mass.: Belknap Press of Harvard University Press, 1960.

Hawthorne, Nathaniel. *The Scarlet Letter.* 1850. Vol. 1 of *The Centenary Edition of the Works of Nathaniel Hawthorne,* edited by William Charvat et al. Columbus: Ohio State University Press, 1962.

Melville, Herman. *"Moby-Dick," "Billy Budd," and Other Writings.* New York: Library of America, 2000. Includes *Moby-Dick* (1851) and "Bartleby, the Scrivener: A Story of Wall-Street" (1853).

Poe, Edgar Allan. *Edgar Allan Poe: Poetry and Tales.* Edited by Patrick F. Quinn. New York: Library of America, 1996. Includes "The Fall of the House of Usher" (1839), "The Tell-Tale Heart" (1843), "The Black Cat" (1843), "The Raven" (1845), and "The Cask of Amontillado" (1846).

Sedgwick, Catharine Maria. *Hope Leslie; or, Early Times in the Massachusetts.* 1827. Edited by Carolyn Karcher. New York: Penguin, 1998.

Stowe, Harriet Beecher. *Uncle Tom's Cabin.* 1852. Introduction by Alfred Kazin. New York: Knopf, 1995.

Thoreau, Henry David. *Walden.* 1854. Edited by J. Lyndon Shanley. Princeton, N.J.: Princeton University Press, 1971.

Warner, Susan. *The Wide, Wide World.* 1850. Afterword by Jane Tompkins. New York: Feminist Press, 1987.

Whitman, Walt. *Walt Whitman: Poetry and Prose.* Edited by Justin Kaplan. New York: Library of America, 1982. Includes "Song of Myself" (1855).

Secondary Works
Asselineau, Roger. *The Evolution of Walt Whitman.* Expanded ed. Iowa City: University of Iowa Press, 1999.

Baym, Nina. *The Shape of Hawthorne's Career.* Ithaca, N.Y.: Cornell University Press, 1976.

Baym, Nina. *Woman's Fiction: A Guide to Novels by and about Women in America, 1820–1870.* 2nd ed. Ithaca, N.Y.: Cornell University Press, 1993.

Douglas, Ann. *The Feminization of American Culture.* New York: Knopf, 1977.

Fisher, Philip. *Hard Facts: Setting and Form in the American Novel.* New York: Oxford University Press, 1985.

Howe, Daniel Walker. *Making the American Self: Jonathan Edwards to Abraham Lincoln.* Cambridge, Mass.: Harvard University Press, 1997.

Howe, Daniel Walker. *The Unitarian Conscience: Harvard Moral Philosophy, 1805–1861*. Cambridge, Mass.: Harvard University Press, 1970.

Kelley, Mary. *Private Woman, Public Stage: Literary Domesticity in Nineteenth-Century America*. New York: Oxford University Press, 1984.

Levin, Harry. *The Power of Blackness: Hawthorne, Poe, Melville*. New York: Knopf, 1958.

Matthiessen, F. O. *American Renaissance: Art and Expression in the Age of Emerson and Whitman*. New York: Oxford University Press, 1941.

Robinson, David M. *Apostle of Culture: Emerson as Preacher and Lecturer*. Philadelphia: University of Pennsylvania Press, 1982.

Robinson, David M. *Natural Life: Thoreau's Worldly Transcendentalism*. Ithaca, N.Y.: Cornell University Press, 2004.

Samuels, Shirley, ed. *The Culture of Sentiment: Race, Gender, and Sentimentality in Nineteenth-Century America*. New York: Oxford University Press, 1992.

Sundquist, Eric. *To Wake the Nations: Race in the Making of American Literature*. Cambridge, Mass.: Belknap Press of Harvard University Press, 1993.

Tompkins, Jane. *Sensational Designs: The Cultural Work of American Fiction, 1790–1860*. New York: Oxford University Press, 1985.

Wellek, Rene. "The Concept of Romanticism in Literary History." In *Concepts of Criticism*, edited by Stephen G. Nichols Jr., pp. 128–198. New Haven, Conn.: Yale University Press, 1963.

Zoellner, Robert. *The Salt-Sea Mastodon: A Reading of Moby-Dick*. Berkeley: University of California Press, 1973.

David M. Robinson

RUTH HALL

Fanny Fern (Sara Payson Willis Parton, 1811–1872) was not an activist—she never made a speech or attended a women's rights convention—yet her novel *Ruth Hall* (1855) is one of the most significant feminist documents of the nineteenth century. In this autobiographical novel she takes what at the time was a revolutionary position, advocating women's economic independence and portraying a woman who—like Fern herself—realized the American Dream. Unlike other fictional heroines, for whom marriage is the only route to economic advancement, Fern's female protagonist gains monetary success through her own perseverance and self-reliance. Yet the inherent maleness of the concept of independent financial achievement

was so embedded in the culture that no conventional reviewers recognized Fern's novel for what it was—a female success story. Instead, she was called "unfeminine" and criticized for "self-love" while the novel was decried as "abominable," "monstrous," and "eminently evil in its tendencies and teachings" (*New York Tribune*, 16 December 1854; *Protestant Episcopal Quarterly Review*, April 1885; *Putnam's Monthly*, February 1855; *Olive Branch*, 30 December 1854 and 13 January 1855). Commenting on this financial double standard, Fern wrote in the *New York Ledger* on 8 June 1861:

> There are few people who speak approbatively of a woman who has a smart business talent or capability. No matter how isolated or destitute her condition, the majority would consider it more "feminine" would she unobtrusively gather up her thimble, and, retiring into some out-of-the-way place, gradually scoop out her coffin with it, than to develop that smart turn for business which would lift her at once out of her troubles; and which, in a man so situated, would be applauded as exceedingly praiseworthy.

What brought Fern to this radical position? Fern, as an avid newspaper reader, was clearly very much aware of issues and events. The first women's rights convention was held in Seneca Falls, New York, in 1848, and Fern would have read news of it and of succeeding conventions, as well as accounts of the speeches of women's rights activists and the ridicule heaped upon them by conventional sources. In her columns she often responded to items she had read in the newspaper, and these responses included satirical comment on critiques of women's rights' positions. But although Fern was aware of and sympathetic to developments in the feminist movement at the time, her own feminism was essentially a practical feminism, deriving primarily from her own experience.

Born Sara Payson Willis in 1811, Fern followed a traditionally feminine path until her husband, Charles Eldredge, died of typhoid fever in 1846, leaving her with two children and no money. Dependent on a begrudging father and father-in-law, she tried unsuccessfully to support herself as a seamstress. In 1849 she capitulated to her father's attempts to coerce her into remarrying as a means of support. Her second husband, Samuel Farrington, proved to be violently abusive, and in January 1851 she left him. Her relatives were scandalized, and her father and father-in-law, hoping to starve her into submission, refused to help her, while Farrington and his brother spread fraudulent stories labeling her as sexually promiscuous—stories which were later retracted by his brother. Unable to obtain a teaching position (probably because of the scandal), she began writing for the newspapers.

It was Fern's own experience that taught her that if a woman does not have money of her own, she is vulnerable to the whims and cruelties of those who do. Fern's position derived from her realization that men had used their control of money to exert power over her. First of all, her father, in his zeal to avoid having to support her and her children, had pressured her into marriage with Samuel Farrington, a man she did not love and who was repulsive to her. Second, during their marriage, Farrington had withheld money for her and her children's necessities in order to bend her to his will. Third, when she left Farrington, her father and father-in-law refused to support her and her children, in an attempt to force her to return to her abusive husband. But the most egregious example of the use of money as a means of exerting power was her father-in-law's will. After she left Farrington, her father-in-law rewrote his will, leaving all of his money—and he was a wealthy man—to her two children (his only grandchildren) *if* she gave them up to him and his wife and agreed never to see them again. If she did not, all of his money would go to charity. It was the cruelty of this will that was the catalyst that created Fanny Fern. Knowing that if she did not earn enough money to support her children, she would either have to give them up or sentence them to a lifetime of poverty, Fern was driven to succeed. The publication of her first article and the signing of the will took place within eighteen days of each other.

Fern's recognition of the necessity of economic independence was also a result of her change in class status. Her descent into poverty after her husband died showed her that middle-class definitions of womanhood were not universal. It would be suicidal for the working-class woman to adopt the submissive dependency and ingenuousness that society prescribed for "true womanhood"; her survival depended on independence and knowledge of the world. Yet advice books for women unilaterally demanded piety, dependence, and submission. As William Andrus Alcott (1798–1859) wrote in *The Young Wife* in 1837, woman was created to be "man's assistant": "The very act of entering into the married state," he said, required complete "submission" (pp. 27–29). Ralph Waldo Emerson (1803–1882) in a speech before the women's rights convention in Boston in 1855 asserted that the proper function of woman was to "embellish trifles" and urged woman not to seek independence but to trust in a "good man" to be her guardian (*Complete Works* 11:403–404). Fern knew that not all women had a "good man" to rely on, and, after her drop in class, she saw that women without class status could not count on men to be their protectors. In *Ruth Hall* she shows how the boardinghouse loungers regard Ruth as sexual prey once they perceive that she is poor and alone (pp. 73–74). As Fern noted in the *Olive Branch* on 29 May 1852, the upper- or middle-class man who might see himself as a protector of women in his own class was often a "highwayman" in relation to working-class women: he took advantage of them, she said, *because* they were "alone and unprotected."

CAREER

Fern's first article was published in June of 1851 in the Boston *Olive Branch*. She was paid fifty cents for it, and in November of the same year she began writing for the Boston *True Flag* as well. Her articles were immediately reprinted in newspapers all over the United States and Britain, and, although she did not receive any compensation for the pirated articles, the publicity brought her fame. In 1853 she published a collection, *Fern Leaves from Fanny's Port-Folio*, which became an instant best-seller, selling 100,000 copies in one year. The Boston editors refused to increase her pay (by then she was earning four and five dollars a column), even though their papers' circulation had soared after she began writing for them, and in late 1853 when a New York editor offered her twelve dollars a column for her articles she accepted his offer and moved to New York.

In 1855 *Ruth Hall* was published, bringing Fern more celebrity. The Mason Brothers, who published the book, had promised to use "extraordinary methods" to promote the novel, and they undertook one of the first examples of a modern advertising campaign—inundating newspapers and magazines with advertisements and creating a need for and a public image of the book. Before the publication of *Ruth Hall*, Fern's identity was unknown, but in December 1854 one of the exploitative editors whom she had satirized in the novel (William Moulton of the *True Flag*) spitefully revealed her identity in his paper, and the novel became a roman à clef. Readers were particularly interested to see Fern's satiric portrayal of her brother, the writer and editor Nathaniel Parker Willis (1806–1867), as the fop and social climber, Hyacinth Ellet. Although the revelation of her identity was painful for Fern, who had written the satirically autobiographical novel in the belief that her identity was safe, the publicity boosted sales of the book: more than 70,000 copies of the novel were sold in the United States in one year, and the book was translated into French and German. Stores began carrying the "Ruth Hall bonnet"; a popular song, "Little Daisy," was written about Ruth Hall's child in the novel; and the composer Louis Jullien wrote "The Ruth Hall

Fanny Fern. Illustration from the sheet music for "The Ruth Hall Schottische" by Louis Jullien. COURTESY OF JOYCE W. WARREN

Schottische," a dance tune dedicated to Fanny Fern, the sheet music of which bore a lithograph of a woman who very much resembled Fern (Warren, *Fanny Fern,* p. 124).

Fern having become a "hot commodity," Robert Bonner (1824–1899), the enterprising editor of the *New York Ledger,* who was seeking to expand the circulation of his fledgling weekly, attempted to persuade Fern to write for his paper. He offered her twenty-five dollars a column, and when she refused, he increased his offer until she finally accepted at one hundred dollars a column—making her the most well-paid newspaper writer of her time. Her serialized novella, *Fanny Ford,* appeared in 1855, after which she signed a contract to write an exclusive weekly column for the *Ledger,* which began in January 1856 and ran continuously until her death in 1872.

ECONOMIC INDEPENDENCE

The overarching theme in all of Fern's work is women's economic independence. The protagonist of *Ruth Hall* pursues the goal of economic independence, as did Fern herself. After she finds that her

culture's prescription of submissive dependency does not work, Ruth begins to assert her independence. When her brother, Hyacinth, refuses to help her, she vows that she will succeed on her own: "I *can* do it, I *feel* it, I *will* do it" (p. 116). The author describes Ruth as a ship "steering with straining sides, and a heart of oak, for the nearing port of Independence" (p. 133). Unlike most traditional nineteenth-century novels, *Ruth Hall* does not end with the heroine's marriage; in fact, there is not even an eligible man on the scene. The novel concludes, not with the picture of a new husband but with the picture of a certificate for ten thousand dollars in bank stock made out to Ruth Hall. That this is the only illustration in the book is indicative of the certificate's significance.

In addition to dramatizing this theme in the novel, Fern stated it explicitly in her newspaper articles. Writing in the *New York Ledger* on 19 December 1857, she called upon women to follow her independent example, in spite of the criticism they might receive from "conservative old ladies of both sexes." As she said of Harriet Hosmer (1830–1908), the sculptor, she was glad that Hosmer "had the courage to assert herself . . . even at the risk of being called unfeminine, eccentric, and unwomanly." Moreover, said Fern in another article, once women become successful, they need not worry about their critics: "They can stand the spiteful criticism with a good house over their independent heads, secured and paid for by their own honest industry" (*Ledger,* 8 December 1866). Not only would success silence or ameliorate the criticism, she said, but the financially independent woman would receive better treatment: "She won't *have* rough usage. She will be in a position to receive good treatment from *motives of policy.* . . . She will, in short, stand on her own blessed independent feet as far as 'getting a living' is concerned, as I do to-day" (*Ledger,* 18 September 1869). On 16 July 1870 she wrote in response to a newspaper writer who had criticized female physicians:

> Why shouldn't women work *for pay?* Does anybody object when women *marry for pay?*—without love, without respect, nay with even aversion? . . . How much more to be honored is she who, hewing out her own path, through prejudice and narrowness and even insult, earns honorably and honestly her own independence.

The most revolutionary aspect of Fern's belief in women's economic independence was her assertion that such independence could be continued after marriage. Many nineteenth-century novels by women portray an impoverished young woman who is able to earn her own living. However, her independence is seen only as a stopgap measure, and by the end of the

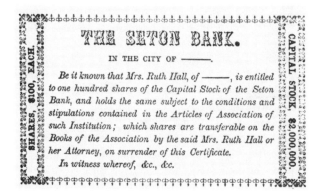

The stock certificate illustration from *Ruth Hall*.

COURTESY OF JOYCE W. WARREN

novel, she always gives up her independent career for marriage and motherhood. This is the plot of such novels as Susan Bogert Warner's *Queechy* (1852), Maria Susanna Cummins's *The Lamplighter* (1854), and Augusta Jane Evans Wilson's *St. Elmo* (1866). Fern, however, did not see marriage and economic independence as incompatible. It might be difficult to combine career and marriage, she said, but she believed that independence in marriage, such as she herself had attained, was not only possible but preferable to dependency (*Ledger,* 8 July 1871). On 18 September 1869 she wrote in the *New York Ledger:*

> Woman, be she married or single, being able to earn her own living independent of marriage—that often hardest and most non-paying and most thankless road to it—will no longer have to face the alternative of serfdom or starvation, but will marry, when she does marry, for love and companionship, and for cooperation in all high and noble aims and purposes, *not* for bread and meat and clothes.

Although *Ruth Hall* ends with the protagonist's acquisition of economic independence rather than the acquisition of a husband, Fern herself did remarry. In January of 1856 she married the writer James Parton (1822–1891), a man eleven years younger than she. However, before the marriage, she had him sign a prenuptial agreement in which she made certain that all of the money she had earned prior to her marriage and all of the money she earned after her marriage would remain hers alone. Such a document was even more necessary then than it is today because in 1856 all of a wife's earnings automatically belonged to her husband.

Fern had had a close call in her second marriage. In 1853, before her identity became known, Samuel Farrington had obtained a divorce in Chicago on grounds of desertion. In September of that year, after

her first book was published, Fern dispatched a lawyer to Chicago to determine what the effect of the divorce would have on her earnings. She must have been elated to read the lawyer's report that the divorce was absolute and that Farrington could not claim "any rights as husband . . . either in person or in property." Farrington was probably not very happy to learn this, however. When he had obtained the divorce he had been unaware that his estranged wife was the famous Fanny Fern, and if he had not divorced her, all of the money she earned as Fanny Fern would have been legally his. Although the Farrington marriage is left out of *Ruth Hall,* in Fern's second novel *Rose Clark* (1856) she portrays a woman whose experience was very much like hers with Farrington. The character, Gertrude, becomes wealthy after her divorce, and her ex-husband, John Stahl, attempts to get money from her. When his friend reminds him that because he has divorced her, the law will not allow him to touch her money, he says confidently: "All women are fools about law matters" (p. 345). Gertrude, however, is more astute than he had thought, and she sends him packing. It is probable that Farrington similarly attempted to get money from Fern, and if he did, she would have been fully armed with a copy of the lawyer's letter. That she was not a "fool about law matters" is apparent in the prenuptial agreement she had drawn up before she married James Parton; she made sure that she would never be financially vulnerable again.

LEGAL POSITION OF MARRIED WOMEN

Of particular importance here is the legal situation of married women in nineteenth-century United States. American law derived from British common law, and according to common law a married woman did not have an identity separate from her husband. As William Blackstone (1723–1780) wrote in the classic *Commentaries on the Laws of England* (1765–1769): "By marriage, the husband and wife are one person in law: that is, the very being or legal existence of the woman is suspended during the marriage" (1:430). A woman could not sue or be sued, own property separately, retain guardianship of her children, or keep any money that she earned. Tapping Reeve (1744–1823), the influential American justice, wrote in *Law of Baron and Femme* in 1816: "The husband, by marriage, acquires an absolute title to all the personal property of the wife" (p. 49). In England, wealthy families had long used marriage settlements to establish a separate estate for a married daughter through equity courts, but many of the American states did not have equity courts, and, even when the courts did exist, the process was expensive and complicated. In the 1840s some states began to pass Married Women's Property Acts, but these laws only dealt with inherited property, not the money that a woman earned; they did nothing for working- or middle-class women who did not have a wealthy father to leave money to them. The laws were designed primarily to protect wealthy fathers, who did not want a spendthrift son-in-law to spend a daughter's inheritance. In some cases—particularly in the South—the laws were a response to the Panic of 1837 and were designed to provide a way to shield property from a man's creditors. Before the Civil War only four states had passed laws protecting a married woman's own earnings. New York passed such a law in 1860, four years after Fern's marriage to Parton, but such laws were not retroactive.

Even after the laws were passed, a conservative judiciary continued to apply common-law principles in the interpretation of the laws. The courts ruled that, unless a wife was abandoned by her husband, her paid labor was "housework," or work done to benefit the household, and, as such, her earnings belonged to her husband as head of household. In *Birkbeck v. Ackroyd* (New York, 1878) the judge ruled, "The bare fact that she [the wife] performs labor for third persons, for which compensation is due, does not necessarily establish that she performed it under the act of 1860, upon her separate account" (see, e.g., Basch, pp. 206–223).

The Seneca Falls Convention in 1848 had passed resolutions asserting that "woman is man's equal" (Stanton et al. 1:72), and the resolutions at the convention in Worcester, Massachusetts, in 1850 were more explicit with respect to women's economic rights, asking that all "avenues of civil and professional employments" be open to women and stating that "the laws of property, as affecting married parties, demand a thorough revisal, so that all rights may be equal between them; that the wife may have, during life, an equal control over the property gained by their mutual toil" (Stanton et al. 1:821). In 1854 Elizabeth Cady Stanton, in a speech to the New York Legislature, urged passage of a Married Women's Property Act that would enable women to "control the wages they earn—to own the land they buy—the houses they build" (Stanton et al. 1:605).

In advocating women's economic independence, Fanny Fern, however, was far in advance of her day. Most women's rights activists supported married women's property rights, but even they were divided on the issue of women's economic independence, particularly after marriage. Similarly, women writers, even those who were economically independent, did not advocate such a role for women—particularly married women—in their published work. The problem was that the concept of women's financial independence was associated with sexual promiscuity. Even such a liberal editor as Robert Bonner, who employed economically independent women like Fanny Fern and E. D. E. N. Southworth (1819–1899), did not publicly advocate economic independence for women. In an editorial in the *New York Ledger* on 14 May 1859 he wrote that if a woman was transplanted from the home to the marketplace, she became a "monster, a man-woman," a condemner of marriage, and an advocate of the "'largest liberty' in the indulgence of the passions." It was not until the late nineteenth and early twentieth centuries with the publication of Charlotte Perkins Gilman's works, particularly her *Women and Economics* (1898), that a woman writer pursued the issue of woman's economic independence, even of married women, in as systematic or outspoken a way as Fanny Fern. As Fern wrote in the *New York Ledger* on 26 June 1869, "I want all women to render themselves independent of marriage as a mere means of support."

See also Autobiography; Banking, Finance, Panics, and Depressions; Editors; Female Authorship; Feminism; Labor; Literary Criticism; Literary Marketplace; Marriage

BIBLIOGRAPHY
Primary Works
Alcott, William Andrus. *The Young Wife*. Boston: George W. Light, 1837.

Blackstone, William. *Commentaries on the Laws of England*. 4 vols. 1765–1780. Chicago: University of Chicago Press, 1979.

Emerson, Ralph Waldo. *Complete Works*. 12 vols. Edited by Edward W. Emerson. Boston: Houghton Mifflin, 1903–1904.

Fern, Fanny. *Rose Clark*. New York: Mason Brothers, 1856.

Fern, Fanny. *Ruth Hall and Other Writings*. 1855. Edited by Joyce W. Warren. New Brunswick, N.J.: Rutgers University Press, 1986.

Reeve, Tapping. *The Law of Baron and Femme*. 1816. New York: Source Book Press, 1970.

Stanton, Elizabeth Cady, Susan B. Anthony, and Matilda Joslyn Gage. *History of Woman Suffrage*. 6 vols. 1881–1992. New York: Source Book Press, 1970.

Secondary Works
Basch, Norma. *In the Eyes of the Law: Women, Marriage and Property in Nineteenth-Century New York*. Ithaca, N.Y.: Cornell University Press, 1982.

Hoff, Joan. *Law, Gender, and Injustice: A Legal History of U. S. Women*. New York: New York University Press, 1991.

Hart, James David. *The Popular Book: A History of American Literary Taste.* New York: Oxford University Press, 1950.

Warbasse, Elizabeth Bowles. *The Changing Legal Rights of Married Women, 1800–1861.* New York: Garland, 1987.

Warren, Joyce W. *Fanny Fern: An Independent Woman.* New Brunswick, N.J.: Rutgers University Press, 1992.

Warren, Joyce W. *Women, Money, and the Law: Nineteenth-Century Fiction, Gender, and the Courts.* Iowa City: University of Iowa Press, 2005.

Joyce W. Warren

SAME-SEX LOVE

For much of the early nineteenth century, same-sex love in America was neither secretive nor subject to social oppression. Indeed what now appear to be surprisingly explicit examples of affection between members of the same sex were often understood, in this earlier period, as legitimate and socially acceptable alternatives to traditional heterosexual unions. Hence Calvin Stowe, husband of Harriet Beecher Stowe, the author of *Uncle Tom's Cabin* (1852), could describe to his famous wife without guilt or shame the solace he found in another man's company during an extended separation from her: "When I get desperate, & cannot stand it any longer, I get dear, good kind hearted Br[other] Stagg to come and sleep with me, and he puts his arms round me & hugs me to my hearts' content" (Hedrick, p. 180).

If such manifestations of same-sex affection (and physical contact) seem unambiguously homoerotic to modern sensibilities, this is due, in part, to changing social and historical definitions of same-sex desire. Until the latter part of the nineteenth century, modern conceptions of homosexuality and homoeroticism did not exist. Indeed many social historians note that "homosexuality," as a scientific term, did not emerge until roughly 1869. Before that time, homosexual acts were not associated with distinct "types" of people, and thus it is only a comparatively recent cultural tendency to link specific sexual practices with specific social identities. In this view it is historically inaccurate to assume that gay and lesbian men and women existed in the same way in all eras and in all cultures.

Love between men in ancient Greece, for example, simply did not have the same social meaning as it does in contemporary society. As a result to speak of homosexual people and practices before the term "homosexual" was even invented may misrepresent the nature of same-sex love in the early decades of the nineteenth century.

To understand desire as historically relative presents both opportunities and difficulties for scholars of gay and lesbian studies. On the one hand, if it cannot be assumed that same-sex love has existed in the same way in all societies, neither can it be assumed that the appropriate social response to such affection is fear, disgust, or violence—reactions that are often promulgated as "natural" in modern culture. On the other hand, the quest for historical precision may bring with it the risk of losing the comforts of generational continuity. To note that same-sex love has meant different things at different times can prove frustrating to those seeking an identifiable tradition of homosexual desire. Adding to this historical challenge is the basic problem of evidence. Unlike the children produced through heterosexual unions, there exists no comparable physical proof of homosexual relations.

Nevertheless, it might reasonably be presumed that the existence of heterosexual relationships points also to the likelihood of same-sex eroticism, even if contemporary definitions of homosexuality do not translate easily into earlier historical periods. In this regard literature provides one way to identify the presence of same-sex love before the category "homosexual" emerged in the late nineteenth century. One should pay close attention, for example, to those works (and authors) that reject traditionally heterosexual concerns, such as marriage or romantic love between men and women. Through such absences, these texts may well signal the presence of a proto-homosexual sensibility. While thus acknowledging the need for historical relativism, one might identify in these earlier texts some of the issues and themes that prefigure contemporary understandings of homoerotic desire.

ROMANTIC FRIENDSHIPS BETWEEN WOMEN

The potential for same-sex love in the early nineteenth century was encouraged by the social organization of American culture itself. During this era, men and women were understood as possessing fundamentally different social capabilities due to differences in biology. Men were seen as logical and rational, ideally suited to the public world of business and commerce. Women, by contrast, were seen as emotional and maternal, naturally adapted to the private, domestic world of the home. Nineteenth-century society thus tended to be divided into separate, gender-specific social spheres. As a result of these divisions, intense attachments often developed between members of the same sex, forging what social historians have termed "romantic friendships." While the possibility of eroticism within these relationships certainly existed, they were thought to be essentially nonsexual, particularly because American culture's interest in identifying (and policing) homosexuality developed only in the latter years of the century. Calvin Stowe's remarks to his wife about his intimate physical contact with Brother Stagg therefore would have raised very few eyebrows.

Women were seen in antebellum America as inherently pure beings; as a result their relationships with other women were believed to be naturally asexual. Intimate, affectionate connections between women were thus socially acceptable facets of everyday life in the early nineteenth century. Such relationships were often encouraged as preferable substitutes to the unwanted advances of men with dubious romantic motives. With the full support of their culture, then, many women formed lifelong, committed partnerships with other women. Often termed "Boston marriages," these relationships were seen as culturally legitimate alternatives to heterosexual marriage and remained so until an increased interest in identifying lesbian "perversion" cast female-female unions as newly suspect at the dawn of the twentieth century. For much of the nineteenth century, however, women could express their affection for each other with great openness and with very little fear of social retribution.

The historian Carroll Smith-Rosenberg has described romantic relationships between women as part of what she terms the "female world of love and ritual," the specifically female social groups that developed in response to the gender-segregated culture of the eighteenth and nineteenth centuries. From birth through schooling and into adulthood, women of the era often experienced their closest emotional bonds with other women. Whether these attachments also included erotic physical contact is not known. On the one hand, historians are careful to note that modern understandings of lesbian sexuality are quite different from the same-sex connections women formed in the early nineteenth century. On the other hand, it seems reasonable to presume that sex between women could occur within such passionate relationships. As historians of women's history have argued, the cultural supposition that women in antebellum America were asexual simply because their era defined them as such should not be accepted at face value.

Identifying same-sex eroticism in literature written by women at this time is thus a complex matter. In countless letters, diaries, short stories, poems, and novels, women detailed their affection and love for each other with unusual candor. But what appears overtly homoerotic from a modern perspective would not have been understood as such in earlier eras. Even those works produced in the late nineteenth century that depict intense female-female relationships, such as Louisa May Alcott's *Work: A Story of Experience* (1873) and Margaret Fuller's *Woman in the Nineteenth Century* (1845), were not seen as "lesbian" texts at the time of their respective publications. Consequently one must approach literature about female same-sex romantic friendships with careful consideration of the cultural context in which these works were produced.

Such concerns, for example, inform contemporary study of the work of Emily Dickinson (1830–1886), one of the most important poets of the nineteenth century. Although she never married, critics frequently have pointed to Dickinson's strong relationships with men (such as her father, her brother, and her mentor Thomas Wentworth Higginson) as evidence of her heterosexuality. Scholarship, however, has increasingly focused on Dickinson's relationship with her sister-in-law Susan ("Sue") Gilbert Dickinson (1830–1913), the person with whom the poet shared what appears to be her most intense emotional bond. While it is not known whether Dickinson and Sue's friendship was sexual, the fact that early editions of Dickinson's work minimized this relationship speaks, perhaps, to an intimacy that transgressed even the nineteenth century's usual tolerance of female-female bonding.

In her poems and letters, Dickinson details fantasies of kissing, caressing, and holding Sue; she describes Sue as her "absent Lover" and refers to herself as "Susan's Idolator [who] keeps a Shrine for Susan." While the extent to which Sue reciprocated this affection is not known, it is clear that she served for Dickinson as one of her primary sources of poetic inspiration. Dickinson repeatedly links her literary gifts with Sue's influence and often utilizes similar imagery to comment both on her writing and her love for Sue. One letter to Sue, for example, begins:

> Dear Sue,
> Your—Riches—
> taught me—poverty!
> Myself, a "Millionaire"
> In little—wealths—as
> Girls can boast—
> Till broad as "Buenos Ayre"—
> (Dickinson, Open Me Carefully, p. 105)

This letter forms the basis for a later poem:

> Your Riches—taught me—Poverty.
> Myself—a Millionaire
> In little Wealths, as Girls could boast
> Till broad as Buenos Ayre—
>
> You drifted your Dominions—
> A Different Peru—
> And I esteemed all Poverty
> For Life's Estate with you—
> (Dickinson, Complete Poems, p. 140)

As the letter and the poem it inspired demonstrate, important facets of Dickinson's writing have their roots in her relationship with Sue Gilbert. While remaining sensitive to the anachronisms inherent in defining this bond as "lesbian," it is possible to identify the centrality of same-sex love to much of Dickinson's poetic genius. In this way her writing helps modern-day readers both to appreciate the nature of women's relationships with other women in this era and to recognize how such relationships form an essential part of the American literary tradition.

ROMANTIC FRIENDSHIPS BETWEEN MEN

Like their female counterparts, many of the nineteenth century's most well-known male authors also experienced the personal significance of same-sex romantic friendships. Ralph Waldo Emerson (1803–1882), for example, the leading proponent of the transcendentalist movement in America, had been attracted to a fellow classmate at Harvard University in the 1820s, an experience that scholars see as formative to some of his subsequent writing. In his essay "On Friendship" (1841), for instance, Emerson notes a "select and sacred relation" between friends "which is a kind of absolute, and which even leaves the language of love suspicious and common, so much is this purer, and nothing is so much divine" (p. 118). While not overtly homoerotic,

Important examples of female romantic friendships are the letters Emily Dickinson wrote to her most intimate friend, and sister-in-law, Sue Gilbert. One letter reads in part:

Susie, will you indeed come home next Saturday, and be my own again, and kiss me as you used to? . . . I hope for you so much, and feel so eager for you, feel that I *cannot* wait, feel that *now* I must have you—that the expectation once more to see your face again, makes me feel hot and feverish, and my heart beats so fast—

Dickinson, *Open Me Carefully*, p. 36.

these comments nonetheless describe the vital importance of same-sex attachments, even naming them as superior to heterosexual unions.

Emerson's friend and fellow transcendentalist Henry David Thoreau (1817–1862) expressed a similar appreciation for intimate connections between men. In a passage from his masterpiece, *Walden* (1854), for example, Thoreau records the arrival of a woodchopper at his cabin, a man described as both effortlessly masculine and aesthetically refined. This visitor brings to the cabin a keen interest in the ancient Greeks, and at his request Thoreau translates from Homer's *Iliad* a scene in which the great warrior Achilles rebukes his bosom friend Patroclus for weeping on the battlefield. The choice of passage is not neutral. In recounting this conversation between male companions who are also lovers, Thoreau tacitly reminds his readers that not all male-male relations are strictly platonic. Achilles's bond to Patroclus (and Thoreau's implicit connection to his unnamed visitor) demonstrates that even within the conventionally masculine worlds of ancient soldiers and contemporary woodchoppers, tender compassion between men is not only possible but also personally enriching.

The erotic potential of male romantic friendship in the nineteenth century finds its fullest expression in the work of Walt Whitman (1819–1892). More than any other author of the period, Whitman gave voice to the range of emotional possibilities within men's relationships with other men. To define these attachments, Whitman used the term "adhesiveness" and clearly distinguished them from the bonds that formed between men and women (which he called "amativeness"). Like Emerson and Thoreau, Whitman saw

Walt Whitman's relationship with Peter Doyle, a streetcar conductor in Washington, D.C., offers one instance of same-sex love between men in the nineteenth century. Years after their first encounter, Doyle described the moment he met Whitman.

He was the only passenger, it was a lonely night, so I thought I would go in and talk with him. Anyway, I went into the car. We were familiar at once—I put my hand on his knee—we understood. He did not get out at the end of the trip—in fact went all the way back with me.

D'Emilio and Freedman, *Intimate Matters: A History of Sexuality in America,* p. 128.

romantic friendships between men as personally transformative and spiritually moving. Unlike that of his transcendental colleagues, however, Whitman's work often concentrates explicitly on the physical attributes of the male body, describing in detail the sensual satisfaction to be gained from an appreciation of "Blacksmiths with grimed and hairy chests," and young men swimming who "float on their backs, their white bellies swell to the sun" (p. 42). For Whitman, attachments between men exist not only in the spiritual realm of transcendental friendship but also in the earthy, corporeal pleasures of the flesh.

His most famous work, "Song of Myself," one portion of the extensively revised *Leaves of Grass* (1855), celebrates this understanding. Whitman sees all aspects of the individual as divine, and hence he glories in his descriptions of the self as "disorderly fleshy and sensual . . . eating drinking and breeding" (p. 56). This sequence of poems details a growing self-awareness of the body as sacred, and Whitman particularly notes the powers his own body contains:

> I believe in the flesh and the appetites,
> Seeing hearing and feeling are miracles, and
>   each part
> and tag of me is a miracle
> Divine am I inside and out, and I make holy
>   whatever I
> touch or am touched from;
> The scent of these arm-pits is aroma finer than
>   prayer,
> This head is more than churches or bibles or creeds.
>
> *(P. 57)*

In describing the magnificence of his body and its desires, the poet implicitly asks that his readers recognize (and appreciate) similar traits in themselves and in those around them. Whitman thus shows his readers how a celebration of the self can (and should) substitute for shame and self-loathing, and he demonstrates, further, how such self-acceptance permits love to grow between men. In so doing "Song of Myself" offers a powerful alternative message to those social scripts that would either demonize same-sex love or force it into hiding.

The transformative power of "adhesive love," according to Whitman, ultimately does more than provide personal gratification; it also has the potential to restore the nation to its democratic potential by correcting the cultural tendency toward materialism and selfish egoism. Thus in *Democratic Vistas* (1871), his trenchant critique of American society, Whitman describes the role same-sex love between men will play in the future prosperity of the United States: "Intense and loving comradeship, the personal and passionate attachment of man to man—which, hard to define, underlies the lessons and ideals of the profound saviours of every land and age," offers "the most substantial hope and safety of the future of these States" (p. 369).

Here, as in "Song of Myself," Whitman defines love between men in explicitly positive terms. By emphasizing the political ramifications of same-sex desire, and by depicting such desire as socially beneficial, Whitman anticipates (and effectively contradicts) many of the objections society makes to gay and lesbian relationships. Same-sex love, in Whitman's view, does not threaten the moral fabric of the United States; on the contrary, it is precisely through this love that American society will be delivered from its moral decay. Through such characterizations of male-male relationships, Whitman's writing has served as a beacon for innumerable gay readers, inspiring American poets, such as Hart Crane and Allen Ginsberg, and several generations of men searching for affirmation of their relationships with other men.

HISTORICAL LESSONS OF SAME-SEX LOVE

One of the primary lessons to be learned from literary examples of same-sex love is that cultural responses to such affection have varied tremendously over time. Because homosexuality, as a category, emerged only in the last quarter of the nineteenth century, the emotions (and sexual activities) identified in the twenty-first century as gay and lesbian were merely part of the general social fabric in this earlier era. Nineteenth-century culture did not observe a strict one-to-one correlation between specific sexual activities and specific social identities, and it is in this respect, ironically, that antebellum America might be seen as more accepting of sexual difference than is present-day American culture. Consequently such an understanding may spur a reconsideration of presumptions about the moral repressiveness of the nineteenth century and of contemporary responses to same-sex desire.

The following example serves as a case in point. The historian C. A. Tripp's research on Abraham Lincoln (1814–1865) suggests that the president's relationships with other men—most notably with his close friend, Joshua Speed (1814–1882)—went beyond the boundaries of mere friendship. The pair shared a bed for several years, and Speed himself noted that "no two men were ever so intimate" (Tripp, p. xx). Because their union predated the term "homosexual," however, to identify Lincoln and Speed as gay misrepresents the specific cultural context in which their relationship developed. Like Emily Dickinson and Sue Gilbert, Lincoln and Speed formed an attachment entirely within the bounds prescribed (and even encouraged) by antebellum society. Consequently the pair's relationship, while intense, would not have been thought improper within the mores of nineteenth-century culture.

Lincoln's apparent comfort with same-sex intimacy serves as an important reminder of the historical lessons to be learned from antebellum culture. Relationships that would likely be seen in the early twenty-first century as unambiguously homoerotic (and thus subject to social critique) existed in the nineteenth century as legitimate alternatives to more traditional heterosexual unions. In this respect the examples of Whitman, Emerson, Dickinson, and Thoreau demonstrate that cultural reactions to same-sex love are neither inevitable nor unchanging. The historical perspective offered by the nineteenth century may thus reveal as much about American culture's future as it does about its past.

See also Friendship; "Hawthorne and His Mosses"; New York; Sexuality and the Body; "Song of Myself"; Transcendentalism

BIBLIOGRAPHY

Primary Works

Dickinson, Emily. *The Complete Poems of Emily Dickinson.* Edited by Thomas H. Johnson. Boston: Little, 1961.

Dickinson, Emily. *The Letters of Emily Dickinson.* 3 vols. Edited by Thomas H. Johnson and Theodora Ward. Cambridge, Mass.: Belknap Press of Harvard University Press, 1958.

Dickinson, Emily. *Open Me Carefully: Emily Dickinson's Intimate Letters to Susan Huntington Dickinson.* Edited by Ellen Louise Hart and Martha Nell Smith. Ashfield, Mass.: Paris, 1998.

Dickinson, Emily. *The Poems of Emily Dickinson.* Edited by R. W. Franklin. Cambridge, Mass.: Belknap Press of Harvard University Press, 1999.

Emerson, Ralph Waldo. *The Collected Works of Ralph Waldo Emerson.* Vol. 2. Edited by Alfred R. Ferguson and Jean Ferguson Carr. Cambridge, Mass.: Belknap Press of Harvard University Press, 1979.

Whitman, Walt. *The Portable Walt Whitman.* Edited by Mark Van Doren. New York: Penguin, 1977.

Secondary Works

Bennett, Paula. *My Life, a Loaded Gun: Female Creativity and Feminist Poetics.* Boston: Beacon, 1986.

D'Emilio, John, and Estelle B. Freedman. *Intimate Matters: A History of Sexuality in America.* Chicago: University of Chicago Press, 1997.

Faderman, Lillian. *Surpassing the Love of Men: Romantic Friendship and Love between Women from the Renaissance to the Present.* New York: Morrow, 1981.

Foucault, Michel. *The History of Sexuality.* Vol. 1, *An Introduction.* 1978. Translated by Robert Hurley. New York: Vintage, 1980.

Hedrick, Joan D. *Harriet Beecher Stowe: A Life.* New York: Oxford University Press, 1994.

Katz, Jonathan Ned. *Love Stories: Sex between Men before Homosexuality.* Chicago: University of Chicago Press, 2001.

Martin, Robert K. *The Homosexual Tradition in American Poetry.* Austin: University of Texas Press, 1979.

Moon, Michael. *Disseminating Whitman: Revision and Corporeality in Leaves of Grass.* Cambridge, Mass.: Harvard University Press, 1991.

Smith-Rosenberg, Carroll. *Disorderly Conduct: Visions of Gender in Victorian America.* New York: Knopf, 1985.

Tripp, C. A. *The Intimate World of Abraham Lincoln.* Edited by Lewis Gannett. New York: Free Press, 2005.

Michael Borgstrom

SAN FRANCISCO

The discovery of gold in the mid-nineteenth century transformed the small fogbound coastal trading post of Yerba Buena into the sophisticated, cosmopolitan, crowded, and often violent city of San Francisco. The men and women who passed through or settled in the city included poets and reporters, novelists and historians—superb storytellers who soon created a vibrant literary culture. To set them in context it is useful to look at three eras of San Francisco history and literature: the precontact period, the colonial age, and the exuberant decades during and after the gold rush.

THE COSTANOANS

By the time of contact with Europeans at the beginning of the seventeenth century, California had the largest (from 250,000 to a million) and most varied indigenous population in North America. The Costanoans, Spanish for "coast dwellers," who inhabited the bay area by 500 C.E. (Pritzker, p. 123) lived in small tribelets, trading and occasionally fighting with other communities. They communicated their values, beliefs, and warm, sometimes ribald, sense of humor in a rich oral literature. It was not the object of the Spanish missionaries who arrived in 1769 to decimate the California Indians, but that was the result. In *Literary San Francisco* (1980), Nancy J. Peters states that,

> The missions were to convert Indians, integrating them as peon labor. . . . The missions extinguished a centuries-old economic and social life. Stripped of their language and identity, deprived of freedom, rounded up by soldiers and kept under guard, the tribes . . . died from European diseases and despair. (Ferlinghetti, p. 8)

In addition, "between 1770 and 1832, the Costanoan population fell by more than 80 percent" (Pritzker, p. 123).

ALTA CALIFORNIA

The area that became the state of California was known to its Spanish conquerors as Alta California. San Francisco Bay remained hidden behind a curtain of fog until José Francisco Ortega discovered it in 1769 and returned in 1776 with Father Junipero Serra and a group of settlers. At the entrance to the bay they built a *presidio* (army post), which remained a working post through the Spanish, Mexican, and American eras, and a few miles inland they founded the Mission of San Francisco de Asís, or Mission Dolores. Serra's fellow Franciscan, Father Francisco Palóu (c. 1722–c. 1789), consecrated the mission and served there for nine years. Palóu became San Francisco's first writer when he wrote Serra's biography, published in Mexico in 1787, and the chronicles of his own California years, *Notícias de la Nueva California,* first published as part of the multivolume *Documentos para la Historia de Mexico* in 1857.

In the early 1800s, Alta California was a ranching society with an economy based on agriculture and raising cattle for beef and hides. Towns were small,

professionals few (one writer applauded the absence of lawyers), and industry so lacking that California at great expense imported its manufactured goods (for example, shoes made in New England from California hides). The Californios' thriving families and communities, the athleticism and zest of life lived on horseback were admired by some American visitors whose letters contributed to the enduring but too often unjustified hope that California could cure physical and spiritual ills. But most felt contempt for the Californios. Both attitudes can bee seen in the experience of Richard Henry Dana Jr. (1815–1882), a Harvard student weakened by measles who decided that shipping out as a sailor aboard a Boston ship trading hides and manufactured goods off the California coast (1835–1836) was what he most needed to recover. He was right. Dana survived an experience so brutal that he devoted much of his life to improving the condition of sailors. The book he wrote when he returned to Boston, *Two Years before the Mast,* became a best-seller when it was published in 1840, and is considered the first California literary classic. Dana admired San Francisco Bay, which he saw briefly, but was appalled at the lack of industry and what he thought was the Californios' laziness and bad morals. Were California to be settled by Protestant and puritanical Americans, he felt, what might they make of it!

IMMIGRATION AND MANIFEST DESTINY

In fact the Americans were slowly on their way. In 1821 Mexico became Independent from Spain and began encouraging immigration, offering land to anyone willing to convert to Catholicism, marry a Californio, and take Mexican citizenship. From the East Coast came explorers in the spirit of what would after 1845 be called Manifest Destiny. In 1835 Captain William Richardson and his family settled on San Francisco Bay in a spot called Yerba Buena, meaning "good herb." When Dana saw Yerba Buena from the deck of his ship there was a lone hut for trade with the ships and Indians. But in 1845 after the United States annexed Texas, and with the South and the Pacific West opening for settlement, increasing numbers of emigrants trekked west, the most infamous being the unfortunate Donner Party, which, trapped and starving in the snows of the Sierra Nevada in the winter of 1846–1847, resorted to cannibalism to survive.

In 1846 war broke out between the United States and Mexico, and Yerba Buena was seized by the Americans; the first American *alcalde,* a sort of combined mayor and justice of the peace, was elected. Alfred Robinson (1807–1895), a trader who had married into a Californio family, published *Life in California during a Residence of Several Years in That*

Sacramento Street, San Francisco, c. 1855. GETTY IMAGES

Territory, in which he predicted that gold and silver mining and an influx of new emigrants would create a populous and thriving city. That year the population indeed more than doubled when Samuel Brannan (1819–1889), a printer, newspaperman, and Mormon leader, landed in town with 238 Mormon pioneers from New York. In 1847 he founded the *California Star,* the first newspaper of the city of San Francisco—for so the new *alcalde,* Washington A. Bartlett, had renamed the town. And in 1848 Brannan, upon learning of the discovery of gold in the American River, about eighty miles northeast of San Francisco, cornered the market in mining implements and other necessary supplies, opened a store, and then sparked gold fever by running about town crying out the news. Ironically in June of that year Brannan had to close down his newspaper because his staff all left for the goldfields.

The 1848 Treaty of Guadalupe Hidalgo allowed the United States to annex the rest of the Southwest. Clearly the gold discovered that year did not bring California into the American fold, but the discovery did forever change San Francisco. Occurring in a decade of famine in Ireland and China, revolution in much of Europe, and industrial unrest in Britain, it gave hope to hundreds of thousands.

SAN FRANCISCO CULTURE AND NOTORIETY

When San Francisco's second *alcalde,* Edwin Bryant (1805–1869), recorded the opening of the gold rush in *What I Saw in California* (1848), San Francisco had become a mix of civilization and vigilantism. By late 1849 the population had skyrocketed to more than thirty thousand and was still growing. All kinds of people poured into California: the sophisticated, the greedy, the thoughtful, the violent.

In 1849 the first theatrical performance in San Francisco was held, and the first English-language book was published. That January Brannan's defunct *California Star* combined with another paper to became San Francisco's first daily, the *Alta California*. In 1850 California was admitted as a free state into the Union, and Bayard Taylor (1825–1878), a prolific travel writer and novelist, published his readable and still popular impressions of gold rush San Francisco in *Eldorado; or, Adventures in the Path of Empire*. The year 1851 saw the first performance in San Francisco of grand opera, Vincenzo Bellini's *La Sonnambula* (*The Sleepwalker*). In 1852 a Philharmonic Society performed in a twelve-hundred-seat hall, and the following year the California Academy of Sciences was founded. In 1856 the historian Hubert Howe Bancroft (1832–1918) opened a bookstore and publishing house. Bancroft eventually employed a staff of researchers and ghostwriters who produced, among other works, a seven-volume *History of California* (1886–1890). Bancroft's enormous personal collection of western Americana eventually became the Bancroft Library at the University of California in Berkeley.

The same year that *La Sonnambula* played in San Francisco, four people were hanged, one whipped, and twenty-eight sentenced to be deported by a Committee of Vigilance, comprised of prominent citizens, including Sam Brannan, who were fed up with an ineffectual municipal government. The year 1853 marked the appearance of the notorious Lola Montez, famed for her dancing, love affairs, and outsize personality. Lola's protégé, "Lotta" Crabtree (1847–1924), would later become the highest paid actress in the country, and in 1875 she generously gave San Francisco an ornate fountain—still there—on Market Street.

The first Chinese men arrived in San Francisco in 1848. In 1855 the first African American journal, the *Mirror of the Times,* appeared, to be followed by the more militant *Elevator* in 1865. San Francisco in 1854 had a "polyglot population . . . with thirty-seven resident foreign consuls to serve them. There were twelve daily papers in several languages, more magazines than in London, and theaters in English, French, Spanish, German, and Chinese" (Ferlinghetti, p. ix).

LITERATURE OF THE GOLD RUSH

Until the 1860s, San Francisco literature consisted primarily of travel books and memoirs, journals and newspapers. In 1854 two important works about the California experience were published. John Rollin Ridge (1827–1867), the son of a Cherokee chief who was stabbed to death by fellow tribesmen for urging acquiescence to U.S. removal policies, wrote *The Life and Adventures of Joaquín Murieta, the Celebrated California Bandit*. Ridge, writing under his Indian name, Yellow Bird, transformed the possibly fictional folk character Joaquín Murieta, a gold-country bandit, into a Robin Hood, a hero dispensing justice to those who had violated his lover and humiliated his family, a Romantic avenger on behalf of the victims of the American onslaught.

And beginning in January 1854 the memoir of Louise Amelia Knapp Smith Clappe (1819–1906), who used the pen name Dame Shirley, appeared as the "Shirley Letters" in the *Pioneer,* a monthly literary journal. In twenty-three letters, ostensibly the private correspondence of Shirley to her sister back east, Clappe describes the diggings—the violence, the miners' homesickness, the beauty of the mountains—from the perspective of a supposedly timid and fastidious wife. Not published in book form until 1922, *The Shirley Letters* is now considered the best of gold rush writing.

The world craved writing about about goldfield adventurers. *California, In-doors and Out* (1856) is the feminist and social reformer Eliza W. Farnham's memoir of chaperoning a group of single educated women to the diggings. The Scottish artist John David Borthwick (1825–1870) wrote and illustrated *Three Years in California* (1857), which not only recounts his experiences mining gold and quartz but also provides detailed descriptions of mining techniques and of life in the camps. Three San Francisco journalists used newspaper reports to compile *Annals of San Francisco,* a history from the age of the explorers until the book's publication in 1855.

SAN FRANCISCO'S CULTURAL HEYDAY

In 1858 the Overland Stage began its run between San Francisco and the East, just in time for the 1859 silver rush, the Comstock Lode, in Nevada. That year Richard Henry Dana Jr. returned by sea to visit the places he saw as a young man; the forlorn shed on the beach had exploded into a city of a hundred thousand. Late in 1862 direct telegraph service was established between San Francisco and New York.

In the 1860s California had the largest number of college graduates in the nation—some from the new University of San Francisco, founded in 1855—and a Normal School opened to train teachers. The city was now sufficiently mature to support a thriving literary community. The writers working and socializing together included Bret Harte (1836–1902) and Mark Twain (1835–1910), who credited Harte with teaching him how to write well; the witty and sarcastic social critic Ambrose Bierce (1842–1914?), who wrote for various San Francisco newspapers and literary magazines "with outrageous black humor . . . capable of ferreting out hypocrisy, fraudulence, and the tyranny that sleeps in the heart of ideologies" (Ferlinghetti, p. 64); Ina Coolbrith (1841–1928), who in 1915 became the first poet laureate of California; Charles Warren Stoddard (1843–1909), a poet and writer of travel books about Hawaii and Tahiti that lured Robert Louis Stevenson into visiting those islands; and Cincinnatus Hiner Miller (1837–1913), a poet of modest talent but great showmanship, who changed his name to Joaquin Miller, after the legendary Murieta, and conquered Europe by swaggering around in a western costume and behaving as Europeans imagined gold miners would. These writers' style was called "local color"—stories so rooted in a particular place that they could not occur elsewhere, rich in details, using the idiosyncrasies of regional speech.

By 1865 Bret Harte, who began as a typesetter and freelance writer for literary journals, had a sufficient reputation to be offered a job editing *Outcroppings,* the first anthology of California poetry. Whatever success or failure emigrants had achieved at the mines, many believed themselves talented poets, and Harte had to choose between mediocre and downright bad submissions. *Outcroppings* created an astonishing furor. Within a few hours of its publication by Anton Roman, hundreds of poets besieged Roman's bookstore to see if they were included in the book. Scathing reviews were widespread, making Harte nothing but enemies. Harte's next project was more successful: in 1868 Roman persuaded him to edit the new *Overland Monthly,* which Roman ambitiously hoped would rival the eastern literary magazine, the *Atlantic Monthly.* Harte asked Coolbrith and Stoddard to join him on the staff; they so enjoyed working together that they called themselves the Golden Gate Trinity.

There was still a large market for gold rush stories, but by the 1860s it was possible to sentimentalize what had been a rugged experience. Twain wrote "The Celebrated Jumping Frog of Calaveras County" (1867), and Harte began what would be a long career spinning stories about a gold rush increasingly softened from the gritty reality. Since then, the world's image of the gold rush and the so-called Argonauts who braved hardships to seek California gold is Bret Harte's: the infant who redeems a community of roughnecks ("The Luck of Roaring Camp"), the plucky prostitute who retires to care for a paralyzed customer ("Miggles"), the loyalty (or is it?) of claim partners who can overlook even wife-stealing ("Tennessee's Partner"), and enough secretly noble gamblers and prostitutes ("The Outcasts of Poker Flat") to keep Harte's career going strong into the twentieth century.

A COMPLICATED LANDSCAPE

In 1863 the newly formed Central Pacific Railroad began work on the western half of the transcontinental railroad. In the *Overland Monthly* in October 1868, the economist Henry George's (1839–1897) essay "What the Railroad Will Bring Us" warned that the new railroad was as likely to bring overpopulation and poverty as prosperity. The railroad certainly brought publications from the East which overshadowed the local production—and took away Twain in 1868 and Harte. Because of the fame Harte earned writing for the *Overland,* the *Atlantic* offered him an amazing ten thousand dollars a year to write a poem or story for each issue, and Harte moved east in 1870. After his writing no longer captivated easterners, he moved to Europe, living mostly in England, where his gold rush tales remained popular.

In 1868 a young man arrived in San Francisco, walked right through town, and lit out for the wilderness. John Muir (1838–1914) spent the summer of 1869 herding sheep in the Sierra Nevada, where he found an Eden he would spend the rest of his life defending. His first essays were published in the *Overland Monthly.* That year the city bought sand dunes in the western section of the city, which William Hammond Hall and John McLaren began to transform into Golden Gate Park. In 1873 Andrew Hallidie created the cable car. Sacramento may have been the seat of the state government, but the 149,473 San Franciscans supported their own popular emperor, the eccentric Joshua A. Norton (c. 1818–1880), a failed businessman who proclaimed himself Norton I, Emperor of the United States and Protector of Mexico. They even (or eventually) obeyed some of his commands, such as the one in 1872 to build a suspension bridge across the bay.

In 1870 the future philosopher Josiah Royce (1855–1916) was a teenager; he would eventually graduate from the new university across the bay and write the definitive history *California from the Conquest in 1846 to the Second Vigilance Committee in San Francisco: A Study of American Character* (1886). And in 1870 the novelist Frank Norris was born; he and such writers as George Sterling and Jack London would create a second wave of great writing set in San Francisco, no longer merely the gateway to the goldfields, but the center of a financial, agricultural, and creative empire facing east and west.

See also California Gold Rush; "The Celebrated Jumping Frog of Calaveras County"; Chinese; Exploration and Discovery; *The Life and Adventures of Joaquín Murieta;* Manifest Destiny; Mexican-American War; *Two Years before the Mast*

BIBLIOGRAPHY

Primary Works

Bancroft, Hubert Howe. *History of California.* 1886–1890. Introduction by Edmund G. Brown. Santa Barbara: W. Hebberd, c. 1963–1970.

Borthwick, John David. *Three Years in California. 1857.* With foreword by Joseph A. Sullivan. Oakland, Calif.: Biobooks, 1948.

Byrant, Edwin. *What I Saw in California.* 1848. Introduction by Thomas D. Clark. Lincoln: University of Nebraska Press, 1985.

Clappe, Louise Amelia Knapp Smith. *The Shirley Letters from the California Mines, 1851–1852.* San Francisco: Thomas C. Russell, 1922. Reprint, edited with an introduction by Marlene Smith-Baranzini, Berkeley, Calif.: Heyday Books, 1998.

Dana, Richard Henry, Jr. *Two Years before the Mast: A Personal Narrative of Life at Sea.* New York: Harper & Brothers, 1840. Reprint, edited with an introduction by Thomas Philbrick, New York: Penguin, 1981.

Farnham, Eliza W. *California In-Doors and Out.* 1856. Introduction by Madeleine B. Stern. Nieuwkoop, Netherlands: De Graaf, 1972.

George, Henry. "What the Railroad Will Bring Us." *Overland Monthly* 1, no. 4 (October 1868). Available at http://www.grundskyld.dk/1-railway.html.

Harte, Bret. *The Luck of Roaring Camp and Other Sketches.* Boston: Fields, Osgood, 1870. Reprint, *The Luck of Roaring Camp and Other Tales,* edited with an introduction by Gary Scharnhorst, New York: Penguin, 2001.

Hicks, Jack, et al., eds. *The Literature of California: Writings from the Golden State.* Vol. 1, *Native American Beginnings to 1945.* Berkeley: University of California Press, 2000.

Palóu, Francisco. *Francisco Palou's Life and Apostolic Labors of the Venerable Father Junípero Serra, Founder of the Franciscan Missions of California.* Introduction and notes by George Wharton James. English translation by C. Scott Williams. Pasadena, Calif.: G. W. James, 1913.

Palóu, Francisco. *Historical Memoirs of New California.* Translated into English from the manuscript in the archives of Mexico, edited by Herbert Eugene Bolton. Berkeley: University of California Press, 1926.

Robinson, Alfred. *Life in California during a Residence of Several Years in That Territory, including a Narrative of Events Which Have Transpired since That Period When California Was an Independent Government.* With an introduction by Andrew Rolle. Santa Barbara, Calif.: Peregrine Publishers, 1970.

Royce, Josiah. *California, from the Conquest in 1846 to the Second Vigilance Committee in San Francisco, 1856: A Study of American Character.* 1886. Introduction by Robert Glass Cleland. New York: Knopf, 1948.

Royce, Sarah. *A Frontier Lady: Recollections of the Gold Rush and Early California.* Edited by Ralph Henry Gabriel. New Haven, Conn.: Yale University Press, 1932. Reprint, Lincoln: University of Nebraska Press, 1977.

Soulé, Frank, John H. Gihon, and James Nisbet. *The Annals of San Francisco.* With a new introduction by Herbert Ely Garcia. Berkeley: Berkeley Hills Books, 1998.

Taylor, Bayard. *Eldorado: Adventures in the Path of Empire.* Berkeley: Heyday Books, 2000.

Twain, Mark. *The Jumping Frog and 18 Other Stories.* Escondido, Calif.: Book Tree, 2000.

Secondary Works

Brands, H. W. *The Age of Gold: The California Gold Rush and the New American Dream.* New York: Doubleday, 2002.

Brechin, Gray. *Imperial San Francisco: Urban Power, Earthly Ruin.* Berkeley: University of California Press, 1999.

Ferlinghetti, Lawrence, and Nancy J. Peters. *Literary San Francisco: A Pictorial History from Its Beginnings to the Present Day.* San Francisco: City Lights Books and Harper and Row, 1980.

Holliday, J. S. *The World Rushed In: The California Gold Rush Experience.* New York: Simon and Schuster, 1981.

Hart, James David. *A Companion to California.* New York: Oxford University Press, 1978.

Limerick, Patricia Nelson. "Will the Real Californian Please Stand Up?" In her *Something in the Soil: Legacies and Reckonings in the New West.* New York: Norton, 2000.

Margolin, Malcolm. *The Ohlone Way: Indian Life in the San Francisco–Monterey Bay Area.* 25th anniversary ed. Berkeley: Heyday Books, 2003.

Pritzker, Barry M. *A Native American Encyclopedia: History, Culture, and Peoples.* New York: Oxford University Press, 2000.

Rathmell, George. *Realms of Gold: The Colorful Writers of San Francisco, 1850–1950.* Berkeley: Creative Arts, 1998.

Starr, Kevin. *Americans and the California Dream, 1850–1915.* New York: Oxford University Press, 1973.

Harriet Rafter

SATIRE, BURLESQUE, AND PARODY

If one were to take note only of the most popular and notable satires from the beginning and end of the period 1820 to 1870—which would include the gentle mockery of Washington Irving in *A History of*

New York . . . by Diedrich Knickerbocker (first edition, 1809; second edition, 1812) and the sly subversiveness of Mark Twain in *The Innocents Abroad* (weekly dispatches, 1867–1868; in book form in 1869)—it might appear that satire in America had not developed appreciably in the middle decades of the century. The opposite, in fact, is true: many strong satiric voices and forms emerged during this time, most of them in relation to political controversies concerning slavery and abolitionism, the Mexican-American War and the Civil War. These new forms of satire influenced political attitudes at the time as well as making a mark on American culture for generations after 1870. Some of the satiric authors, such as Irving, James Fenimore Cooper, and Herman Melville, are well known for their writings in other forms; others remain virtually unknown in the early twenty-first century despite their accomplishments as satirists.

IRVING, COOPER, AND POE

In the early days of the new Republic, political partisans directed ferocious personal attacks against their opponents, but due to a lack of imaginative shaping, such attacks usually remained at the level of invective. The most common object of such vituperation was Thomas Jefferson. Book 4 of Washington Irving's (1783–1859) *History of New York* contains some satire of Jefferson and his administrations (1801–1809), cloaked in the guise of Knickerbocker's account of the administration of an early governor of New Amsterdam, William Kieft. This political satire remains at one remove from the topical, having been written at the end of Jefferson's presidency rather than in the middle of it. Moreover, Irving's temperate and indirect satire of the third president and his policies does not seek to destroy Jefferson personally. Rather, it takes its place alongside the satire of other objects in the work, including the Federalists (Jefferson's opponents), as well as the early Dutch and Swedish settlers, pedantic historians, acquisitive Yankees, slaveholding southerners, and in general the rowdy politics of the new Republic. Irving characteristically communicates all of this satire of the beginnings of New York and of the country's later regional and ethnic groups in a tone of evenhanded good humor. One other kind of satire in the early decades of the nineteenth century criticized those foreign observers who berated citizens of the new country for being vulgar, violent, and yet baselessly proud of their egalitarian institutions and manners. James Kirke Paulding's *John Bull in America* (1825) provides a good example of American responses that satirized these mostly British satirists.

Criticism of the manners and institutions of the Americans did not come only from foreigners,

however. After having written *The Pioneers* (1823), *The Last of the Mohicans* (1826), and several other novels, James Fenimore Cooper (1789–1851) spent eight years overseas and on his return published two novels that agreed with the foreign observers in criticizing the decline in manners and sense of one's own place that he felt had become a widespread problem among Americans. In essays collected in *The American Democrat* (1838), he argued that it was necessary to have men of property and education in a democracy to serve as a counterweight to the unrestrained rule of the majority or the mob. In *Homeward Bound* and *Home as Found* (both 1838), Cooper suggests that in the preceding decade America experienced a leveling downward and an increased regard for the dollar as the only or the ultimate standard of value. He paints satiric portraits of men who have no place but who have the assurance to take on anything. Aristobalus Bragg, for instance, who passed the bar at the age of twenty-one after studying medicine and theology, exhibits a combination of cleverness, vulgarity, kindness, and impudence, wrapped up in shrewdness in all practical matters. A product of the same democratizing pressures, the traveler and writer Steadfast Dodge portrays himself as a confident, optimistic, and knowledgeable commentator, yet he has lost all independence of mind because he lives in fear of disapproval by the majority. In these novels of the late 1830s Cooper satirized what he saw as the America produced by Andrew Jackson's presidency (1829–1837): a leveling of the educated and propertied with the uneducated and unpropertied and an obsessive and vulgar pursuit of the main chance. Cooper's satiric criticism of this America, like Irving's earlier criticism of Jefferson, comes from a conservative cultural position that defends some hierarchies in society as both natural and necessary to preserve a high level of civilization.

Another source of satiric energies at this time undermined very different objects and usually carried no clear political implications. Edgar Allan Poe (1809–1849) originally planned to publish many of his early stories in a volume of parodies to be entitled "Tales of the Folio Club." The stories were not accepted as a whole but in the late 1830s and early 1840s were published separately in different periodicals, where they were almost always taken at face value as straightforward narratives unaffected by ironic countercurrents. Through the exaggeration of conventions, however, and through the self-destructive monomania of their narrators, these and later tales such as "Ligeia," "The Fall of the House of Usher," and "William Wilson" expose and undermine the narrative forms of the time, especially the conventions of the macabre in the gothic and of obsessive love in romanticism. Even Poe's detective stories and tales of ratiocination make use of tricks and parodies to produce an effect of hoaxing and satire that often reverses their surface effect of arrogant certainty. Through this kind of undercutting, Poe's tales typically satirize uncritical or unsuspecting readers. Paradoxically, although these tales appeared in monthly literary magazines such as *Graham's* and *Blackwood's,* they also expose the emptiness of the most popular narrative forms at the time and of the magazines that published them. In effect, they critique the presumptions of contemporary middlebrow literary culture.

DIALECT HUMOR AND POLITICAL SATIRE

A new form of publication encouraged the development of another form of satire during this period. The beginning of penny newspapers around 1830 brought news, opinions, and humor columns within the reach of almost every reader, including those with very little money. The Maine author Seba Smith (1792–1868) appealed to this broad range of readers by creating Jack Downing, a Down-Eastern who reported on political affairs and personalities along the eastern seaboard, especially in Washington, D.C., to the folks back home in Portland, Maine. Downing's letters to the *Portland Daily Courier,* written in New England dialect, conveyed sharp Yankee assessments of Jacksonian politics in an understated way for more than two decades beginning in the early 1830s. Before the days of the telegraph and press services, publishing such a humorous local column could mean success for a small-town paper. Reprinted and imitated in other local papers, the Downing letters set off a movement toward the use of regional humor around the country. Not all of this regional humor was political or satiric; in particular, the two most famous humorous characters of the Old Southwest (which would include Arkansas and Missouri), Sut Lovingood and Simon Suggs (created by George Washington Harris and Johnson J. Hooper respectively), were amoral tricksters who were proud of their deceptions and cheating. These characters may have been entertaining to many readers, but they were not themselves satiric, nor were they satirized by their authors.

By contrast, James Russell Lowell (1819–1891) employed regional dialect humor for strongly satiric and political purposes in the series of poetic letters he wrote for the *Boston Courier* and *Standard* in the persona of Hosea Biglow. The first series of *The Biglow Papers* was written to criticize the war against Mexico in 1846–1847 and appeared in book form in 1848 (with an elaborate apparatus of introductions and notes by the pedantic fictional editor, Reverend Homer Wilbur). Like others who opposed the Mexican-American War (such as Henry David Thoreau), Lowell saw it as an unnecessary conflict provoked by the United States in order to spread slavery through newly acquired territories. Biglow's first letter is directed against a recruiting sergeant whom he portrays as attempting to trick young men into fighting an unjust war. Another sarcastically reports a debate in the Senate in which John C. Calhoun claims that he "stands on" the Constitution in his fierce defense of slavery. A number of letters are written by a fellow New Englander who has gone to the war and reports that conditions for the troops fall far short of what the war's supporters said they would be. In one of the last letters, this soldier, Birdofredum Sawin, reports that he has lost a leg, a hand, and an eye, but rather than criticizing the leaders who started the war, he decides that his physical disabilities may qualify him to become a politician after the war. On the one hand, Lowell thus offers a New England version of the roguish characters in Old Southwest humor. On the other, the soldier's plight resembles that of characters in other satires, such as *Don Quixote* (1604, 1614) and *Candide* (1759), who suffer physical indignities and loss of limbs as a result of their collisions with the world. A later American example of such a character is Lemuel Pitkin in Nathanael West's *A Cool Million* (1934).

Lowell was not a journalist but a member of a prominent Boston family, a poet and critic who went on to become professor of Romance languages and literatures at Harvard (1857–1877) and American ambassador to Spain and then England (1877–1885). His *Biglow Papers* offer a noteworthy example of an intellectual intervening in the public sphere through the use of an innovative form that was both entertaining and political. A second series of *The Biglow Papers,* directed against slaveholders and secessionists during the Civil War, appeared in the *Atlantic Monthly* from 1861 to 1866 (book form, 1867). The second series, however, has somewhat less energy and bite than the first.

The most successful and influential satirical work of the Civil War years and their immediate aftermath was *The Nasby Papers* by David Ross Locke (1833–1888), who built on and extended Lowell's accomplishment in the first series of *The Biglow Papers.* Locke spent most of his career as a journalist associated with papers in Ohio, becoming editor and eventually owner and publisher of the *Toledo Blade.* He was just short of thirty when the first of the Nasby letters appeared in 1862. A collection was published in book form in 1864, and five more volumes followed in the next four years. In Petroleum V. Nasby, Locke constructed a caricatural portrait of a northern Democrat—a proslavery political operative, a lazy office seeker, a cruel, callous,

This is the first stanza of a poem in James Russell Lowell's The Biglow Papers *(first series, no. 5). The occasion was the unsuccessful attempt of two antislavery men, Drayton and Sayres, to lead seventy men and women from slavery. They were prevented by the district attorney of Washington, D.C., and the Africans were returned as the property of their owners. Senator John C. Calhoun of South Carolina (1782–1850) angrily asserted that the Constitution provided for slavery and that the federal government and the northern states had no right at all to interfere with the institutions of the southern states. For Calhoun and his southern followers, any attempts to restrict slavery or aid fugitive slaves constituted tyranny and were preludes to a dissolution of the Union. For Lowell and other northern abolitionists, the institution of slavery violated the most basic human right to freedom.*

"Here we stan' on the Constitution, by thunder!
It's a fact o' wich ther 's bushils o' proofs;
For how could we trample on 't so, I wonder,
Ef 't wor n't thet it 's ollers under our hoofs?"
Sez John C. Calhoun, sez he;
"Human rights haint no more
Right to come on this floor [of the Senate],
No more 'n the man in the moon," sez he.

Lowell, *The Biglow Papers,* p. 111.

and cowardly man, and a self-proclaimed Christian minister, "Lait Paster uv the church uv the Noo Dispensashun." The misspellings in his letters—"ez" for "as," "wuz" for "was," "ablishn" for "abolition," and so on—are supposed to indicate a generalized dialect, but because most of the changes barely affect pronunciation, they work mostly to designate Nasby as an uneducated and unintelligent but dangerous bigot. Like Simon Suggs and Sut Lovingood, Nasby is always on the make, looking out for a free ride, but unlike these predecessors, he is the constant object of his author's satire and serves as the vehicle for the satire as well. Thus, employing the satiric technique of praise by blame, Locke makes clear that those whom Nasby praises one is to blame and condemn, and those whom Nasby attacks rise in one's estimation. Nasby's arguments reveal his inconsistency, illogicality, and hypocrisy: he has almost constant recourse to a language of liberty, "democricy," and "tirany," but the only freedom he is interested in is the slave owner's freedom to do as he wants with his slaves and his

own freedom to obtain a do-nothing job as the local postmaster. Any attempt to obstruct either of these goals he considers tyrannical.

Nasby is not a complicated character; neither is the message that Locke implies throughout the *Papers,* which consistently accords with the positions of the Republican Party. Still, Locke employs a variety of satiric techniques and forms in the letters: some recount dreams, some transcribe interviews, some consist of Nasby's lamentations over the course of events. A letter from 1 June 1862 gives an account of Nasby's interview with Clement Vallandigham, a proslavery Copperhead Democrat who was exiled for sedition by Abraham Lincoln. In the interview, Vallandigham tells Nasby that to win elections in Ohio, the Democrats should push to prohibit "holesail" voting by blacks, should sow fears of a huge immigration of freed blacks into the state, and should raise the specter of an amalgamation of the races, although, as even Nasby points out, none of these is remotely possible any time soon. Locke's point, of course, is that elections are often won by playing to bigotry and fear. He also knew that abolition would not end the oppression of Africans in America. Immediately after the approval of Emancipation (6 January 1866), he has a Southerner console Nasby by pointing out that the South and the Democrats will now actually be stronger politically than before the war: slaves used to count for only three-fifths of a person, but since each now counts for one, the increased population of the South will lead to increased representation in Congress. Southerners can observe the letter of the emancipation law yet still keep blacks in a condition of servitude by imposing restrictions on their movements, their ability to own property and vote, and their other civil rights. Some of Nasby's letters employ comic satire, but Locke does not turn away from also portraying the grisly violence caused by racial hatred after Reconstruction. On such occasions his satire has an effect like that of Mark Twain's later in "The United States of Lyncherdom" (written 1901): both record the casual perpetration of atrocities in a country that claims to be dedicated to equal protection of the law for all.

In Nasby's letters Locke harnessed satiric techniques to a strong indignation at racial injustice and exercised a significant effect on his own time. Both Abraham Lincoln and Ulysses Grant believed that *The Nasby Papers* strengthened the Union cause and helped the North win the war. For the concept and the execution of these papers, Locke acknowledged his debt to Lowell's *Biglow Papers,* and Lowell was pleased that Locke thus extended his work. Another writer to whom Locke gave credit as a predecessor was

Artemus Ward, the pseudonym of Charles Farrar Browne (1834–1867). Like Locke, Browne wrote for an Ohio newspaper, the *Cleveland Plain Dealer*. Artemus Ward, his fictional creation, was the proprietor of a wax figure show that toured small towns around the country. Ward's writing was one of the first to use phonetic misspellings that did not indicate dialect pronunciations. His columns usually presented comic observations of a scene, a town, or an event; his satire avoided politics but could be both sharp and humorous when directed at religious sects such as Quakers, Mormons, and Free Lovers.

MELVILLE AND OTHER SATIRISTS, 1855–1865

Not all satire in the late 1850s and 1860s took shape through regional dialect humor, however. For example, critics agree that *The Confidence-Man: His Masquerade* (1857), the last novel by Herman Melville (1819–1891) to be published in his lifetime, is a satiric work, although they have reached little agreement on the objects or the meaning of the satire. The narrative recounts a series of conversations that take place during one day on a steamboat going down the Mississippi River. One set of these conversationalists can be identified as confidence men—they all appear on a list that one of them provides of his "friends" on the ship—although, strikingly, they do not seem to be interested mainly in taking money from the other passengers. Those to whom they address their appeals for confidence prove themselves to be either gullible believers or hard-hearted cynics whose resistance to such appeals comes close to an asocial misanthropy. The implication of these tortuous philosophical exchanges remains enigmatic in the extreme. Helen Trimpi has argued that every character in the novel is patterned on a political figure from the 1840s or 1850s who can be identified by comparison with political caricatures of the time. Others have maintained that the confidence men are different incarnations of the divinity or of the devil or that the narrative presents a satiric critique of the kind of faith required of participants in a capitalist society. Perhaps all these patterns of meaning contribute to the ultimate significance of this suggestive work, which appears to have been as cryptic in its own day as in ours: only two hundred copies of it were sold.

For another satire that sees satanic forces at work in the United States in the late 1850s but that articulates a very definite point of view on the subject, one could turn to *The Devil in America* (1860), by R. S. Gladney (Lacon, 1806–1869). In this proslavery narrative in blank verse set in Pandemonium—like the first books of John Milton's *Paradise Lost* (1666)—

various subordinate demons report to their leader on the progress they have made sowing discord and division around the country. These lieutenants include the demons of superstition, atheism, sectarianism, alcohol, fanaticism, and abolition. By fanaticism, the author chiefly means agitation for women's rights, and he strongly links such a program with the abolitionist movement: the speakers at a women's rights convention include Miss Free-Love and Miss Free-Soil. In contrast, according to this long poem, slavery is natural and in accord with divine law. Although the Union has thus been brought to the verge of dissolution by the demons' activities, the work concludes with a vision of the defeat of Satan's forces and the establishment of a millennium based on technological progress in which there will be no need for prisons, hospitals, or wars. The narrative thus moves abruptly from an extended satiric representation of contemporary America to a wishful utopian conclusion.

The last satiric work to be considered here returns in form to the series of letters published a week or a few weeks apart, in this case throughout the course of the Civil War. Unlike the other collections already discussed, it is not in dialect—though its use of language is remarkable—and it takes as the object of its satire neither slavery nor abolitionism. The letter writer of Robert Henry Newell's (1836–1901) *Orpheus C. Kerr Papers* (1861–1865) is named for the large number of office seekers who came to Washington, D.C., during the Lincoln administration, but Newell directs his satire primarily at the Union military and their conduct of the Civil War. Kerr casts his reports on the doings of the Mackerel Brigade in an inflated language of empty magniloquence, making regular use of circumlocution and mythological reference to describe the incapacity, stupidity, delays, and retreats that seem to be ubiquitous in the army. Thus whiskey drinking is always "taking the Oath," and Kerr's bony and starving horse is "my Gothic Pegasus." The same techniques of exaggeration reveal the hollowness of the officially established lines of the government and the press: the latter is "the Palladium of the Republic" which is always reporting on the condition of "our distracted nation." Aside from research and development on ridiculous new super-artillery weapons, the most nefarious plan of attack the Union comes up with is to let "the celebrated Confederacy" capture their supply wagons and eat the Union rations: doing so will make it sick on the spot, and the Mackerel Brigade will capture it alive (Confederate soldiers are never referred to in the plural but always as "the Confederacy"). Occasionally Abraham Lincoln appears in his "anecdotage" as a cracker-barrel philosopher telling long, pointless stories when decisions about military matters urgently need to be taken. *The Orpheus C. Kerr Papers* harnesses surreal absurdity to produce scathing antiwar satire of the kind that Joseph Heller was to achieve later in *Catch-22* (1961).

BURLESQUES

Theatrical burlesques or travesties that shorten, simplify, and adapt a well-known play to other circumstances, often to the contemporary lives of lower classes or other ethnic groups or races, came to be popular on the English stage in the first decades of the nineteenth century. Many of these burlesques made their way to the United States in the 1830s and 1840s, when American burlesques on the English model began to be written and performed. Both in England and in America, Shakespeare's plays provided the most frequent source of burlesques, with the best-known plays—*Hamlet, Macbeth, Othello*—being the most frequently travestied. Burlesques presupposed a wide acquaintance with the originals, because without such familiarity, the humor and satire of the takeoff could not be appreciated. The object of such burlesques could be to satirize the actors and the productions of the original plays in the serious theater; to satirize a contemporary political figure or development; to mock the ethnic or racial group being represented; or some combination of all three. Thus, for example, in *Much Ado about a Merchant of Venice* (1868), Portia's most famous speech begins

> The quality of mercy is so strained
> In this our day, and all the prisons drained
> By legislative pardons.
>
> *(Wells 5:113)*

Such topical references, as well as mentions of familiar places in the city of performance, made these plays entertaining to wide audiences that included working-class and middle-class, educated and uneducated theatergoers. Such a mixing of audiences became rarer as the period wore on, however, especially after the Astor Place riot in New York City in May 1849, when twenty-two working-class people were killed at a demonstration of about ten thousand against the "aristocratic" style of an English actor who was performing *Macbeth* at the Astor Place Opera House at the time. From that point on, high or elite culture defined itself more and more in opposition to, rather than in conjunction with, popular culture. Especially in America, burlesques written for blackface minstrel shows became significant elements of the culture in the 1840s and remained so for several decades. The dominant, though not the only, effect of these works was to mock black bodies and black people's ways of acting and of speaking. Indeed, these derogatory and

---

The letter from which the following selections are taken was written after the first battle of Bull Run (21 July 1861), which ended in defeat for the Union. To counteract the demoralization that followed the defeat, Orpheus C. Kerr goes to the navy yard in Washington, D.C., to witness the testing of newly invented cannon. The first weapon fails to fire, but the government orders forty of the guns anyway. The second is a revolving cannon, which pivots as it shoots two balls simultaneously but which the gunner refuses to fire because he "has a large family dependent on him for support"; the government still orders six of the guns "to be furnished in time for our next war."

The last weapon subjected to trial was a mountain howitzer of a new pattern. The inventor explained that its great advantage was, that it required no powder. In battle it is placed on the top of a high mountain, and a ball slipped loosely into it. As the enemy passes the foot of the mountain, the gunner in charge tips over the howitzer, and the ball rolls down the side of the mountain into the midst of the doomed foe. The range of this terrible weapon depends greatly on the height of the mountain and the distance to its base. The Government ordered forty of these mountain howitzers at a hundred thousand apiece. . . .

Last evening a new brigadier-general, aged ninety-four years, made a speech to Regiment Five, Mackerel Brigade, and then furnished each man with a lead-pencil. He said that, as the Government was disappointed about receiving some provisions it had ordered for the troops, those pencils were intended to enable them to draw their rations as usual. I got a very big pencil, my boy, and have lived on a sheet of paper ever since.

Newell, *The Orpheus C. Kerr Papers*, pp. 85–87.

---

stereotyped representations have exerted a lasting influence in American culture down to the present.

Thus, although *The Innocents Abroad* (1869) by Mark Twain (1835–1910) returns to a kind of subtle and understated satire like Irving's in his *History of New York*, it does so after, and no doubt partly in response to, a period of energetic, innovative, and hard-hitting satire. In *The Innocents Abroad,* Twain participates in the world and the discourse of travel even as he quietly dismantles or undercuts the conventions of behavior and writing by travelers. In *The Gilded Age* (1873, with Charles Dudley Warner), Twain offers a more wide-ranging and explicit satire of American types such as the corrupt politician, the ineffectual but voluble dreamer, and the young woman determined to attend medical school. Even though the title of this novel gave its name to the era, however, the satire of Twain and Warner remains humorous, affectionate, and accommodating. A more searching, bitter, and tragic satire would have to wait until *Adventures of Huckleberry Finn* (1885), *A Connecticut Yankee in King Arthur's Court* (1889), and the late essays and stories. In the same decades, Ambrose Bierce was honing his incisive wit and satire in the short works that would be collected in book form as his *Fables* (1898) and *The Devil's Dictionary* (1906). Such works belong to the next chapter in the history of satire in America.

See also Dialect; Humor; Tall Tales

BIBLIOGRAPHY
Primary Works
Cooper, James Fenimore. *Home as Found.* 1838. New York: Capricorn, 1961.

Irving, Washington. *A History of New York . . . by Diedrich Knickerbocker.* 1809. New York: Harcourt, Brace, 1927.

Locke, David Ross. *The Nasby Papers.* Indianapolis: C. O. Perrine, 1864.

Lowell, James Russell. *The Biglow Papers.* 2 vols. Boston: Houghton Mifflin, 1885.

Newell, Robert Henry. *The Orpheus C. Kerr Papers.* 4 vols. 1862–1868. New York: AMS Press, 1971.

Secondary Works
Austin, James C. *Petroleum V. Nasby (David Ross Locke).* New York: Twayne, 1965.

Carlisle, Henry C., Jr., ed. *American Satire in Prose and Verse.* New York: Random House, 1962.

Cox, James M. *Mark Twain: The Fate of Humor.* Princeton, N.J.: Princeton University Press, 1966.

Eddings, Dennis W., ed. *The Naiad Voice: Essays on Poe's Satiric Hoaxing.* Port Washington, N.Y.: Associated Faculty Press, 1983.

Harrison, John M. *The Man Who Made Nasby, David Ross Locke.* Chapel Hill: University of North Carolina Press, 1969.

Levine, Lawrence. *Highbrow/Lowbrow: The Emergence of Cultural Hierarchy in America.* Cambridge, Mass.: Harvard University Press, 1988.

Lott, Eric. *Love and Theft: Blackface Minstrelsy and the American Working Class.* New York: Oxford University Press, 1993.

Palmeri, Frank. *Satire in Narrative: Petronius, Swift, Gibbon, Melville, Pynchon.* Austin: University of Texas Press, 1990. Contains a chapter on Melville's *Confidence-Man* as a narrative satire.

Trimpi, Helen P. *Melville's Confidence Men and American Politics in the 1850s.* Hamden, Conn.: Archon, 1987.

Wells, Stanley, ed. *Nineteenth-Century Shakespeare Burlesques.* 5 vols. Wilmington, Del.: Michael Glazier, 1978. Vol. 5 includes American burlesques of Shakespeare, among them *Much Ado about a Merchant of Venice* (1868) and *Hamlet the Dainty* (1870).

Frank Palmeri

THE SCARLET LETTER

Nathaniel Hawthorne's (1804–1864) novel *The Scarlet Letter* (1850) raises important questions about the relationship between literature and history. A historical novel set in seventeenth-century New England, it offers Hawthorne's interpretation of the meaning and legacy of the Puritan culture that defined the region. Like many nineteenth-century American authors, including Henry Wadsworth Longfellow, James Fenimore Cooper, and Lydia Maria Child, Hawthorne looks to America's colonial past as a source of subject matter in a country that he lamented (in the preface to his 1860 novel *The Marble Faun*) had "no shadow, no antiquity, no mystery, no picturesque and gloomy wrong, nor anything but a common-place prosperity" (p. 854). As did his contemporaries, Hawthorne saw in an exploration of the past an opportunity to evaluate how that past shaped the character and culture of America in his own day. Through this interpretation of the past, however, Hawthorne could also consider issues that were important to mid-nineteenth-century America, including the relationship between the individual and the community, the impact of a society's codes and values upon its members, the place of women in American culture, and the difficult position of the artist or independent thinker in any society, past or present.

"THE CUSTOM-HOUSE"
Hawthorne raises some of these concerns in "The Custom-House," which serves as a preface to the novel proper. "The Custom-House," set during Hawthorne's day, provides insights into Hawthorne's

own relationship with the state, as he had been a public employee at the Custom House of Salem for three years prior to writing his novel. Turned out of office when the presidential administration changed in 1849 and the anti-Jacksonian Whigs came to power, Hawthorne defended his record as an employee but also revealed his uneasiness over the conditions that arise when individuals remain too long dependent upon the state. He presents his former coworkers as marked by "the lack of energy that distinguishes the occupants of alms-houses" (p. 124), suggesting that lifetime government appointments undermine the self-reliance and personal initiative valued in Hawthorne's culture. Hawthorne had depended on patronage appointments himself, for until the success of *The Scarlet Letter,* he had been unable to support his family on the proceeds of his writing career. But he claims that his powers of imagination and creativity were diminished while under public employ, returning only after he had been dismissed and no longer had to conform to a particular political identity.

Hawthorne also makes use of his position as a "surveyor" in the Custom House to assess the traditions from the past that have given rise to the concept of an "American" identity. Hawthorne explores the ways in which individual identity is shaped by family, place, and the past, suggesting that his own identity is bound up with the tales of his ancestors and the town of Salem. He describes the attachment to place as an "instinct" that impels an individual to return after periods of absence, an instinct that comes into play for *The Scarlet Letter*'s Hester Prynne at the end of the novel. In addition to the questions he poses about individual identity, Hawthorne, like many of his contemporaries, looks to the Puritan past of New England as the source of America's democratic impulse. Sacvan Bercovitch has pointed out the way that Hawthorne, in common with many mid-nineteenth-century historians, saw in the early settlers' desire to create a new order that separates itself from Old World hierarchies and institutions the foundation for the balance between individual liberty and the consent to compromise that allows for both America's progress and stability (pp. 36–38).

Hawthorne links the preface to the novel proper through the explanation of his discovery in the Custom House of a manuscript and the remnants of an embroidered letter *A* supposedly left behind by one of his predecessors, the surveyor Jonathan Pue. These materials, Hawthorne suggests, provided him with the substance of the narrative that follows and lend it authenticity. This claim of physical evidence for the story that unfolds emphasizes its ties to history, but Hawthorne also

explores his fascination with the idea of the scarlet letter, his desire to discern its meaning, to solve its riddle. He speaks of the letter as a "mystic symbol" that demands interpretation and that offers a multiplicity of meanings. He suggests that his own "imagining [of] the motives and modes of passion that influenced the characters" (p. 147) gives access to a truth that may be found when "the Actual and the Imaginary . . . meet, and each imbue itself with the nature of the other" (p. 149), indicating his view that the romance allows its author to engage in imaginative reconstruction, to tell the stories of the past that may not be part of the official public record but that have a bearing on personal and cultural identity and on the specific historical circumstances of the writer's own time.

HAWTHORNE AND NEW ENGLAND'S HISTORY

Hawthorne was well steeped in New England history, having spent a number of years in his early adulthood studying the works of various historians who examined and interpreted the colonial era. He was also well read in texts that were popular during the colonial period, such as the Puritan theologian and religious leader Cotton Mather's *Magnalia Christi Americana* (1702), a history of New England that celebrates the evidences of Christ in the New World. Hawthorne's own family background had made this period of interest to him, for he traced his paternal lineage back to Puritan officials and judges, including John Hathorne, who served during the Salem witchcraft trials. Hawthorne felt uneasy about the harsh judgmental aspects of this godly form of governance, seeing in his ancestors stern and inflexible men who seemed to show little mercy toward those they deemed in the wrong, meting out harsh punishment to those who violated the laws and codes of their community. Hawthorne admired his ancestors' strength of purpose and industriousness but wondered what they would think of a descendant who spent his time writing fiction instead of competing openly in the marketplace to build his fortune and provide for his posterity.

Hawthorne does not provide the exact dates for the action of *The Scarlet Letter,* but he sets the scene during one of the governorships of Richard Bellingham, most likely that of 1641–1642, and no later than 1654, since Bellingham's sister, Anne Hibbins, who makes brief appearances in the novel, was executed for witchcraft in 1656. In the 1640s the Puritans were still establishing their colonies and making inroads into the wilderness that surrounded them. Their plans for settlement were founded in the hope of establishing communities that would exemplify the religious and moral rigor they deemed necessary for salvation. In the words of John Winthrop, the first governor of the Massachusetts Bay Colony, they were to be "as a city upon a hill," modeling righteousness and a social order defined by religious precepts ("A Modell of Christian Charity," quoted in Miller and Johnson 1:199). Winthrop urged his fellow settlers to sacrifice personal ambitions for the good of the community, to place the needs of the whole above those of the individual. The Puritans followed strict codes of conduct and severely punished anyone who was thought to threaten the cohesiveness of the group. Their anxieties about the success of their "errand" and the role they were to play in the unfolding of God's Providence were intensified in the 1640s and 1650s by the events occurring in England, as Puritans there came to power during the English Civil War. Some New Englanders feared that the emergence of a Puritan Commonwealth at home made their own experiment extraneous. This time of insecurity for the Puritans in New England makes it a perfect era in which to set a historical novel, for moments of cultural conflict are those that produce changes for individuals and for a society as a whole. Hawthorne's own day marked another period of cultural conflict, both in light of the revolutions and political upheaval occurring in Europe and in the growing anxiety over the impact slavery and sectional conflict would have on the state of the union in America. In addition, various reform movements of the 1840s and 1850s, including women's rights and temperance, challenged cultural assumptions while people continued to adjust to changes wrought by the expansion of industry, especially in the Northeast.

The Puritan settlements of New England were troubled by discord at home as well as by political upheaval abroad. The so-called antinomian controversy, which erupted in the late 1630s, centered around the actions and ideas of Anne Hutchinson, a figure to whom Hawthorne often compares his main character, Hester Prynne. Hutchinson was well acquainted with church teaching and with Puritan theology. She began to hold meetings in her home to instruct other women, and she asserted that individuals could realize their salvation through direct revelation from God, an idea that some felt eliminated the need for clergy to interpret the word of God to their congregations. Her views were labeled "antinomian," meaning contrary to the law, and she was accused of crimes against the church and the state. Hutchinson was banished from the Massachusetts Bay Colony in 1638, eventually moving to New York, where she died during an Indian raid in 1643. Hawthorne's comparisons of Hester Prynne to Anne Hutchinson underscore Hester's role as a figure who tests her culture's ideas and values; Hutchinson's

exile suggests what might befall Hester should she speak her thoughts in public.

The other domestic threat to the stability and security of the colony was the supposed presence of witchcraft. The witchcraft hysteria that gripped Salem and other Massachusetts Bay towns did not occur until about fifty years after the events recounted in *The Scarlet Letter*, commencing in 1692. But fear of witchcraft was present in the colony from its founding, as was fear of Satan's attempts to undermine the efforts of settlers to carry out God's will in the New World. Witches were perceived as threats to the social and spiritual order because of their supposed relationship with the devil, a relationship that gave them access to supernatural powers and dangerous knowledge. Those accused of witchcraft were often independent thinkers or individuals who had provoked their neighbors through contentious behavior. In *The Scarlet Letter*, Mistress Hibbins hints at dark knowledge and secret meetings in the forest, suggesting both the presence of witchcraft and the way that Hester's own knowledge and journey into the forest might be perceived.

HESTER'S SIN

By drawing on the historical past and the romance tradition to shape his narrative, Hawthorne feels free to "claim a certain latitude," to focus on circumstances of his "own choosing and creation" (as he phrases his approach in the preface to his 1851 novel *The House of the Seven Gables*, p. 351), determining which characters and events will occupy the foreground of his narrative and which will provide only background context. In *The Scarlet Letter*, Hawthorne makes mention of officials within the Puritan colony, but he uses them as secondary, though powerful, players in the conflicts that unfold. In the novel, Hawthorne is more concerned with the lives and relationships of his four central characters—Hester Prynne; the Reverend Arthur Dimmesdale; Roger Chillingworth; and Hester's daughter, Pearl—figures who are not historical personages but whose thoughts and actions are affected by the culture that surrounds them. Each of these characters struggles with questions of identity, both in terms of self- and public perception. Their relationships to each other and the patterns of concealment and revelation that emerge from their interactions allow Hawthorne to explore how identity evolves and how individuals construct public personae to suit their own needs. His characters' interactions with the larger Puritan community raise questions about the nature of patriarchal culture and its control of women, the tension between individual freedom and community standards, and the potential for reintegration into the social order.

Hester Prynne's punishment. Hester stands on the town's scaffold holding her daughter, Pearl. GETTY IMAGES

Individual freedom is clearly a foreign idea to the colony, for Hawthorne opens the narrative proper with a chapter entitled "The Prison-Door." This door, "studded with iron spikes" (p. 158), asserts the power of the civil authority and its willingness to use physical force to coerce individuals to conform their behavior and their thinking to the standards of the community. By beginning with this image of enclosure and punishment, Hawthorne emphasizes the oppressive restriction of the world his characters inhabit. Each of the public settings he uses—the jail, the marketplace, and the scaffold—are infused with meaning by the culture that has constructed them, particularly the scaffold, which is seen as an instrument conducive to good citizenship. Against this darkness and gloom, Hawthorne contrasts the wild rosebush that grows alongside the prison door, a thing of beauty that he claims "has been kept alive in history" (p. 159); he associates the rosebush with Anne Hutchinson and through her with independence of thought, something that persists despite the efforts to eradicate it. Hester Prynne's story unfolds with the opening of the prison door, but her entrance into the narrative is not a step into freedom but a movement initially toward further punishment.

Hester Prynne re-enters the public world from which she has been secluded until after the birth of her child. The marketplace is peopled by various members of the community: government officials, members of the clergy, and local townsfolk, who view Hester as a criminal and source of scandal, a scandal that affects not only her personally but the community as a whole. In this Puritan culture, marriage is viewed as one of the foundations of social order, and a crime that violates the bonds of marriage threatens order itself. The demand for punishment of Hester's crimes is evident in the words of some of the female spectators, who feel she has not suffered enough, that the civil authorities "should have put the brand of a hot iron on Hester Prynne's forehead" (p. 162). This desire to see Hester physically marked for her crime reflects what the modern French theorist Michel Foucault has identified as the law's need to display its triumph visibly on the body of the transgressor; it also reflects the Puritan distrust of the flesh, which is perceived as a source of temptation. Initially this scene suggests a uniformity of vision among the community, but Sacvan Bercovitch calls attention to the multiple viewpoints actually present in the crowd; he sees this as evidence of "pliancy" within the Puritan community, creating the possibility for evolving views of Hester Prynne and, on a larger scale, an evolving culture that will eventually lead to the successful American Revolution (pp. 55–56).

When Hester emerges from the prison carrying Pearl, the evidence of Hester's guilt, she cannot escape the charge of adultery. As she climbs to the scaffold, Hester is placed in a position that emphasizes her isolation from those around her. Questioned by the civil and religious authorities, Hester refuses to name her partner in adultery, even though she recognizes him among the dignitaries before her. In doing so, Hester takes the responsibility for what has happened upon herself, intensifying her isolation and loneliness. By positioning her as he does in this scene, Hawthorne calls attention to Hester's oppositional role against the patriarchal authorities of Puritan church and state. He uses her silence in ironic ways; Hester's culture expects women to keep silent, yet her silence here functions as an act of resistance against an authority she does not accept. As punishment for her choices, Hester faces exile to the edge of the settlement, emphasizing her position as an outcast, but for Hester this marginalization allows her to engage in further resistance to authority as she speculates on the possibilities of freedom and self-realization unhampered by the close scrutiny of neighbors.

At the end of chapter 3, "The Recognition," Hester Prynne is interrogated by church authorities. The passage reveals Hester's strength and determination, her willingness to resist the pressure brought to bear upon her to name her partner in adultery.

"Woman, transgress not beyond the limits of Heaven's mercy!" cried the Reverend Mr. Wilson, more harshly than before. "That little babe hath been gifted with a voice, to second and confirm the counsel which thou hast heard. Speak out the name! That, and thy repentance, may avail to take the scarlet letter off thy breast."

"Never!" replied Hester Prynne, looking, not at Mr. Wilson, but into the deep and troubled eyes of the younger clergyman. "It is too deeply branded. Ye cannot take it off. And would that I might endure his agony, as well as mine!"

"Speak, woman!" said another voice, coldly and sternly, proceeding from the crowd about the scaffold. "Speak; and give your child a father!"

"I will not speak!" answered Hester, turning pale as death, but responding to this voice, which she too surely recognized. "And my child must seek a heavenly Father; she shall never know an earthly one!"

"She will not speak!" murmured Mr. Dimmesdale, who, leaning over the balcony, with his hand upon his heart, had awaited the result of his appeal. He now drew back, with a long respiration. "Wondrous strength and generosity of a woman's heart! She will not speak!"

Discerning the impracticable state of the poor culprit's mind, the elder clergyman, who had care-fully prepared himself for the occasion, addressed to the multitude a discourse on sin, in all its branches, but with continual reference to the ignominious letter. So forcibly did he dwell upon this symbol, for the hour or more during which his periods were rolling over the people's heads, that it assumed new terrors in their imagination, and seemed to derive its scarlet hue from the flames of the infernal pit. Hester Prynne, meanwhile, kept her place upon the pedestal of shame, with glazed eyes, and an air of weary indifference. She had borne, that morning, all that nature could endure; and as her temperament was not of the order that escapes from too intense suffering by a swoon, her spirit could only shelter itself beneath a stony crust of insensibility, while the faculties of animal life remained entire. In this state, the voice of the preacher thundered remorselessly, but unavailingly, upon her ears. The infant, during the latter portion of her ordeal, pierced the air with its wailings and screams; she strove to hush it, mechanically, but seemed scarcely to sympathize with its trouble. With the same hard demeanour, she was led back to prison, and vanished from the public gaze within its iron-clamped portal. It was whispered, by those who peered after her, that the scarlet letter threw a lurid gleam along the dark passage-way of the interior.

Hawthorne, *The Scarlet Letter,* in *Novels,* pp. 176–177.

THE TWO INTERVIEWS

In the world that Hester Prynne inhabits, a woman is defined by two principal roles in her life, as wife and mother. Each role entails a set of culturally defined obligations and duties, conventions of a patriarchal culture that defines woman only through her relationship to man and to reproduction. Hawthorne uses a pair of "interviews" to explore the expectations held for women in colonial New England and Hester's ambivalence toward them. Hawthorne structures these interviews to underscore how Hester is defined by external forces, despite her desire to pursue self-realization. In each interview, Hester's participation as a speaking subject is curtailed, her voice eclipsed by those of others who exercise outward control over her. The first interview takes place within her prison cell, when the elderly scholar and physician Roger Chillingworth, who is ransomed from Indian captivity just in time to see Hester on the scaffold, comes to see her. Having sent Hester ahead of him to New England and delayed in his own arrival, Chillingworth expresses dismay at what his wife has done. Hester knows that by law she has wronged her husband, yet she argues that she did not love him when they married. For Hester, love has a power that is equal to the law, and it is the tension between these two powers that energizes her resistance to what the law and the scarlet letter demand: her submission to authority, her consent to be governed by a power outside herself. Although Hester makes her protest to Chillingworth, he reminds Hester of her duty to him and asserts his authority when using the term "wife" in asking her to keep the secret of his identity. By concealing his identity he eliminates his public link to Hester and to any paternal claim that Pearl might make upon him. He also shields himself from the shame of cuckoldry, retaining respect and authority within the community, rather than being perceived as a figure of diminished masculinity who could not control his wife.

The second interview, which takes place at the governor's house before many of the same men who questioned her on the scaffold, focuses on Hester's role as a mother and the questions that arise within the Puritan community about Hester's ability to instill in her child proper values and respect for the law given her own immoral conduct. That Hester gives Pearl freedom to explore her world and to express herself stands in sharp contrast to the standard practice within the Puritan community that strictly regulated a child's actions and strove to break a child of willfulness. Emily Miller Budick suggests, however, that Hester experiences ambivalent feelings about the way her role as a mother inhibits her will toward freedom, so that in her relationship to Pearl, her refusal to answer many of Pearl's questions and her stern responses to the child in effect silence Pearl much the way Hester feels silenced by her culture. Whatever ambivalence she feels, Hester fears that Pearl will be taken from her, denying her the one human bond that provides some solace and normalcy in her isolation. Again in this interview, Hester discovers that her own words do not carry authority, that her voice is negated by those of the officials who question her and even by her child's. Pearl informs the ministers that she was not made by God but "plucked by her mother off the bush of wild roses" (p. 213), a statement that recalls the allusions to Anne Hutchinson and the threat of anarchy associated with her. This startling announcement, which Pearl makes out of her own capricious willfulness, convinces Wilson and the others that Hester has failed in her duty as a mother, that her child is as wayward as its mother. Despite Hester's emotional pleas, they remain fixed in their objective to take Pearl away, until Hester admits her ineffectiveness before them by asking Dimmesdale to speak for her. Dimmesdale's calm and logical argument makes the case that Hester could not make for herself, even though his words echo the claims that she has asserted, because his authority among his peers remains unquestioned.

Hawthorne plays upon irony in having Dimmesdale speak for Hester, as Dimmesdale, the father of Hester's child, has engaged in his own pattern of silence and resistance from the novel's opening. Dimmesdale's motivation differs from Hester's, however, for while she remains silent in part to protect him, his silence is self-serving, shielding him from the public ignominy and rejection that Hester has suffered, preserving his authority and right to speak in a community that respects him. While he cultivates a public persona as a devout minister, Hester's partner in adultery wrestles in private with his guilt, seeking expiation not through public confession, as his Puritan tradition endorses, but through bloody scourging in his private chamber. In effect attempting to mark his flesh with the sign of the law's triumph, Dimmesdale finds no relief because he refuses to answer the law's public demands. Unlike Hester, he does not believe that their love for one another legitimated their actions, but he resists accepting the consequences of those actions (including Pearl), not out of principle but out of pride and fear. His role in the community provides him cover, and Dimmesdale himself is aware of the irony in his growing reputation as a powerful and ardent preacher who moves others toward greater piety. At the midpoint of the novel, Dimmesdale stands upon the scaffold, as though he is rehearsing his public confession, but he does so at night, with no crowd present to witness his "exposure." Only Pearl, who with her mother has joined Dimmesdale on the scaffold, seems ready to take him to task, asking him to stand with her and Hester on the scaffold at noon the next day. Dimmesdale engages in evasion to avoid confronting the real questions Pearl asks: Will he own her as his child, in his heart and in public? Will he acknowledge his own human nature and the consequences of his actions?

Hester too has cultivated a public persona that conceals her inner life. Her charitable works and quiet ways gradually win the sympathy of most of those who originally scorned and condemned her. They assume that her outward actions signify that she accepts the authority exercised over her, feels remorse for her wrongdoing, and admits the need for redemption and reintegration into the community. But Hester's public silence continues to be an act of resistance rather than a sign of consent. Beneath her calm exterior, Hester grapples with radical ideas about her own nature as an individual and the position of women in her culture. Her place at the margin of her community has allowed her to contemplate the restructuring of society, "the whole system . . . to be torn down, and built up anew" (p. 260), with relations between men and women established on more equal footing. Through his sympathetic treatment of Hester, Hawthorne endorses a critique of patriarchal culture, but he expresses reservations about the implications of Hester's radicalism for women and for society, reflecting his ambivalence toward the women's rights movement of his own day.

This passage that concludes The Scarlet Letter *reveals the changes wrought in Hester and her acceptance of a more subdued life than she had once imagined.*

But there was a more real life for Hester Prynne, here, in New England, that in that unknown region where Pearl had found a home. Here had been her sin; here, her sorrow; and here was yet to be her penitence. She had returned, therefore, and resumed,—of her own free will, for not the sternest magistrate of that iron period would have imposed it,—resumed the symbol of which we have related so dark a tale. Never afterwards did it quit her bosom. But, in the lapse of the toilsome, thoughtful, and self-devoted years that made up Hester's life, the scarlet letter ceased to be a stigma which attracted the world's scorn and bitterness, and became a type of something to be sorrowed over, and looked upon with awe, yet with reverence too. And, as Hester Prynne had no selfish ends, nor lived in any measure for her own profit and enjoyment, people brought all their sorrows and perplexities, and besought her counsel, as one who had herself gone through a mighty trouble. Women, more especially,—in the continually recurring trials of wounded, wasted, wronged, misplaced, or erring and sinful passion,—or with the dreary burden of a heart unyielded, because unvalued and unsought,—came to Hester's cottage, demanding why they were so wretched, and what the remedy! Hester comforted and counselled them, as best she might. She assured them, too, of her firm belief, that, at some brighter period, when the world should have grown ripe for it, in Heaven's own time, a new truth would be revealed, in order to establish the whole relation between man and woman on a surer ground of mutual happiness.

Earlier in life, Hester had vainly imagined that she herself might be the destined prophetess, but had long since recognized the impossibility that any mission of divine and mysterious truth should be confided to a woman stained with sin, bowed down with shame, or even burdened with a life-long sorrow. The angel and apostle of the coming revelation must be a woman, indeed, but lofty, pure, and beautiful; and wise, moreover, not through dusky grief, but the ethereal medium of joy; and showing how sacred love should make us happy, by the truest test of a life successful to such an end!

So said Hester Prynne, and glanced her sad eyes downward at the scarlet letter. And, after many, many years, a new grave was delved, near an old and sunken one, in that burial-ground beside which King's Chapel has since been built. It was near that old and sunken grave, yet with a space between, as if the dust of the two sleepers had no right to mingle. Yet one tombstone served for both. All around, there were monuments carved with armorial bearings; and on this simple slab of slate—as the curious investigator may still discern, and perplex himself with the purport—there appeared the semblance of an engraved escutcheon. It bore a device, a herald's wording of which might serve for a motto and brief description of our now concluded legend; so sombre is it, and relieved only by one ever-glowing point of light gloomier than the shadow:—

"On a field, sable, the letter A, gules."

Hawthorne, *The Scarlet Letter*, in *Novels*, pp. 344–345.

He suggests that something essential to woman's wholeness is lost when she devotes all her energies to thought and reform at the expense of feeling and connection with others.

Hester's inner resistance to the demands of her culture have inspired thoughts of literal escape from its control, thoughts she shares with Dimmesdale when they meet in the forest. Hawthorne treats the forest as a space not subject to the laws and codes of the Puritan community, a space in which the characters give voice to ideas and emotions that have been repressed through much of the narrative. This makes sense in the Puritan context, as Puritans viewed their world allegorically—they thought that every earthly aspect had a higher, more "real" spiritual analog—and the forest, for Puritans, was the devil's workshop. In keeping with his own spirit of compromise between independence and conformity, however, Hawthorne temporizes that the feeling of freedom that the forest evokes may prove elusive, like the sunlight that flickers in and out of the scene. Hester asserts her continuing belief that love has sanctioned their relationship and sexual union, despite community codes and social consequences. Emboldened by thoughts of escape, she removes the letter from her dress and takes the cap from her head, symbolically lifting the oppression she has endured, revealing the beauty and sexuality that have remained at her core, a transformation that hinges on her reconnection to Dimmesdale. Confident that she can sustain the weakened Dimmesdale and circumvent the power of the patriarchal authority that has kept them apart, Hester beckons Pearl to join in their reunion. Pearl refuses to approach until Hester resumes the cap and letter, a response that reconnects actions and consequences, that reasserts the primacy of the social codes that govern their world and that have shaped both Hester's and Pearl's identities.

The climax of the novel draws all of the characters back to the marketplace and the scaffold, underscoring the public nature and context of the events that transpire. Having resolved to end his silence, Dimmesdale needs this public context as he seeks catharsis by exposing his sin and by owning his actions and his child before the community and before God. In a reversal of their roles in the forest, Dimmesdale struggles to convince Hester that his course is better than the escape she had planned, for it acknowledges their relationship and transgression before the eyes of the community and their consent to be governed by the laws of God and man. For Dimmesdale, this consent initiates a reintegration into their social and moral world, from which both have been separated by the earlier choices they have made. Initially Hester is not willing to accept such an idea, for to do so is to renounce all she has thought and come to believe in her period of exile, to renounce the woman who had spoken with such confidence in the forest meeting. Dimmesdale's death at the close of this scene and his refusal to hold out the promise of reunion in the afterlife leave Hester bereft of the relationship that had meant most to her, that had kept her tied to the settlement at Boston.

The last chapter of the novel focuses on Hester, who after a period of absence returns to New England and the community she had once hoped to escape. Throughout the novel, Hawthorne has praised Hester's strength, her independence of thought, her willingness to own her actions, but he sees her inflexibility as leading to a form of absolutism that inhibits compromise and the resolution of conflict, the same absolutism he mistrusts in the reform movements of his own day, particularly abolition and the more radical elements of the women's rights campaign. Upon her return, Hester voluntarily resumes wearing the scarlet letter, which she comes to see as a badge of membership in a community in which she participates. Hawthorne's ideal of a "true woman" who finds balance between her individual needs and her obligations to the community influences how he shapes Hester's choices, especially that of relinquishing a leadership role in any movement toward dramatic social change. While he may have questioned the power of a patriarchal culture and hoped to see changes in the relationship between men and women, Hawthorne believed such change would come slowly, through modulated, not radical, social evolution.

See also The Bible; "The Birth-mark"; *The Blithedale Romance;* Courtship; Crime and Punishment; "The Custom-House"; "Hawthorne and His Mosses"; *The House of the Seven Gables;* Individualism and Community; Marriage; Nature; Puritanism; Religion; The Romance; Sexuality and the Body; "Young Goodman Brown"

BIBLIOGRAPHY
Primary Work
Hawthorne, Nathaniel. *Novels.* New York: Library of America, 1983.

Secondary Works

Bell, Michael Davitt. *Hawthorne and the Historical Romance of New England.* Princeton, N.J.: Princeton University Press, 1971.

Bercovitch, Sacvan. *The Office of the Scarlet Letter.* Baltimore: Johns Hopkins University Press, 1991.

Budick, Emily Miller. *Engendering Romance: Women Writers and the Hawthorne Tradition, 1850–1990.* New Haven, Conn.: Yale University Press, 1994.

Colacurcio, Michael J. *The Province of Piety.* Cambridge, Mass.: Harvard University Press, 1984.

Colacurcio, Michael J., ed. *New Essays on* The Scarlet Letter. Cambridge, U.K.: Cambridge University Press, 1985.

Foucault, Michel. *Discipline and Punish: The Birth of the Prison.* Translated by Alan Sheridan. New York: Pantheon, 1977.

Johnson, Claudia Durst. *Understanding* The Scarlet Letter. Westport, Conn.: Greenwood Press, 1995.

Kennedy-Andrews, Elmer, ed. *Nathaniel Hawthorne:* The Scarlet Letter. New York: Columbia University Press, 2000.

Kesterson, David B. *Critical Essays on Hawthorne's* The Scarlet Letter. Boston: G. K. Hall, 1988.

Mellow, James R. *Nathaniel Hawthorne in His Times.* Boston: Houghton Mifflin, 1980.

Miller, Perry, and Thomas H. Johnson, eds. *The Puritans: A Sourcebook of Their Writings.* 2 vols. New York: Harper and Row, 1963.

Pennell, Melissa McFarland. *Student Companion to Nathaniel Hawthorne.* Westport, Conn.: Greenwood Press, 1999.

Reynolds, David S. "Hawthorne's Cultural Demons: History, Culture, and *The Scarlet Letter.*" In *Novel History: Historians and Novelists Confront America's Past (and Each Other),* edited by Mark C. Carnes, pp. 229–234. New York: Simon and Schuster, 2001.

Reynolds, Larry J. "*The Scarlet Letter* and Revolutions Abroad." *American Literature* 57, no. 1 (1985): 44–67.

Ryskamp, Charles. "The New England Sources of *The Scarlet Letter.*" *American Literature* 31 (November 1959): 257–272.

Scharnhorst, Gary, ed. *The Critical Responses to Nathaniel Hawthorne's* The Scarlet Letter. Westport, Conn.: Greenwood Press, 1992.

Melissa McFarland Pennell

SCIENCE

The nineteenth century was the great age of science: within just two generations, science was consolidated as a profession, having anchored itself in the industrializing urban centers of Europe and America and spread to connect the globe's farthest reaches into a single unified structure of knowledge. Paradoxically, however, the more nineteenth-century science aspired to unity, the more it proliferated in specialties, as the reach of global exploration and laboratory experimentation opened new questions and whole new fields of inquiry. The newly emerging knowledge changed the very character of the universe: intellectuals active in mid-century had been born in a closed and balanced universe governed by Newtonian mechanical principles. The self-evident design of nature had pointed directly to nature's designer, God, and the study of nature was warranted as a path to understand humankind's place in a universe where natural and moral truth had the same divine source. In the span of a single lifetime, this harmonious picture was strained by astronomy's discovery of deep space and by geology's growing insight into deep time, both difficult to reconcile with Genesis. Once the implications of Charles Darwin's (1809–1882) theory of evolution had been widely absorbed, the sciences that a generation before had helped to explicate religion were instead superseding it, and their once cozy relationship had fallen apart. At the same time, the comfortable assumption that science formed part of a single, coherent intellectual culture was also coming apart. Early in the century, science seemed accessible to all. Public figures such as Benjamin Franklin and Thomas Jefferson had moved easily across the boundaries dividing science from general literate culture, and education in basic science was deemed essential to a democratic citizenry. By 1870 science had become fully professionalized. Its practitioners needed special training, and its institutions denied access to nonspecialists, leading to tension over the role such an elite enterprise should play in a democratic society.

THE NATURE OF AMERICAN SCIENCE

The great unifying force in nineteenth-century American science was geography, the exploration of new landscapes that in turn opened new worlds of knowledge, from the Lewis and Clark expedition of 1803–1806 to the mid-century's exploring expeditions to the Far West and beyond. "Geography" then had not yet acquired the far more limited meaning of the early twenty-first century: as seen in *Cosmos,* Alexander von Humboldt's (1769–1859) popular work in physical geography (published in English in 1850), it encompassed astronomy, geology, natural history, geophysics, meteorology, and anthropology in a grand synthesis that sought a total physical description of the earth as a planetary body. American science in this period is often accused of being practical or even utilitarian, excluding pure research, and of being strictly empirical or Baconian, compelled to gather ever more facts and to refuse hypotheses in a naive belief that the facts alone would add up to truth. Such terms only make sense if projected back from the twentieth century, when science was dominated by theoretical research in chemistry and physics. These fields were nascent in the nineteenth-century United States, but the high cost of equipment and limited access to the necessary training meant that the leading work in such fields was still performed in Europe. By contrast, the leading edge of American science was spatial and temporal, as an avalanche of new data forced a broad-based restructuring of knowledge, from a static, balanced, and closed Newtonian universe to a universe that was dynamic, developmental, and organic. In short, science—particularly American science—was not opposed to but was part of the global movement called Romanticism.

In the early 1800s, Americans could claim only a handful of men—perhaps twenty in all—who made their living in science. The only way to make science pay was to teach it, and the only full-time science positions were in medical colleges. Hence medicine was the only realistic career path for a young man interested in science. By 1870 the institutional structures of science had taken shape, and science was a paying profession open to middle-class men (and a few women). Even the very word "scientist," coined in 1833 by William Whewell, had come into common usage with the emergence of a distinct class of scientific workers all taking part in a collective, organized enterprise.

THE GROWTH OF SCIENTIFIC INSTITUTIONS

A number of institutions had to take shape if a community of scientists was to be created and supported. First, they needed to be able to find each other. There were scientists in frontier towns and far-flung territories, but until transportation and communication networks improved, their lives were lonely and their interests hard to sustain. By contrast, scientists in urban centers were able to found small scientific societies. In villages these might be little more than local gatherings of a handful of amateur enthusiasts, but cities could multiply the points of contact to create an information center: arranging meetings; housing books, scientific apparatus, and natural history collections; sponsoring lectures and publications; raising money from civic-minded citizens for more ambitious projects. Such groups were open to—even dependent on—amateurs, hence they tended to be egalitarian and democratic, in contrast to exclusive organizations such as Philadelphia's American Philosophical Society. For example, Henry David Thoreau's (1817–1862) interest in natural history led him to join one such group founded in 1830, the Boston Society of Natural History; Thoreau traveled often to the society's rooms to borrow books and chat with fellow members.

Whereas Thoreau's Concord was an easy train ride from Boston, scientists without such easy access to cities had to create their own societies. In 1840 several geologists from rural areas across the Northeast and Midwest met in Philadelphia to form the Association of American Geologists, with annual meetings that floated from city to city; soon they expanded their membership base to include natural historians, and in 1848 they flung the doors open to become a national science society, the American Association for the Advancement of Science (AAAS, modeled on the British equivalent, the BAAS). An early membership drive tried to net Thoreau, who declined their offer on the basis that he could not attend their meetings (while fulminating in his journal that they would not understand the kind of science he was interested in pursuing), thus turning down the opportunity to participate in a new phenomenon, the nationalization of American science.

A handful of scientific societies attempted to publish transactions of their meetings, an expensive process that met with limited success. What was needed was a truly national journal that could connect all American scientists with each other and communicate American science to the rest of the world. This was the achievement of Benjamin Silliman (1779–1864), who in 1818 founded the *American Journal of Science and Arts*. "Silliman's Journal," as it was called, probably did more than any other single factor to found and sustain a national community of American scientists and bring American science to the attention of Europe, pointing to the essential role of writing in creating and communicating what would come to be accepted as scientific knowledge.

If science were to grow as an information system, it had to find a place in American colleges. The standard curriculum already included a certain amount of science: natural philosophy or physics, astronomy, often some natural history, all within the overarching rubric of natural theology, the study of the grand design of nature insofar as it proved the existence and attributes of God. Separate schools of science began to emerge at mid-century: in 1847 a grant by the cotton manufacturer Abbott Lawrence funded the formation of Harvard's Lawrence Scientific School, which scored a tremendous coup by hiring Louis Agassiz (1807–1873), the Swiss zoologist who came to give a few lectures and stayed to reshape American science into a profession on the European model. Other science schools followed (New York's Cooper Union in 1858, the Sheffield Scientific School at Yale in 1861), and science increasingly found its way into the general university curriculum, opening new teaching jobs for young scientists. Once they attained a firm institutional base, professors of science could establish massive research collections, such as the herbarium established by the botanist Asa Gray (1810–1888) at Harvard or Louis Agassiz's Museum of Comparative Zoology. Nor were museums restricted to higher education: the lack of a national repository for natural history specimens was addressed in 1858, when the new Smithsonian Institution in Washington, D.C., accepted the collections gathered by the federally funded Wilkes expedition of 1838–1842. Another kind of opportunity arose in 1864 with the burning of New York's natural history collection (which had included the ornithologist and artist John James Audubon's birds). This national tragedy led to a fund-raising campaign and the founding of the new public American Museum of Natural History—housed in a fireproof building. Astronomical observations also needed to be made, collected, and housed: in 1836 Williams College established America's first observatory,

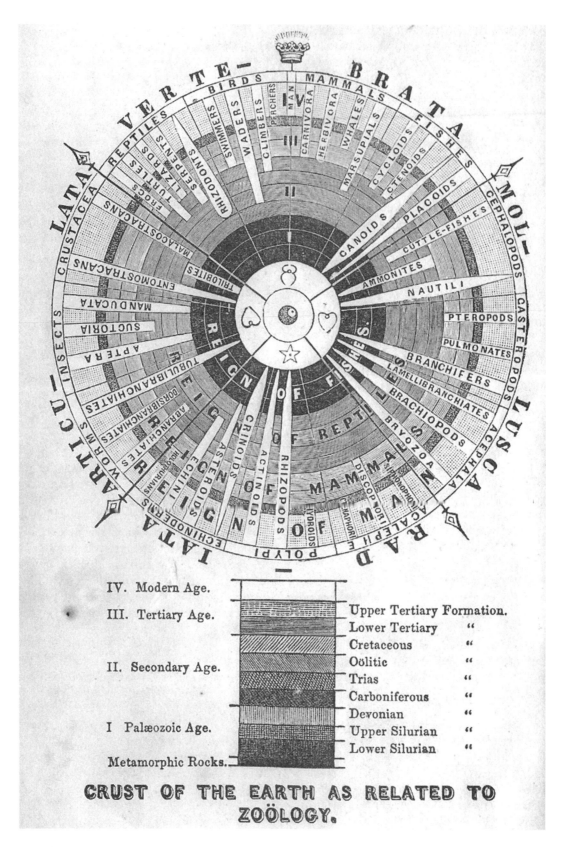

Frontispiece to *Principles of Zoölogy*, by Louis Agassiz and A. A. Gould. Agassiz extrapolated a time sequence from the fossil record. COURTESY OF LAURA DASSOW WALLS

and by 1860 America could claim eight first-class observatories and at least twenty more with good-quality instruments.

This tremendous growth in science was funded in part by higher education, as professors built academic bases for science. Government support played a huge role at both state and federal levels: starting in the 1830s, numerous states conducted surveys of geological and other natural resources, employing a whole cadre of young scientists; by 1860 twenty-nine of the thirty-three states had sponsored surveys. Starting with Meriwether Lewis (1774–1809) and William Clark (1770–1838), the federal government poured its resources into exploring expeditions, such as the force sent out in 1838 under the command of Charles Wilkes (1798–1877) to survey the Pacific Ocean and its coasts and investigate geology, natural history, and anthropology; and the expeditions led by Charles Frémont and William H. Emory in the 1840s to map and survey the unknown territories west of the Mississippi. One historian estimates that a third of antebellum American scientists were on the government payroll and another that up to one-third of the American government's total income was invested in funding explorations. Finally, private industry employed a growing number of scientists to turn knowledge into practical products, and private philanthropy turned American businessmen like Abbot Lawrence and wealthy Englishmen like James Smithson into patrons of American science.

Such growth, however funded, would still have been impossible without a parallel growth in networks of transportation and communication. While visiting the United States in 1841, the British geologist Charles Lyell (1797–1875) and his wife Mary had to endure crowded, dirty, and bumpy carriages, long waits for erratic steamboats, even long rides in borrowed canoes. By their return trip in 1852 the Lyells marveled at the speed and ease with which the new railroads whisked them across the same country. Mass distribution of journals and books was impractical until printing costs dropped, and mailing them was ruinously expensive until postal rates dropped too: only when specimens, data, publications, and the scientists themselves could travel easily would science grow exponentially, built as it is on the exchange of ideas and the collection of texts and objects. Nor could science flourish in a democracy without public interest and support. By mid-century popular science books were easily available for sale even in midwestern villages such as Milwaukee, and periodicals and newspapers regularly fed the public appetite for science with popular articles and reports on the latest wonders. Public lectures were the main channels for disseminating information about science: starting in the 1830s, the lyceum movement—in which both Ralph Waldo Emerson (1803–1882) and Thoreau were active—spread rapidly across the United States (in 1839 Horace Mann counted 137 in Massachusetts alone). One historian estimates that about one-fifth of lyceum platform time was given over to scientific subjects. Lecture series could also reach huge numbers of people. Lyell and Agassiz were both induced to come to the United States by the large fees offered by the Lowell Institute lectures, funded in 1837 by a bequest from the industrialist John Lowell. Benjamin Silliman inaugurated the institute in 1839 with a lecture series on geology, and a second on chemistry was so popular the crowds overflowed into the streets. Demand for Agassiz's lecture course was so great that it had to be offered twice, to an estimated audience of five thousand.

THE EMERGENCE OF POPULAR SCIENCE

The Reverend William Ellery Channing observed in 1841 that science had left its retreats to begin the work of instructing the race: "Through the press, discoveries and theories, once the monopoly of philosophers, have become the property of the multitudes. . . . Science, once the greatest of distinctions, is becoming popular" (quoted in Zochert, p. 448). Yet the very popularity of science pointed to a source of tension: lectures and popular articles could give the public only the most superficial of overviews, and often audiences were entertained more with wonders and marvels than with deeper scientific reasoning. In August 1851 Thoreau grumbled in his journal about a visit to a menagerie at which not a cage was labeled, and instead of some descendent of Baron Georges Cuvier there to lecture on natural history, a ring was formed for "Master Jack & the poney" (*Journal* 3:351).

Optimistically speaking, perhaps acquaintance with wonders would awaken interest and lead to deeper theoretical understandings, but even then the theoretical frameworks developed by scientists were moving ever farther from widespread public comprehension. For example, the major reform in botanical and zoological classification was the "natural" system, which examined a number of overall relations that could be judged only by someone with specialized training. By contrast, the older Linnaean system had relied on obvious characteristics that could be easily grasped, such as the number of stamens in a flower. Whereas the old system had made botany readily available to a family on an educational outing, the new system turned botany into a specialty suitable only for trained scientists.

Into the breach flowed popularizing texts, such as the botany textbooks by Asa Gray and Almira Phelps,

Cover of Asa Gray's *Popular Botany for Children.* At mid-century, practicing scientists often wrote popularizing texts such as this one to enhance public understanding of science and the support for their work. This introduction to botany by America's leading botanist was published in New York in 1864. COURTESY OF LAURA DASSOW WALLS

which sought to keep the gap from widening. At mid-century, such texts were often written by the scientists themselves in an effort to enhance public understanding of and support for their work: Alexander von Humboldt, John Herschel, Mary Somerville, Asa Gray, Louis Agassiz, Charles Darwin, and Thomas Henry Huxley, for instance, all wrote books aimed at a wide audience. However, starting in the 1840s popularizers of science moved into the marketplace, offering secondary accounts rather than original science. That such writers could have a powerful impact is suggested by the career of Edward Livingston Youmans (1821–1887), the popular science writer who roomed with Walt Whitman (1819–1892) in the 1840s and to whom Whitman owed much of his understanding of science, particularly electricity and evolution. Thus Youmans's vision of science lives on in Whitman's poetry, long after readers have forgotten its original sources in scientists like Humboldt, Hermann Ludwig

Ferdinand von Helmholtz, and Darwin. Popular science writing also opened a career in science to women, who were otherwise excluded: although unable to produce science, women such as Almira Phelps, Sarah Hale (editor of *Godey's Lady's Book*), Susan Fenimore Cooper, and Elizabeth Cary Agassiz affiliated themselves with science by disseminating it to a wider public, helping science to acquire and maintain its position in the competitive marketplace of democratic America.

ASTRONOMY

The foundational notion that the universe was harmoniously ordered by a designing deity was most obvious if one looked to the heavens. As one popular astronomy text proclaimed, "An undevout astronomer is mad" (Ferguson 1:1–2). American schoolchildren were taught astronomy as part of natural philosophy, making astronomical facts a part of basic education. The craft of practical astronomy was essential to navigation and to explorers of both land and sea, who used celestial observations to plot coordinates and draw accurate maps. Periodically public interest in astronomy was excited by marvels such as comets: the Great Comet of 1843, which confirmed to the millenarian William Miller and his followers that the end of the world was at hand, generated a fad that lasted for the duration of its passage. More sustained interest was generated by John Herschel's (1792–1871) best-selling *Treatise on Astronomy* (1833), which introduced modern astronomy to America and was responsible for a meteoric rise in its popularity. Herschel's readers were shocked to learn that America had not a single fixed observatory, and in the next three decades Americans built nearly thirty observatories, several of them first-class.

The astronomy boom was encouraged by improved telescope technology and the increasing availability of good instruments. Maria Mitchell became the only woman to achieve recognition in science in this period for her discovery of a comet in 1847 as part of Alexander Ballas Bache's far-flung U.S. Coast Survey. At the other extreme, Thoreau noted with pride in his journal his 1854 purchase of a telescope for eight dollars. When turned to the heavens, the telescopes revealed exciting new insights into the physical structure of the universe: the immensity of deep space, as measured by the newly calculated speed of light; the astonishing variety of celestial objects; a new perspective on earth as itself a planetary body; the intriguing thought that intelligent life might be found on other worlds. Perhaps most exciting of all was the visual evidence for Pierre Laplace's (1749–1827) nebular hypothesis, proposed in 1796 but not popularly known until the 1840. According to Laplace, the earth and other planets had coalesced out of clouds of matter surrounding the sun in a process that for many was the first hint of evolutionary science.

GEOLOGY

All of these discoveries widened God's universe infinitely, yet none was seen as a threat to religion—even the nebular hypothesis could be embraced as a model for God's primal creation. The same could also be said for geology, which seemed at first to fit comfortably with theology. American geologists were making great advances on European theories of stratigraphy by successfully working out long sequences of geological succession. Yet the discontinuities between formations seemed to point to periods of disruption, even to periodic catastrophes when all life had been wiped out to start anew. The Massachusetts geologist Edward Hitchcock (1793–1864) used such evidence to defend

against the view of a mechanistic universe operating by eternal law rather than by God's providence. According to Hitchcock, the geologic record showed that God had repeatedly erased the earth of its creatures and populated it with new life; the biblical account of creation in Genesis recorded only the most recent erasure. By contrast, Benjamin Silliman claimed that Genesis portrayed the whole of creation, for the "days" were really long ages, corresponding to the vast periods of time evident in geological history. The evidence of the rocks clearly showed that creation had occurred not in six days but over untold millennia, and although no geologist questioned this evidence, such differences of opinion pointed to unresolved problems over how to reconcile geology and Genesis. For, as James Hutton had said in the eighteenth century, geology showed "no vestige of a beginning,—no prospect of an end" (Hutton, p. 304). By the 1830s Charles Lyell had updated this view by emphasizing that natural laws operating in the present could explain all the phenomena of the past. Americans geologizing in the West who observed the power of erosion used Lyellian thinking to speculate that it was this force of nature, rather than a destructive God, that caused the breaks in the geological record.

THE EVOLUTIONARY DEBATE IN AMERICA

Emerson began reading Lyell in 1826 and immediately saw the evolutionary implications of a universe unfolding according to law across deep time. Thoreau used Lyell to assert that careful observation of the present was the key to understanding the past, an insight he used to deduce the history of the Massachusetts forest and to assert in *Walden* (1854) that creation had not happened once for all time but was continuous, that humans live in "not a fossil earth, but a living earth" (p. 309). American earth proved indeed to be rich in fossils, such as the enormous mammoth bones unearthed in New York. These deepened the puzzle even more: Thomas Jefferson had believed that Lewis and Clark would surely find mammoths grazing in the West, for the notion that a whole species might go extinct seemed a clear violation of the balance of nature. Meanwhile, German scientists were just beginning to theorize that certain forms of life had become extinct in the past, an idea taken up by Georges Cuvier (1769–1832), who used fossils to characterize entire geological periods. As evidence mounted that life forms were not static but had an immensely long history of development, the problem of how to account for species change became ever more pressing.

The French naturalist Jean-Baptiste Lamarck (1744–1829) offered one theory: individual organisms could create new capabilities, which would then be inherited by their descendants. Lamarck was roundly rejected by British scientists, and Lyell offered a contrasting view of life forms cycling eternally in and out of existence in response to changing climates. The first popular theory of evolution was offered by Robert Chambers (1802–1871) in his best-selling *Vestiges of the Natural History of Creation,* published anonymously in 1844. According to *Vestiges,* evolution occurred when a developing embryo developed just a bit more than the usual, so that succeeding generations rose incrementally through the ranks of ever higher and more complex life forms, replaced at the bottom by the spontaneous generation of new life. Scientists attacked *Vestiges* as both unscientific and ungodly with such ferocity that Darwin shelved his own theory and lived in terror that his colleagues would learn of his own, equally scandalous ideas. Yet the scorn heaped on *Vestiges* by the scientific community only encouraged popular fascination with evolution, including such enthusiasts as Emerson, who drew on *Vestiges* to refine his own evolutionary theory of "arrested and progressive development" (*Journals* 11:158), and Walt Whitman, whose "Song of Myself" gave to Chambers's abstract evolutionary process poetic expression.

In the years of public controversy over *Vestiges,* support for evolution was coming from all directions, particularly from American scientists. Comparative morphologists from Cuvier on drew attention to the way both animal and plant forms seemed to converge on certain fundamental patterns or plans. This insight had major implications for classification, as taxonomists strove to create a "natural" system that would group species by resemblance and structure rather than a few arbitrarily chosen characteristics. Such natural groupings would soon provide Darwin with some of his most compelling evidence. American scientists such as John Torrey and Asa Gray were instrumental in gaining acceptance for the natural system, even as scientific explorers compounded the problem by flooding taxonomists with new species. As the number of new species rose, the very definition of a species came into question, and variations collected from different geographical locations made the once clear boundaries between species increasingly difficult to define. Darwin would use such evidence from American scientists to break down the species concept altogether, suggesting instead that species intergraded continuously and variations were new species just coming into being.

In addition, the geographical scope from which scientific specimens were being collected raised some puzzling problems of distribution. On the one hand, why were certain species suited to, say, a dry climate not found wherever the climate was dry? Instead, regions with similar climates were populated, oddly enough, with different species. On the other hand, why were similar or even the same species found in widely separated locations? In the 1850s, Asa Gray and Louis Agassiz entered into a heated debate over this issue. Agassiz declared that all species had been separately created by God in their present numbers and location, whereas Gray dismissed such a view as unscientific and offered the alternative theory that species had migrated, spreading from one location to others. Thoreau, who knew Agassiz personally and owned Gray's works, followed the debate closely. In June 1858, when he encountered frogs on the "bare rocky top" of Mount Monadnock, he wondered how they had got there: Could they possibly have hopped up, as Gray might suggest? Or had they been created on the spot, as Agassiz would have insisted? (*Journal* 10:467–468).

Darwin would provide the breakthrough theory that resolved these puzzles—one reason his theory of evolution was accepted so swiftly by American scientists. Only Agassiz held out, and in a few years even his own son Alexander Agassiz had gone over to Darwin's side. Darwin argued that because more individuals were born than could possibly survive to adulthood, nature must select only a few for survival. Because every individual shows chance variations—in size or color, for example—some individuals would by accident of birth have some slight advantage that made their survival more likely, and survivors would pass those advantages on to their offspring. Over the course of many generations, a new variety would form that could, over still more generations, become distinct enough to make a new species. Darwin had hesitated to publish his ideas, but as the *Vestiges* controversy subsided, he began to air his thoughts to selected friends. Asa Gray's articles in "Silliman's Journal" caught Darwin's eye, and in 1857 he wrote to tell Gray of his radical new theory while swearing him to secrecy. Thus when *On the Origin of Species* was published in 1859, Gray had already helped lay the groundwork, and in a series of essays he took on the task of presenting Darwin's ideas to the American public. Agassiz, furious, leapt to the opposition, and the ensuing controversy acquainted Americans with advanced scientific theories that might otherwise have slept on in the technical journals. Another of Darwin's earliest converts was Thoreau, who read *Origin* early in 1860 and immediately began incorporating its insights into his own theories of plant distribution and forest succession, on which he was working at the time he contracted the illness that led to his death in 1862.

As he wrote in his journal in 1860, "The development theory implies a greater vital force in nature, because it is more flexible and accommodating, and equivalent to a sort of constant *new* creation" (*Journal* 14:147).

Thoreau had no objections to Darwin on religious grounds, having long since abandoned conventional Christianity. But for those who held to a conventional Christianity, Darwin seemed to rupture forever the long friendship between religion and science. Individual scientists did find ways to reconcile the two. Gray, for instance, accepted Darwin's theories as an explanation of how God's power was manifested in nature. Yet the consensus of science no longer relied on theological reasoning, and young clergymen increasingly ignored or rejected science, which only a generation earlier had been cast as religion's most powerful ally. Science and religion had been definitively separated.

SLAVERY AND RACE

In the United States the evolutionary debates were at their height during the years leading up to the Civil War, and one of the most vexed questions of the time was what the new theories meant for humanity. Some scientists de-emphasized race as a meaningful category: the English ethnologist James Cowles Prichard argued that there were so many dozens of races that the real emphasis should be on the unity of humankind, and the scientist Charles Pickering returned home from the Wilkes expedition with a complex picture of human diversity, migration, and cross-cultural exchange. Yet for others, the powerful progressive narrative of evolution, with Caucasian people so evidently at the summit, suggested irresistibly that the various races were either evolutionary stages in humanity's upward progression or else degenerations from an earlier state of perfection. Louis Agassiz used his prominent position to argue for "polygenesis": in his view the races of humans were so different as to be the result of multiple separate creations, hence different species. The hard truth was that science proved Genesis wrong. With the support of Samuel George Morton's cranial studies, which had shown the brains of nonwhite races to be distinctly smaller, and the racist theories of Josiah Nott and George Gliddon, Agassiz wrote that science proved the black race to have advanced mentally little beyond the chimpanzee and gorilla.

Polygenesis made little popular headway in the slave-owning South, for it too openly defied the Genesis account of human descent from one couple, Adam and Eve. However, the scientific response to polygenesis was remarkably weak—only South Carolina's John Bachman, a zoologist who had worked with Audubon, publicly argued against it—and it left a legacy of racial stereotypes that lasted through the twentieth century. When Emerson became a prominent speaker for abolitionism, he set about examining the full range of scientific theories for support. Even though the weight of science seemed to be against him, ultimately he repudiated all theories of racial inferiority to insist that evolution showed all races had the capacity to advance equally; hence science, when truly understood in the full context of modern geology and physical geography, lent its support to the abolition of slavery and the political equality of all the races.

SCIENCE AND AMERICAN LITERATURE

The intense interest in science shown by such American literary figures as William Cullen Bryant, Emerson, Thoreau, Whitman, Emily Dickinson, and Edgar Allan Poe belies the once common myth that Romantic writers rejected science in the name of poetry and emotion. Their oft-quoted expressions of dismay at science turn out to be, on closer examination, either admonishments to scientists for having forgotten their true path or expressions of disgust at the mechanistic materialism of eighteenth-century science, associated with the cold rationalism of deism and the violence of the French Revolution. By contrast, the new science of the nineteenth century was fundamental to Romanticism, for it opened an exciting vision of nature as dynamic process and organic interconnectedness. Poe (1809–1849) brought his wide reading in astronomy, physics, mathematics, psychology, and medicine to bear in his fictions, and he dedicated his book *Eureka* (1848) to the German scientist Alexander von Humboldt. As Poe's very name suggests, however, there were darker visions of the new science as well. Its imaginative and explanatory power could tempt the unwary explorer into satanic defiance, like Herman Melville's Ahab, using compass, quadrant, and charts to hunt the oceans for the White Whale; or Mary Shelley's Dr. Frankenstein, creating the monster that threatens all of humanity. Shelley's Faustian *Frankenstein* (1818) became the dominant literary story of science, one that Nathaniel Hawthorne explored repeatedly in such narratives as "The Birth-mark," "Rappacini's Daughter," and *The Scarlet Letter* (1850). A young Henry Adams speculated ominously in a letter of 1863, "Some day science may have the existence of mankind in its power, and the human race commit suicide by blowing up the world" (Adams 1:135).

Even the writers who most celebrated science expressed ambivalence at its possible misuse. Emerson warned constantly that science should be, as he put it in an 1836 lecture, "humanly studied," and should the scientist become the "slave of nature," science would become "unhallowed, and baneful" (*Early Lectures* 2:36, 37); in the same year he warned, in *Nature* (1836), of the dangers of "this half-sight of science" (*Collected Works* 1:41). Thoreau worried about the "inhumanity of science" (*Journal* 8:162) that demanded he kill a snake to learn its species, and when he had to kill a box turtle for Agassiz's collection, he berated himself as a murderer. Whitman was capable of walking out in disgust from the lecture of the "learn'd astronomer" to look up "in perfect silence at the stars" (p. 409–410), but the more remarkable fact may be that he attended the lecture at all. For Whitman, science was the "fatherstuff" that begot "the sinewy races of bards" (p. 15); the poet who seeks to reconnect fact with spirit can recover the original power of poetry only by starting with science.

THE BEGINNINGS OF ENVIRONMENTALISM

As Adams's eerily prescient speculation suggests, there were good reasons for ambivalence. That humans could alter the face of nature—could tinker with, even destroy, the balance of nature—was an idea just dawning in these years. In 1811 Humboldt had pointed to the role deforestation played in shrinking Mexico's great Lake Texcoco and changing the climate of its high interior plateau to hotter and drier. Following up on Humboldt's insight, the American George Perkins Marsh showed, in *Earth and Man* (1864), that deforestation had destroyed the soils of Greece and Italy, rendering them permanently arid and barren. As the United States too leveled its forests, would not the same thing happen there? Thoreau's detailed studies of forests, plant distribution, and hydrology led him to become a pioneer of ecology a full generation before that science came into existence. His calls for the preservation of wild nature, together with his and his friend Emerson's demonstrations of nature's redemptive power, gave rise to a new environmental awareness and the new tradition of American nature writing, developed by their followers John Muir and John Burroughs. As ecology dwindled toward century's end from a central integrative concept uniting humanity and nature to yet another scientific specialty beyond the reach of most Americans, it fell to the nature writers of the twentieth and twenty-first centuries to sustain the rich poetry of the material and factual world of nature.

CONCLUSION

By the nineteenth century's end, scientists had disciplined themselves into the rigors of scientific method, erecting ideological demands that the character of sci-

entific knowledge must be objective, uninfected by the needs and desires of the self. Meanwhile literature too had begun to seek authority by erecting the same structures of professionalization and institutionalization that had proved so effective in science: academic training, learned journals, professional societies, academic centers in colleges and universities. Matthew Arnold, the Victorian architect of the new profession of literature, told an American audience in 1883 not that poet and scientist should each seek in the other's work their best complement and corrective, as Emerson had insisted, but rather that humane letters would do for humanity precisely what science could not: relate knowledge to human concerns, "to the sense in us for conduct, and to the sense in us for beauty" (p. 391). Hence the proper focus for education should be not the sciences, as the new scientific professionals such as Huxley were claiming, but the humanities. In effect, literature secured its own status as a discipline by separating itself from science, concealing from view much of what makes nineteenth-century American writers distinctive: their fascination with science's reconstruction of their physical and conceptual world and their energy in seeking to participate in that process, to make its power their own.

See also Colleges; Ethnology; Exploration and Discovery; Lyceums; Nature; Popular Science; Religion; Romanticism; Technology

BIBLIOGRAPHY
Primary Works

Adams, Henry. *A Cycle of Adams Letters, 1861–1865.* 2 vols. Edited by Worthington C. Ford. Boston, 1920.

Arnold, Matthew. "Literature and Science." In *Poetry and Criticism of Matthew Arnold,* edited by Dwight Culler, pp. 381–396. Boston: Houghton Mifflin, 1961.

Emerson, Ralph Waldo. *The Collected Works of Ralph Waldo Emerson.* 6 vols. Edited by Alfred R. Ferguson. Cambridge, Mass.: Harvard University Press, 1971–.

Emerson, Ralph Waldo. *The Early Lectures of Ralph Waldo Emerson, 1833–1842.* 3 vols. Edited by Stephen E. Whicher, Robert E. Spiller, and Wallace E. Williams. Cambridge, Mass.: Harvard University Press, 1959–1972.

Emerson, Ralph Waldo. *The Journals and Miscellaneous Notebooks of Ralph Waldo Emerson.* 16 vols. Edited by William Gilman et al. Cambridge, Mass.: Harvard University Press, 1960–1982.

Emerson, Ralph Waldo. *Nature.* Boston: J. Munroe, 1836.

Ferguson, James. *Ferguson's Astronomy Explained upon Sir Isaac Newton's Principles.* 2 vols. Edited by David Brewster. Philadelphia, 1917.

Hutton, James. "Theory of the Earth." *Transactions of the Royal Society of Edinburgh* 1 (1785): 209–305.

Thoreau, Henry David. *Journal,* vol. 3, *1848–1851.* Edited by Robert Sattelmeyer, Mark R. Patterson, and William Rossi. Princeton, N.J.: Princeton University Press, 1990.

Thoreau, Henry David. *Journal,* vol. 8, *1854.* Edited by Sandra Harbert Petrulionis. Princeton, N.J.: Princeton University Press, 2002.

Thoreau, Henry David. *The Journal of Henry David Thoreau.* 1906. 14 vols. Edited by Bradford Torrey and Francis Allen. New York: Dover, 1962.

Thoreau, Henry David. *Walden.* 1854. Edited by J. Lyndon Shanley. Princeton, N.J.: Princeton University Press, 1973.

Whitman, Walt. *Complete Poetry and Collected Prose.* Edited by Justin Kaplan. New York: Library of America, 1982.

Secondary Works

Baym, Nina. *American Women of Letters and the Nineteenth-Century Sciences: Styles of Affiliation.* New Brunswick, N.J.: Rutgers University Press, 2002.

Bozeman, Theodore Dwight. *Protestants in an Age of Science: The Baconian Ideal and Ante-Bellum American Religious Thought.* Chapel Hill: University of North Carolina Press, 1977.

Bruce, Robert V. *The Launching of Modern American Science, 1846–1876.* Ithaca, N.Y.: Cornell University Press, 1988.

Crawford, T. Hugh. "Networking the (Non)Human: Moby-Dick, Matthew Fontaine Maury, and Bruno Latour." *Configurations* 5, no. 1 (1997): 1–21.

Daniels, George H. *Science in American Society: A Social History.* New York, N.Y.: Knopf, 1971.

Daniels, George H., ed. *Nineteenth-Century American Science: A Reappraisal.* Evanston, Ill.: Northwestern University Press, 1972.

Goetzmann, William H. *New Lands, New Men: America and the Second Great Age of Discovery.* New York: Viking, 1986.

Goetzmann, William H. "Paradigm Lost." In *The Sciences in the American Context: New Perspectives,* edited by Nathan Reingold, pp. 21–34. Washington, D.C.: Smithsonian Institution Press, 1979.

Gossin, Pamela, ed. *Encyclopedia of Literature and Science.* Westport, Conn.: Greenwood Press, 2002.

Greene, John C. *American Science in the Age of Jefferson.* Ames: Iowa State University Press, 1984.

Hovenkamp, Herbert. *Science and Religion in America, 1800–1860.* Philadephia: University of Pennsylvania Press, 1978.

Reingold, Nathan. *Science in America since 1820.* New York: Science History Publications, 1976.

Reingold, Nathan, ed. *Science, American Style.* New Brunswick, N.J.: Rutgers University Press, 1991.

Reingold, Nathan, ed. *The Sciences in the American Context: New Perspectives.* Washington, D.C.: Smithsonian Institution Press, 1979.

Scholnick, Robert J. "'The Password Primeval': Whitman's Use of Science in 'Song of Myself.'" In *Studies in the American Renaissance,* edited by Joel Myerson, pp. 385–425. Charlottesville: University Press of Virginia, 1986.

Scholnick, Robert J., ed. *American Literature and Science.* Lexington: University Press of Kentucky, 1992.

Walls, Laura Dassow. *Emerson's Life in Science: The Culture of Truth.* Ithaca, N.Y.: Cornell University Press, 2003.

Walls, Laura Dassow. *Seeing New Worlds: Henry David Thoreau and Nineteenth-Century Natural Science.* Madison: University of Wisconsin Press, 1995.

Zochert, Donald. "Science and the Common Man in Ante-Bellum America." *Isis* 65 (1974): 448–473.

Laura Dassow Walls

SECOND GREAT AWAKENING

See Evangelicals; Mormons; Religion

SELF-PUBLISHING

See Amateurism and Self-Publishing

"SELF-RELIANCE"

"Self-Reliance" is the most widely known—and perhaps the most misunderstood—essay by Ralph Waldo Emerson (1803–1882). The most casual reader can identify as Emerson's the dozens of affirmative aphorisms from the essay, pithy sayings used widely in greeting cards and in advertisements. "Trust thyself: every heart vibrates to that iron string" (*CW* 2:28); "Whoso would be a man must be a nonconformist" (p. 29); "live ever in a new day" (p. 33); "A foolish consistency is the hobgoblin of little minds" (p. 33); "An institution is the lengthened shadow of one man" (p. 35). Countless readers have turned to this essay for encouragement and personal validation since it was first published in Emerson's *Essays: First Series* in 1841. One hundred years later, the poet Edgar Lee Masters paid tribute to the liberating force of Emerson on youth in the intellectually repressive atmosphere of rural Illinois: "Under his influence we felt that we were not hostile to the good life by free thinking about religion, or about anything else" (p. 2). More recently, the musician and environmentalist Don Henley declared that "Self-Reliance" was "one of the primary forces that motivated me to become a song writer. It gave me confidence in myself" (quoted in Mott, p. 64).

THE CRITICAL DEBATE

Despite such testimonials to the appeal of Emerson's message of self-reliance, the nature and the legacy of "Self-Reliance" are matters of perennial dispute. Generations of readers like Masters and Henley have found in Emerson reassurance that their lives are inherently worthy and encouragement to hold to personal convictions or to cultivate talents. The very matter of self-reliance, however, has been a battleground on which critics of American culture have argued over whether Emerson's most characteristic principle is an innocuous mode of individual reflection or something more sinister and dangerous—a mantle for selfish and predatory forms of capitalism, a high-sounding cloak for aggressive expansionist and militarist impulses, a sign of the failure of community in the United States, an illusion masking loneliness and alienation at the very heart of the national psyche. The argument began immediately, among conservative religious thinkers who already suspected Emerson of being a heretic after his "Divinity School Address" (1838), and among writers with a darker, more tragic view of human nature. Nathaniel Hawthorne's tales of sin and *The Scarlet Letter* (1850), with its penetrating analysis of the human heart, and Herman Melville's portrait of Captain Ahab's intellectual pride and isolation in *Moby-Dick* (1851) are often seen as implicit quarrels with Emersonian self-reliance and optimism.

Criticism of Emersonian self-reliance grew more pointed in the second half of the twentieth century. In *The Imperial Self* (1971), Quentin Anderson argued that the boisterous competitiveness of the Age of Jackson—accompanied by its disruption of social arrangements and economic instability—drove many intelligent young Americans in upon their own private resources. He regarded Emerson as chief among those who, in privileging moments of insight, fell back on personal integrity as the only secure value in a volatile world. But this posture, Anderson insisted, was ultimately desperate and selfish, a rejection of community and history and the psychological and moral equivalent of antinomianism—the Puritan heresy asserted by Anne Hutchinson (1591–1643) that placed the regenerate individual above the constraints of theological and social law that govern everyone else. In 1981 Yale president A. Bartlett Giamatti extended the charges against Emerson, announcing at a commencement ceremony that Emerson's essay "Power" helped unleash a mean-spirited incivility in the United States, providing our political leaders with a rationale for ruthless abuse of power. Robert N. Bellah's sociological study of the loss of community in America, *Habits of the Heart* (1985), offered a less biting critique but still decried the damage caused by the culture's celebration of a free-floating, unattached "self"—a tradition he found popularized by Emerson and alive in the selfishness of the 1980s "Me Generation." But what was the cultural climate in which Emerson began to conceive of self-reliance?

THE CONTEMPORARY CONTEXT OF SELF-RELIANCE

"Self-Reliance" is the culmination of Emerson's attempt to name and describe the role of individualism in an age of unsettling change causing both hope and fear in the young nation. As a Unitarian minister at Second Church in Boston (1829–1832), Emerson had begun formulating a concept of character that would withstand the vagaries of life. Fascinated by Stoic ideas of self-control, he initially referred to this quality as "self-respect," "self-command," and "self-trust." In a sermon of 1830 he also called it "self-reliance" (*CS* 2:266). He noted in an 1831 sermon, however, the "limits of self-reliance": *"the origin of self"* is God (*CS* 3:202). By 1833 he was lecturing from material that would find its way into his great 1841 essay. Emerson's attempt to explain and inculcate self-reliance mirrored the growing impulse of common people in the 1830s to control their own destinies, to assert their autonomy in political, social, and economic spheres of life. Such mobility required them to establish internal structures of self-control in place of external social structures. The rapid spread of evangelical religion—though it was more emotional than Emerson's more temperate and cultured form of Unitarianism—embodied the same democratic spirit. Zealous preachers leveled doctrinal and denominational barriers to God, arousing in average folk a stirring, immediate, personal religious experience.

The national life of the 1830s was marked by such public confidence that the characteristic slogan of the decade was "Go ahead!"—a phrase made popular by the self-promoting frontiersman and politician Davy Crockett. New York, Boston, and Philadelphia were engaged in vigorous commercial competition. States in the Northeast were newly connected by a network of canals that embodied the nation's robust, entrepreneurial economic system. Emerging as a source of astonishment and pride was the railroad, which in Henry David Thoreau's *Walden; or, Life in the Woods* (1854) became an ambiguous symbol of progress. Americans were pushing inexorably west. The new nation was undergoing dynamic transformation. Fortunes were to be made by men capable of shrewd investments and driving a hard bargain, and anyone, it seemed, could create a new life by removing to new territory, by working hard, by seizing opportunity. Sixty years earlier, in the throes of the American Revolution, Thomas Paine had envisioned in *Common Sense* (1776) that on these shores we had it in our power to begin the world anew. Now in the 1830s it seemed that Americans were quite literally refashioning their *selves*.

Foreign visitors in the 1830s noted the influence of democratic political and economic forces on the American character and sought a new vocabulary to describe the phenomenon. The first literary use of the term *self-reliance* noted by the *Oxford English Dictionary* was by the English social critic and reformer Harriet Martineau (though Emerson had been using the term for several years). In *Society in America* (1837) she observed the destructive influence of socially approved gender stereotypes, declaring, "Women are, as might be anticipated, weak, ignorant and subservient, in as far as they exchange self-reliance for reliance on anything out of themselves" (3:117). The French writer Alexis de Tocqueville in *Democracy in America* (1835, 1840) offered a more political sense of the related term *individualism*, which he contrasted with the older term *egoism*. Individualism, he suggested, is a product of democratic disruption of social order and relationship found in older aristocratic societies. The condition of "social equality," he believed, encourages people to "imagine that their whole destiny is in their own hands," which threatens to confine each person "in the solitude of his own heart" (p. 478)—a danger averted in America only by the vigor of the electoral system and local control.

The nation's mood was embodied by its seventh president, Andrew Jackson—the first president from a state outside of Massachusetts and Virginia—whose two terms (1829–1836) ushered in new political opportunities for common folk even as the country witnessed the introduction of the spoils system and a festering of social and moral problems. The nation's bounding spirit indeed masked tensions and contradictions. Land hunger was accompanied in the Southeast by the cruel and tragic policy of Indian removal. Settlement in Texas provoked conflict with Mexico, and Crockett was martyred at the Alamo in 1836. War fever against Mexico would culminate in 1846–1848 in a conflict opposed as jingoistic by many Americans, including Thoreau, whose "Resistance to Civil Government" ("Civil Disobedience," 1849) was triggered by his refusal to pay a tax that he claimed would underwrite an illegal war that was an underhanded scheme to carve out a new slave territory. A sense that

society as well as individuals had the ability to change fueled a reform spirit that was beginning to press for the improved conditions of those who, owing to racism, gender, physical disability, or other constraints, were denied the opportunities that were fundamental to the country's pride. The emergence of abolitionism, the woman's movement, education reform, temperance, penal reform, and improved treatment of the blind, the deaf, and the mentally ill would cause the 1840s to be called the Age of Reform. Already in the 1830s these reform movements were evidence that boastful nationalism could not conceal abusive and immoral social conditions. But the real blow to public as well as personal confidence was the economic panic of 1837, which wiped out fortunes and stirred up insecurity about the very conditions and promise of American life.

Before he published "Self-Reliance," Emerson, as well as his associates in the Transcendental Club and other reformers, had already begun to criticize the pervasive materialism of American culture. His "The American Scholar" was later called "our intellectual declaration of independence" by Oliver Wendell Holmes. But when he gave this Phi Beta Kappa address at Harvard on 31 August 1837 he was challenging the intellectual stagnation afflicting his own generation and the rising one in the United States, and he attacked a major cause of this ennui: the dominance of the "so-called 'practical men'" (*CW* 1:59) whose sneering disdain of thinking and all activity that cannot be measured by the accumulation of wealth and power had skewed the nation's values. The current economic panic should have made manifest the fragility of mere materialism.

Emerson had other more personal reasons to want to hitch his wagon to values more enduring than those of the marketplace. Ever since he was a child, his family had been afflicted by calamitous illness and early death. Most recently he had lost his young wife to consumption (1831), followed by the deaths of his brothers Edward and Charles (in 1834 and 1836). He was introverted by nature, and his early career in the ministry and his new venture into the vocation of lecturing and writing, though certainly means of making a living, involved intellectual talents not weighed merely in the countinghouses of Boston. Three important forces had further shaped his sense of individualism: the American Revolution, whose legacy Massachusetts had keenly memorialized; the liberal Christianity, or Unitarianism, in which he had been raised; and the international Romantic movement that had attracted him as a youth. Each of these three traditions encouraged kinds of individualism that transcended aggressiveness in the political and economic arenas. The Revolution and its aftermath introduced influential new families into New England society, as independence spurred new ambition and wealth. But the dream of continually redefining and extending the benefits of liberty in the new republic kindled the imaginations of Emerson's generation. Unitarianism in Boston had evolved into the rather staid denomination of the cultural elite in Emerson's day. But Unitarianism's stress on self-culture involved not just development of one's bank account but intellectual, aesthetic, and spiritual growth; and for reform-minded transcendentalists, self-culture was no license to withdraw into self-involvement but carried a moral imperative: to alleviate the suffering of others who struggled under the weight of institutional or other barriers to the achievement of personal dignity and selfhood. British and European Romanticism offered works of art and philosophy (and the example of dynamic lives such as those of Byron and Goethe) to inspire those who sought to assert the importance of the individual—of mind, emotion, and imagination—in a world of convention, political oppression, deadening reason, and rampant materialism.

Against this backdrop of political, religious, and artistic idealism the publication of "Self-Reliance" in 1841 coincided with the founding at West Roxbury, Massachusetts, of Brook Farm (1841–1847), which was to be one of the most successful communitarian experiments in the United States. Emerson, who followed the reforms of the age with interest and was increasingly drawn into abolitionist activities, was attracted to the principles of Brook Farm and thought seriously of joining. But in the end he chose to maintain his own domestic circle and to emphasize what was called self-culture, or the regeneration of the individual. "Self-Reliance" is his major expression of that self-reform.

VISION AND STYLE

"Self-Reliance" cannot be reduced to a social treatise or blueprint for personal success. Emerson's response to the spirit of his age is far too subtle. His prose, moreover, is famously nonlinear. His essays typically lack formal thesis statements, road maps of what lies ahead, reassuring autobiographical detail, smooth transitions, or formal summaries and conclusions. Grasping for intellectual anchors, most readers eagerly seize upon his engaging maxims, as though to quote them is to capture the essence of an essay. But Emerson's prose purpose is—as he told the audience of his "Divinity School Address" of 1838—to provoke, to entice the reader into engaging with an idea and to see a familiar term in strange and challenging contexts.

In reading Emerson, context is everything—starting with the placement of an essay in relation to other essays in a book. "Self-Reliance" is preceded in the 1841 *Essays* by "History," whose first sentence declares that "There is one mind common to all individual men" (*CW* 2:3); it is followed by "Compensation," which seeks to uncover the unalterable moral equilibrium underlying all things. Accordingly, in "Self-Reliance," Emerson calls us not to be arrogantly self-defining or self-assertive but to be alert to our own resources, which means having the courage to accept and act out the "divine idea" in each person. Out of context, Emerson's maxims can sound cocky, aggressive, self-promoting, willful, or simply contrary; but his assertion of the ancient maxim "Trust thyself" is followed in the essay by the injunction to "Accept the place the divine Providence has found for you; the society of your contemporaries, the connexion of events" (*CW* 2:28). The universal law of true freedom, he implies, consists in engaging with the facts and situations of our specific lives. Because life is in the present moment, intuition is more valuable than "consciousness" (p. 29) otherwise our actions are extraneous and not integral to our character. Integrity consists not in withdrawing from the hurly-burly of life but in spiritual equipoise that is tested "in the midst of the crowd" (p. 31). It is not a random or chaotic phenomenon but "cumulative" (p. 34). The twin threats to our integrity are external and internal—"the multitude" and our own "consistency" or "reverence for our past act or word" (p. 33) for our past acts—both of which tempt us with conformity and loss of spontaneity.

But how to fix "meaning" or even paraphrase such a fluid essay? Emerson typically tempts us with a stunning image or a claim that seems finally to codify, or at least capture, his essential idea—only to shift the very ground of image or claim. For example, early in the essay he asserts the imperative, in the face of social pressure, to express his own "nature." Then he exemplifies his stance as "nonconformist" by yoking two declarations that must have struck contemporary readers as flirting with irreverence. The first is Byronically defiant and willful: "'if I am the Devil's child, I will live then from the Devil.'" The second is a cavalier, profane appropriation of the Old Testament account of the Passover (Exodus 12:22–23) and Moses' injunction to record God's commandments (Deuteronomy 6:9): "I would write on the lintels of the door-post, *Whim.* I hope it is somewhat better than whim at last, but we cannot spend the day in explanation" (*CW* 2:30). Such statements establish a tone of urgency, a feeling that the implications of the essay press beyond printed words to life to be lived outside the pages. Yet even this is only part of Emerson's vision. Seven pages later he defends the stance of self-reliance against the charge of narcissistic arrogance by reversing the very terms of his earlier whimsicality. "When we discern justice, when we discern truth," he writes, "we do nothing of ourselves, but allow a passage to its beams. . . . [Thoughtless people] fancy that I choose to see this or that thing. But perception is not whimsical, but fatal" (p. 37–38). In the most famous passage in the essay, Emerson had warned that "A foolish consistency is the hobgoblin of little minds" (p. 33); Emerson refuses to fall into this trap himself, especially when playing with as volatile a concept as whim. Having earlier evoked the giddy sense of freedom from conformity, he now goes to great length to show that self-reliance is finally no frivolous disregard of moral responsibility but a continually demanding response to hard truth.

If only one could sustain such alertness! Emerson has encouraged us by holding out the democratic promise that we may find ourselves to be "true prince[s]" because, as he saucily notes, the great men of history did not "wear out virtue" (p. 36). But we are not allowed to rest on these noble heights, for Emerson uses a rhetorical give-and-take strategy throughout the essay, keeping us oscillating between glowing affirmations about human *potential* and deflating reminders about the *actual* state of affairs. The "soul is light" itself; yet now "Man is timid and apologetic" (p. 38). "God is here within"; "But now we are a mob" (p. 41).

Emerson devotes much of the essay to explaining what self-reliance is—and is not. It is personal but not idiosyncratic, as it derives from a universal source, an "aboriginal Self" (p. 37; identified as God in the sermon a decade earlier); it renders one "godlike" (p. 43) but is not "mere antinomianism" (p. 42). Definitions—words themselves—are finally inadequate to convey fully what is at stake in self-reliance. "To talk of reliance," in fact, "is a poor external way of speaking. Speak rather of that which relies, because it works and is" (p. 40). It is a delusion to think that we must squeamishly withdraw from falsehood and moral contamination, for our "isolation . . . must be elevation" (p. 41). Acting with integrity is done "not selfishly, but humbly and truly" (p. 42). The affliction of "our age," we are reminded, is that individuals have "become timorous desponding whimperers" (p. 43). Lacking the resiliency of rural youth who, like cats, land on their feet, privileged youth are desiccated and expect quick results. Self-reliance, however, is not a badge or an easy fix but character and life itself. It does not justify a feeling of moral superiority, nor is it license to ignore injustice or to dominate others.

The essay ends with brief mention of contemporary ills: society's skewed values, the culture's "rage of travelling" (p. 46), the imitative strain that taints individuals and institutions. Criticizing the shallow optimism of the day, he declares that we are no better today than people in Plutarch's age. The nineteenth century's materialism—its "reliance on Property" and quantification (p. 49)—is evidence that history is not a record of continual improvement of the human condition and that as yet America is unexceptional. The only antidote to both arrogance and blind confidence in the future is a kind of stoic integrity defined as "yourself" and "the triumph of principles" (p. 51).

Emerson's nonlinear prose and rhetorical strategies unsettle logical expectations and conventional ways of defining terms. Demanding, disorienting, and even disturbing, his vision and style are also, as he intended, liberating. Even as Emerson refuses to provide a pat definition of self-reliance and thwarts us from settling comfortably into a new orthodoxy—even as we are thrown on our own imaginative resources— we achieve a sense of mastery. We are compelled to supply personal experience to exemplify Emerson's aphoristic claims, becoming in the process not recipients of secondhand wisdom but co-creators of meaning.

SELF-RELIANCE IN EMERSON'S LATER WRITINGS

Throughout his career Emerson wrote pointedly about the psychological and social dangers of isolation, abuse of power, and narcissism—all perversions of genuine self-reliance. In his essay "Intellect" (1841) he warns that in a merely self-regarding mind, a single obsessive thought is a kind of "prison" (*CW* 2:201). His portrait of Napoleon in *Representative Men* (1850) is a devastating exposé of individualism turned tyranny. Napoleon is the epitome of the practical man—driven, focused, charismatic—but in the end an egotistical, mean, untrustworthy liar. And in "Culture," in the later, more pragmatic *The Conduct of Life* (1860), Emerson reflects on a paradox: that nature instills individualism in each person, yet many talented people are "shut . . . up in a narrower selfism" (*W* 6:133), afflicted by the "goitre of egotism" (*W* 6:134). The broadening corrective to "solitude and repulsion" is afforded by culture. Indeed, in this essay Emerson contradicts his own advice from "Self-Reliance": In the 1841 essay he had chided the contemporary passion for travel as "a fool's paradise" (*CW* 2:46); in 1860 he admits that travel can be one of the treasured activities of culture that leavens narrow egotism in the provincial individual. And so Emerson, in changing times and contexts, still has the courage to resist "foolish consistency" in his own thinking.

Despite Emerson's nuanced treatment of self-reliance, readers continue to plunder his works to prop up all manner of political and philosophical stances and to praise him or blame him for what they take to be the qualities or the defects of his vision. Emerson has long been one of the handiest straw men in debates over national value, the term "Emersonian" usually implying, for good or ill, one's take on the implications of self-reliance. Lacking careful definition, "Emersonian" is as charged and flexible (and thus perhaps as meaningless) an adjective as such comparable cultural signifiers as "Puritan," "Victorian," and "modern." It is a critical commonplace that readers find what they are seeking in Emerson, and wise readers step cautiously before using Emerson for ulterior purposes. Emerson's protean style and his strong sense of paradox have always made paraphrasing him, let alone using his writings as support for ideological positions, a slippery affair. Self-reliance, as Emerson knew, is hard to define and even harder to live out. The challenge of "Self-Reliance"—as he intended—is renewed with each fresh reading.

See also "The American Scholar"; "Experience"; "The Poet"; *Nature;* Transcendentalism

BIBLIOGRAPHY

Primary Works

Emerson, Ralph Waldo. *The Collected Works of Ralph Waldo Emerson.* 6 vols. to date. Edited by Alfred R. Ferguson, Joseph Slater, and Douglas Emory Wilson. Cambridge: Harvard University Press, 1971–. Cited in the text as *CW;* "Self-Reliance" is in volume 2.

Emerson, Ralph Waldo. *The Complete Sermons of Ralph Waldo Emerson.* 4 vols. Edited by Albert J. von Frank et al. Columbia: University of Missouri Press, 1989-1992. Cited in the text as *CS.*

Emerson, Ralph Waldo. *The Complete Works of Ralph Waldo Emerson.* 12 vols. Edited by Edward Waldo Emerson. Boston: Houghton Mifflin, 1903–1904. Cited in the text as *W.*

Martineau, Harriet. *Society in America.* 3 vols. London: Saunders & Otley, 1837.

Tocqueville, Alexis de. *Democracy in America.* 1835, 1840. Edited by J. P. Mayer. Translated by George Lawrence. New York: Harper and Row, 1966.

Secondary Works

Anderson, Quentin. *The Imperial Self: An Essay in American Literary and Cultural History.* New York: Knopf, 1971.

Bellah, Robert N., et al. *Habits of the Heart: Individualism and Commitment in American Life.* New York: Harper and Row, 1985.

Bloom, Harold. "Emerson: Power at the Crossing." In *Ralph Waldo Emerson: A Collection of Critical Essays,* edited by Lawrence Buell, pp. 148–158. Englewood Cliffs, N.J.: Prentice Hall, 1993.

Giamatti, A. Bartlett. *The University and the Public Interest.* New York: Atheneum, 1981.

Howe, Daniel Walker. *Making the American Self: Jonathan Edwards to Abraham Lincoln.* Cambridge, Mass.: Harvard University Press, 1997.

Masters, Edgar Lee. *The Living Thoughts of Emerson.* London: Cassell, 1947.

Mitchell, Charles E. *Individualism and Its Discontents: Appropriations of Emerson, 1880–1950.* Amherst: University of Massachusetts Press, 1997.

Mott, Wesley T. "'The Age of the First Person Singular': Emerson and Individualism." In *A Historical Guide to Ralph Waldo Emerson,* edited by Joel Myerson, pp. 61–100. New York: Oxford University Press, 2000.

Swart, Koenraad W. "'Individualism' in the Mid-Nineteenth Century (1826–1860)." *Journal of the History of Ideas* 23 (January–March 1962): 77–90.

Wesley T. Mott

SENECA FALLS CONVENTION

A touchstone moment and fulcrum point of both literal and symbolic significance, the Seneca Falls Convention of 1848 is considered to have begun the organized first wave of the feminist movement in America. The nineteenth-century women's rights movement focused women's discontent about their social and legal situations and introduced the imperative of political change.

ABOLITION'S INFLUENCE ON WOMEN'S RIGHTS

Elizabeth Cady Stanton (1815–1902), the most important philosopher among the women's rights advocates in the nineteenth-century United States, was born into a conservative family. She married an abolitionist lecturer, Henry Brewster Stanton (1805–1887), in 1840, and together they attended the World's Anti-Slavery Convention in London during their honeymoon. The movement for gaining women's right to vote can be dated back to that event, for the refusal to allow women delegates to participate challenged the activist women "to confront their own oppression," according to the historian Judith Wellman (p. 63). And it was in London that Elizabeth Stanton met the Quaker minister Lucretia Mott (1793–1880), who was to become one of Stanton's most important mentors.

After Elizabeth Stanton moved to the village of Seneca Falls, New York, in 1847, she and Lucretia Mott determined to hold a local convention to discuss women's rights. The necessary cultural conditions had been arising during public discussion about the implications of changing the laws against women's ownership of property. New York passed its first Married Women's Property Act in April 1848, allowing married women to control and acquire property legally. The stage was also set by events in June 1848, including the creation of a new group called the Congregational Friends, started by adherents of the Quaker faith in nearby Waterloo, New York, and by the formation of the Free-Soil Party, which sought to eliminate slavery in the United States western territories.

As the lives of Elizabeth Cady Stanton and Henry Stanton demonstrate, the women's rights movement is linked significantly with the abolition cause. But it is not merely that women compared their oppression with that of slaves and used the metaphor of "slavery," because women also learned through participation in the antislavery movement how to turn their perceptions of injustice into a widespread political movement. As Ellen Du Bois explains, abolitionism provided women "with a way to escape clerical authority, an egalitarian ideology, and a theory of social change" (p. 32). When abolitionism grew beyond its evangelical origins and began challenging institutional Protestant religion, William Lloyd Garrison (1805–1879), editor of *The Liberator*, emphasized whites' and blacks' common, shared humanity. Abolitionist feminists applied this concept to women, and the philosophy that "women were essentially human and only incidentally female liberated them from the necessity of justifying their own actions in terms of what was appropriate to women's sphere" (Du Bois, p. 36). Furthermore, the Seneca Falls Convention shows that the emphasis on overcoming public apathy by raising and agitating sentiment about one's cause was a prominent method among advocates of both abolition and women's rights.

THE CONVENTION AT SENECA FALLS

Although the first announcement appeared only eight days before the meeting, approximately three hundred people attended the Seneca Falls Convention, held at the Wesleyan Chapel of the Wesleyan Methodist Church, an abolitionist denomination, on 20 and 21 July 1848. The object of the meeting, as stated in their public call, was to discuss "the social, civil, and religious condition and rights of women." Women and men gave speeches, read aloud and discussed the content of the Declaration of Sentiments, made some revisions, and approved the document. The Declaration

This passage is from Elizabeth Cady Stanton's memoir Eighty Years and More: Reminiscences 1815–1897. *It shows the underpinnings of Stanton's thinking about women's rights and her interest in agitating public awareness of the cause. Stanton was also, like Ralph Waldo Emerson, a philosopher of her era.*

Emerson says, "A healthy discontent is the first step to progress." The general discontent I felt with woman's portion as wife, mother, housekeeper, physician, and spiritual guide, the chaotic conditions into which everything fell without her constant supervision, and the wearied, anxious look of the majority of women impressed me with a strong feeling that some active measures should be taken to remedy the wrongs of society in general, and of women in particular. My experience at the World's Anti-slavery Convention, all I had read of the legal status of women, and the oppression I saw everywhere, together swept across my soul, intensified now by many personal experiences. It seemed as if all the elements had conspired to impel me to some onward step. I could not see what to do or where to begin—my only thought was a public meeting for protest and discussion.

In this tempest-tossed condition of mind I received an invitation to spend the day with Lucretia Mott, at Richard Hunt's, in Waterloo [New York]. There I met several members of different families of [Quaker] Friends, earnest, thoughtful women. I poured out, that day, the torrent of my long-accumulating discontent, with such vehemence and indignation that I stirred myself, as well as the rest of the party, to do and dare anything. My discontent, according to Emerson, must have been healthy, for it moved us all to prompt action, and we decided, then and there, to call a "Woman's Rights Convention."

Stanton, *Eighty Years and More*, pp. 147–148.

of Sentiments was a rewriting of the Preamble of the U.S. Declaration of Independence to declare men and women equal and to criticize the specific "injuries and usurpations on the part of man toward woman."

Signing continued on both days of the convention, but the reasons that only one-third of the persons present signed the document remain unknown. For

The Seneca Falls Convention. Illustration from *Harper's Weekly,* 11 June 1859. The cartoonist emphasizes popular opinions of early feminists as angry, humorless fanatics. THE LIBRARY OF CONGRESS

instance, Quakers held egalitarian principles about men and women, but they might not have supported participation by either sex in the corrupt world of politics. Others may have sympathized but been reticent to sign publicly in support of women's political rights. All resolutions in the Declaration of Sentiments passed. Disagreement concerned whether men as well as women should sign the declaration and whether the convention should demand the elective franchise for women, or the right to vote; both questions were answered affirmatively. The only known African American to sign the declaration was Frederick Douglass (1818–1895), author of the most famous autobiography by an escaped American slave (1845), who spoke out for both women's suffrage and abolition.

Many other conventions, regional and national, followed this first convention, and national women's rights organizations were also formed. It is valuable to remember that these early women's rights activists had to teach themselves how to be instigators of a rebellion because their lives of domesticity had not trained them for such civic participation. Female friendships were thus an essential resource of the movement. Among the

more supportive and enduring activist friendships was the relationship begun in 1851 between Stanton and Susan B. Anthony (1820–1906), who is considered to have been the most effective recruiter and organizer of the women's rights advocates.

With the passage of the Nineteenth Amendment to the Constitution in 1920, giving women the right to vote, some people heralded the completed success of the goals motivating the Seneca Falls Convention. But more leaders believed that the work of feminism's "second wave" was just beginning and that there was much more work to do for achieving women's equality. There is no consensus on whether full parity has been achieved by the early twenty-first century.

LITERARY REFLECTIONS OF THE ISSUES AT SENECA FALLS

Without dramatizing the event itself, creative literature throughout the latter half of the nineteenth century regularly addressed the concerns expressed at the Seneca Falls Convention. Exploring what women's "rights" should be provided the conflicts

Elizabeth Cady Stanton (left) with Susan B. Anthony, c. 1881. © BETTMANN/CORBIS

for many novels, and the 1850s mark a turning point of heightened awareness and frequent contesting of the limited roles and living conditions previously assigned to American women. Many writers chose to advance or condemn progressive issues indirectly through their fiction. The inclusion of intellectually curious heroines in many popular novels by authors of all political leanings of this time period attests to the increased interest in women's minds and not just their bodies. The educational attainments of these female characters, in both their own learning and their employment as teachers, shows that the abilities of women extended beyond domestic management and that they could achieve success in the public sphere. However, best-selling authors usually ended books with the heroine's marriage, thus returning their women to the domestic sphere.

James Fenimore Cooper (1789–1851), author of the Leatherstocking series of books, including *The Last of the Mohicans* (1826), reacted against the tide of support for women's rights. Cooper's *The Ways of the Hour* (1850) expresses his disagreement with New York's Married Women's Property Act, which he

feared would bring chaos and destroy families. Emma Dorothy Eliza Nevitte (E. D. E. N.) Southworth (1819–1899) much more favorably addressed property laws and women's rights in *The Discarded Daughter; or, The Children of the Isle*, serialized during 1851 and 1852. Yet Southworth is best known for establishing a new type of heroine: the adventurous young woman who defies gender restrictions, struggles for the people and causes she loves, and outwits villainy, often while disguised as male. Southworth's most famous character is "Capitola the Madcap" from *The Hidden Hand*, a serialized tale that became a best-selling novel in 1888. Capitola performs typically masculine feats, such as rescuing a woman from a forced marriage, fighting a duel, and capturing a criminal and determining his just retribution. Another popular Southworth adventure novel, serialized under the title *Britomarte, the Man-Hater* (1865–1866), includes a heroine who is an outspoken women's rights activist. The literary critic Karen Tracey explains how Southworth used the "double-proposal plot" structure with a renegotiation of marriage customs to show that "the political and the personal are intertwined" (p. 133) and that women deserved the additional responsibilities they proved they could manage during the Civil War. The novel was republished as two books with milder titles, *Fair Play; or, the Test of the Lone Isle* (1868) and *How He Won Her: A Sequel to "Fair Play"* (1869), emphasizing the romantic endings.

Laura Curtis Bullard (1831–1912), a novelist and journalist, publicly promoted universal suffrage and reforms to improve women's lives, but her experimental novels reached comparatively few popular readers. In *Christine; or, Woman's Trials and Triumphs* (1856), the heroine initially rejects marriage and devotes herself to women's rights but ultimately combines marriage with her career in lecturing, writing about feminist issues, and training professional women workers. In 1870 Bullard took over the editorship of the *Revolution*, a feminist periodical begun by Anthony and Stanton to publish fiction and nonfiction on behalf of women's rights.

Henry James's novel *The Bostonians* (1886) features characters advocating women's rights, including a charismatic young public speaker romantically pursued by a southern man who believes women belong only in the private sphere of the home; he ultimately removes her from the activist community, keeping her from the lecture stage. Hester Prynne in Nathaniel Hawthorne's (1804–1864) *The Scarlet Letter* (1850) may be the quintessential American heroine, a character bringing unity to the fragmented women's roles in antebellum America and dreaming of a revolution in religious interpretation and relations between men and women. Hawthorne's *The Blithedale Romance* (1852) severely critiques feminists and reformers, but his creation of memorable and complex female characters contributes to his stature as one of America's most important authors.

Humorists were also inspired by the beginnings of feminism. In 1855 George Pickering Burnham's *History of the Hen Fever: A Humorous Record* in part parodied the women's rights movement. Newspapers also responded immediately with ridicule of the Seneca Falls Convention, which, added to family pressures, caused many signers of the original Declaration of Sentiments to withdraw their names if not their agreement. Softening her social commentary with comedy, Sara Payson Willis Parton (1811–1872), known as Fanny Fern, used her novel *Ruth Hall* (1855) and a weekly newspaper column from 1853 to 1872 to satirize social problems, lampoon male tyranny, and demand economic independence for women. From the 1870s to the early twentieth century, the satirist Marietta Holley (1836–1926) used the persona of Samantha, "Josiah Allen's wife," to endorse the causes of feminism and women's suffrage.

See also Abolitionist Writing; Declaration of Sentiments; Female Authorship; Feminism; Friendship; History; Marriage; Quakers; Reform; Suffrage

BIBLIOGRAPHY

Primary Works

Bullard, Laura Curtis. *Christine; or, Woman's Trials and Triumphs.* New York: DeWitt and Davenport, 1856.

Burnham, George Pickering. *The History of the Hen Fever: A Humorous Record.* Boston: James French, 1855.

Fern, Fanny [Sara Payson Willis Parton]. *Ruth Hall, a Domestic Tale of the Present Time.* 1855. Introduction and notes by Susan Belasco Smith. New York: Penguin, 1997.

Southworth, E. D. E. N. *Fair Play; or, The Test of the Lone Isle.* Philadelphia: T. B. Peterson, 1868.

Southworth, E. D. E. N. *How He Won Her: A Sequel to "Fair Play."* Philadelpha: T. B. Peterson, 1869.

Stanton, Elizabeth Cady. *Eighty Years and More: Reminiscences, 1815–1897.* 1898. Boston: Northeastern University Press, 1993.

Secondary Works

Bardes, Barbara, and Suzanne Gossett. *Declarations of Independence: Women and Political Power in Nineteenth-Century American Fiction.* New Brunswick, N.J.: Rutgers University Press, 1990.

Du Bois, Ellen Carol. *Feminism and Suffrage: The Emergence of an Independent Women's Movement in America,* 1848–1869. 1978. Ithaca, N.Y.: Cornell University Press, 1999.

Reynolds, David S. *Beneath the American Renaissance: The Subversive Imagination in the Age of Emerson and Melville.* New York: Knopf, 1988.

Tracey, Karen. *Plots and Proposals: American Women's Fiction, 1850–90.* Urbana: University of Illinois Press, 2000.

Wellman, Judith. *The Road to Seneca Falls: Elizabeth Cady Stanton and the First Women's Rights Convention.* Urbana: University of Illinois Press, 2004.

Amy Cummins

SENSATIONAL FICTION

Sensational fiction of the 1820–1870 period consisted largely of inexpensive, mass-produced pamphlet novels, many of them in yellow paper jackets emblazoned with racy titles in lurid dark lettering and melodramatic lithographs that ranged from the titillating to the horrific. Designed as ephemeral entertainment for a mobile readership, this fiction was an important barometer of popular taste and a revelation of such issues as class relations, gender, ethnicity, and the contexts of major American literature.

The heyday of yellow-covered sensational novels was the two decades from 1840 to 1860. Before then, sensational stories appeared mainly in newspapers. Although all societies since ancient times have hungered for sensationalism, antebellum America developed unique ways of satisfying this hunger. The 1830s witnessed a newspaper revolution. Improvements in technology and transportation facilitated the rapid dissemination of newspapers designed for the masses. Richard M. Hoe's cylinder press, introduced in 1832, greatly increased the speed of newspaper production. Previously, newspapers had been primarily political sheets that went for the relatively high price of six cents. The printing innovations of the 1830s brought about a drastic price reduction and wide distribution among a mass readership. The penny paper—the one- or two-cent sheet that appealed to the masses with its unabashedly sensational contents—began in 1833 with Benjamin H. Day's *New York Sun* and Horatio David Sheppard's *New York Morning Post,* followed shortly thereafter by the *Boston Daily Times,* the *Philadelphia Public Ledger,* the *Baltimore Sun,* and, most notoriously, James Gordon Bennett's *New York Herald.*

Bennett spoke for all the penny-press editors when he declared that American readers "were more ready to seek six columns of the details of a brutal murder, or the testimony of a divorce case, or the trial of a divine for improprieties of conduct, than the same amount of words poured forth by the genius of the noblest author of our times" (Pray, p. 255). A "Secret Tryst," a "Horrible Accident," a "Bloody Murder," a "Lamentable Business Failure"—anything lively was fodder for the penny newspaper, which was hawked on the sidewalks of America's fast-growing cities by shouting newsboys. Ralph Waldo Emerson noted in his journal that his countrymen spent their time "reading all day murders & railroad accidents" in newspapers (p. 433). Henry David Thoreau, likewise, spoke of "startling and monstrous events as fill the daily papers" (p. 267).

America was hardly alone among nations whose popular press was rapidly changing, but it was known for the excessiveness of its newspaper sensationalism. In 1847, Walt Whitman (1819–1892), as editor of the *Brooklyn Daily Eagle,* noted "the superiority of tone of the London and Paris press over our cheaper and more diffused press," emphasizing: "Scurrility—the truth may as well be told—is a sin of the American newspaper press." Foreign commentators made a similar point. In 1842 the London *Foreign Quarterly Review* generalized: "The more respectable the city in America, the more infamous, the more degrading and disgusting, we have found to be its Newspaper Press." By the 1850s, a writer for the *Westminster Review* could declare: "*Our* press is bad enough. . . . But its violence is meekness and even its atrocities are virtues compared with that system of *brutal and ferocious outrage* which distinguished the press of America" (Wilmer, p. 398).

Also fanning the public's interest in sensationalism were nonfictional trial pamphlets and criminal biographies. This period saw the rapid publication of pamphlets about notorious American murderers, robbers, pirates, swindlers, and sex fiends. Nathaniel Hawthorne (1804–1864), an avid reader of crime narratives, in his 1844 allegorical tale "Earth's Holocaust," described such literature as an irresistible swarm that had suddenly appeared "in the shape of a cloud of pamphlets from the press of the New World" (p. 398). Herman Melville (1819–1891) in his 1857 novel *The Confidence-Man* (his own version of the swindler genre) described someone aboard a riverboat peddling "the lives of Meason, the bandit of Ohio, Murrel, the pirate of the Mississippi, the brothers Harpe, the Thugs of the Green River country, in Kentucky" (p. 841).

It was a short step from such nonfiction narratives to the sensational fiction that surged to the fore of American publishing in the 1840s and 1850s. Such fiction, churned out by mass publishers such as Gleason of Boston and T. B. Peterson of Philadelphia, often took the form of cheap pamphlet novels about pirates, corsairs, freebooters, mythic monsters, and so forth, answering a growing demand for what Whitman called "blood and thunder romances with alliterative titles and plots of startling interest" (*Uncollected Poetry and Prose*, pp. 20–21). Typical titles (with the inevitable descriptive subtitles) included Maturin Murray Ballou's *Fanny Campbell; or, The Female Pirate Captain* (1845); Frank Forrester's *Pierre, the Partisan: A Tale of the Mexican Marches* (1847); Harry Halyard's *Wharton, the Whale-Killer!; or, The Pride of the Pacific* (1848); and Johannes Adrianus Block's *Mary Bean, the Factory Girl; A Domestic Story, Illustrative of the Trials and Temptations of Factory Life* (1850).

THE QUAKER CITY

The most important sensational novel of the period— and one of the landmarks of American popular culture—was George Lippard's (1822–1854) *The Quaker City; or, The Monks of Monk Hall: A Romance of Philadelphia Life, Mystery, and Crime*, which detailed secret sexual depravity and drunken excess among Philadelphia's ruling class. Nightmarish, erotic, and fiercely egalitarian, *The Quaker City* had instant appeal for the masses. It first appeared in ten paper-covered installments published between fall 1844 and spring 1845. By the time a few sections of it had appeared, it had divided Philadelphia along class lines: many workers became fans of Lippard, whereas their wealthier fellow citizens objected to his thinly veiled portrayal of local celebrities and denounced his depictions of sex and violence. In November 1844 a performance of a play based on the novel had to be canceled owing to fears of violence between admirers and opponents of the work. Lippard received death threats. A thin man with long black curls, he cut a Byronic figure as he walked black-caped around Philadelphia carrying a sword-cane for protection.

The furor over the novel provided wonderful publicity, and when the expanded edition appeared in May 1845 as a single volume, the publishers claimed that more than sixty thousand copies had been sold within a year. For a decade thereafter the novel's annual sale averaged ten thousand. The best-selling American novel before Harriet Beecher Stowe's *Uncle Tom's Cabin* (1852), *The Quaker City* passed through twenty-seven American "editions" by 1849 and became, as Lippard boasted, "more attacked, and more read, than any other work of American fiction ever published" (p. 2). Lippard went on to produce

George Lippard. Author of *The Quaker City*. THE LIBRARY OF CONGRESS

several more urban-exposé novels, including *The Empire City* (1849), *Memoirs of a Preacher* (1849), and *New York: Its Upper Ten and Lower Million* (1853), all of which dramatized social injustices and upper-class corruption in American cities.

The main plot of *The Quaker City* was based on a famous seduction case of 1843 in which a Philadelphian named Singleton Mercer was acquitted after killing Mahlon Heberton, who had enticed Mercer's sister into a house of assignation and allegedly seduced her on a promise of marriage. In his novel, Lippard enriched this real-life tale through multiple ironies. Irony controls the story of Byrnewood Arlington, who, despite the eventual disgust over the seduction of his sister, had actually facilitated the seduction by encouraging and laying a bet on Gustavus Lorrimer's plans for a sexual escapade. Also ironic is that Byrnewood is a seducer in his own right: Annie, the young servant he has impregnated, haunts his mind even as he tracks down and kills his sister's seducer. This sister, Mary Arlington, seems like a conventional heroine but comes close to being the obverse of one: she lies to her parents, gullibly swallows Lorrimer's talk about a pastoral Wyoming home,

and at the end croons longingly for her lost "Lorraine," even after he has been exposed as a fraud.

Into this main plot Lippard weaves two others. In one, the beautiful Dora Livingstone, reared in poverty and now married to the wealthy merchant Albert Livingstone, tries to rise even higher socially by taking up with Algernon Fitz-Cowles, who pretends he is an English lord who will give her royal rank. Dora's husband, alerted to her infidelity by Dora's former lover, Luke Harvey, vows revenge, finally poisoning her in his country estate and dying there in a fire. The third plot revolves around a young woman, Mabel, who was the illegitimate daughter of the monstrous pimp Devil-Bug but was raised by the Reverend F. A. T. Pyne (originally Dick Baltzar). The lecherous, hypocritical Pyne drugs Mabel in an effort to rape her, but she is rescued by Devil-Bug, who wants to portray her to the world as the daughter of the rich Livingstone so that she will gain wealth and status. Mabel is temporarily inveigled into becoming the main "priestess" of a cult led by a mad sorcerer, Ravoni, but Devil-Bug frees her; she becomes known to the world as the rich Izole Livingstone, and she marries Luke Harvey.

The central action takes place in the labyrinthine den of iniquity known as Monk Hall, where Philadelphia's elite gather nightly to indulge in drunken revelry, illicit sex, and financial double-dealing. Supervising this depravity with demonic glee is the keeper of Monk Hall, Devil-Bug. No mere criminal, Devil-Bug is an "Outlaw of hell," a "deplorable moral monstrosity," "a wild beast, a snake, a reptile, or a devil incarnate—anything but a man" (pp. 106–107).

The novel runs with blood and reeks of murder and madness. It is filled with freakish characters who swing between cold sarcasm and crazed terror and who are described in a wryly imaginative style that often becomes almost surrealistic in its zany distortions and weird juxtapositions. Even as the novel parodies penny papers through its portrait of the editor Buzby Poodle (known as Count Common Sewer because of the opportunistic sensationalism of his paper, the *Daily Black Mail*), it is itself a kind of massive penny paper, piling hair-raising events on top of each other with dizzying speed. It is of a piece with the commercialized freaks and overall violence that characterized antebellum life in the United States.

If *The Quaker City* has the atmosphere of nightmare, it is because Lippard, a labor reformer with views akin to those of his German contemporary Karl Marx, regarded American society as a dark realm of class divisions, economic uncertainty, and widespread corruption. America's rapidly growing cities were suddenly strange, overwhelming places. Without effective sanitation, they were squalid and disease prone. Garbage was heaped on unpaved streets that quickly turned to mud or dust. The tenement areas where the poor lived were filled with overcrowded, ramshackle houses. Huge hotels, department stores, and mansions stood in stark contrast to the humble homes of the poor. Lippard's novel describes "a mass of miserable frame houses [that] seemed about to commit suicide and throw themselves into the gutter, and in the distance a long lines of dwellings, offices, and factories, looming in broken perspective, looked as if they wanted to shake hands across the narrow street" (p. 42).

The success of Lippard's novel gave impetus to a whole school of popular fiction about the "mysteries and miseries" of American cities. Some fifty American novels of city life, most of which exaggerated Lippard's sensationalism while deemphasizing his reformist purpose, appeared between 1845 and 1870: Ned Buntline, Henri Foster, and George Thompson established themselves as the most prolific authors in the field. The corrupt aristocracy and squalid poverty of New York, Boston, and Philadelphia were the most popular topics, though the city novelists probed the "mysteries" of a remarkable range of other cities, including Rochester (New York), Lowell (Massachusetts), and Nashua (New Hampshire), as well as St. Louis, San Francisco, and New Orleans.

GEORGE THOMPSON

By 1855 an entire book, anonymously published as *Confessions and Experience of a Novel Reader,* was devoted to excoriating sensational "Yellow-Jacket Literature." The author estimated that in the United States, with its population of 24 million, there was "an enormous circulation of over 2.5 million volumes, extending their deleterious influence, and diffusing their pernicious principles throughout society" (p. 39). The author wrote, "If any one has any doubts as to the fearfully rapid increase of this public poison—a demoralizing literature, the real 'Pandora's box of evil passions'—the flood-gate, from beneath whose slimy jaws runs a stream of pollution, sending forth its pestilential branches to one great ocean of immorality, let such a one take a walk with me through the length and breadth of our land" (p. 27).

The most productive writer of such fiction was George Thompson (b. 1823), a paunchy, peripatetic man who divided his time between editing racy newspapers in eastern cities and writing pamphlet novels, including *Venus in Boston; City Crimes; New York Life; The Gay Girls of New York;* and *The Mysteries of Bond-Street.* Thompson boasted in his autobiography that he had written "a sufficient quantity of tales, sketches,

poetry, essays, and other literary stock of every description, to constitute half a dozen cartloads" (*Venus in Boston,* p. xi). Evidence of sixty different titles survives.

In Thompson's hands, the city mysteries genre became an expansive medium. From penny newspapers and true-crime pamphlets, Thompson derived images of crime and violence with proven appeal for the American masses. From the exhibitions of P. T. Barnum he inherited an interest in the freakish and bizarre. From British and French pornography, he gleaned erotic themes, such as the sexually voracious woman and the reverend rake.

Thompson was the most sexually explicit author of the day. His work contains scene after scene in which taboo or outré sex is suggested, if not described in detail. Among the kinds of sexual activity Thompson depicts are adultery, miscegenation, group sex, incest, child sex, and gay sex. In *City Crimes* he described the below-ground Dark Vaults, where "the crime of incest is as common . . . as dirt! I have known a mother and a son—a father and a daughter—a brother and a sister—to be guilty of criminal intimacy" (p. 131). In the same novel Lucretia Franklin becomes so bored and sexually frustrated by her proper husband that she murders him; she and her daughter Josephine then lead lives of unrestrained nymphomania, using men (and boys) solely for sexual gratification and disposing of them. In another plot in *City Crimes,* the aristocratic, outwardly prudish Julia Fairfield coyly resists the advances of her fiancé, Frank Sydney, while she secretly carries on a torrid affair with her black servant Nero, by whom she is pregnant. Frank discovers the affair and spurns her, but, with the prospect of complete sexual freedom before her, she tells him, "I tell you that I consume with desire—but not for enjoyment with such as *you,* but for amours which are recherché and unique," such as that "with my superb African" (p. 152).

CULTURAL AND LITERARY INFLUENCE OF SENSATIONALISM

Sensational fiction deepens our understanding of the major American literature. For example, the reverend rake, a standard figure in sensational writing, provides a backdrop to Hawthorne's Arthur Dimmesdale, the hypocritical clergyman of *The Scarlet Letter* (1850). Lecherous clergymen were often featured in newspaper stories with racy titles such as "The Reverend Seducer," "More Religious Hypocrites," "The Reverend Rascal," and so forth. Thompson, who coined the phrase "reverend rake" to describe the modern preacher, generalized in *The Countess* (1849): "Within the pale of every church, hypocrisy, secret and damning hypocrisy, is a predominating quality" (p. 19). In Thompson's novels clergymen and moral reformers are singled out as being especially libidinous. Thompson was equaled in this regard only by Lippard, whose Reverend F. A. T. Pyne of *The Quaker City* is a debauchee who nightly applies his ministerial earnings to the purchase of wine, women, and opium at Monk Hall. The reverend rake was so common a figure in sensational writing that Hawthorne could hardly overlook it in his search for a main male character for *The Scarlet Letter*. Hawthorne notably enriched this standard character by placing him in a bygone Puritan setting described with sympathy and seriousness. Were Dimmesdale merely a reverend rake, he would be like any coarse, lip-smacking clergyman in sensational fiction. Were he solely a virtuous Puritan preacher, he would be a dreary anachronism for many of Hawthorne's readers. Because he is *both* a devout Puritan and a reverend rake, he is at once sincerely tormented and explosively ironic. Since he is a believing clergyman, he is honestly tortured and humane in a way that F. A. T. Pyne and the other reverend rakes cannot be.

Edgar Allan Poe's (1809–1849) fiction, too, is illuminated by consideration of the sensational writings of the day. Poe was a close friend of Lippard, with whom he shared an interest in horror and diseased psychology along with a rationalist regard for puns, careful plot construction, and the minutiae of mechanical contrivances. There appear to be particular connections between *The Quaker City* and "The Cask of Amontillado" (1846), the horror tale Poe wrote shortly after Lippard's novel appeared. The Dead Vault below Monk Hall, dripping with moisture and filled with skeletons, wine casks, and hidden niches, is much like the skeleton-filled, dripping wine cellar into which Montresor lures Fortunato. The portrait of Devil-Bug, spade in hand, preparing to bury alive Byrnewood Arlington and taunting him with black jokes and screeching laughter looks forward to that of Montresor, spade in hand, burying alive Fortunato while torturing him psychologically with jokes and screams.

A number of other major authors were also influenced by sensational literature. The fleeting, deceptive appearances Melville conjures up in *The Confidence-Man* had precedent in popular novels like Ned Buntline's (c. 1823–1886) *The G'hals of New York* (1850), which contains a character called "the Confidence Man" and which portrays a world in which, as Buntline writes, one "must make up his mind whether he will cheat or be cheated, whether he will dupe or be duped, whether he will pluck or be plucked" (p. 25). Whitman noted the great popularity

of sensational literature, in which he saw "various forms and preparations of only one plot, namely, a sickly, scrofulous, crude, amorousness" (*Notebooks*, 4:1604). He asked in a newspaper article, "Who will underrate the influence of a loose popular literature in debauching the popular mind?" (*I Sit and Look Out*, p. 113). Alarmed by the bald prurience of much popular writing, Whitman in his poetry tried to restore sex to the level of naturalness, honesty, and genuine emotion. Mark Twain (1835–1910), who is known to have read Lippard in the early 1850s, showed Lippard's influence in *Innocents Abroad* (1869), where he names his ship of fools *The Quaker City*, and in *Adventures of Huckleberry Finn* (1885), in which his depiction of human savagery in Pap (who recalls Devil-Bug), his cynical vision of conventional society, and his parody of sentimental literature through his portrait of the lachrymose poetess Emmeline Grangerford all have Lippardian overtones.

Bold, zestful, and, at its best, stylistically experimental, sensational fiction was a significant presence on the nineteenth-century scene, one that richly merits the increasing attention it is receiving among literary and cultural historians.

See also Book Publishing; Gothic Fiction; Pornography; Reform; Urbanization

BIBLIOGRAPHY
Primary Works
Buntline, Ned. *The G'hals of New York*. New York: Robert M. DeWitt, 1850.

Confessions and Experience of a Novel Reader. Chicago: William Stacy, 1855.

Emerson, Ralph Waldo. *Emerson in His Journals*. Edited by Joel Porte. Cambridge, Mass.: Harvard University Press, 1982.

Foster, George G. *New York by Gas-Light*. 1850. Reprint. *New York by Gas-Light and Other Urban Sketches*. Edited by Stuart M. Blumin. Berkeley: University of California Press, 1990.

Hawthorne, Nathaniel. *Mosses from an Old Manse*. 1846. Columbus: Ohio State University Press, 1974.

Lippard, George. *George Lippard, Prophet of Protest: Writings of an American Radical, 1822–1854*. Edited by David S. Reynolds. New York: Peter Lang, 1986.

Lippard, George. *The Quaker City; or, The Monks of Monk Hall*. 1845. Edited by David S. Reynolds. Amherst: University of Massachusetts Press, 1995.

Melville, Herman. *Pierre, Israel Potter, The Piazza Tales, The Confidence-Man, Uncollected Prose, Billy Budd*. New York: Library of America, 1984.

Pray, Isaac Clark. *Memoirs of James Gordon Bennett and His Times*. New York: Stringer and Townsend, 1855.

Thompson, George. *The Countess; or, Memoirs of Women of Leisure*. Boston: Berry and Wright, 1849.

Thompson, George. *The Gay Girls of New York; or, Life on Broadway*. New York, 1853.

Thompson, George. *Venus in Boston and Other Tales of Nineteenth-Century City Life*. Edited by David S. Reynolds and Kimberly R. Gladman. Amherst: University of Massachusetts Press, 2002. Contains *Venus in Boston* (1849), *City Crimes* (1849), and Thompson's autobiography, *My Life* (1854).

Thoreau, Henry David. *The Journal of Henry David Thoreau*. Edited by Bradford Torrey and Francis H. Allen. New York: Dover, 1965.

Whitman, Walt. *I Sit and Look Out: Editorials from the Brooklyn Daily Times*. Edited by Emory Holloway and Vernolian Schwartz. New York: AMS Press, 1966.

Whitman, Walt. *Notebooks and Unpublished Prose Manuscripts*. Edited by Edward H. Grier. New York: New York University Press, 1984.

Whitman, Walt. *The Uncollected Poetry and Prose of Walt Whitman*. Edited by Emory Holloway. Gloucester, Mass.: Peter Smith, 1972.

Wilmer, Lambert A. *Our Press Gang: or, A Complete Exposition of the Corruptions and Crimes of American Newspapers*. Philadelphia: J. T. Lloyd, 1859.

Secondary Sources

Cohen, Daniel A. *Pillars of Salt, Monuments of Grace: New England Crime Literature and the Origins of American Popular Culture, 1674–1860*. New York: Oxford University Press, 1993.

Davis, David Brion. *Homicide in American Fiction, 1798–1860*. Ithaca, N.Y.: Cornell University Press, 1957.

Denning, Michael. *Mechanic Accents: Dime Novels and Working-Class Culture in America*. London: Verso, 1987.

Looby, Christopher. "George Thompson's 'Romance of the Real': Transgression and Taboo in American Sensation Fiction." *American Literature* 65, no. 4 (1993): 651–672.

Noel, Mary. *Villains Galore: The Heyday of the Popular Story Weekly*. New York: Macmillan, 1954.

Reynolds, David S. *Beneath the American Renaissance: The Subversive Imagination in the Age of Emerson and Melville*. New York: Knopf, 1988.

Reynolds, David S. *George Lippard*. Boston: Twayne, 1982.

Siegel, Adrienne. *The Image of the American City in Popular Literature, 1820–1870*. Port Washington, N.Y.: Kennikat Press, 1981.

Streeby, Shelley. *American Sensations: Class, Empire, and the Production of Popular Culture*. Berkeley: University of California Press, 2002.

Streeby, Shelley. "Opening Up the Story-Paper: George Lippard and the Construction of Class." *boundary 2* 24, no. 1 (1997): 177–203.

David S. Reynolds

SENTIMENTALISM

Emerging in England in the mid- to late eighteenth century, and reflecting a similar trend in continental literature at the time, literary sentimentalism or "sensibility" prioritized feeling. It developed primarily as a middle-class phenomenon, reflecting the emphasis on compassion or feeling as a desirable character trait in the newly emergent middle class. Although, on the one hand, the reader might take pleasure in feeling itself, in England by the 1770s the rise of sensibility was also linked to a growing activism—the awareness of and concern for the suffering of others reflected in, for example, the antislavery movement, concerns about child labor, and the campaigns for better hospitals, prison reform, and charity schools as well as in the response to the suffering associated with the rapid rise of industrial capitalism and the urban misery caused by exploitative labor practices.

The following lines from Hannah More's (1745–1833) poem "Sensibility" (1782) sum up the varied attitudes involved in sensibility: the pleasure that one derives from feeling; the heartfelt moral dictate to do the right thing; and the way in which feeling inspires activism:

> Sweet Sensibility! Thou keen delight!
> Thou hasty moral! Sudden sense of right!
> Thou untaught goodness! Virtue's precious seed!
> Thou sweet precursor of the gen'rous deed!
> *(Ll. 337–340)*

The word "sentimental" is first known to have appeared in print in English in the 1740s. Becoming almost immediately popular, the term was used to describe the emotional state of a sensitive and "genteel" person, and sentiment began to play an important role in literature. As Louis Bredvold notes, "Drama and fiction had discovered that pathos could best soften the heart and raise the tear that betokens humanity" (pp. 416, 433). Among the earliest British novels that heralded the rise of sentimentalism were Samuel Richardson's *Pamela; or, Virtue Rewarded* (1740) and *Clarissa* (1747–1748); Oliver Goldsmith's *The Vicar of Wakefield* (1766); Laurence Sterne's *A Sentimental Journey* (1768); and Henry Mackenzie's *The Man of Feeling* (1771). According to Paul Langford, Mackenzie's novel was a "deliberate attempt to portray the sentimentalist as a benevolent man" (p. 481).

To be a "man of feeling" became a desirable goal even among middle-class men of business.

The sentimental novel first made its way across the Atlantic in the form of the seduction narrative. After William Hill Brown's *The Power of Sympathy* appeared in 1789, Susanna Rowson's (1762–1824) *Charlotte Temple* (1794) became America's first best-seller. Rowson's novel inspired feeling, and generations of readers, men and women from all classes, wept over the hapless Charlotte's fate. Many of those readers were so moved by the novel that they made the pilgrimage to the heroine's presumed grave in Trinity Churchyard in New York, leaving flowers and other mementos. Yet as Cathy Davidson points out, it is a mistake to think of the novel as only sentimental. Subtitled *A Tale of Truth,* it portrays an all-too-common and very realistic situation: the seduction and betrayal of an innocent and ignorant young girl and her subsequent death in childbirth. Addressing the young female reader, Rowson assures her that, as Davidson notes, "she is not alone in a world in which she has no legal or political identity," where women are trivialized, and where the sexual double standard prevails ("Introduction," p. xvii). As Rowson says in her preface, compassion inspired her to write the novel, and she hopes that her words will help to prevent some of the miseries that she chronicles (p. 6).

During certain periods in American history, sentimentalism has been particularly evident in literature. One such period was the Progressive Era of the late nineteenth to early twentieth centuries, during which, as Jaime Harker points out, the "muckrakers" used a sentimental appeal to feeling in order to bring about social and economic reform (p. 56). Upton Sinclair's 1905 novel *The Jungle,* for example, vividly portrays moving scenes of the miserable working and living conditions of immigrants in the unregulated meat-packing industry. Essentially a middle-class movement, Progressivism was promoted by Protestant ministers, and Progressives often used religious rhetoric to attack the injustices of industrial capitalism.

MID-NINETEENTH-CENTURY SENTIMENTALISM

The period in American history that is most commonly associated with sentimentalism is the mid-nineteenth century. The sentimentalism of this period has been defined in various ways. Some have characterized it as conservative, a rationalization of the status quo, while others have characterized it as radical and a means of effecting social change. But most sources agree that it is associated with femininity and domesticity, its primary characteristic being an emphasis on feeling and the affective bonds among human beings.

What differentiates mid-nineteenth-century sentimentalism from that of other periods, however, is that it is generally characterized as wholly female. Although women writers did not have a monopoly on feeling during this period, and their books were read by men as well as women, sentimentalism fit nicely into contemporary definitions of domestic womanhood. Also largely middle-class and incorporating religious rhetoric into their writing, the sentimental writers of this period were criticized by later, more secular critics seeking a "virile" masculine ethos. Twentieth-century critics wrote contemptuously about mid-nineteenth-century women writers, often without even reading their works. Fred Lewis Pattee characterized the period as "The Feminine Fifties" in his 1940 book by that title and called even so cynical and down-to-earth a writer as the satirical Fanny Fern the "most tearful and convulsingly 'female' moralizer" of the period (p. 110). Herbert Ross Brown's study of the antebellum period, *The Sentimental Novel in America* (1940), labeled sentimentality a "disease" and castigated women writers of the period for not dealing with what for him were the "real" issues: the [masculine] "national drama" of Manifest Destiny and the "rise of the common man" (pp. 358–359, 369–370). Following in this tradition, Ann Douglas in *The Feminization of American Culture* (1977) maintained that the intellectual "toughness" of the male-dominated Calvinism of the Puritan theologian Jonathan Edwards (1703–1758) had been undermined by the sentimentalism of feminized ministers and middle-class women writers. Dismissing the writers' attempts to effect social change, she held them responsible for the country's "introduction to consumerism" and mass culture (see, for example, pp. 5–7, 10–13). Other critics similarly criticized the sentimental novelists as essentially conservative writers who implicitly reified the values of the dominant bourgeois culture.

In contrast to critics like those cited above, more recent studies, particularly among feminist critics, have explored the cultural and aesthetic value of mid-nineteenth-century sentimentalism. Jane Tompkins's book *Sensational Designs* (1985) is a specific attack on Douglas's thesis that mid-nineteenth-century women writers destroyed a superior Puritan "male-dominated" tradition and advanced consumer culture and the status quo. Instead, says Tompkins, the sentimental novelists used the established value system to "effect a radical transformation of . . . society" (p. 145). Describing "sentimental power" as "a political enterprise" that spoke to "large masses of readers," Tompkins asserts that the sentimental novelists reached

In an article in the New York Ledger titled "What Shall We Do?" (2 February 1867) Fanny Fern expressed her own determination to do what she could to address social and political issues. Even though, as a woman, she had no political power, she did what many other women writers did at the time: she used her pen.

What if you are so constituted that injustice and wrong to others rouses you as if it were done to yourself? What if the miseries of your fellow beings, particularly those you are powerless to relieve, haunt you day and night? . . . What if you cannot carry out the practically atheistic creed of so many of the present day? Of so many young men—to their shame, be it said—who with a man's chances fold their supine hands over all these abuses? . . . Well, rather than be that torpid thing, and it a man, I would rather be a woman tied hand and foot, bankrupt in chances, and worry over what I am powerless to help. At least I can stand at my post, like a good soldier, because it is my post; meantime—I had rather be taken off that by a chance shot, than rust in a corner with ossification of the heart.

Fern, Ruth Hall and Other Writings, pp. 336–337.

Harriet Beecher Stowe, Fanny Fern, Maria Cummins, E. D. E. N. Southworth, Frances Harper, Elizabeth Stoddard, Elizabeth Stuart Phelps, and Augusta Evans Wilson are among the mid-nineteenth-century writers whose names were on everyone's tongue during this period but who a hundred years later had seemingly been erased from history. Until the last two decades of the twentieth century the only nineteenth-century woman writer that American college students read was Emily Dickinson. Part of the reason for this was the literary movement called the New Criticism, which dominated literary scholarship and pedagogy during the 1940s, 1950s, and 1960s. Eschewing any discussion of social or cultural issues or emotion, and focusing wholly on the work of art as a "well-wrought urn" divorced from history, the New Critics looked for irony and ambiguity, not feeling and social reform.

Literary scholars determined what books were published and what books were read, but in terms of attitudes toward sentimentalism, the cultural climate of the time was also significant. In the 1940s and 1950s postwar American liberals, disillusioned by Joseph Stalin's purges in the Soviet Union, came to associate sentimentalism with naive ideology and turned to the pragmatic vision of a masculine America. Thus the American historian Arthur Schlesinger Jr., in his 1949 book The Vital Center, condemned the "persistent and sentimental optimism [that] has endowed Doughface progressivism with what in the middle of the twentieth century are fatal weaknesses: a weakness for impotence" (p. 40). The "man of feeling" was no longer to be admired—in politics or in literature. And sentimentality, identified as "soft," feminine, and emasculating, whether that of the mid- or late nineteenth century, was seriously out of fashion. Literary critics were repelled by or afraid of emotion and evinced what Susan Harris in Nineteenth-Century American Women's Novels (1990) calls a "deep-seated revulsion from the feminine" (p. 5). As Suzanne Clark notes in Sentimental Modernism (1991), this "reversal against the sentimental helped to establish avant-garde intellectuals as a discourse community defined by its adversarial relationship to domestic culture" (p. 1).

It was not until the late twentieth century that feminist scholars, having recovered the works of a number of nineteenth-century women writers, began to deal with the question of sentimentality. Some were embarrassed by the sentimentalism in the works, but instead of condemning the works as Douglas had done, they either ignored it or attempted to explain away the sentimentality as "subversive." Others were not bothered by the sentimentality, while still others, like Tompkins, found it a strength rather than a weakness.

down to the "cultural realities" that modernist criticism has disdained (pp. 126, xiv, xiii). According to Tompkins, twentieth-century critics deliberately established literary standards that denigrated everything that nineteenth-century women writers represented: "In reaction against their world view, and perhaps even more against their success, twentieth-century critics have taught generations of students to equate popularity with debasement, emotionality with ineffectiveness, religiosity with fakery, domesticity with triviality, and all of these, implicitly, with womanly inferiority" (p. 123).

During most of the second half of the twentieth century, the concept of "sentimentality" had indeed taken on negative connotations. The works by nineteenth-century women writers—even those with important cultural and literary significance—were totally excluded from high school and college syllabi, and for the most part were out of print. Alice Cary, Lydia Sigourney, Lydia Maria Child, Susan Warner,

These latter critics have looked at sentimentalism both for its cultural significance and for its aesthetics.

CULTURAL CRITICISM

Like Tompkins, who asserted the transformative power of sentimental texts, cultural critics have analyzed specific works in terms of the authors' efforts at social reform. Although some scholars have criticized mid-century writers for buying into the status quo of the dominant society, such criticism cannot be applied to all writers. Moreover, such criticism fails to recognize the complexity of sentimentalism: a writer who believed strongly in the religious teachings of her culture could also oppose other aspects of that culture which she felt did not live up to those teachings. If a writer took seriously the dictates of religion and conscience as well as the democratic teachings about equality, the writer could be inspired to attack inequities that she saw in the system. The basic rule of thumb in sentimentalism was that one had to "feel right." Using a deliberate appeal to feeling, sentimental writers spoke out strongly against slavery, for example. As Harriet Beecher Stowe (1811–1896) wrote in the preface to *Uncle Tom's Cabin* (1852), her intention in the novel was "to awaken sympathy and feeling for the African race" (p. 3). And Harriet Jacobs (1813–1897) wrote in the preface to *Incidents in the Life of a Slave Girl* (1861), "I do earnestly desire to arouse the women of the North to a realizing sense of the condition of two millions of women at the South, still in bondage, suffering what I suffered" (p. 1).

In addition to their efforts with respect to bringing about an end to slavery, sentimental writers also weighed in on gender issues, revealing such injustices as married women's property laws, women's legal infirmities, and cultural attitudes demeaning to women. Fanny Fern (1811–1872) in *Ruth Hall* (1855) and E. D. E. N. Southworth (1819–1899) in *The Hidden Hand* (1859), for example, used conventional strategies to reveal inequities in the situation of women. By portraying the fact that sane women could be locked away in insane asylums with impunity, that women had no control over any money that they earned or brought into a marriage, that their employment opportunities were limited to exploitative labor or prostitution, and that they were expected to obey without question even the most wrongheaded or cruel husband, such texts, by gaining the sympathy of readers and their admiration for a gritty heroine, advanced the cause of women's rights even without seeming to. A hundred years later, critics might ask why such texts were so popular. But it is important to remember that sentimentality was the principal frame of reference of the time. As Michael Riffaterre and other students of

narrative have pointed out, a text's verisimilitude is dependent upon references to the "sociolect," that is, the "myths, traditions, ideological and esthetic stereotypes, commonplaces, and themes" that are harbored by its audience (p. 130). Thus, nineteenth-century writers' portrayals of people and situations that contemporary readers could relate to, in a language and within a frame of reference that all readers were familiar with, reached a wider audience and could be more persuasive than any abstract treatise.

Even the most "sentimental" of the sentimental novelists used the appeal to feeling to provide a guide for women who might be floundering in a society that accorded them little respect as individuals. Certainly the reason why Susan Warner's (1819–1885) *The Wide, Wide World* (1850) and Maria Cummins's (1827–1866) *The Lamplighter* (1854) were such blockbusters was because they spoke to such women. In spite of the fact that the dominant culture had no use for higher education for women (Walt Whitman in 1857 argued against the establishment of public high schools for girls because, he said, women's function was simply to be good wives and mothers, and Dr. Edward Clarke reflected long-standing popular prejudices when he warned in 1873 that too much education would damage a woman's reproductive organs), both novels emphasize the intellectual development of their heroines. And in spite of the fact that the dominant culture decreed that women should never question male authority (a story in *Godey's Lady's Book* in 1850—ironically titled "Woman's Rights" praises a young woman for silently and passively bowing her head in acquiescence to the blows and verbal abuse from her ill-tempered father), both heroines not only question male authority, but Gertrude in *The Lamplighter* actively defies her guardian and leaves home in order to follow her conscience. The lesson of sentimentalism was that one had to do what made one "feel right"— whether it meant defying one man's rule or a nation's laws—and this was a powerful lesson for the legally and socially powerless.

In this sense Christianity, rather than being only an opiate to lull women into passive acceptance of an unjust system as some critics would claim, was often used by women—who had no political rights and whose opinions were trivialized—to support a position that was contrary to national law or their culture's mores. Thus, Ruth Hall in Fern's novel finds in religion the courage to defy her relatives and the whole social structure in order to seek economic independence—then an ignominious role for a middle-class woman (p. 123). Frances Harper (1825–1911) in her 1859 short story "The Two Offers" uses religion to defend her anti-social position defending productive spinsterhood

We Both Must Fade, 1869. Painting by Lilly Martin Spencer. Spencer was one of the most popular American women painters of the nineteenth century, known in particular the sentimentalism of her works. Here she evokes the evanescence of beauty. SMITHSONIAN AMERICAN ART MUSEUM, WASHINGTON, DC, USA/ART RESOURCE, NY

against the misery of a failed marriage and urging education for women, including African American women: "scope should be given to [woman's] Heaven-endowed and God-given faculties. The true aim of female education" should be the development of "all the faculties of the human soul" (p. 109). Mrs. Bird in *Uncle Tom's Cabin,* in disagreeing with her senator husband who has voted in favor of the Fugitive Slave Law, asserts, "I don't know anything about politics, but I have read my Bible" (p. 89). Similarly, Stowe in writing *Uncle Tom's Cabin* gained credence—and clearly also courage—from her appeal to a higher authority, invoking God in her attack on America's law. The novel concludes with the powerful warning: "Both North and South have been guilty before God; and the *Christian Church* has a heavy account to answer . . . for, not surer is the eternal law by which the millstone sinks in the ocean, than that stronger law by which injustice and cruelty shall bring on nations the wrath of Almighty God!" (p. 485).

THE AESTHETICS OF SENTIMENT

Although analysis of sentimental texts has focused primarily on cultural criticism, a number of scholars have also looked at the aesthetics of the genre. What such scholars have recognized is that sentimental texts must be looked at within the context of their own value system. Modernist criteria have only served to denigrate the sentimental. For most of the twentieth century it was impossible to undertake literary analysis of sentimental texts because they were considered by modernism to be inherently nonliterary. Developments in other disciplines also helped to pave the way for the feminist reevaluation of nineteenth-century women's writings. With the New Historicism and Foucauldian theory asking questions about authority and challenging the concept of objective truth, scholars began to question the modernist criteria that had consigned sentimental literature to the dustheap. In the 1980s and 1990s, following Tompkins's assertion in *Sensational Designs* that sentimental writing is "complex and significant" and the titular question in Susan Harris's 1991 essay "But Is It Any Good?" critics began to look at sentimental texts as one might look at texts in any genre—examining the text within a specific set of conventions and assessing the literary techniques employed by the author.

In her 1997 essay "Reclaiming Sentimental Literature," Joanne Dobson focuses on two aspects of sentimental rhetoric: the use of language and troping practices, both of which, she says, illustrate the "effectiveness of sentimentalism's rhetoric" and the "authenticity of its sentiment" (p. 269). The language, she says, is accessible and understated, almost conversational, because the goal of sentimental literature is communication. The most common tropes are metaphors for the threat of the destruction of human connections. These tropes are consistent with the thematic concerns of sentimental literature, which, she says, emphasize "relational experience and the consequences of its rupture" (p. 268).

Some scholars have traced the historic beginnings of aesthetic theory and its relationship to sentimentalism. Wendy Dasler Johnson looks to the eighteenth century in her 1999 study of nineteenth-century American male sentimentalists in relation to Julia Ward Howe's (1819–1910) poetry. Using Howe as what she calls a "heuristic" for men's sentimental poetry, she found that Howe and John Greenleaf Whittier, for example, both used eighteenth-century belletristic rhetorical codes "designed to produce sympathetic identification" with their readers in order to move them to social action, while Henry Wadsworth Longfellow shared with Howe the use of the literary device of the eroticized woman writer imported from nineteenth-century Europe (p. 18). Elizabeth Maddock Dillon in "Sentimental Aesthetics" (2004) traces the history of aesthetic studies, showing its historic closeness to sentimentalism. Aesthetics, she points out, "developed in response to the revolutions of the eighteenth century," which ushered in the liberal idea of self-government and brought to sentimentalism the concept of individual autonomy or "liberal subjectivity" (p. 497). Looking at nineteenth-century American texts in relation to the writings of Friedrich Schiller, she discusses the moral sense of aesthetic theory that bound the sentimental subject to the community through sympathy and led to the exercise of political agency (pp. 498–499, 508). Thus, she says, the moral tone of sentimental writing can be seen as the "product of aesthetic theory rather than solely the language of Christian reform" (p. 509).

Scholars who have analyzed the literary effectiveness of sentimental texts have found that, just as in any genre, some writers are more skillful than others and some works are more successful than others, but for the most part they have found that, once rid of modernism's prejudices, one can find enduring thematic value and talented literary expression in sentimental writing. To Harris's question "Is it any good?" the answer more often than not is an unqualified "yes."

Although sentimental literature—like the literature of any genre—was sometimes used inauthentically, and although some of its assumptions are no longer intellectually fashionable, the values of sentimentalism still resonate today. As Joanne Dobson wrote in 1997, "In a world of mortality, of absolute and certain loss—the universal and immutable human condition—a body of literature giving primacy to affectional connections and responsibilities still reflects the dilemmas, anxieties, and tragedies of individual lives" (p. 280).

See also Abolitionist Writing; Domestic Fiction; Education; English Literature; Female Authorship; Feminism; Manhood; Reform; Religion

BIBLIOGRAPHY

Primary Works

Bennett, Paula Bernat, ed. *Nineteenth-Century American Women Poets.* Malden, Mass.: Blackwell, 1998.

Clarke, Edward A. *Sex in Education; or, A Fair Chance for Girls.* 1873. Boston: Houghton, Mifflin and Co., 1892.

Cummins, Maria. *The Lamplighter.* 1854. Edited by Nina Baym. New Brunswick, N.J.: Rutgers University Press, 1988.

Fern, Fanny. *Ruth Hall and Other Writings.* 1855. Edited by Joyce W. Warren. New Brunswick, N.J.: Rutgers University Press, 1986.

Harper, Frances Ellen Watkins. "The Two Offers." 1859. In *A Brighter Coming Day: A Frances Ellen Watkins Harper Reader,* edited by Frances Smith Foster, pp. 105–114. New York: Feminist Press, 1990.

Jacobs, Harriet A. *Incidents in the Life of a Slave Girl.* 1861. Edited by Jean Fagan Yellin. Cambridge, Mass.: Harvard University Press, 1987.

Kilcup, Karen L., ed. *Nineteenth-Century American Women Writers: A Critical Reader.* Malden, Mass.: Blackwell, 1998.

Lane, Haddie. "Woman's Rights." *Godey's Lady's Book* 40 (April 1850): 269–273.

Rowson, Susanna. *Charlotte Temple.* 1794. Edited by Cathy N. Davidson. New York: Oxford University Press, 1986.

Southworth, E. D. E. N. *The Hidden Hand.* 1859. Edited by Joanne Dobson. New Brunswick, N.J.: Rutgers University Press, 1988.

Stowe, Harriet Beecher. *Uncle Tom's Cabin.* 1852. Edited by Darryl Pinckney. New York: Signet, 1998.

Warner, Susan. *The Wide, Wide World.* 1850. New York: Feminist Press, 1987.

Whitman, Walt. "Free Academies at Public Cost." *Brooklyn Daily Times,* 9 July 1857.

Secondary Works

Baym, Nina. *Woman's Fiction: A Guide to Novels by and about Women in America, 1820–1870.* Ithaca, N.Y.: Cornell University Press, 1978.

Bredvold, Louis I. "The Literature of the Restoration and the Eighteenth Century." In *A History of English Literature,* edited by Hardin Craig et al., pp. 322–459. New York: Oxford University Press, 1950.

Brewer, John. *The Pleasures of the Imagination: English Culture in the Eighteenth Century.* Chicago: University of Chicago Press, 1997.

Brodhead, Richard H. *Cultures of Letters: Scenes of Reading and Writing in Nineteenth-Century America.* Chicago: University of Chicago Press, 1993.

Brown, Gillian. *Domestic Individualism: Imagining Self in Nineteenth-Century America.* Berkeley: University of California Press, 1990.

Brown, Herbert Ross. *The Sentimental Novel in America, 1789–1860.* Durham, N.C.: Duke University Press, 1940.

Clark, Suzanne. *Sentimental Modernism: Women Writers and the Revolution of the Word.* Bloomington: Indiana University Press, 1991.

Davidson, Cathy N. "Introduction." In *Charlotte Temple,* by Susanna Rowson, pp. xii–xxxiii. Oxford: Oxford University Press, 1986.

Davidson, Cathy N., and Jessamyn Hatcher, eds. *No More Separate Spheres!* Durham, N.C.: Duke University Press, 2002.

Dillon, Elizabeth Maddock. "Sentimental Aesthetics." *American Literature* 76 (September 2004): 495–523.

Dobson, Joanne. "Reclaiming Sentimental Literature." *American Literature* 69 (June 1997): 263–288.

Douglas, Ann. *The Feminization of American Culture.* New York: Avon, 1977.

Gould, Philip. "Revisiting the 'Feminization' of American Culture." *Differences: A Journal of Feminist Cultural Studies* 11, no. 3 (1999–2000): i–xii.

Harker, Jaime. "'Pious Cant' and Blasphemy: Fanny Fern's Radicalized Sentiment." *Legacy* 18 (January 2001): 52–64.

Harris, Susan K. " 'But Is It Any Good?': Evaluating Nineteenth-Century American Women's Fiction." *American Literature* 63 (March 1991): 42–61.

Harris, Susan K. *Nineteenth-Century American Women's Novels: Interpretive Strategies.* Cambridge, U.K.: Cambridge University Press, 1990.

Johnson, Wendy Dasler. "Male Sentimentalists through the 'I—s' of Julia Ward Howe's Poetry." *South Atlantic Review* 64 (autumn 1999): 16–35.

Kaplan, Fred. *Sacred Tears: Sentimentality in Victorian Literature.* Princeton, N.J.: Princeton University Press, 1987.

Lang, Amy Schrager. "Slavery and Sentimentalism: The Strange Career of Augustine St. Clare." *Women's Studies* 12, no. 1 (1986): 31–54.

Langford, Paul. *A Polite and Commercial People: England 1727–1783.* New York: Oxford University Press, 1992.

Pattee, Fred Lewis. *The Feminine Fifties.* New York: D. Appleton-Century, 1940.

Riffaterre, Michael. *Fictional Truth.* 1990. Baltimore: Johns Hopkins University Press, 1993.

Samuels, Shirley, ed. *The Culture of Sentiment: Race, Gender, and Sentimentality in Nineteenth-Century America.* New York: Oxford University Press, 1992.

Schlesinger, Arthur M., Jr. *The Vital Center: The Politics of Freedom.* 1949. New Brunswick, N.J.: Transaction, 1998.

Solomon, Robert. "In Defense of Sentimentality." *Philosophy and Literature* 14 (1990): 304–323.

Tompkins, Jane. *Sensational Designs: The Cultural Work of American Fiction, 1790–1860.* New York: Oxford University Press, 1985.

Warren, Joyce W. *Women, Money, and the Law: Nineteenth-Century Fiction, Gender, and the Courts.* Iowa City: Iowa University Press, 2005.

Warren, Joyce W., ed. *The (Other) American Traditions: Nineteenth-Century Women Writers.* New Brunswick, N.J.: Rutgers University Press, 1993.

Joyce W. Warren

SEX EDUCATION

On 26 February 1835 a Boston mob chased the popular health lecturer Sylvester Graham (1794–1851) into hiding and harangued the women leaving the hall where he had spoken. One witness saw "about one thousand mobbers" confronting Graham "for lecturing to the Ladies *alone* and not even their husbands admitted!!!" The previous summer, a mob in Portland, Maine, had attacked Graham while he lectured on chastity to a female audience. Why did such an apparently conservative sex educator draw the crowds' moral outrage? The Graham mobs illustrate major themes of nineteenth-century sex education. First, discussions about sex took place in conspicuously public venues: lecture halls, newspapers, and peer education societies. Second, even adult sex education was highly contested terrain, and people on all sides of the podium engaged actively in conflicts over sexual knowledge. Thus the Boston women vehemently defended their presence at Graham's lecture: "one of the ladies hissed the mob with all vengeance" while another "addressed several of the men." Finally, certain topics that might not seem erotic to twenty-first-century minds struck contemporaries as sexually fraught. When Graham lectured on chastity the mobbers viewed him as an interloper in their sexual relationships with their wives. Segregating the class by gender enhanced its claims to modesty. But by admonishing women to limit the frequency of marital sex, Graham challenged the assumption of husbands' unlimited sexual access to their wives that both underwrote women's *feme covert* legal status and circulated loudly in popular culture. The speaker later recalled that his remarks on "the frequency of connubial commerce" had "given more offence" than any other topic he broached. Additionally, married women may have sought birth control advice within a "chastity" lecture. Periodic abstinence within marriage, or the rhythm method, grew in prominence as a contraceptive strategy after the 1840s when lecturers and writers popularized the newest scientific explanations of ovulation and the menstrual cycle.

ORAL AND VERNACULAR TRADITIONS

New forms of sex education boomed in the United States from 1820 to 1870, when diverse sources of printed information began to supplement face-to-face conversations among family members and peers. The transportation revolution of the 1820s moved the cultural products of public sex education beyond the urban North. While residents of burgeoning cities could most easily access the new media, canvasing agents also sold domestic medical manuals and health journals throughout the hinterlands. Manuals often contained information about sexual behavior and pregnancy, instructions for assisting childbirth, and recipes for treating sexually transmitted infections (STI). However, word of mouth continued as the primary form of sex education for many through mid-century. For example, enslaved people educated each other secretly in herbal knowledge that may have included abortifacients. In addition, spiritual traditions such as *vodoun* included herbal methods for treating many diseases, including STI.

From the later seventeenth century until the 1830s, one pseudonymous midwifery manual titled *Aristotle's Masterpiece* (1741) offered the most accessible written information on sex in North America. The book recorded Anglo-American oral culture and may have been read aloud in groups. *Aristotle's Masterpiece* differed from much of the later sex education literature in several ways. First, it devoted bawdy passages to sexual sensation, offering descriptions of clitoral sensitivity and female ejaculation as evidence that women's pleasure counterbalanced men's lust. It also posited female orgasm (and therefore consent) as necessary for conception to occur, a theory that undermined the rape accusations of pregnant women. Second, no mention of contraception accompanied this view of conception. However, the pseudo "Aristotle" cautioned women against seeking herbal emmenagogues (agents that promote the menstrual discharge) if pregnant—a coded but recognizable abortion reference. Finally, *Aristotle's Masterpiece* privileged penile-vaginal penetration, but unlike later sex manuals, the text ignored practices that deviated from its sexual ideal.

FREE THOUGHT AND CONTRACEPTIVE ADVICE LITERATURE

Throughout the late 1820s and 1830s a band of radical intellectuals known as freethinkers became the major purveyors of new information about sex. Skeptical of organized religion, committed to eradicating poverty, and optimistic about the possibilities of human agency, the free-thought tradition profoundly shaped nineteenth-century American sex education. Its proponents were the first to encourage interventions in the seemingly inevitable process of conception. As contraceptive literature proliferated, the marital birthrate among white adults born in the United States declined dramatically, reduced by almost half over the course of the nineteenth century. Freethinkers also introduced "physiology" as a rubric for sex education. By the end of the 1830s consumers could assume that popular physiology lectures and texts included sexual information. Three freethinkers

engaged most famously with sexuality: Robert Dale Owen, Frances "Fanny" Wright, and Charles Knowlton. Beginning with them, physiologically framed contraceptive advice became a major feature of sex education literature.

In early 1831 Robert Dale Owen (1801–1877) published the first American contraceptive advice pamphlet, *Moral Physiology*. The tract described vaginal sponges and condoms but primarily advocated coitus interruptus, ushering into public dialogue lasting debates over the efficacy and morality of withdrawal. *Moral Physiology* argued that even unmarried women should have the requisite information enabling them to control their fertility, debunking the double standard that allowed male seducers to escape the consequences of extramarital pregnancies. Yet while Owen wrote for women as well as men, his preference for withdrawal as a technique preserved male control over contraception and militated against the use of contraception in casual or commercial sex. Owen explicitly addressed working-class people, arguing that decreased family size would ameliorate poverty until property relations could be revolutionized. Some working-class readers wrote letters of appreciation for the information provided in *Moral Physiology*, but others angrily insisted that labor activism should address wages and conditions of work in industrial society rather than focusing on the sexual practices of workers.

Fanny Wright (1795–1852), a brilliant Scottish heiress and Owen's publishing colleague, became the first woman to address American audiences about sexuality. Wright unabashedly embraced sexual pleasure as "the best source of human happiness" and advocated free physiology lessons for all workers, especially women. She affirmed women's desires, insisted on the necessity of consent, and—most explosively—advocated interracial sex. With visionary optimism, Wright believed that consensual interracial sex would purge the society of racism. Coupled with her critiques of the marriage relation, such ideas enraged conservatives and alienated erstwhile financial supporters. Opponents of women's sexual autonomy used Wright's name as a slur to dissuade other women from speaking in public. Decades later, even women whose ideas about sex hardly resembled hers earned reputations as "Fanny Wrightists," an association that continued to carry severe social consequences. Although Wright mainly contributed to sex education as a speaker, her controversial messages touched important literary figures: Walt Whitman, among others, recalled the impact of her oratory.

In 1832 her fellow freethinker Charles Knowlton (1800–1850) introduced genital anatomy into American sex education and faced legal persecution as a result. His book *Fruits of Philosophy* drew Massachusetts obscenity charges four times between 1832 and 1835, resulting in one conviction and a sentence of three months of hard labor. Allies organized a spirited defense, and at least one of his trials drew large crowds. Knowlton's understanding of reproductive physiology, particularly the motility of sperm, offered evidence against the old claim that conception required female orgasm and also led him to promulgate spermicidal douching as the most effective contraceptive method. Knowlton thought pleasure a legitimate goal of sex and argued that in order to be realistically effective, contraception should not impede sensation. *Fruits of Philosophy* urged women to take power in reproductive decision making (including an explicit defense of abortion). Thus, in the developing sex education literature, free-thought physiology added a proto-feminist ethos and contraceptive focus to pseudo-Aristotle's emphasis on pleasure. Both traditions assumed a largely nonprofessional and working-class readership.

RESPECTABLE PHYSIOLOGY AND THE NEW DEVIANCE

During the 1830s the free-thought tenet that bodily processes could be strategically managed coalesced with a social movement that strove to democratize medicine by educating ordinary people about self-healing. The popular health movement promoted disease prevention, critiquing the medical establishment for charging exorbitant fees and administering dangerous treatments for illnesses that could have been avoided. Hundreds of lecturers and healers itinerated throughout the North and West during the second third of the century, often drawing crowds that numbered in the thousands. But the emphasis on preventing chronic diseases as well as pregnancy drew invidious distinctions within popular sex education. Beginning in the 1830s in the United States, physiological arguments began to distinguish "healthy" sex from "unnatural" genital behaviors. The practice of pathologizing particular sexual behaviors while simultaneously promoting others bore lasting and contradictory implications for sex education. Ironically, scientific categories of sexual normativeness and deviance grew out of a popular movement that rejected intellectual elitism.

Graham most famously promoted a popular science of sexual restraint based on a distinction between natural and unnatural behaviors. He maintained that the body needed equilibrium to function properly and that excessive stimulation destroyed harmonious cooperation among the organs. Masturbation, defined

inherently as artificial stimulation, appalled him. By overstimulating the nervous system, it led to debility, mental illness, and death. It also carried social consequences. Graham frequently worried that male masturbators rendered themselves impotent as husbands and fathers. In at least one lecture, he associated female masturbation with lesbianism. Sex education became a form of prophylaxis against deviance. Youth required special instruction in "nature's laws" to encourage them to abstain. Graham compiled an entire book of lectures to young men, but he also claimed that masturbation "appears to be still more common among girls." Including—and targeting—youth in public discussions of sex constituted a significant innovation. Graham exerted tremendous influence on the emergent culture of American sex education, achieving fantastic fame especially among middle-class and upwardly mobile reformers. After his career, few sex educators avoided the topic of masturbation and none until the twentieth century argued that it could be part of healthy sexual function.

Yet ironically, Graham's words inspired younger writers to develop a language of sex education that challenged the institution of marriage and promoted sexual self-sovereignty for everyone who had reached puberty. Two of the most noteworthy mid-century sex educators, Mary Gove Nichols and Frederick Hollick, radically reworked Graham's message.

Mary Gove (1810–1884) educated women primarily to achieve sexual independence from husbands and doctors. In publications and lectures she provided information about pregnancy, birth, and contraception to married and unmarried women. After leaving a violent first marriage, she turned the Grahamite focus on self-restraint into a tool to encourage women to resist all external controls on their sexual and reproductive lives—especially nonconsensual sex and compulsory motherhood. During the 1840s Gove moved within literary circles in New York City, most notably befriending Edgar Allan Poe. While these intellectual peers introduced her to the utopian socialism of Charles Fourier, Gove developed her hydropathic (water-cure) practice. She and her second husband, Thomas Low Nichols, author of a risqué sex education book titled *Esoteric Anthropology* (1853), began to urge the abolition of marriage from a physiological standpoint. Their sex radicalism eventually alienated them from mainstream sex educators.

Frederick Hollick's (1812–1900) more reformist influence on American sex education peaked during the 1840s and 1850s, when his two most popular books went through hundreds of editions and at least three translations. Like Gove, Hollick used physiology to critique contemporary marriage, but he stopped short of calling for free love. He invited young, unmarried readers to explore his highly explicit sex manuals *The Origin of Life* (1845) and *The Marriage Guide* (1850), both of which celebrated coital pleasure while providing clear contraceptive instructions. Hollick argued that all people who had reached puberty needed sexual information and services. *The Marriage Guide* advertised condoms, aphrodisiacs, and genital therapies; later works instructed readers in STI cures. Hollick's extreme popularity probably resulted from his ability to titillate and challenge readers without overtly calling for a sexual revolution.

INTERACTIVE SEX EDUCATION: WHO WAS LISTENING?

The penny press, ubiquitous handbills, and wheat-pasted broadsides introduced most urbanites to the existence of sex education lectures. But popular health lectures attracted only those with leisure time and money to spare. The average price for a lecture averaged twelve and a half to twenty-five cents; publications ranged from twenty-five cents to a dollar. Cheaper sources of information about prophylaxis, STI cures, abortion, and contraception were available in proprietary pamphlets and newspaper advertisements. Among lecture attendees, petition signatures and testimonials of skilled craftspeople, clerks, and merchants outnumbered but did not fully eclipse those of laborers and servants. Sex education lectures were frequently segregated by gender; they were likely often de facto segregated by race. However, Grahamite sex education touched listeners within free black activist communities: abolitionist and African American newspapers carried notices and articles about popular health speakers. The middle-class African American lecturer Sarah Mapps Douglass (1806–1882) taught physiology to working-class and formerly enslaved black women in courses that likely included information about sex. Students engaged actively in the lectures, sometimes participating as anatomical demonstrators or querying the teacher according to their own interests. Douglass's career spanned several decades, continuing through Freedmen's Aid efforts in the mid-1860s. Given dominant racist stereotypes that hypersexualized black women, Douglass may have consciously chosen to desexualize her lecture notices. White writers included sexualized, racist imagery in their sex education material, exacerbating the hostile environment that African American speakers faced. Nearly all sex educators perceived themselves as vulnerable to censure, but white lecturers—women and men—defended their right to speak about needed information with social and scientific justifications.

Black teachers refrained from making public statements about the sexual content of their work overall.

In general, mid-century readers of openly sexual literature developed a sense of personal involvement and shaped its educational content. Thousands wrote testimonials to announce their approval of popular writers and to recount their own discoveries, priorities, and experiences. The careers of Gove and Hollick illuminate the interactive workings of sex education during this period. Gove inspired and even trained women to speak to each other about sexual physiology. She gave her first public lecture (1838) at the behest of Grahamite women in Boston, and in the wake of her lecture tours into the 1840s, audience members formed peer education groups known as Ladies' Physiological Societies from Maine to Ohio. Ordinary women also defended embattled lecturers. When Hollick faced obscenity charges in Philadelphia during 1845 and 1846, hundreds of women campaigned on his behalf, at once demanding sex education and defining its respectability. In this context, Lydia Maria Child (1802–1880), an icon of female literary activism, urged women to pursue sex education without shame.

THE END OF AN ERA

As the Civil War consumed the nation, widespread involvement in sex education waned. The diversity of available information declined further during the conservative postwar decades. In 1873 Anthony Comstock (1844–1915), a dry goods salesman turned anti-vice lobbyist, won national legislation that outlawed the transmission of "obscene" information through the mails. As obscenity charges effectively silenced dissenters, sex educators increasingly both professed institutional expertise—anathema to antebellum popular health writers—and articulated a conservative sexual consensus that presupposed marriage, disparaged female desire, criminalized abortion, and called for increased monitoring of youth.

See also Crime and Punishment; Education; Feminism; Free Love; Marriage; Miscegenation; Same-Sex Love; Science; Sexuality and the Body

BIBLIOGRAPHY
Primary Works
Aristotle. *Aristotle's Works: Containing the Master-Piece, Directions for Midwives, and Counsel and Advice to Child-bearing Women, with Various Useful Remedies.* 1741. London: Published for the booksellers, 1830.

Gove, Mary S. *Lectures to Ladies on Anatomy and Physiology.* Boston: Saxton & Pierce, 1842.

Graham, Sylvester. *A Lecture to Young Men, on Chastity Intended also for the Serious Consideration of Parents and Guardians.* Boston: Light & Stearns, 1837.

Hollick, Frederick. *The Marriage Guide.* New York: T. W. Strong, 1850.

Hollick, Frederick. *The Origin of Life: A Popular Treatise on the Philosophy and Physiology of Reproduction, in Plants and Animals Including the Details of Human Generation, with a Full Description of the Male and Female Organs.* New York: Nafis & Cornish, 1845.

Knowlton, Charles. *Fruits of Philosophy; or, The Private Companion of Adult People.* 1832. Edited with an introductory notice by Norman E. Himes with medical emendations by Robert Latou Dickinson. Mount Vernon, N.Y.: Peter Pauper Press, 1937.

Nichols, Thomas Low. *Esoteric Anthropology: A Comprehensive and Confidential Treatise on the Structure, Functions, Passional Attractions and Perversions, True and False Physical and Social Conditions, and the Most Intimate Relations of Men and Women. Anatomical, Physiological, Pathological, Therapeutical, and Obstetrical; Hygienics and Hydropathic.* Cincinnati: Valentine Nicholson, 1853.

Secondary Works

Brodie, Janet Farrell. *Contraception and Abortion in Nineteenth-Century America.* Ithaca, N.Y.: Cornell University Press, 1994.

Fett, Sharla. *Working Cures: Healing, Health, and Power on Southern Slave Plantations.* Chapel Hill: University of North Carolina Press, 2002.

Silver-Isenstadt, Jean L. *Shameless: The Visionary Life of Mary Gove Nichols.* Baltimore: Johns Hopkins University Press, 2002.

Horowitz, Helen Lefkowitz. *Rereading Sex: Battles over Sexual Knowledge and Suppression in Nineteenth-Century America.* New York: Knopf, 2002.

April Rose Haynes

SEXUALITY AND THE BODY

The project of writing, thinking, and talking about nineteenth-century bodies and sexualities may seem like a relatively recent innovation within the fields of literary and social history. But it is important to begin by recognizing that this type of inquiry is not in fact altogether new. In 1923 the British modernist author and critic D. H. Lawrence surveyed the field of what he referred to as "classic American literature" with similar themes in mind. Authors such as Benjamin Franklin, Hector St. John de Crèvecoeur, James Fenimore Cooper, Edgar Allan Poe, Nathaniel Hawthorne, Richard Henry Dana, Herman Melville, and Walt Whitman could be characterized according to Lawrence in his *Studies in Classic American Literature* by their collective attempt to give expression to what he referred to as "IT": "You have got to pull the democratic and idealistic clothes off American utterance, and see what you can of the dusky body of IT underneath" (p. 14). Two decades later, the literary critic Leslie Fiedler shocked his academic audience by asserting in his 1948 essay "Come Back to the Raft Ag'in, Huck Honey!" that one of the most revered of all American novels, Mark Twain's *Adventures of Huckleberry Finn* (1885), was held in such high esteem largely because it told the archetypically American story of "a white and a colored American male flee[ing] from civilization [and] into each other's arms" (p. vi). Never bashful about his claims (and always ready to push the most tender of his audience's many buttons), Fiedler added "brother-sister incest and necrophilia" (p. vi) to his list of American archetypes when, a decade later, he revised and expanded his argument concerning interracial homoeroticism in his book-length study *Love and Death in the American Novel* (1960).

If these less-than-conventional takes on nineteenth-century U.S. literary and social history were the exceptions that proved the rules of an earlier and more genteel scholarly establishment, then it is indisputable that the emergence of feminist and gender studies in the 1970s and 1980s and lesbian-gay and queer studies in the 1980s and 1990s turned the tide decisively toward a sustained critical interest in questions of how sex, gender, sexuality, and diverse forms of embodiment appeared in nineteenth-century culture and literature. For scholars who aligned themselves with the feminist political activism of the 1960s and 1970s, these questions focused primarily on the ways in which large- and small-scale social relationships were pervasively organized through what the anthropologist Gayle Rubin in "The Traffic in Women" called the "sex-gender system." Feminist literary critics discovered evidence of this system—and the ways in which its cultural front worked to maintain patriarchal control over women's sexual and reproductive power—everywhere in the largely male-authored nineteenth-century literary canon endorsed (and criticized) by Lawrence and Fiedler. Lesbian-gay and queer scholars of U.S. literary and social history were also inspired by contemporary movements for social justice—in this case, the increasingly vocal and effective demands for social recognition and political rights by sexual minorities during the 1970s and 1980s. And they too walked the path of reinterpretation and recovery. On the one hand, they could simply reread and reevaluate the canon of "classic American literature" because it required no great interpretive leap to position its more unorthodox moments—Whitman's writings on same-sex male love in his *Calamus* poems (1860) or Melville's lighthearted eroticization of the relations among sailors in *Moby-Dick* (1851)—at the center of an emerging lesbian-gay or queer canon. On the other hand, the same group of scholars reconstructed the rich homoerotic worlds of nineteenth-century men and women by unearthing and archiving previously neglected (or repressed) journal entries and personal letters that described and celebrated physical intimacies between same-sex friends.

These new fields of inquiry clearly drew on the insights of their predecessors such as Lawrence and Fiedler. Yet they also diverged from them in important ways. The "IT" that Lawrence longed to disrobe in his *Studies in Classic American Literature* was a multivalent concept, but it referred most directly to the primal sexual drive that had been recently mistranslated as the "id" (from the German pronoun *es*) in the writings of Lawrence's contemporary, Sigmund Freud—a mistranslation that resulted from an attempt to make Freud appear more "scientific," and less "literary," to his English-speaking audience. Similarly influenced by Freudian understandings of sexuality, Fiedler's reconstruction of U.S. literary history adopted as its starting point the premise that sex is essential to any narrative of either individual or social development. In contrast, many of the feminist and queer critics who followed in the wake of Lawrence and Fiedler did more than locate IT at the heart of social and literary history. They also pressed their readers to think critically and historically about the Freudian tendency to isolate the topics of sexuality and the body from broader questions of how power is exercised and represented. As the French philosopher and historian Michel Foucault put it in the first volume of his immensely influential *The History of Sexuality* (which first appeared in French in 1976), scholars of sexuality and the body have often been misled by the "repressive hypothesis" (pp. 17–49)—the theory that IT is a natural (or organic) drive located within the body, and that IT relates to power solely through dynamics of repression. Foucault does not deny the obvious ways in which the practices and writings of sexual minorities have been repressed and censored, both historically and today. But he presses literary and social historians to begin with a more fundamental series of questions about how we have come to isolate sex from other forms of bodily pleasure and appetite, to assume that sexuality has a history of its own, and to imagine that the proper telling of that history will lead to our liberation. Answers to these questions can be found in the archives of nineteenth-century literary and social

history. Before moving to those answers, however, it is first necessary to take a detour in order to explain how the body itself became a source of literary and social interest.

BEGINNING WITH THE BODY

The history of the body and its political significance is tremendously complicated, but it is possible to trace two dominant influences. The first concerns the rise in the seventeenth century of empiricism as a theory and practice of knowledge production. In most histories, this move is associated with John Locke, the British philosopher who argued in his 1690 treatise *An Essay concerning Human Understanding* that all human knowledge is grounded in experience and that experience itself is accessible only through the senses. This "sensationalist psychology"—the theory that sensory experience is the means by which we come to know ourselves and the world—turned away from theological ways of knowing. In doing so, it informed the thinking of a wide range of subsequent speakers and writers interested in transforming their audiences' relations to themselves and their worlds. Partly due to Locke's influence, Jonathan Edwards (1703–1758), the eighteenth-century New England evangelical minister, kicked off the great American tradition of hellfire preaching by attempting through his fire-and-brimstone sermons to make his listeners not only know that the flames of hell burned hot but also to feel the effects of those flames as they licked against the flesh

A century later, Lydia Maria Child (1802–1880), the nineteenth-century abolitionist and women's rights advocate, wrote a series of tear-jerking, blush-inducing sentimental novels in which she pulled at her readers' heartstrings in an attempt to mobilize support for a wide variety of liberal social and political reforms. George Lippard (1822–1854), Child's contemporary and fellow reformer, published sensational fiction intended to elicit shudders, groans, and screams from its readers by dwelling on the devious schemes and violent crimes of America's upper class, all in the name of advancing the cause of mid-century labor radicalism. In each case, these authors joined leagues of other writers and activists in turning toward the body and its sensations as a means of pushing for the reform of social and political relations that they perceived as unjust. Even Ralph Waldo Emerson (1803–1882), one of the most abstract of the nineteenth-century proponents of the philosophy of transcendentalism, worried in a 1836 lecture on the topic of "love" that his audience might find his comments "unjustly cold" and then responded by staging his own "shrink[ing] at the remembrance of such disparaging words" in order to reassure his listeners that he too valued the "warmth" provided by the body and its sensations (p. 99).

The second major influence that contributed to the intensification of the political significance of the body in the nineteenth century concerned the rise of the scientific and popular discourse known as "comparative anatomy." Again, the important contrast here is to earlier theological justifications of political and social hierarchy through appeals to concepts such as divine right kingship and the biblical curse of Ham. (The first posed the rule of the monarch as the will of God; the second explained the bondage of dark-skinned peoples by portraying them as inheritors of Ham's divinely ordained curse.) Like their predecessors, most practitioners of "comparative anatomy" assumed the need for race, class, and gender hierarchies, but they adapted their supporting arguments to more secular and democratic times by focusing on the body and its anatomy as the key to understanding the "natural" differences and inequalities between and among the "species" and "subspecies" of humanity. One of the best known of these arguments appeared in Samuel Morton's *Crania Americana* (1839), a treatise that attempted to naturalize Anglo-American imperialism, plantation slavery, gender subordination, and class stratification by measuring and comparing "craniological" differences between male and female Native, African, and Anglo-Americans. Similar thinking pervaded the writings of more historically reputable figures. Thomas Jefferson included his observations on the innate mental and aesthetic inferiority of Africans (and the superiority of Europeans) in his *Notes on the State of Virginia* (1784–1785), while a succession of prominent nineteenth-century Supreme Court justices endorsed the social institutions of slavery, segregation, and white supremacy by viewing them as expressions of inherent racial differences or, to use the period's dominant metaphor for the interweaving of race, biology, and reproduction, "blood." There are, of course, important distinctions to be drawn between these influential theorists of race, class, and gender. But they share an interest in and commitment to shielding the social inequalities indexed by these categories from political debate by grounding them in the putatively natural—anatomical or biological—differences between and among bodies.

As an example of these paired influences and how they intersected, consider the final chapter of the most famous antislavery novel of the nineteenth century, Harriet Beecher Stowe's *Uncle Tom's Cabin* (1852). Throughout the novel, Stowe (1811–1896) casts her "African" characters—Uncle Tom in particular—as having a natural penchant for the same brand of liberal Christianity that Stowe strove to practice. This naturalization of Africans as a racial type prone to Christian spirituality and benevolence produced two major effects in the novel. First, it allowed Stowe to follow the racializing logic of the comparative anatomists by asserting a natural racial difference between Africans and Europeans while also inverting the white supremacist conclusions that typically accompanied that logic. Second, it produced a narrative structure in which Christ-like Africans could act as both moral victims and spiritual redeemers, thus enabling the sensitive reader to experience bodily sensations of guilt, outrage, and remorse at the tragedy of Uncle Tom's Christ-like death. Stowe's final chapter brought these two discourses of the body together. In response to a hypothetical question concerning the fate of the former slaves after emancipation, Stowe advised that they be sent to the African colony of Liberia, where they "may put in practice the lessons they have learned in America" (p. 386). Though Stowe later withdrew this recommendation, her initial suggestion is remarkable both for its recasting of the experience of American slavery as an education in Christian civility and for its inability to imagine a national future in which racially divergent bodies could mix. In response to a second question about how readers could expedite this future free of slavery (and freed slaves), Stowe recommended that they "*feel right*" (p. 386)—a phrase that tethered the mid-century belief that readers could be best motivated to act through the experience of bodily sensation (or "feeling") to the assertion that those sensations must be stimulated only by what is morally and spiritually correct (or "right"). Where the answer to the first question aligned Stowe with the comparative anatomists and their racializing belief in discrete body types (Uncle Tom's body as racial evidence of his unassimilatability), the answer to the second committed her to the sensationalist psychology that underwrote the period's faith in sensory experience as the only sure way of motivating and reforming either the individual or the society of which that individual was a part (Uncle Tom's bodily suffering as a physical catalyst for the reader's spiritual and moral advancement).

FROM THE BODY TO SEXUALITY

Given the intensification of the body as a site of political contestation by the mid-nineteenth century, the answer to the question of the relation between the body and sexuality might initially seem obvious. If the body, its sensations, and its anatomy became increasingly significant in the late eighteenth and early nineteenth centuries, then surely sexuality must have become more significant as well. Yet it is crucial to recognize that it was not until the mid-nineteenth century that terms like "sex," "sexual," and (even later) "sexuality" began to take on the meanings that they have for us in the early twenty-first century. This does not imply that early-nineteenth-century writers did not speak of the body and its physical relations with other bodies. In fact, their texts were obsessed with that topic. But the vocabulary that they used to understand those relations—"lust," "licentiousness," "wantonness," "chastity," "purity"—tended to be drawn from religious sources, ethnographic surveys, and health-reform debates. And while it might be tempting to assume that early-nineteenth-century writers were merely too repressed (socially or psychologically) to speak straightforwardly about sex and sexuality, such an approach misunderstands the strange and different ways in which those writers (and their readers) talked about and experienced their bodies. Take "lust" as an example. Whereas an early-twenty-first-century literary critic might simply translate "lust" as "sexual desire," an early-nineteenth-century writer would be more likely to think of it in relation to either religious concepts such as "infidelity" and "impurity" or proto-racial concepts such as "savagery" and "barbarity," both of which figured "lust" as a form of social and physical degeneracy that could be countered only through self-discipline and spiritual refinement. (The afterglow of this history can be seen in Lawrence's description of "IT" as having a specifically "dusky body.") The important point here is not that separate religious, racial, and sexual discourses came together in the term "lust" but that the "three" discourses were not separable in the first place. "Sex" and "sexuality," in other words, were not yet names for (and policed as) isolable forms of social practice and individual desire.

A close reading of one of Walt Whitman's best-known poems demonstrates how this historical difference worked in literary practice. In one of his many engagements with the religious and health-reform discourses of the mid-1850s, Whitman (1819–1892) adopts and parodies the anti-onanist or, to use a more familiar term, the anti-masturbation writings of his contemporaries. (Onan is the biblical figure who sins in Genesis 38:7–10 by "spilling his seed upon the ground.") The "villain touch" passage from "Song of Myself" in the 1855 edition of *Leaves of Grass* begins with the question "Is this then a touch? . . . quivering me to a new identity," then moves toward an answer as Whitman's speaker externalizes desire in an attempt to distinguish inclination from will. "Prurient provokers" attack the poet's "I," "stiffening [his] limbs, / Straining the udder of [his] heart for its withheld drip, / Behaving licentious," "Depriving [him] of [his] best for a purpose," "Unbuttoning [his] clothes," "Immodestly sliding the fellow senses away," showing "No

consideration, no regard for draining strength" (p. 55). Next, the speaker racializes desire through reference to the military geography of U.S. imperialism in the mid-century. The "provokers" leave him defenseless, deserted by "sentries," "helpless to a red marauder," "given up by traitors" (pp. 55–56). Finally, the speaker identifies with this racialized and treasonous desire, abandoning his will and mapping a geography of "licentiousness" onto his own body: "I talk wildly. . . . I have lost my wits. . . . I and nobody else am the greatest traitor, / I went myself first to the headland . . . my own hands carried me there" (p. 56). As elsewhere in "Song of Myself," this passage equivocates on two critical points: the number of actors in the scene ("You," "I," "provokers," "marauders"), and the bodily location of the speaker's desire ("straining udder," "dripping heart," "sliding senses"). But it clearly ends by identifying will and desire through a celebration of the speaker's ecstatic self-abandon. "You villain touch!" the passage concludes, "what are you doing? . . . my breath is tight in its throat, / Unclench your floodgates! you are too much for me" (pp. 55–56). The passage focuses on what is now thought of as an isolatable "sexual practice," but Whitman presents that practice only through the racial, religious, and health reform discourses of his period.

If "sexual practice" cannot be said to stand on its own here and elsewhere in the nineteenth century, then how did the isolation of concepts of "sex" and "sexuality" come into being? Again, this question opens onto a tremendously complicated history. But three major factors stand out. The first concerns the rise of industrial capitalism in the United States during the first half of the nineteenth century. In contrast to agrarian economies where slaves, apprentices, and servants tended to be integrated hierarchically into households in which men and women played vital roles in the manufacture of domestic and commercial goods, the new industrial economy created separate urban and semi-urban neighborhoods for the laboring classes who were free—in theory—to live outside of those households by selling the labor power of their bodies to the highest bidder. In practice, this freedom was curtailed in at least two ways: by structural inequalities within labor markets dominated by the owners of capital and by legal limits placed on what types of labor could be bought and sold.

The literary response to labor inequalities focused on class antagonisms and the policing of "vice" in neighborhoods where laborers lived and socialized, whereas the response to illegal labor was writing that scrutinized "prostitution" as *the* social problem of the nineteenth-century urban world. *New York by*

Whitman, *Walt Whitman: Poetry and Prose*, pp. 55–56.

"VILLAIN TOUCH"

The following passage from Walt Whitman's 1855 version of "Song of Myself" marks one point of origin for twentieth-century understandings of sexuality and the body.

Is this then a touch? . . . . quivering me to a new
   identity,
Flames and ether making a rush for my veins,
Treacherous tip of me reaching and crowding to
   help them,
My flesh and blood playing out lightning, to
   strike what is hardly different from myself,
On all sides prurient provokers stiffening my
   limbs,
Straining the udder of my heart for its withheld
   drip,
Behaving licentious toward me, taking no denial,
Depriving me of my best as for a purpose,
Unbuttoning my clothes and holding me by the
   bare waist,
Deluding my confusion with the calm of the sun-
   light and pasture fields,
Immodestly sliding the fellow-senses away,
They bribed to swap off with touch, and go and
   graze at the edges of me,
No consideration, no regard for my draining
   strength or my anger,
Fetching the rest of the herd around to enjoy
   them awhile,
Then all uniting to stand on a headland and
   worry me.

The sentries desert every other part of me,
They have left me helpless to a red marauder,
They all come to the headland to witness and
   assist against me.
I am given up by traitors;
I talk wildly. . . . I have lost my wits. . . . I and
   nobody else am the greatest traitor.
I went myself first to the headland. . . . my own
   hands carried me there.

You villain touch! what are you doing? . . . . my
   breath is tight in its throat;
Unclench your floodgates! you are too much
   for me.

Gas-Light, the journalist George Foster's 1850 exposé of murder and mayhem in New York City's Five Points district, typifies the interweaving of these two responses. Originally serialized in the *New-York Daily Tribune*, Foster's sketches portrayed the city's gambling dens and oyster cellars as a savage underworld nurturing among men and women of all races "the monster vice of humanity . . . licentiousness" (p. 120). There can be no doubt that Foster knowingly marketed these sketches to the voyeuristic impulses of the *Tribune*'s middle-class readership, but he claimed to write them in an attempt to gather the knowledge necessary for the moral reform of prostitution in New York's vice districts. To the latter end, he followed his reformist predecessors in isolating "licentiousness" as the cause of social disorder and dissent, but he also gave that cause a new name: "sexual appetite" (p. 82). Though familiar to twenty-first-century readers, this naming of the "sexual" as the linchpin of moral reform and regulation would have impressed Foster's audience with its novelty.

The second major factor influencing the isolation of sex and sexuality from a broader range of desires and practices is really the structural complement to the the rise of industrial capitalism. Where lower-class men and women were represented as appropriately housed in urban vice districts where bodies and sexual appetites spiraled dangerously out of control, their middle-class counterparts increasingly inhabited class- and race-segregated neighborhoods in which men were expected to leave home during the day to "work" and "produce" while women were supposed to stayed at home to "consume" and "reproduce." This familiar social geography resulted in (and from) the development of what historians now call the "cult of domesticity"—the mid-century sex-gender system that idealized the middle-class home as a refuge where "true women" practicing the "feminine" virtues of piety and sentiment could prevail against "true men" and the "masculine" countervirtues of profit and rationality. These complementary gender ideals created many effects, but one of the most notable is the slippery slope of sexual normalization that we still live with (and on) today. The ideals of "true womanhood" and "true manhood" could never be fully embodied in everyday life (even among those with the social and economic means of doing so), but they could link one's gender identity and class status more and more tightly to one's ability to control what Foster called the "sexual appetite." When Foster's sketches landed on the early morning doorsteps of New York's middle-class homes, they contributed to this system of sexual regulation both a warning and a promise. Any individual man or woman, Foster advised, could "pervert" the "operation of the sexual appetite" by falling prey to the seductions of urban vice; yet men and women could also transform that "appetite" into the "purest and holiest passion implanted in the heart" if they properly managed its effects (p. 82). While it is possible to understand this linkage of class, gender, race, and sex as indicative of a specifically middle-class dynamic of repression, it is more accurate to think of it as a sign of that class's increasingly serious investment in the isolation and refinement of its newly sexualized body as a means of asserting and morally justifying its social privilege.

While the concepts of sex and sexuality were thus in the process of being isolated and refined in the crucible of urban class formation, similar dynamics were at work in the context of the capitalist expansion and settler colonialism that characterized U.S. nation-building projects of the period. Read carefully, mid-century novels, political tracts, and sermons did more than choose sides in the battle between demonized lower-class neighborhoods and idealized middle-class domiciles. They also linked those battles to the consolidation of the nation and the rapid expansion of its territorial borders. Stowe, for instance, consistently argued for the national abolition of slavery by portraying the plantation economies that dominated the U.S. South and Southwest as a breeding ground for (interracial) sensuality and vice (a claim that advocates for slavery reversed by painting industrial capitalism as responsible for the development of urban vice districts). Margaret Fuller similarly sprinkled throughout her feminist treatise *Woman in the Nineteenth Century* (1845) allusions to the exotic perils of "savage sensualism" (p. 285), women "enslaved by an impassioned sensibility" (p. 302), "Oriental" polygamy (p. 320), metropolitan "sty[es] of sensuality" (p. 324), and "Turkish slave-dealers" (p. 324). Though marshaled in a variety of contexts and to diverse political ends, these metaphors consistently suggested that battles fought over (and against) the "sexual appetite" were also battles for racial and national purity. Almost three decades later, the Page Act of 1875, the prototype for the turn-of-the-century onslaught of racially restrictive immigration legislation, realized these metaphorical associations by invoking the threat of prostitution in order to bring the immigration of Chinese women (and the settlement of many Chinese men) to a virtual standstill. In each of these complexly interrelated cases, popular and literary discourses of the body and its newfound sexuality provided authors and reformers with the rhetorical terrain upon which they could map their competing visions of the nation's past, present, and future.

BEYOND SEXUALITY

So what does it mean to take on the project of writing, thinking, and talking about the literary and social history of nineteenth-century bodies and sexualities today? One effect of scholarship attentive to this question has been to make our current usage of the terms "body," "sex," and "sexuality" less familiar. And while this skeptical turn can be viewed as a radical departure from the Freudian assumptions of early- and mid-twentieth-century writers and critics such as Lawrence and Fiedler (as well as some feminist and queer scholars today who still write of IT as either "repressed" or "liberated"), it also resonates strongly with the literary and historical archives of the nineteenth century.

For this reason, it might be best to return in conclusion to that century's greatest poet of bodies and their diverse sensualities, Walt Whitman. Looking back over his long career in his essay "A Backward Glance o'er Travel'd Roads" (1888), Whitman recognized that questions focused on sexuality and the body had become increasingly significant across a wide spectrum of social and political contexts. But he also knew that the related tendency to isolate discussions of sexuality from those contexts would only lead to misunderstandings of the politics of the body and its social relations. When discussing objections to his poems as obscene (and efforts to censor them as such), Whitman thus responded by defending his right to speak of the "fact of sexuality, as an element in character, personality, the emotions, and a theme in literature" (p. 669). Yet he also distanced himself from contemporary writers and critics who were beginning to isolate the "sexual fact" from its social and political contexts when he added that he would not "argue the question by itself; it does not stand by itself. The vitality of it is altogether in its relations, bearings, significance—like the clef of a symphony" (p. 669). In many respects, Whitman's twofold strategy—his insistence on speaking simultaneously of and against the isolation of sexuality—is as astute a form of literary body politics today as it was when he originally published it in 1888.

See also Ethnology; Labor; *Leaves of Grass;* Proslavery Writing; Psychology; Reform; Sensational Fiction; Urbanization

BIBLIOGRAPHY
Primary Works

Emerson, Ralph Waldo. *Essays: First and Second Series.* New York: Vintage, 1990.

Foster, George. *New York by Gas-Light and Other Urban Sketches.* 1850. Edited by Stuart M. Blumin. Berkeley: University of California Press, 1990.

Fuller, Margaret. *The Essential Margaret Fuller.* Edited by Jeffrey Steele. New Brunswick, N.J.: Rutgers University Press, 1992.

Jefferson, Thomas. *Notes on the State of Virginia.* 1784–1785. Edited by Frank Shuffleton. New York: Penguin, 1999.

Lawrence, D. H. *Studies in Classic American Literature.* 1923. New York: Penguin, 1977.

Locke, John. *An Essay concerning Human Understanding.* 1690. Oxford: Clarendon Press, 1947.

Melville, Herman. *Moby-Dick.* 1851. New York: Penguin, 2001.

Morton, Samuel George. *Crania Americana; or, A Comparative View of the Skulls of Various Aboriginal Nations of North and South America.* Philadelphia: J. Dobson, 1839.

Stowe, Harriet Beecher. *Uncle Tom's Cabin; or, Life among the Lowly.* 1852. Reprinted in *"Uncle Tom's Cabin": Authoritative Text, Backgrounds and Contexts, Criticism,* edited by Elizabeth Ammons. New York: Norton, 1994.

Whitman, Walt. *Walt Whitman: Poetry and Prose.* New York: Library of America, 1996.

Secondary Works

Fiedler, Leslie. *Love and Death in the American Novel.* 1960. Rev. ed. New York: Dell, 1966.

Foucault, Michel. *The History of Sexuality.* Vol. 1, *An Introduction.* Translated by Robert Hurley. New York: Vintage, 1990. First appeared as *Histoire de la sexualité,* vol. 1, *La volonte de savoir* (1976).

Rubin, Gayle. "The Traffic in Women." In *Toward an Anthropology of Women,* edited by Rayna R. Reiter, pp. 157–210. New York: Monthly Review Press, 1975.

Bruce Burgett

SHORT STORY

In a sketch by Washington Irving (1783–1859) titled "The Mutability of Literature" (from the 1819–1820 *Sketch Book of Geoffrey Crayon, Gent.*), the narrator converses with a cranky talking quarto, a small book embittered by two centuries of neglect in the library of Westminster Abbey. By way of consolation, the narrator explains to the volume that in the age of modern printing "the stream of literature has swollen into a torrent—augmented into a river—expanded into a sea." At this rate of growth, he says, in spite of the best efforts of critics, "it will soon be the employment of a lifetime merely to learn [the] names" of the world's good books (p. 134). While fearing for the fate of any writer's posterity in the face of increasingly numerous and prolific authors, the narrator concedes that at least a few writers will continue to find longevity in the minds of readers. Though speaking about writing of all kinds, the narrator may as well be discussing the American short story, for in Irving's era the waters of short fiction began to quickly rise. From the widening river of published sketches, tales, and stories in the mid-nineteenth century, critics have identified Irving, Nathaniel Hawthorne (1804–1864), Edgar Allan Poe (1809–1849), and Herman Melville (1819–1891) as among the major authors of the period's short fiction. While there is undoubtedly consensus as to the makeup of this canonized group, the ranks of remembered names have begun to grow. Renewed attention to formerly neglected texts has allowed more nineteenth-century short story authors—regionalists and women writers, among others—to be heard again.

BEGINNINGS AND THE IDEA OF A DISTINCTLY AMERICAN GENRE

Given the importance of beginnings and endings to the short story form, it might seem unfitting to simply bracket this discussion by the round-numbered years of 1820 and 1870. Auspiciously for this volume, however, the story that critics tell about the American short story very often begins precisely in 1819–1820 with the publication of Irving's *The Sketch Book of Geoffrey Crayon, Gent.* The collection, which contains such famous tales as "Rip Van Winkle" and "The Legend of Sleepy Hollow" alongside sketches like "The Mutability of Literature," garnered wide critical acclaim on both sides of the Atlantic, a truly exceptional feat for a work by an American author at the time. In the mid-nineteenth century the terms "sketch," "tale," and "story" were often used interchangeably. Beginning in the twentieth century, short-fiction critics, who are rarely uninterested in the taxonomy of short prose works, have tended to identify an evolutionary lineage from the brief descriptive sketch to the more plot-driven tale to the modern short story. In histories of American short fiction dating back to the 1920s, Irving secures his position as literary pioneer for penning among the very first examples of the modern short story and engaging—to an unprecedented degree—with decidedly American topics and themes. In short, Irving's short stories inaugurate what many scholars call a distinctly American genre. Objections to this description have been emphatic and numerous, but the question of the genre's Americanness is rarely absent from critical debate. Andrew Levy notes that "it is difficult to find a period or venue in the past one hundred years in which the belief that the short story is an American art form was not widespread" (pp. 27–28). That American writers were the first to fully develop the short story form, that the short story gives a record of American life, and that the genre is particularly adaptable to American life are all reasons for the distinct American-ness of the short story given by critics dating back to William Dean Howells (1837–1920). To begin this discussion in 1820, then, not only affords a useful point of entry to the slate of major American short-fiction writers of the nineteenth century but also prompts an awareness of the literary nationalism that lies at the center of so many critical responses to the American short story.

During a twenty-year sleep that passes as quickly as but one night, a young nation appears before Rip Van Winkle fully formed, replete with new citizens, new fashions, and of course new government, signi-fied by a portrait of General George Washington in place of King George. The American short story, how-ever, did not spring up as if out of a dream. Stories had been published in the United States as early as the late eighteenth century; most were reproductions of, adaptations of, or tales written in the style of British and continental pieces. Short fiction of this period, like its longer incarnations, often weathered criticism for fostering immorality. In this climate, stories fre-quently offered a moral lesson, though in imparting such lessons they sometimes delighted readers by describing various threats to virtue in vivid detail. Many critics—especially those most invested in the distinctly American nature of the short story—describe a steady evolution from stories merely copied from overseas sources to stories that contain only the remnants of borrowed elements and rely more heavily on new plots specific to the United States. "Rip Van Winkle," which draws its most basic premise from German folklore but dramatically pivots upon life before and after American independence, is sometimes offered as an example of a piece on the American end of such a spectrum. Employing the transatlantic approach to early American literature, however, leads to no shortage of examples of ongoing cross-pollina-tion between short fiction in England and America during the early decades of U.S. history. *The Sketch Book* itself, which was published almost concurrently in England and America and which frequently por-trays the flow of people and information across the Atlantic, begins to demonstrate the porous national boundaries of the literary marketplace.

The Sketch Book made Irving's reputation, but it was not his first literary effort. Irving, a New York native, began publishing in magazines and newspapers while earning his living in law and business. Writing under the pen name Diedrich Knickerbocker—from whose papers several pieces from *The Sketch Book* are purportedly borrowed—Irving published in 1809 *A History of New York from the Beginning of the World to*

the End of the Dutch Dynasty, a popular mock history. In the years following the 1819–1820 serial publica-tion of *The Sketch Book,* Irving produced two more volumes of "Geoffrey Crayon's" observations: *Bracebridge Hall* (1822) and *Tales of a Traveller* (1824). Irving, who would go on to publish more nonfiction, released the bulk of his short fiction during the 1820s, reaching his audiences not only through these book collections but also in periodicals.

AMERICAN PERIODICALS AND MAJOR SHORT STORY WRITERS OF THE PERIOD

It is impossible to talk about the nineteenth-century American short story or sketch without highlighting the history of American magazines; the popularity of each fostered the rise of the other. Some scholars even question whether the American short story would have thrived in the absence of these publishing out-lets. Dramatic increase in periodical circulation during the nineteenth century was part and parcel of the advent of mass culture. Under the new conditions of the literary marketplace, writers, for the first time, could live as professional authors. Magazines had begun to appear in the colonies in the 1740s. Andrew Bradford's *American Magazine* and Benjamin Franklin's *General Magazine* were first issued within three days of each other in 1741. In the years follow-ing the American Revolutionary War, the number of successful titles rose. By 1820, Eugene Current-García recounts, despite the existence of only the most basic publishing facilities in the United States, "more than a hundred magazines had come into being, flourished for a time, and then disappeared, leaving behind in their files many hundreds of pieces of short fiction" (p. 3). The number of periodicals only rose from there. The 1830s saw the first issues of several magazines that would enjoy lengthy runs, including *Godey's Lady's Book* (founded in 1830) and the *Southern Literary Messenger* (1834). "Gift books," annual collections of short pieces, were also popular. The number of avail-able American magazines climbed steadily until the Civil War and proliferated dramatically toward the end of the century, when the rise of print advertising and the drop in postal fees lowered issue prices suffi-ciently to allow mass circulation. For the better part of the nineteenth century, magazines remained a primary venue for the publication of short stories. Already in the 1820s to the 1850s, major writers such as Irving, Hawthorne, and Poe, along with scores of now-forgotten short story authors, filled the pages of numerous magazines in response to the great demand for new short fiction.

It is in the pages of *Graham's Magazine* (founded 1841) that Poe published perhaps the most

FROM "THE TELL-TALE HEART"

Edgar Allan Poe's famous story "The Tell-Tale Heart" was first published in January of 1845 in The Pioneer *and reprinted in the* Broadway Journal *on 23 August 1845. Below are the final paragraphs of this dark tale of murder and guilt.*

The officers were satisfied. My *manner* had convinced them. I was singularly at ease. They sat and while I answered cheerily, they chatted of familiar things. But, ere long, I felt myself getting pale and wished them gone. My head ached, and I fancied a ringing in my ears; but still they sat, and still chatted. The ringing became more distinct : I talked more freely to get rid of the feeling: but it continued and gained definitiveness—until, at length, I found that the noise was *not* within my ears.

No doubt I now grew *very* pale; but I talked more fluently, and with a heightened voice. Yet the sound increased—and what could I do? It was *a low, dull, quick sound—much such a sound as a watch makes when enveloped in cotton.* I gasped for breath, and yet the officers heard it not. I talked more quickly, more vehemently but the noise steadily increased. I arose and argued about trifles, in a high key and with violent gesticulations; but the noise steadily increased. Why *would* they not be gone? I paced the floor to and fro with heavy strides, as if excited to fury by the observations of the men, but the noise steadily increased. O God! what *could* I do? I foamed—I raved—I swore! I swung the chair upon which I had been sitting, and grated it upon the boards, but the noise arose over all and continually increased. It grew louder—louder—louder! And still the men chatted pleasantly, and smiled. Was it possible they heard not? Almighty God!—no, no? They heard!—they suspected!—they *knew*!—they were making a mockery of my horror!—this I thought, and this I think. But anything was better than this agony! Anything was more tolerable than this derision! I could bear those hypocritical smiles no longer! I felt that I must scream or die!—and now—again—hark! louder! louder! louder! *louder*!—

"Villains!" I shrieked, "dissemble no more! I admit the deed!—tear up the planks!—here, here!—it is the beating of his hideous heart!"

Poe, *Great Short Works*, p. 389.

important—or at least the most frequently cited—document in the early development of the American short story, his April and May 1842 review of Nathaniel Hawthorne's short story collection *Twice-Told Tales* (1842 edition). If many critics deem Irving the earliest writer of the American short story, as many if not more scholars ascribe to Poe the title of founder of the genre, largely on account of the self-conscious consideration of the form that he offers in this review. For Poe, "the unity of effect or impression" (*Great Short Works*, p. 521) is the most important element of a composition, and this unity may be accomplished only in pieces short enough for a reader to absorb in one sitting. "Without a certain continuity of effort—" Poe writes, "without a certain duration or repetition of purpose—the soul is never deeply moved" (p. 521). Conceding that the short rhymed poem affords an author the greatest opportunity to produce his best and most important work, Poe declares the "short prose narrative" to be the next best form, the prose piece that "should best fulfil the demands of high genius" (p. 521). He selects for celebration the tale and not the novel, for the latter, because of its length, "deprives itself, of course, of the immense force derivable from *totality*" (p. 522). And if the rhythms of the short poem are particularly useful for expressions of beauty, Poe writes, the tale surpasses the poem when its goal is "Truth," or "terror, or passion, or horror, or a multitude of such other points" (p. 523). From the first to the last, each word and every sentence of a short story needs be in the service of the story's preconceived single effect, Poe states in his review. Only then can a tale give its reader the fullest possible satisfaction.

According to Poe's essay, the only American authors who had so far excelled in this most important of genres were Irving and Hawthorne. The Massachusetts-born Hawthorne graduated from Bowdoin College in 1825 and right away began the uphill climb toward professional authorship, a summit yet reached by few, if any, American fiction writers besides Irving. After self-publishing a gothic romance called *Fanshawe* (1828)—which he would later disavow—Hawthorne set to work writing tales. He had in mind three separate collections, each with its own design. But finding no publisher willing to put out his work in book form, Hawthorne placed the stories separately. By 1837 around thirty such pieces had been published—often anonymously—in gift books, newspapers, and magazines. Finally, backed by his friend Horatio Bridge, Hawthorne published his first collection of short fiction, *Twice-Told Tales*, in 1837. The book contained eighteen tales, sketches, and essays, most of which had been previously "told" in periodicals. A two-volume edition, expanded to include

FROM POE'S REVIEW OF HAWTHORNE'S *TWICE-TOLD TALES*

One of the earliest critical pieces about the American short story, Edgar Allan Poe's review of Nathaniel Hawthorne's Twice-Told Tales *is cited often in discussions of the development of the genre. It was originally published in the April and May 1842 issues of* Graham's Magazine.

Were we called upon, however, to designate that class of composition which, next to such a poem as we have suggested, should best fulfil the demands of high genius—should offer it the most advantageous field of exertion—we should unhesitatingly speak of the prose tale, as Mr. Hawthorne has here exemplified it. We allude to the short prose narrative, requiring from a half-hour to one or two hours in its perusal. The ordinary novel is objectionable, from its length, for reasons already stated in substance. As it cannot be read at one sitting, it deprives itself, of course, of the immense force derivable from *totality*. Worldly interests intervening during the pauses of perusal, modify, annul, or counteract, in a greater or less degree, the impressions of the book. But simple cessation in reading would, of itself, be sufficient to destroy the true unity. In the brief tale, however, the author is enabled to carry out the fulness of his intention, be it what it may. During the hour of perusal the soul of the reader is at the writer's control. There are no external or extrinsic influences—resulting from weariness or interruption.

A skilful literary artist has constructed a tale. If wise, he has not fashioned his thoughts to accommodate his incidents; but having conceived, with deliberate care, a certain unique or single *effect* to be wrought out, he then invents such incidents—he then combines such events as may best aid him in establishing this preconceived effect. If his very initial sentence tend not to the outbringing of this effect, then he has failed in his first step. In the whole composition there should be no word written, of which the tendency, direct or indirect, is not to the one pre-established design. And by such means, with such care and skill, a picture is at length painted which leaves in the mind of him who contemplates it with a kindred art, a sense of the fullest satisfaction. The idea of the tale has been presented unblemished, because undisturbed; and this is an end unattainable by the novel. Undue brevity is just as exceptionable here as in the poem; but undue length is yet more to be avoided.

Poe, *Great Short Works*, pp. 521–522.

twenty-one additional tales, followed in 1842. Four years after that, Hawthorne published *Mosses from an Old Manse* (1846), which featured new stories such as "The Birth-mark" and "Rappaccini's Daughter" alongside the older but yet uncollected standouts "Young Goodman Brown" and "Roger Malvin's Burial." Released the same year as Hawthorne's third edition of *Twice-Told Tales* was *The Snow Image and Other Tales* (1851), a miscellaneous grouping of pieces written during the span of Hawthorne's career to date. "My Kinsman, Major Molineux" is among the better-known stories included in this, Hawthorne's final collection of short fiction. Like Irving and other nineteenth-century authors, Hawthorne displays in much of his work a keen interest in the gothic and the supernatural. Stories like "Young Goodman Brown," which describes a man's journey into a dark and evil wood, delve into the moral and spiritual lives of its characters. "The Birth-mark," the tale of a scientist's

tragic obsession with removing a blemish from his wife's otherwise perfect visage, is but one story that employs the symbolism and allegory so central to Hawthorne's literary project. And as he would later do in *The Scarlet Letter* (1850), Hawthorne also turned to New England history for inspiration in his short fiction. In the last sentence of his *Graham's* review, Poe praises Hawthorne for his originality and style, calling him "one of the few men of indisputable genius to whom our country has as yet given birth."

Poe, who worked at *Graham's* in 1841 and 1842, supported himself throughout his career with editorial positions on several other American periodicals, including the *Southern Literary Messenger, Burton's Gentleman's Magazine,* and the *Broadway Journal*. Aware even then of the importance of magazines to the early development of short fiction and to American literary culture more generally, Poe aspired to found, edit, and publish his own cutting-edge literary journal, a project that never quite came to fruition. The poet, literary critic, and fiction writer followed through on his high regard for the short prose form and earned his reputation as a master of the short story, publishing in total about seventy tales, mostly in the 1840s, many of which appeared in his two short-fiction collections *Tales of the Grotesque and Arabesque* (1840) and *Tales* (1845). Critics have long been interested in Poe's biography and its relationship to the bent of his fiction; orphaned at three and later witness to his tubercular wife's painful death, he was well acquainted with sickness and loss—as well as addiction—long before his own death at age forty. The uncanny and the gruesome, the ghostly and the ghastly, are all key features of Poe's work, much of which, like that of his predecessors and contemporaries, is gothic in nature. The plots of "The Cask of Amontillado" and "The Pit and the Pendulum," for example, hinge upon characters' imprisonment in crypts or dungeons. Poe is frequently deemed the originator of detective fiction for tales such as "The Murders in the Rue Morgue," "The Mystery of Marie Roget," and "The Purloined Letter," in which his character C. Auguste Dupin, a mastermind of perception and reason, effortlessly solves crimes of violence and extortion. Hoaxing was also one of Poe's favored modes—and even when not directly hoaxing, the author frequently took in his tales a comic or satirical turn.

Like Poe, Herman Melville offered high praise of Hawthorne's short fiction. His 1850 review of *Mosses* was published in the *Literary World* soon after Hawthorne and Melville became friends. Melville had earned only limited recognition for his novels—*Moby-Dick* (1851), which he dedicated to Hawthorne, was a commercial failure—when he somewhat reluctantly turned to short stories in a relatively unsuccessful attempt to avoid fading into obscurity and insolvency. It was not until the 1920s that a Melville renaissance launched that author into the literary canon, bringing to readers' attention not only the now-famous novel of the white whale but also Melville's small but distinctive body of short stories. Melville published more than a dozen tales in *Putnam's Monthly* and *Harper's New Monthly Magazine* during the period 1852–1856, some of which were included in his only short-fiction collection, *The Piazza Tales* (1856). "Bartleby, the Scrivener" and "Benito Cereno" are perhaps the most-anthologized titles from the six-story volume.

A DEMOCRATIC FORM AND NINETEENTH-CENTURY LOCAL COLOR WRITERS

Melville's belated canonization demonstrates how the reputations of short story writers of the nineteenth century, like authors of all genres and periods, have waxed and waned. It is a commonly voiced claim—clearly not unconnected to the idea of a distinctly

Illustration for Poe's "Murders in the Rue Morgue." Engraving by Eugene Michel Abot after a painting by Daniel Urrabieta Vierge. Widely regarded as the progenitor of the detective story, Poe's tale of murders by an orangutan was a radical departure from previous forms of fiction. BIBLIOTHEQUE NATIONALE, PARIS, FRANCE, LAUROS/GIRAUDON/ THE BRIDGEMAN ART LIBRARY

American form—that the American short story is a uniquely democratic genre, an idea invoked in examinations of both celebrated and lesser-known story writers. The form is said to be democratic for clearing less traditional paths between obscurity and lasting renown. The literary careers of the authors discussed above, for example, show how, in the nineteenth century, one did not need to be an established writer to publish short stories but could instead publish stories in order to become known or earn a living as a fiction writer. The short story is also called democratic for facilitating the publication of work by writers from demographics less likely to find an audience. If Irving, Hawthorne, Poe, and Melville, all white males from the Northeast, are the short-fiction writers to have earned a place in the eyes of critics as major figures of the period, they are but a tiny sampling of those whose tales and sketches were released widely during the years 1820 to 1870. Indeed, the American magazine made publishing short fiction a much easier prospect for writers of many backgrounds and levels of literary experience. Kristie Hamilton explains:

> As readership of periodicals grew rapidly, the market for sketches was opened to writers who might otherwise have been unable to gain access to a national audience (Euro-American women, African Americans, Westerners, Southerners), and these authors recognized in the sketch the opportunity for revision of its heretofore dominant voice—the disinterested (white, urban, Northeastern) gentleman. (P. 16)

Some of these authors, often under the auspices of a critical interest in local color or women's writing, have earned increased attention in recent scholarship. Short stories that capture the peculiar customs, dialects, and landscapes of various regions filled periodicals in record numbers during the mid-nineteenth century. In singling out for mention only a few local color writers of this time, however, it is important not to overlook the great number of authors who, responding to the demand for this genre, translated knowledge of the country's various regions into numerous sketches and tales. Several writers, however, have received a greater degree of attention, especially those penning southern and western "frontier humor" writing, a popular subgenre. William Gilmore Simms's (1806–1870) tales of the South are among the earliest popular examples of writing in this tradition. Bret Harte's (1836–1902) local color fiction about California—in addition to southern locales—combines humor with sentiment. Also writing in this vein was the Missouri-born author of *Adventures of Huckleberry Finn* (1885), Mark Twain (1835–1910), whose satirical sketches employ folklore in a manner characteristic of local color.

Women published short stories throughout this period, especially in such female-targeted venues as ladies' magazines. And the number of published women writers began to grow after mid-century as local color gained momentum. Judith Fetterley and Marjorie Pryse have been leading voices in a surge of scholarship since the late twentieth century about women regionalist writers, for whom the short story or sketch was the primary form. Women regionalists, according to these critics, tend to undermine stereotypical depictions of the region that local color sometimes advances. Short fiction by *Uncle Tom's Cabin* (1852) author Harriet Beecher Stowe (1811–1896), Alice Cary (1820–1871), and Rose Terry Cooke (1827–1892) are among those from the period singled out by Fetterley and Pryse for renewed attention. Local color from the period aims to capture in writing the variegated landscape of the United States, often preserving scenes that were fading rapidly with modernization. And stories of local color, like much nineteenth-century short fiction, are deeply indebted to an oral, folkloric tradition.

Short-fiction authors of the nineteenth century—canonized, recovered, or infrequently remembered—who wrote updated folklore, gothic tales, didactic allegories, humorous satires, and local color sketches, began a rich tradition of short story writing that has thrived, unabated, right up into the twenty-first century.

See also "Bartleby, the Scrivener"; "Benito Cereno"; "The Birth-mark"; "The Celebrated Jumping Frog of Calaveras County"; "The Fall of the House of Usher"; Literary Marketplace; Literary Nationalism; Periodicals; "Young Goodman Brown"

BIBLIOGRAPHY
Primary Works
Fetterley, Judith, and Marjorie Pryse, eds. *American Women Regionalists 1850–1910*. New York: Norton, 1992.

Hawthorne, Nathaniel. *Twice-Told Tales*. 1837. Expanded ed. 1842. New York: Modern Library, 2001.

Hawthorne, Nathaniel. *Young Goodman Brown and Other Short Stories*. New York: Dover, 1992.

Irving, Washington. *The Sketch Book of Geoffrey Crayon, Gent.* 1819–1820. Reprinted as *"The Legend of Sleepy Hollow" and Other Stories in "The Sketch Book."* New York: Signet, 1981.

Melville, Herman. *The Piazza Tales*. 1856. Northwestern-Newberry edition. Evanston, Ill.: Northwestern University Press, 2000.

Poe, Edgar Allan. *Great Short Works of Edgar Allan Poe: Poems, Tales, Criticism*. Introduction by G. R. Thompson. New York: Perennial, 2004.

Secondary Works
Current-García, Eugene. *The American Short Story before 1850: A Critical History*. Boston: Twayne, 1985.

Hamilton, Kristie. *America's Sketchbook: The Cultural Life of a Nineteenth-Century Literary Genre*. Athens: Ohio University Press, 1998.

Lee, A. Robert, ed. *The Nineteenth-Century American Short Story*. London: Vision Press, 1985.

Levy, Andrew. *The Culture and Commerce of the American Short Story*. New York and London: Cambridge University Press, 1993.

Pattee, Fred Lewis. *The Development of the American Short Story: An Historical Survey*. New York and London: Harper & Brothers, 1923.

Tallack, Douglas. *The Nineteenth-Century American Short Story: Language, Form, and Ideology.* London and New York: Routledge, 1993.

Voss, Arthur. *The American Short Story: A Critical Survey.* Norman: University of Oklahoma Press, 1973.

Rebecca Berne

SLAVE LAWS

See Compromise of 1850 and Fugitive Slave Law

SLAVE NARRATIVES

In 1856 the fugitive slave John Thompson (b. 1812) published an autobiographical account of his life in slavery and his escape to freedom titled *The Life of John Thompson, a Fugitive Slave; Containing His History of Twenty-five Years in Bondage, and His Providential Escape. Written by Himself.* The title and contents of Thompson's narrative establishes it as a representative text of the antebellum slave narrative genre. In its broadest sense the slave narrative genre includes any narrated, nonfictional account of an individual's life in slavery. Thompson's work is similar in its scope to the thousands of other autobiographical accounts published by, and on behalf of, enslaved and formerly enslaved African Americans.

A careful reading of one specific narrative allows one to see how, as a literary genre, slave narratives are in fact pieces of history and community memory. Slave narratives represent a space in which a collective African American identity is able to emerge, despite the devastating and dehumanizing effects of chattel bondage. However, along with acknowledging this shared identity, the reader must also recognize the individual slave narrator's quest for personal agency in the telling of his or her story. Slave narrators cherish their identities as individuals and human beings apart from the "peculiar institution" of slavery, an institution that specifically sought to deny them both humanity and individuality. Slave narratives fill in the gaps and silences about African American history and identity. And these narratives also chronicle the quest for black personhood: the struggle to be recognized as a human being within a system that renders slaves as property and as "three-fifths" of a whole person.

PRODUCTION, RECEPTION, AND PUBLICATION

In the title to his narrative, John Thompson firmly declares his name and status as a fugitive slave and juxtaposes those labels with the phrase "written by himself." His fugitive status is a proud declaration of his successful escape from slavery, even as his actual name is an admission of the far-reaching tentacles of slavery; he is a "Thompson" because he and his family are born the property of a white slaveholding family with the surname "Thompson." As John Thompson's name, and thus his identity, is intertwined with his status as property, the declaration that his narrative is "written by himself" allows Thompson ownership of something that does rightfully belong to him: the story of his life. Of the hundreds of slave narratives written and published in the antebellum period, the term "written by himself" is a distinguishing feature of those stories in which the writer claims authority over both the means and the rights to tell the story of his own life. The term "written by himself" is about textual authority, meant to assure the reader that the subsequent narrative was not "ghostwritten" by white hands, and is indeed the product of someone who has lived the harsh reality of a life in slavery.

So much of the information disseminated about slavery in the nineteenth century reflected the proslavery agenda of white historians, journalists, and chroniclers. Both northern and southern white writers published accounts that depicted slaves as content, well-kept, and happy with their roles as lifelong servants to white families. John Thompson cites the Reverend Nehemiah Adams's famous 1854 *A South-Side View of Slavery* as a typical example of an attempt by a white writer to paint "slavery in such glowingly beautiful colors" (Thompson, p. 441). One of the most significant contributions of the slave narrative genre is that it gives the victimized and oppressed a space to tell their own stories and to forcefully contradict prevailing myths that African Americans were satisfied with their status as perpetual servants.

The issue of who has the means and opportunity to "set the record straight" concerning slavery is a complex one, as there are many examples of texts that are not authentic first-person autobiographies produced by the hand of a slave narrator but are still considered "slave narratives." In both the antebellum and postbellum periods, white writers produced written accounts of orally dictated life stories of slaves with varying degrees of accuracy. Some of these writers and "editors" crafted a complete retelling of a slave's particular life story. Particularly in the earlier antebellum slave narratives, an amanuensis would take great liberties and literary license in his or her depictions of a slave's life, even while making the claim that the resulting narrative was a faithful depiction of the slave narrator's story. Yet because the subjects of these narratives either could not speak or were not allowed to speak for themselves, the reader should rightfully question both the validity of the story being told and the motivations of the amanuensis.

In Nat Turner's 1831 *Confessions,* the extraordinary events of an armed slave insurrection, as well as the biographical material of Turner's life, are not penned by Turner (1800–1831), but by Thomas Ruffin Gray. Gray was a local white attorney who helped to prosecute Turner for his role in this rebellion and who also financially profited from the publication and sale of this sensational story. In this "slave narrative," Gray attempts to allay fears of local whites by downplaying the scope of the planned rebellion even as he demonizes Nat Turner for daring to take up arms against his oppressors. The narrative of the most significant slave insurrection in American history might have read very differently if Nat Turner's narrative had been "written by himself."

Prevailing nineteenth-century cultural sentiment argued that the enslaved person did not have the higher reasoning and intellectual skills capable of producing a sustained piece of literature. Thus, the existence of a multitude of authentic first-person slave narratives helped to shatter racist cultural and pseudo-scientific conventions. To have the mental facilities to write one's own autobiography elevated the slave narrator from the status of "chattel" to the status of "human being;" the creation of literary texts challenged the traditional place African Americans occupied on the "Great Chain of Being." Because of widespread disbelief that those deemed mentally inferior could in fact produce detailed analyses of their lives, many slave narratives contain documents, prefaces, supporting letters, or introductions written by prominent white citizens. These sources were intended to authenticate the extraordinary fact that not only were some slaves and former slaves literate but also the horrific stories they revealed about slavery in their narratives were true.

The existence of these "authentication documents" gives the slave narrative real textual authority for its nineteenth-century white readership; the slave narrator is certified as a "truth teller" when there is corroborating evidence presented by a white source. This "objective" outside voice was required to lend credence to what many white Americans considered to be extraordinary and unbelievable stories about the brutality of slavery. For a nation that believed slavery was a benign institution, slave narrators' tales of rape, murder, and brutality were almost impossible to believe unless a "trustworthy" authority could vouch for the writer's veracity. In addition to verifying a particular person's life story, these supporting documents by prominent whites were instrumental in increasing the marketability and sale of these slave narratives, as is the case in Frederick Douglass's (1818–1895) 1845 autobiography, *Narrative of the Life of Frederick Douglass.* Both William Lloyd Garrison (1805–1879) and Wendell Phillips (1811–1884), two of the most famous abolitionists, provide their stamp of approval for Douglass's best-selling narrative. Douglass's fame as a writer and an orator is directly related to his (sometimes troubled) relationship with these two men.

John Thompson's 1856 narrative does not contain any outside documents. As was the case for many slave narrators who self-published, Thompson wrote his own preface and addressed it to the reader. This preface provides some clues as to why enslaved and formerly enslaved men and women would want to write their stories, despite the great personal risks of doing so. Many slave authors wrote their autobiographical accounts while they were still fugitives, risking discovery that they could be captured and remanded back to slavery. Thompson indicates that he writes because "it may be permitted to one who has worn the galling yoke of bondage, to say something of its pains, and something of . . . freedom" (p. 416). He also writes that he "found many of my brethren from other and remote states, had written on the subject," but decides to pen his story in order to relate his own unique experiences (p. 416). There is an awareness for Thompson, even in 1856, that in writing and publishing his narrative, he is participating in an established African American literary and intellectual tradition and that he is filling in the gaps of ignorance concerning slave life.

Slave narrators crafted their stories for public consumption for a wide variety of reasons. Solomon Bayley's 1825 work, *A Narrative of Some Remarkable Incidents, in the Life of Solomon Bayley, Formerly a Slave,* is a remarkable preservation of his family history as well as a glimpse into the domestic lives of enslaved families. In his narrative Bayley preserves the details of the lives of his African-born grandmother; his first generation American-born mother; his own children; and the entire family's participation in the colonization and settlement of Liberia. Slave narratives were often the only documents that spoke about a person's or a family's entire existence; Thompson indicates that he and his family are recorded in a farming ledger along with the livestock. The written word provides a legacy of the hardships and endurance of enslaved people who were denied other legacies, including the right to own property or to parent their own children.

In her 1861 narrative *Incidents in the Life of a Slave Girl*, Harriet Jacobs (1813–1897) indicates that she pens her narrative to provide a financial legacy, as well as a written family history, for her children. With so few economic opportunities available to former slaves, particularly slave women, it is Jacobs's hope that her story has an economic value. The motivations for writing slave narratives may have differed significantly according to gender. As Frances Smith Foster indicates in her work *Witnessing Slavery: The Development of Ante-Bellum Slave Narratives*, less than 12 percent of extant slave narratives are written by women, and few of these are produced within the antebellum era. Few slave women had the means or opportunity to become literate and thus produce narratives. Slave or formerly enslaved women who were literate and wanted to write may have been silenced by male authority (both black and white). Slave women performed manual labor in the fields, in addition to their domestic duties, making leisure time in which to write a virtual impossibility. The perceived value of black women was in their capacity to breed, to literally reproduce chattel slavery from their wombs, either voluntarily or involuntarily. And yet writers like Harriet Jacobs, Elizabeth Keckley (1818–1907), and Amanda Berry Smith (1837–1915) give birth to written texts of their own accord, taking on the role of "writer," and thereby participating in a male-dominated space and marketplace. All three of these women explicitly express their hope that their writing would have social, as well as economic, value.

It is uncertain whether any slave narrators significantly profited from their autobiographical works, but it is clear that slave narratives were wildly popular with their predominately white reading audience. In his introduction to *I Was Born a Slave: An Anthology of Classic Slave Narratives*, Yuval Taylor reports that Solomon Northup's 1853 narrative, *Twelve Years a Slave: Narrative of Solomon Northup*, sold twenty-seven thousand copies; Douglass's 1845 text, *Narrative of the Life of Frederick Douglass*, went through seven American and nine British printings in five years, with over thirty thousand copies sold; and William Wells Brown's (c. 1814–1884) 1847 narrative, *Narrative of William W. Brown, a Fugitive Slave*, sold ten thousand copies in the United States and sold an additional eleven thousand copies in England (Taylor, p. xx). These numbers, which far exceed the sales of books by white American writers publishing about the same time, including Nathaniel Hawthorne, Henry Thoreau, Herman Melville, and Walt Whitman,

demonstrate that there was an almost insatiable desire for these first-person accounts of slavery.

These sales numbers, which may in fact be low estimates, raise the question as to why slave narratives were such popular reading material. Who read these narratives and why? For the predominately white readership, these stories could be titillating and sensationalistic; slave narratives provide a voyeuristic view into a world of slavery that is depraved and yet also highly exotic. Thinly veiled acts of miscegenation and heroic escapes from sadistic overseers appear in most slave narratives, along with the primary antislavery message. Even as these works fit into the rubric of abolitionist propaganda, the material is still sensational. Perhaps no narrative illustrates this more than the 1860 William and Ellen Craft narrative, *Running a Thousand Miles for Freedom; or, The Escape of William and Ellen Craft from Slavery*. The married couple makes their ingenious escape from slavery with Ellen Craft posing as a wealthy, white male slaveholder, attended to by her faithful male slave, who in reality is her husband, William Craft. The publication of this narrative is accompanied by a portrait of Ellen Craft, fully outfitted in her male, slaveholding garb. This bold transgression of supposedly fixed racial, gender, and class categories is shocking to its audience.

While prurient details generate an initial interest in a particular slave narrative, the reader must confront the decisive antislavery message at the heart of all of these texts. There is little doubt that the majority of these nineteenth-century readers—white, northern, professing Christians—were already sympathetic or inclined toward the abolitionist cause prior to reading slave narratives. And yet, most slave narratives adapt sentimental literary forms in order to directly appeal to the hearts and consciences of even these already sympathetic readers. By presenting the brutal realities of slavery forcefully enough, slave narratives could not only incite emotions but also stir their readers into action for the antislavery cause. As a tool of antislavery propaganda, the slave narrative's form is remarkably effective, as is evidenced by one of the most widely read and influential works of American literature, Harriet Beecher Stowe's (1811–1896) 1852 novel, *Uncle Tom's Cabin*. This novel is partially the product of Stowe's reading and "borrowing" of details from the life story of former slave Josiah Henson (1789–1883), who initially published his own slave narrative in 1849 under the title *The Life of Josiah Henson, Formerly a Slave, Now an Inhabitant of Canada, as Narrated by Himself*. If Stowe is the "little woman" who started a "big war" (as Lincoln said when they first met), then the slave narrative must be recognized as the kindling that sustained the antislavery fire. Because it offers direct appeals to the moral values of its readership, the slave narrative genre is embraced enthusiastically by a religious audience that reads these documents as testimonies of Christian faith and models of spiritual salvation. Many slave narratives are explicitly crafted as proselytizing tools, which is logical given that most slave narratives are published under the auspices of churches or religious organizations, particularly the Methodists, Presbyterians, and Religious Society of Friends (Quakers).

While the typical reader profile is that of a white, Christian northerner, a fair number of African Americans, enslaved and free, also read slave narratives, as John Thompson indicates that he had done. Throughout his account, he specifically addresses his brothers and sisters in bondage, articulating the fact that only these men and women truly understand his plight. And while the black literate population in the antebellum era was small, published slave narratives become invaluable for these readers. Slave narratives were blueprints to freedom for the black reader as they offered proof that a successful flight from slavery was possible, confirmed the existence of the Underground Railroad and other escape routes, provided strategies for achieving literacy, and urged men and women in chains to seek both their spiritual and personal freedom.

THEMATIC CONTENT

Slave narratives ranged from two- or three-page documents published by local churches to several-hundred-page autobiographical tomes produced in installment. Some writers of slave narratives achieved fame and notoriety within their lifetimes, like Frederick Douglass and Elizabeth Keckley, author of the 1868 narrative *Behind the Scenes, or, Thirty Years a Slave, and Four Years in the White House*. Most slave narrators published their stories and then faded into historical obscurity. Some managed to escape or were emancipated from slavery while in the prime of their lives; others felt the yoke of bondage well into their old age. Despite the vastly different stylistic forms of these narratives, as well as the wide variety of circumstances under which these writers labored, slave narratives have a fairly formulaic structure: a linear and chronological account of the subject's life, with emphasis on articulating family history, "coming to religion," attaining literacy, and gaining freedom—all actions that refute typical proslavery rhetoric.

"I was born" is the phrase that Thompson uses to begin his narrative, and that is often the introductory phrase for slave writers. Like Thompson's naming of himself in his title, "I was born" becomes a declarative

act of writing himself into existence. If self-awareness is one condition that separates humans from animals, the reader can no longer believe Thompson is an animal if he is able to confirm his own existence. Likewise, Thompson gives voice to his family members by naming them, recalling specific information about them, and making it clear to his audience that genuine ties of love and affection bond him with his family, countering the commonly accepted belief that African Americans were incapable of sustained familial relationships. Henry Bibb's (1815–1854) 1849 narrative, *Narrative of the Life and Adventures of Henry Bibb, an American Slave, Written by Himself,* is the tale of a man so passionately committed to his family that despite successfully escaping slavery more than six times, he keeps returning to the South to try to rescue his wife and child. Without such autobiographical information gleaned from slave narratives, there would be no accurate historical documentation of slave family life, plantation traditions, or evidence of the survival of African rituals and customs. This autobiographical information emphasizes commonalities between the reader and the writer, as the reader most likely has family members from whom he or she could not bear to be parted. Is not then the slave a "man and a brother?"

This notion of "brotherhood," particularly the question of who has access to "Christian brotherhood" is an issue examined by black writers in almost every written document about slavery. Some nineteenth-century white Christians fought against slaves having access to religious teaching, fearing the consequences of exposure to "radical" messages about freedom and salvation. Others believed that religion would help slaves to be more content in their biblically ordained status as descendants of Ham, and thus perpetual servants. Some proslavery advocates simply argued that as beasts of burden, slaves had no souls that could be saved. Given these sentiments, it is no surprise that "coming to religion" is a prominent feature of slave narratives, a process whereby the narrator is made aware of his innately sinful nature; he endures various trials as his godly spirit battles his sinful flesh; and he emerges cleansed of his sin as a full-fledged member of the Christian community. In reality, slaves were denied membership or full participation in most churches; this provided the impetus for the founding, and later the institutionalization, of all-black denominations. Slave narratives detail whippings by "Christian" overseers that are accompanied by recitations of scripture. The biblical justification of slavery becomes the single most important rhetorical argument upholding the bondage of an entire race. Despite this, almost every single slave narrative affirms embracing a devout

Christian faith as necessary for African Americans, enslaved and free. Why?

Certainly slave narrators are aware that their acceptance as human beings rests on proof that unlike animals, they have souls that can receive salvation. These conversion accounts force the question as to whether it is morally justifiable to enslave a fellow Christian brother or sister. The authors of slave narratives understand their audience: religion represents social, political, and economic currency. Religion renders the more unsavory details of slavery more palatable to the white Christian reader; it again establishes bonds of common experiences, linking the reader and the writer; and it provides a common language and reference point for black and white alike. Slave narratives couch revolutionary sentiments and subversive acts in Christian code, as religion is almost the only acceptable political construct available to slaves.

Most important, accounts of "coming to religion" mark the slave narratives as carefully crafted literary works in which the writers are keenly aware of how to use the language and rhetoric of Christian scripture to create a new racial paradigm in which African Americans are no longer the most wretched of the earth but are instead identified with God's chosen people. Slave narratives often specifically reference Old Testament prophets and parables, as they parallel the experience of blacks in bondage with the history of the Israelites' enslavement and subsequent exodus. By retelling and reworking these biblical stories, slave narratives create a distinctly African American literary form, rooted and grounded in Christian tradition but specific to the cultural experiences of a people whose heritage is intertwined with slavery. The last chapter of John Thompson's narrative is an elegantly crafted sermon in which he parallels his sailing knowledge with his religious life. He deliberately draws comparisons between the story of his life and that of the Old Testament prophet, Jonah. While Jonah is best known for the three days he languished in the belly of the whale, Thompson chooses to emphasize the extraordinary deliverance experience in Jonah's story. He leaves the reader to conclude that if Jonah can be rescued from his impossible situation, deliverance of African Americans from bondage is not only possible, but imminent.

Thompson's personal deliverance from slavery is intimately connected to his literacy. Similar to the account Douglass relates in his narrative, Thompson is taught to read as a child by a sympathetic white boyhood friend. Most slave narratives give some brief account as to how its authors attained literacy, as this was a significant feat for African Americans in the

nineteenth-century. Some "stole learning," by using a variety of tricks to get others to teach them to read. Others, like Harriet Jacobs, were fortunate enough to be taught alongside the children of the slaveholders. Others write that they experience "miraculous" and "instantaneous" literacy. Severe penalties existed for those slaves and freed blacks who dared to learn how to read, as well as for those bold enough to teach them. Many slave narrators depict their achievements of literacy as their moment of true freedom, even if they are still legally slaves when they become literate. Freedom and literacy are inextricably linked in the slave narrative tradition as the shackles of ignorance are no less binding than the yoke of slavery.

The quest for freedom takes many forms in the slave narrative tradition. Henry Box Brown's 1849 text, *Narrative of Henry Box Brown,* depicts a man so desirous of freedom that he encloses himself in a three-foot-long and two-foot-wide box and mails himself out of slavery. Freedom is literacy for some; for others, freedom is Christian salvation. Freedom is making sure your children do not have to endure chattel bondage. Freedom is walking away from slavery at any cost, even if it means leaving behind parents or children. The slave narrative is a documentary history showing that African Americans never wavered in their collective and individual quests for freedom. Thompson concludes his narrative with the thought: "for freedom, like eternal life, is precious, and a true man will risk every power of body or mind to escape the snares" (p. 479).

LITERARY IMPACT AND LEGACY

Slave narratives were influenced by but also significantly affected many other literary forms, including the confessional narrative, the autobiography, the sentimental novel, the spiritual narrative, the picaresque novel, the travel narrative, and the sermon and jeremiad traditions. Writers of slave narratives were also readers influenced by particular key texts—including *Pilgrim's Progress, The Columbian Orator,* the King James Bible, and John Wesley's hymns—on the style and content of slave narratives. In addition to the impact of these Western literary forms, there is an undeniable African literary and cultural impact on the slave narratives as well. Jacob Green's 1864 book, *Narrative of the Life of J. D. Green, a Runaway Slave, from Kentucky, Containing an Account of His Three Escapes,* employs the extended use of the trickster-hero motif. In William Grimes's 1825 text, *Life of William Grimes, the Runaway Slave. Written by Himself,* traditional folk beliefs, otherwise labeled as "witchcraft," are explicitly discussed. Grimes's narrative is open-ended and circular; there is no explicit antislavery resolution such as that found in almost all other slave narratives. In addition, the earliest

The Resurrection of Henry Box Brown at Philadelphia. Lithograph, c. 1850. Henry Brown escaped slavery by having himself shipped to Philadelphia. Here he is shown emerging from the crate with the help of Frederick Douglass (holding a pry bar). Brown recounted his story in an 1849 narrative. BROWN RARE BOOKS AND SPECIAL COLLECTIONS DIVISION, THE LIBRARY OF CONGRESS

of the antebellum slave narratives offer mythic imagery, musical references, ritual religious practices, and allusions to secret societies that can be traced to specific African sources. In a thorough examination of slave narrative tradition, the "African" elements in this progenitor of African American literature cannot be neglected. Whether employing the neo–slave narrative form, or addressing thematic issues of freedom, agency, and identity, all subsequent black literature owes its debt to the slave narrative genre, the first sustained written documents created by first- and second-generation Americans of African descent.

In addition to being literary texts, slave narratives are also historical monuments; without this material, some of the most painful moments in American history would be forever lost. There would be no documentary evidence proving that slaves resisted their condition of bondage. Without this material, there would be no written legacy of a people's survival. It is not known when John Thompson died; as is the case for so many other "minor" writers of slave narratives, no information about his life after the publication of

his narrative exists. Like most slave narratives, his story is not particularly extraordinary. What is remarkable is that this "ordinary" story itself has survived, leaving a historical and literary legacy of a singular individual and the community from which he emerged.

See also Abolitionist Writing; Autobiography; The Bible; Blacks; Compromise of 1850 and Fugitive Slave Law; *The Confessions of Nat Turner;* Female Authorship; *Incidents in the Life of a Slave Girl; Narrative of the Life of Frederick Douglass;* Slavery; *Uncle Tom's Cabin;* Underground Railroad

BIBLIOGRAPHY
Primary Works

Taylor, Yuval, ed. *I Was Born a Slave: An Anthology of Classic Slave Narratives.* Chicago: Lawrence Hill, 1999.

Thompson, John. *The Life of John Thompson, A Fugitive Slave; Containing His History of Twenty-five Years in Bondage, and His Providential Escape, Written by Himself.* Worcester, Mass.: J. Thompson, 1856.

Secondary Works

Andrews, William L., ed. *African American Autobiography: A Collection of Critical Essays.* Englewood Cliffs, N.J.: Prentice Hall, 1993.

Davis, Charles T., and Henry Louis Gates Jr., eds. *The Slave's Narrative.* Oxford and New York: Oxford University Press, 1985.

Genovese, Eugene D. *Roll, Jordan, Roll: The World the Slaves Made.* New York: Pantheon, 1974.

Fleischner, Jennifer. *Mastering Slavery: Memory, Family, and Identity in Women's Slave Narratives.* New York: New York University Press, 1996.

Foster, Frances Smith. *Witnessing Slavery: The Development of Ante-Bellum Slave Narratives.* 2nd ed. Madison: University of Wisconsin Press, 1994.

McDowell, Deborah E., and Arnold Rampersad, eds. *Slavery and the Literary Imagination.* Baltimore: Johns Hopkins University Press, 1989.

Olney, James. "I Was Born: Slave Narratives, Their Status as Autobiography and as Literature." *Callaloo* 20 (winter 1984): 46–73.

Pierce, Yolanda. *Hell without Fires: Slavery, Christianity, and the Antebellum Spiritual Narrative.* Gainesville: University Press of Florida, 2005.

Raboteau, Albert J. *Slave Religion: The "Invisible Institution" in the Antebellum South.* New York: Oxford University Press, 1978.

Sekora, John. "Black Message/White Envelope: Genre, Authenticity, and Authority in the Antebellum Slave Narrative." *Callaloo* 32 (summer 1987): 482–515.

Yolanda Pierce

SLAVE REBELLIONS

Slave rebellions in the United States will probably always be impossible to enumerate exactly for the period 1820 to 1870. Slave owners tried whenever possible to conceal the uprisings and their extent, both to deter other slaves and to maintain, for northerners' benefit, the "happy plantation" myth. It is even difficult to define exactly what constituted such a rebellion. For example, the historian Herbert Aptheker's definition of slave insurrection requires a minimum involvement of ten slaves, freedom as their objective, and contemporaneous references to the incident as a seditious event; according to this definition he finds approximately 250 rebellions to have taken place (p. 162). Other scholars argue that this figure is inflated, or they employ different definitions, according to which one must then claim that many additional rebellions on a much smaller scale

took place. Two things were clear: slaves lived in a state of constant restiveness, and the happy plantation was indeed a myth.

Resistance to slavery took many forms. Some slaves rebelled on an individual basis and ran north, sometimes with spouses or other family members. Despite the iconic status of Harriet Tubman (c. 1820–1913), the Underground Railroad's most famous escapee and conductor, the vast majority of these fugitives were men. Women and men alike, however, engaged in smaller, everyday acts of rebellion calculated to destabilize and infuriate, such as petty theft, arson, strikes, and temporary truancy. For some indeed, the truancy was more than temporary, as communities of runaway slaves, often allied with Native Americans, established themselves in then-obscure regions (such as Virginia's Great Dismal Swamp or the Florida Everglades) within slave states. When survival made it necessary, they conducted raids, sometimes violent, on white settlements. These fugitives, known as "outlyers" or maroons, lived in a kind of tenuous freedom within slavery that was common in the Caribbean, whence the term "maroon" originates.

INFLUENCE OF HAITI ON EARLY-NINETEENTH-CENTURY U.S. SLAVERY

The Caribbean in fact had recently been the site of an event that profoundly affected the way both slaves and slaveholders in the United States came to view their "peculiar institution." Between 1791 and 1803 a massive rebellion in Saint-Domingue (now Haiti) had brought about the rise of the black leaders Toussaint L'Ouverture (c. 1743–1803) and Jean-Jacques Dessalines (c. 1758–1806) followed by the overthrow of slavery and the declaration of Haiti's independence as a black republic. Not surprisingly the success of this revolt (itself spurred by the French Revolution) horrified U.S. slave owners and brought hope to their slaves, despite attempts by southern authorities to suppress the news. Almost immediately, as the nineteenth century began, the revolutionary fervor seemed to have spread to U.S. slaves: in 1800 a potential rebellion in Virginia led by Gabriel Prosser (c. 1776–1800) was betrayed but if effected could have involved as many as a thousand slaves, all prepared to use violence if necessary. After Haiti's rebellion, such U.S. slave rebellions were increasingly aimed, as the historian Eugene D. Genovese puts it, "not at secession from the dominant society but at joining it on equal terms" (*From Rebellion to Revolution*, p. xx). Haiti had raised the potential stakes. As many scholars note, however, there were still far fewer rebellions in the United States than in the Caribbean and Latin America for various reasons, including the relative

***Blow for Blow,* c. 1863.** Lithograph by H. L. Stephens, from a series of cards depicting aspects of slavery. THE LIBRARY OF CONGRESS

black-white ratio, the difference between owners' absenteeism and paternalism as methods of control, and the availability of arms.

The Haitian revolution, followed so soon by Prosser's conspiracy and the general concept of chattel property demanding societal equality and freedom, alarmed slave owners into adopting the self-defeating pattern of repression that they would enforce ever more harshly after subsequent rebellions. Slaves' freedom of movement and assembly were further restricted; the Fugitive Slave Law was reworked and tightened; by 1850 literacy was forbidden to slaves in every southern state, to prevent the transmission of notions of freedom; free blacks were "encouraged" to leave their states, and preferably the South, lest they give

ideas to the unfree; the American Colonization Society, established in 1816, attempted to remove the free black population to Liberia.

DENMARK VESEY

Such constantly reinforced repressive measures almost guaranteed that slaves would continue to rebel. The next major insurrection was that organized by Denmark Vesey (c. 1767–1822) in Charleston, South Carolina, in 1822. Vesey himself was free, having bought his freedom with lottery winnings. For him, a deeply religious man, the incitement of slave insurrection was largely a matter of principle, and like many of his successors, he invoked the Founding Fathers, appealing to the rights of man. His plan relied on secrecy, with a small group of lieutenants—none of whom knew the plot in its entirety—responsible for recruitment. Jack Pritchard, known as Gullah Jack, was responsible for recruiting maroons, for instance; Peter Poyas, a capable organizer, was Vesey's deputy. There was no difficulty in enlisting recruits, especially as rumors were circulating that the 1821 Missouri Compromise debate in Congress had ended by making all the slaves free, and it was also the beginning of a decade when the African American population was rapidly increasing and the economy as a whole weakening. Although the total number of recruits ascribed to Vesey may have included many slaves whose eventual participation the leaders merely assumed, nevertheless as many as nine thousand slaves are said finally to have been involved in what the abolitionist Thomas Wentworth Higginson (1823–1911) described as "the most elaborate insurrectionary project ever formed by American slaves" (p. 107).

The uprising was first scheduled for July 1822 (on the French revolutionary holiday Bastille Day, as Genovese points out) with the apparent aim of taking Charleston by force, then sailing to freedom in the Caribbean. Betrayal by a house slave caused the date to be advanced, but then additional betrayal led to the revelation of the plot, the arrest of more than three hundred people, including free blacks, and the hanging of Vesey and his lieutenants. Yet their plan had come so close to fruition that Charleston and the South in general remained for some time in a state of terror, which was followed by a new wave of repression. In this case repression included the outlawing in South Carolina of the African Methodist Episcopal Church, which had been regarded with suspicion since its founding: any place that encouraged slave assembly was suspect, but the fact that the legislature took the extreme measure of banning the church entirely underlines the increasingly important part that religion was playing in slave rebellions.

DAVID WALKER AND NAT TURNER

This religious factor was clear in one of the most influential texts of the abolitionist movement, David Walker's (1785–1830) *Walker's Appeal, in Four Articles: Together with a Preamble, to the Coloured Citizens of the World, but in Particular, and Very Expressly, to Those of the United States of America, September 28, 1829,* usually known as *Walker's Appeal.* This militant work written by a free black warned of God's vengeance if slavery was not ended, invoked the Declaration of Independence and the rights of man, denounced plans for colonization, and called upon people of color to take their fate into their own hands. *Walker's Appeal* was widely disseminated throughout the country and was viewed with alarm even by major northern abolitionists, such as William Lloyd Garrison (1805–1879). Its incendiary ideas spread among slaves, even those who were unable to read it, and although there is no known direct link between *Walker's Appeal* and the most successful and famous slave rebellion in U.S. history two years later, there is no doubt that *Walker's Appeal* helped to shape the spirit of the times and to foment all the smaller rebellions that continued unabated. It was in this turbulent context that Nat Turner's rebellion took place.

The slave Nat Turner (1800–1831) of Southampton County, Virginia, has been variously described as a prophet, a lunatic, a hero, and a religious fanatic; he was certainly a deeply religious man, who, like the Puritans before him, read the "signs" of the world. He interpreted them to mean that he was destined to lead his people in revolt, which he did in August 1831, relying like Vesey on a small number of initial associates. His strategy was to begin by killing all the white people at a series of farms, starting with his own home farm, and to gather followers along the way, with a view to taking the county seat of Jerusalem. By the height of the revolt, Turner had seventy to eighty followers, and approximately fifty-seven white people had been killed (although many historians and contemporary commentators alike, including Higginson, were at pains to point out that no rapes had been perpetrated). However, encounters with the local militia caused Turner's supporters to become disorganized, and they were all except Turner captured or killed the next day. Turner hid out in the immediate vicinity for two months until he was finally captured and executed. The whole of the South had been traumatized by Turner's insurrection, especially as it was better-documented than most, thanks to a series of jailhouse confessions dictated to and published by a local lawyer; the extent of the bloodshed was also unprecedented. The usual repressions followed, notably including restrictions on religious practices: Virginia law banned blacks, whether slave or free, from practicing religious observances without their white families. As Kenneth S. Greenberg notes, Nat Turner had "personified the threat of an independent African American religion" (Turner, *Confessions of Nat Turner,* p. 23).

Rebellions continued, however. John Brown's (1800–1859) raid on the arsenal at Harpers Ferry in 1859 (which included a number of African Americans among the insurgents) indicated that, right up to the eve of the Civil War, Americans of all races were willing to shed blood to end slavery and frequently did so out of a religious belief in a higher order of freedom. Although it is impossible to be sure when these rebellions finally ended, Herbert Aptheker lists an unfulfilled plot in Troy, Alabama, in 1864 as the last slave conspiracy in the United States. By this time slaves were also able to express resistance by joining the Union army.

SHIPBOARD REBELLIONS

Not all slave conspiracies took place on U.S. soil, however. Mutinies took place on ships carrying Africans destined to become slaves in the Americas or carrying slaves from one location to another. Often these

---

Nat Turner was for a time the most feared man in the South. This extract from the Norfolk Herald, *Norfolk, Virginia, for 4 November 1831 illustrates both slave owners' relief at recapturing Turner before his revolt escalated and their contempt that he should even contemplate seizing the personal freedom that they felt the Founding Fathers had clearly earmarked for white Americans only:*

He is said to be very free in his confessions, which, however, are no further important than as shewing that he was instigated by the wildest superstition and fanaticism, and was not connected with any organized plan of conspiracy beyond the circle of the few ignorant wretches whom he had seduced by his artifices to join him. He still pretends that he is a prophet, and relates a number of revelations which he says he has had, from which he was induced to believe that he could succeed in conquoring *the county of Southampton!* (what miserable ignorance!) as the white people did in the revolution.

Turner, *Confessions of Nat Turner,* pp. 88–89.

---

rebellions, like those on land, took the form of minor acts of individual resistance, although it was also not uncommon for a potential slave to commit suicide by deliberate self-starvation. The two most noteworthy organized mutinies of the period were those aboard the *Amistad* in 1839 and the *Creole* in 1841. The *Amistad* was a Spanish-owned ship bound for a port in Cuba when the slaves, Africans mostly from Mende, took over the ship under the leadership of Joseph Cinqué (c. 1814–c. 1879). It was eventually recaptured in August 1839 by U.S. forces made suspicious of what contemporaneous media accounts called "the Long, Low Black Schooner" by the fact that it appeared to be manned by armed black sailors. The ship was brought into port in Connecticut. The ensuing three trials made the case notorious, especially when former president John Quincy Adams (1767–1848) became involved, arguing for the Africans before the Supreme Court. They were finally freed after two and a half years on the grounds that the laws of Spain did not permit any legal property claims to the captives. The trials forced discussions of the legality of slavery and its role in international relations, making the Mendians valuable to the abolitionist cause.

The circumstances of the *Creole* rebellion, about which Frederick Douglass (1818–1895) wrote his only work of fiction, *The Heroic Slave* (1853), were different. The *Creole* was a U.S.–owned ship on its way from Richmond, Virginia, to New Orleans in November 1841, when the slaves—led by Madison Washington, a name whose evocation of the Founding Fathers Douglass emphasized—took over the ship. They sailed to British-controlled Nassau in the Bahamas, and Britain by then having outlawed the slave trade, they were ultimately released after initial detention. The case of the *Creole* was not nearly as celebrated as that of the *Amistad,* but it did cause diplomatic problems with Britain and provoked considerable comment in the press.

SLAVE REBELLIONS IN LITERATURE

Douglass's *The Heroic Slave* was, as the title perhaps suggests, basically a fictionalized general biography of Madison Washington, including other acts of rebellion, such as his flight to Canada in 1840 and his subsequent recapture when trying to rescue his wife; the account of the *Creole* mutiny is in fact the novel's climax. As a writer, though, Douglass was and is even more well-known for his autobiography recounting his own acts of rebellion and escape from slavery, published as *Narrative of the Life of Frederick Douglass, an American Slave, Written by Himself* in 1845, revised as *My Bondage and My Freedom* in 1855 and as *Life and Times of Frederick Douglass* in 1881 and 1892. The last part of the initial title is telling: many slaves told their stories of resistance and escape to white abolitionists, who shaped the accounts into an "as-told-to" format, but Douglass and Harriet Jacobs (1813–1897), author of *Incidents in the Life of a Slave Girl* (1861), were among the few to write their own stories in their own words. These nonfiction narratives were the form in which individual slave rebellions most often entered literature at this time, organized rebellions entering via newspapers; most fictional accounts emerged after the Civil War era. However, in 1853 the fugitive slave William Wells Brown (c. 1814–1884) published the first version of the novel then titled *Clotel; or, The President's Daughter: A Narrative of Slave Life in the United States*. This first African American novel deals with the flight from slavery of the title character and incorporates Nat Turner's rebellion, a veteran of which the heroine's daughter marries. Martin Robison Delany (1812–1885), whose family escaped slavery in 1822 and who became (among other achievements) a newspaper editor, a political activist, and an explorer, finally published his only novel in complete form in 1861–1862, although the ending is now lost. *Blake; or, the Huts of America* argues the necessity of militant slave resistance, taking a nationalist stance that envisions ultimate freedom in a free black Cuba. In this latter respect, it ironically uses many of David Walker's arguments to promote opposite viewpoints.

White American authors who addressed slave rebellions include Herman Melville (1819–1891), whose "Benito Cereno" (1856), another tale of shipboard slave mutiny, was based on the experiences of Captain Amasa Delano (1763–1823), who published his account in 1817. Delano had encountered a Spanish slave ship that the slaves had taken over, but the slaves forced the remaining Spanish crew to feign continued control for Delano's benefit. In Melville's hands, the story becomes a nuanced tale of subversion and imposture, which has led to considerable critical debate over whether it reinforces or undermines racial stereotypes and abolitionist positions. Critics have also frequently commented on the physical similarity of the Spanish ship in the tale (the *Tryal,* renamed by Melville the *San Dominick*) to the *Amistad*. Harriet Beecher Stowe's (1811–1896) best-selling *Uncle Tom's Cabin,* published serially in 1851 and 1852, addressed slave rebellion mostly in the form of the escape North of the light-skinned George and Eliza Harris and their son, with their imminent departure for Liberia forming the "happy ending." More controversial and much less popular was Stowe's next novel, *Dred: A Tale of the Great Dismal Swamp* (1856). The title character is the son of Denmark Vesey, whose story the novel incorporates; he is also based on Nat Turner and as such is described as resembling "one of the wild old warrior prophets of the heroic ages" (p. 241). An "intensely black" (p. 240), powerful, and passionate man, he and his form of rebellion, hiding out in the swamp, were inevitably found by readers to be much more unsettling than George Harris.

SCHOLARSHIP ON SLAVE REBELLIONS

Over the last fifty years of the twentieth century much scholarly work on slave rebellions, sometimes controversial in nature, appeared. Herbert Aptheker's *American Negro Slave Revolts*, which first appeared in 1943, was and still is an immensely useful resource, countering the earlier notion of the happy plantation full of contented slaves. Aptheker perhaps stresses the opposite position too strongly in fact. Other scholars have often accused him of exaggerating the extent of slave resistance, but his scholarship is nevertheless valuable. Also valuable is the work of Eugene D. Genovese, especially *From Rebellion to Revolution* (1979) and *Roll, Jordan, Roll* (1974), and earlier C. L. R. James's *The Black Jacobins: Toussaint L'Ouverture and the San Domingo Revolution* (1938). These historians situate U.S. slave revolts in the broader context of the Caribbean and Latin America. Their Marxist stance must be taken into account, as must Aptheker's, but the broad perspective is productive. Thomas Wentworth Higginson's collection of studies of slave rebellions, originally published in the *Atlantic Monthly* in the 1850s and 1860s, is the closest to being contemporaneous with the rebellions themselves and is based on primary sources. *The Slumbering Volcano: American Slave Ship Revolts and the Production of Rebellious Masculinity* by Maggie Montesinos Sale (1997) contains useful analysis of both mutinies and the rhetoric of mutiny. *Rebels against Slavery* by Patricia C. McKissack and Fredrick L. McKissack (1996) is an accurate, clearly written book for young adults that covers most aspects of slave rebellion and would also be a suitable introduction for the general reader.

See also Abolitionist Writing; *An Appeal in Favor of That Class of Americans Called Africans;* "Benito Cereno"; *Blake; Clotel;* Compromise of 1850 and Fugitive Slave Law; *The Confessions of Nat Turner;* Harpers Ferry; *Incidents in the Life of a Slave Girl; Narrative of the Life of Frederick Douglass;* Slave Narratives; Slavery

BIBLIOGRAPHY
Primary Works

Brown, William Wells. *Clotel; or, the President's Daughter.* 1853. In *Three Classic African-American Novels*, edited by William L. Andrews, pp. 71–283. New York: Mentor, 1990.

Delany, Martin Robison. *Blake; or, the Huts of America.* 1861–1862. Introduction by Floyd J. Miller. Boston: Beacon, 1970.

Douglass, Frederick. *Narrative of the Life of Frederick Douglass, an American Slave, Written by Himself.* 1845. Edited with an introduction by Houston A. Baker Jr. New York: Penguin, 1982.

Hendrick, George, and Willene Hendrick, eds. *Two Slave Rebellions at Sea.* New York: Brandywine, 2000. Contains commentary and the texts of "Benito Cereno," *The Heroic Slave*, and chapter 18 of *A Narrative of Voyages and Travels* by Amasa Delano.

Higginson, Thomas Wentworth. *Black Rebellion: Five Slave Revolts.* c. 1860. Introduction by James M. McPherson. New York: Da Capo, 1998. Republication of 1969 Arno edition, consisting of last five chapters of *Travellers and Outlaws.*

Jacobs, Harriet. *Incidents in the Life of a Slave Girl, Written by Herself.* 1861. Edited by Lydia Maria Child. Introduction by Jean Fagan Yellin. Cambridge, Mass.: Harvard University Press, 1987.

Stowe, Harriet Beecher. *Dred: A Tale of the Great Dismal Swamp.* 1856. 2 vols. Grosse Pointe, Mich.: Scholarly Press, 1968.

Stowe, Harriet Beecher. *Uncle Tom's Cabin.* 1852. Introduction by Alfred Kazin. New York: Knopf, 1995.

Turner, Nat. *The Confessions of Nat Turner and Related Documents.* Edited and with an introduction by Kenneth S. Greenberg. Boston: Bedford/St. Martin's, 1996.

Walker, David. *Walker's Appeal.* 1829. In *The Ideological Origins of Black Nationalism*, compiled by Sterling Stuckey, pp. 39–117. Boston: Beacon, 1972.

Secondary Works

Aptheker, Herbert. *American Negro Slave Revolts.* 1943. 50th anniversary edition. Foreword by John H. Bracey. New York: International, 1993.

Camp, Stephanie M. H. *Closer to Freedom: Enslaved Women and Everyday Resistance in the Plantation South.* Chapel Hill: University of North Carolina Press, 2004.

Genovese, Eugene D. *From Rebellion to Revolution: Afro-American Slave Revolts in the Making of the Modern World.* Baton Rouge: Louisiana State University Press, 1979.

Genovese, Eugene D. *Roll, Jordan, Roll: The World the Slaves Made.* New York: Pantheon, 1974.

James, C. L. R. *The Black Jacobins: Toussaint L'Ouverture and the San Domingo Revolution.* 1938. New York: Vintage, 1963.

McKissack, Patricia C., and Fredrick L. McKissack. *Rebels against Slavery: American Slave Revolts*. New York: Scholastic, 1996.

Sale, Maggie Montesinos. *The Slumbering Volcano: American Slave Ship Revolts and the Production of Rebellious Masculinity*. Durham, N.C.: Duke University Press, 1997.

Helen Lock

SLAVERY

The practice of forcing people to work without compensation can be traced to societies across the globe, and accounts of slavery can be found among the earliest writings and records from some of the oldest known civilizations. The Bible, the text that for millions of Americans is the sacred foundation of national principles, offers numerous allusions to slavery. The Old and New Testaments acknowledge master-and-slave relationships with a general proclivity of acceptance. Throughout the Old Testament the prevalence of slavery is evident through the numerous references to slaves and masters. Celebrated patriarchs such as Abraham, Moses, and Solomon held slaves. For Moses the rules of enslavement are in part divinely sanctioned. It is God who instructs Moses that servants who are bought must be circumcised before they can be accepted at the Passover meal (Exodus 12:43–44). God further instructs Moses that he can buy bonds men and bondswomen from among the heathens, but of his fellow Israelites who are poor, he can only hire them as servants—they cannot be bought as bondservants (Leviticus 25:39–46).

The pervasiveness of slavery in the Bible is a reminder that while slavery is almost universally proclaimed unjust and inhuman today, it has a long and somewhat remarkable history. While the Bible and Christianity served as the foundation of American abolitionist rhetoric, they just as readily served the rhetoric of proslavery advocates. Proponents of slavery frequently alluded to the New Testament call for servants to be obedient to their masters (Titus 2:9). These apparent biblical sanctions of slavery were cast against other scriptures cited by critics of slavery to show the un-Christian nature of the practice. However, reminders of Christ's call to treat others as you would have them treat you (Matthew 7:12) or the proclamations in the Old and New Testaments of God's deliverance of the meek did little to disturb the convictions of proslavery advocates. In addition to the ambiguous contribution of religion to the reading of slavery in America, the classical civilizations that influenced American thought further clouded this discussion. While ancient Greek and Roman societies were the foundation of neoclassical notions of civilization that informed colonial American thought, the Greeks and Romans also sanctioned slavery while they concurrently espoused high ideals about citizenship and the human spirit.

With the practices and ideals of the ancient world as their guide, early Americans created and negotiated a world of contrasting realities. One was the reality of a post–Revolutionary War call to guarantee liberty and equal rights for citizens of the new nation; the other was the reality of a social and legal system that relegated slaves (who by the close of the eighteenth century were overwhelmingly black) to bondage and exploitation. The master-slave dichotomy that emerged in America was, at least in its form, not unlike the hierarchy Moses outlined in Leviticus: those who were among the chosen or privileged were protected from bondage, but those who ranked among the outsiders (blacks in the case of American society, heathens in the case of Moses' society) were candidates for bondage. The social hierarchy that emerged out of American slavery was reminiscent of the caste societies in numerous slaveholding civilizations; however, in America the centrality of race and the generational nature of slavery produced a system of bondage unparalleled in its time for longevity and for its brutal legacy.

In ancient civilizations of the Middle East, the Far East, and Africa as well as Greece and Rome, slavery was commonly the consequence suffered by prisoners of war, convicted criminals, and victims of personal and political disputes. The enslaved could find themselves relegated to any number of duties, including work as house servants, concubines, soldiers, and laborers. While the enslaved in the ancient world and in the Middle Ages were usually condemned to life-long servitude, in general their plight was not transgenerational. In fact, in some instances slaves were educated and could serve as tutors and teachers or, as in the case of the ancient Roman playwright Terence, could become celebrated and revered members of society. Slavery in America was different, however. American slavery did not begin as a race-based caste system, but by the close of the seventeenth century Native Americans and whites were no longer good candidates for the long-term, labor-intensive needs of plantation owners. Given their darker skin and their alienation, Africans proved better suited to the planters' labor needs. With their contrasting physical appearance and the absence of kinship or community roots in the New World, enslaved Africans could not easily escape. Moreover, with laws that decreed slavery

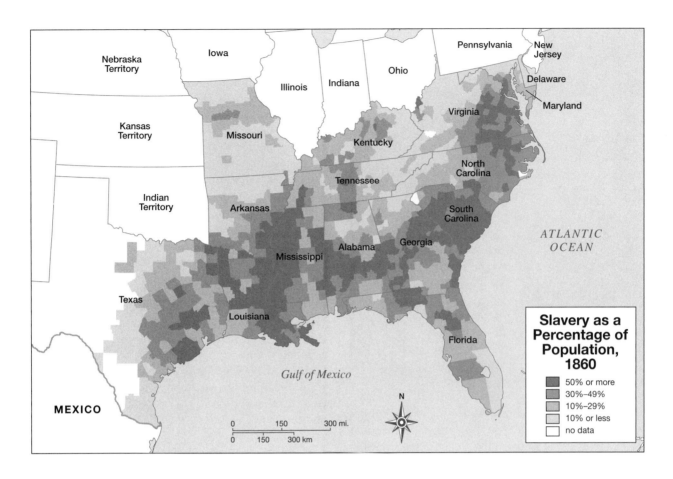

Nebraska Territory

Iowa

Pennsylvania

New Jersey

Kansas Territory

Illinois

Indiana

Ohio

Delaware

Maryland

Missouri

Kentucky

Virginia

Indian Territory

Arkansas

Tennessee

North Carolina

South Carolina

Texas

Mississippi

Alabama

Georgia

ATLANTIC OCEAN

Louisiana

Florida

Gulf of Mexico

N

MEXICO

0   150   300 mi.
0   150   300 km

Slavery as a Percentage of Population, 1860

50% or more
30%–49%
10%–29%
10% or less
no data

a lifetime condition that was passed on to offspring, black slaves became a regenerating source of free workers for America's plantations.

TRANSATLANTIC SLAVE TRADE AND RACIALIZED SLAVERY

The transatlantic slave trade did not mark the birth of slavery on the African continent or the removal of enslaved Africans to distant places. Arab traders predated their Iberian trade rivals by centuries in the trafficking of Africans. When the Portuguese and Spanish began transporting blacks to Europe as slaves in the 1500s, Arabs had been exporting African slaves across the Sahara for centuries. Up to this point these dealings in African slave trading resembled those that took place throughout Africa, Europe, and the Middle East. Slaves were the product of various circumstances, and they varied in ethnicity and skin color. Arabs did not limit their trade to dark-skinned Africans, for example, and at varying times they enslaved and traded people from Africa to Europe to Asia.

On the African continent slavery was commonplace. Among sub-Saharan Africans the enslaved were often the products of war. In contrast to the slave system that emerged in the Americas, slavery here was not an agricultural chattel system instituted to maintain plantation estates. It was not based on skin color, and its effect was not generational; indeed, the offspring of these slaves were not cast into slavery and in many instances the slaves were integrated into the family and community. With the influx of Portuguese traders along the west coast of Africa in the 1500s and the succeeding centuries of western trade and colonization on the continent, African slavery became the wellspring of horrors for those in Africa as well as those forced to make the transatlantic voyage. Those enslaved on the continent faced the ever-increasing threat of being thrown into the transatlantic slave market. As the demand for laborers escalated in the Americas, the chances increased dramatically for those enslaved in Africa to become cargo on one of the many voyages between Africa and the Americas.

The transatlantic slave trade fueled the slave market in Africa and the removal of millions from Africa to the Americas, a centuries-long human ill maintained in order to answer the labor needs of white planters in the New World. The United States was not the leading agent in the trafficking of Africans;

Slaves aboard the ship *Wildfire*. Illustration from *Harper's Weekly,* 2 June 1860. The importation of slaves had been declared illegal in the United States in 1808, but the practice nevertheless continued. The slave ship pictured here was intercepted and the African captives set free. THE LIBRARY OF CONGRESS

however, slavery in America grew into a major economic and social system. By the dawn of the nineteenth century the economy of the southern states, and thus that of the nation, was rooted in the agricultural system of chattel labor. The economic health of plantations rested in the right of planters to hold fellow humans without their consent and to demand their labor without paying them wages. This tenuous master-slave relationship informed the emergence of American society in both the North and the South. In the South, most blacks were enslaved and most worked as agricultural laborers. While they lived in close proximity to their masters and other whites, legal and social codes relegated blacks to outcast status. In general, whites did not recognize blacks as having fundamental human rights and needs and presumed that they did not have the intellectual and moral capacity to comprehend the motives and actions of their white enslavers.

Though slavery had ended in the North by the 1820s, the experience of northern free blacks was not overwhelmingly better than that of their southern counterparts. At the conclusion of the colonists' fight for independence there were free blacks able to trace their ancestry back to several generations of free blacks. This, however, left them no more secure than those freed blacks of less impressive ancestry, nor did it distinguish them significantly from first-generation slaves or their offspring. Free blacks had the burden of proving they were free; they were excluded from long-standing and meaningful employment; and in the North and South, they faced restrictions in housing and education. Whether free in the North or the South, blacks in the United States suffered the effects of a slave system that created a monolithic identity of blackness and whiteness. Whiteness signaled freedom and privilege, while blackness marked the opposite; whether slave or free, the place of blacks in American society grew out of this black-white dichotomy. Free blacks faced constant reminders that their freedom was limited: from laws that restricted their movement, that excluded them from legal protection and privileges, and that often against reality gave them their identity, free blacks understood well that their status was simply a step above those in bondage. In America, slavery and blackness were considered one and the same.

AMERICAN SLAVERY: THE MAKING OF AN UNEASY SOCIETY

While the authors of the Constitution proclaimed the new nation a united one, the issue of slavery was a point of divisiveness from the start. From the removal of Thomas Jefferson's criticism of British participation in the slave trade in his early draft of the Declaration of Independence to the North-South compromise of determining legislative representation (agreement to give slaves a three-fifths count in state population tallies), northern and southern interests were not one on the issue of slavery. Moreover, with objections to slavery articulated by Quakers and free blacks long before colonists declared themselves the United States, abolitionism was bound to become a powerful political and social force. With their outpouring of appeals to the public as well as the support that many offered the Underground Railroad, antislavery proponents made a long-lasting, peaceful compromise impossible.

In general, the very presence of free blacks further heightened the uneasy existence of slavery in America. In a society that equated slavery to blackness, the presence of a free black—and oftentimes vocal—population threatened constructed boundaries of place and identity. How could slaves be made to be content with their lot when free blacks served as a constant and real reminder that blackness did not mean one was

Picking cotton on a Georgia plantation. Wood engraving from *Ballou's Pictorial Drawing Room Companion,* 1858. During the 1850s, newspaper coverage of slavery helped increase public awareness of the issue, but it was not until southern states began to threaten succession that northern publications voiced strong support for the abolitionist position. THE LIBRARY OF CONGRESS

inherently destined or suited only for servitude? This circumstance also fueled a fear of slaves that would provoke many masters to treat slaves in ways unimaginably harsh. Slavery served to highlight the distinct divide between rhetoric and reality in America's national identity. The Founding Fathers' proclamations of a hardworking, ambitious, and self-made American citizenry clashed severely with the aristocratic picture of wealthy white planters whose fortunes were derived from the involuntary labor of blacks. It was difficult to distinguish between the wealthy gentry of Britain and their planter counterparts in America. The freedom, liberty, and inalienable rights claimed with such conviction by the Founding Fathers was notably denied to slaves, and it was this blatant hypocrisy that nineteenth-century black writers would repeatedly highlight in their works.

SLAVERY, AMERICANNESS, AND LITERATURE

An ever-present reminder of America's inhumanity and hypocrisy, slavery has haunted the imaginations of American writers from pre-Revolutionary days to the present. The musings of early writers and thinkers—black, Native American, and white—on the subject of slavery informed the discourse on slavery in the nineteenth century. In poetry, letters, diaries, short stories, biographies, folktales, and essays, slavery was repeatedly a subject of reflection and contention, and in politics it marked America's continued struggle to negotiate the differences between rhetoric and reality. With the dawn of Jacksonian democracy in the election of 1828, Andrew Jackson's claims of allegiance to democratic principles and work ethics once again highlighted the exclusion of slaves and Native Americans from these noble ideals. Touting himself as a common man and a representative of the masses, Jackson was a popular two-term (1829–1837) president. A slave owner himself, however, Jackson supported the slaveholding interests of the wealthy and powerful circle in which he lived.

Today the most widely read and celebrated nineteenth-century writings on slavery are those that highlighted the evils of the institution. There is little readership, even in institutions of higher learning, for nineteenth-century proslavery writings. Modern readers should remember, however, that antislavery publications were a response not only to the practice of slavery but also to the denigrating representations of blacks in books, magazines, and newspapers. E. N. Elliott's 1860 collection of essays *Cotton Is King, and Pro-Slavery Arguments* was among numerous such proslavery publications. In works such as Elliott's, blacks were regularly represented as docile, content, childlike beings content with their lot. Plantation owners were often depicted as paternal figures who provided the slaves the necessary material provisions for daily living. Many essayists, poets, and fiction writers represented slavery as an innocuous oddity in American life, and many others were simply silent on this practice. Silence could have been the result of any number of factors. Some authors may have decided that the muddied logistics of slavery threatened the distinct division of good and evil they hoped to portray; for others, slavery and slaves were simply topics that did not warrant artistic or philosophical introspection. The inattentiveness to slavery in some northern writings may have been informed by the lack of physical proximity. Distance often insulates communities from practices and ideals they might find unacceptable, thereby leaving their thinkers and artists free to focus on more regional or abstract matters. For many New England writers, however, the geographical distance between New England and the South was not enough to lull them into silence.

In addition to the persistent spirit of abolitionism in early-nineteenth-century America, the active and vocal free black community in the North helped to keep slavery at the forefront of social and moral discourse. Early in their history as slaves in the New World, blacks passed on orally their stories of enslavement, and some, who were either literate or worked through transcribers, were able to have their experiences written. These accounts of slaves and former slaves became known as slave narratives. The most celebrated of these works was Frederick Douglass's (1818–1895) *Narrative of the Life of Frederick Douglass* (1845). Douglass's personal account became the hallmark abolitionist publication, but it was by no means the first. Although few in number, manuscripts and publications of slave accounts dating back to colonial America demonstrate the early efforts of blacks to give voice and history to their experiences. The length of these documents varies from a few pages to a few hundred pages. In a few cases these written voices were not in English but in the Arabic language that some slaves spoke and wrote.

By the beginning of the nineteenth century blacks were writing and publishing poetry, narratives, and speeches, demonstrating their capacity for literacy and their understanding of its importance. It was not until 1827, however, that the first African American newspaper was founded. *Freedom's Journal* was a significant accomplishment and contribution to the future of African American activism. In contrast to the individual emphasis of single-authored works, a newspaper made possible the publication of multiple voices and experiences and provided an additional medium to disseminate news and information throughout black communities. *Freedom's Journal* was born as Jacksonian democracy began its rise; it represented the determination of blacks to have a voice in a world and under a leadership that continued to deny their humanity.

In 1829 the black activist David Walker published *Walker's Appeal*, a tract that simultaneously called on enslaved blacks to rise up against slavery and answered the rising democratic rhetoric among whites of this era. Organized in four articles with a preamble, *Walker's Appeal* instantly called to mind the U.S. Constitution. Walker placed particular emphasis on answering Thomas Jefferson's published denunciations of blacks and his speculations on their humanness. He challenged Jefferson's allegedly objective observations and charged that, on the contrary, as arbiters of a democracy that was not catholic in practice, Jefferson and America's Founding Fathers compromised their own constructs of white civility and humanity. Walker reminded his readers of America's failure to live up to its proclamations of liberty and freedom. Like the Founding Fathers who called for revolution against the tyrant mother country, Walker called on his brethren in bondage to rebel. In the same year of Walker's riotous tract, the less fiery George Moses Horton (c. 1798–c. 1880), a slave poet of North Carolina, composed "On Liberty and Slavery." While absent the revolutionary call found in *Walker's Appeal,* Horton's poem nevertheless suggests that the slave's appeal is connected to a fundamental constitutional ideal. In six of ten stanzas Horton identifies liberty at the core of the slave's yearning. It is "Dear Liberty" that will come and free him from bondage and open the door to opportunity.

In the midst of black voices indicting America for its hypocrisy and Jacksonians singing the praises of their liberty-granting nation, a circle of northern white women activists emerged. These women merged their interests in women's rights and abolitionism and became a formidable force in the fight against slavery. While New England's leading writer and public intellectual, Ralph Waldo Emerson (1803–1882), did not at first appear especially inclined to

GANG OF 25 SEA ISLAND
COTTON AND RICE NEGROES,
By LOUIS D. DE SAUSSURE.

On *THURSDAY* the 25th Sept., 1852, at 11 o'clock, A.M., will be sold at RYAN'S MART, in Chalmers Street, in the City of Charleston,

A prime gang of 25 Negroes, accustomed to the culture of Sea Island Cotton and Rice.

CONDITIONS. — One-half Cash, balance by Bond, bearing interest from day of sale, payable in one and two years, to be secured by a mortgage of the negroes and approved personal security. Purchasers to pay for papers.

No.	Age.	Capacity.	No.	Age.	Capacity.
1 Aleck,	33	Carpenter.	16 Hannah,	60	Cook.
2 Mary Ann,	31	Field hand, prime.	17 Cudjoe,	22	Prime field hand.
3—3 Louisa,	10		3—18 Nancy,	20	Prime field hand, sister of Cudjoe.
4 Abram,	25	Prime field hand.	19 Hannah,	34	Prime field hand.
5 Judy,	24	Prime field hand.	20 James,	13	Slight defect in knee from a broken leg.
6 Carolina,	5		21 Richard,	9	
7 Simon,	1½		22 Thomas,	6	
5—8 Daphne, infant.			5—23 John,	3	
9 Daniel,	45	Field hand, not prime.			
10 Phillis,	32	Field hand.	1—24 Squash,	40	Prime field hand.
11 Will,	9				
12 Daniel,	6		1—25 Thomas,	28	Prime field hand.
13 Margaret,	4				
14 Delia	2				
7—15 Hannah,	2 months.				

Broadside advertisement for a slave auction. The image is part of the Broadsides Collection of the Emergence of Advertising in America website, http://scriptorium.lib.duke.edu/eaa/.

encourage public criticism of slavery, many of his female counterparts thrust themselves into the debate with little constraint. Four years prior to "The American Scholar" (1837), Emerson's now celebrated address before a Cambridge audience, his fellow New Englander Lydia Maria Child (1802–1880) published *An Appeal in Favor of That Class of Americans Called Africans* (1833). In this pamphlet Child did not simply appeal to her audience's Christian sensibilities; more provocatively, she proclaimed the equality of blacks and indicted fellow northern whites for their part in an institution that defied fundamental principles of Americanness. Child maintained that with their systematic denial of citizenship rights to blacks in the North, northern whites were no less unprincipled than southern planters. The denial of citizenship rights to blacks in the North reified denigrating perceptions of them that validated proslavery propaganda.

Child was among the more radical of her circle; nevertheless, appeals from numerous New England women activists would follow. Among these were Angelina Grimké's 1836 pamphlet *Appeal to the Christian Women of the South* and, more than a decade later, Harriet Beecher Stowe's *Uncle Tom's Cabin* (1851–1852), the fictional appeal that Abraham Lincoln lauded for garnering northern sentiment for the slaves. The abolitionist enthusiasm of his female contemporaries did not take root in Emerson, whose most celebrated works failed to address the more pressing and controversial issues of his day. In his hallmark meditations on the American self, "The American Scholar" and "Self-Reliance" (1841), Emerson criticized Americans for their failure to distinguish themselves from their former tyrants (British) and from the stifling ways and ideas of the Old World (Europe). He called on Americans to find their own way, search their own hearts, to discover what was uniquely American. He argued that the core of the American self was that individual who explored his own soul, his own mind, and then, by his own labor, brought his visions to reality. While Emerson chided Americans for their dependence on Europeans for their understanding and vision, he ignored one of America's most pervasive and striking practices of dependency. Slavery, the dependence on the forced labor of others for the realization of one's vision, was a glaring contradiction to self reliance. In the two works that would become his signature treatise on Americanness, however, Emerson was remarkably silent on this matter.

While many of his female contemporaries in 1830s and 1840s New England were outspoken abolitionists, Emerson's public addresses that touched on the issue of slavery were for the most part guarded and indirect. In this respect, Emerson's celebrated transcendentalist contemporary Henry David Thoreau (1817–1862) offered a more resonant abolitionist voice. Among his numerous antislavery tracts, Thoreau's "Slavery in Massachusetts" (1854) and "Resistance to Civil Government" (1849; often referred to by the title "Civil Disobedience") highlight his strict criticisms of America for its participation in and support of what he deemed an innately undemocratic and uncivilized institution. Among Emerson's other celebrated literary contemporaries, however, the critique of slavery was mute at best. The New Englander Nathaniel Hawthorne and the southerner Edgar Allan Poe were not abolitionist sympathizers. While there are critics of Herman Melville's "Benito Cereno" (1856) who argue that it is a criticism of the transnational evil into which slav-

ery had grown, the story's ending leaves an ambiguous read at best. The world is restored to white order with the slaves horrifically put to death. While the Spanish captain, Benito Cereno, has been disturbed to the point of self-imposed isolation, his American counterpart, Captain Delano, seems especially relieved that his world has been reclaimed. Were the slaves justified in their insurrection and killing of the Spanish captain, or were their acts simply the manifestation of their nature? Melville offers no certain answer, thereby leaving proponents of slavery a handy and often used anecdote about black-white violent encounters.

Walt Whitman (1819–1892), the self-proclaimed bard of Emerson's call for a unique American poetics, answered Emerson in 1855 with the publication of *Leaves of Grass*. Whitman's work was not an abolitionist endeavor, but his poetic portrait on the diversity of the American self included blacks as equals among God's great human creations. Whitman does not make explicit antislavery appeals; however, in lines 183–192 of "Song of Myself," Whitman's narrator recalls his encounter with a runaway slave. Undoubtedly the narrator's offer of refuge to the runaway stood out for many readers in the mid-1800s. Whitman's suggestion of the rightness of such an act was not an uncontroversial stand. The Fugitive Slave Law of 1850 had created a greater rift between northerners and southerners. The enactment of this law affirmed the right of southerners to pursue and apprehend runaway slaves in free states. Whitman's passing tale of an offer of refuge to a runaway highlighted the sentiment of many abolitionists who disregarded the law and continued to assist runaways.

By the mid-1800s slavery's most important literary legacy was the slave narrative. Published slave narratives in antebellum America became almost formulaic: the story told was the narrator's journey from slavery to freedom, and this outer layer of narrative usually consisted of additional narrative layers. This could include the narrator's concurrent spiritual narrative, the narrator's journey from intellectual darkness to enlightenment, or the narrator's bildungsroman. Although preceded and followed by numerous others, Douglass's 1845 *Narrative* has remained one of the most recognized works in American literature. Perhaps part of *Narrative*'s popular appeal for its early white readership was its recognizable form. Readers were more easily drawn in because his was the story of a male slave: this offered the convenience of avoiding the more delicate and distasteful details of sexual exploitation that might surface in the accounts of female slaves. *Incidents in the Life of a Slave Girl* (1861), Harriet

Jacobs's (1813–1897) autobiographical account of enslavement, highlights the alienation awarded black women narrators who failed to gloss over this slave experience. Unlike Douglass, who simply offered speculation that his father was his master, Jacobs recorded with some detail her familial connection to whites of respectable ancestry. Moreover, Douglass's tale ends in marriage to a black woman, so that even if his father was white, his marriage confirms his place among blacks. Jacobs's story does not end in marriage, but it does conclude with Jacobs as mother of two illegitimate children, fathered by her white lover—a well-respected member of the community.

Rebecca Harding Davis's (1831–1910) short novel *Life in the Iron Mills* (1861) exemplifies the entrenched place of slavery in the American psyche. In this story of immigrant mill workers in West Virginia, Davis painted the picture of their despairing and exploited lives by drawing parallels to chattel slavery. The mill workers are white and free, but Davis wanted to show that their victimization bore uncomfortable resemblances to that of slaves in the south. Davis set her tale in a slave-bordering state, reminding readers of the close proximity between those who were supposedly white and free to those who were black and enslaved. With descriptions of the environment and the immigrants that also inspire images of slavery and the enslaved, Davis challenged America's noble claims of liberty and opportunity for its citizens. If whites were being relegated to conditions that almost collapsed their identity into blackness/servitude, what was the future of Americanness and the American dream? Davis's pondering was not singular, nor was it confined to an isolated historical moment. Many white authors of her time would ask this question through their works, and many after have continued to cast questions about white identity and privilege against the backdrop of American slavery and its legacy.

See also Abolitionist Writing; *An Appeal in Favor of that Class of Americans Called Africans; Incidents in the Life of a Slave Girl; Life in the Iron Mills; Narrative of the Life of Frederick Douglass;* Proslavery Writing; Slave Narratives; Slave Rebellions; *Uncle Tom's Cabin*

BIBLIOGRAPHY
Secondary Works

Bennett, Lerone Jr. *Before the Mayflower: A History of Black America.* 6th ed. Chicago: Johnson, 1987.

Braxton, Joanne M. *Black Women Writing Autobiography: A Tradition within a Tradition.* Philadelphia: Temple University Press, 1989.

Bruce, Dickson D., Jr. *The Origins of African American Literature, 1680–1865.* Charlottesville: University Press of Virginia, 2001.

Conniff, Michael L., and Thomas J. Davis. *Africans in the Americas: A History of the Black Diaspora.* New York: St. Martin's, 1994.

Dillon, Merton L. *Slavery Attacked: Southern Slaves and Their Allies, 1619–1865.* Baton Rouge: Louisiana State University Press, 1990.

Diouf, Sylviane A. *Servants of Allah: African Muslims Enslaved in the Americas.* New York: New York University Press, 1998.

Eltis, David. *The Rise of African Slavery in the Americas: The English in Comparative Perspective.* New York: Cambridge University Press, 1999.

Franklin, John Hope, and Alfred A. Moss, Jr. *From Slavery to Freedom: A History of Negro Americans.* 6th ed. New York: McGraw-Hill, 1988.

Genovese, Eugene D. *Roll, Jordan, Roll: The World the Slaves Made.* New York: Pantheon, 1974.

Gomez, Michael A. *Exchanging Our Country Marks: The Transformation of African Identities in the Colonial Antebellum South.* Chapel Hill: University of North Carolina Press, 1998.

Inikori, Joseph E. "Slavery in Africa and the Transatlantic Slave Trade." In *The African Diaspora,* edited by Alusine Jalloh and Stephen E. Maizlish, pp. 39–72. College Station: Texas A&M University Press, 1996.

Levine, Lawrence W. *Black Culture and Black Consciousness: Afro-American Folk Thought from Slavery to Freedom.* New York: Oxford University Press, 1978.

Meier, August, and Elliott M. Rudwick. *From Plantation to Ghetto.* New York: Hill and Wang, 1969.

Melish, Joanne Pope. *Disowning Slavery: Gradual Emancipation and "Race" in New England, 1780–1860.* Ithaca, N.Y.: Cornell University Press, 1998.

Morgan, Edmund S. *The Birth of the Republic 1763–1789.* 3rd ed. Chicago: University of Chicago Press, 1992.

Kolchin, Peter. *American Slavery 1619–1877.* New York: Hill and Wang, 1993.

Sanders, Ronald. *Lost Tribes and Promised Lands: The Origins of American Racism.* New York: HarperCollins, 1992.

Segal, Roland. *Islam's Black Slaves: The Other Black Diaspora.* New York: Farrar, Straus and Giroux, 2001.

Stamp, Kenneth M. *The Peculiar Institution: Slavery in the Antebellum South.* New York: Vintage, 1989.

Sundquist, Eric J. *To Wake the Nations: Race in the Making of American Literature.* Cambridge, Mass.: Harvard University Press, 1993.

Thornton, John K. "The African Experience of the '20 and Odd Negroes' Arriving in Virginia in 1619." *William and Mary Quarterly* 50, no. 3 (1998): 421–434.

Elizabeth J. West

SOCIOLOGY FOR THE SOUTH

By the 1850s southerners had been wrestling with the moral problem of slavery for a long time. In 1776 a southern slaveholder, Thomas Jefferson (1743–1826), had declared that all men were created equal; six years later, in his *Notes on the State of Virginia,* he contemplated the institution of slavery as practiced in his state, a brutal contradiction of that idea, and said "I tremble for my country when I reflect that God is just, that his justice cannot sleep forever" (p. 289). Many of his contemporaries eased their consciences by freeing their own slaves and devising plans for general emancipation. Later, when such plans came to seem unrealistic, their descendents turned to special pleading, trying to explain to themselves why southern slaves should be considered exceptions to the self-evident truths of the Declaration of Independence. By then Jefferson had summarized these truths in a single proposition: "the mass of mankind has not been born with saddles on their backs, nor a favored few booted and spurred, ready to ride them legitimately, by the grace of God" (p. 1517). Two generations of southerners spent their thinking lives caught between that ideal and the intransigent fact of slavery. So the effect was startling when, in a book published in 1854, another Virginian announced that "men are not 'born entitled to equal rights!' It would be far nearer the truth to say, 'that some were born with saddles on their backs, and others booted and spurred to ride them,'—and the riding does them good" (Fitzhugh, p. 179). Southerners knew they were seeing, as one reviewer of the book wrote, "something new under the sun" (*De Bow's Review* XIX, 1855).

FITZHUGH AND THE PROSLAVERY ARGUMENT

The Virginian was an obscure forty-eight-year-old lawyer named George Fitzhugh (1806–1881); the book was *Sociology for the South.* It was a polemical defense of slavery, one of many such published in the south between 1830 and the Civil War. This defense had become the main (though never the only) preoccupation of southern intellectuals during these years, and the project stimulated a remarkable flurry of thought and writing. By 1860 these thinkers had worked out their arguments thoroughly enough that a kind of canon of representative texts could be established in a thick

anthology entitled *Cotton Is King.* The book's editor, E. N. Elliott, made room for essays by political economists, social theorists, Bible scholars, and reputed experts in the new science of ethnology—but he made none for Fitzhugh, whose views were considered needlessly eccentric and extreme. Even a friendly reviewer of *Sociology for the South* warned that it was full of statements that must be taken with a grain of salt; a decidedly unfriendly reviewer, the abolitionist William Lloyd Garrison (1805–1879), called Fitzhugh "the Don Quixote of slavedom" (Wish, p. 200). Yet Garrison thought him important enough to be worth arguing with. So did his fellow abolitionist Wendell Phillips (1811–1884), who publicly debated the Virginian, and so did Abraham Lincoln (1809–1865), who borrowed one of his most famous statements, that the nation could not endure half slave and half free, from an unsigned editorial written by Fitzhugh. Many recent scholars have agreed with these northern foes, treating Fitzhugh as among the most important proslavery thinkers, perhaps the clearest spokesman for what one of them, the historian Eugene Genovese, has called "the slaveholders' philosophy" (p. v).

Fitzhugh called such attention to himself by being more radical and uncompromising, and also more philosophically abstract, than almost any other southern defender of slavery. He was never content to mark off southern slavery as a "peculiar institution," a singular exception to the rule of liberty and equality. Fitzhugh insisted that, far from being "peculiar," southern slavery was the current manifestation of a universal, immemorial, natural, and benevolent idea, the only humane relationship possible between weak people and strong ones. Liberty and equality were the historical anomalies, bizarre and destructive aberrations in social thought, coined only recently (during the Enlightenment) and already on their way to extinction.

THE FAILURE OF FREE SOCIETY

Thus Fitzhugh gave his tract the subtitle "The Failure of Free Society." By that term he meant democratic capitalism, founded on the idea of the private, autonomous individual. Fitzhugh believed that this individual was in effect a fictional character created by John Locke (1632–1704), and therefore the founding idea of free society was false. Fitzhugh also believed that the economy set in motion by this theory, a system of unrestrained competition, was inevitably destructive, turning neighbors into enemies and society into a field of warfare, and inevitably ending with the strong crushing the weak. And he thought that he had discerned the shape of "free society's" history and could see that it was coming to an end right before his eyes. "The ink was hardly dry," he observed, "with which Adam Smith wrote his *Wealth of Nations,* lauding the benign influences of free society, ere the hunger and want and nakedness of that society engendered a revolutionary explosion that shook the world to its centre" (pp. 39–40).

The explosion in Paris in 1789 was not the last one; as recently as 1848 Europe had once more been shaken by political revolution, a shock wave Fitzhugh traced to its source in the continuing collapse of free society. The northern section of the United States was hardly better off; its cities were crowded with the desperate poor, victims of a heartless industrial order, and its academies and lyceums thronged with crazed reformers—socialists, Fourierists (followers of the French social theorist Charles Fourier), agrarians, and others—whose very existence was proof of a society on its last legs. But the American South, he maintained, was a different story: "Whilst all this hubbub and confusion is going on in France and England, occasioned by the intensest suffering of the free laborers, we of the South . . . have been 'calm as a summer's evening,' quite unconscious of the storm brewing around us" (p. 65).

The reason for this southern exceptionalism, Fitzhugh proposed, was slavery. Unlike free laborers, who were helpless victims of the marketplace, "slaves never die of hunger; seldom suffer want" (p. 48). The free laborer was bound to his employer only by a temporary contract; he could be fired as soon as he ceased to be useful. The slave, however, was the permanent responsibility of his master, who was bound by law and morality to care for him, or else to sell him to someone who could. Therefore the slave, "when night comes, may lie down in peace. He has a master to watch over and take care of him" (p. 167). "It is domestic slavery alone," Fitzhugh concluded, "that can establish a safe, efficient and humane community of property. It did so in ancient times, it did so in feudal times, and does so now, in Eastern Europe, Asia and America" (pp. 47–48). He in fact understood southern slavery as a latter-day incarnation of the feudal system, in which lords and serfs were bound to each other by unbreakable ties of mutual obligation. The displacement of that humane system by "free society" was for him a historical catastrophe from which the Western world was still reeling.

THE CRITIQUE OF CAPITALISM

Now "free society" in the North and Europe had its own social critics, who had identified many of the same problems that Fitzhugh noted and had offered their own solutions. Fitzhugh prided himself on his knowledge of these advanced thinkers—Charles Fourier (1772–1837), the French emperor Louis-Napoleon (1808–1873), the English novelist Charles Kingsley (1819–1875), and many others—whom he tended to lump together under the label "socialist." He never cited his contemporary Karl Marx (1818–1883), but the two breathed the same intellectual air during their formative years, and it is important to recognize that Marx's world, the world of European radicalism, was the one that fascinated Fitzhugh.

Although he was a conservative, Fitzhugh wanted a voice in that radical conversation, and although he was a provincial Virginian who had rarely left his home state, he felt entitled to one. For he and his neighbors, he believed, had all but unwittingly solved the problems that vexed those thinkers. "Slavery is a form, and the very best form, of socialism," he explained, and "a well-conducted farm in the South a model of associated labor that Fourier might envy" (pp. 27–28, 45). "Socialism proposes to do away with free competition; to afford protection and support at all times to the laboring class; to bring about, at least, a qualified community of property, and to associate labor. All these purposes, slavery fully and perfectly attains" (p. 48). "Toward slavery," therefore, "the North and all Western Europe are unconsciously marching" (p. 45). Previous apologists for southern institutions had worried that the region was straggling in civilization's march to modernity. Fitzhugh's novel claim was that it had simply and prophetically struck out in a more promising direction, where the rest of the world must eventually follow. The task of *Sociology for the South*—and Fitzhugh was among the first Americans to employ that neologism, or to try practicing the science it named—was to make southerners aware of their own wisdom, to raise their unconscious habits to the level of doctrine.

Such is Fitzhugh's argument in a nutshell. Perhaps not surprisingly, it has been treated ever since 1854 with both interest and dismay. Southerners, accustomed to thinking of themselves as the heirs of Jefferson and Washington, were puzzled to learn that they were actually the peers of Fourier and Louis Napoleon. Abolitionists, comfortable as the enlightened critics of a backward region, were nonplussed at finding the tables turned. Neither group knew quite what to make of Fitzhugh and subsequent readers have not had much more luck. To many he has seemed an anomaly, an inexplicable throwback to the age of throne and altar, set down in democratic, capitalist America. But Fitzhugh was recognizably a man of his own time and place, an antebellum American writer.

In his critique of the marketplace Fitzhugh harmonized with a chorus of better-known contemporaries: with Nathaniel Hawthorne (1804–1864), who noted that "In this republican country, amid the fluctuating waves of our social life, somebody is always at the drowning point" (*The House of the Seven Gables*, pp. 383–384), and with Henry David Thoreau (1817–1862), who in *Walden* (another book of 1854), argued that Americans lived in "quiet desperation" (p. 329) because they blindly accepted a flawed political economy. He might have envied Thoreau the quip that under capitalism, "if some have the pleasure of riding on a rail, others have the misfortune to be ridden upon" (*Walden*, p. 396) and he would have applauded Ralph Waldo Emerson's remark that modern capitalists, though lacking a feudal lord's power of life and death over his laborers, would nonetheless "in all love and peace eat them up as before" ("Historic Notes on Life and Letters in New England"). And when Fitzhugh claimed that slavery was sustained not by force but by an emotion called "domestic affection," when he insisted that the southerner was in fact "the Negro's friend, his only friend," he positioned his book within a vast nineteenth-century literature idealizing home, hearth, and family as havens in a heartless, capitalist world (pp. 105–108, p. 95). It would not be far-fetched to say that *Sociology for the South* sentimentalized slavery just as *Uncle Tom's Cabin*, two years before, had sentimentalized abolition.

The Civil War of course rendered all Fitzhugh's arguments moot and cost him his audience. Although he may have cared more about presenting his general social vision than about preserving southern slavery (he was a lawyer, not a planter, and owned few slaves himself), it was the defense of that institution that gave him his pulpit; abolition took it away. When he died in 1881 he left no true intellectual heirs in the south or elsewhere. He was too intellectually isolated to have made disciples and too eccentric to have found kindred spirits. If his ideas lived on after his death, it was in the person of a fictional character, Basil Ransom, the protagonist of Henry James's 1886 novel *The Bostonians*. A southerner living like a fish out of water in postbellum New York, a gleeful reactionary, a lover of the Middle Ages, a hater of the triumphant capitalist world around him, and an eloquent defender of community, hierarchy, and order, Ransom must have been inspired by Fitzhugh's tracts. But James makes him a hopeless and nearly helpless anachronism, irrelevant to the bustling world around him, and treats him with a mixture of pity and amusement. Fitzhugh's actual fate was a little kinder; he was briefly acknowledged in his own time, and continues to be in ours, at least as the most articulate and quotable spokesman for ideas that deserved to lose, and did.

See also Ethnology; *The Impending Crisis of the South;* Labor; Proslavery Writing; Slavery

BIBLIOGRAPHY
Primary Works
Elliott, E. N. *Cotton Is King, and Pro-Slavery Arguments.* Augusta, Ga.: Pritchard, Abbott & Loomis, 1860.

Emerson, Ralph Waldo. "Historic Notes on Life and Letters in New England," in *The Complete Works of Ralph Waldo Emerson*, vol. 10, *Lectures and Biographical Sketches.* Boston: Houghton Mifflin, 1911.

Fitzhugh, George. *Sociology for the South; or, the Failure of Free Society.* Richmond, Va.: A. Morris, 1854.

Hawthorne, Nathaniel. *Novels.* New York: Library of America, 1983.

Jefferson, Thomas. *Writings.* New York: Library of America, 1984.

Thoreau, Henry David. *Walden.* 1854. New York: Library of America, 1985.

Secondary Works
Genovese, Eugene D. *The World the Slaveholders Made: Two Essays in Interpretation.* New York: Pantheon Books, 1969.

Gilmore, Michael T. *American Romanticism and the Marketplace.* Chicago: University of Chicago Press, 1985.

Grammer, John M. *Pastoral and Politics in the Old South.* Baton Rouge: Louisiana State University Press, 1996.

O'Brien, Michael. *Conjectures of Order: Intellectual Life and the American South, 1810–1860.* Chapel Hill: University of North Carolina Press, 2004.

Wish, Harvey. *George Fitzhugh, Propagandist of the Old South.* Baton Rouge: Louisiana State University Press, 1943.

John M. Grammer

SOME ADVENTURES OF CAPTAIN SIMON SUGGS

A classic of the genre that critics label southwestern or frontier humor, *Some Adventures of Captain Simon Suggs* recounts the antics of a confidence man with the motto "IT IS GOOD TO BE SHIFTY IN A NEW COUNTRY." Although its thirty-year-old author Johnson Jones Hooper (1815–1862) was a newspaper editor and lawyer in the village of Lafayette, Alabama, all of the book's printings issued from northern presses that offered paperbound books for the popular market. Suggs's *Adventures* appeared over a dozen times between its first publication in 1845 and the end of the Civil War in 1865. It never earned the author much money, but it gained a widespread reputation for him and the fictional Captain Suggs.

Simon Suggs was an early American example of a familiar type: the scoundrel who evokes more laughter than scorn. Defying law and convention, he lives by his wits in a society where nothing is settled. At a time when the American future seemed unbounded, Hooper's humor played upon people's hopes for the best and fears about the worst. It also captured, in exaggerated form, the anxious optimism of migrants like the author, a well-born North Carolinian who had moved to Alabama in 1837 to make a name for himself in the newer part of the South.

In some respects Suggs's *Adventures* built upon the foundation of Augustus Baldwin Longstreet's *Georgia Scenes,* an 1835 collection of stories often identified as the first important work of southwestern humor. Longstreet, Hooper, and other humorists often recounted their stories of rough characters from the perspective of an educated narrator. This mix of high and low reflected their experiences in a peripatetic fraternity of lawyers and journalists that roamed the rural South—working, drinking, gambling, and swapping tall tales to relieve the pressures of their scrambles to get ahead in the world. The narrative frame of the gentlemanly observer appears everywhere in southern writing, from ubiquitous newspaper tales to stories by the South's most prolific author, William Gilmore Simms. While it owed something to European literary forms, it gained vitality from oral practice in the United States, and it was an important step in the evolution of distinctive nineteenth-century American styles.

NARRATIVE FORM AND LANGUAGE

Some Adventures of Captain Simon Suggs contributed to this evolution. Although Hooper uses an educated narrator, he subverts the gentleman and makes the charlatan Suggs the center of his book. In the opening pages the unidentified narrator announces that his purpose is to write a campaign biography of Captain Suggs, a candidate for local office. It quickly becomes obvious that the candidate is a fraud. The narrator describes Suggs's "adventures" as he roams Alabama in search of profit, and Suggs's cleverness, energy, and enthusiasm dominate the accounts. The narrator quotes Suggs soliloquizing about his intentions, talking his victims into cunning traps, and pronouncing the (im)moral lessons of his swindles. As the books ends, the relationships among the narrator, the Captain, and the author become hopelessly entangled when a long letter from Suggs, which constitutes most

Simon Suggs. Frontispiece illustration from the first edition. COURTESY OF JOHANNA SHIELDS

of the last chapter, effectively becomes the narrative. Suggs addresses his biographer as Johns Hooper, "eeditur of the eest Allybammyun'" referring to Hooper's *East Alabamian* (p. 141). Suggs praises the episodes that had already appeared, in fact, in the New York periodical *Spirit of the Times,* and he negotiates with Johns about which exploits will appear in the full-length biography (actually, the one in the reader's hands). With these shifting perspectives, Hooper thoroughly obscured the line between truth and fiction. In the process he created an original example of comic realism and further moved southwestern fiction away from conventional forms.

Hooper's use of language further widened the distance between the literary tradition American writers inherited and the one they were making. Language in the *Adventures* fills its usual role as a marker for social class; however, it has other purposes. The narrator's inflated speech helps discredit him. Suggs's earthy language conveys his keen mother wit. And throughout the book, exaggerated language makes all of the confidence games seem funny rather than criminal. Hooper's parody works because he had a remarkable ear for the rhythms in spoken language: the slimy posturing of a

Tensions between town and country have always been part of American experience. Although Simon Suggs lived in rural eastern Alabama, he makes visits elsewhere, and the following scene shows him at the state's capital in Tuscaloosa. He is there to make a run at Faro—variously called the "Tiger" or the "beast"—the one game he usually loses. In the opening to this episode, the narrator spoofs the civilized life of towns from the perspective of the backwoodsman Suggs. Whigs like Johnson Hooper thought that the lower classes did not properly appreciate education, and his ideas are reflected here in Suggs's words. It is also true, however, that Hooper was fond of drinking and that he never attended college, so the humor has a double edge. The narrator speaks first, describing Suggs's entry into the town.

As he hurried along . . . with the long stride of the back-woods, hardly turning his head, and to all appearance, oblivious altogether of things external, he held occasional "confabs" with himself in regard to the usual objects which surrounded him—for Suggs is an observant man, and notes with much accuracy whatever comes before him. . . . On the present occasion, his communings with himself commenced opposite the window of the drug-store,—"Well, thar's the most deffrunt speerits in *that grocery* ever *I* seed! That's koniac, and old peach, and rectified, and lots I can't tell thar names! That light-yaller bottle tho'; in the corner thar, that's Tennes*see*! I'd know that *any whar*! And that tother bottle's rot-gut, ef I know myself—bit a drink, I reckon, as well's the rest! What

a power o' likker they do keep in this here town; ef I warn't goin' to run against the bank, I'd sample some of it, too, I reether expect. But it don't do for a man to speerets much when he's pursuin' the beast—"

"H-ll and scissors! Who ever seed the like of the books! Aint thar a pile! Do wonder what sort of a office them fellers in thar keeps, makes 'em want so many! They don't read 'em *all*, I judge! Well, mother-wit kin beat book-larnin, at *any* game! . . . Human natur' and the human family is *my* books, and I've never seed many but what I could hold my own with. . . . As old Jed'diah [his father] used to say, book larnin spiles a man ef he's got mother-wit,, and ef he aint got that, it don't do him no good—."

Hooper, *Some Adventures of Captain Simon Suggs*, pp. 52–53.

banker feeding at the public trough, the stern admonitions of a stupid parent, the obsequious fawning of ambitious young men, and above all, the rhetorical flourish of the editor and the vulgar performances of Simon Suggs. To create the overall rhythm of his work, Hooper constantly set one form of language against another with the voices of Johns and Suggs dominant and other voices interspersed. Through skillful manipulation of the many rhythms he heard, Hooper gave the *Adventures* another kind of American reality.

Hooper's achievement can readily be seen in "The Captain Attends a Camp-Meeting," perhaps the most outrageous of Suggs's adventures. The narrator sets up the story by relating Suggs's need for cash and introducing a backwoods revival to meet his need; then the action begins, conveyed mostly through dialogue. A preacher displays a convert, saying: "I tuk him, fust in the Old Testament—bless the Lord!—and I argyed him all thro' Kings—then I throwed him into Proverbs.—and from that, here we had it up and down, kleer down to the New Testament" (p. 121). A woman falls down in ecstasy, shouting "Glo-o-*ree*!" Watching it all, Suggs sizes up his prey:

"Well now," said he, as he observed the full-faced brother who was "officiating" among the women, "that ere feller takes *my* eye! thar's he's been this half-hour, a-figurin amongst them galls, and's never said the fust word to nobody else. Wonder what's the reason these here preachers never hugs up the old, ugly women? Never seed one do it in my life—the sperrit never moves 'em that way! It's nater tho'. . . . Nater will be nater, all the world over, and I judge ef I was a preacher, I should save the purtiest souls fust, myself!" (Pp. 120–123)

Armed with this insight, Suggs captivates the congregation by faking a conversion, complete with tears, acrobatics, and sexual imagery. The onlookers' credulity sets up the real scam, when Suggs gathers the customary offering by cleverly exploiting the status anxieties of his listeners: "ef you aint able to afford anything, jist give us your blessin' and it'll be all the same!" (p. 130). Of course he shortly absconds, depriving the lusty preachers of their usual cash returns. Many years later, Mark Twain would adapt this story for an episode in the career of his con men the King and the Duke in *Adventures of Huckleberry Finn*.

THEMES

Some Adventures of Captain Simon Suggs was distinctly southern in its setting, characters, and oblique defense of slavery. However, its themes reveal more about the similar values of northerners and southerners in 1845 than about their differences. It is impossible to say precisely which themes resonated with what people, but the evidence suggests that the book had a national audience. Moreover, the themes of ruthless individualism, excesses of capitalism, and commercialization of politics still ring true in modern popular culture.

According to the French observer Alexis de Tocqueville, Americans were the most individualistic people in the civilized world, and Hooper thoroughly satirizes that trait. In spite of their own individualism, many educated Americans worried that freedom might unleash selfish forces, and Hooper constantly plays upon the resulting ambivalence. Johns jokingly portrays Suggs as a predatory animal, claiming that if nature "made him, in respect to his moral conformation, a beast of prey, she did not refine the cruelty by denying him the fangs and claws" (p. 13). Extreme individualism—something like the law of the jungle—reigns in Suggs's Alabama, a fictional extension of American life.

Americans were also ambivalent about the excesses of capitalism, as people prone to self-interested behavior nonetheless fretted about reckless speculation, especially when others did it. The humor in the *Adventures* plays upon this tension too, for many of Suggs's scams concern the marketplace. Details about wildcat banking, land frauds, and similar ventures may escape modern readers, but anyone living under a capitalist system will recognize its underside as a prominent feature in the *Adventures*.

The commercialization of politics was still new and frightening in the 1840s. On an unprecedented scale, the two major parties used patronage to reward their loyal supporters, dispensing the spoils of victory—government jobs and contracts—as if they were private property. Modern readers may miss some of the Whig editor Hooper's shots at the Democratic Party and its founder Andrew Jackson. For example, the book's narrator is likened to Amos Kendall, Jackson's biographer, and Suggs earns the rank of captain in a phony war set near the site of Jackson's 1814 defeat of the Creek Indians at Horseshoe Bend. By 1840 Whigs had skillfully adapted Democratic tactics. Hooper's book was more than a partisan critique. It satirized the selling of a candidate, a practice that was becoming thoroughly American.

While modern readers may respond sympathetically to the satires of individualism, capitalism, and democracy in the *Adventures*, they are not likely to appreciate its humor about inequality—prejudices of class, race, and gender that scholars have identified everywhere. Hooper used derogatory stereotypes about backwoods people, African Americans, Native Americans, and women, suggesting that while slavery was southern, racism and other forms of prejudice were national. However, Hooper did not aim his satire only at the downtrodden. Suggs's favorite targets are white southern males, the people a wandering rascal might really meet and those most likely to put cash in his pockets.

Indeed, Suggs cons people of all classes because he sees their "soft spots," the kinds of flaws that, in Hooper's skeptical view, belong to human nature. The deepest theme in the *Adventures* provides a kind of existential affirmation: despite their flaws, people can know themselves and share, through laughter, their mutual humanity. Although he is a scoundrel, Suggs is not truly evil, for he constantly unmasks the pretenses through which people hide their flaws. In that way he embodies a perverse kind of justice. It is likely that Hooper hoped Americans would moderate their individualism, tame capitalism, and reform democracy. It is clear, though, that he intended for people not only to laugh at Suggs and his kind but also to laugh at human nature, including what they saw in themselves.

CRITICAL RECEPTION

Since its first publication in 1845, *Some Adventures of Captain Simon Suggs* has had a mixed reputation. While some readers appreciated its liveliness and originality, many asserted that such crude writing was acceptable for men only. In any case, most contemporary critics paid popular American humor little attention. The literary qualities of works like Hooper's first gained widespread critical attention in the 1930s. Although critics variously described such writing as simply funny, praised its masculinity, or equated it with the adventurous spirit of the frontier—appraisals that seemed naive by the century's end—they also recognized the creativity of its authors. By the mid-twentieth century, critical attention began to shift, especially with the appearance of Kenneth Lynn's influential work *Mark Twain and Southwestern Humor*. Since then critics have echoed Lynn's claims that the humorists' use of vernacular language and some of their themes influenced Twain, and they have added evidence about influences upon Herman Melville and William Faulkner.

In the late twentieth century, as interest in popular culture grew, more literary theory seeped into discussions of southwestern humor, but mixed responses continued. Some theoretical critics see Hooper's book as a subtle example of bourgeois social control; others find pre-bourgeois patterns of carnival in this and other humor about commoners; and still others suggest that Suggs's nihilistic ethos anticipates the universal anomie of modern life. In his important study, *Fetching the Old Southwest: Humorous Writing from Longstreet to Twain*, James Justus has demonstrated the relationship between Suggs's fictional world and the modernizing impulses of nineteenth-century America, suggesting how a full-scale reappraisal of Hooper's book might reflect theoretical interpretations when they are appropriately contextualized. Substantially modifying Lynn's earlier assertion that the humorists separated themselves from their environment, Justus places Suggs and his fellow southwesterners securely in the American cultural tradition.

Literary theory and historical context must be combined to understand popular texts like the *Adventures*, for successful humor rests not only an artful text but on values so embedded in readers that laughter seems spontaneous. As long as some readers find it funny, Hooper's work affirms continuities in the American experience—continuities rooted, for better and for worse, in persisting traits of human nature itself.

See also Borders; Confidence Men; Humor; Tall Tales

BIBLIOGRAPHY

Primary Work

Hooper, Johnson Jones. *Some Adventures of Captain Simon Suggs, Late of the Tallapoosa Volunteers; Together with "Taking the Census" and Other Alabama Sketches.* 1845. Introduction by Johanna Nicol Shields. Tuscaloosa and London: University of Alabama Press, 1993.

Secondary Works

Beidler, Philip D. *First Books: The Printed Word and Cultural Formation in Early Alabama.* Tuscaloosa and London: University of Alabama Press, 1999.

Hoole, William Stanley. *Alias Simon Suggs: The Life and Times of Johnson Jones Hooper.* University: University of Alabama Press, 1952. Dated and marred by the author's sympathies for the Confederate States of America but more detailed than any other biographical treatment.

Justus, James H. *Fetching the Old Southwest: Humorous Writing from Longstreet to Twain.* Columbia: University of Missouri Press, 2004.

Lenz, William E. *Fast Talk and Flush Times: The Confidence Man as a Literary Convention.* Columbia: University of Missouri Press, 1985.

Lynn, Kenneth S. *Mark Twain and Southwestern Humor.* Boston: Little, Brown, 1959.

Morris, Christopher. "Southern Humorists and the Market Revolution." In *Southern Writers and Their Worlds,* edited by Christopher Morris and Stephen G. Reinhardt. College Station: Texas A&M University Press, 1996.

Reynolds, David S. *Beneath the American Renaissance: The Subversive Imagination in the Age of Emerson and Melville.* New York: Knopf, 1988.

Shields, Johanna Nicol. "A Sadder Simon Suggs: Freedom and Slavery in the Humor of Johnson Hooper." In *The Humor of the Old South,* edited by M. Thomas Inge and Edward J. Piacentino. Lexington: University of Kentucky Press, 2001. First published in *Journal of Southern History* 56 (November 1990): 641–664.

Somers, Paul, Jr. *Johnson J. Hooper.* Boston: Twayne, 1994.

Johanna Nicol Shields

THE SONG OF HIAWATHA

"Sanborn brought me your good gift of Hiawatha," wrote Ralph Waldo Emerson (1803–1882) on 25 November 1855 to Henry Wadsworth Longfellow. He had not been able to finish it before yesterday, he admitted, but then he knew that a book by Longfellow one could dip into whenever one wanted. No need to rush the reading experience: "I have always one foremost satisfaction in reading your books that I am safe—I am in variously skilful hands but first of all they are safe hands." *Too* safe, perhaps? Emerson claimed he had enjoyed the book his friend Franklin Sanborn had so kindly delivered to him. He found it, as he said, redundantly, "very wholesome, sweet & wholesome as maize very proper & pertinent to us to read." However, what bothered him about Longfellow's American Indian poem, was, well, the *Indian* part of it: "The dangers of the Indians are, that they are really savage, have poor small sterile heads,—no thoughts, & you must deal very roundly with them" and not as lovingly as Longfellow had. "I blamed your tenderness now & then, as I read, in accepting a legend or a song, when they had so little to give" (*Letters*, p. 386).

It is useful to remember that Emerson, the icon of anti-establishment thought in mid-nineteenth century America, found *The Song of Hiawatha*, now regarded as the epitome of nineteenth-century conventionality and sentimentalism and as a covert endorsement of Native American removal, too provocative because apparently too sympathetically "Indian." A strange claim when one considers that Longfellow himself had not had much personal exposure to Native Americans. In October 1837, when he had just begun his appointment as the new Professor of Modern Languages at Harvard University, he witnessed a gathering of a dozen Sauk and Fox Indians, who had come to Boston to attend a peace conference. They visited City Hall, performed some war dances on the Common, and then went to see a performance by Edwin Forrest at the Tremont Temple, where they unsettled the audience by letting out a war whoop when one of the characters fell dying. The Fox and Sauk impressed Longfellow: "one carries a great war-club, and wears horns on his head," he told his sister-in-law back in Portland, "another has his face painted like a gridiron, all in bars: —another is all red, like a lobster; and another black and blue, in great daubs of paint, laid on not sparingly" (*Letters* 2:45). These "hard customers," as Longfellow called them, were so visibly different from the white Anglo-Saxon norm, and yet, as Longfellow also noticed, one of them, make-up and all, was puffing a cigar!

In the late 1840s Longfellow was frequently seen around town with the Ojibwa chief Kah-ge-ga-gah-bowh or George Copway, a Christian convert and a "good-looking young man" (S. Longfellow 2:145), who gave Longfellow his autobiography, *The Life, History, and Travels of Kah-ge-ga-gah-bowh (George Copway)* (1847). On 27 January 1851, in a particularly poignant moment, he took Copway to the Armory Hall in Boston, where the poet and Native American chief both admired the new sculpture *The Wounded Indian* by Peter Stephenson (1823–1861), one of the key artistic expressions of the popular belief that "savage" native America was destined to vanish. In his journal, Longfellow misrepresented the name of Stephenson's sculpture as "The Dying Indian," a slip that speaks to what many consider one of the primary themes of the poem Longfellow was to write a few years later. *The Wounded Indian* catapulted Stephenson to fame, increased the number of his commissions, and allowed him to open his own studio. Likewise, *The Song of Hiawatha*, which ended with the native protagonist drifting off compliantly and resignedly into a "fiery sunset" (*The Song of Hiawatha*, p. 159), yielded royalties of over $7,000 in its first ten years and helped Longfellow, who had sent his letter of resignation to the Harvard Corporation on 16 February 1854, to secure his new position as a professional popular poet.

On the poem's official publication date, 10 November 1855, 4,000 of the 5,000 copies printed had already been sold, and a new edition of 3,000 was already underway. Interestingly, Whitman's *Leaves of Grass* had appeared on 4 July the same year, with a print run of just 795 copies, only a few of which were actually sold (Loving, p. 213).

In time, steamships were named after Longfellow's Native American protagonists; "Hiawatha pencils," or sleighs decorated with scenes from the poem, became

Henry Wadsworth Longfellow. © BETTMANN/CORBIS

available for purchase; and a New York bar served a Hiawatha drink, which promised "to make the imbiber fancy himself in the happy hunting grounds" (Moyne, "Parodies of Longfellow," p. 94). No wonder that Lawrence Buell, one of the poet's most sympathetic modern readers, called *Hiawatha* "a pleasant-anthropological tour de force but nothing more" (Buell, p. xxix).

SOURCES FOR *HIAWATHA*

Longfellow began working on a poem about the Ojibwa trickster-hero Manabozho in late June 1854, just a few weeks after two hundred guards had marched the convicted fugitive slave Anthony Burns through streets lined with shocked onlookers, beneath windows darkly draped in mourning and a black coffin labeled "Liberty" suspended from ropes, to the ship that would return him to Virginia. The event appalled and disgusted Longfellow: "Hung be the Heavens with black!" he wrote in his diary (26 May 1854). But Longfellow saw himself as a healer, not as a political agitator. The same month, he happened to be reading *Kalevala* by Elias Lönnrot (1802–1884), a collection of the songs sung by the peasants of northern Finland, which the author hoped would be understood as the belated Finnish answer to the *Iliad* or the *Edda*, a thought that must have seemed attractive to Longfellow as he was looking for a subject as well as a form that would address and alleviate the crisis of a nation rent apart by the issue of slavery. On 22 June 1854, he wrote in his journal:

> I have at length hit upon a plan for a poem on the Indians that seems to be the right one, and the only. It is to weave together their beautiful traditions into a whole. I have hit upon a measure, too, which I think is the right and only one for such a theme.

A few days later, he changed his protagonist's name to that of an Iroquois political leader Hiawatha (pronounced "Hee-a-wa-tha," as Longfellow insisted).

In his 22 June journal entry, Longfellow represents *The Song of Hiawatha* as an organic whole. But the finished product makes one think less of an intricately woven fabric than of something Longfellow's distant relative Ezra Pound (1885–1972) would later say about his own epic poem, *The Cantos,* namely that it was a "ragbag" stuffed with bits and scraps of whatever he found that seemed to belong there (Pound, p. 318). "This Indian Edda—if I may so call it," Longfellow wrote in the notes he added to his poem, "is founded upon a tradition prevalent among the North American Indians" (p. 161). But Longfellow goes far beyond mixing Norse poetry and Native American lore. The title of his poem alludes to the *Chanson de Roland* as well as to the beginning of the *Odyssey.* The magic mittens and enchanted moccasins of Longfellow's hero remind the reader of the seven-league boots and other magic gifts extended to the heroes of fairy tales, and his adventures ever so faintly resemble the labors of Hercules, the daring deeds of Beowulf, as well as the trials of Prometheus. Like many heroes of epic proportions, Hiawatha is the product of a god's rape of a mortal woman, and like many of them he goes into the underworld to prove his mettle, fighting the evil king of the serpents, Pearl-Feather, and spending time, like Jonah, inside the belly of a big sea creature—not a whale in this case, but a fish, the giant sturgeon Nahma. There are similarities between Hiawatha's courtship of Minnehaha, the beautiful girl from the hostile tribe of the Dakotahs, and the story of Romeo and Juliet, of course without the tragic outcome. His associates are the Hercules-like Kwasind and the beautiful Chibiabos, who, like Orpheus, teaches nature how to make music: "All the many sounds of nature / Borrowed sweetness from his singing" (p. 44).

In twenty-two cantos of varying length, Longfellow leads us through the life of his protagonist. He begins with Hiawatha's birth and childhood and then takes the reader through the various tests of his strength to which he subjects himself (a period of ritual fasting as well as battles with with his father, the evil

magician Pearl-Feather, and the unpredictable trickster Pau-Puk-Keewis). Several cantos detail Hiawatha's love for his friends and his wife Minnehaha. But Hiawatha's good work on behalf of his people (as described in Cantos XIII and XIV) cannot last: a period of famine ends with Minnehaha's death, and the final two cantos herald the inevitable arrival of the white colonizers. The plots Longfellow has cobbled together (an origin myth and a coming-of-age story at the beginning, a love story in the middle, and a version of King Arthur's departure from Camelot at the end) reinforce the unfavorable impression that *Hiawatha* is a hodgepodge of cultural references rather than a cohesive work of the poet's imagination.

Even the native "tradition" mentioned in Longfellow's notes is not a unified whole. Longfellow had in fact mixed a mythical story told by the Ojibwa but shared by several tribes—that of Manabozho, "a personage of miraculous birth, who was sent among them to clear their rivers, forests and fishing grounds, and to teach them the arts of peace" ("Notes," p. 161)—with other "curious legends," notably that of the legendary founder of the Iroquois nation, Hiawatha. He had discovered these and other stories in the books of the Bureau of Indian Affairs officer and amateur ethnographer Henry Rowe Schoolcraft (1793–1864), "to whom the literary world is greatly indebted for his indefatigable zeal in rescuing from oblivion so much of the legendary lore of the Indians" (*The Song of Hiawatha,* p. 161). Margaret Fuller (1810–1850), for one, thought that Schoolcraft's retellings of Indian legends were seriously deficient, arguing in her *Summer on the Lakes, in 1843* (1844) that the "flimsy graces" and "bad taste" of his style had retained little of the "Spartan brevity and sinewy grasp of Indian speech" (p. 88). But Longfellow went ahead and sanitized the Manabozho myth even further.

Much of the fun of the legend derives from the native trickster's flouting of rules and the unpredictability of his character. Manabozho is a "dirty fellow" and an "evil genius" (Schoolcraft 1:145, 165), a mere mortal as well as a supernatural being, never better and often worse than the people among whom he appears. Deception and suspicion play a prominent part in Schoolcraft's narrative, whereas Longfellow has carefully eliminated such duplicity from his version, notably the episode in which Hiawatha's grandmother Nokomis sleeps with a long-haired bear. Always "fond of novelty" (Schoolcraft 1:156), Schoolcraft's Manabozho has no mission except his own advantage: "He felt himself urged by the consciousness of his power to new trials of bravery, skill, and necromantic prowess" (1:154), whereas Longfellow's saintly Hiawatha thinks not about himself but "for profit of the people, / For advantage of the nations" (*The Song of Hiawatha*, p. 35). The one trickster figure left in Longfellow's poem is Hiawatha's antagonist, the "mischief-maker" Pau-Puk-Keewis, who assumes some of the original Manabozho's attributes, by transforming himself, for example, into the largest of beavers, just as Manabozho once asked to be turned into the largest of wolves. But Pau-Puk-Keewis is killed off in rather dramatic fashion: having his head beaten to a pulp and dropping from the sky like a malevolent Icarus, he ends up buried under a huge pile of sandstone.

LONGFELLOW'S POLITICAL PURPOSE

Hiawatha's altruistic nature defines Longfellow's political purpose in the poem. His intention was not to "tame" the savages but to integrate native themes and cultural references into the larger system of shared cultural meanings that, for him, was the business of American literature. None of Longfellow's readers in 1855 would have failed to perceive the importance of the first canto, where a multitude of native tribes from both the North and the West—separated not only by geography but also by "hereditary hatred" (*The Song of Hiawatha*, p. 7)—come together to hold a council meeting and listen to the prophecy of Gitche Manito, "the creator of the nations" (p. 7) that he will send them a prophet who will show them how to live together as brothers.

The messianic Hiawatha, a pacifist like his creator Longfellow, brings a golden age of happiness and peace to his people, teaching them, in the pivotal Canto XIV ("Picture-Writing"), how to remember their own past by drawing their ancestral totems on gravestones and how to transcribe their songs on reindeer skins. The most potent of these songs, "dangerous more than war or hunting," is, of course, the love song: "Naked lies your heart before me, / To your naked heart I whisper!" (p. 105). Significantly, for all his traditional heroic bravado, Hiawatha's own most intense emotional relationships in the book are with men, his beloved friend Chibiabos, who is brave as a man but also soft as a woman, and the strong man Kwasind, who has more brawn than brain: "Long they lived in peace together, / Spake with naked hearts together" (p. 47). Strikingly, the death of Chibiabos causes Hiawatha to moan and wail for "seven long weeks," whereas he spends only seven days and nights mourning the passing of his wife Minnehaha. Readers would also have noticed the sexual overtones of Hiawatha's ritual struggle with the golden-haired corn-god Mondamin, whose touch sends throbs of "new life and hope and vigor" (p. 37) through Hiawatha's body. After Mondamin's death, Hiawatha,

as if he were Mondamin's lover, makes a soft bed in the ground for his naked body, waiting for the maize to sprout from it. Minnehaha's father, the Old Arrowmaker, laments that the heroes of the olden days are gone—"Now the men were all like women, / Only used their tongues for weapons" (p. 70), a charge that also applies to Hiawatha, "the youth with flaunting feathers" (p. 73), who never misses the opportunity for a good speech.

Arguably, Hiawatha's sensitive or, put negatively, compliantly feminine side leaves him ill-prepared for the advent of the whites at the end of the poem, which is usually cited as an example of Longfellow's ideological blindness and his adherence to the popular stereotype of the "vanishing Indian." Indeed, Hiawatha's final vision seems to underwrite the notion of Manifest Destiny:

> I beheld the westward marches
> Of the unknown, crowded nations.
> All the land was full of people,
> Restless, struggling, toiling, striving,
> Speaking many tongues, yet feeling
> But one heart-beat in their bosoms
>
> (P. 152)

But then he also anticipates another, sadder westward movement, that of his own people scattered, dying, and deaf to all the counsel he has given them. "Weakened, warring with each other" they drift away, "like the withered leaves of Autumn" (p. 153). In Hiawatha's dream, unknown flowers appear to be springing up beneath the feet of the advancing colonists, "the White man's Foot in blossom" (p. 152). But most of Longfellow's readers would have known that this generous vision refers to a troublesome European weed, the broadleaf plantain, also known as the cart-track plant, examples of which Louis Agassiz had pointed out to Longfellow on an after-dinner walk on 13 December 1849. It does matter, too, that the whites that force Hiawatha to depart at the end of the poem are the "Black Robes"—Catholic priests—known, unlike the Puritans, for their normally more informed approach to native cultures. But in Longfellow's poem, they are struggling with Hiawatha's language: "And the Black-Robe chief made answer, / Stammered in his speech a little, / Speaking words yet unfamiliar . . ." (p. 156).

Longfellow's achievement in *The Song of Hiawatha* is precisely that he defamiliarizes the white world and forces his audience to enter the unfamiliar world of native culture, where humans swim like beavers, ghosts walk at night, the stars, glaring like the eyes of wolves, seem hungry, and snowflakes hiss among withered oak-leaves. The odd, monotonous trochaic meter of the poem (one stressed syllable followed by one unstressed syllable), whether or not it sounds to the reader like a primitive drumbeat, imposes a kind of barrier between the reader and the text, reminding her or him that while the landscape of the poem (the southern shore of Lake Superior, between Grand Sable Dunes and the Pictured Rocks) might be familiar, its original inhabitants are not. In the world of the Ojibwa, a squirrel is called "Adjidaumo," the grasshopper "Pah-puk-kee'na," and the robin "Ope'chee," while the blueberry is known as "Meenah'ga" and the spearmint as "Nah'ma-wusk"—all reminders that these creatures and plants are both the same as, and different from, the ones Longfellow's readers would have encountered in their own backyards and fields. Drenched with original Ojibwa phrases, *The Song of Hiawatha* often reads like the draft of a translation deliberately left unfinished, a text that is neither fully English nor really Native American.

Longfellow had his reasons for the cultural mish-mash he offered his readers. His "Indian Edda" (*The Song of Hiawatha*, p. 161), as diverse and disparate as its sources are, reflects a fairly coherent attempt to deconstruct conventional notions like authority, authorship, and cultural authenticity. Several times in the "Prologue" to the poem Longfellow's narrator imagines the question a reader would ask of him ("Should you ask me, whence these stories?" [p. 1]), only to refuse any information about his sources and to suggest that the very idea of an origin is ludicrous when applied to a text that essentially tells itself. Interestingly, Hiawatha himself, who has "neither father nor mother" (Schoolcraft 1:139), is driven by a desire to know more about his origins. He goes out to confront the "heartless" abuser Mudjekeewis, who raped and effectively killed his mother, on the "gusty summits" of the Rocky Mountains. The fight between father and son that now follows assumes mythic pro-portions—"the earth shook with the tumult and confusion of the battle, / And the air was full of shout-ings, / And the thunder of the mountains, / Starting, answered: 'Baim-wawa!'" (p. 31)—and ends only when Hiawatha has driven Mudjekeewis into a corner. Having exorcized the ghost his own father and asserted his self-sufficiency, Hiawatha can go on to be an effective leader of his people. He is no one's son and no one's father, neither a coward nor a patriarchal tyrant, but a friend and brother to his people, a fellow-sufferer and healer, a true shaman. Longfellow's nar-rator nowhere promises—as Whitman famously did at just about the same time—that one would only need to "stop" with him for a while to "possess the origin of all poems" (Whitman, p. 663). Instead, he wanted his poem to be like the "rude inscription[s]" (*The Song of Hiawatha*, p. 4) Hiawatha has taught his people to leave on their gravestones, a series of images left on the reader's mind: Hiawatha flanked by his two friends, the poet and the strong man; the nude Minnehaha, "unashamed and unaffrighted," dancing around the cornfield; the sun setting like a blood-red flamingo settling into her nest at nightfall (p. 31).

IMITATIONS AND PARODIES

Inevitably, a poem intended to convey the idea that it was shared cultural property rather than an author's individual creation spawned a number of imitations and parodies. An anecdote widely circulated at the time had a lover respond to a marriage proposal *Hiawatha*-style: "I will answer, I will tell you; I will have you, I will wed you" (Moyne, "Parodies of Longfellow," p. 95). Everyone these days, sighed Nathaniel Hawthorne in a letter to his publisher Ticknor, seemed to be "seized with an irresistible impulse to write verses in this new measure" (Moyne, "Parodies of Longfellow," p. 96). Parodying *Hia-watha* became an almost athletic challenge, and even Longfellow kept track himself of the many knockoffs, satirical and otherwise, his poem was generating. When his friend Charles Sumner sent him a parody titled "Miseh-Ko-da-sah," Longfellow recommended that he should read the much better one by Shirley Brooks that had just come out in *Punch*. Among the many satirical spin-offs with titles like *Milkanwatha*, *The Song of Drop o' Wather*, and *The Song of Higher-Water*, one stands out that seems less good-natured than the rest: *Plu-ri-bus-tah: A Song That's-By-No-Author* (1856). This is a bitter satire produced by a writer with a particularly unforgiving disposition, "Q. K. Philander Doesticks," a pseudonym for the *New York Tribune* journalist Mortimer Neal Thomson (1831–1875). In his defiant "Author's Apology," Doesticks declares that his main intent was to "break things" and, more specifically, to "slaughter the American Eagle, cut the throat of the Goddess of Liberty, annihilate the Yankee nation" (p. x). And that is exactly what his poem did: *Plu-ri-bus-tah* begins with the mighty Jupiter emitting thick clouds of smoke through his meerschaum pipe, an ironical allu-sion to the peace pipe smoked at the beginning of *Hiawatha*. The Indians are too busy to notice because they are attending a "Red republican mass-meeting," sponsored by Hiawatha, who has given out free tick-ets "over all the lakes and rivers" (p. 31). Meanwhile, their ruler, the goddess Miss America, is complaining to Jupiter that the pretty playthings he had given her, the cute Indians who had so entertainingly "shot, and killed, and scalped each other, / Roasted, broiled and

𝔜ᵉ 𝔟𝔢𝔯𝔶 𝔯𝔞𝔭𝔞𝔠𝔦𝔬𝔲𝔰 𝔜𝔢𝔫𝔯𝔶 𝔞𝔟𝔡𝔲𝔠𝔱𝔰 𝔶ᵉ 𝔖𝔞𝔩𝔟𝔞𝔤𝔢𝔰 𝔣𝔯𝔬𝔪 𝔶ᵉ 𝔇𝔦𝔰𝔠𝔬𝔫𝔰𝔬𝔩𝔞𝔱𝔢 𝔄𝔪𝔢𝔯𝔦𝔠𝔞.

"Ye very rapacious Henry abducts ye Salvages from ye Disconsolate America." Illustration from the satire *Plu-ri-bus-tah: A Song That's-By-No-Author*, 1856, by "Q. K. Philander Doesticks." COLLECTION OF CHRISTOPH IRMSCHER, BALTIMORE

stewed each other" (p. 34) have all been captured by "the poet Henry Wadsworth":

> He took all my Indian subjects,
> All my pretty, playful warriors,
> With their toys, the knife and war-club,
> With their pretty games of scalping
> . . . .
> Took them all to make a book of.
>
> *(P. 36)*

The silhouette drawing for the book by John McLenan (credited as "John M'Lenan") shows a tall, thin, spindly-legged figure with a long nose—a "long fellow" indeed—carrying away several miniature Indians with nose-rings while clutching a copy of *Hiawatha* under his left arm. In the background a screaming Miss America is raising her arms.

CONCLUSION

As his "Indian" trochees invaded the consciousness of the American reading public, Longfellow could be certain that at least one of his messages had been understood. *Hiawatha*, the "song that's by no author," had acquired multiple authors; it had become truly everybody's poem. To some extent, this is still true today. One of the more recent spoofs is *The Song of Hakawatha*, written by the pseudonymous F. X. Reid. *Hakawatha*, a computer hacker's irreverent take on Longfellow's melancholy Indian story, is said to have originated at the University of Glasgow in the early 1980s, but the lines, which closely imitate Longfellow's numbing rhythms, still speak to every computer user's experience today:

> First, he sat and faced at the console
> Faced the glowing, humming console
> Typed his login at the keyboard
> Typed his password (fourteen letters)
> Waited till the system answered
> Waited long and cursed its slowness
> (Oh that irritating slowness—
> Like a mollusc with lumbago) . . .

Less charitably inclined readers might contend that the number of *Hiawatha* parodies proves how hopelessly obsolete Longfellow's work became in the United States in a matter of a just few decades. But one could also take the opposite position and argue that parodies like the one above attest to how much Longfellow still is part of American popular culture.

See also Fireside Poets; Indian Wars and Dispossession; Indians; Lyric Poetry; Popular Poetry

BIBLIOGRAPHY
Primary Works

Doesticks, Q. K. Philander [Mortimer Neal Thomson]. *Plu-ri-bus-tah: A Song That's-By-No-Author: A Deed without a Name.* New York: Livermore and Rudd, 1856.

Emerson, Ralph Waldo. *The Selected Letters of Ralph Waldo Emerson.* Edited by Joel Myerson. New York: Columbia University Press, 1997.

Fuller, Margaret. *The Essential Margaret Fuller.* Edited by Jeffrey Steele. New Brunswick, N.J.: Rutgers University Press, 1995.

Longfellow, Henry Wadsworth. Journal, 1 November 1850–31 December 1851. Longfellow Papers, MS Am 1340 (203). Houghton Library, Harvard University.

Longfellow, Henry Wadsworth. Journal, 1 September 1853–31 December 1855. Longfellow Papers, MS Am 1340 (206). Houghton Library, Harvard University.

Longfellow, Henry Wadsworth. *The Letters of Henry Wadsworth Longfellow.* 6 vols. Edited by Andrew Hilen. Cambridge, Mass.: Belknap Press of Harvard University Press, 1966–1982.

Longfellow, Henry Wadsworth. "Notes for *Hiawatha*: Indian Words and Names." c. 1854. Longfellow Papers, MS Am 1340 (92). Houghton Library, Harvard University.

Longfellow, Henry Wadsworth. *The Song of Hiawatha.* 1855. Edited by Daniel Aaron. London: J. M. Dent, 1992.

Lönnrot, Elias. *The Kalevala; or, Poems of the Kalevala District.* Translated by Francis Peabody Magoun, Jr. Cambridge, Mass.: Harvard University Press, 1963.

Pound, Ezra. *Poems and Translations.* New York: Library of America, 2003.

Reid, F. X. *The Song of Hakawatha.* http://www.cis.strath .ac.uk/∼sinclair/hakawatha.html.

Schoolcraft, Henry Rowe. *Algic Researches, Comprising Inquiries Respecting the Mental Characteristics of the North American Indians; First Series: Indian Tales and Legends.* 2 vols. New York: Harper & Brothers, 1839.

Whitman, Walt. *Leaves of Grass and Other Writings.* Edited by Michael Moon. New York: Norton, 2002.

Secondary Works

Arvin, Newton. *Longfellow: His Life and Work.* Boston: Little, Brown, 1963.

Buell, Lawrence. "Introduction." In *Selected Poems,* by Henry Wadsworth Longfellow. New York: Penguin, 1988.

Calhoun, Charles C. *Longfellow: A Rediscovered Life.* Boston: Beacon, 2004.

Fiske, Christabel F. "Mercerized Folklore." *Poet Lore* 31 (1920): 538–575.

Irmscher, Christoph. *Longfellow Redux.* Champaign: University of Illinois Press, forthcoming.

Jackson, Virginia. "Longfellow's Tradition; or, Picture-Writing a Nation." *Modern Language Quarterly* 59, no. 4 (December 1998): 471–496.

Legler, Henry E. "Longfellow's *Hiawatha:* Bibliographical Notes Concerning Its Origins, Its Translations, and Its Contemporary Parodies." *The Literary Collector* 9 (November–December 1904): 1–19.

Longfellow, Samuel. *Life of Henry Wadsworth Longfellow, with Extracts from his Journals and Correspondence.* 3 vols. Boston: Houghton Mifflin, 1891.

Loving, Jerome. *Walt Whitman: The Song of Himself.* Berkeley: University of California Press, 1999.

Moyne, Ernest J. "Parodies of Longfellow's *Song of Hiawatha.*" *Delaware Notes* 30 (1957): 93–108.

Moyne, Ernest J. *Hiawatha and Kalevala: A Study of the Relationship between Longfellow's "Indian Edda" and the Finnish Epic.* Helsinki: Suomalainen Tiedeakatemia, 1963.

Christoph Irmscher

"SONG OF MYSELF"

"Song of Myself" is the final title Walt Whitman gave to his long, changing, remarkably fluid poem that he originally published as "Leaves of Grass" in the first edition of *Leaves of Grass* (1855).

It was renamed "Poem of Walt Whitman, an American" in the 1856 edition and was called simply "Walt Whitman" in the editions of 1860, 1867, and 1871. Only in the final edition of *Leaves of Grass* in 1881 did the poem become "Song of Myself." Not just the title but many other features of the poem changed over the years: Whitman radically altered the punctuation, added some sections and deleted others, tinkered with many individual lines, and divided up the poem in very different ways. In its original form, the poem had unnumbered stanzas that varied from a single line to over eighty lines; by 1860 Whitman had numbered these stanzas from 1 to 372; and by 1867 he had further divided the poem into fifty-two numbered sections, still keeping the stanza numbers; only in 1881 did he drop the stanza numbers and retain just the fifty-two sections. In addition to the internal changes, Whitman altered the position of the poem in *Leaves of Grass,* placing it first among the twelve poems in the 1855 edition but dropping it into second position in 1860 and moving it farther back in each succeeding edition. The poem thus plays a different role in each edition of *Leaves,* and its meanings shifted as Whitman revised it and recontextualized it over nearly three decades. He would never again write a poem anywhere near as long as "Song of Myself."

ORIGINS

The origins of "Song of Myself" have remained a mystery. Whitman was an inveterate keeper of notebooks, a habit that began during his days as a newspaper reporter and editor in the 1840s. He used these notebooks to record the names of people he met, to keep financial ledgers, and to jot down notes about sights, sounds, and ideas. In one notebook, now known as "Talbot Wilson" (after the name that appears at the top of the first page), Whitman records many ideas and images that eventually make their way into "Song of Myself." There has been a long debate over when these notebook entries were made; for many decades, critics dated the notebook from the late 1840s, thus suggesting that Whitman had been working on "Song of Myself" for seven or eight years before its publication in 1855. The mystery was intensified during World War II, when the notebook, then housed at the Library of Congress, was shipped for safekeeping to a midwestern university. When the box containing the notebooks was returned to the Library of Congress, the Talbot Wilson was missing. In 1998 it was discovered in the attic of a book collector. Examinations of the notebook showed conclusively that, while Whitman did use it in the 1840s, he cut out the earlier pages and began reusing it in the early 1850s, perhaps as late as 1854. All the notes leading to "Song of

Myself" date from the 1850s, thus indicating a much quicker development of the poem than had previously been assumed.

The later dating allows us to see more clearly how "Song of Myself" had its genesis and rapid gestation during the explosive decade of the 1850s, following the Missouri Compromise and the introduction of the Fugitive Slave Law, which increased federal oversight of the process of returning runaway slaves to their owners. Many Americans who resisted this law strenuously objected to the imposition of federal jurisdiction over what had previously been state decisions, and many argued that the enforcement of the law made all Americans complicitous in slavery and, even worse, coerced all Americans into becoming slave catchers. The controversies surrounding this law boiled over in 1854 when the escaped slave Anthony Burns was retained in Boston, Massachusetts, and ordered back to the South by federal marshals and by President Franklin Pierce. Pierce provided hundreds of U.S. troops to escort Burns through the streets of Boston, where twenty thousand angry residents demonstrated against his forced return, and stationed a navy boat in Boston harbor to take him back to Virginia. Whitman wrote an angry, sarcastic poem that he later called "A Boston Ballad" about this incident. In the poem, he chastised the people of the North for allowing this injustice to occur, and he imagined hauling King George III's bones out of his coffin, reassembling them, and putting a crown on the corpse's head, since such cowardice indicated Americans had become subservient to tyrannical power once again. But now the tyrannical power was seen as the U.S. government itself, which was imposing an unjust law on individual states. Whitman included "A Boston Ballad" in the first edition of *Leaves of Grass,* but this was hardly the only mention of the slavery issue in *Leaves:* of the twelve poems appearing in the first edition, nine dealt with slaves, including the three longest poems, "The Sleepers," "I Sing the Body Electric," and "Song of Myself."

Whitman's involvement with the slavery issue dated back to the 1846 Wilmot Proviso, which prohibited slavery in territories the United States acquired from Mexico; the proviso had split the Democratic Party, and Whitman became a Barnburner, a Democrat who opposed the extension of slavery to western territories. But it was not until early 1848 that Whitman came into direct contact with the institution of slavery. Acting impulsively on an unexpected offer to edit the New Orleans *Daily Crescent,* he abruptly left Brooklyn for Louisiana, where for three months he experienced southern culture, witnessed slave auctions, and absorbed the multilingual mix of the Creole city. His sojourn there would have lasting

effects, ranging from his use of occasional French terms in "Song of Myself" to his powerful evocation of the slave market in "I Sing the Body Electric" and his detailed descriptions of slaves in "Song of Myself." He carried back with him a slave auction poster, which he kept in his room from then on as a stark reminder of what he had witnessed. Once back in Brooklyn, Whitman founded and edited for a short time a free-soil newspaper he called the *Freeman;* then, during the years leading up to the appearance of the first edition of *Leaves of Grass,* he gave himself time to read, to write incessantly in the small notebooks he always carried with him, and to allow his roiling ideas to evolve. In a burst of creative energy, still discernible in the notebooks he left behind, he discovered his revolutionary new vehicle, a long-lined free verse organized by a vast and absorptive "I" who would speak for all of America in a brash and nondiscriminating voice.

Whitman's notebooks and surviving manuscripts reveal the intensity and fluidity of the development of his poetic style. Images, phrases, and whole lines of what would become "Song of Myself" can be found in his prose jottings, and only a year or two before *Leaves* appeared, Whitman was unclear what shape—even what genre—his new expression would take. In one notebook from the early 1850s, which contains prose lines that would later take their place in "Song of Myself," Whitman writes: "Novel? Work of some sort/Play? . . . Plot for a Poem or other work . . . A spiritual novel?" (*Daybooks,* p. 775). For a while, he thought about turning his notes into speeches and going on the lecture circuit. Only gradually do the notebooks edge toward his discovery of his line, but once that discovery comes, he moves quickly toward the finished poem. In the Talbot Wilson notebook, we find some of Whitman's earliest proto-lines for "Song of Myself":

> I am the poet of slaves and of the masters of slaves
> I am the poet of the body
> And I am
> I am the poet of the body
> And I am the poet of the soul
> I go with the slaves of the earth equally with
>   the masters
> And I will stand between the masters and the slaves,
> Entering into both so that both shall under-
>   stand me alike
> I am the poet of Strength and Hope
>   (*Notebooks, p. 67*)

From the beginning, Whitman was busy embedding deep in his poem impossible contradictions, and he always wedded opposites with his omnipresent "and." He would not be the poet of slaves or the poet of masters but rather the poet of slaves *and* masters. Whatever democratic voice he invented would have to speak for both, or it was doomed to be partial and thus not representative. And to stand *between* masters and slaves was to stand in a politically and sexually charged space, historically a place of rape and torture, but a place also where mixing and hybridity began. There is no easy space to inhabit in American history, and Whitman was courageous enough to insist on speaking for the full range of American identities, from the most powerful to the powerless, and to recognize that there are no slaves without masters, no masters without slaves, and that only when every individual begins to recognize the slave *and* the master within could a democratic voice begin to merge and emerge.

And it was nothing less than the creation of a democratic voice that Whitman was after; he sought in "Song of Myself" to voice an "I" that would for the first time articulate just what a nonhierarchical sensibility would sound like. He was not speaking in his poem as the Walt Whitman of the mid-1850s but rather as a Whitman projected far into a more perfectly realized democratic future. He was teaching Americans how to think and speak democratically, in a freer and looser idiom, in a more conversational and less formal tone. He achieved an uncanny combination of oratory, journalism, and scripture—haranguing, mundane, and prophetic—all in the service of identifying a new American attitude, an accepting voice that would catalog the diversity of the country and manage to hold it all in a vast, single, unified identity: "I am large. . . . I contain multitudes" (*Leaves,* p. 55). This new voice spoke confidently of union at a time of deep division and tension in the culture, only five years short of the outbreak of the Civil War, and it spoke with the assurance of one for whom everything, no matter how degraded, could be celebrated as part of itself: "What is commonest and cheapest and nearest and easiest is Me" (p. 21). His work echoed the lingo of the American urban working class and took pride in an American language that was forming as a tongue distinct from British English.

Part of that new American speech involved a much more open acknowledgment of sexuality and the body than the culture was accustomed to. "Song of Myself" was fueled by erotic energy—"Urge and urge and urge, / Always the procreant urge of the world" (p. 2)—and the narrator initiates his journey with a bizarre sex act:

> I mind how we lay in June, such a transparent
> summer morning;
> You settled your head athwart my hips and gently
> turned over upon me,

> And parted the shirt from my bosom-bone, and
> plunged your tongue to my barestript heart,
> And reached till you felt my beard, and reached
> till you held my feet.
>
> (P. 15)

The physical encounter here has been variously read as a homosexual act, heterosexual intercourse, or a kind of charging up of the body by the soul. Whitman is sometimes categorized as a transcendentalist but his beliefs are more "descendentalist," with the soul entering the body to energize the senses instead of the soul transcending the physical world. For Whitman, soul without body was unthinkable, and in this generative scene, the tongue is plunged into the heart, initiating a union of physical voice and heart—both the seat of love and emotion *and* the organ of life, pumping blood to the head and hands and genitals. In "Song of Myself," the narrator's body speaks and sees and hears and touches and tastes and smells, absorbing the world through heightened senses: "Welcome is every organ and attribute of me . . . / Not an inch nor a particle of an inch is vile" (p. 14). This erotic drive would urge the democratic self to cross boundaries of race and gender and class: "Who need be afraid of the merge? / Undrape . . . you are not guilty to me" (p. 17). All human beings inhabit bodies, and democracy starts, Whitman believed, with a full acknowledgment of the body's desires and drives: they are what unify us.

FIRST PUBLICATION

In the spring of 1855, Whitman took his manuscript, still in flux, to his friend Andrew Rome, a Scottish immigrant who ran a small print shop in Brooklyn and specialized in printing legal documents. Published around 4 July, the first edition of *Leaves,* with its legal-sized paper, large typeface, and rough finish, looks like what it is: a declaration of literary independence, a proclamation of a new kind of literature fit for a new democracy. Since Andrew Rome did not normally print books but only legal forms, the large-sized paper was what he would have had in stock. Whitman would have loved the resonance and suggestiveness of printing his poems on legal-sized paper. This was, after all, poetry printed to be posted like a legal notice, a contract between the author and reader, between the "I" and "you": "what I assume you shall assume" (p. 13). When you open this book, Whitman seems to be saying, you enter into a binding agreement with the poet: "Gentlemen I receive you, and attach and clasp hands with you" (p. 28). The legal language continues throughout "Song of Myself": "I *bequeath* myself to the dirt to grow from the grass I love" (p. 56; emphasis added), he writes at the end of the poem.

Whitman included as a frontispiece an engraving of himself in laborer's garb, staring at the reader with a challenging look, wearing a "wide-awake" hat (a hat associated with abolitionists and later with supporters of Abraham Lincoln's candidacy for president, a group known as the "wide-awakes"). The portrait is unlike any previous frontispiece representation of an author: the full-body pose, with the torso as the center of focus, suggests that *this* poetry emerges not just from the intellect but from the experience of a body at work in the world, hat on, shirt open, ready to be inspired and ready to perspire. The engraving by Samuel Hollyer turns out to be a collage made from an earlier daguerreotype of Whitman dressed in more formal attire—Whitman the flaneur, the well-dressed young dandy aspiring to be part of the nation's rising professional middle class—melded with another shot of Whitman as day laborer, proud to speak for the working class and identifying himself more with "Bowery b'hoys" than with newspaper editors. Whitman's absorptive identity in "Song of Myself" was built on this fluidity, this ease in crossing all the class and gender and even racial barriers that separated Americans. At a key point in the poem, the narrator pauses to name himself and in doing so brings the frontispiece engraving alive:

> Walt Whitman, an American, one of the roughs,
>   a kosmos,
> Disorderly fleshy and sensual . . . eating drinking
>   and breeding . . .
> Through me many long dumb voices
> Voices of the interminable generations of slaves.
>
> *(P. 17)*

In the very act of identifying himself, Whitman emphasizes his unashamed sexuality and easy sensuality, simultaneously making it clear that the whole point of his poem is to give voice to the previously voiceless, to let the slaves speak as part of the democratic conversation.

This idiosyncratic engraving would remain for Whitman the emblem of "Song of Myself." After 1856 he stopped using it as the frontispiece for *Leaves of Grass,* but in the 1881 final edition of *Leaves,* he reprinted it opposite the first page of "Song of Myself," as if to emphasize that the engraving illustrated the "I" of that poem. In the first edition of *Leaves,* the poem occupied forty-three pages, beginning with "I celebrate myself / And what I assume you shall assume, / For every atom belonging to me as good belongs to you" (p. 13), and ending with "Failing to fetch me me [*sic*] at first keep encouraged, /

Walt Whitman. Engraving from the frontispiece to *Leaves of Grass,* 1855. ©CORBIS

Missing me one place search another, / I stop some where waiting for you" (p. 56). This long poem became his best-known work, an epic of American individualism, setting out to expand the boundaries of the self to include, first, all fellow Americans, then the entire world, and ultimately the cosmos. Throughout the poem, Whitman probes the question of how large the new democratic self can become before it dissipates into contradiction and fragmentation, and each time he seems to reach the limit, he dilates even more: "My ties and ballasts leave me . . . I travel . . . I sail . . . my elbows rest in the sea-gaps, / I skirt sierras . . . my palms cover continents, / I am afoot with my vision" (p. 35). Cataloging a huge array of urban and country scenes, portraying people at work in myriad occupations, incorporating vast geographical stretches, redefining life and death as one continuous and evolving dynamic process, Whitman's "I" takes the reader on a dizzying journey through American history, biological evolution, and a variety of religions, absorbing everything and rejecting nothing. His plea is that we all learn to accept and live in plurality, difference, and contradiction: "Do I contradict myself? / Very well then . . . I contradict myself" (p. 55).

STRUCTURE AND STYLE

Whitman creates two great characters in this poem: "I" and "you." The "I" becomes a model voice of American democracy. The "you" becomes an identity space the reader is invited to occupy. It is possible to hear the "you" in "Song" as addressed to the entire nation or the entire world, and it is also possible to hear it as intimately addressed only to the individual reader at a particular moment. "Song" opens with "I" and ends with "you," and the poem enacts a transfer of the absorptive energy from poet to reader, who by the final lines is sent off alone to continue the journey the poem began.

The deep structure of the poem seems to be a half-submerged slave-escape narrative, in which the speaker is seeking to liberate the reader from every kind of enslavement—religious, philosophical, moral, social, as well as physical. Chattel slavery was only the most conspicuous and blatant form of soul-killing coercion operating in mid-nineteenth-century America, and Whitman knew the culture was generating other forms, including the emerging "wage slavery" brought on by incipient capitalism, which had already begun to sap the individuality and pride that Whitman had admired in the artisanal culture he grew up in. Instead of using their hands in creative and skilled work, more and more Americans were becoming hired hands, selling their labor in a demeaning marketplace that treated humans as interchangeable machine parts and paid them by the hour. So "Song of Myself" takes the reader on what the poet calls "a perpetual journey" (p. 51), one that turns into an escape narrative for those who need to liberate themselves from the enslaving beliefs and possessions that prevent individual growth, need to put "creeds and schools in abeyance" (*Complete Poetry,* p. 188) and embark on a new road: "Not I, not any one else can travel that road for you, / You must travel it for yourself" (*Leaves,* p. 52).

An actual slave-escape narrative surfaces in the poem at key points, as when the speaker states "The runaway slave came to my house" (p. 19), was welcomed in, given a room that opened onto the narrator's room, and shared the table with the "I," who gave the slave food, water, a bath, clean clothes, and hope. Soon, a kind of utopian space seems to open up as the "I" watches white workers taking part in a "shuffle and breakdown" (p. 20), black dances that seem to be loosening up and liberating the white laborers. Then the narrator describes in detail a working

"negro" who "holds firmly the reins of his four horses" and has a "glance" that "is calm and commanding" as the sun "falls on the black of his polish'd and perfect limbs" (p. 20). As the democratic escape narrative progresses, racial boundaries are crossed and blacks acquire agency, pride, and beauty. Later, more distinctions collapse as the "I" literally gives itself over to a runaway slave who is captured, and speaks *as* the slave instead of *for* or *to* or *of* the slave: "I am the hounded slave . . . I wince at the bite of the dogs" (p. 39).

Whitman's free verse picked up the rhythms of American speech and issued in vast, flowing sentences that ran over his lengthy lines, each one an extended exhalation of breath, complete with an early "stream of consciousness" effect produced by Whitman's idiosyncratic use of ellipses instead of more standard punctuation. His poetry, he announced at the beginning of "Song of Myself," was based on "respiration and inspiration" (p. 13), the breathing in of the world around him in all its diversity and the breathing out again in words that echoed that world. Whitman invents a style that captures the easy influx of sensory experience, and, throughout "Song of Myself," he pictures himself as the ultimate absorber of physical sensations, his five senses wide open, allowing each moment to redefine who and what he is: "In me the caresser of life wherever moving" (p. 11); "I am of old and young, of the foolish as much as the wise" (p. 23); "I resist anything better than my own diversity" (p. 24); "To me the converging objects of the universe perpetually flow, / All are written to me, and I must get what the writing means" (p. 26). The speaker of "Song" is someone whose senses are charged up, heightened, electric:

> I have instant conductors all over me whether
>   I pass or stop,
> They seize every object and lead it harmlessly
>   through me.
> I merely stir, press, feel with my fingers, and am
>   happy,
> To touch my person to some one else's is about
>   as much as I can stand.
> Is this then a touch? . . . quivering me to a new
>   identity.
>
>   (P. 32)

Whitman turns the impersonal act of reading into an intimate sensory experience and talks to his reader as if the print on the page were itself a sentient being aware of the reader's presence: "Listener up there! Here you . . . what have you to confide to me?" (p. 55). We as readers are being addressed more directly than we are used to by a writer, and we are even being asked to respond, to confide to the "I" of this poem our secrets, dreams, anxieties. Whitman's exclamation to the reader—"Listener up there!"—comes as a shock because it expresses awareness of the physical position of the reader in relation to the text, of the reader's face hovering above the page. Whitman creates, in other words, a new democratic act of reading, where the author is not so much the "authority" as the companion, someone not only to be listened to but also talked to. Whitman always believed that a democracy would have to develop new, more rigorous reading habits, and readers would have to learn to wrestle with authority and never passively accept what persons in authority claimed. Democracy would require a new concept of "author" and "reader," a more intimate interaction between the "I" and the "you" of any text. "Song of Myself" sets out to enact this new relationship and in so doing, to forge a democracy.

Three versions of "Song of Myself" (1855, 1856, and 1860) appeared before the Civil War, three more (1867, 1871, and 1881) after. After the Emancipation Proclamation and Reconstruction, the historical currency of "Song of Myself" changed dramatically, and the poem, when read in the context of Whitman's later work, receded into a nostalgia for a dreamed-of democracy that was never realized, that was shattered by the war, by the persistent racial strife in the culture after emancipation, and by growing class disparities. In each new edition, Whitman tamed "Song" a bit more, channeling the original nonstop flow into numbered sections and replacing the innovative use of ellipses with more standard punctuation. By the twentieth century, most people had stopped reading "Song" as a poem growing out of the specific turbulent social history of 1850s America, and many began reading it as primarily a spiritual or mystical text. But in the late twentieth and early twenty-first century, "Song of Myself" was examined anew as a key text in nineteenth-century American cultural studies, a poem that responds acutely to the tensions of class, race, and sexuality—as well as to linguistic, religious, and scientific issues—that defined the United States in the years leading up to the Civil War.

See also "Crossing Brooklyn Ferry": *Leaves of Grass;* Lyric Poetry; "Out of the Cradle Endlessly Rocking"; "When Lilacs Last in the Dooryard Bloom'd"

BIBLIOGRAPHY

Primary Works
Folsom, Ed, and Kenneth M. Price, eds. The Walt Whitman Archive. http://www.whitmanarchive.org.

Whitman, Walt. *Complete Poetry and Collected Prose.* Edited by Justin Kaplan. New York: Library of America, 1982.

Whitman, Walt. *Daybooks and Notebooks.* Vol. 3. Edited by William White. New York: New York University Press, 1978.

Whitman, Walt. *Leaves of Grass.* Brooklyn, N.Y.: Andrew H. Rome, 1855. Available in facsimile at www.whitman archive.org. Except where otherwise noted, page citations in text are to this edition.

Whitman, Walt. *Leaves of Grass: A Textual Variorum of the Printed Poems.* Vol. 1. Edited by Sculley Bradley, Harold W. Blodgett, Arthur Golden, and William White. New York: New York University Press, 1980.

Whitman, Walt. *Notebooks and Unpublished Prose Manuscripts.* Vol. 1. Edited by Edward F. Grier. New York: New York University Press, 1984. Includes the Talbot Wilson notebook. A digital reproduction of the Talbot Wilson notebook is also available at the Library of Congress American Memory website at http://memory.loc.gov/ammem/wwhtml/wwhome.html.

Secondary Works
Erkkila, Betsy. *Whitman the Political Poet.* New York: Oxford University Press, 1989.

Folsom, Ed, and Kenneth M. Price. *Re-Scripting Walt Whitman: An Introduction to His Life and Work.* Oxford: Blackwell, 2005.

Greenspan, Ezra, ed. *Song of Myself: A Sourcebook and Critical Edition.* New York: Routledge, 2005.

Higgins, Andrew C. "Wage Slavery and the Composition of *Leaves of Grass:* The 'Talbot Wilson' Notebook." *Walt Whitman Quarterly Review* 20, no. 2 (2002): 53–77.

Klammer, Martin. *Whitman, Slavery, and the Emergence of Leaves of Grass.* University Park: Pennsylvania State University Press, 1995.

Levine, Herbert J. "Union and Disunion in 'Song of Myself.'" *American Literature* 59, no. 4 (1987): 570–589.

Loving, Jerome. *Walt Whitman: The Song of Himself.* Berkeley: University of California Press, 1999.

Mack, Stephen John. *The Pragmatic Whitman: Reimagining American Democracy.* Iowa City: University of Iowa Press, 2002.

Martin, Robert K. "Whitman's Song of Myself: Homosexual Dream and Vision." *Partisan Review* 42, no. 1 (1975): 80–96.

Miller, James E., Jr., ed. *Whitman's "Song of Myself": Origin, Growth, Meaning.* New York: Dodd, Mead, 1964.

Warren, James Perrin. "'The Real Grammar': Deverbal Style in 'Song of Myself.'" *American Literature* 56, no. 1 (1984): 1–16.

Ed Folsom

SOUTHERN LITERARY MESSENGER

See Periodicals

SPANISH SPEAKERS AND EARLY "LATINO" EXPRESSION

Spanish speakers have been present and writing in what is today the United States since the late sixteenth century, when Spanish explorers and colonizers described their experiences in chronicles, prose, poems, and epistolary exchanges. But it was not until the nineteenth century that Spanish speakers from various Latin American countries and Spain began to develop a cultural identity within the United States that was linguistically, racially, and culturally distinct from the Anglo-American majority culture. In the nineteenth century Spanish speakers comprised three principal groups: American citizens of Spanish ancestry, Spanish-speaking immigrants from the Americas, and exiled political figures in the United States who fought for Latin American independence from Spain. The presence of these Spanish speakers transformed the American cultural landscape at a time when the United States was defining its own cultural and national identity in response to its rapid continental and hemispheric expansion. The most significant polemic of and about Spanish speakers in the United States came as a result of the Mexican-American War (1846–1848). After the war Mexico lost almost half of its territories to the United States, including modern-day California, Utah, and Nevada and parts of New Mexico, Colorado, and Wyoming as well as Mexico's claim to Texas, which had been under U.S. occupation since 1836. The massive acquisition of territory meant that the country's cultural, ethnic, linguistic, and religious makeup would undergo considerable transformation. Yet how is it that American literary history has not been able to register this important incorporation of a people, their cultural history, and the literature that charts this transformation? This essay seeks to provide the basis from which to understand what has been conceived as a "recent" cultural and literary phenomenon borne out the 1960s civil rights movements.

SPANISH SPEAKERS AFTER "THE AMERICAN 1848"

Scholars (Michael Paul Rogin, Shelly Streeby) have referred to the period after the Mexican-American War as "the American 1848" in order to emphasize how the United States's acquisition of Mexican territories signaled a new age of expansionism driven by monopoly capitalism. The American 1848 also aggravated the tenuous balance held between northern free states and southern slave states that would culminate in the Civil War. These tensions arose with the signing of the Treaty of Guadalupe Hidalgo (1848), which ended the Mexican-American War. The acquisition of land also meant the incorporation of the territory's inhabitants as well as their culture, customs, and modes of being.

When the treaty was finally signed on 2 February 1848, Mexico sought to protect its citizens by negotiating three articles that referred specifically to Mexicans who would remain in the newly conquered territory. These three articles informed both the legal status of Mexicans in the United States as well as their role as future U.S. citizens in the making. Mexican familiarity with Anglo-American law is evident in the drafting of these articles insofar as they acknowledge an ethnically marked subject of citizenship as well as the symbolic preconditions for asserting differential (but not deferential) citizenship: namely, the protection of cultural, religious, and linguistic difference. The articles in question, Articles 8, 9, and 10, sought to ensure U.S. citizenship, free practice of religion (the protection of Catholicism in a predominantly Protestant country), and recognition of Mexican land grants, respectively. The articles were heavily contested on the Anglo-American side before the treaty was signed. On 4 January 1848, almost four weeks prior to the signing, Senator John Calhoun (1782–1850) of South Carolina appeared before the Senate floor to state his disdain for the annexation of Mexican territories to the United States. Calhoun, though an expansionist, vehemently expressed racially motivated concerns in an effort to thwart the signing of the treaty. He noted how the United States had "never dreamt of incorporating into our Union any but the Caucasian race—the free white race" (pp. 98–99). Calhoun's conflation of racial identity with ethnic, national, and linguistic identities was a strategic move meant to prevent what he and many others saw as the incorporation of potentially free states into the union.

Only Article 8 (citizenship) of the treaty survived intact when it was ratified by the Senate on 19 March 1848. By striking Article 10 completely, the Senate placed a serious impediment to the "guarantee" of Mexican American citizenship it had bestowed: the full exercise of citizenship could be achieved only if one was a landowner. As a result of various poll-tax and literacy laws that were already in effect prior to the signing of the treaty, Mexican Americans and many Spanish speakers in previously Mexican territories had limited possibilities for entry into civic life as their U.S. citizenship became largely symbolic. The question of land title was therefore of paramount importance if Mexican Americans were to exercise full citizenship. Yet Mexican American possibilities for resolving land disputes were fraught with lengthy and costly battles. After the California Land Act of 1851, which established the procedures for confirming land titles for Mexican and Spanish grants, the average time for settlement of a claim in California was seventeen years (Robinson, p. 106). Not surprisingly, Mexican Americans began to redress their second-class citizenship in both the court of law and the court of public opinion. For many Spanish speakers, the rise of print culture made publishing a viable medium for redressing the injustices occasioned by the American 1848. Spanish speakers writing in both English and Spanish attempted to reach their own communities as well as English-speaking communities. The responses to cultural, political, and material dispossession were class codified and could be divided into four principal—though not exclusive—literary modes of historical and self-representation. These four principal modes were the *corrido* (a border ballad, usually about a struggle or border conflict); plays that emerged from an older tradition of *autos* (devotional plays) from the Spanish colonial period; the novel (the historical novel in particular); and the *crónica* (opinion pieces, editorials, and essays). Each of these modes of literary-historical and cultural recordation reached various class strata and relied on either print culture or oral transmission for the representation of group-specific concerns.

THE *CORRIDO*

The *corrido* emerged in the nineteenth century along the U.S.-Mexican border after the Texas Revolution of 1836, which provided ample historical and personal material from which to relate stories of valor in the face of Anglo-American encroachment. Transmitted and sung along the border, the most famous *corridos* were reproduced in broadsides and in Spanish-language newspapers throughout the Southwest. The *corrido* was transmitted orally and required no literate reading public since it was performed to a community of listener-observers who were in turn witnessing the staging of an event from a decidedly Mexican perspective. The *corrido* provided an easy-to-understand, though often variable, counterrepresentational medium because it did not require a literate public. Unlike the novel and the *crónica,* the *corrido* allowed history and counterhistories to filter through various class strata. The Spanish *romance* eight-syllable line structure also facilitated rote memorization and dissemination and explains the *corrido*'s continuing popularity.

The *corrido,* however, was ultimately bound to iteration in and among various Spanish-speaking communities; transmitted almost always in Spanish, its resonance in the American public sphere was therefore limited. This was not the case with the plays, novels, or *crónicas* whose counterhistorical resonance attempted to sway Anglo-American sentiment about the Mexican-American War and, even more broadly, about the various Spanish-speaking groups in the country and their respective concerns regarding an ever-expanding United States.

STAGING DISSENT

Though the literary historiography is scant, the historical record indicates that in the nineteenth century plays by and for Spanish speakers were written, performed, and often improvised. Many of these plays have been lost, and all we have are mentions of them in newspapers, playbills, and broadsides. The extant material that we do possess and are still recovering from this period come from the pioneering work of Chicano scholars. The Chicano literature scholar Raymund A. Paredes notes how one of the earliest and most interesting plays from the period is the anonymous *Los Tejanos* (The Texans), which appears to have been written around 1846 (p. 1082). No doubt inspired by the nickname given to Texas Rangers by Mexicans, *los diablos tejanos* ("the Texan devils" or, more felicitously, "the devilish Texans"), the play tells the story of the Santa Fe expedition of 1841 when some three hundred Texans attempted to "free" New Mexico from Mexican control. The play, though incomplete, charts this factual military and cultural intrusion by recalling how the "liberators" were captured or killed as a result of their hubris and cultural incompetence. The Texans presume to know the Mexican character, and it is their belief in the prevailing negative stereotypes about Mexicans that causes their downfall. These stereotypes consisted of racialized associations that posited the Mexican as sinister, conniving, and lazy "greasers." Falling prey to these stereotypes, the Texan General McLeod is outsmarted by the New Mexican Jorge Ramírez, who leads the general and his band into a cultural and military ambush. He pretends to be a traitor to his fellow Mexicans only to have General McLeod follow him into Santa Fe, all the while being oblivious to Ramírez's scheme. Once in New Mexico, Ramírez's men ambush the bewildered Anglo-Americans and thereby prevent New Mexico from being usurped by the United States.

The play is emblematic of the cultural conflicts between Mexican Americans and Anglo-Americans that would also manifest themselves in other literary genres of the period. The Mexican American is caught in a contentious and consistently confrontational

Illustration from Colonel Frank Triplett's *Conquering the Wilderness*, 1883. After 1848, the stereotype of Mexicans as sinister characters became commonplace in the public imagination. This engraving labels Mexicans as "Greasers"; a nearby illustration carried the caption "Murderous Mexicans." CLEMENTS LIBRARY, UNIVERSITY OF MICHIGAN

engagement with Anglo-Americans over the right to determine what public identity the dispossessed are to assume: the identity imposed by the aggressor or the one clamoring for representational justice. The figure of Jorge Ramírez was significant to the degree that he symbolically assured Mexican Americans that they would ultimately prevail. The tensions would also be evident in the literature of Mexican Americans as well as in that of other Spanish speakers.

HISTORICAL MEMORY

One of the most important novels from the period is María Amparo Ruiz de Burton's (1832–1895) historical romance *The Squatter and the Don* (1885), a text destined to oblivion were it not for the intervention of the Chicana scholars Beatrice Pita and Rosaura Sánchez, who reedited the novel and provided an important introduction to the historical circumstances

that produced it. Ruiz de Burton's novel narratively stages in English how Mexicans became second-class citizens after the war. The "Don" in the title refers to Mariano Alamar, a patrician rancher whose wealth has been encroached upon by an eastern squatter, William Darrell. The Darrells, well-to-do easterners, have found themselves caught in a moral dilemma involving the legitimacy of Mexican-Spanish land grants and the right to stake claims to those grants that may or may not be binding in the reconstruction's judicial system. The Alamars watch as entrepreneurs such as Charles Crocker, Mark Hopkins, Collis P. Huntington, and Leland Stanford successfully promote underdevelopment in the don's southern California by successfully blocking a southern transcontinental railroad with a terminus in San Diego from being built, thereby forcing the Mexicans to sell their land as nearby Los Angeles is developed to the detriment of the Mexican stronghold of San Diego. Ruiz de Burton's Californio blue-eyed protagonist, Don Alamar, notes:

> When I first read the text of the treaty of Guadalupe Hidalgo, I felt a bitter resentment against my people; against Mexico, the mother country, who abandoned us—her children—with so slight a provision of obligatory stipulations for protection. But afterwards, upon mature reflection, I saw that Mexico did as much as could have been reasonably expected at the time. In the very preamble of the treaty the spirit of peace and friendship, which animated both nations, was carefully made manifest. . . . The treaty said that our rights would be the same as those enjoyed by all American citizens. But, you see, Congress takes very good care not to enact retroactive laws for Americans. . . . I think but few Americans know or believe to what extent we have been wronged by Congressional action. (P. 67)

Don Alamar's recourse to historical memory presents the personalized narrative of an *hombre de razón*, literally "a reasonable man" but connotatively a "white man," who has weighed the injustices of empire and found Congress, and by extension the nation itself, wanting in its legally binding responsibility to honor the agreements set forth in the Treaty of Guadalupe Hidalgo. Ruiz de Burton's conscious construction of Don Alamar as "white," however, evinces a palliative strategy of racial and linguistic accommodation—one that she must have found to be successful because of, and not in spite of, its assimilative cultural grounding. To date there is no conclusive evidence regarding the public-sphere resonance of her counterhistorical novel after it was published. The evidence is clear, however, about how she was received in the political sphere.

After the onset of the American Civil War (1861–1865), concern over her husband, the Union army captain Henry S. Burton (and perhaps even concern over her pension), made her request a meeting with President Abraham Lincoln (Aranda, p. 64). After several attempts she secured a meeting with Lincoln, whom she finally met in person in 1861. (She would fictionally reconstruct this meeting in her first novel, *Who Would Have Thought It?*, 1872.) She discussed her husband's service to the Union and requested his promotion to colonel, a request that did not fall on deaf ears. Lincoln wrote to his secretary of war, Simon Cameron, and asked him to promote her husband "if it could be done without injustice to other officers"; six months later the Senate formally approved the promotion of Henry S. Burton (Aranda, p. 64).

Ruiz de Burton's counterhistorical agency—her willingness to sway public opinion in favor of Mexican Americans—as ultimately dependent upon a literate English-speaking public, and the cultural, political, and historical memory her novel attempted to redress was an important though largely symbolic gesture since discrimination against Mexicans did not cease but intensified. The representation of Mexicanness that she wanted to redress as *gente de razón* (as reasonable "white" people) did not achieve any resonance in the public sphere. That was not the case with the various Spanish-speaking media outlets that sought mass circulation in an attempt to increase sales, widen their sphere of influence, and provide an accurate forum for Spanish speakers and their group-specific concerns.

THE RISE OF "LATINO" EXPRESSION

Mid-nineteenth-century New Orleans provided a propitious environment for various multi-language print media. Kirsten Silva Gruesz, in her pioneering *Ambassadors of Culture*, asserts that since the inception of the "first Spanish-language newspaper in the United States, *El Misisipí*," New Orleans was "the undisputed capital of Hispanophone print production" with at least twenty-three different Spanish-language periodicals; its nearest contender, New York, had only thirteen (p. 110). She notes how important French-language newspapers like *L'Abeille* and the *L'Avenir du peuple* were by the 1830s already printing Spanish-language sections; by the 1840s nearly half the items in *L'Avenir du peuple* were written in Spanish. The 1840s also saw the Spanish-language press in New Orleans thrive and supersede the French-language press, not only for the Spanish-speaking expatriate communities but for Latin Americans as well. Important newspapers such as *El independiente, Diario del gobierno, La verdad, La patria,* and its predecessor *El hablador* were distributed throughout the

United States via express courier, steamboat, and railway as well as the rudimentary but fast-spreading technology of the telegraph, allowing almost immediate access to important news in and out of the United States (Silva Gruesz, p. 112). The war with Mexico was covered with singular interest in the Spanish-language press since many Spanish speakers (citizens, expatriates, émigrés, and travelers) saw Anglo-American expansion in Mexico as but a precursor to Anglo-American expansion into the other Americas—a fundamental concern for the Cuban writer José Martí as he noted in his essay *Nuestra América* (Our America).

RACIAL AND ETHNIC CONFLATION IN THE PUBLIC SPHERE

In the eastern United States, the feared expansionist zeal attributed to the United States after the war with Mexico and interventions elsewhere in the Americas forced Spanish-speaking communities, particularly in the Atlantic cultural centers of Philadelphia and New York City, to fight two principal representational battles: one racial and the other political as jingoist rhetoric saturated public media. The Cuban independence leader José Martí (1853–1895), who lived fourteen years of his life in exile in the United States, spearheaded the drive to form what today would be considered a "Latino" counterpublic, a community-specific attempt to counter prevailing stereotypes and media inaccuracies of and about Spanish speakers and their descendants.

Martí was a champion of liberatory projects and left a substantial body of writing that reasoned through the possibilities for racial parity as a condition of democracy, as he argued in *Nuestra América*. Though he spent most of his time in New York City while he was in the States, he often traveled to Key West and the Tampa Bay region, where Cuban communities had established themselves in mid-nineteenth century. In New York he was also associated as a writer with various English, Spanish, and bilingual newspapers. He wrote for the *New York Sun* as well as for *Patria*, the paper of the Cuban independence party (not to be confused with *La patria* of New Orleans, though his essays in Spanish appeared there as well), and his *crónicas* appeared in major newspapers throughout the United States and the Americas, as did his many important political essays and belletristic works.

When Martí first arrived in the United States he was in awe of a country where the experiment of democracy inspired him to dream of a Cuba free from Spanish colonial rule. His exuberance was short-lived, however, as he steadily witnessed the struggles of working people in cities like New York and Philadelphia. Martí was also concerned with what the Spanish-speaking press had acknowledged about U.S. expansionism in Latin America since the war with Mexico: that it was imperial expansionism driven by a belief in "Manifest Destiny." With the memory of the annexation of Mexico close to the heart, Martí and many other Latin American intellectuals living in the United States saw how American expansionism was threatening the newly liberated, or soon to be liberated, republics of Latin America, which had been under Spanish colonial rule. Martí was especially concerned about what he saw as U.S. encroachment upon Cuba and the Caribbean.

In 1889 Martí wrote the editor of the *New York Evening Post* after the paper reproduced an article that appeared in the *Philadelphia Manufacturer*. The article was characterized by Martí as an attack on Cubans in the United States and on the island alike. Articulating sentiments similar to those levied against Mexican's inferior racial composition on the human scale by the likes of Calhoun, the *Philadelphia Manufacturer* article depicted Cubans as "destitute vagrants" and "moral pigmies"; "effeminate"; people "unfitted by nature and experience to discharge the obligations of citizenship in a great and free country" like the United States (*José Martí Reader,* p. 210). Writing in English, Martí responded by interweaving Cuba's Ten Years' War (1868–1878) with Cuban American civic intervention in the United States. Martí noted that these claims against Cubans and Cuban Americans "cannot be justly said of a people who possess, besides the energy that built the first railroad in Spanish dominions and established against the opposition of the government all the agencies of civilization, a truly remarkable knowledge of the body politic" (p. 210). He went on:

> Never was ignorance of history and character more pitifully displayed. . . . We need to recollect, in order to answer without bitterness, that more than one American bled by our side, in a war that another American was to call a farce. A farce the war that has been by foreign observers compared to an epic, the upheaval of a whole country, the voluntary abandonment of wealth, the abolition of slavery in our first moment of freedom. (P. 211)

Martí was quick to note that the Cuban independence movement was premised on the very ideals of democratic institutions that were worth fighting for alongside Americans who believed in these ideals.

For Martí the *crónica* provided an immediate and useful tool for both his work as the architect of the Cuban independence movement and the early Latino expression that emerged in the nineteenth century

after the American 1848. That today we do not consider the likes of Ruiz de Burton or Martí part of the American literature canon is instructive of the degree to which the decidedly American creation of "difference" (especially with regard to its connotatively related racial, ethnic, gender, and linguistic markers) has served as one of the organizing principles of American identity from the nineteenth century to the present. That the United States does not recognize difference as its own creation should not obfuscate our need to reexamine the foundational conceits of American literary history and cultural memory.

CONCLUSION

The demise of an exilic consciousness on the part of Latin Americans in major Latino centers and Mexican responses to dispossession from the protocols of citizenship resulted in the commonality of Latino expression that scholars in the U.S. academy have only recently begun to chart. The direct engagement with the strictures of Anglo-American political representation was a primary concern for Spanish speakers that found expression organized around two principal fronts: first, the local—that is, the manifestations of homeland concerns at the immediate local level—and second, what has come to be termed the "glocal," meaning the impact of American policies in the country of origin (even if the country of origin was the United States, newly conceived after 1848, as was the case for Mexicans). The fundamental generative moment when it became necessary to articulate what today we call a Latino-specific subjectivity and identity was in 1848 and was fashioned by the ensuing polemic that registered the transition from Mexican to Anglo-American territorial dominance. The Latino subject surfaced along that literal and metaphorical divide between Mexico and the United States—a divide that fractured alliances, elided ethnic identities, and disembodied subjects from the protocols of citizenship. The literal divide was a trope of a rising U.S. nationalism, and its complicit metaphorical weight and accompanying truth claims were perpetuated in the public sphere through various print media on both sides of the cultural divide.

The current emphasis and ostensible novelty associated with Latino cultural production and identity is but a recent manifestation of a larger and unresolved cultural conflict that arose after the Mexican-American War. The various conceits associated with American democratic participation and the unfulfilled promise of equality created competing forms of cultural citizenship that vied for legitimacy and human access to cultural capital in the public sphere. These competing forms of "*being* American" appealed to the ontological status of Latino citizens (the purportedly knowable core of their "being"), where strategic whiteness and claims to a distinctive ethnic identity born of proto-colonialism renegotiated the nature of Hispanicity, often to near-collusive ends, as with Ruiz de Burton's blue-eyed protagonist. The public-sphere resonance of Latino responses to the loss of political influence, like Ruiz de Burton's novel, resulted in a publicly rendered identity that elided ethnic particularisms in favor of assimilative forms of national belonging. Like most projects marked by strategic essentialism, the politics of nineteenth-century Latino identity positioned itself as racially white for political gain, all the while lamenting the symbolic loss of cultural and ethnic particularisms. Its alternative, the noncritical embrace of a Latino-specific ethnic identity, did not prove to be a worthwhile strategy in the public sphere as civic influence diminished in measure with the singular dependence on Spanish-language accounts of "glocal" and local concerns. Spanish-language prominence and Anglo-American cultural and linguistic discrimination during this period ultimately facilitated the disintegration of a viable bilingual cultural identity for Spanish speakers. These negotiations surrounding civic identity constituted subject positions that altered the way Spanish speakers understood themselves in relation to the American body politic and the way that they were imagined as a community by the culture writ large.

See also Borders; Catholics; Democracy; Ethnology; Manifest Destiny; Mexican-American War; New Orleans

BIBLIOGRAPHY
Primary Works
Calhoun, John. *Congressional Globe.* Senate, 30th Cong., 1st sess., 1848.

Martí, José. *José Martí Reader: Writings on the Americas.* Edited by Deborah Schnookal and Mirta Muñiz. New York and Melbourne, Australia: Ocean Press, 1999.

Martí, José. *Nuestra América.* 1881. Buenos Aires: Editorial Losada, 1939.

Ruiz de Burton, María Amparo. *The Squatter and the Don: A Novel Descriptive of Contemporary Occurrences in California.* 1885. Edited by Rosaura Sánchez and Beatrice Pita. Houston, Tex.: Arte Público Press, 1992.

Ruiz de Burton, María Amparo. *Who Would Have Thought It?* 1872. Edited by Rosaura Sánchez and Beatrice Pita. Houston, Tex.: Arte Público Press, 1995.

Secondary Works
Aranda, José F. "Breaking All the Rules: María Amparo Ruiz de Burton Writes a Civil War Novel." In *Recovering the U.S. Hispanic Literary Heritage,* vol. 3, edited by María Herrera-Sobek and Virginia Sánchez Korrol. Houston, Tex.: Arte Público Press, 2000.

Espinosa, Aurelio M., and J. Manuel Espinosa. "The Texans." *New Mexico Quarterly Review* 13 (1943): 299–308.

Paredes, Raymund A. "Early Mexican American Literature." In *A Literary History of the American West,* edited by J. Golden Taylor and Thomas Lyon. Fort Worth: Texas Christian University Press, 1986.

Robinson, W. W. *Land in California: The Story of the Mission Lands, Ranchos, Squatters, Mining Claims, Railroad Grants, Land Scrip, Homesteads.* Berkeley: University of California Press, 1948.

Rogin, Michael Paul. *Subversive Genealogy: The Politics and Art of Herman Melville.* New York: Knopf, 1983.

Silva Gruesz, Kirsten. *Ambassadors of Culture: The Transamerican Origins of Latino Writing.* Princeton, N.J.: Princeton University Press, 2002.

Streeby, Shelley. *American Sensations: Class, Empire, and the Production of Popular Culture.* Berkeley: University of California Press, 2002.

Taylor, J. Golden, and Thomas Lyon, eds. *A Literary History of the American West.* Fort Worth: Texas Christian University Press, 1986.

Lázaro Lima

SPIRITUALISM

In 1848 in a Hydesville, New York, farmhouse, mysterious noises were heard in the daughters' bedroom. Harriet Beecher Stowe (1811–1896), author of *Uncle Tom's Cabin* (1852), would later ridicule those noises as "tippings and tappings and rappings" (p. 130). Thirteen-year-old Margaret Fox and twelve-year-old Kate Fox concluded that the noises were the ghost of a deceased peddler telling them that he had been murdered in the house and buried in the cellar. The girls tapped on the bedstead, the ghost tapped back, their mother interpreted, and this conversation with the dead inspired a vast movement that converted thousands in the United States to a metaphysical belief in the communication between the dead and the living: spiritualism. The first half of the nineteenth century was a time when many Americans had begun to doubt their Christian faith and consequently to despair of an afterlife; they looked for alternative routes. The more sensational aspects of the movement had abated by 1870, but a spiritualist influence continued in works such as William Dean Howells's critique of spiritualism, *The Undiscovered Country* (1880); Henry James's satire of the movement, *The Bostonians* (1886); Mark Twain's "Mental Telegraphy," an 1891 anecdotal essay that verified the source of psychic phenomena as natural science as opposed to the ghostly world of the supernatural; and *Of One Blood; or, The Hidden Self* (1901–1902) by the African American editor and writer Pauline Elizabeth Hopkins, who took her subtitle from an essay by the philosopher William James on the connection between the supernatural and science.

THE VOICE OF SPIRITUALISM

In its heyday spiritualism depended on "mediums," who were individuals employed by departed spirits to convey their sentiments. Mediums such as the Fox sisters were considered earthly gifted souls who both evoked and mediated the language of the dead speaking from beyond the grave; the knocks would not occur unless a medium was in the room. Women were considered especially apt mediums because mediumship was conceived as passive receivership of the spiritual world—an analog to the gender roles of the time. Nevertheless women asserted themselves through spiritualism, eventually taking to the wearing of veils and exploiting the theatricality of their position. That spiritualism gave unique opportunities to women was a fact not missed by the misogynistic satirist Q. K. Philander Doesticks (Mortimer Thomson, 1871–1875), who attacked those "accommodating 'spirits' [who filter] through the 'Medium' of those crack-brained masculine women, or addle-headed feminine men who profess to act as go-betweens from Earth to the Spirit World" (p. 13). Money was an especially unusual dividend for female professionals of the time; Margaret and Kate Fox earned $100 a night in mediumistic demonstrations in New York in 1850. The famous trance speaker Cora Hatch not only managed to make quite a bit of money from an early age, she had amassed enough power at age seventeen to be granted something virtually unheard of during the time—a divorce.

Communication with spirits took place at interpretive séances; in the early days, spirits could only say yes or no or provide a numerical answer according to a medium's predetermined code of rappings. The exception to this was the Fox sisters, who spelled out words laboriously by calling out letters and waiting for verification by a corresponding rap. By the 1860s trance speaking and spirit writing (often enhanced by the aid of the planchette) allowed for much longer and more coherent messages. Séances continued throughout the movement's heyday into the 1870s. Many famous people participated in the spirit world of table rappings. For example, Rufus Griswold, a prominent editor, held a séance with the Fox sisters and included

among the guests the editor Nathaniel Parker Willis; James Fenimore Cooper, author of the Leatherstocking Tales; the poet William Cullen Bryant; and the transcendentalist philosopher George Ripley. Lest one assume that all great men of the time were skeptics, it is interesting to note that this séance made quite an impact. Willis wrote it up in the *Home Journal* and Ripley in the *New York Tribune*. Sir Arthur Conan Doyle, author of the Sherlock Holmes tales, claimed that Cooper thanked the Foxes on his deathbed for the peace that they had brought him by putting him in touch with his dead sister.

THE PHILOSOPHY OF SPIRITUALISM

Whereas women were more often the mediums, men were usually the ones to argue in print for the movement's legitimacy. Andrew Jackson Davis (1826–1910), a former mesmerist, or hypnotist, wrote *The Principles of Nature, Her Divine Revelations, and a Voice to Mankind* (1847). Davis constructed an optimistic metaphysics of ever-evolving immortal spirits desirous of rapport with mortals who would themselves subsequently evolve through the contact. In ideas like his some saw a connection between spiritualism and Unitarianism and Swedenborgianism. (Mesmerism originated in the 1840s and was most notably fictionalized in Nathaniel Hawthorne's *The House of the Seven Gables* and *The Blithedale Romance*.)

Along with Davis, another convert to spiritualism was Judge John Edmonds of the New York Supreme Court, who edited *Spiritualism*, a collection of séance communications in two volumes that was published in 1853. Another distinguished spiritualist was the radical reformer and educator Robert Dale Owen (1801–1877), although Owen rejected the more sensationalized aspects of spiritualism, such as table rapping. His introspective *Footfalls on the Boundary of Another World*, published in Philadelphia in 1860, sold two thousand copies in a week and four thousand in the first three months. The son of an English reformer, Owen had edited labor newspapers in the United States and was at the time the best-known American to write a spiritualist treatise. Owen was known for careful investigation and cautious conclusions. The most concrete contemporary account of the historical sequence of spiritualist table-rapping incidents is Eliab Capron's *Modern Spiritualism: Its Facts and Fanaticisms, Its Consistencies and Contradictions* (1855). Capron recounts a prolific number of spiritualist events that he claims to transcribe directly from sources including newspapers, journals, and direct testimony, providing his own transitions and occasional commentary on the events.

The Boston planchette. "I saw as the name denotes, a little board of varnished wood, fashioned in the shape of a heart, seven inches long and five inches wide, that formed a sort of table by means of two pentagraph wheels at the broad end of the heart, and the lead-pencil inserted in a socket, one inch and a-quarter from the pint of the heart" (Field, *Planchette's Diary*, p. 7). COURTESY AMERICAN ANTIQUARIAN SOCIETY

In addition to the works above, a number of spiritualist journals were published, including the *Spiritual Telegraph, Light from the Spirit World*, and *Disclosures from the Interior and Superior Care for Mortals*. Invariably these periodicals included examples of automatic writing, such as selections from Lizzie Dotten's *Poems from the Inner Life* (1869). Automatic writing was the involuntary transcription by the medium of often lengthy messages from those

in the afterworld. Quickly the spiritualist movement diversified through automatic writing into longer treatises than the blunt question and answer sessions produced by table rappings or the planchette. Mediums who did automatic writing were frequently visited by the spirits of Romantic poets and other literary greats. Dotten, for example, alleged that her poems were transcriptions of new work as well as sage messages from Shakespeare, Edgar Allan Poe, and Robert Burns. Thomas Lake Harris believed that his work came to him through the Romantic poets Lord Byron, Samuel Taylor Coleridge, John Keats, and Percy Bysshe Shelley. The gothic caste of his own poetry, coupled with his mysterious death, made Poe a particular magnet for spiritualists. Even the spiritualist poet Thomas Holley Chivers, who had infamously accused Poe of plagiarizing "The Raven" and "Ulalume" from him, felt it necessary to defend the poet after his death from the claims of Mrs. Lydia M. Tenney that she was trance-writing Poe. Sarah Helen Whitman, Poe's onetime fiancée and the subject of his second "To Helen" poem, became a famous Poe medium with claims to legitimacy. In 1853 she published *Hours of Life and Other Poems,* a testament to her spiritualist attachment to Poe.

Whitman claimed that she and Poe shared a common bloodline, and she used Poe's reputation as a source by which to gain public recognition. Throughout the nineteenth century, spiritualist women extended their feminism beyond woman suffrage to include broader concerns, such as economics, women's dress, and marriage laws. By 1871, when the future suffragist Victoria Woodhull combined her leadership of the National Convention of Spiritualists with a meeting of the National Woman Suffrage Association, it was clear that a legendary merger between women's liberation and spiritualism had finally occurred, although spiritualist feminists would continue to push beyond the suffragists' advocacy of the woman's vote.

LITERARY ATTACKS AGAINST SPIRITUALISM

As one might expect, humorists and sometime humorists had a field day with what they alleged to be the pretensions of spiritualism, especially its pomposity, imposition on the gullible, undeserved profitability, and as seen in the quote from Mortimer Thomson above, the elevation of at least certain women to positions of power and influence during a time when men were supposed to rule the business sphere. One jibe at the movement's pomposity came from the New England sage James Russell Lowell (1819–1891), whose "The Unhappy Lot of Mr. Knott" was a long narrative parody of the Fox incident. In the Lowell version poor A. Gordon Knott, who has shown dubious architectural taste in fashioning his faux medieval mansion and worse judgment in choosing a certain Colonel Jones to wed his daughter Jenny, is snookered into thinking his house is haunted by "Those raps that unwrapped mysteries / So rapidly in Rochester" (p. 96). The poem is full of bad puns, including one about Knott's dead wife, who, "to rule him from her urn" might "have taken a peripatetic turn / For want of exorcising" (p. 97). Lowell pokes fun at alphabetical rapping and insinuates that the Fox sisters manufactured their sounds through toe cracking, a common accusation that Margaret ultimately confirmed in her old age. Even the Foxes' murdered peddler shows up in Lowell's poem, murdered by Colonel Jones. In the end Jenny and her real lover, Dr. Slade, marry as a result of staging the whole event.

Although the larger-than-life newspaper editor Horace Greeley vouched for spiritualism, P. T. Barnum, famous stager of spectacles and circuses, dismissed spiritualists as "humbugs" and took glee in revealing their behind-the-scenes tricks. The philosopher Oliver Wendell Holmes called spiritualism a "plague," and the editor of the *Knickerbocker*, Lewis Gaylord Clark, staged a hoax of his own to expose the fraudulence of séances. In "Among the Spirits," published in 1858, the humorist Artemus Ward uses a gullible narrator, so uneducated that he speaks in dialect, to mock Andrew Jackson Davis's concept of spiritual evolution in the afterlife. At a séance the narrator calls up the "Sperret" of his old pal William Tompkins to find out that, incredibly, the semiliterate Tompkins is with the seventeenth-century religious poet John Bunyan, Shakespeare, and the poet and playwright Ben Jonson in a circus. Tompkins disappears when the narrator asks about the money his dead friend owes him, to be replaced by the narrator's father, who says he is ashamed of his son's writing career because "Litteratoor is low" (p. 42). The narrator concludes that "Sperret rappers . . . air abowt the most ornery set of cusses I ever encountered in my life" (p. 43).

The longest parody of spiritualism is the story "The Apple-Tree Table; or, Original Spiritual Manifestations" (1856) by Herman Melville (1819–1891). The tale of a table haunted by 150-year-old bugs is based on an incident in the Berkshires that Henry David Thoreau also used in *Walden* as a symbol of resurrection. Hawthorne's "The Custom-House" is also evoked at the opening by the narrator's description of finding the table, upon which is a "ghostly, dismantled old quarto" (p. 9), in a closed garret of his home thought by popular sentiment to be haunted. As the narrator reads in the parlor at night from *Magnalia*,

the Puritan minister Cotton Mather's work on witchcraft, he is terrified to observe the "cloven feet" (p. 9) of the table. Soon, after an obvious allusion to the "Fox Girls," the table begins to "tick!" (p. 21). When they hear the ticking, the narrator's daughters immediately assume the table is haunted. The narrator occupies a midway ground between doubt and credulity and establishes his wife as the commonsense skeptic whose "naturalist" perspective wins out over his irrational fears and the daughters' insistence that they "consult Madame Pazza, the conjuress" (p. 49). "Conjuress" is an intriguing possible reference to African spiritualism; the Quaker abolitionists and ardent spiritualists Amy Post and Isaac Post may have found inspiration for their beliefs in their contact with the spiritual tales of African American slaves in the Underground Railroad. The famous African American radical thinker W. E. B. Du Bois writes that all "American fairy tales and folk-lore are Indian and African" (p. 14) and that native Africans had a "profound belief in invisible surrounding influences, good and bad" (p. 141). The scholar Ann Braude notes that white spiritualists were welcomed into African American churches.

Though "The Apple-Tree Table" is lighthearted, Melville implies within it a link between spiritualism and demonism, declaring in the wife's voice that "all good Christians" have nothing to fear (p. 28). In this he echoes what many religious leaders of the time were saying about the movement. In 1854 the former transcendentalist Orestes Brownson published a novel called *The Spirit-Rapper* in which the first-person narrator converts from mesmerism to spiritualism and later denounces the movement as the work of Satan. Brownson reiterates here his own personal conversion to Roman Catholicism. Harriet Beecher Stowe's brother Charles also connected spiritualism with demonism in his 1853 "Review of the 'Spiritual Manifestations.'" The famous Beecher family, seldom a united front, is always interesting to watch as its members take adamant stands on cultural issues only to recant them, sometimes in ambiguous ways. Isabella Beecher Hooker was an ardent advocate of spiritualism, as she was of free love (love without legal restrictions) and feminism—three movements that were intimately associated during this period. But her sister Harriet Beecher Stowe published three condemnations of spiritualism in her brother Henry Ward Beecher's *Christian Union* in 1870, complaining that spiritualism's promise of easy immortality had preempted faith in "the great beneficent miracles recorded in Scripture" (p. 130). Stowe's ambivalence about spiritualism can be seen in the fact that only two years earlier Stowe had approved the planchette. Her neighbor Mark Twain echoed

Stowe's later sentiments that this Ouija device was too easy a purchase of heaven.

SPIRITUALISM AND DOMESTICITY

Stowe's earlier plans to write an essay in 1868 approving the planchette did not materialize, perhaps because she was anticipated in that same year by the actress and journalist Kate Field (1838–1896), whose *Planchette's Diary* is a much more lighthearted publication than Stowe would have intended. Unlike Stowe's somber approach to the spiritualist movement, Field's work is a cheerful account of her relationship with what she drolly calls "Madam" Planchette even though the planchette is controlled by the spirit of Field's dead father. The father's staunch character serves Field in defending "Madam" against the most common accusation that spiritualism is a fraud. As he rather irascibly responds to the questions of Field's associates, the father asks how he can be expected to know the answers when they are outside his experience and unrelated to the interests and sentiments of his daughter, whom he uses as his medium. Field's entertaining accounts of a number of her soirees cleverly bat away, as if they were irritating gnats, every conceivable objection to the workings of the planchette. The planchette does not always get names right, for example, because "The mind never dwells upon names in spiritual life" (p. 16). Names do come up, however, and often the planchette reveals surprising results. Field uses only initials—Mr. O., Miss C.—in her recounting of her numerous planchette evenings. But one clue suggests that all these evenings really happened and with famous participants. Mr. G., for example, uses initials, but the planchette is able to discern that his unused first name is Richard and his middle name is Watson; Field discloses Mr. G. is an editor, and the surmise must be that this is the then assistant editor of *Century Magazine*, Richard Watson Gilder.

Another possible reason for Harriet Beecher Stowe's ambivalence about spiritualism was that her good friend and fellow writer Elizabeth Stuart Phelps (1844–1911) published two works in 1868 that touched positively on spiritualist themes. Her novel *The Gates Ajar* features the heroine's search for consolation after the death of her brother in the Civil War and the reassurance of her aunt that the dead are still in the mortal sphere. The book does not profess spiritualism per se but certainly opens the door to communication between the living and the dead. Aunt Winifred's conviction is that the dead are still around one, aiding one, in corporeal form; the novel even suggests that Aunt Winifred can commune with her own dead husband.

Phelps treats spiritualism more overtly in "The Day of My Death," an inverted mirror image of Melville's "The Apple-Tree Table." Here the mother, Allis, is credulous about the onslaught of rappings in her new home, while her husband Fred's skepticism leads him to exhaust all natural explanations until he finally believes the rappings and levitations are actually happening. They accelerate when Allis's spiritualist cousin Gertrude arrives for a visit wearing the standard medium's garb, a green barege veil. Gertrude, interpreting the uncanny from a spiritualist perspective, predicts that Fred is to die on a particular soon-approaching day. Although Phelps writes her tale as fiction, she claims that it actually occurred and that she has reliable witnesses to verify it. In her fictionalized version, however, the husband's prophesied death is proven inaccurate. Phelps's unwillingness to turn spiritualism morbid at the end is fueled by her instincts for what will sell.

What remains most surprising about the mid-century beginnings of the spiritualist movement in America is the manner in which it captured the entire nation, both in popular culture and in the realms of the most respected writers. During these years the waning faith in traditional religion and consequent unfulfilled longing for an afterlife, together with spiritualism's tie-in between faith and the scientific empiricism engendered by burgeoning technologies equally obsessed with fields of electrical magnetism, lent an integrity and fervor to the spiritualist movement that may never have again.

See also Death; Feminism; *The Gates Ajar;* Journals and Diaries; Philosophy; Religion; Satire, Burlesque, and Parody; Theater

BIBLIOGRAPHY
Primary Works
Barnum, P. T. "The Spiritualists." In his *The Humbugs of the World,* pp. 49–109. Detroit: Singing Tree Press, 1970.

Doesticks, Q. K. Philander [Mortimer Thomson]. "How Doesticks Came to Think of It." In *Doesticks What He Says,* pp. 13–17. New York: Edward Livermore, 1855.

Du Bois, W. E. B. *The Souls of Black Folk.* New York: Library of America, 1990.

Field, Kate. *Planchette's Diary.* New York: J. S. Redfield, 1868.

Lowell, James Russell. "The Unhappy Lot of Mr. Knott." In *The Complete Writings of James Russell Lowell,* vol. 12, pp. 91–120. Cambridge, Mass.: Riverside, 1904.

Melville, Herman. "The Apple-Tree Table; or, Original Spiritual Manifestations." 1856. In *The Apple-Tree Table and Other Sketches,* pp. 9–51. New York: Greenwood, 1969.

Phelps, Elizabeth Stuart. "The Day of My Death." In *Men, Women, and Ghosts,* pp. 113–160. Boston: James R. Osgood, 1873.

Stowe, Harriet Beecher. "Spiritualism." *Christian Union* 2 (3 September 1870): 129–130.

Ward, Artemus. "Among the Spirits." In *Complete Works of Artemus Ward,* pp. 40–43. New York: Burt Franklin, 1970.

Secondary Works

Braude, Ann. *Radical Spirits: Spiritualism and Women's Rights in Nineteenth-Century America.* Bloomington: Indiana University Press, 1989.

Kerr, Howard. *Mediums, and Spirit-Rappers, and Roaring Radicals: Spiritualism in American Literature, 1850–1900.* Urbana: University of Illinois Press, 1972.

Owen, Alex. "Power and Gender: The Spiritualist Context." In *The Darkened Room: Women, Power, and Spiritualism in Late Victorian England,* pp. 1–40. Philadelphia: University of Pennsylvania Press, 1990.

Pattee, Fred Lewis. *The Feminine Fifties.* New York: D. Appleton–Century, 1940.

Janet Gabler-Hover

SUFFRAGE

Nineteenth-century suffrage movements can be best understood both within the history and culture of the period and as part of a broader set of social reform movements. For the most part, between the turn of the century and the Civil War, voting rights became increasingly defined in terms of whiteness and manhood. Early in the century, New Jersey law had allowed "all 'inhabitants' who otherwise were qualified" to vote, which was "interpreted locally to mean that property-owning women could vote" (Marilley, p. 54). In 1807, however, the New Jersey legislature established that only free white men could vote, thus enacting voting-rights criteria more in line with the rest of the nation. As for free African Americans, few states immediately denied them the vote following the Revolution, but by the time of the Civil War, only Massachusetts, Vermont, New Hampshire, Maine, and Rhode Island failed to discriminate against free blacks (Keyssar, p. 55). Enslaved blacks were denied the vote, as were many Native Americans and a number of new immigrants, including Chinese immigrants in the West and Irish immigrants in the East. It was within this political context that the suffrage movements developed and operated.

Despite the success of these antiprogressive voting laws, an environment for progressive social and political reform was being established. In the late 1820s the Englishwoman Frances (Fanny) Wright (1795–1852) began a lecture tour of the United States, speaking before audiences of both men and women. By speaking in front of mixed audiences, a violation of contemporary notions about what constituted the women's sphere, Wright established a precedent. In 1829 David Walker (1785–1830) published *Walker's Appeal . . . to the Coloured Citizens of the World,* in which he argued that slaves should revolt against their owners. He also condemned antislavery colonization efforts that would send freed slaves to Africa. Two years later, William Lloyd Garrison (1805–1879) established *The Liberator,* an abolitionist weekly that became a champion of other radical social reforms, including women's rights. In the early 1830s Maria W. Stewart (1803–1879), a free African American woman living in Boston, was published in *The Liberator* and delivered speeches before mixed-sex black audiences, arguing for universal rights and the abolition of slavery. These examples served as early moments in a developing reform culture that would have increasing if often indirect influence on American politics in the decades preceding the American Civil War.

THE DEVELOPING SUFFRAGE MOVEMENTS

The suffrage movements of this period were thus an aspect of larger reform movements that targeted a broad expansion of rights for Americans who were denied the benefits associated with citizenship. The most prominent of these movements began in the 1830s and focused on antislavery reform; as a supporter of the movement, the radical abolitionist Garrison greatly affected suffrage reform. Garrison not only advocated freedom and full citizenship rights for enslaved African Americans but also encouraged female participation in the movement, thus providing the foundation for the first organized women's rights movement in the United States. Garrison's *The Liberator* offered a forum for radical social reformers including Sarah Moore Grimké (1792–1873), Angelina Emily Grimké (1805–1879), Frederick Douglass (1818–1895), and Wendell Phillips (1811–1884) to advocate a progressive agenda organized around a radical expansion of rights, including suffrage, for the disenfranchised. The formation in 1833 of the American Anti-Slavery Society also proved to be a significant moment in antebellum social reform, providing the organizational foundation for the antislavery movement while also creating an environment in which a philosophy for women's rights could develop. Early on, women were among the most active abolitionists, organizing petition drives and raising the money needed to sustain the movement. Some of these

***The Age of Brass; or, The Triumphs of Woman's Rights,* 1869.** Lithograph by Currier & Ives. Fears of female dominance resulting from women's suffrage are expressed in this cartoon. THE LIBRARY OF CONGRESS

women also became increasingly visible in their abolitionism by publishing their antislavery arguments and by speaking before mixed-sex and mixed-race audiences. Following Wright and Stewart, the most notable early examples of this were the Grimké sisters, daughters of a wealthy slave-owning family, who became two of the most vocal of the Garrisonian antislavery activists in the late 1830s. Both wrote against slavery and spoke to audiences composed of both men and women. The participation of women in the abolition movement provided them with experience that would later become essential in planning women's rights organizations and running conventions, but it also underscored the need for an independent women's rights movement. At the 1840 World Anti-Slavery Convention in London, female delegates from the United States were denied the opportunity to participate because they were women, which convinced Lucretia Mott (1793–1880) and Elizabeth Cady Stanton (1815–1902) that the time for the reform of women's rights had arrived.

In 1838 Sarah Grimké published *Letters on the Equality of the Sexes,* which grew out of her developing political beliefs and the criticism she and her sister had received for their very public abolitionism, which was perceived as transgressing the appropriate female sphere. Earlier in 1837 the General Association of Congregational Ministers of Massachusetts had issued their "Pastoral Letter," a response to the public political activity of the Grimkés. In this letter, the ministers urged women to reject the public sphere and to instead embrace the private, encouraging "the cultivation of private Christian character, and private efforts for the spiritual good of individuals." Grimké challenged this position by advocating greater rights and freedoms for women. In 1843 a second founding work of the American women's rights movement was published, Margaret Fuller's (1810–1850) essay "The Great Lawsuit; Man versus Men, Woman versus Women," which Fuller later expanded into a book, *Woman in the Nineteenth Century* (1845). Less overtly political than Sarah Grimké and other women's rights activists, Fuller advanced ideas that were nonetheless crucial to the developing women's rights movement. Fuller argued that women should have access to the same paths in life as those available to men and should be responsible for their own choices.

While Fuller does not specifically champion suffrage—her arguments are more philosophically abstract than overtly political, reflecting an approach rooted in transcendentalism—her work helped provide an ideological basis for later women's rights efforts, which included the vote for women. The 1848 Seneca Falls Convention drew on Fuller's work for a philosophical foundation for women's rights. The Seneca Falls Convention stands out as perhaps the most important moment in the nineteenth-century women's rights movement, in part because it was the first meeting in the United States organized exclusively for the advancement of women's rights but also because of its Declaration of Sentiments. Written by Elizabeth Cady Stanton and modeled on the Declaration of Independence, this document details how men have historically wronged women, echoing Thomas Jefferson's litany of England's abuses of the colonies. Included in Stanton's declaration was a list of resolutions, the ninth of which claimed that it is "the duty of the women of this country to secure to themselves their sacred right to the elective franchise" (1:70). This resolution proved to be the most controversial, even within the convention itself, as opponents condemned it, arguing that it was impractical and that it would undermine women's rights as a whole. The resolution passed, however, when Frederick Douglass argued that the vote was an essential component of freedom that should be denied based neither on sex nor race. Following the Seneca Falls Convention, female suffrage became an important element in the drive for expanded women's rights, with Stanton and Susan B. Anthony (1820–1906) often taking the lead. However, while most of these reformers believed that suffrage was a crucial element of women's rights, other issues related to property rights, divorce rights, and child custody sometimes were deemed of greater significance for women; part of the reason for this was that the reform of these laws would provide immediate relief for women, but it was also a question of what was most pragmatic, as female suffrage faced considerable entrenched opposition.

ABOLITIONISM IN THE 1850S

As a women's rights movement developed, abolitionists continued their efforts to end the practice of slavery in the United States. A key moment occurred in 1845 when *Narrative of the Life of Frederick Douglass, an American Slave,* an autobiography detailing Douglass's years as a slave and his escape to the North, was published. Douglass had for several years been among the most effective antislavery speakers, but it was his first autobiography that most firmly established his abolitionist credentials and public identity,

and it has endured as one of the most important works of antebellum literature. In the decades following the *Narrative,* Douglass remained active as a reformer, publishing his own abolitionist paper, the *North Star,* which later became *Frederick Douglass' Paper,* and advocating universal suffrage.

The 1850s proved to be one of the most politically contentious decades in American history, largely because of the slavery issue. Early in the decade, two novels, Harriet Beecher Stowe's (1811–1896) *Uncle Tom's Cabin* (1852) and William Wells Brown's (c. 1814–1884) *Clotel* (1853), reflected the politically charged environment. Stowe's novel, first serialized in the moderate antislavery newspaper the *National Era,* became the most successful novel in American history. Stowe had intended that *Uncle Tom's Cabin* would peacefully end slavery in America by revealing to the public the moral horrors associated with the institution. While the novel clearly fell short of this goal, it did shape the antebellum discourse on slavery and advance the antislavery sentiment in the North. Brown's *Clotel* may have had a lesser social impact than *Uncle Tom's Cabin,* but it is nevertheless significant both for cultural and literary reasons. The first published novel by an African American writer, it details the travails of the daughters of Thomas Jefferson and an African American slave, exploring how the intersection of Jefferson's two legacies—that of the rhetoric of freedom invoked in the Declaration of Independence and that of his own slave progeny—revealed conflicting American belief systems that were reflected in the ongoing ideological clash between northern freedom and southern slavery. Both novels represent the antebellum era's spirit of reform, specifically in antislavery terms, and both advanced the emphasis on individual rights advocated by radical reformers.

During the 1850s this conflict became more heated as politicians attempted to maintain the compromise on slavery between North and South written into the constitution while antislavery reformers advanced their own agendas and northerners and southerners became increasingly mutually suspicious. The Fugitive Slave Act (1850), the Kansas-Nebraska Act (1854), and the Supreme Court's *Dred Scott* decision (1857) were pivotal moments in the ongoing attempt to maintain this delicate balance, and each reinforced the belief of many northerners that slave power had increasing authority in their lives. From this situation emerged John Brown's (1800–1859) violent attacks on proslavery settlers in Kansas and his later raid on Harpers Ferry. Widely condemned throughout the nation, Brown nonetheless gained the respect of many northerners even if they objected to his violent tactics, largely because he provided a challenge to what they perceived as the spread of slave power, which is reflected in Henry David Thoreau's "A Plea for John Brown" (1859). In the realm of politics, the formation and rapid growth of the Republican Party demonstrated the increasing importance of political abolitionism and a movement away from apolitical reform societies as the center of the antislavery movement. John Brown's acts in 1859 and the founding of the Republican Party in 1854 reflected the growing antislavery sentiment in the North; this sentiment would lead to the election of Abraham Lincoln to the presidency, which in turn offered southern states the rationale to secede, prompting the beginning of the Civil War.

SUFFRAGE AND THE POSTWAR PERIOD

The Civil War caused social reformers to pause in their reform efforts and shift their focus to the war. Following the Union victory, suffrage activists recognized the opportunity to press their case. The alliance between women's rights reformers and abolitionists had been established in the early years of Garrison's *The Liberator,* but long-developing tensions between the two movements were exacerbated following the war. For decades, this alliance had been threatened by the unwillingness of many antislavery activists to accept the very public roles that women had occupied. While male Garrisonians largely embraced the women's contribution and supported women's rights, more conservative reformers identified their behavior as a violation of the women's sphere and a threat to the antislavery cause.

When it became clear after the war that new laws would be established providing rights and protections to newly free African Americans, including possible amendments to the constitution involving voting rights, suffrage activists could see both opportunity and potential danger. While Stanton and Anthony continued to call for suffrage for women, other reformers, including Frederick Douglass, Lucy Stone (1818–1893), and Lydia Maria Child (1802–1880), argued that such advocacy at this crucial moment would endanger suffrage for black men, with potentially disastrous consequences. For Douglass, it was a question of survival for African Americans, as the racially charged postwar milieu in the South and the riots targeting blacks in northern cities revealed. Suffrage, Douglass believed, would provide a form of protection that had long been denied to African Americans. For Stanton and others, failure to achieve suffrage for women would be a defeat and would indicate that decades of effort had been squandered. The passage of the Fourteenth Amendment proved especially vexing, as the inclusion of the word "male" three times in

Section 2 made the fears of suffragists real; the constitution had now clearly excluded women from voting in federal elections.

Suffragists held out hope that a subsequent amendment would grant women the vote, but the later passage of the Fifteenth Amendment, which declared that "The right of citizens of the United States to vote shall not be denied or abridged by the United States or by any State on account of race, color, or previous condition of servitude," dashed these hopes, as well, as the language made it clear that women would continue to be denied the elective franchise. Women's suffrage was thus deferred, and it would take nearly fifty years before women gained the vote, with the passage of the Nineteenth Amendment. What initially appeared to be a victory for African Americans was, however, complicated by widespread systematic efforts to deny them the vote for decades following the war. It would take the civil rights movement of the mid-twentieth century to finally ensure that the Fourteenth and Fifteenth Amendments would truly be enforced.

See also Declaration of Sentiments; *Letters on the Equality of the Sexes; The Liberator;* Oratory; Reform; Seneca Falls Convention; *Woman in the Nineteenth Century*

BIBLIOGRAPHY
Primary Works

Brown, William Wells. *Clotel; or, The President's Daughter.* 1853. New York: Arno Press, 1969.

Fuller, Margaret. *Woman in the Nineteenth Century and Other Writings.* 1845. Edited and with an introduction by Donna Dickenson. Oxford and New York: Oxford University Press, 1994.

General Association of Congregational Ministers of Massachusetts. "Pastoral Letter." 1837. In *American Rhetorical Discourse,* edited by Ronald F. Reid, pp. 365–367. Prospect Heights, Ill: Waveland Press, 1995.

Grimké, Sarah. *Letters on the Equality of the Sexes and Other Essays.* Edited and with an introduction by Elizabeth Ann Bartlett. New Haven, Conn.: Yale University Press, 1988.

Stanton, Elizabeth Cady, Susan B. Anthony, and Matilda Joslyn Gage. *History of Woman Suffrage.* 6 vols. 1881–1922. New York: Arno Press, 1969.

Stowe, Harriet Beecher. *Uncle Tom's Cabin; or, Life among the Lowly.* Boston: J. P. Jewett; Cleveland: Jewett, Proctor, and Worthington, 1852.

Walker, David. *David Walker's Appeal to the Coloured Citizens of the World.* 1829. Edited and with a new introduction by Peter P. Hinks. University Park: Pennsylvania State University Press, 2000.

Secondary Works

Du Bois, Ellen Carol. *Feminism and Suffrage: The Emergence of an Independent Women's Movement in America, 1848–1869*. Ithaca, N.Y.: Cornell University Press, 1978.

Isenberg, Nancy. *Sex and Citizenship in Antebellum America*. Chapel Hill: University of North Carolina Press, 1998.

Keyssar, Alexander. *The Right to Vote: The Contested History of Democracy in the United States*. New York: Basic Books, 2000.

Marilley, Suzanne M. *Woman Suffrage and the Origins of Liberal Feminism in the United States, 1820–1920*. Cambridge, Mass.: Harvard University Press, 1996.

Yellin, Jean Fagan. *Women and Sisters: The Antislavery Feminists in American Culture*. New Haven, Conn.: Yale University Press, 1989.

James R. Britton

SWALLOW BARN

John Pendleton Kennedy (1795–1870) published *Swallow Barn; or, A Sojourn in the Old Dominion*, his first and finest novel, in May 1832. He left his name off the title page, allowing his first-person narrator, Mark Littleton, to stand in as author. But Kennedy was already well established as a man of letters, and knowledge of his authorship of *Swallow Barn* spread quickly. The novel met with widespread acclaim. As a contributor to the *Southern Literary Messenger* noted some years later, *Swallow Barn* was "read and enjoyed, from the Chesapeake to the Ohio" (p. 764). Actually, the popularity of the work extended even further. A London edition appeared in August 1832, and a two-volume Swedish translation was published in Stockholm in 1835. *Swallow Barn* is considered the foremost example of a minor genre of antebellum American literature known as the plantation novel.

THE STORY

The narrator begins the story of his sojourn in Virginia with an introductory epistle to a friend back in his home state of New York. Kennedy thus situated *Swallow Barn* in a tradition of travels through the South written by northerners that included such works as *Letters from the South* (1817), by James Kirke Paulding (1778–1860). In its literary style, its closest antecedent is *Bracebridge Hall* (1822) by Washington Irving (1783–1859). Implicitly, Kennedy uses his narrative to bridge the gap between sectional differences and to inform northerners of the delights of Virginia.

The casual tone and leisurely pace of the introductory epistle prepare readers for the narrative to follow. Over the first hundred pages of the book, he introduces all the major characters who people the James River plantation known as Swallow Barn: Frank Meriwether, the master of the plantation; Lucretia, his dutiful and affectionate wife; Prudence, the eccentric spinster sister; Parson Chub, the stereotypical cleric who is fond of food, drink, and books; Ned Hazard, the cousin who has invited Mark Littleton to Swallow Barn; Bel Tracy, the neighboring beauty whom Ned loves; Carey, the banjo-playing slave who is described as "a perfect shadow of his master" (p. 36); and numerous other characters who visit the plantation during Mark's stay.

One of the most delightful episodes in the book concerns Frank Meriwether's library. Since the seventeenth century, Virginia gentlemen had been known for having fine collections of books. When Parson Chub suggests a book-buying expedition, Frank likes the idea and agrees to finance the parson's excursion to New England. After Parson Chub returns with great masses of old folios, he and Frank retire to the library every evening for long hours of undisturbed study. Or so it would seem. One evening, Ned discovers their secret upon entering the library accidentally:

> When he entered the library, both candles were burning in their sockets, with long, untrimmed wicks; the fire was reduced to its last embers, and, in an armchair on one side of the table, the parson was discovered in a sound sleep over Jeremy Taylor's Ductor Dubitantium; whilst Frank, in another chair on the opposite side, was snoring over a folio edition of Montaigne. And upon the table stood a small stone pitcher containing a residuum of whisky-punch, now grown cold. (P. 67)

CRITICAL RECEPTION

When *Swallow Barn* first appeared, praise of the novel was almost universal in the southern press. Remarkably, the book received many positive comments from northern reviewers as well. Noticing the book for the staid Boston quarterly the *North American Review*, Edward Everett (1794–1865) began with a pronouncement: "This is a work of great merit and promise" (p. 519). Not all northerners appreciated *Swallow Barn*, however. The reviewer for the *New-England Magazine* thought the author was satirizing plantation life and called the book "a gentle satire on the pride, aristocratic feeling, and ignorance of a certain class, rather numerous in the south. . . . His principal characters are humorously conceived, pompous, ignorant and dogmatic. He has succeeded admirably in showing them in a ridiculous light" (p. 76).

Frontispiece from the 1851 illustrated edition of *Swallow Barn*. THOMAS COOPER LIBRARY, UNIVERSITY OF SOUTH CAROLINA.

Kennedy's next novel, *Horse-Shoe Robinson* (1835), gave reviewers the opportunity to cite his previous one, and the success of *Horse-Shoe Robinson* reinforced the critical appreciation of *Swallow Barn*. Edgar Allan Poe (1809–1849), to name the book's most distinguished contemporary reviewer, recalled reading *Swallow Barn* with great fondness. Speaking in the editorial plural, Poe observed, "We have not forgotten, nor is it likely we shall very soon forget, the rich simplicity of diction—the manliness of tone—the admirable traits of Virginian manners, and the striking pictures of still life, to be found in *Swallow Barn*" (p. 648).

REVISIONS AND LATER EDITIONS

Two decades later, Kennedy significantly revised his plantation novel. G. P. Putnam and Company published the new edition of *Swallow Barn* in 1851. Kennedy made his most significant alterations in the later portions of the work. The first edition had contained a lengthy appreciation of Captain John Smith (1580–1631) toward its end, a digression that, though heartfelt, greatly taxed the reader's patience at a point when the story was already starting to seem too long. Kennedy greatly abbreviated his discussion of Smith for the revised edition. In a chapter entitled "The Quarter," which describes life among the slaves,

Kennedy also sharpened his defense of the practice of slavery to suit the 1850s. The new edition was illustrated by David Hunter Strother (1816–1888). Contemporary readers appreciated Strother's illustrations, but his depiction of a plantation peopled by barefoot, wide-eyed, happy-go-lucky slaves now seems cloyingly racist.

The revised edition was received with much enthusiasm. The introduction to a prepublication extract in the *International Magazine,* for example, called Kennedy "the best painter of manners who has ever tried his hand at their delineation in America" and *Swallow Barn* "one of the most charming compositions in the literature of the present time" (p. 151). The Putnam edition went through numerous reprints in the 1850s and stayed in print through the nineteenth century, though its popularity waned considerably after the Civil War. But many *Swallow Barn* enthusiasts could still be found after Reconstruction, even in the North. Writing in the 1870s, Robert C. Winthrop (1809–1894) said that the novel's "sketches of Virginia life and manners, including a very notable chapter on Slavery, entitled 'The Quarter,' furnish the best picture we have even now of that section of the Union at the period to which they relate, and possess not a little of historical interest and permanent value" (p. 71).

The Putnam edition went out of print in the first decade of the twentieth century, and *Swallow Barn* remained out of print until 1929, when Harcourt, Brace published a new edition with an introduction by Jay B. Hubbell (1885–1979) as part of its American Authors series. This new edition reinforced the status of *Swallow Barn* as a classic of American literature, and some readers were grateful for the opportunity to reread it. Edward M. Gwathmey (1891–1956), for one, commented,

> We greet Kennedy's *Swallow Barn* upon its republication with the same pleasure that we feel in greeting a friend of our youth who has been absent from our midst for a long time and who suddenly reappears. . . . It is a book to be read for relaxation. In it Kennedy does not burden his readers with an intricate plot; so that it may be read with equal pleasure either in parts or in its entirety. I can think of no book which I should prefer to have for a traveling companion on a wearisome journey. (P. 225)

DEPICTION OF SLAVERY

Not all shared Gwathmey's enthusiasm, however. Many have found *Swallow Barn* difficult to read, not only because of its leisurely pace and lengthy digressions but also because of Kennedy's partisan defense of slavery. Some passages of the book are hard to receive with anything but scorn today. In "The Quarter," for example, Kennedy identifies slavery as a transition state between savagery and civilization, observing that "no tribe of people have ever passed from barbarism to civilization whose middle stage of progress has been more secure from harm, more genial to their character, or better supplied with mild and beneficent guardianship, adapted to the actual state of their intellectual feebleness, than the negroes of Swallow Barn" (p. 453).

The novel is now recognized more as a cultural artifact than a classic work of literature. Beginning in the 1960s, *Swallow Barn* was largely read for its depiction of African American life and culture and, as a result, was more often denigrated than appreciated. Later, however, some scholars recognized *Swallow Barn* as an important reflection of American attitudes toward family, community, and place. The international reputation promised by the early Swedish translation never materialized, but a Russian study written

by Louisa P. Bashmakova in the late 1990s found that *Swallow Barn* exemplifies the role of the South as the cradle for a poetic mythology central to the American literary imagination.

See also Proslavery Writing

BIBLIOGRAPHY

Primary Work

Kennedy, John Pendleton. *Swallow Barn; or, A Sojourn in the Old Dominion.* 1832. Edited by Lucinda H. MacKethan. Baton Rouge: Louisiana State University Press, 1986.

Secondary Works

Bakker, Jan. "Time and Timelessness in Images of the Old South: Pastoral in John Pendleton Kennedy's *Swallow Barn* and *Horse-Shoe Robinson.*" *Tennessee Studies in Literature* 26 (1981): 75–88.

Bashmakova, Louisa P. *Pisateli Starago Iuga.* Krasnodar: Ministerstvo Bysshego i Professional'nogo Obrazovaniia Possiia Federatsii, 1997.

Bohner, Charles H. *John Pendleton Kennedy, Gentleman from Baltimore.* Baltimore: Johns Hopkins Press, 1961.

[Everett, Edward.] "*Swallow Barn.*" *North American Review* 36 (1833): 519–544.

Gwathmey, Edward M. Review of *Swallow Barn. American Literature* 1 (1929): 225–226.

Hare, John L. *Will the Circle Be Unbroken?: Family and Sectionalism in the Virginia Novels of Kennedy, Caruthers, and Tucker, 1830–1845.* New York: Routledge, 2002.

"Literary Notices." *New-England Magazine* 3 (1832): 76–79.

"Notices of New Books." *Southern Literary Messenger* 17 (1851): 764.

Poe, Edgar Allan. *Essays and Reviews.* Edited by G. R. Thompson. New York: Library of America, 1984.

Romine, Scott. *The Narrative Forms of Southern Community.* Baton Rouge: Louisiana State University Press, 1999.

"Rural Life in Virginia: The *Swallow Barn.*" *International Magazine of Literature, Art, and Science* 4 (1851): 151–156.

Winthrop, Robert C. *Addresses and Speeches on Various Occasions, from 1869 to 1879.* Boston: Little, Brown, 1879.

Kevin J. Hayes

TALL TALES

Tall tales, oral and written, and one of America's oldest and most popular narrative forms, flourished in the nineteenth century, especially on the frontier. A combination of reality and fantasy, usually told in the first person as a true story and frequently disguised as a personal narrative or anecdote, the tall tale typically depends on the storyteller assuming a straight-faced pose, purporting to be relating fact but enlarging the plot with fictive and outlandish details, which cumulatively create an incredible and fanciful yarn. The intent of the tall tale is humorous, its humor stemming from absurd situations intended to entertain through amusing stretchers or comic lies. Moreover, according to Henry B. Wonham, tall tales promote communal identity, solidifying the connection between the yarn spinner and his listeners when the latter "respond instantaciously with appropriate recognition and understanding to the rhetorical game he is playing" ("Character Development of the Ring-Tailed Roarer," p. 272) Those who catch on, comprehending and appreciating the tale as fiction rather than as truth, who enjoy the storyteller's artful reconfiguring and embellishment of details in creating the preposterous, and who thereby subsequently avoid embarrassment and humiliation, comprise the tale's in-group. The victim, on the other hand, often an outsider and naïf, hears the tall tale as fact and regards it as true and plausible. And his gullibility contributes to the amusement of the tale's narrator and of the rest of the knowing audience.

An antecedent of the tall tale is the seventeenth- and eighteenth-century promotional tract, books like William Wood's *New England Prospect* (1634), John Josselyn's *New England Rarities Discovered* (1672) and *An Account of Two Voyages to New England* (1675), George Alsop's *A Character of the Province of Maryland* (1666), and John Lawson's *A New Voyage to Carolina* (1709), which feature deliberately exaggerated and spurious descriptions of flora, fauna, climate, and Native Americans. For example, Lawson describes the fertility of the Carolina soil, humorously noting that "eating peaches in our Orchards makes them come up so thick from the kernel that we are forced to take a great deal of care to weed them out; otherwise they make our Lands a Wilderness of Peach trees" (p. 115); Josselyn reports among New England's rarities radishes that grow "as big as a man's arm" (p. 336), a frog as large as a man, a goose with three hearts, and a wild cat with six whole geese in his stomach. Exercises in humorous hyperbole, these promotional tall tales not only accentuated American self-identity that came to be associated with the American frontier but also satirized English ignorance and gullibility about America. Earmarks of the tall tale also show up occasionally in William Byrd's 1728 *The History of the Dividing Line* when he describes alligators that swallow rocks to make themselves heavy enough to pull cows underwater to drown them and then afterward to regurgitate the rocks and squirrels that cross a river on pieces of bark, using their tails as sails.

MUNCHAUSEN'S INFLUENCE

While oral tall tales flourished on the American frontier in the late eighteenth and nineteenth centuries, a crucial development in the evolution of the tall tale in its written form was a foreign import, the widely popular pamphlet *Baron Munchausen's Narrative of His Marvellous Travels and Campaigns in Russia* (1785), by the German Rudolph Raspe. By 1800 *Baron Munchausen's Narrative* had been translated into five languages, and by 1835 it had gone through twenty-four editions in the United States, the latter a reliable indicator of its popularity here. In fact, early editions of the baron's fantastic adventures and exploits were brought to America and reprinted, but with some distinctive Americanizations added. Numerous nineteenth-century American yarn spinners seemed to imitate some of Raspe's tall-talish methods in their stories, including featuring deadpan prevaricators who were purporting to be recounting their tales orally to a community of listeners comprised of persons gathering around campfires, congregating on steamboats or in saloons, or attending political barbeques. Moreover, many of these raconteurs, among them James Kirke Paulding's Nimrod Wildfire, Thomas C. Haliburton's Sam Slick, Thomas Bangs Thorpe's (1815–1878) Jim Doggett, Hardin E. Taliaferro's Fisher's River story-tellers, George Washington Harris's (1849–1869) Sut Lovingood, and William Gilmore Simms's Sam Snaffles, sometimes adopted variants of narrative techniques, appropriated plots and motifs, and in some cases even produced reincarnations of Munchausen tales. As a catalyst for the emergence of the written tall narrative in America, Walter Blair has observed, "the baron's tales about hunting and fishing in Russia . . . were ready made for American appropriation and naturalization" ("A German Connection," p. 133).

The southwestern humorist Hardin E. Taliaferro (1811–1875), the author of *Fisher's River (North Carolina) Scenes and Characters* (1859) who was born in Surry County, North Carolina, but who spent most of his adult life as a Baptist minister in Alabama, has the affable Uncle Davy Lane, an actual Surry County story-teller, recount two tales in this collection, "The Pigeon's Roost" and "Ride in the Peach Tree," which employ folklore motifs first popularized in the Munchausen tales. In "The Pigeon's Roost," Uncle Davy relates how his horse, which he has hitched to the limb of a tree where a large flock of pigeons is roosting, is suddenly lifted forty feet into the air after he begins shooting at the birds, a variation of the Munchausen story where the baron, when caught in a snowstorm, ties his horse to what he believes is the stump of a tree, only to discover the next morning when the snow has melted that he had tied his horse to the weathercock of a church steeple. In "Ride in a Peachtree" Uncle Davy recounts a hunting story, built on a popular Munchausen motif, in which he describes having shot at a deer, using a peach stone for ammunition (the

Baron had used cherry stones) and discovers sometime later that the deer he shot has a peach tree growing behind its shoulders.

Another widespread appropriation from Munchausen by American storytellers is the motif of the wonderful hunt, an element recast in numerous nineteenth-century American tall tales featuring hunting adventures, one of the best of which is William Gilmore Simms's (1806–1870) "How Sharp Snaffles Got His Capital and Wife," published posthumously in *Harper's Magazine* in 1870. Based on an actual hunting excursion in the autumn of 1847 when Simms and some of his friends traveled to the Balsam range in southwestern North Carolina, "Sharp" (Sam) Snaffles seems to be drawing, if only indirectly, on the wonderful hunt pattern established in some of the Munchausen tales. In Simms's variant, he has Sam Snaffles describe in a straight-faced manner how he snared twenty-seven hundred geese by placing a large net on a pond, and when the geese get entangled, they fly away with him, eventually dropping Sam into a hollow stump loaded with honey. Then when a bear comes down the stump and threatens Sam's life, he kills it, the bear providing him with four hundred and fifty pounds of meat. With geese, two thousand pounds of honey, and an enormous quantity of bear meat, Sam has, with little intentional effort on his own, managed to acquire the capital to attain respectability and ultimately to marry the woman he desires for his wife.

DAVY CROCKETT AND MIKE FINK

Through their adventures and exploits on the American frontier, Mike Fink (1770–1823) and David Crockett (1786–1836), both real-life frontiersmen, literally invented themselves as larger-than-life characters. Furthermore, their fictionalization in numerous tall tales, many by anonymous journalists, helped to popularize Fink and Crockett as mythic heroes. Tales featuring them were widely circulated both orally and in print, the print versions appearing in almanacs, plays, gift books, newspapers, and magazines. In 1828 Morgan Neville in "The Last of the Boatmen" featured Fink as a half horse, half alligator kind of man, and Timothy Flint, Thomas Bangs Thorpe, John S. Robb, and anonymous authors of the *Crockett Almanac* sketches further enlarged Fink to legendary status. Born in Fort Pitt on the Pennsylvania frontier where he served as an Indian fighter and scout in the 1770s, Fink later migrated to the Mississippi and Ohio Rivers where he worked as a keelboatman and eventually moved to the Rocky Mountains to become a hunter and trapper. In actuality a rowdy, fearless, reckless roughneck, violently cruel and already a legend before he died, Fink, in fictionalized accounts, was reconfigured as a man who could drink a gallon of whiskey in twenty-four hours but without impairing his physical mobility or slurring his speech, who boasted that he "could out-run, out-jump, out-shoot, out-brag, out-drink, and out-fight, rough an' tumble . . . any man on both sides the river from Pittsburgh to New Orleans an' back ag'in to St. Louiee," who could ride a moose like a horse, and who even beat Davy Crockett in a shooting match ("Mike Fink's Brag," p. 2056; "Mike Fink Hunting a Moose," p. 211; "Col. Crockett Beat at a Shooting Match," p. 65).

Crockett was born on the Tennessee frontier, fought in the Creek War, served in the Tennessee legislature and in the United States Congress, and later fought heroically for Texas independence before being killed at the battle of the Alamo. Through self-promotion and as a subject of numerous tall tales he was elevated to iconic status, even while still alive. Acknowledging his mythic status, in part attributable to his own invention in his pseudo-autobiography and the imaginative lore featured in biographies and in tall tales by anonymous folk journalists and almanac writers, Congressman Crockett wrote,

> I have met with hundreds, if not thousands of people who have formed their opinions of my appearance, habits, language, and every thing else. . . . They have almost in every instance expressed the most profound astonishment at finding me in human shape, and with the *countenance, appearance,* and *common feelings* of a human being. (Blair and Hill, p. 122)

Tall tales, many the work of anonymous writers in the *Crockett Almanacs* (1835–1856), comically and hyperbolically celebrated Davy Crockett's exploits, including such fabricated boasts that he drank dry the waters of the Gulf of Mexico, rode his pet alligator up Niagara Falls, unfroze the earth frozen in its axis with hot bear oil, escaped a tornado by mounting a streak of lightning, and saved the United States from destruction by wringing the tail off Haley's Comet and throwing it back into outer space.

The *Crockett Almanacs* also featured frontier women, aptly designated as "riproarious shemales," an "inversion of the then current ideal of femininity," according to Michael A. Lofaro ("Riproarious Shemales," p. 117). Though not given voice so as to be able to celebrate their own superhuman exploits orally, these women, almost all of whom were single, displayed extraordinary abilities, such as independence, physical strength, courage, and self-confidence, typically the attributes ascribed to legendary frontier men. Lotty Ritchers, "The Flower of Gum Swamp,"

A Tongariferous Fight with an Alligator. Woodcut from the *Crockett Almanac*, 1837. THE LIBRARY OF CONGRESS

who would rather fight and gouge out men's eyes than court them romantically; Katy Goodgrit, who "could grin a wild cat out of countenance" (p. 156); and Sal Fink, the "Mississippi Screamer," who, when six years old, "used to play see-saw on the Mississippi snags, and after she war done she would snap 'em off, an' so cleared a large distinct of the river" are some of the more memorable extraordinary female characters featured ("Sal Fink," pp. 171–172).

THE TALL TALE: AT HOME IN THE SOUTH

The chief period of prominence of the tall tale was 1830 to 1860, and the principal practitioners were professional men living in the South, typically only writers by avocation, who were known as the humorists of the Old Southwest. Many tall tales in this tradition—humorous sketches, mock letters, and anecdotes—began appearing in the 1830s in newspapers such as William T. Porter's the *Spirit of the Times, New Orleans Picayune, St. Louis Reveille, Montgomery Mail, Louisville Courier, Cincinnati News,* and *Columbia South Carolinian.* Writers of southern frontier tall tales usually adopted a frame or box structure, which re-created the oral tale-telling situation and which featured a refined and educated narrator who would establish the preparatory social context for the tale and introduce the vernacular storyteller, often a colorful backwoodsman and an artful and likable liar, who would then recount the tall tale. Moreover, many tales were so outlandish and incredible that most readers did not readily identify with the backwoods raconteur, nor did they vicariously attach themselves sympathetically to him.

One of the best known, most entertaining, and most absurd Old Southwestern tall tales that employs the frame device is Phillip B. January's "That Big Dog Fight at Myers's," which appeared originally in the *Spirit of the Times.* In it, Uncle Johnny graphically and retrospectively recounts an action-packed, fictive adventure about Old Irontooth, who, when drunk, amused a tavern crowd by getting down on all fours and fighting Myers's dog with his teeth and hands. In confronting the dog before the fight, Old Irontooth, Uncle Johnny humorously observes, assumes doglike characteristics, "walkin' backards and forards, pitchin' up the dust and bellerin like bull," but when Myers's dog begins to "see *our* animal strut up to the gate and begin to smell, then, like another dog, he got fairly crazy to git thru at him; rarin', cavortin', and *tarin'* off pickets" of the fence (Cohen and Dillingham, p. 250).

An even better example of the written frontier tall tale that replicates the zestful and hyperbolic quality of oral storytelling and that employs both frame and vernacular narrators is Thomas Bangs Thorpe's "The Big Bear of Arkansas" (1841), which was also published in Porter's *Spirit of the Times.* Jim Doggett, Thorpe's tall-talking raconteur from Shirt-tail Bend, masterfully manipulates a crowd of male gentlemen travelers on a Mississippi River steamboat with amusing and extravagant claims about how large everything is in Arkansas, including potatoes, beets, corn, mosquitoes, turkeys, and especially bears. One bear, in particular, Jim describes as eluding him during a hunt that lasted for three years. In the surprising, perfectly timed, and skillfully executed anticlimactic moment of Jim's story, when Jim's "creation" bear, which by this point has assumed mythic proportions, suddenly appears, Jim is literally caught with his pants about his ankles, engaging most inappropriately and unheroically in a bowel movement in the woods. Jim's listeners have become so engrossed in his story that they set themselves up to be deceived by their own vanity and preconditioned expectations concerning how they believe Jim's tale will end.

The tall tales of George Washington Harris feature improbable incidents as told by an untutored East Tennessee mountaineer and prankster named Sut Lovingood who is given dominant voice with little or no intrusion from the authorial narrator. In fact, Sut has full control of the fictive world he describes as in "Sut Lovingood's Daddy, Acting Horse" when, after the family's one plow horse has frozen to death, Sut's father has himself harnessed to plow the corn patch (Cohen and Dillingham, p. 203). Moreover, the frame in a typical Sut Lovingood yarn, such as this one, emphasizes that Sut is only telling a story rather than performing an action and that he is encouraging both his frame audience listeners as well as the readers outside the narrative to participate vicariously, becoming, if only in an imaginative sense, a part of the oral tale's audience.

In one of the more significance developments in the evolution of the Southwestern humorous tall tale, Taliaferro in *Fisher's River (North Carolina) Scenes and Characters* gives an actual marginalized character, Charles Gentry, a Surry County, North Carolina, African American slave preacher, extended narrative voice in two comic oral folk sermons, "The Origin of Whites" and "Jonah and the Whale." In the frame, Taliaferro presents Gentry in a highly complimentary manner, mentioning his goodness, cleverness, and originality and showing a respectable understanding of and toleration for his extreme revisionist theology. For example, in his tall-talish alteration of the standard biblical text of the Cain and Abel story, Gentry voices a comically original, liberating, and imaginative alternative script, fabricating a dialogue between God and Cain concerning the whereabouts of Cain's brother

Abel, whom he has killed. In Gentry's version, Cain reacts to God's query by turning "white as bleach cambric in de face, and de whole race ob Cain dey bin white ebber since" (p. 189) Beneath the surface of Gentry's lively and inventive yarn is Taliaferro's affirmation of the black man's capability as a storyteller.

AFRICAN AMERICANS AND THE TALL TALE
The use of African American narrators of tall tales was more widespread in local color writing of the 1880s. Uncle Remus is employed cautiously yet subversively by Joel Chandler Harris (1848–1908) to challenge the racial status quo in the South in allegorical, comical tales pitting small animals like Brer Rabbit against predators like Brer Fox, animals who talked and acted like people. Charles W. Chesnutt's (1858–1932) Uncle Julius, in tall tales like "The Goophered Grapevine," which Julius humorously narrates in dialect, cloaks or detracts from the story's subtext, which offers a serious social commentary on the economic exploitation of slaves. Jake Mitchell, another African American storyteller, likewise cleverly told entertaining tall tales to white people, sometimes to manipulate situations outside the narrative to his personal advantage and empowerment. Mitchell's collaborator Robert Wilton Burton, a white Auburn, Alabama, bookseller, wrote the frames to the thirty-six Jake stories published in Alabama newspapers from 1886 to 1891.

MARK TWAIN
The major beneficiary of the legacy of the Old Southwestern tall tale was Mark Twain (1835–1910), who also represents the culmination of this tradition in nineteenth-century American literature. Some of Twain's most memorable writings display tall-talish features that Twain has refashioned and refined into creditable literary art. Among these are "The Notorious Jumping Frog of Calaveras County" (1867), featuring Simon Wheeler, who, in a spontaneous recollection tells about the compulsive bettor Jim Smiley's fantastic animals; some of the episodes from *Roughing It* (1872), including the amazing tale in which George Bemis recounts being chased up a tree by a wounded buffalo and Jim Blaine's loose and rambling tale purporting to be about his grandfather's old ram but is not; "Baker's Blue-jay Yarn" in *A Tramp Abroad* (1880) in which Jim Baker, a lonely California miner, humanizes blue jays and recounts a blue jay's attempt to fill a hole in the roof of a cabin with acorns; and "The Raft Chapter," originally intended as a section in *Adventures of Huckleberry Finn* (1885), showcasing competitive verbal boasts of two ring-tailed roarers. In these texts, modifications of the

frontier tall tale, Mark Twain created some lively, engaging characters who are masters of spinning an oral yarn and/or of replicating tall talk. Twain's tall tale raconteurs masterfully adopt a deadpan pose, realistically mimicking the orality of backwoods yarn spinners as they accentuate events to incredible, hyperbolic proportions, using vernacular dialect to create incongruous comparisons and embellished descriptions in their accounts.

CONCLUSION
With the beginning of the Civil War in 1861, the same year of the demise of the *Spirit of the Times,* which for thirty years had been the leading outlet for humorous backwoods tall narratives, and the close of the southwestern frontier, which had formerly provided conditions conducive to the creation and proliferation of humorous yarns, the prominence of the literary tall tale was greatly diminished. But in Mark Twain, William Faulkner, William Price Fox, Fred Chappell, Roy Blount Jr., Garrison Keillor, and other American writers, the tall tale has enjoyed resurgence and has continued to remain a vital and engaging literary form.

See also "The Big Bear of Arkansas"; "The Celebrated Jumping Frog of Calaveras County"; Folklore; Humor; *Some Adventures of Captain Simon Suggs*

BIBLIOGRAPHY
Primary Works
Chesnutt, Charles Waddell. *The Conjure Woman and Other Conjure Stories.* Edited by Richard H. Brodhead. Durham, N.C.: Duke University Press, 1993.

"Col. Crockett Beat at a Shooting Match." 1839. In *Half Horse, Half Alligator: The Growth of the Mike Fink Legend,* edited by Walter Blair and Franklin J. Meine. Chicago: University of Chicago Press, 1956.

De Remnant Truth: The Tales of Jake Mitchell and Robert Wilton Burton. Edited by Kathryn Sport and Bert Hitchcock. Tuscaloosa: University of Alabama Press, 1991.

"The Flower of Gum Swamp." 1841. In *Davy Crockett's Riproarious Shemales and Sentimental Sisters: Women's Tall Tales from the Crockett Almanacs, 1835–1856,* edited by Michael A. Lofaro. Mechanicsburg, Pa.: Stackpole Books, 2001.

Harris, Joel Chandler. *The Complete Tales of Uncle Remus.* Boston: Houghton Mifflin, 1955.

Harris, George Washington. "Sut Lovingood's Daddy, Acting Horse." 1854. In *Humor of the Old Southwest,* edited by Hennig Cohen and William B. Dillingham. Athens: University of Georgia Press, 1994.

January, Phillip B. "That Big Dog Fight at Myers's." 1845. In *Humor of the Old Southwest*, edited by Hennig Cohen and William B. Dillingham. Athens: University of Georgia Press, 1994.

Josselyn, John *An Account of Two Voyages to New England*. 1675. Reprinted in *Collections. Massachusetts Historical Society, Boston*, 3rd series, 23 (1833).

"Katy Goodgrit." 1842. In *Davy Crockett's Riproarious Shemales and Sentimental Sisters: Women's Tall Tales from the Crockett Almanacs*, 1835–1856, edited by Michael A. Lofaro. Mechanicsburg, Pa.: Stackpole Books, 2001.

Lawson, John. *A New Voyage to Carolina*. 1709. Edited by H. T. Lefler. Chapel Hill: University of North Carolina Press, 1967.

"Mike Fink's Brag." In *The Heath Anthology of American Literature*, vol. 1, edited by Paul Lauter et al. Boston: Houghton Mifflin, 2002.

"Mike Fink Hunting Moose." In *Half Horse, Half Alligator: The Growth of the Mike Fink Legend*, edited by Walter Blair and Franklin J. Meine. Chicago: University of Chicago Press, 1956.

"Sal Fink, the Mississippi Screamer, How She Cooked Injuns." 1854. In *Davy Crockett's Riproarious Shemales and Sentimental Sisters: Women's Tall Tales from the Crockett Almanacs, 1835–1856*. Edited by Michael A. Lofaro. Mechanicsburg, Pa.: Stackpole Books, 2001.

Taliaferro, Hardin E. *Fisher's River (North Carolina) Scenes and Characters, By "Skitt" Who Was Raised Thar*. New York: Harper & Brothers, 1859.

Thorpe, Thomas Bangs. "The Big Bear of Arkansas." 1841. *Humor of the Old Southwest*, edited by Hennig Cohen and William B. Dillingham. Athens: University of Georgia Press, 1994.

Secondary Works

Blair, Walter. "A German Connection: Raspe's Baron Munchausen." In *Critical Essays on American Humor*, edited by William Bedford Clark and W. Craig Turner, pp. 123–139. Boston: Hall, 1984.

Blair, Walter, and Hamlin Hill. *America's Humor: From Poor Richard to Doonesbury*. New York: Oxford University Press, 1978.

Brown, Carolyn S. *The Tall Tale in American Folklore and Literature*. Knoxville: University of Tennessee Press, 1987.

Caron, James E. "The Violence and Language of Swapping Lies: Towards a Definition of the American Tall Tale." *Studies in American Humor* 5 (1986): 27–37.

Cohen, Hennig, and William B. Dillingham. Introduction to *Humor of the Old Southwest*, edited by Hennig Cohen and William B. Dillingham, pp. xv–xl. Athens: University of Georgia Press, 1994.

Lofaro, Michael A. "Riproarious Shemales: Legendary Women in the Tall Tale World of the Crockett Almanacs."

In *Crockett at Two Hundred: New Perspectives on the Man and the Myth*, edited by Michael A. Lofaro and Joe Cummings, pp. 114–152. Knoxville: University of Tennessee Press. 1989.

Lofaro, Michael A. "Shemales, Sentiment, and Stereotypes: A Long View of the Crockett Almanacs." In *Davy Crockett's Riproarious Shemales and Sentimental Sisters: Women's Tall Tales from the Crockett Almanacs, 1835–1856*, edited by Michael A. Lofaro, pp. 5–92. Mechanicsburg, Pa.: Stackpole Books, 2001.

Wardenaar, Leslie A. "Humor of the Colonial Promotional Tract: Topics and Techniques." *Early American Literature* 9, no. 3 (1975): 286–300.

Wonham, Henry B. "Character Development of the Ring-Tailed Roarer in American Literature." *Southern Folklore* 46 (1989): 265–279.

Wonham, Henry B. "In the Name of Wonder: The Emergence of the Tall Narrative in American Writing." *American Quarterly* 41 (1989): 284–307.

Wonham, Henry B. *Mark Twain and the Art of the Tall Tale*. New York: Oxford University Press, 1993.

Yates, Norris W. *William T. Porter and "The Spirit of the Times": A Study in the Big Bear School of Humor*. Baton Rouge: Louisiana State University Press, 1957.

Ed Piacentino

TASTE

Few issues circulated more consistently—or more nervously—within American culture during the 1820–1870 period than those regarding issues of taste and sensibility. Novels and plays, poems and stories in magazines such as *Godey's Lady's Book* and newspapers such as the *New York Tribune* and the *New York Herald,* conduct manuals for men and women, and even the pulpiest dime novels and the most wrenching slave narratives were involved in the dissemination of a seemingly endless series of texts in which characters negotiate the vexed terrain of cultural consumption and sensibility. What modes of conduct or affect best became a woman or man seeking certain forms of class distinction? What were the proper standards of reading and writing? How might leisure activity and aesthetic consumption mark one as tasteful in ways that were either positive or negative? Were there tasteful ways to spend money? And more abstractly, what sort of body came with varying degrees of taste and class? These and myriad similar questions act as the backdrop for a great deal of the literary and cultural production during this period. Indeed in a very real way fiction and theater, in particular, were the space in which American standards of taste were taking shape in relation to categories of class and culture.

TASTE AND THE MIDDLE CLASS

This cultural influence was particularly evident in the forms of taste and awareness taking shape in the emergent middle classes. Though still fragmentary, heterogeneous and contradictory, the middle class saw in the mirrored reflection of these literary narratives an increasingly coherent version of itself and its cultural preferences, especially as these preferences were defined in relation to the polar extremes of "high" and "low" culture. The term that later came to be used to define this sensibility is "middlebrow," and certainly one of the most fascinating dimensions of the literary and cultural production of this era is the way it models a zone of taste and sensibility located—often quite anxiously—somewhere between these two more obvious sites of distinction. Following the magisterial work of the French sociologist Pierre Bourdieu, American academics such as Lawrence Levine, Janice Radway, and Jonathan Freedman have shown how the American middlebrow sought increasingly to legitimize itself by invoking the authority of taste, aesthetics, and "culture" even as it struggled with intense feelings of insecurity in the face of "true" or "real" high culture. "The petit bourgeois is filled with *reverence* for high culture," Bourdieu writes with perhaps a hint of sympathetic irony. "He bows, just in case, to everything which looks as if it might be culture" (p. 323). But Bourdieu suggests, even such reverence is doomed to failure. Lacking the cultural and educational advantages of the aristocratic classes, the middlebrow is forever conscious of the fact that "legitimate culture is not made for him (and is often made against him) so that he is not made for it; and that it ceases to be what it is as soon as he appropriates it" (p. 327).

MIDDLE-CLASS TASTE AND THE THEATER

Bourdieu's analysis is of particular use in examining the forms of taste and sensibility emerging in nineteenth-century America, a period marked by the seemingly tireless efforts of the middlebrow to carve out a space for itself somewhere between the more rarified sphere of highbrow taste and distinction and the cruder, usually sensational, world of working-class (and necessarily lowbrow) culture. This is perhaps best exemplified in the fraught cultural transition taking place in American theaters from the 1820s to the 1870s, as operas, symphonies, and even performances of Shakespeare became increasingly rarified and hostile to lower-class audiences. This transition was highlighted by the 1849 Astor Place riot, in which a working-class mob of some five

thousand assaulted the Astor Place Opera House in New York City as part of a running feud over its ostensibly elitist and highbrow production of Shakespeare's *Macbeth*. The actual riot, in which twenty-two people were killed, was sparked by a rivalry between Edwin Forrest (1806–1872), a working-class "Jacksonian" actor championed by the rowdy and voluble crowd of "Bowery b'hoys" who filled the Chatham, Bowery, and other theaters for his melodramas, and William Macready (1793–1873), a British actor who expressed withering distain for such audiences. As Levine explains, Macready described Forrest's audiences as "vulgar," "coarse," "underbred," "disagreeable," and "ignorant" (p. 66)—epithets that became much stronger on 7 May 1849, when Macready was booed and pelted with eggs and rotten vegetables by a crowd filled with Forrest sympathizers. The riot that occurred three nights later was the culmination of tensions between these classes, but it was also a watershed in the shaping of middlebrow taste and culture in America. Indeed Levine reports that by the 1870s audiences had learned to become much more docile and cooperative in their expressing their tastes, agreeing to remain seated until the end of a performance and limiting applause to appropriate moments. As a contemporary of the conductor Theodore Thomas wrote in 1872, "When the audience relapses into barbarism . . . he quietly but firmly controls them. I have seen him . . . leave the stand and quietly take a seat in the corner of the orchestra, remaining there until he has carried his point" (Levine, p. 192).

Even as these transitions were taking place, American culture often displayed a knowing, even playful kind of meta-awareness of the problematic of taste in the mid-century. This can be seen, for example, in the extreme popularity of Anna Mowatt's (1819–1870) hit comedy of manners, *Fashion; or, Life in New York*. Opening in 1845 to immediate critical and financial success, Mowatt's play is a satire of America's obsession with highbrow taste and cultural distinction. An early line from the culturally insecure Mrs. Tiffany suggests the ways in which Mowatt is staging bad taste for her theater audience: "Ah," she says prior to the social visiting hour she has arranged, "very elegant, very elegant indeed! There is a *jenny-says-quoi* look about this furniture,—an air of fashion and gentility perfectly bewitching" (p. 7). Obsessed with things European—she complains that even the English language is "decidedly vulgar" (p. 8)—Mrs. Tiffany is clearly offered as one who consumes culture and taste in ways that are overdetermined and indeed comical. Like the taste-anxious petit bourgeois described by Bourdieu, Mrs. Tiffany bows before all that appears to bear the stamp of cultural legitimacy. Nor is this insecurity an isolated cultural condition. As Millinette, Mrs. Tiffany's French lady's maid, puts it in an ironic aside: "De money is all dat is *necessaire* in dis country to make one [a] lady of fashion. Oh, it is quite anoder ting in *la belle France*!" (p. 6).

Tellingly Mrs. Tiffany's absurdity is highlighted here by the presence of her new black servant, Zeke, whose dandyish attitudes mirror her own. "Dere's a coat to take de eyes ob all Broadway!" he proclaims in the play's opening lines as he regards his new livery outfit. "It am the fixin's dat make de natural *born* gemman. A libery forever! Dere's a pair of insuppressibles to 'stonish de colored population" (p. 5). Zeke's extreme ignorance is of course part of antebellum culture's deeply ingrained racism. This racism, however, is in fact a crucial component of the game of culture Mowatt is staging for her audience. For what Zeke provides is a site onto which to displace concerns about bad taste. Far more than Mrs. Tiffany, Zeke's is a body the audience would have understood as inherently vulgar and thus incapable of acquiring the modes of taste and sensibility they themselves were seeking to establish and maintain. In this sense Zeke is an extension of the logic of taste and culture seen in stock "black dandy" minstrel characters such Dandy Jim and Zip Coon. As the cover of an 1843 songbook titled *Dandy Jim, from Carolina* suggests, such characters are locked in a narcissistic gaze in which surface modes of consumption (clothes, hair, other modes of fashion) are misunderstood as the equivalent of more internal modes of selfhood (delicacy, refinement, whiteness) that were the true markers of taste at mid-century.

Characters such as Zeke and the rowdy audiences at the Astor Place Opera House indicate that, as the term itself implies, taste was a concept that reflected profound awareness of and concern about embodiment—about, that is to say, the kind of body that came with the various standards, preferences, and sensibilities that went into the shaping of the tastes that informed the middlebrow mindset. Another quote from Bourdieu is useful in this context:

> Taste, a class culture turned into nature, that is, *embodied,* helps to shape the class body. It is an incorporated principle of classification which governs all forms of incorporation, choosing and modifying everything that the body ingests and digests and assimilates, physiologically and psychologically. It follows that the body is the most indisputable materialization of class taste. (P. 190)

Bourdieu's emphasis on the reciprocity between the physiological and the psychological is especially crucial here, for what mid-nineteenth-century American literature and culture reflects over and over again is the deeply emotional and psychologized nature of the effort to establish and maintain the kind of taste-sensitive "class body" he describes. And nowhere is

Dandy Jim from Carolina. Songbook cover, c. 1843. The irony of attempts by excluded groups to achieve good taste was a common subject in the mid-nineteenth century. THE LIBRARY OF CONGRESS

this more evident than in the focus of so many mid-nineteenth-century texts on a process one might refer to as middle-class self-fashioning.

TASTE IN ANTEBELLUM FICTION

While the middlebrow aesthetic taking shape at mid-century might be understood as standing in anxious or perhaps even ambivalent relation to "culture," the fiction of this period provided a space in which to work out such unease. Working to provide the legitimation that established culture was withholding and that low-brow culture was threatening to undermine, many of the writers of this period provided in their work a kind of aesthetic chart by which readers could map out the terrain of sensibility and taste that would answer to the anxious needs of the middlebrow.

The career of Jo March in Louisa May Alcott's (1832–1888) best-selling *Little Women* (1868–1869) marks a didactic high point of this process: Alcott here offers a gradual process of reform in which Jo learns the forms of discipline and restraint—"the sweetness of self-denial and self-control" (p. 82)—necessary to the formation of a tasteful "little woman" in nineteenth-century America. Most telling perhaps is Jo's short career as a writer of lowbrow sensational literature—"bad trash," as Jo's eventual husband, the kindly Professor Bhaer, calls it (p. 355). "She was living in bad society; and imaginary though it was, its influence affected her," readers are told in one of the many moments of direct address provided by Alcott's narrator. "Unconsciously, she was beginning to desecrate some of the womanliest attributes of a woman's character" (p. 349). Jo's dalliance with lowbrow pulp is an object lesson for Alcott's readers, especially the middlebrow reading audience most likely identify with her as they read *Little Women*. For what it implies is a connection to the tastes and sensibilities of the lowbrow crowds assaulting the Astor Place Opera House, forms of consumption that must be cast off and repressed in the name of fashioning the kind of taste appropriate to a properly middlebrow sensibility. Indeed Jo's later fiction is praised precisely because it purportedly rejects such sensibilities. "You wrote with no thought of fame or money," Jo's mother tells her, "and put your heart into it" (p. 436).

Jo's lesson here is twofold. In addition to rejecting the debasing and distasteful world of lowbrow sensationalism, she earns the respect of her soon-to-be husband, Professor Bhaer, whose excessively middlebrow sensibilities (he possesses cultural rather than financial currency) are marked as quite different from the highbrow tastes of Jo's other suitor, her wealthy young neighbor Laurie. "You and I are not suited to each other," Jo says in rejecting Laurie's long-delayed overtures to her (p. 364), a comment that has as much (if not more) to do with taste and sensibility than actual temperament or attraction. For the life that awaits Jo—schoolteacher and mother—is one that requires the modest income and modulated tastes of the middlebrow. In an amazing passage late in the novel, Laurie says that he would like to give some of his money to Professor Bhaer and Jo. "Out-and-out beggars get taken care of, but poor gentlefolks fare badly" he says (p. 459). In fact, however, Alcott's novel suggests that "gentlefolks"—represented by Jo and her husband—do perfectly well as residents of the tasteful middlebrow territory Alcott has carved out for them.

A similar logic of middlebrow self-fashioning—one might call it "middlebrow romance"—informs Nathaniel Hawthorne's (1804–1864) gothic novel *The House of the Seven Gables* (1851). The backdrop for this text is the long and bitter property dispute between the aristocratic Pyncheon family and the working-class Maules, but Hawthorne makes it clear that, as staged in the novel's present, this feud is played out in the arena of taste and cultural production. This is particularly evident in the depiction of the last descendent of the Maule family, a young man named Holgrave. Daguerreotypist, short story writer, and sometimes mesmerist, Holgrave is, like Jo March, a producer of mass culture that is decidedly lowbrow in orientation. As he explains to Phoebe Pyncheon upon learning that she has not read any of the fiction he has published:

> Well, such is literary fame! Yes, Miss Phoebe Pyncheon, among the multitude of my marvellous gifts, I have that of writing stories; and my name has figured, I can assure you, on the covers of Graham and Godey, making as respectable an appearance, for aught I could see, as any of the canonized beadroll with which it was associated. In the humorous line, I am thought to have a very pretty way with me; and as for pathos, I am as provocative of tears as an onion. (P. 186)

Holgrave's stories occupy space alongside more established writers in middlebrow venues such as *Graham's* magazine and *Godey's Lady's Book*, but—and ominously—they are also manipulative of their reader's affective states. This is reflected not only in Holgrave's ability to produce tears in his readers but more profoundly when he manages to mesmerize Phoebe by the very act of reading his pulpy and sensational story to her. Here is how Hawthorne describes the moments immediately following Holgrave's reading:

> Holgrave gazed at her, as he rolled up his manuscript, and recognized an incipient stage of that curious psychological condition, which, as he himself had told Phoebe, he possessed more than an ordinary faculty of producing. A veil was beginning to be muffled about her, in which she could behold only him, and live only in his thoughts and emotions. (P. 211)

What better description of the putatively debasing or regressive effects of lowbrow culture at mid-century, effects that have their root in the very notion of "bad taste?" "I consider myself as having been very attentive," Phoebe says (p. 212), but in fact she has been immobilized—mesmerized—by the seductive "magic" of lowbrow sensationalism. Phoebe, it can be said, is on the receiving end of the "bad trash" that threatens to "desecrate" Jo March in Alcott's *Little Women*.

As critics have suggested, Hawthorne ultimately seems uncomfortable with this scenario. Seeing that Phoebe has been partially mesmerized by listening to his story, Holgrave resists the urge to take advantage of Phoebe's vulnerability. Instead, he suggests that he will burn his short story: "The manuscript must serve to light lamps with," he says (p. 212). More dramatically still, Holgrave and Phoebe become romantically involved, a plot shift that hastens the "developement of emotions" necessary to secure middlebrow distance from the outside world of cultural production (p. 305). An exchange between the two characters late in the novel sums up the dramatic shifts that take place in the wake of Holgrave's reading of his magazine story to Phoebe: "How wonderfully your ideas are changed!" she says, to which Holgrave replies: "You find me a conservative already! Little did I think ever to become one" (p. 315). Holgrave and Phoebe thus take up a posture not at all unlike that modeled by Jo March and Professor Bhaer in *Little Women*. Here too is a "middlebrow romance," a form structured around the repression of bad taste, lowbrow culture, and its attendant working-class associations; it advocates instead the "developement of emotions" that are tasteful and middlebrow in nature.

"TASTE" IN SENSATIONAL FICTION

Significantly, however, even the lowbrow sensationalism of this period—the "bad trash" offered in penny newspapers such as the *New York Herald* and the *New York Sun* and in dime novels such as George Lippard's (1822–1854) best-selling *The Quaker City* (1845) and George Thompson's (b. 1823) *Venus in Boston* (1849)—stages scenes of middlebrow self-fashioning, this despite what is often the stated resistance to the kinds of taste offered in narratives such as *House of the Seven Gables* and *Little Women*. As the influential editor James Gordon Bennett (1841–1918) put it in his outlandishly sensational (and enormously successful) *New York Herald* essay titled "Penny Literature versus Loafer Literature" (30 September 1836):

> By a singular perversity in the taste of the age, the monthly and weekly periodical literature—the Magazines, the Mirrors, the Knickerbockers, and such like trashy publications, have degenerated into vehicles of mere sickly sentimentalism, fit only for the kitchen or the laundry. The daily press and the cheap periodicals appear to possess the only strength—the only nerve—the only real talent and genius. Conversant in matters of real business—engaged in active life, the mind is taken away from itself, and its egotism and vanity are rubbed over severely by the unfanciful buffetings of the world.

For Bennett, in other words, publications that promote middlebrow taste are themselves guilty of offering "trashy" fare that shies away from the grittier, more unpleasant realities of life at mid-century. Lippard offers a similar posture in *The Quaker City*, the best-selling novel in America prior to the publication of Harriet Beecher Stowe's *Uncle Tom's Cabin* in 1852. As he puts it in a defensive direct address to the "shallow pated critic" whose "white kid-gloves" suggest his middle- or highbrow sensibility, "Our taste is different from yours. We like to look at nature and at the world, not only as they appear, but as they are!" (p. 305). For Lippard as for Bennett, middlebrow taste, emphasizing as it did an anxiety about the more visceral pleasures of the class body, was silly and out of touch with reality.

Despite such claims, however, much of the period's lowbrow sensationalism stages narratives that turn on the very forms of taste and sensibility favored by Alcott and Hawthorne. A particularly useful example of this is offered in Theodore Winthrop's (1828–1861) popular "urban gothic" novel *Cecil Dreeme* (1861), seventeen editions of which were published by 1864. Usually offered as pulpy, often silly dime novels devoted to excessive violence, sexual titillation, and extreme racism, urban gothic sensationalism provided audiences with a widely disseminated and inexpensive medium for engaging with and challenging the inequalities of class in America from the 1830s onward. Yet this material also provides some of the most direct and affective commentary on the nation's issues of taste and sensibility, especially as the notion of taste applied to the emerging category of the middlebrow.

The narrative of *Cecil Dreeme* revolves around a young man named Robert Byng, a twenty-six-year-old professional who is returning to America after ten years of study abroad and who is staged fairly clearly as someone who must negotiate the forms of taste and sensibility that have been taking shape in America during his absence. This is particularly evident in the interactions between Byng and a "Hebrew-ish" (p. 23) and wealthy financier named Densdeth, an older man who wields considerable power over Byng and a number of other characters in the novel. At times the relationship between the two seems fairly one-sided, with Densdeth aggressively pursuing Byng in a manner that suggests the desire for economic and perhaps even sexual domination. At other times the attraction is more reciprocal, suggesting that Byng is himself drawn to Densdeth and the form of submission he demands. As Byng puts it at one point: "'What does it mean,' thought I, this man's strange fascination? When his eyes are upon me, I feel something stir in my heart, saying, 'Be Densdeth's! He knows the mystery of life.' I begin to dread him. Will he master my will? What is this potency of his?" (p. 65).

As Byng's comment about Densdeth's "strange fascination" makes clear, Densdeth is associated here with sensibilities that Byng himself feels with real intensity—he later describes himself as "a youth . . . dragged along by an irresistible attraction" (p. 180). And what this suggests is that Densdeth as exotic Jew embodies a set of pleasures that, though marked as deviant, also seem to stand in for the pleasures and affects of the rarified highbrow culture Densdeth seems intended to represent. "I love luxury for its own sake," Densdeth tells Byng early on. "I mean to have the best for all my senses. I keep myself in perfect health, you see, for perfect sensitiveness and perfect enjoyment" (p. 63). As this and a variety of similar passages suggest, Densdeth represents the kind of sensuous voluptuousness so often associated with the stereotypical figure of the highbrow Jew. But as Densdeth's influence over the various men in the novel suggests, these are desires inherent within all of the male characters in *Cecil Dreeme,* projected outward onto the excessive, the Jew. Byng's confusion, that is to say, is a thoroughly ambivalent effort to organize the pleasures and tastes of middlebrow sensibility: attracted to but put off by the excesses of Densdeth as highbrow pleasure seeker, Byng embodies the uncertainty and ambivalence of the middlebrow seeking to establish cultural assurance in the uncertain game of taste and cultural consumption.

It is therefore telling that the form of pleasure Densdeth offers is one that Byng comes to understand as slightly vulgar, as if Densdeth fails to understand the nuances of cultural distinction necessary to the formation of middlebrow sensibility. "Densdeth was a little too carefully dressed," Byng observes at one point.

> His clothes had a conscious air. His trousers hung as if they felt his eye on them, and dreaded a beating if they bagged. His costume was generally quiet, so severely quiet that it was evident that he desired to be flagrant, and obeyed tact rather than taste. In fact, taste always hung out a diamond stud, or an elaborate chain or eye-glass. (P. 75)

Such moments suggest that Byng's discomfort with Densdeth is negotiated by means of reference to forms of taste and sensibility that are specifically middlebrow and thus inaccessible to one such as Densdeth. Indeed one of the moments in which Byng grows wary of Densdeth is at the opera, which he designates as a problematic cultural space. "It was thoroughly debilitating, effeminate music," he says.

> No single strain of manly vigor rose, from end to end of the drama. . . . Emasculated music! Such music as tyranny over mind and spirit calls for, to lull its unmanned subjects into sensual calm. . . . Between the acts, I saw Densdeth moving about, welcome everywhere. . . . All the salable people, and, alas!, that includes all but a mere decimation, threw open their doors to Densdeth. Opera-box and the tenants of the box were free to him. (Pp. 256–257, 259)

Byng's concerns about the unmanning and emasculating effects of the cultural milieu in which Densdeth operates are related to the cultural politics of the Astor Place incident. Though certainly not one of the Jacksonian-style "b'hoys" said to have taken part in the earlier riot, Byng seeks to distance himself from Densdeth by recourse to a language of cultural distinction in which he seeks to understand his own more middlebrow sensibilities as superior to (as well as more masculine than) those of the highbrow elite—this despite the fact that Byng is so clearly drawn to Densdeth and the forms of culture and pleasure he seems to embody.

This ambivalence about the Jew as a register of competing forms of taste and sensibility is something Jonathan Freedman points out in his discussion of du Maurier's infamous Jewish mesmerist, Svengali. Both artistic genius and debased villain, Svengali, like Densdeth, is simultaneously a figure both of high and low culture. And in both instances this ambivalence centers on the interchangeable Otherness of these characters. As Freedman explains in a passage that seems quite useful for understanding the cultural situation Winthrop is staging in Robert Byng:

> In the middlebrow imaginary, to be cultured is to be dangerously (or pleasurably) touched with the alien force and sexual energy socially ascribed to the Jew; it is also to be, however temporarily and within reason, to be touched with the aura of specialness, distinction and superiority that is also ascribed to that figure. Yet, at one and the same time, to be middlebrow (rather than highbrow) is to be saved from the fate of being *too* Jewish, too outré, too extreme, too powerfully connected to this model of identity and response that is so visibly connected with the powers of otherness. (P. 113)

The aspiring middle-class and middlebrow citizen, Byng sees in Densdeth a model of taste and manhood he both desires and disavows. For as culturally sophisticated Jew, Densdeth offers an opportunity both to indulge in the very desires and pleasures of culture that afford one a sense of cultural superiority and, simultaneously, an opportunity to confirm one's status as middling by understanding the Jew as a form of Otherness that makes such indulgence excessive and overwhelming.

In *Cecil Dreeme* the highbrow Densdeth is eventually killed by one of the men he has persecuted, an event that allows Byng to marry a young woman who has long hidden from an arranged marriage with Densdeth in a small apartment in New York City. Needless to say, perhaps, this woman is an artist; even better, she is uninterested in selling her work, a fact that suggests she is able to resist the potentially debasing lure of a market culture that peddles largely in bad taste. The union thus provides yet another example of the way the period's fiction imagines for its readers a space in which the middlebrow might see himself or herself reflected in narratives that stage dilemmas of class and taste only to resolve them in the form of the middlebrow romance.

This is not to say, however, that the threat of excessive desire embodied in Densdeth no longer has an effect upon Byng. Indeed Densdeth has this power even in death. As Byng puts it in the closing pages, with Densdeth lying prostrate on the ground before him:

> The strange fascination of his face became doubly subtle, as he seemed still to gaze at me with closed eyelids, like a statue's. I felt that, if those cold feline eyes should open and again turn their inquisition upon my soul, devilish passions would quicken there anew. I shuddered to perceive the lurking devil in me, slumbering lightly, and ready to stir whenever he knew a comrade was near. (P. 330)

On the one hand, this is urban gothic melodrama at its silliest; it is what Alcott's narrator would, in a moment of taste-anxious middlebrow anxiety, term "bad trash." On the other hand, it also provides a useful example of the game of projection involved in negotiations of middlebrow sensibility. For the dead body of the highbrow Jew is here the embodiment of the desire for cultural attainment that is very much alive within Byng as aspiring middlebrow. In this sense Winthrop's narrative simply extends a sensibility that permeates various other texts produced at mid-century. For although each author seeks to depict the middlebrow (and her tastes) as necessitating a class body drained of excessive passion and desire, each also manages to reveal the way this figure is decidedly ambivalent: knowing what it most desires (access to either high or low culture) but committed to not having it, the middlebrow of mid-nineteenth-century America offers a form of taste that can only be defined in terms of ambivalence and anxiety.

See also Ethnology; *The House of the Seven Gables;* Jews; *Little Women;* Periodicals; Sensational Fiction; Sexuality and the Body

BIBLIOGRAPHY

Primary Works

Alcott, Louisa May. *Little Women* 1868–1869. Edited by Elaine Showalter. New York: Penguin, 1989.

Bennett, James Gordon. "Penny Literature versus Loafer Literature." *New York Herald*, 30 September 1836.

Hawthorne, Nathaniel. *The House of the Seven Gables.* 1851. New York: Penguin, 1981.

Mowatt, Anna Ogden. *Fashion; or, Life in New York.* 1845. Boston: Walter H. Baker, 1935.

Winthrop, Theodore. *Cecil Dreeme.* New York: Dodd, Meade, 1861.

Secondary Works

Bourdieu, Pierre. *Distinction: A Social Critique of the Judgement of Taste.* Cambridge, Mass.: Harvard University Press, 1984.

Freedman, Jonathan. *The Temple of Culture: Assimilation and Anti-Semitism in Literary Anglo-America.* New York: Oxford University Press, 2000.

Levine, Lawrence. *Highbrow/Lowbrow: The Emergence of Cultural Hierarchy in America.* Cambridge, Mass.: Harvard University Press, 1988.

Radway, Janice. *A Feeling for Books: The Book-of-the-Month Club, Literary Taste, and Middle-Class Desire.* Chapel Hill: University of North Carolina Press, 1997.

David Anthony

TECHNOLOGY

"The splendors of this age outshine all other recorded ages," Ralph Waldo Emerson (1803–1882) wrote in his journal in 1871, adding a list of recent innovations that he saw as important driving forces of modern history: "In my lifetime, have been wrought five miracles, namely, 1. the Steamboat; 2. the railroad; 3. the Electric telegraph; 4. the application of the Spectroscope to astronomy; 5. the photograph; five miracles which have altered the relations of nations to each other" (*Journals* 16:242). Though one may argue about the actual role of these inventions in changing the course of modern history, there is no doubt that for the eminent New England philosopher technological progress represented not just a revolution of "improved means to an unimproved end," as his disciple Henry David Thoreau (1817–1862) sarcastically put it (p. 192), but the ambivalent legacy and future of modern society at large. Given the increasing presence of the machine in early-nineteenth-century America, the extent to which technical inventions shaped the minds and attitudes of its people can hardly be overrated. What is more, it was during these important stages of the nation's growing political and cultural self-awareness that the very concept of "technology" as independent from other areas of rational investigation such as philosophy, literature, and the arts had first been introduced. When the Harvard professor Jacob Bigelow (1787–1879) published his influential study *Elements of Technology* (1829), the term and its underlying differentiation between the so-called useful and the fine arts became known to a wider public. Despite its utilitarian etymology (from the Greek word *techne,* meaning a systematic way of doing things), technology for Bigelow signified not merely a method or a new tool but a particular mindset—a rational, scientific approach by which men cope with the complexity of nature and by which they try to master the vagaries of human existence.

Technically Bigelow defined "technology" as a wedding of two already established disciplines: the application of science to the useful arts. Yet in view of what had already been achieved in this new field he was convinced that once technology was instituted as a common practice there would be no return to an earlier state of being, that it was a force administering its own laws and following its own logic. "The augmented means of public comfort and of individual luxury, the expense abridged and the labor superseded, have been such," he explains with regard to possible public skepticism about technology's rapid progress, "that we could not return to the state of knowledge which existed even fifty or sixty years ago, without suffering both intellectual and physical degradation" (p. 6). In a similar vein, Emerson's friend the English critic Thomas Carlyle, while brandishing the age's mechanical orientation in his influential essay "Signs of the Times," published the same year as Bigelow's *Elements*, outlines his hopes for the future by explicitly approving of the progress made in learning and the arts:

> Doubtless this age also is advancing. . . . Knowledge, education are opening the eyes of the humblest; are increasing the number of thinking minds without limit. This is as it should be; for not in turning back, not in resisting, but only in resolutely struggling forward, does our life consist. . . . Indications we do see . . . that Mechanism is not always to be our hard taskmaster, but one day to be our pliant, all-ministering servant. (Pp. 485–486)

What such diverse writers as Bigelow, Carlyle, and Emerson thus have in common is a feeling that with the staggering number of mechanical inventions, an irrevocable shift—a transition from a pretechnological state to a society continuously producing and being shaped by technology—has occurred.

By and large, early-nineteenth-century Americans welcomed the introduction of new devices and means of transportation, and they generally understood the importance of technology for the pressing task of exploring and settling the vast continent. Contrary to Carlyle and other European critics of mechanization they rarely discussed technology as a companion to industrialization. So much did the idea of an "industrialized" society seem out of place in America that the nation readily embraced mechanical contrivances such as steamboats, the McCormick automatic reaper, and the power loom while at the same time denouncing industrialization for its obvious negative consequences—the establishment of an impoverished, morally weak proletariat and the pollution of the natural environment. What could be observed in England,

---

In a letter to Thomas Jefferson on 28 June 1813, John Adams highlights the importance of technology in shaping modern society. As he points out, the changes occasioned by new inventions during the early decades of the nineteenth century had been dramatic:

The invention in mechanic arts, the discoveries in natural philosophy, navigation, and commerce, and the advancement of civilization and humanity, have occasioned changes in the condition of the world and the human character which would have astonished the most refined nations of antiquity.

Lester J. Cappon, ed., *Adams-Jefferson Letters*, 2 vols., (Chapel Hill: University of North Carolina Press, 1959), 2:340.

Germany, or France as a result of large-scale manufacturing simply did not apply to the conditions in the New World. Given the scarcity of its population, the abundance of nature and wilderness, and the great distances that separated individual settlements, instituting improved means of transportation, communication, and production appeared more of a practical necessity than a social evil. "With abundant resources but few people to exploit them," the historian of technology Carroll Pursell reminds us, "Americans who aspired to surpass quickly the splendor and power of the old British Empire soon realized that machines would have to replace hands if the job were to be done" (p. 2).

DO MACHINES MAKE HISTORY? TECHNOLOGY AND AMERICA'S MANIFEST DESTINY

While "Yankee ingenuity" soon became synonymous with the pioneering efforts to build the nation, it also spelled out an unflinching belief in the essential power of knowledge. In line with fundamental ideas of the Enlightenment and the premium it placed on the human capacity to better social conditions and to envision a future perfected state of society, the founding fathers actively endorsed the invention of labor-saving machinery and other useful contrivances. Though apprehensive of the negative impact of the machine on communal life, technological expertise was essential not only as a means to serve the needs of the individual

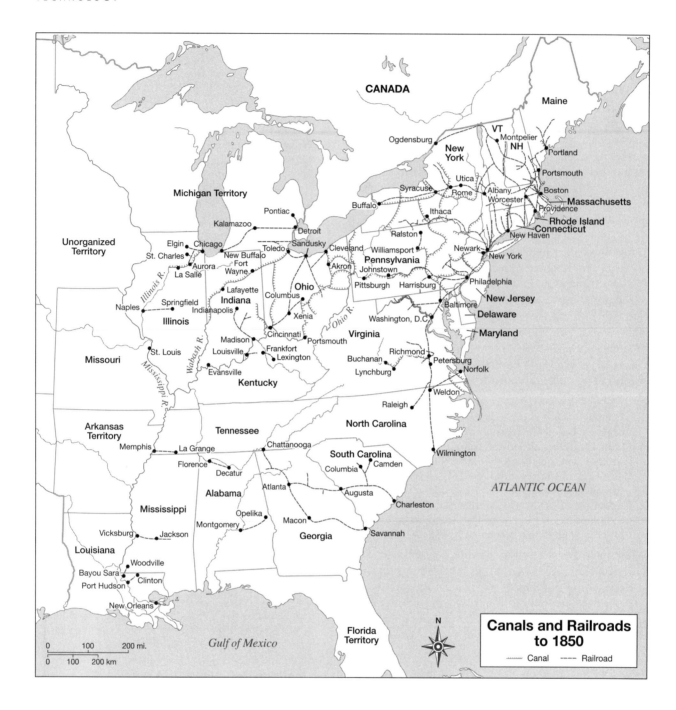

Canals and Railroads to 1850

citizen but also to promote the Republic's higher humanitarian goals. Even Thomas Jefferson (1743–1826), who in his *Notes on the State of Virginia* (1785) promulgated a pastoral America immune to the social and moral corruption of industrial production, eventually conceded that technology could well be a major ingredient of historical progress. To Robert Fulton, the successful inventor of a new steamboat, he wrote in 1810: "I am not afraid of new inventions or improvements, nor bigoted to the practices of our forefathers.

It is that bigotry which keeps the Indians in a state of barbarism in the midst of the arts" (Meier, p. 219). For Jefferson and his fellow Americans the importance of technology was thus actually twofold. First, technological advancement figured, in a very literal sense, as a means to conquer and eventually possess the whole of the continent. Second, it was taken to vindicate synecdochically the historical destiny of America and the accompanying exploitation of natural resources that led to the extinction of its native population.

Two famous literary authors, Edgar Allan Poe (1809–1849) and Nathaniel Hawthorne (1804– 1864), took issue with this widespread metaphorical conflation of technology and historical progress. In his political satire "The Man That Was Used Up" (1839), Poe turned the tables on Americans' naive readiness to assume an intrinsic connection between progress and technology. By relating the creation of the republic and the violence associated with its geographical expansion to an authentic historical figure, who literally is made of and, later, "wasted" by modern technology, Poe launches a scathing critique of historical progress as the fulfillment of America's special destiny. In the story technological progress is tied up with this character to such a degree that his very name calls forth commendations on the age's inventiveness and mechanical expertise. Whenever the narrator mentions General John A. B. C. Smith, supposedly a veteran Indian fighter of the late Bugaboo and Kickapoo campaign and alias of former Vice President Richard M. Johnson, the general's friends and acquaintances invariably reiterate a paean to the "wonderful age" of invention (p. 381). Though the general seems to be well recognized among his contemporaries as a living emblem of the marvelous prospects of modern times, the enthusiastic responses to the narrator's query about his actual identity remain strikingly evasive and tautological. With each interlocutor, the fabulous soldier becomes increasingly entangled in a skein of elliptic discourses that are bound to mystify rather than uncover the history of his mysterious personality. In the end General Smith remains but a narrative construct, a hollow (and horrible) signifier of both technological ingenuity and historical myth.

If "The Man That Was Used Up" questioned antebellum Americans' love affair with machinery by exposing its inherent (self-) destructive powers, Hawthorne took a different, yet in no way less critical, approach. In his famous short story "The Celestial Railroad" (1843) he satirizes the historical driving role that many ascribed to the onrush of technology and material inventions by making technology the center of a burlesque rewriting of John Bunyan's *The Pilgrim's Progress.* Machines clearly abound in this allegorical tale. Not only does the modern Christian alleviate the burden of his pilgrimage to the Celestial City by riding on the newly established railroad, he also encounters such engineering achievements as, for example, a daring bridge whose foundations have been secured by "some scientific process," a tunnel lit by a plethora of communicating gas lamps, and a steam-driven ferryboat.

Significantly, Hawthorne's adoption of technological metaphors in the story blurs with his critical stance on specific cultural practices and religious trends. When

---

In his short story "The Man That Was Used Up," Edgar Allan Poe ridicules the enthusiasm for technological progress rampant among his fellow-Americans by using hyperbole and satire:

"There is nothing at all like it," he would say; "we are wonderful people, and live in a wonderful age. Parachutes and railroads—man-traps and spring-guns! Our steam-boats are upon every sea, and the Nassau balloon packet is about to run regular trips (fare either way only twenty pounds sterling) between London and Timbuctoo. And who shall calculate the immense influence upon social life— upon arts—upon commerce—upon literature— which will be the immediate result of the great principles of electro magnetics! Nor, is this all, let me assure you! There is really no end to the march of invention. The most wonderful—the most ingenious . . . the most truly *useful* mechanical contrivances, are daily springing up like mushrooms."

Thomas Ollive Mabbott, ed., *The Collected Works of Edgar Allan Poe,* 3 vols. (Cambridge, Mass.: Harvard University Press, 1978), 2:381–382.

---

the narrator finally arrives at the present-day Vanity Fair, where "almost every street has its church and . . . the reverend clergy are nowhere held in higher respect" (p. 139), he ridicules the traveling lecturers of these burgeoning sects as "a sort of machinery" designed to distribute knowledge without the encumbrance of true learning. On the surface a critique of facile latitudinarianism—a prominent, pseudo-rational strain of thought within the Anglican church—and the contemporary fad of providing instruction through oral rather than literary discourse, the passage also betrays Hawthorne's anxiety about the ongoing mechanization of American society in general. Moreover, the "etherealizing" of literature that appears to be the bottom line of his complaint epitomizes the difficult position of literary authors within an increasingly technological, differentiated sphere of cultural production. Much as Hawthorne tries to defend the superior quality of the literary text (versus the sheer "machinery" of trivial lectures), his rhetorical strategy also lays bare the degree to which he himself has become a part of the new machine environment. If he dismisses the shallow libertarian sects as a movement inevitably leading to moral and intellectual destruction, to use machinery as an emblem of such inevitability attests to the symbolic power of modern

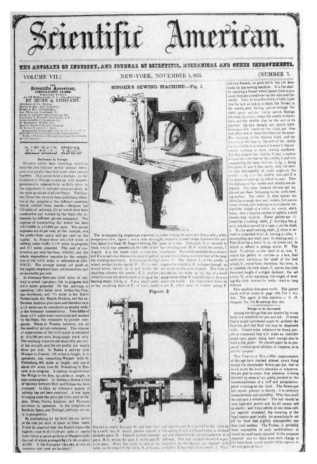

The cover of the journal *Scientific American*, 1 November 1851, heralding Isaac Singer's invention of the continuous stitch sewing machine. Although Singer was only one of the inventors involved in the development of the sewing machine, his company came to dominate the manufacture of models for domestic use, which were welcomed by American women as great labor-saving devices. GETTY IMAGES

technology, a power that held enthralled even the most conservative of antebellum writers.

TECHNOLOGY AND THE ROMANTIC POLITICS OF DISEMBODIMENT

This ambiguity of the literary writer vis-à-vis an increasingly technological environment can be traced throughout the major works of the period. The establishment of the literary profession within the socioeconomic network of nineteenth-century American society required its differentiation from other specialized professions such as engineering or manufacturing, and it rested on a rationalization of the inventive process as exempted from the materialist exigencies of industrial production. The notion of modern authorship, in other

words, developed along the lines of strong antimaterialist biases that emphasized the spiritual over the physical implications of writing. Romantics often conceived of their work as a disembodied process that turned on an effort to transcend both the bodily confines of the writer and the material constraints of the text to be produced. That the Romantic poetics of disembodiment were closely tied to contemporary discussions of technology can be seen in Hawthorne's metafictional short story "The Artist of the Beautiful" (1844). The story effectively juxtaposes the materialist foundations of modern technological society and the ethereal, disembodied work of the Romantic writer. Resonating with references to early industrial manufacturing and the emphasis that Jacksonian America placed on punctuality and the utilitarian ideal of the "useful" arts, "The Artist of the Beautiful" aptly reflects the cultural changes concurrent with rapid technological advancement and the burgeoning of the antebellum American economy. Not only does Hawthorne apprize the conflict between the *practical* and the *beautiful* by creating a character who is both watchmaker and artist; he also has his protagonist, Owen Warland, embark on a highly symbolic project. Searching for a material form that will communicate his aesthetic ideals, the watchmaker builds a synthetic creature, a mechanical butterfly, which combines his artistic ambitions and the difficulties arising from his ambivalent professional status.

Hawthorne's text cogently portrays the human body as the antithesis to everything that is beautiful and aesthetically important. Having set his heart upon the realization of an abstract concept, biological life matters only as conditional to the accomplishment of Warland's task. Whereas the technological—and the body as its physical-material counterpart—operates in direct opposition to the artist's ethereal strivings, the story as a whole might well be taken as an attempt to amalgamate the divergent forces of creativity and materiality. The ironic and ambiguous ending, which has left many readers puzzled as to the true relation of art, nature, and material culture in the story, could thus be read as a plea for the inclusion—rather than exclusion—of technology into the realm of artistic production. In keeping with the organic principle of Romantic writing, Hawthorne provides his watchmaker with the power to animate, to spiritualize, machinery. Warland's ambition is not "to be honored with the paternity of a new kind of cotton machine" but to produce a "new species of life and motion" (pp. 453, 466). It is thus not by imitating nature but by competing with her, by putting forth "the ideal which nature has proposed to herself in all her creatures, but has never taken pains to realize" (p. 466) that the watchmaker becomes an artist. However frail and transient his imaginative child may be, as carrier of an original idea it takes on a quality more real than reality itself. "When the artist rose high enough to achieve the beautiful," as we learn in the concluding paragraph of the story, "the symbol by which he made it perceptible to mortal senses became of little value in his eyes while his spirit possessed itself in the enjoyment of the reality" (p. 475).

The historian Daniel Boorstin has remarked that capitalist "America has been the laboratory and the nemesis of romanticism" (p. 173). Though Boorstin's use of the term "romanticism" was rather figurative, the bifurcation of values expressed in his statement—one ringing with promises of new insights, the other gloomy and apocalyptic—underscores the complex self-representations of American Renaissance writers and their contradictory relations with antebellum society. His critical satires notwithstanding, Poe overall responded positively to the wave of new technology. Despite his emphasis on the exceptional cognitive status of creative work, his definition of authorship was utterly technological. Given the fervor with which Poe embraced, for example, "anastatic printing" (also known as "relief etching" that reproduced a facsimile impression of the original) as a way of experimenting with and ultimately increasing the representational value of written texts, he impressively foreshadows the constructivist tradition within modern arts that is mainly identified with early-twentieth-century avant-garde movements. Rather than figuring as the downfall of the writer's profession, science and technology provided for Poe a "laboratory" of new ideas from which he concocted the symbols and metaphors that are now closely associated with his literary oeuvre.

Nor would Hawthorne or Herman Melville (1819–1891) conceive of the contemporary technological environment as the "nemesis" of literary creativity. Aware of the ubiquitous presence of the machine in antebellum America, these writers examined the changing conditions under which they labored in sometimes excruciating detail. However, the numerous representations of literary work in both their shorter fiction and in many of their full-fledged romances should rather be read as part of an imaginative search for professional identity. Far from advocating the writer's withdrawal from society, they addressed the processes of modernization in a quite pragmatic manner. To find a place of their own within America's dramatic shift from agrarian virgin land to a Tartarus of industrial labor, Hawthorne and Melville often had recourse to highly symbolic modes of self-representation that helped to deflate the rising tensions between, on the one hand, the materiality of the printed text, and on the other, the original ideas it conveyed. Since the conflict between

modern authors and the economic and technological environment often turned on the rival ideologies of idealism and materialism, cybernetic imagery, as we have seen in "The Artist of the Beautiful," offered a perfect screen onto which the writer's struggle for social recognition could be projected.

THE AUTHOR IN PAIN: TECHNOLOGY AND THE CIVIL WAR

Complex images of humans-turned-machine (or vice versa), which abound in antebellum literature, reflect the authors' attempt to avoid the social trapdoors of their idealist self-definitions and thereby to narrow the gap between literary work and other modern professions. Yet, however widespread the urge to compete on the marketplace of specialized labor, American Renaissance writing is also marked by the somber prospects of the author's inevitable alienation from society. In Melville's "Bartleby, the Scrivener," isolation and estrangement of the literary worker sets in after a period of extreme productivity. Since Melville's literary reputation was already flagging when the story first appeared in 1853, the text encapsulates, on one level, its author's doomed struggle for public recognition. On another level, however, it instances the first in a row of mid-nineteenth-century American texts in which authorship appears to be entirely overwhelmed by technology. There is no escape for Bartleby from the prison house of Wall Street and the mass production of written texts; mired in physical deterioration and increasing muteness, the scrivener's initial resistance to the growing mechanization of his office environment eventually turns into a hollow gesture of all-encompassing passivity.

Melville's symbolic depiction of the artist's fragmented, immobilized body in "Bartleby" ties in with concerns traceable in the work of two other contemporary Americans, Rebecca Harding Davis (1831–1910) and Walt Whitman (1819–1892). To bring into conjunction writers as structurally different as Melville, Davis, and Whitman is by no means an easy task. If Davis's social realism already differs considerably in both its form and its setting from Melville's Romantic self-representation, Whitman's democratic, all-embracing pose seems to be even farther from the latter's deeply pessimistic stance. However, in Davis's *Life in the Iron Mills* (1861) and in Whitman's *Drum-Taps,* a cluster of poems about the Civil War first published in 1865, the besieged artist is rendered as being as muted and paralyzed when confronted with modern technology as the starving scrivener. What thus began as the self-conscious claim of Romantic artists to a voice of their own is transformed, under the influence of war technology and its disfigured, amputated victims, into painful dramatizations of the writer's speechlessness and despair.

See also "Bartleby, the Scrivener"; Popular Science; Science; Urbanization

BIBLIOGRAPHY

Primary Works

Adams, John, and Thomas Jefferson. *The Adams-Jefferson Letters.* Vol. 2. Edited by Lester J. Cappon. Chapel Hill: University of North Carolina Press, 1961.

Bigelow, Jacob. *Elements of Technology.* Boston: Hilliard, Gray, Little and Wilkins, 1829.

Carlyle, Thomas. "Signs of the Times." *Edinburgh Review* 49 (1829): 439–459.

Davis, Rebecca Harding. *Life in the Iron Mills and Other Stories.* New York: Feminist Press, 1972.

Emerson, Ralph Waldo. *Journals and Miscellaneous Notebooks of Ralph Waldo Emerson.* Vol. 16. Edited by Ronald A. Bosco and Glen M. Johnson. Cambridge, Mass.: Harvard University Press, 1982.

Hawthorne, Nathaniel. "The Celestial Railroad" and "The Artist of the Beautiful." 1843, 1844. In *Mosses from an Old Manse,* vol. 10 of *The Centenary Edition of the Works of Nathaniel Hawthorne,* edited by William Charvat, Roy Harvey Pearce, and Claude Simpson. Columbus: Ohio State University Press, 1974.

Melville, Herman. *The Piazza Tales and Other Prose Pieces, 1839–1860.* Vol. 9 of *The Writings of Herman Melville.* Edited by Harrison Hayford et al. Evanston, Ill.: Northwestern University Press, 1987.

Poe, Edgar Allan. "The Man That Was Used Up: A Tale of the Late Bugaboo and Kickapoo Campaign." 1839. In *Collected Works of Edgar Allan Poe,* vol. 2, *Tales and Sketches, 1831–1842,* edited by Thomas Ollive Mabbott, pp. 376–392. Cambridge, Mass.: Harvard University Press, 1978.

Thoreau, Henry David. *Walden.* 1854. Edited by J. Lyndon Shanley. Princeton, N.J.: Princeton University Press, 1971.

Whitman, Walt. *Leaves of Grass.* 1855. Edited by Harold W. Blodgett and Scully Bradley. New York: New York University Press, 1965.

Secondary Works

Benesch, Klaus. *Romantic Cyborgs: Authorship and Technology in the American Renaissance.* Amherst: University of Massachusetts Press, 2002.

Boorstin, Daniel. *The Genius of American Politics.* Chicago: University of Chicago Press, 1953.

Bromell, Nicholas K. *By the Sweat of the Brow: Literature and Labor in Antebellum America.* Chicago and London: University of Chicago Press, 1993.

Kasson, John F. *Civilizing the Machine: Technology and Republican Values in America, 1776–1900.* New York: Grossman, 1976.

Matthiessen, F. O. *American Renaissance: Art and Expression in the Age of Emerson and Whitman.* London: Oxford University Press, 1941.

Marx, Leo. *The Machine in the Garden: Technology and the Pastoral Ideal in America.* London and New York: Oxford University Press, 1964.

Meier, Hugo A. "Thomas Jefferson and a Democratic Technology." In *Technology in America: A History of Individuals and Ideas,* edited by Carroll W. Pursell Jr., pp. 17–33. Cambridge, Mass.: MIT Press, 1981.

Pease, Donald E. *Visionary Compacts: American Renaissance Writing in Cultural Context.* Madison: University of Wisconsin Press, 1987.

Pursell, Carroll W., Jr. "Introduction." In *Technology in America: A History of Individuals and Ideas,* edited by Carroll W. Pursell Jr. Cambridge, Mass.: MIT Press, 1981.

Klaus Benesch

TEMPERANCE

The antebellum period was famously a time of social reform. Reformers agitated for the abolition of slavery and the expansion of women's rights, but they also renovated prisons and poorhouses and instituted mental asylums and schools for the deaf and the blind. They passed out religious tracts and insisted that the Sabbath be observed. They improved sewers and drains, inspected the homes of the poor, and campaigned against the death penalty and for world peace. They lived in communes, rejected fashion in favor of rational dress, and took all sorts of water cures. But above all else, they advocated temperance reform. Antebellum temperance reform was the largest mass movement in United States history—and certainly one of the most influential.

Temperance reform unfolded in five sometimes overlapping phases: (1) the licensing movement of the eighteenth century, (2) the moderationist societies of the early nineteenth century, (3) the temperance societies of the early to mid-nineteenth century, (4) the teetotal societies of the mid-nineteenth century, and (5) the prohibitionist movement of the mid-nineteenth century. The essay that follows will sketch out the history of temperance reform, pausing to consider four milestone temperance texts, and will conclude by discussing the effects that temperance reform had on the non-canonical and canonical literary texts of the antebellum period.

THE PREHISTORY OF TEMPERANCE
REFORM: LICENSING

Throughout the seventeenth century and much of the eighteenth, drinking was frequent and alcohol was abundant. Beer or cider was served at every meal, to children as well as adults, and various liquors and cordials were used as medicines; many families distilled their own spirits and brewed their own beer. Church meetings, town elections, and militia trainings were all occasions for drinking, while the tavern was the site for all the communal activities that could not take place in the church, from business meetings and newspaper reading to cockfighting and bear baiting. Historians estimate that Americans drank more than twice as much alcohol in the colonial period as they do now, but no one at the time thought of this as a problem. On the contrary, alcohol was celebrated as salutary and drinking as convivial. Alcohol was understood not only to deaden pain and induce sleep but also to cure colds, break fevers, aid digestion, and, more generally, sustain the body's constitution; moreover, it served as a reliable alternative for an often impure water supply. The drinking of alcohol was understood to reaffirm communal ties—on holidays, at harvest time, and during all the rituals that punctuate a life, such as baptisms, weddings, and funerals. Communal ties were reaffirmed daily as well in the informal political debates that sprang up among the men who gathered every evening in taverns, gatherings that were as democratic as the revolution such debates would ultimately foment.

This happy conception of alcohol and drink was first challenged in the United States in 1673, when the Puritan minister Increase Mather published a pair of sermons entitled "Wo to Drunkards: Two Sermons Testifying against the Sin of Drunkenness." Mather voices the then current view of alcohol when he takes for granted the fact that "drink is in itself a good creature of God," but he attempts to alter the contemporary view of drinking by arguing that "the abuse of drink is from Satan" (p. 23). In introducing the category of "abuse" Mather is drawing a new distinction between moderate and excessive drinking. The consequences of excessive drinking fall on individual drunkards: their reason is destroyed and their souls are imperiled; their time and money are wasted, and they are often drawn into crime. But the fate of individual drunkards has become a concern for the Puritan community more generally because, Mather believes, excessive drinking has recently become more prevalent. For this reason, he exhorts the elders of Boston to monitor the drinking of others in order to ensure that it does not become excessive; more specifically, he calls on the elders to regulate the number of taverns and alehouses in the city and to supervise them more closely. In emphasizing regulation and supervision,

Mather is anticipating the form that temperance activity would take throughout the eighteenth century, when the so-called licensing movement would seek to ensure that drinking houses and the drink trade remained in the hands of a respectable elite.

Toward the end of the eighteenth century two texts argued that licensing was not enough: Anthony Benezet's *The Potent Enemies of America Laid Open* (1774) and Benjamin Rush's *An Inquiry into the Effects of Spirituous Liquors on the Human Body* (1790). The two texts are medical treatises that differ from Mather's sermons both in argument and in rhetoric. Where Mather had drawn a distinction between excessive and moderate drinking, Benezet and Rush instead distinguish among forms of alcohol: they condemn distilled spirits while praising beer, wine, and hard cider. Where Mather had relied on scriptural authority for his arguments, quoting Isaiah's attack on drunkards, Benezet and Rush rely instead on the authority of medicine and science. And where Mather had focused on the spiritual and moral effects of drunkenness, Benezet and Rush attend to the effects that spirits have on the body as well as on the mind and the character. Indeed, Rush establishes a remarkably precise set of correlations between various alcoholic and nonalcoholic drinks and various bodily and moral states. He depicts these correlations visually through what he calls the "Moral and Physical Thermometer," which arranges drinks according to their specific "hotness," from water through punch to pepper in rum, and then displays the specific "diseases," "vices" and "punishments" to which the hotter drinks give rise (p. 4). A toddy, for instance, leads to gout, idleness, and debt, while morning drams lead to melancholy, "hatred of just gov't" and jail or the whipping post (p. 4).

MODERATIONISM AND TEMPERANCE

Taken together, Mather's sermons and Benezet's and Rush's treatises laid the conceptual foundation for temperance reform. But reform did not seize the public imagination until the early nineteenth century, when people became troubled by a sudden rise in drinking rates. In the seventeenth and eighteenth centuries people had drunk at a rate more than double our own; in the first third of the nineteenth century, however, they suddenly began drinking at a rate more than triple. More specifically, the annual per capita consumption of distilled alcohol was six gallons a year; with the rise of temperance reform at mid-century, that rate would fall to two gallons a year, where it has held steady ever since. What these numbers obscure, however, is the fact that many women, children, and slaves did not drink at all in the period, which means that the

The Drunkard's House. Illustration from the book *The National Temperance Offering and Sons and Daughters of the Temperance Gift,* edited by S. F. Cary and published in 1850. Such visual imagery greatly enhanced the message of temperance literature. BROWN UNIVERSITY LIBRARY

typical drinker was consuming nearly half a pint of distilled alcohol every day.

Historians argue that the causes of this sudden rise in alcohol consumption were largely agricultural. A number of farmers had moved west, across the Allegheny mountains, only to find that the nation's infrastructure was not adequate to transporting their crops back to the cities and ports of the east. As a result, they needed to convert the grain they grew into something more portable: some began feeding their grain to livestock, while many more began distilling it into spirits. Spirits were easily transported back to the East, and they also circulated widely in the western territories, where a shortage of hard money made alcohol the most common currency. At the same time as the spread of agriculture was caus-

ing a national drinking binge, however, the rise of industrialization was making sobriety seem newly necessary. In the colonial period, labor had been spasmodic: agricultural labor followed cycles of activity and rest, harvest time followed by harvest festival; and artisanal labor too was oriented to tasks rather than time. Factory work, by contrast, required a disciplined labor force, one that would show up for work on time, every day—and sober.

Agricultural expansion thus created a situation that industrialization felt compelled to control. The first attempt to do so took the form of the moderationist movement of the early to mid-nineteenth century. This movement began in 1813, with the founding of the Massachusetts Society for the Suppression of Intemperance and the Connecticut Society for the Reformation of Morals. These groups emerged, historians argue, in response to the depression that was caused in New England by the War of 1812 and the consequent naval embargo; there was a fear that the newly unemployed would fall into drunkenness, and the moderationists sought to forestall this possibility by instilling what they called the habits of moderation. Moderation was defined in one of two ways: either as moderate, rather than excessive, drinking, or more commonly, as the drinking of fermented, rather than distilled, alcohol. That these two distinctions were sometimes confused with one another points to the fact that the moderationist societies were far more deeply concerned with a third distinction, the distinction of class. The moderationist societies drew their leaders and most of their members from the traditional New England elite, from the ranks of men who belonged to the Federalist Party and to the Congregationalist or the Unitarian Church. These men viewed alcohol and drinking through the lens of their own elite status, and as a result they tended to believe that problematic drinking—whether it be excessive drinking or the drinking of spirits—was a phenomenon particular to the lower classes. In the event, neither moderationist society proved to be very influential, and both had faded away by the early 1820s.

In 1826 a new group emerged, the American Temperance Society (ATS), which drew its members from a variety of evangelical denominations and included nearly as many women as men. The ATS followed the moderationists in taking excessive spirit-drinking to be primarily a lower-class phenomenon, but it argued that the responsibility for having caused this drinking, and thus the responsibility for ending it, lay squarely with the moderate drinkers of the upper classes. These drinkers had set an example that the lower classes were following at great peril; they were therefore obligated, the ATS argued, to set a new and better example by abstaining from spirits entirely. In this way, the third phase of temperance reform, temperance proper, began. The ATS was remarkably influential, in large part because many of its evangelical members had already been involved in mission work of various kinds and therefore knew how to disseminate their message much more broadly than previous reformers had been able to do. Where Mather addressed the church fathers of Boston and Benezet and Rush addressed the political leaders of the emerging United States, the ATS spoke directly, through illustrated tracts and weekly newspapers, to the moderate drinkers it was attempting to persuade. And persuaded they were: by 1833 more than six thousand local societies were affiliated with the ATS

and more than a million men and women had signed the temperance pledge.

Temperance was quickly radicalized in two different ways. Some ATS groups began arguing that the sale of spirits should simply be outlawed, and in this way they inaugurated the prohibitionist phase that would come into prominence in the 1850s. Others began arguing that beer and wine—ultimately, even communion wine—were as dangerous as spirits. This latter line of argument gave rise, in 1836, to a group that ultimately replaced the ATS, the American Temperance Union; more generally, it gave rise to teetotalism, the fourth phase of temperance reform.

TEETOTALISM AND PROHIBITION

One of the earliest and most influential teetotal texts is Lyman Beecher's *Six Sermons on the Nature, Occasions, Signs, Evils, and Remedy of Intemperance* (1827). In these sermons Beecher erases all the distinctions that Mather, Benezet, and Rush had carefully drawn. There is no difference, for Beecher, between the strongest spirits and the weakest wine, no difference between a binge and a sip, because the weaker lead inevitably to the stronger and the sip leads inevitably to the binge. For this reason, Beecher insists on total abstinence from all forms of alcohol for everyone. "A flag must be planted at the entrance of [the drunkard's] course," he writes, "proclaiming in waving capitals—THIS IS THE WAY TO DEATH!!" (p. 39). Even as Beecher radicalizes temperance reform, he also borrows and combines the rhetorical strategies that had been used by earlier temperance texts. Specifically, he combines a medical analysis of what alcohol does to the body with religious claims about what it does to the soul, and he exhorts the nation to begin collecting the data that will reveal what alcohol is doing to the economy as well. He insists, in particular, on statistics, which he believes have a unique power to make visible "the height, and depth, and length, and breadth of this mighty evil" (p. 71).

Beecher and the American Temperance Union focused on saving the sober, just as earlier reformers had focused on saving the moderate drinker, in large part because no one believed that confirmed drunkards could be reclaimed. In 1840 a group called the Washingtonians began to do just that. Begun by six formerly hard-drinking artisans and laborers who agreed to support one another in their efforts to remain sober, the Washingtonian movement made a place not only for reformed drunkards but also for working-class men and women within temperance reform. The effects were astonishing: by 1843 the Washingtonians could claim 500,000 members. The Washingtonians differed from other groups not only in the focus of their efforts but also in their methods. Where the members of other temperance and teetotal societies gathered to listen to professional lecturers, the Washingtonians held what they called "experience meetings." In these meetings, the speakers were reformed drunkards who described in often harrowing detail what their lives had been like when they were drinking, why they decided to abstain, and what their lives had been like since—a narrative model that continues to structure Alcoholics Anonymous meetings even today. These meetings were supplemented by teetotal fairs and picnics, teetotal concerts and balls, and most popular of all, Fourth of July celebrations in which men and women would declare their independence from King Alcohol.

From the beginning, the more established temperance and teetotal societies were shocked by the Washingtonians: they condemned the vulgarity of the teetotal festivities and, even more, the luridness of the experience meetings. Increasingly, some of the Washingtonians themselves came to share this view. Many working-class men and women had turned to teetotalism in the hopes of improving their social and economic status, and they began to want the meetings they attended to display the respectability to which they aspired. In response to this desire, the Sons of Temperance emerged in 1842 and gradually took the place of the Washingtonians. Eschewing experience speeches and teetotal songs, the Sons of Temperance offered less entertainment but more concrete aid. Indeed, they remade temperance reform according to the model of the mutual aid societies that working-class men and women had first started forming in the 1830s.

Because the Washingtonians, and later the Sons of Temperance, believed that drunkards could be reclaimed by example, they continued to rely on the power of moral suasion. By contrast, the middle-class temperance and teetotal societies, believing as they did that drunkards were beyond redemption, increasingly began to argue that sobriety would be possible only when alcohol was outlawed. Prohibition first emerged as a possibility in the 1830s, when temperance societies in New England sought to deny licenses to taverns that sold liquor, but it came into real prominence in the 1850s. By 1850 Massachusetts had succeeded in transforming itself, county by county, into a teetotal state, and in 1851 Maine was the first state to vote itself teetotal all at once. Twelve states and territories had followed by 1855. That year, however, marked the high point of nineteenth-century

prohibition—and of nineteenth-century temperance reform more generally. In the 1860s a number of states repealed their so-called Maine Laws; by the late 1870s only New Hampshire, Vermont, and Maine itself remained dry. The Maine Laws were repealed in part because they proved impossible to enforce, given the very rudimentary state of police forces in the period, but more importantly because they had failed to fulfill the promise of temperance reform. Once the sale of alcohol was made illegal, it became increasingly clear that drinking was not in fact the sole cause of declining morals, rising crime, and growing unemployment. Some temperance activity persisted throughout the postbellum period, but for the most part the nation would not begin to think of alcohol and drinking as uniquely dangerous for another fifty years—until the early-twentieth-century agitation that would lead to fourteen years of national prohibition.

TEMPERANCE IN LITERATURE

In 1865 the National Temperance Society established its own publishing house. "The demand of the present is *books,* Books, BOOKS!," its members proclaimed. "Men *must* have books, women *will* have books, and children *should* have books." In making this proclamation the National Temperance Society was implicitly acknowledging that books had already played an enormous role in antebellum temperance reform. The illustrated tracts and newspapers that the American Temperance Society had begun distributing in the 1820s and 1830s had quickly been joined by a huge number of texts from a wide range of genres: there were novels, stories, poems, and plays as well as magazines directed to various ages and even alphabet books. The most popular temperance texts proved to be Timothy Shay Arthur's *Ten Nights in a Bar-room* (1854), a best-selling novel, and John Gough's *Autobiography* (1845), which recorded the life story of one of the Washingtonians' most famous speakers. Arthur's play focuses on the damaging consequences of drinking: its protagonist decides to open a tavern, and, as a result, his daughter is killed in an accident, his wife is driven mad, and he is himself killed by his own son. Gough's *Autobiography,* by contrast, focuses on the benefits of sobriety. His own conversion from drinking and his subsequent career as a temperance speaker demonstrates the peace and prosperity that sobriety brings.

The effects of temperance reform on literature are not confined, however, to these explicitly didactic texts; nearly all the canonical authors of the period stand in some kind of relation to temperance reform. Some were straightforward advocates of teetotalism,

The Drunkard's Progress. Lithograph by Nathaniel Currier, c. 1846. Currier depicts what many believed was the all-too-common fate of those who consumed alcohol: escalating consumption and degradation culminating in a miserable death. THE LIBRARY OF CONGRESS

among them the daughter of Lyman Beecher, Harriet Beecher Stowe. Particularly devoted to teetotalism were antislavery writers, who equated drunkenness with other forms of bondage. Indeed, Frederick Douglass argued, in his autobiography, that owners encouraged their slaves to drink on the rare days of holiday so as to "disgust their slaves with freedom" (p. 115). And Frances Harper, in her novel, *Iola Leroy* (1892), argued for temperance on the grounds that "the colored man has escaped from one slavery" and should be careful not "to fall into another" (p. 170). Other writers, specifically the transcendentalists, were drawn to some idea of temperate living or moderation, even as they were repelled by certain aspects of the cause. Ralph Waldo Emerson, for instance, saw the value of regulating the bodily appetites, but he also recognized that the careful distinctions of temperance reform could serve as a distraction from more fundamental issues: "The curious ethics of the pledge, of the Wine-question [is]," he wryly observed, "a gymnastic training to the casuistry and conscience of the time." And Henry David Thoreau's *Walden* (1854) can be read as an idiosyncratic celebration of

cool, clear water by a lifelong water drinker, one who has retreated to the woods in large part to escape from the organized activities of reform.

Other authors made drunkenness and temperance an explicit topic in their own writing. Some did this for cynical reasons, writing didactic temperance fiction solely in order to make money or to ensure the publication of their work. Nathaniel Hawthorne, for instance, wrote a temperance short story early in his career, "A Rill from a Town Pump" (1835), but later parodied the representational practices of temperance reform in his anti-reformist novel, *The Blithedale Romance* (1852). Walt Whitman wrote temperance stories, as well as an entire temperance novel, *Franklin Evans* (1842); later in his life he would insist not only that he had written the novel solely for money but also that he had done so entirely drunk. Still other authors treated temperance reform as one remarkable social phenomenon among others, as when Herman Melville satirized it mildly in *Moby-Dick* (1851) and exposed its inadequacies in *Redburn* (1849). Finally, some authors used drunkenness to articulate seemingly unrelated concerns, as when Emily Dickinson, in "I taste a liquor never brewed—," used drunkenness as a figure for visionary experience or when Elizabeth Stoddard, in *The Morgesons* (1862), used it to figure sexual desire and generational decline. The protagonist of *The Morgesons* first feels desire when she first drinks mulled wine, and she will later insist that her lover conquer his inherited tendency to dissipation before she agrees to marry him. In all of these ways, temperance reform left its mark not only on cultural attitudes toward drinking and alcohol but also on the nation's literature.

See also Evangelicals; Health and Medicine; Puritanism; Reform; Religion; Sensational Fiction; Unitarians

BIBLIOGRAPHY

Primary Works

Arthur, Timothy Shay. *Ten Nights in a Bar-room, and What I Saw There.* Chicago: M. A. Donohoe, 1854.

Beecher, Lyman. *Six Sermons on the Nature, Occasions, Signs, Evils, and Remedy of Intemperance.* 1827. New York: American Tract Society, 1845.

Benezet, Anthony. *The Potent Enemies of America Laid Open: Being Some Account of the Baneful Effects Attending the Use of Distilled Spirituous Liquors; and the Slavery of the Negroes.* Philadelphia: Joseph Crukshank, 1774.

Douglass, Frederick. *Narrative of the Life of Frederick Douglass, an American Slave.* 1845. Edited by Houston A. Baker Jr. New York: Penguin, 1986.

Emerson, Ralph Waldo. "Lecture on the Times." 1841. In *Nature; Addresses and Lectures.* Boston: James Munroe, 1849.

Gough, John Bartholemew. *The Autobiography of John Gough.* 1845. Boston: J. B. Gough, Gould, and Lincoln, 1852.

Harper, Frances E. W. *Iola Leroy, or, Shadows Uplifted.* 1892. Oxford: Schomburg Library, Oxford University Press, 1988.

Mather, Increase. *Wo to Drunkards: Two Sermons Testifying against the Sin of Drunkenness.* Cambridge, Mass.: Marmaduke Johnson, 1673.

Rush, Benjamin. *An Inquiry into the Effects of Spirituous Liquors on the Human Body, to Which Is Added, a Moral and Physical Thermometer.* Boston: Thomas & Andrews, 1790.

Secondary Works

Lender, Mark Edward, and James Kirby Martin. *Drinking in America: A History.* 1982. Rev. ed. New York: Free Press, 1987.

Reynolds, David S. *Beneath the American Renaissance: The Subversive Imagination in the Age of Emerson and Melville.* Cambridge, Mass.: Harvard University Press, 1988.

Reynolds, David S., and Debra J. Rosenthal. *The Serpent in the Cup: Temperance in American Literature.* Amherst: University of Massachusetts Press, 1997.

Rorabaugh, W. J. *The Alcoholic Republic: An American Tradition.* New York: Oxford University Press, 1979.

Tyrell, Ian R. *Sobering Up: From Temperance to Prohibition in Antebellum America, 1800–1860.* Westport, Conn.: Greenwood Press, 1979.

Walters, Ronald G. *American Reformers, 1815–1860.* New York: Hill and Wang, 1978.

Amanda Claybaugh

THEATER

Most American writers of the nineteenth century had an important stake in the theater. Edgar Allan Poe, whose parents were actors, wrote theater reviews, had a story adapted to the stage, and refers to himself in "The Philosophy of Composition" as a "literary *histrio*" (p. 530). Many others, including Washington Irving, Henry Wadsworth Longfellow, Walt Whitman, Mark Twain, Bret Harte, Louisa May Alcott, William Dean Howells, and Henry James were, at some point, professional drama critics or playwrights. Specific references to theater of their day may also be found in the writings of Nathaniel Hawthorne, Herman Melville, and James Fenimore Cooper. "I ought to acknowledge my debt to actors, singers, public speakers, conventions, and the Stage in New York," Whitman (1819–1992) confessed toward the end of his life, "and to plays and operas generally" (*Complete Poetry and Collected Prose*, p. 1289).

For Whitman the importance of the antebellum stage is wrapped up with all of the public culture of the 1830s and 1840s, the speeches and sermons, political rallies, circuses, songs, and parades. As Rosemarie Bank has written, for dignitaries and even presidents, visiting theaters to receive acclamations or to address the people was a common use of these places of assembly (p. 12). And Whitman did not hesitate to lump together performers as diverse as the actors Fanny Kemble and Junius Booth, the Quaker demagogue Elias Hicks, and the seaman-preacher Father Taylor, who was also the model for Melville's Father Mapple (Emerson called him "the Shakespeare of the sailor & the poor"). So in spite of Whitman's acknowledgment of "theatricals in literature" and his memory of the leading authors, poets, editors, and other important cultural figures of the times in the audiences, theater of this period can also seem unliterary. Theater was social in a sense that disappeared by the end of the century. The ability of the public to applaud at any time, to holler, and to throw fruits and nuts was regarded as a "right" not to be infringed. As theater riots in the first half of the nineteenth century attest, audiences felt licensed to give or withhold consent to a performance; such theater required charismatic performers more than subtle texts. For Whitman, the actors Junius Booth and Edwin Forrest were foremost among the "dramatic artists" of his youth (*Complete Poetry and Collected Prose*, pp. 1185–1192).

THE PLAYWRIGHTS

The playwrights of the mid-nineteenth century— Robert Montgomery Bird (1806–1854), Nathaniel Parker Willis, George Henry Boker, Anna Cora Mowatt, George Aiken, Augustin Daly, Dion Boucicault, and many others—are virtually unread in the early twenty-first century. As a drama critic for the *Brooklyn Daily Eagle* in 1847, even Whitman derided the drama of his day in an article titled "Miserable State of the Stage—Why Can't We Have Something Worth the Name of American Drama!" (*Gathering of the Forces*, pp. 310–314). He complained of the vulgarity of audiences, the problems of a "starring system" of dominant actors, the timidity of American authors who produced derivative versions of English and French dramas, and the New York press who were "slaves of the paid puff system." Yet the drama and theater of the time are socially, politically, and at times aesthetically significant. Between 1820 and 1870 hundreds of Americans wrote plays for public and private (parlor) performances, and many more of all classes attended them. In *The Guide to the Stage*, a handbook for would-be actors first published in 1827, Leman T. Rede lists well over eighty permanent theaters scattered across America, not to mention the churches, steamboats, and homes in which plays were also performed.

However, dramatists commonly complained that it was impossible to make a living writing plays. Before new copyright protection pushed by Bird, Boker, and Boucicault passed Congress in 1856, no law protected the staging of any play. Moreover, a manager could translate or adapt a first-rate French or British comedy and be assured of success. An original piece by an American, on the other hand, could cost ten times the price of a translation. So most plays produced in America were translations of French and German texts or British plays. The sentimental domestic plays and spectacular, heroic dramas of the German August von Kotzebue (1761–1819) were

among the most popular works on the American stage. The operas of the Italians Gioacchino Rossini (1792–1868) and Vincenzo Bellini (1801–1835) were also immensely popular. Ironically, one of the most successful Americans writing for the theater in this period was a Louisiana-born Creole of color, Victor Séjour (1817–1874), who expatriated himself to Paris where his acclaimed dramas, such as *Diégarias* (1844) and *La tireuse de cartes* (1859) were performed at the Théâtre Français and the Théâtre de la Porte Saint-Martin respectively. The latter, based upon the recent kidnapping of a Jewish child, Edgardo Mortara, by the Vatican, was performed before an audience that included the emperor Napoleon III and Empress Eugénie and generated considerable controversy in the Catholic press throughout Europe.

On the other hand, the Irish-born Dion Boucicault (1820–1890) adapted the plot of a French play, *Les pauvres de Paris* (1856), to create *The Poor of New York* (1857), which then became *The Poor of Liverpool*, *The Poor of Leeds*, *The Poor of Manchester*, *The Streets of Islington*, and *The Streets of London*. The originality of the plot was less important than the new standard Boucicault set for sensationalism, lighting a house on fire in the last act and bringing a real fire truck on stage to put it out. Perhaps Boucicault's most famous and controversial "American" play, *The Octoroon; or, Life in Louisiana* (1859), like Séjour's *Diégarias*, which is about Christians and Jews, depicts the tragic fate of a child of a racially mixed union. Boucicault's drama seeks to capture "local color" of a southern plantation while also employing a variety of racial, ethnic, and class stereotypes. Like all of Boucicault's plays, *The Octoroon*, aims at a mass audience and so takes an ambiguous position on the issue of slavery. The central female character, the beautiful "tragic mulatta," Zoe, is the child of a white plantation owner and his slave mistress. Like numerous novels and plays of the period concerned with miscegenation, *The Octoroon* presents a highly sympathetic heroine who is compelled to die rather than consummate a love that transgresses racial barriers.

In addition to probing the limits of racial identity, the drama proved to be a richly transnational commodity in the nineteenth century, one in and through which national identity might be both insisted on and questioned. Bird's 1834 play *The Broker of Bogota* exhibits the ambivalence of a society (urban, capitalist, American) in conflict with inherited forms of art, courtship, and of economy, but the play is set in New Grenada. South America is a space in which the concerns of nineteenth-century Americans are recognizable but defamiliarized. For Bird, as for President James

Monroe in 1823, South America is a space always geographically continuous and politically aligned with the United States. Bird, who set numerous works south of the border, was not alone in having a deep interest in the Spanish colonies. One of the most popular plays of the 1820s was Kotzebue's *Pizarro in Peru,* and many other plays with noticeably American themes, including speeches about democracy and opposition to kings, were set in Europe (ancient and modern). Popular British and French novels were also a rich mine for theatrical productions. The works of Sir Walter Scott, the elder Alexandre Dumas, and Charles Dickens were quickly adapted to the stage, but so were many American works (often before they were finished being serialized), such as "Rip Van Winkle" and *Uncle Tom's Cabin.*

SHAKESPEARE AND BLACKFACE MINSTRELSY

By far the most popular playwright in America of this period was Shakespeare. *Richard III* was the most commonly performed of Shakespeare's plays in the nineteenth century and was lampooned frequently in such versions as *Bad Dicky.* The tragedies *Hamlet, Macbeth, King Lear,* and *Othello* went through countless productions, adaptations, and parodies (as can be seen in Twain's *Huckleberry Finn*), not to mention provoking a wide range of pseudo-Elizabethan verse tragedies, culminating in the Shakespearean scenes and characters of Melville's *Moby-Dick.* Contributing to Shakespeare's popularity was the flow of great British actors to North America. In 1846 Charles Kean brought his visually elaborate, historically "accurate" *King John, Henry VIII,* and *Richard III* to New York. *King John* alone cost an extraordinary $12,000 to stage and set a new standard for spectacular stagings in America (Odell 5:252). Edmund Kean, Junius Brutus Booth, Charles Kemble, Fanny Kemble, and William Charles Macready all had significant tours in the United States and some stayed. Junius Booth's sons Edmund and John Wilkes Booth were both actors whose names live on, the former becoming the greatest Hamlet of the nineteenth century and the latter assassinating President Abraham Lincoln in Ford's Theater during a performance of the comedy *Our American Cousin.*

As Lawrence Levine has shown, Shakespeare was popular entertainment in nineteenth-century America, when an entire evening generally consisted of a long play, an afterpiece (usually a farce), and a variety of between-act specialties (p. 21). Shakespeare was presented with and in the same spirit as magicians, dancers, singers, acrobats, minstrels, and comics. And Shakespeare parodies, such as *Julius Sneezer, Hamlet and Egglet,* and *Much Ado about a Merchant of Venice,* frequently took the form of short skits and satirical songs performed by minstrels, white actors in blackface.

The relationship between American performances of Shakespeare and minstrelsy also indicates a central problem of theatrical practice in America, an underlying anxiety about the originality of American culture. Theater in America drew upon Old World dramatic models, most notably the plays of Shakespeare, while also acknowledging the importance of slavery and race in the New, specifically in complicated appropriations of African American music and dance by white actors in blackface. The origins of such racial representations do not reside solely with whites or blacks but in relationships between the two, and the fact that Shakespeare and minstrels occupied the same stages indicates the cultural melting pot that the mid-century stage had become. African Americans, however, did not perform in theaters for whites in this period, with the exception of productions at the short-lived but important African Grove Theater in New York founded by William Henry Brown (1808–1883) in 1821. The brilliant black actors James Hewlett and Ira Aldridge (who later moved to London) performed Shakespeare's *Richard III* there as well as Brown's *Drama of King Shotaway* (1823). Aldrich's influence was felt subsequently when, for instance, the African American author and abolitionist, William Wells Brown (1818–1884), who saw Aldrich in London, gave powerful and romantic readings of his antislavery melodrama *The Escape; or, a Leap for Freedom* (1858). In 1823, however, the African Grove was closed by city authorities, and for most of the century blacks on stage were played or caricatured by whites.

Blackface minstrelsy originated with the white actor Thomas Dartmouth Rice, who began to perform his "Jim Crow" song and dance in 1830. Minstrel performances, the portrayal of generally happy slaves and supposed plantation culture through songs, farces, skits, mock oratory, and satire, became one of the most popular cultural forms of the century, preeminently in Stephen Foster's "Plantation Melodies." George Aiken's (1830–1876) 1852 adaptation of Harriet Beecher Stowe's *Uncle Tom's Cabin,* the period's greatest financial success, also drew on blackface performance and, in the character of the slave girl Topsy, on minstrel humor. In the play, unlike Stowe's novel, Topsy sings and "dances a breakdown" (Richards, p. 391). Played by a white woman in burnt cork, she speaks in black dialect, "grins," and is the source of most of the play's stage business in addition to her musical bits. Like Jim Crow and the urban dandy Zip Coon, the characters of Topsy and Uncle Tom became stock figures in minstrel performances of the nineteenth century.

Representing old and new, indigenous and foreign, Shakespeare and slavery, American theater was a crucible for the young nation's most contentious issues. As Eric Lott points out, the moment of minstrelsy's greatest popularity (1846–1854) was also a time of bitter political controversies: labor struggles in New York and other major cities, debates over the extension of slavery, the Seneca Falls women's rights convention, and the Astor Place theater riot. In short, minstrelsy and Shakespeare spoke to aspirations and anxieties of the working-class public in the urban Northeast in the years between 1830 and 1850, especially in the large playhouses in the Bowery district of lower Manhattan.

THE ASTOR PLACE RIOT, THE BOWERY AUDIENCE, AND EDWIN FORREST

No single event reflected more deeply the complexity of the American public's relationship to topics of class and national identity than the Astor Place riot in 1849. Rival productions of *Macbeth* were being staged, one at the Astor Place Opera House featuring the Englishman William Charles Macready, known for his cerebral acting style, aristocratic demeanor, and allegedly anti-American comments; and one at the Broadway Theatre, featuring America's own flamboyantly patriotic Edwin Forrest. The venues themselves were weighted with ideological significance. The architecture and interior design of the two theaters reflected important class as well as artistic differences. The Astor Place, which had opened only two years earlier, was one of the most fashionable theaters in the city. It was capable of seating eighteen hundred people in the pit, dress circle, family circle, and gallery. The Broadway Theatre, on the other hand, could accommodate forty-five hundred people and had an immense pit to which only men and boys were admitted. Macready's second performance at the Astor Place Opera House (the first had been abortive) was disrupted by a large crowd of blue-collar workingmen, loafers, and "Bowery b'hoys," many allegedly supporters of Forrest. The Astor Place riot climaxed as the militia fired into a crowd that had thrown paving stones at the theater. More than twenty died, and over one hundred were injured. Aspects of the Astor Place riot inform Melville's (1819–1891) novels *White-Jacket* and *Moby-Dick*, both of which Melville wrote later that year. In *White-Jacket*, theatricals are actually staged on deck by the crew, and a riot ensues.

Edwin Forrest (1806–1872), generally considered the first great tragedian of the American stage, was not only a popular favorite in the United States among the working people but also was himself deeply patriotic and frequently made extravagant expressions of love for the American people. Unlike

Edwin Forrest as Metamora. Engraving after the photograph by Mathew Brady. THE GRANGER COLLECTION, NEW YORK

foreign stars who seemed indifferent to the development of American drama, Forrest also was famous for encouraging American dramatists by sponsoring playwriting competitions (though in controlling rights to the plays, he deprived writers of the chance to make a living beyond prize money from their work). Several important plays were written for Forrest, which he performed throughout his career. One of the most famous was John Augustus Stone's (1800–1834) Indian play *Metamora; or, Last of the Wampanoags* (1829). Like plays that depicted (or misrepresented) African Americans, "Indian plays" reached their highest popularity between 1829 and 1838. They represented political and national themes in terms of family drama, typically through "the traditional comedy motif of a daughter torn between her father's command and the voice of her heart with the serious theme of the end of American Indian legitimacy—the vanishing Indian" (Sollors, p. 104). Yet the lofty renditions of dying Indian chiefs also came in for burlesque, most brilliantly by the Irish immigrant John Brougham (1810–1880) who, in *Metamora; or, The Last of the Pollywogs* (1847), actually humanized the Indian character by portraying him in a less noble and pathetic manner. Forrest's other star vehicles included three winners by Bird: a drama of a slave revolt in ancient Rome, *The Gladiator* (1831); *Oralloossa* (1832), a play about Pizarro set in South America; and *The Broker of Bogota* (1834). The playwright Robert T. Conrad (1810–1858) won with *Jack Cade* (1841), a spin-off play about the rebel leader of the people in Shakespeare's *Henry VI, Part Two*.

The comic actor and pantomimist George Lafayette Fox (1825–1877) also appealed to male audiences of the Bowery, and his performances were considered to be among the greatest of his time. Unlike the performances of Forrest, Fox's generally were not interpretations of scripts. Earlier in the nineteenth century, theaters had featured spectacular pantomimes and acrobatics generally as afterpieces to more serious productions. However, in the 1830s, the Ravels, a highly acclaimed troupe of pantomimists, arrived from France to revolutionize pantomime in America, transforming it into a popular form of entertainment in its own right. In 1850 Fox, whose early roles included phrenological lecturer, hypnotist, and a proliferation of comic Irishmen, made his way to the Bowery theaters, which were gradually becoming more proletarian as the Broadway venues were becoming increasingly upscale. According to Laurence Senelick, Fox's greatest success and most lasting fame came as Humpty Dumpty. Supposed by many to be the funniest man of his day, his violent physical humor represented the brutal street life of the Bowery. His face painted with a white lead makeup that later led to his insanity and death, Fox's staging of the pantomime *Humpty Dumpty* at the Olympic Theatre in 1867 especially excited its audience by familiar representations of the neighborhood; the scenes included the new, as yet unfinished, courthouse in City Hall Park and even a view of the Olympic Theatre itself by night. The blend of topical humor, patriotism (the orchestra playing "Independence Day Has Come" and an old-fashioned Yankee dance, among other things), spectacular scenery, violent slapstick comedy, and ballet ensured the play's success. As Senelick remarks, "Thus was the English harlequinade assimilated to the *mores* of Boss Tweed's New York" (p. 141).

WOMEN OF THE AMERICAN THEATER

If Forrest and Fox sought through their acting styles and choice of plays to portray America through an overdetermined masculine ethos, there were also important women performing and writing American plays. Charlotte Cushman (1816–1876), who had originally trained as an opera singer, was generally regarded as the first great tragic actress of the American stage, often playing opposite Forrest. Cushman was well known for roles ranging from Lady Macbeth to a cross-dressed Romeo and other male parts. A different kind of actress, the sensationalistic Adah Isaacs Menken (1835–1869) was internationally famous for her starring role in the equestrian melodrama *Mazeppa*, which she first performed in 1861. Menken was stripped onstage to a flesh-colored body stocking, lashed to the back of the "wild horse of Tartary," and sent flying up a narrow ramp to the peak of a papier-mâché mountain. Mark Twain (1835–1910), a young newspaper reporter in the audience at one of those performances, later described how "the Great Menken came flaming out of the heavens like a vast spray of gas-jets" (p. 153). One of the most glamorous celebrities of the 1860s, Menken also wrote poetry and cultivated a literary following, befriending Walt Whitman, Charles Dickens, Algernon Swinburne, and the elder Alexandre Dumas, with whom she was rumored to have had an affair.

Most "respectable" women stayed away from the theater in the first half of the nineteenth century, unless escorted by men. Anna Cora Mowatt (1819–1870), who was born in France to a wealthy family, first attended the theater in 1831 when she saw the great English actress Fanny Kemble touring the United States. Like many young women of her class, Mowatt wrote and performed plays for her family. Private theatricals increased in popularity over the next few decades. The March family in Louisa May Alcott's *Little Women* (1868–1869) entertain themselves at home with an *Operatic Tragedy,* and many such plays were published, one example being a collection titled *Amateur Theatricals and Fairy-Tale Dramas: A Collection of Original Plays, Expressly Designed for Drawing-Room Performance* (1868) by Sarah Annie Frost. As Karen Halttunen has written: "Nowhere was the new direction of middle-class culture more evident than in the vogue of private theatricals that swept the parlors of America in the 1850s and 1860s. But this cultural transformation was already underway by 1845, when middle-class audiences began to gather at the Park Theatre to enjoy an evening of laughing at themselves and at each other for their increasingly fashionable social lives" (p. 153). In 1841, when her husband was financially ruined and became almost completely blind, Mowatt was convinced to read Shakespeare in public for money. She wrote and produced her most enduring work in 1845, *Fashion,* a comedy of manners and satire of the nouveau riche Tiffany family in New York, which also presented

Actress Adah Isaacs Menken in her most famous role, the Tartar Mazeppa, c. 1862. Menken wore a fleshcolored costume in the final act of the play to simulate nudity and titillated audiences worldwide. GETTY IMAGES

one of the few American dramatic types, the stage Yankee, here called Adam Trueman. At the premier the owner of the Park Theatre, John Jacob Astor, closed the third tier of side boxes to prostitutes in deference to Mowatt's high-class sensibilities. The third tier, which was later replaced by a balcony or "family circle," had been designed with semiprivate bars and separate entrances to accommodate "unescorted ladies" or "single gentlewomen" and their clientele. Properly escorted ladies sat in more prestigious, private boxes, though often still with some trepidation. Harriet Beecher Stowe, for instance, went veiled, and with her book agent as guardian, to see a performance of *Uncle Tom's Cabin*. The theater was regarded as a dangerous place of seduction for women and men

alike, and, in the minds of many, there was a relationship between the profession of the actress and that of the prostitute. It was, therefore, especially remarkable when Mowatt herself later turned to acting and became for nearly a decade one of America's foremost and highly respected actresses.

Between 1850 and 1870 new museum theaters built in New York, Boston, and Philadelphia cultivated an aura of "respectable" theatergoing. In particular they aimed to attract women and children with plays designed to inform and instruct. As Bruce McConachie writes, the American Museum of P. T. Barnum in New York and the Boston Museum of Moses Kimball appealed to the middle class, banning liquor and prostitution and presenting plays in lecture halls that eliminated the hierarchical arrangement of the pit, boxes, and gallery (pp. 162–176). The moral dramas performed in these venues ranged from temperance plays, such as William H. Smith's wildly popular melodrama *The Drunkard* (1844) to the abolitionist vehicle *Uncle Tom's Cabin*, both of which Barnum first produced. In his memoir *A Small Boy and Others*, Henry James (1843–1916) reflects on the excitement he experienced at Barnum's museum in New York, where he watched an early production of *Uncle Tom's Cabin* in 1853. The pleasant boyhood memories include the deep aromas of peppermint and orange peel and the crowded hall in which lights were now dimmed.

MELODRAMA AND AMERICAN LITERATURE

Most dramatic literature written before 1870, from romantic "tragedy" to moral reform drama to nationalistic comedy, has some marks of what in the early twenty-first century is thought of as melodrama, a dramatic form imported from postrevolutionary France. Peter Brooks has argued that melodrama be understood in the context of the collapse of a hierarchically cohesive society, the liquidation of the traditional sacred in France (p. 15). In the world of melodrama, traditional truths have been thrown into question and thus become personalized. Many American plays are concerned with the failure of the visible world to reflect a predictable and stable "reality." The problem of trust or the ability to know others, which resonates throughout Boker's *Francesca da Rimini* and Bird's *Broker of Bogota*, finds its fullest expression in Melville's *The Confidence-Man: His Masquerade* (1857). Melville makes use of theatrical forms, from highly ostentatious Shakespearean acting to blackface, to represent the social and economic uncertainties of his market-driven age. Central chapters of *Moby-Dick* are written in dramatic form, with dialogue and stage directions, and the nature of Ahab's dramatic excess is better understood when read in the context of contemporary acting and writing for the stage.

The hyperbolic rhetoric of melodrama indicates not only the tenuous relationship between appearance and reality but also the inadequacy of language itself to express emotional or moral truths. Melodrama privileges stage effect, grand gesture, powerful vocal utterance, and scenic display over text and, consequently, over the psychological coherence of character. As David Grimsted notes, melodrama "made light of rationality" and replaced it with "a concept of feeling or intuition" (p. 20). In Stone's *Metamora* tears and sighs "speak more than language could relate." This kind of theater was not so much antiliterary as it was at odds with traditional literary forms. The authors of the nineteenth century, though often ambivalent about contemporary audiences and plays, recognized in the popular theater their own chaotic world and often saw their world as theater. Whitman's close friendships with actors (he felt "almost one of their kind") and his passionate love of theater culminated in his appreciation of the great Shakespearean actor Junius Booth. Booth's "genius was to me one of the grandest revelations of my life, a lesson of artistic expression," he wrote. Nearly every American author of the nineteenth century thought deeply about theater and represented aspects of it in other literary forms. American theater was a barometer of the culture's concerns and a microcosm of American democracy.

See also Circuses and Spectacles; Cross-Dressing; English Literature; Humor; Satire, Burlesque, and Parody; Sensational Fiction; Taste; *Uncle Tom's Cabin*

BIBLIOGRAPHY

Primary Works

Poe, Edgar Allen. *Essays and Reviews.* New York: Library of America, 1984.

Rede, Leman T. *The Guide to the Stage: Containing Clear and Ample Instructions for Obtaining Theatrical Engagements.* 1827. Edited by Francis C. Wemyss. New York: Samuel French, 1861.

Twain, Mark. "A Full and Reliable Account of the Extraordinary Meteoric Shower of Last Saturday Night." In *The Californian: Sketches of the Sixties.* San Francisco: John Howell, 1926.

Whitman, Walt. *Complete Poetry and Collected Prose.* New York: Library of America, 1982.

Whitman, Walt. *The Gathering of the Forces: Editorials, Essays, Literary and Dramatic Reviews and Other Material Written by Walt Whitman as Editor of "The Brooklyn Daily Eagle" in 1846 and 1847.* Vol. 2. Edited by Cleveland Rogers and John Black. New York: Knickerbocker Press, 1920.

Secondary Works

Ackerman, Alan L. *The Portable Theater: American Literature and the Nineteenth-Century Stage.* Baltimore: Johns Hopkins University Press, 1999.

Bank, Rosemarie K. *Theatre Culture in America, 1825–1860.* Cambridge, U.K., and New York: Cambridge University Press, 1997.

Brooks, Peter. *The Melodramatic Imagination: Balzac, Henry James, Melodrama, and the Mode of Excess.* New Haven, Conn.: Yale University Press, 1976.

Grimsted, David. *Melodrama Unveiled: American Theater and Culture, 1800–1850.* Berkeley: University of California Press, 1968.

Halttunen, Karen. *Confidence Men and Painted Women: A Study of Middle-Class Culture in America, 1830–1870.* New Haven, Conn.: Yale University Press, 1982.

Levine, Lawrence W. *Highbrow/Lowbrow: The Emergence of Cultural Hierarchy in America.* Cambridge, Mass.: Harvard University Press, 1988.

Lott, Eric. *Love and Theft: Blackface Minstrelsy and the American Working Class.* New York: Oxford University Press, 1993.

McConachie, Bruce A. *Melodramatic Formations: American Theatre and Society, 1820–1870.* Iowa City: University of Iowa Press, 1992.

Odell, George C. D. *Annals of the New York Stage.* 15 vols. New York: Columbia University Press, 1931.

Quinn, Arthur Hobson. *A History of the American Drama.* 2 vols. New York: Appleton-Century-Crofts, 1923, 1927.

Quinn, Arthur Hobson, ed. *Representative American Plays from 1767 to the Present Day.* 5th ed. New York: D. Appleton–Century, 1917.

Richards, Jeffrey H., ed. *Early American Drama.* New York: Penguin, 1997.

Senelick, Laurence. *The Age and Stage of George L. Fox, 1825–1877.* Hanover, N.H.: University Press of New England, 1988.

Shattuck, Charles H. *Shakespeare on the American Stage: From the Hallams to Edwin Booth.* Washington, D.C.: Folger Shakespeare Library, 1976.

Sollors, Werner. *Beyond Ethnicity: Consent and Descent in American Culture.* New York: Oxford University Press, 1986.

Alan Ackerman

TOURISM

In the closing months of 1819 and into the winter of 1820 readers throughout the United States eagerly awaited installments of a provocative travel narrative by one of America's rising literary stars, Washington Irving (1783–1859). His whimsical and thoughtful mix of travel sketches and short fiction would become the first formidable salvo in a battle for an indigenous literature in the young nation. It was no accident that *The Sketch Book,* at its core a travel book, would become such a popular and critically acclaimed work of American literature. It tapped into the essential nature of the country, a culture defined by movement. Irving effectively captivated an audience eager both to celebrate its sense of self and to venture out into the broader world.

Americans would be unable to inundate the rest of the world until technological advances meshed with an increasing economic vitality, which allowed a much broader range of Americans to travel in the second half of the nineteenth century. The tourists and travel writers in the two generations following *The Sketch Book* would nonetheless shape the aesthetic purpose that has since informed American tourism. In the years between 1820 and the Civil War, American tourists, representatives for the most part of the nation's economic and social elite, established the first American identity on the world stage. These tourists were keen to be acknowledged and respected as members of the great hope for a civilized future. If Irving seized on a growing mood of Americans to define themselves as both a part of and apart from the Old World, the growing developments in travel infrastructure began to make such forays possible. Early limitations on travel would be erased at a remarkable rate as steam navigation both on land and sea steadily chipped away at the time, danger, and expense of travel. Until the 1840s, when steam-powered ships began to make regular trips across the Atlantic Ocean in two weeks, the journey to the Old World for Americans demanded at least six weeks in sailing packets. With the advent of steam navigation, the world opened to Americans on a substantially larger scale. No longer wholly subservient to the vagaries of the winds, ocean travel became relatively dependable, and Americans were ready to exploit the new opportunities.

The result of such technological advance was inevitable. By the 1840s the interest in both tourism and travel literature had evolved into an outright phenomenon. In the May 1844 issue of the *United States Magazine and Democratic Review,* for example, Henry Tuckerman notes, "our times might not inaptly be designated as the age of travelling. Its records form no insignificant branch of the literature of the day" (p. 527). The American curiosity about faraway lands combined with the increasing availability of quicker and cheaper transportation, creating a boom in foreign travel. More Americans were physically and economically able to travel abroad, and as the number of commercial and passenger ships sailing the Atlantic Ocean multiplied, so did the number of tourists who could afford to make the trip to the Old World. Christof

Wegelin notes that the steadily increasing numbers from 1820 to 1849 exploded by 1860. U.S. citizens returning yearly to Atlantic and Gulf ports, according to Wegelin, fluctuated between just under 2,000 to just over 8,000 in the three decades following 1820, but in 1860 the returning tourists in the four largest Atlantic ports numbered 19,387 (p. 307). With the dramatic technical advances in steam-powered ships, voyages between the continents became commonplace. Tuckerman continues, "steam is annihilating space. . . . The ocean, once a formidable barrier, not to be traversed without long preparation and from urgent necessity, now seems to inspire no more consideration than a goodly lake, admirably adapted to summer excursions" (p. 527). These new tourists not only wanted to test themselves in a foreign context but they also traveled to learn.

In an age of a democratization of knowledge that glorified self-improvement, the burgeoning, literate middle class clamored toward anything perceived as educational. This social quest was intricately intertwined with tourism. The Unitarian clergyman William Ellery Channing (1780–1842) effectively captured the growing mood in his "Self Culture," a lecture first given in Boston in 1838. Channing defined "self culture" as "the care which every man owes to himself, to the unfolding and perfecting of his nature" (p. 354). He insisted that the goal of the American people should be "to fasten on this culture as our Great End, to determine deliberately and solemnly, that we will make the most and best of the powers which God has given us" (p. 371). The time-honored and socially respected art of traveling, in and of itself connoted self-improvement, whether or not tourists actually changed substantially or learned anything. Tourists could always say—once back at home—that they had been there, wherever "there" was, and no matter the nature of the experience, that fact alone could hold sway in any salon discussion or social occasion. Traveling to learn, at least ostensibly, therefore established itself as a valuable part of touristic performance.

TOURING THE OLD WORLD

Europe offered the strongest lure for American tourists, who sought to understand where they came from in order to know where they were going. The United States had successfully separated itself politically from England, but it had yet to sever the undeniable emotional and intellectual ties to European cultures and institutions. The European travel experience helped these tourists, who were overwhelmingly of European descent, reconcile opposing impulses: to reject the past by concentrating only on an American future or to embrace that legacy and the rich associational identity it fostered. By traveling to Europe, Americans could wander among the accomplishments of their ancestors and celebrate them, all the while affirming their belief through direct comparison that America was a land of the future and Europe of the past.

Washington Irving is the first significant writer to give a resonant voice to this impulse. In the "Author's Account of Himself," the introduction for *The Sketch Book,* Irving wistfully captures a prevailing and enduring sentiment through the voice of his fictional narrator, Geoffrey Crayon:

> But Europe held forth the charms of storied and poetical association. There were to be seen the masterpiece[s] of art, the refinements of highly-cultivated society, the quaint peculiarities of ancient and local custom. My native country was full of youthful promise: Europe was rich in the accumulated treasures of age. Her very ruins told the history of times gone by, and every mouldering stone was a chronicle. I longed to wander over the scenes of renowned achievement—to tread, as it were, in the footsteps of antiquity—to loiter about the ruined castle—to meditate on the falling tower—to escape, in short, from the common-place realities of the present, and lose myself among the shadowy grandeurs of the past. (Pp. 14–15)

Irving makes calculated word choices as he describes the attractions of Europe: "ruins," "times gone by," "mouldering stone," "ruined castle," "falling tower," and "shadowy grandeurs of the past." Taken together, these not-so-subtle associations encouraged readers to view Europe as a culture long past its prime. Irving's tone is that of a romantic dreamer touring a cemetery that is aesthetically charming, perhaps, but marked by death nonetheless. Irving was by no means alone, and subsequent generations of tourists would likewise lose themselves among "shadowy grandeurs," and many would whistle along the way as they echoed his enthusiasm and "youthful promise."

TOURING THE AMERICAN LANDSCAPE

As he had with the American perspective to European charms, Irving reflects a common attitude of nineteenth-century American tourists in relation to the American natural landscape. He writes that "on no country have the charms of nature been more prodigally lavished" and goes on to expound the virtues of those "charms":

> Her mighty lakes, like oceans of liquid silver; her mountains, with their bright aerial tints; her valleys, teeming with wild fertility; her tremendous cataracts, thundering in their solitudes; her boundless plains, waving with spontaneous verdure; her broad deep rivers, rolling in solemn silence to the ocean; her trackless forests, where vegetation puts forth all its magnificence; her skies, kindling with the magic of summer clouds and glorious sunshine;—no, never need an American look beyond his own country for the sublime and beautiful of natural scenery. (P. 10)

The energy of this passage serves as a striking contrast with the "shadowy grandeurs of the past" that dominate his romantic musings of Europe. In his description of the natural beauty of America, he highlights the vitality of life—"teeming with wild fertility" and "spontaneous verdure." If American tourists went out into the rest of the world, especially Europe, with insecurities about their cultural and intellectual status, they could at least be highly confident in the potential of the land itself, a continual source of national pride.

Whereas travel writers and readers looked eastward to the past of the Old World, they looked to the interior of North America and westward to their supposed future. If Europe represented the "treasures of age," then the West promised an "image of perpetual juvenescence" (p. 15), according to James Jackson Jarves, author of *Scenes and Scenery in the Sandwich Islands* (1843). The promise of the New World was embodied most dramatically in the beauty of its natural landscape, which stood in stark opposition to the ruins of the Old World. It was a new Eden of possibilities. One of the most popular travel writers of the century, Bayard Taylor, named the narrative of his journey to the West Coast *Eldorado; or, Adventures in the Path of Empire* (1850). Tourists could take part in this cultural production with a confident imperialistic tone. The American quest for cultural stability influenced the popularization of travel books on the whole. The slow but steady American conquest of the West, moreover, gave epic significance to any journey through the region. The number of travelers who ventured west, as compared to the number of those who visited Europe, was small, however. The infrastructure for travel to the West was virtually nonexistent in the first half of the nineteenth century, and travel beyond the Mississippi River was reserved for comparatively few. Between 1820 and 1840 most continental tourism focused on travel within the original thirteen colonies. Toward the midpoint of the century, of course, many more tourists embarked on tours farther westward, but travel remained dominated by emigrants and entrepreneurs. The message from these early tourists resonated to readers still hugging the eastern shore.

AMERICAN TOURISM AND CULTURAL ASCENDANCY

Americans of the nineteenth century had a powerful need to define their place and identity in relation to, or, more frequently, in opposition to the rest of the world. Many Americans felt a contradiction between wanting to respect the accomplishments of Old World cultures and wanting to debunk them. As is made evident by the quantity of travel books published during the era, American tourists often became obsessed with Europe's past as an object lesson for the idyllic future inherent in the United States. In looking toward the other horizon, tourists to the New World and, by extension, the South Seas, most often sought to define themselves by dismissing the accomplishments and integrity of native cultures, or, in a more benign condescension, viewing them as simplistic and romantically alluring as residents of a new Eden. As self-appointed messengers of a new world order, nineteenth-century American tourists typically patronized the peoples they encountered. As representatives of what they saw as a beneficent civilization on the rise, they provided a strong cultural framework for aggressive late-nineteenth-century political imperialism.

The tourists of the mid-nineteenth century established the dominant cultural perspectives that would continue to define American tourism for generations to come. Although their impact was significant, by 1870 the world of tourism was on the verge of an upheaval that would be driven by the more far-reaching forces of economic and political power weight gained by sheer numbers of tourists. The publication of Mark Twain's *The Innocents Abroad* in 1869 signaled the impending shift to mass tourism and imminent American muscularity. In the concluding pages of his narrative of a highly publicized five-month tour of the Old World, America's first pleasure cruise, Twain noted that he and his fellow tourists "always took care to make it understood that [they] were Americans—Americans!" (p. 645). If the earlier generations of American tourists endeavored to define a young nation, subsequent tourists were increasingly capable of redefining the world.

See also Americans Abroad; Exploration and Discovery; *The Innocents Abroad;* Nature; Travel Writing

BIBLIOGRAPHY
Primary Works
Channing, William Ellery. "Self Culture." In *The Works of William E. Channing, D.D.*, 4th ed., vol. 2, pp. 347–411. Boston: James Munroe, 1845.

Irving, Washington. *The Sketch Book of Geoffrey Crayon, Gent.* 1819–1820. Author's rev. ed. New York: G. P. Putnam, 1860.

Jarves, James Jackson. *Scenes and Scenery in the Sandwich Islands and a Trip through Central America*. Boston: James Munroe, 1843.

Tuckerman, Henry T. "The Philosophy of Travel." *United States Magazine and Democratic Review* 14 (1844): 527–539.

Twain, Mark. *The Innocents Abroad*. 1869. Edited by Shelley Fisher Fishkin. New York: Oxford University Press, 1996.

Secondary Works
Baker, Paul. *The Fortunate Pilgrims: Americans in Italy, 1800–1860*. Cambridge, Mass.: Harvard University Press, 1964.

Buzard, James. *The Beaten Track: European Tourism, Literature, and the Ways to Culture, 1800–1918*. Oxford and New York: Oxford University Press, 1993.

Lueck, Beth L. *American Writers and the Picturesque Tour: The Search for National Identity, 1790–1860*. New York: Garland, 1997.

Mulvey, Christopher. *Anglo-American Landscapes: A Study of Nineteenth-Century Anglo-American Travel Literature*. Cambridge, U.K., and New York: Cambridge University Press, 1983.

Perry, Lewis. *Boats against the Current: American Culture between Revolution and Modernity, 1820–1860*. New York: Oxford University Press, 1993.

Schriber, Mary Suzanne. *Writing Home: American Women Abroad, 1830–1920*. Charlottesville: University Press of Virginia, 1997.

Stowe, William W. *Going Abroad: European Travel in Nineteenth-Century American Culture*. Princeton, N.J.: Princeton University Press, 1994.

Wegelin, Christof. "The Rise of the International Novel." *PMLA* 77, no. 3 (1962): 305–310.

Jeffrey Alan Melton

TRAIL OF TEARS

It is estimated that the Cherokees inhabited the land now known as the states of North Carolina, South Carolina, Georgia, Tennessee, and Alabama for hundreds or even thousands of years prior to European contact. For the most part women farmed, and men hunted. The Cherokees governed themselves through consensus and allowed both men and women to join in debates. It was not until European settlers arrived that the ownership of land became an issue and the Cherokees found it necessary to create laws and treaties to protect their homeland.

THE LOSS OF HOME
On 28 November 1785 the Cherokees signed the first of such treaties, the Treaty of Hopewell. This served as

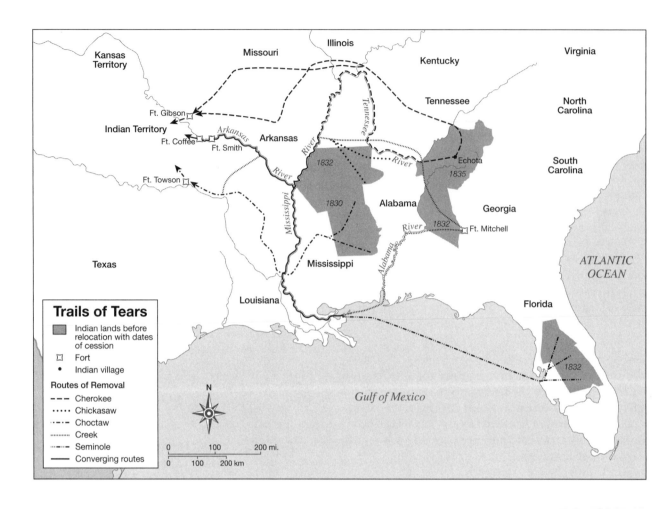

a peace treaty between European settlers and the Cherokees intended to ensure protection of Cherokee land. Yet Georgia refused to acknowledge the treaty; in 1828 Georgia outlawed the Cherokee national government, which by 1827 consisted of a constitution that allowed for a bicameral legislature, a chief executive, and a judicial system. The state of Georgia required a loyalty oath for whites living within the Cherokee Nation and created the Georgia Guard to enforce state law. The fate of the Cherokees' land was ultimately determined once gold was discovered in Dahlonega, Georgia, in 1829. As a result President Andrew Jackson (1767–1845) signed the Indian Removal Act on 28 May 1830.

The Cherokee Nation fought removal by taking their case to the Supreme Court in *Cherokee Nation v. Georgia* in 1831. The Court had to choose whether to uphold the laws of the Cherokee national government or those of the state of Georgia. Chief Justice John Marshall (1755–1835), while declining to rule on the validity of Cherokee law, declared the Cherokee Nation a "domestic dependent nation" that would not be affected by the laws of individual states even though

it was considered part of the United States and so was subject to federal rule.

In late December 1830 Georgia passed a law requiring white men to acquire a license from the state before entering Indian country. After the law took effect on 1 March 1831, eleven missionaries were arrested because they had not sought licenses, and nine received pardons from the governor in exchange for a promise that they would obey Georgia law in the future. Samuel A. Worcester and Elizur Butler, who refused the pardon, were sentenced to prison for four years. Their challenge to the verdict came before the Supreme Court in March 1832 as *Worcester v. Georgia*. The court ruled in favor of the Cherokees and claimed that Georgia law was not valid within the Cherokee Nation. The Georgia Guard continued to enforce state law in the Cherokee Nation in spite of this verdict. When President Jackson did nothing to prevent the guard's attacks on the Cherokee people, some Cherokees began to question the feasibility and success of a continued resistance against removal.

In the midst of Georgia's refusal to recognize the Cherokee Nation, several Cherokees began to lose faith in the idea of resistance. One such figure was Elias Boudinot (1740–1821), who had been educated in a missionary school. Previously Boudinot held the position of editor of the *Cherokee Phoenix,* the national newspaper printed in English and the Cherokee syllabary. The first issue appeared on 21 February 1828 and was widely read by Native Americans and settlers. Initially Boudinot chose to run articles and editorials that championed the idea of resistance to removal from Georgia. In 1832 his views on resistance began to change in light of Georgia's refusal to recognize the decision in *Worcester v. Georgia* and President Jackson's refusal to force the state to comply with the federal ruling. At this point Boudinot opened the issue of Indian removal up for debate. Despite his efforts to garner editorials from both sides, the Cherokee Council refused to allow Boudinot to publish articles questioning the feasibility of resistance. As a result he resigned as editor. Perhaps the most notable pieces of resistance literature were the Cherokee Memorials, documents that held the status of petitions in the nineteenth century. These memorials were written by members of the Cherokee Council and citizens to protest the impending Indian Removal Act of 1830.

The majority of Cherokees sided with John Ross (1790–1866), the chief of their tribe, and his efforts to resist removal. However, Boudinot, Major Ridge (1771–1839), and several other Cherokee leaders chose to negotiate with the U.S. Senate and formed what would be known as the Treaty Party. In December 1835 the Treaty Party signed the Treaty of New Echota despite the absence of John Ross and the Cherokee Council. Out of twenty thousand, only two hundred Cherokees met and ratified the treaty that called for their removal west of the Mississippi. The treaty gave the Cherokees two years to prepare for the removal. General Winfield Scott (1786–1866) was placed in charge of the forced removal that later came to be known as the Trail of Tears. The removal began in the summer of 1838, and many Cherokees died from exhaustion, hunger, and disease. In the winter of 1838–1839 fourteen thousand Cherokees marched twelve hundred miles into what is now Oklahoma. It is estimated that four thousand died. On 22 June 1839 a band of Cherokee assassins killed Major Ridge, his son John Ridge, and Elias Boudinot for signing the Treaty of New Echota.

THE TRANSCENDENTALISTS' RESPONSE

The violent "removal" that came to be known as the Trail of Tears evoked varied responses from the general public and literary world alike. But it was a group of writers who would come to be known as the transcendentalists who seemed to evince the most ardent response. The transcendentalists were drawn to the Cherokees because they perceived them as children of nature and celebrated their primitive connection to the earth. They also found within the Cherokee a character indigenous to American literature. Yet ironically these same authors stressed that the Cherokees should abandon their "primitivism" and assimilate into Western culture if they hoped to escape extinction. The Cherokees' "primitive" nature made for a good read, but in reality this behavior was unacceptable. Many transcendentalists also wrote about the removal of the Cherokees from their homeland. While Ralph Waldo Emerson's (1803–1882) letter to President Martin Van Buren (1782–1862) proves the most direct in his criticism of the Cherokee removals, other transcendentalists such as Henry David Thoreau (1817–1862) and Margaret Fuller (1810–1850) briefly address the Trail of Tears while exploring the impending fate of the Cherokees through their journals and travel writings.

Emerson's letter to President Van Buren was most likely a tribute to his late brother Charles Emerson. Charles wrote several letters to his brothers encouraging them to take a stand on the removals. In 1832 Emerson encountered Major Ridge at Federal Street Church and was captivated by his powerful oratorical abilities (Emerson, "To Charles Chauncy Emerson," p. 346). He wrote Charles informing him that Ridge, in his oratory, took full advantage of the "romance" surrounding the plight of the Indians. In his 1837 lecture "Manners," Emerson romanticizes the "infantile simplicity" of the "Indian in the woods" (p. 135). He also appears to embrace the archetype of the noble savage, a hero who possesses the simplicity of a child. After pressure from his friends and family, Emerson wrote a letter in defense of the Cherokees to President Van Buren on 23 April 1838. In his diary Emerson complains about having to write the letter. He states: "Then is this disaster of Cherokees brought to me by a sad friend to blacken my days & nights. I can do nothing. Why shriek? Why strike ineffectual blows?" (*Journals and Miscellaneous Notebooks* 5:475). Several of Emerson's friends debated the idea of civilizing the noble savage through education and, most importantly, religion. Emerson himself praised the "Apostle" John Eliot, a widely respected missionary responsible for converting many Cherokees to Christianity. Yet in the end the author begins to doubt the Cherokees' ability to assimilate into Western culture based on their own "eternal inferiority." Once Emerson decides to write the letter out of guilt and a sense of duty to his brother, he declares, "I stir in it for the sad reason that no other mortal will move & if I do not, why it is left undone" (*Journals and Miscellaneous Notebooks* 5:477).

In the letter Emerson appeals to the moral sentiment of President Van Buren. He writes in regard to the "sinister rumors" concerning the Cherokees. Emerson acknowledges the achievements of the Cherokees and expresses a sense of indignation at the ratification of the Treaty of New Echota. He refers to it as a "sham treaty" and exposes the egregious circumstances under which it was ratified. Additionally he openly accuses the president and his government of ignoring the crisis of the Cherokee people and shipping them out west. After this declaration, Emerson retreats a bit rhetorically and incredulously asks, "In the name of God, sir, we ask you if this be so?" (p. 543). In addition to appealing to the president's sense of morality, Emerson also introduces the idea of ethics. He claims that never before was there such a "gross misrepresentation" and "denial of justice" (p. 543). Emerson refers to the removals as a crime and suggests that the president will debase his own office and nation if he does not reconsider the removal debate. He claims that he argues on behalf of the people and their sense of duty to civilize the Cherokees. Finally, he warns the president that the citizens have begun to doubt the moral character of their government and have grown despondent. He urges the president in all of his wisdom and authority to adhere to the will of the people and put an end to injustice.

Despite his attempt to alter the fate of the Cherokee, Emerson romanticizes them as a children of nature who merely need to adopt the ways of civilization in order to survive. Similar to Emerson, Thoreau depicted the Native American as possessing a lost innocence. In *A Week on the Concord and Merrimack Rivers* and selected portions of *Walden*, Thoreau celebrates the Native American's primitivism and animal nature. In his *Journal* dated 1837–1846 he suggests that the Cherokees' primitive role as hunters is what will seal their doomed fate. Thoreau suggests that the Cherokee should "forsake the hunter's life and enter into the agricultural, the second, state of man" (p. 444). Here the author expresses frustration over the Cherokees' refusal to evolve as farmers. He claims that "if they had grasped their [plow] handles more firmly, they would never have been driven beyond the Mississippi" (p. 446). Thoreau explains that white farmers would not think twice about taking land that is hunted as opposed to land that is farmed. Thoreau, who spent much of his life as a surveyor in the Concord area, aptly notes that the hunting field lacks clear property boundaries, unlike those around a farm. According to Thoreau, the land is "property not held by the hunter so much as by the game which roams it, and was never well secured by warranty deeds" (p. 446). Thus, according to the author, the Cherokees' refusal to assimilate into an agricultural-based economy that stresses landownership is what led to their removal.

Margaret Fuller, like Emerson and Thoreau, felt pressed to address the plight of the Cherokees. In her 1844 memoir *Summer on the Lakes, in 1843* she comments on the Indian's unique, spiritual appreciation of nature. She also compares him to a Greek tragic hero of sorts. Throughout most of the work, Fuller is most invested in unearthing the plight of the Native American woman and comparing and contrasting her fate to that of the European woman. Fuller also ponders the fate of the Native Americans as a whole and at one point offers amalgamation as the answer. She quickly decides that this is not an option because "those of mixed blood fade early, and are not generally a fine race" (p. 96). Her final suggestion is to allow the Native Americans to govern themselves, yet she questions rather fatalistically that "the designs of such [plans] will not always be frustrated by barbarous selfishness, as they were in Georgia" (p. 101). Here Fuller suggests that even if the Cherokees did have competent leaders to act on their behalf, they would still be confronted with Georgia's oppressive state laws.

Retrospectively Fuller's comments about the future of the Cherokees proved rather prophetic. She felt, as did the members of the Treaty Party, that resistance against the state laws of Georgia would prove futile. Thoreau as well somewhat echoed her sentiments. He felt that the answer to the Cherokee's success could be found in agriculture, yet he still considered them a doomed race. Emerson's letter to President Van Buren and the Cherokee Memorials pose the most convincing arguments for resistance to removal. Ironically the majority of the Cherokees were against removal, yet the few men who signed the Treaty of New Echota ultimately determined the fate of the Cherokee people.

See also Cherokee Memorials; Ethnology; Indians; Indian Wars and Dispossession; Oratory; Romanticism; Transcendentalism

BIBLIOGRAPHY

Primary Works

Emerson, Ralph Waldo. *The Journals and Miscellaneous Notebooks of Ralph Waldo Emerson.* Vol. 5, *1835–1838,* edited by Merton M. Sealts Jr. Cambridge, Mass.: Harvard University Press, 1965.

Emerson, Ralph Waldo. "Manners." In *The Early Lectures of Ralph Waldo Emerson,* vol. 2, *1836–1838,* edited by Stephen E. Whicher, Robert E. Spiller, and Wallace E. Williams. Cambridge, Mass.: Belknap Press of Harvard University Press, 1964.

Emerson, Ralph Waldo. "To Charles Chauncy Emerson, Boston, March 4, 1832." In *The Letters of Ralph Waldo Emerson,* edited by Ralph L. Rusk, pp. 345–347. New York: Columbia University Press, 1939.

Emerson, Ralph Waldo. "To Martin Van Buren, Concord, April 23, 1838." In *Emerson's Prose and Poetry,* edited by Joel Porte and Saundra Morris. New York: Norton, 2001.

Fuller, Margaret. *Summer on the Lakes.* 1844. 2nd ed. Edited by Arthur B. Fuller. New York: Haskell House, 1970.

Marshall, John. *Cherokee Nation v. Georgia.* 1831. Edited by Nathan Aaseng. San Diego, Calif.: Lucent Books, 2000.

Marshall, John. *Worcester v. Georgia.* 1832. In *The Cherokee Removal: A Brief History with Documents,* edited by Theda Perdue and Michael D. Green. Boston: Bedford/St. Martin's, 1995.

Thoreau, Henry D. *The Journal of Henry D. Thoreau, 1837–1846.* 1906. Edited by Bradford Torrey and Francis H. Allen. Boston: Houghton Mifflin, 1949.

Secondary Works

Alexander, Floyce. "Emerson and the Cherokee Removal." *ESQ* 29, no. 3 (1983): 127–137.

Bellin, Joshua David. "Apostle of Removal: John Eliot in the Nineteenth Century." *New England Quarterly* 69, no. 1 (1996): 3–32.

Ehle, John. *Trail of Tears: The Rise and Fall of the Cherokee Nation.* New York: Doubleday, 1988.

Foreman, Grant. *Indian Removal: The Emigration of the Five Civilized Tribes of Indians.* 1932. Norman: University of Oklahoma Press, 1953.

Garvey, Gregory T. "Mediating Citizenship: Emerson, the Cherokee Removals, and the Rhetoric of Nationalism." *Centennial Review* (1997): 461–469.

Johoda, Gloria. *The Trail of Tears.* New York: Holt, Rinehart, and Winston, 1975.

Maddox, Lucy. *Removals: Nineteenth-Century American Literature and the Politics of Indian Affairs.* New York: Oxford University Press, 1991.

McLoughlin, William G. *Cherokees and Missionaries, 1789–1839.* 1984. Foreword by William L. Anderson. Norman: University of Oklahoma Press, 1995.

Perdue, Theda, ed. *Cherokee Editor: The Writings of Elias Boudinot.* Knoxville: University of Tennessee Press, 1983.

Perdue, Theda, and Michael D. Green, eds. *The Cherokee Removal: A Brief History with Documents.* Boston: Bedford/St. Martin's, 1995.

Remini, Robert V. *Andrew Jackson and His Indian Wars.* New York: Viking, 2001.

Rozema, Vicki. *Cherokee Voices: Early Accounts of Cherokee Life in the East.* Winston-Salem, N.C.: J. F. Blair, 2002.

Jennifer M. Wing

TRANSCENDENTALISM

In the mid-1700s, the New England Puritan churches began to divide, as some ministers and congregations in Boston and eastern Massachusetts began to resist key doctrines of Calvinism. These churches had been established during the Puritan migrations of the mid-1600s and were grounded theologically on the doctrines of John Calvin (1509–1564). Calvin's theology, as interpreted by the New England Puritans, stressed the absolute nature of God's sovereignty and the inevitability of human depravity. These churches were the official or sanctioned churches of the Massachusetts Commonwealth, the "parish" churches, retaining their public status and support into the early nineteenth century. While theological controversy of one kind or another had been a regular aspect of Puritanism in both England and New England, and indeed in Protestantism generally, the religious divisions that began to emerge in this period would prove to be of particular significance because they led to the formation of a separate movement of religious liberalism that eventually took the name of Unitarianism. Centered in the well-established churches of Boston and at Harvard College, the liberals gained an intellectual and cultural influence that outstripped their relatively small numbers and helped to shape a powerful American liberal tradition in education, literature, the arts, and politics. It was from this movement of Boston liberal theology that the literary and political movement of transcendentalism evolved in the 1830s and 1840s.

THE EVOLUTION OF A NEW DENOMINATION

As the name "Unitarian" might suggest, the liberals differed with the Calvinists, or orthodox as they were also known, on the doctrine of the trinity. But a more fundamental point of division between the two camps was their conception of human nature. The Calvinists held that men and women were naturally corrupt, and their doctrine of innate depravity expressed this darker view of human motives and capabilities. Furthermore, the Calvinists held that the human will was incapable of changing the condition of the individual, that no human effort of belief or works could of itself produce salvation. Salvation was a work of grace, a gift of forgiveness and redemption given by God and not earned by humans. The liberals increasingly dissented from these views.

Liberal ministers such as Charles Chauncy, Jonathan Mayhew, and Ebenezer Gay offered important articulations of liberalism in the eighteenth century, and in the early nineteenth century the movement was carried on and expanded by Joseph Stevens Buckminster, William Emerson, Henry Ware Sr., and

Andrews Norton. The most influential exponent of liberal religion, William Ellery Channing (1780–1842), emerged as an important voice in the second and third decades of the nineteenth century, advocating a more generous view of human motives and capabilities and a more positive view of the nature of God. The Supreme Being was, for Channing, less a dreadful, judgmental figure than the epitome of the just and compassionate morality for which human beings could strive. Convinced that men and women could and did act out of selfless and compassionate motives, Channing rejected the idea of innate depravity. With Henry Ware Jr. and other liberal theologians, he depicted human life as a period of probation in which each person was tested and thereby encouraged to develop an ever-improving character, one that would take them closer to the moral model of God. Religion thus became an art of developing a growing "Likeness to God" (1826), as Channing put it in one of his most important sermons, a continual process of spiritual devotion and ethical character building.

Controversy between the Calvinists and the liberals continued into the nineteenth century, flaring up in an 1805 dispute over the appointment of the liberal Henry Ware Sr. as Hollis Professor of Divinity at Harvard and again in 1819, when Channing, in his sermon "Unitarian Christianity," declared the principles of liberalism and offered a trenchant refutation of Calvinism. By then, many congregations in Boston had begun to split between Calvinists and liberals, and a legal dispute over the church in Dedham in 1826 helped the liberals retain control of the church buildings and assets. Unitarianism thus became a new religious denomination, still embroiled with its Calvinist opponents but optimistic and ambitious to spread its message of positive spiritual development and human capability.

Early liberal theology was heavily influenced by the English philosopher John Locke and by Scottish Enlightenment philosophers such as Francis Hutcheson, Thomas Reid, and Dugald Stewart. Its orientation was empirical and anti-idealist, positing the reality and primacy of the material world and describing knowledge, following Locke, as chiefly the product of the bodily senses. In defending the reality and truth of the New Testament in his *Evidences of the Genuineness of the Gospels* (1837–1844), the Harvard theologian Andrews Norton placed great emphasis on the New Testament's historical record of the attested miracles, resting biblical truth on the recorded confirmation of the actual eyewitness to these miraculous claims. In other words, he grounded religious truth in presumed material fact and historical event. But this view of the literal truth of the biblical narrative was being steadily undermined by the "Higher Criticism"

of German biblical scholars such as Johann Gottfried Eichhorn (1752–1827), Friedrich Schleiermacher (1768–1834), and Ferdinand Christian Baur (1792–1860). Using methods of historical research and rational analysis to recognize the Bible as a collection of books written by men at different chronological periods, they made positions such as Norton's, which represented the views of many Unitarian ministers of the early nineteenth century, increasingly doubtful and untenable.

If religious certainty could not be secured through the senses and the evidence of the material world, must one then abandon the spiritual life altogether? A number of younger Unitarian ministers began to resist this conclusion in the 1830s, taking instead a wholly different approach to the problem of religious knowledge. If external evidence was weak or inconclusive, perhaps internal evidence was more certain. Perhaps the mind did not passively absorb knowledge from its surroundings but instead possessed innate qualities and powers that provided religious understanding and spiritual experience of another sort. The mind, in fact, might be understood to tally or correspond with the natural world, to possess within itself the same energy or power as that which we see in natural objects and processes. The most arresting proponent of these theories was a young Unitarian minister, recently separated from his Boston pulpit, named Ralph Waldo Emerson (1803–1882). In an original and challenging book titled *Nature* (1836), Emerson propounded a theory of religion based on "intuition" rather than empirical evidence, explaining the religious sentiment as deeply ingrained into the nature of the mind itself. He argued that mind and nature corresponded in fundamental ways—that nature could mirror to us our own identities and potentialities—because they had a common origin and shared a common nature. Both were vehicles of a divine energy that shaped reality and gave it value and significance.

Emerson had listened closely to the preaching of Channing and had sought him out for a list of reading materials when he began his divinity studies. In Channing's conception of religion as a process of continual spiritual advancement and self-culture Emerson found an important new way to consider the religious life. Extending Channing's premises, he began to preach an empowering version of spiritually intense, ethically grounded nonconformity, in which each man and woman was enjoined not to accept passively the religious premises and imperatives of others, or the dictates of a church or other institution, but to rely instead on an innate moral sense. "Souls are not saved in bundles," Emerson wrote. "The Spirit saith to the man, 'How is it with thee? thee personally'?" (*W* 6:214). This philosophy, which rested on the premise of a unifying transcendent or spiritual energy that generated all reality and held it in unity, came to be known as transcendentalism.

By 1836 Emerson had moved from his Boston pulpit into the role of freelance lecturer. He followed *Nature* with two important lectures at Harvard, "The American Scholar" (1837) and the "Divinity School Address" (1838), and summarized his developing philosophy in two volumes, *Essays* (1841) and *Essays: Second Series* (1844). The "Divinity School Address," in particular, was controversial for its pointed critique of the conventional preaching of the day, and its insistence that the "religious sentiment" was not mediated by the church or by the supernatural intervention of Jesus, but was instead a universally available capability. The great achievement and legacy of Jesus was that "alone in all history, he estimated the greatness of man" (*CW* 1:81). With these and other works in the late 1830s and early 1840s, all marked by Emerson's stirring poetic and rhetorical gift, he began to make an important impact on American literature, one that continues into the twenty-first century.

The appearance of *Nature* in 1836 was accompanied by the publication in the same year of several works by others that suggested that a transcendentalist movement had begun to blossom. William Henry Furness (1802–1896), a Unitarian minister in Philadelphia and a friend of Emerson's, published *Remarks of the Four Gospels,* a work that accepted the reality of the biblical miracles but resisted their relevance in the establishment or proof of the truth of Christianity. Convers Francis (1795–1863), a Unitarian minister in Watertown, Massachusetts, and later a member of the Harvard faculty, published *Christianity as a Purely Internal Principle,* which, as its title suggests, made internal or intuitive evidence fundamental to religious belief. It was also in 1836 that Amos Bronson Alcott (1799–1888), who would later become one of Emerson's closest friends, published his *Conversations with Children on the Gospels,* a book that grew out of his work at his experimental Temple School in Boston. Alcott prefaced his work with a treatise titled "The Doctrine and Discipline of Human Culture," which approached Channing's doctrine of the culture and development of the soul from the perspective of education rather than theological doctrine. Alcott's philosophy of education was dialogic and interactive rather than hierarchical. The role of the educator was not to impart facts and ideas to a passive student but to strengthen and cultivate that student's inner strengths and capabilities. What had been essentially a theological movement was thus beginning to open into a more general movement of reform, with

Amos Bronson Alcott on the steps of the Concord School of Philosophy. COURTESY OF THE CONCORD FREE PUBLIC LIBRARY

important implications for education, politics, and social justice, as well as literature and art.

Almost from its beginning, transcendentalism was an embattled movement. Its critique of the more moderate form of liberal religion represented by the Unitarian mainstream generated a counter-critique, and controversy sizzled in Unitarian circles from the middle 1830s to the early 1840s. In 1836 George Ripley (1802–1880), a Boston Unitarian minister and one of the best-read and most incisive theological thinkers among the transcendentalists, published two essays— "Schleiermacher as a Theologian" and "Martineau's Rationale of Religious Inquiry"—in the Unitarian journal *Christian Examiner.* These essays further advanced the view, shared by Emerson, Furness, and other transcendentalists, that acceptance of the biblical miracles was not a necessary element of Christian faith. Andrews Norton, who had been a liberal firebrand in his youth, now found himself in the role of defender of what had

TRANSCENDENTALISM AND NINETEENTH-CENTURY CHRISTIANITY

Two controversial addresses on the nature of Christ and on Christian theology expressed the transcendentalists' critique of the Christian theology of their era. In his 1838 address to the graduates of the Harvard Divinity School, Ralph Waldo Emerson argued that the cult of the personality of Jesus was a barrier to a fuller understanding of the essentially nonpersonal or transpersonal nature of the deity. Emerson preferred to use the "Soul" to indicate those attributes, and later wrote an essay titled "The Over-Soul" (1841) to describe this new religious conception. In "The Transient and Permanent in Christianity" (1841), Theodore Parker argued for an "Absolute Religion" that defined such Christian doctrines as the trinity and belief in the biblical miracles as "transient" attempts to understand and express the nature of religious experience.

From Ralph Waldo Emerson's "Divinity School Address" (1838)

Historical Christianity has fallen into the error that corrupts all attempts to communicate religion. As it appears to us, and as it has appeared for ages, it is not the doctrine of the soul, but an exaggeration of the personal, the positive, the ritual. It has dwelt, it dwells, with noxious exaggeration about the *person* of Jesus. The soul knows no persons. It invites every man to expand to the full circle of the universe, and will have no preferences but those of spontaneous love. But by this eastern monarchy of a Christianity, which indolence and fear have built, the friend of man is made the injurer of man. The manner in which his name is surrounded with expressions, which were once sallies of admiration and love, but are now petrified into official titles, kills all generous sympathy and liking. All who hear me, feel, that the language that describes Christ to Europe and America, is not the style of friendship and enthusiasm to a good and noble heart, but is appropriated and formal,—paints a demigod, as the Orientals or the Greeks would describe Osiris or Apollo.

(CW 1:82)

From Theodore Parker's "The Transient and Permanent in Christianity" (1841)

Any one who traces the history of what is called Christianity, will see that nothing changes more from age to age than the doctrines taught as Christian and insisted on as essential to Christianity and personal salvation. What is falsehood in one province passes for truth in another. The heresy of one age is the orthodox belief and "only infallible rule" of the next. Now Arius, and now Athanasius is Lord of the ascendant. Both were excommunicated in their turn; each for affirming what the other denied. Men are burned for professing what men are burned for denying. For centuries the doctrines of the Christians were no better, to say the least, than those of their contemporary pagans. The theological doctrines derived from our fathers, seem to have come from Judaism, Heathenism, and the caprice of philosophers, far more than they have come from the principle and sentiment of Christianity. The doctrine of the Trinity, the very Achilles of theological dogmas, belongs to philosophy and not religion; its subtleties cannot even be expressed in our tongue. As old religions became superannuated and died out, they left to the rising faith, as to a residuary legatee, their forms, and their doctrines; or rather, as the giant in the fable left his poisoned garment to work the overthrow of his conqueror. Many tenets that pass current in our theology, seem to be the refuse of idol temples; the off-scourings of Jewish and Heathen cities, rather than the sands of virgin gold, which the stream of Christianity has worn off from the rock of ages, and brought in it bosom for us. It is wood, hay and stubble, wherewith men have built on the corner stone Christ laid. What wonder the fabric is in peril when tried by fire?

(Myerson, ed., Transcendentalism: A Reader, *p. 347)*

become a somewhat conservative position on the miracles. Norton attacked Ripley's position and Ripley replied, bringing the transcendentalist controversy, as it has come to be known, into the pages of the *Christian Examiner.*

In this already overheated environment, Emerson's "Divinity School Address" (1838) generated further controversy. Andrews Norton responded to it with his own address, "A Discourse of the Latest Form of Infidelity" (1839), and another Unitarian leader and

Harvard faculty member, Henry Ware Jr. (1794–1843), who had preceded Emerson in the pulpit of the Second Church of Boston, also responded critically to the "Divinity School Address" in an 1838 sermon titled "The Personality of the Deity." Ware's objections, however, were different from those of Norton. He believed that Emerson's emphasis on a more abstract concept of "soul" depersonalized the more commonly held belief in the father-like nature of God. God's "personality" was an essential element, Ware felt, in the possibility of worship and religious devotion. Unless men and women understood God as a "person," they would have no deeply emotional attachment to him and would thus lose the sense of comfort and security that the parental qualities of God provided.

A further, and somewhat more bitter, dispute followed in 1841, when Theodore Parker (1810–1860), minister of the Unitarian church in Roxbury, delivered a sermon titled "The Transient and Permanent in Christianity." Parker's sermon, now regarded as a key text of the transcendentalist movement, made a crucial distinction between the historical trappings and manifestations of religion, which changed from age to age and from culture to culture, and its unchanging spiritual core. His argument, of course, was that theologies, with their particular doctrines and symbols, fade away, while a pure essence of religion—Parker thought of it as "Absolute Religion"—remains an eternal part of human experience. As part of his argument, Parker categorized the accounts of miracles in the Bible with the "transient" elements of religion. Some of the ministers in the audience who did not hold liberal views were alarmed and outraged at Parker's sermon, and they demanded that other Unitarian ministers take a stand on it. A fierce controversy within Boston Unitarian circles ensued, in which most of Parker's fellow ministers distanced themselves from him and maneuvered to exclude him from their group. Parker, stung by the ostracism but hardheadedly determined to continue as a Unitarian minister, resisted their efforts and eventually turned his ostracism into a badge of honor, moving to a new pulpit in Boston and becoming one of the city's most prominent preachers. His fame continued to grow as he embraced the antislavery movement, earning a reputation as one of America's greatest antislavery orators.

KEY FIGURES AND EVENTS

While transcendentalism is usually referred to as a movement, it was in fact a very loose association of individuals, by no means in agreement on all issues, that generated very few institutional structures. One of the few meeting points was the Transcendental Club, which first met in 1836 and continued a series of gatherings in which Emerson, Parker, Ripley, Frederic Henry Hedge, and others played key roles. Composed with only a few exceptions of Unitarian ministers, the club helped to reinforce a shared sense of the need for change within Unitarianism. A clearer record of the thinking of the transcendentalist group can be found in the four-year run of *The Dial* (1840–1844), a journal edited by Margaret Fuller (1810–1850) and Emerson to provide a medium of expression for transcendental writing. Under the editorships of Fuller (1840–1842) and then Emerson (1842–1844), *The Dial* became a literary as well as a theological magazine, publishing poetry, book reviews, and fiction along with sermons and theological writings and commentary on political and social reform. One of the most significant early literary and cultural magazines in the United States, *The Dial* is one of the more important legacies of the transcendental movement. It gave voice to figures such as Ralph Waldo Emerson, Theodore Parker, Amos Bronson Alcott, Margaret Fuller, Jones Very, Christopher Pearse Cranch, and Henry David Thoreau. With the Transcendental Club, it is one of the chief means we have for determining who was counted, and who counted themselves, as part of the transcendental movement. *The Dial* also gave Margaret Fuller a key place in the literary landscape of New England, helping to open the door for her later work for the *New-York Daily Tribune*. Emerson's younger protégé, Henry David Thoreau (1817–1862), often assisted Emerson with the details of copyediting and preparing the magazine for publication and also published some of his early work there. Thoreau's connection with *The Dial* gave him an introduction to publishing operations, exposed him to the writings of many of his contemporaries, and also provided a venue for work that he might not have otherwise completed.

Another series of cultural events that helped to shape the development of transcendentalism, and gave prominence to one of its key figures, were Fuller's public "Conversations," seminars for women held in Boston from 1839 to 1844. Fuller was (like Thoreau) an excellent linguist in both classical and modern languages, and she was one of the best judges of literature among the transcendentalists. She was deeply interested in the work of the German poet Johann Wolfgang von Goethe and published an important assessment of him in *The Dial*. She had been influenced by Amos Bronson Alcott's theory of the use of dialogue in education, and she adapted this technique for her "Conversations," building on an earlier New England tradition of women's reading groups. She hoped to use these formal but nevertheless dialogic events to encourage women's public self-expression, an essential step, she believed, in their full self-development.

Fuller's "Conversations" were important in the development of her advocacy for the rights of women, a process that was also advanced in her editorship and contributions to *The Dial*. Although she had to relinquish her editorship after two years because the magazine did not generate enough circulation to provide her any pay, she learned much in that role, and she also profited from the outlet for her essays that *The Dial* provided. Her 1841 essay "Goethe" was important in making Goethe's achievement known more widely, and it demonstrated Fuller's judgment and her potential as a literary critic. Her most significant *Dial* publication followed in 1843, an essay on women's rights titled "The Great Lawsuit: Man versus Men, Woman versus Women." She expanded this essay into the book *Woman in the Nineteenth Century* (1845), her most important work and a historically significant articulation of the argument for women's rights.

Fuller argued that women, as well as men, should be allowed to develop the full range and capacity of their nature. The process of self-cultivation was a central value of Emerson and other transcendentalists; Fuller used the idea here to bolster her argument for women's rights. She combined this emphasis on self-cultivation with the observation that conventionally "masculine" traits were not necessarily restricted to men, nor were "feminine" traits restricted to women. These artificial barriers of gender definition had to be overcome, for the good of both men and women. Citing many examples of women's strengths and achievements, and of the positive conception of women in myth and history, Fuller defied the rigid division in her historical era between a public sphere restricted to men and a domestic sphere restricted to women. She would herself live this theory out in moving to New York in 1844 to become a columnist for the *New York Tribune* and by going to Europe in 1846, where she both reported on and became an active supporter of the unsuccessful Italian Revolution of 1848 led by Giuseppe Mazzini.

UTOPIAN IDEALS

Fuller's turn toward issues of politics and social reform typified the path that many of the transcendentalists took in the late 1840s and early 1850s. Reacting to the social injustices generated by the competitive market economy and to the malaise of materialism that infected American society, the transcendentalists searched for alternative forms of economic interaction

and cooperation and were drawn to early forms of associationist thought advanced by the French social theorist Charles Fourier and his American disciple and popularizer Albert Brisbane. Under the leadership of George and Sophia Ripley, several transcendentalists helped to establish the Brook Farm commune in 1841. On a farm in Roxbury, just south of Boston, the group began a cooperative work association that included both raising crops and conducting a school. Ripley had been an important voice in the transcendentalists' critique of conventional theology and biblical interpretation. Respected by all the transcendentalists for his learning, he brought both leadership and deep dedication to Brook Farm. He and others became increasingly interested in Fourier's theories of the equitable and harmonious distribution of the labor, and in 1844 they reformulated Brook Farm into a Fourierist "phalanx" in order to pursue those goals. Fourier believed that the necessary work of a community could be divided among its members in such a way that individuals would be required to perform duties for which they had no affinity or attraction. He termed the arrangement of such a community a "phalanx" and saw such communities as the basis of a new social order. The periodical that they founded at Brook Farm, *The Harbinger,* offers an excellent record of the discourse of social theory during the years of the commune's existence.

Though not without its troubles, Brook Farm survived and was in a process of expansion until a fire destroyed a new building into which the commune had poured much of its resources and undermined the farm's financial stability, causing it to disband in 1847. Satirized by a disillusioned former commune member, Nathaniel Hawthorne, in his 1852 novel *The Blithedale Romance,* and generally discounted by historians of the period as a failed experiment, Brook Farm is nevertheless remembered as an important symbol of the tradition of progressive critique that accompanied the development of the American industrial economy at mid-century. Scholarly work on its history by Richard Francis and Sterling F. Delano have shown that it remains an important index of both the hopes for a more just society and the theoretical and pragmatic difficulties of implementing this form of utopian project. In this sense, Brook Farm provides a window into the spirit of dissenting social experimentation in the United States in the period just before the Civil War.

Amos Bronson Alcott's Fruitlands commune, undertaken on a farm near Harvard, Massachusetts, in late 1843, much smaller in scale and much less durable even than Brook Farm, is another example of dissenting experimentation. An inveterate experimenter, Alcott had blazed a trail in teaching with his Temple School in

Boston and had also endured harsh criticism and social ostracism as a result. His contribution to *The Dial*, two collections of aphoristic "Orphic Sayings," also had become, to critics of the transcendentalist movement, targets of derision for their abstraction and portentousness. Alcott undertook the Fruitlands project with the English reformer Charles Lane in his typical spirit of hope, but also as a kind of vocational last stand, an attempt to make his and his family's way in the world while still avoiding the competitive and corrupting ways of the world. Like Brook Farm, Fruitlands became more famous through satiric depictions than through any historical accounts of it. Alcott's daughter Louisa May, who became one of America's most celebrated and widely read novelists, described the experiment through the eyes of a somewhat unwilling child participant (she was ten when the family moved to Fruitlands) in "Transcendental Wild Oats" (1873), a fable in which she depicts her father as the naive victim of the cunning Lane. It was Louisa May Alcott's income from her book sales that finally gave the Alcott family financial stability in the 1860s.

In 1845 Henry David Thoreau undertook a utopian experiment of a different kind when he began to build a cabin for himself at Walden Pond, on land that his friend Emerson had recently acquired. Aware of the Brook Farm and Fruitlands experiments, and sharing the spirit of resistance and experimentation that they embodied, Thoreau instead began an experiment in solitude, hoping to discover, through self-reflection and the close observation of nature, how to live a more wise and fulfilling "natural life." Thoreau stayed at Walden two years, and over the next seven years he worked through an expanding account of his life there. *Walden; or, Life in the Woods* (1854) became a literary and environmental classic, a book that spoke deeply to many American readers, then and now, who felt a gnawing worry that life was sliding by them, out of their control and beyond their ability to comprehend or even enjoy. Thoreau's call to "live deep and suck out all the marrow of life" (p. 91) has remained a challenge to a culture complacently awash in consumer goods and cowed into a pusillanimous conformity. The book charts the flow of the seasons as Thoreau lived at the pond, recording both his private thoughts and aspirations as well as his descriptions of the animal and plant life around him, which he took as his companions and teachers. Deeply spiritual in its sense of nature as a manifestation of transcendent spirit, but also resolutely this-worldly in its practical concerns about how life should be lived day to day, *Walden* reflected Thoreau's dual identity as a poet-seer and a skillful and grounded realist. In scaling back his material wants, and thereby dramatically simplifying his way of life, he established an enduring counterstatement to the development of American cultural values and to a modern style of life characterized by relentless consumption and frantic hurry.

Thoreau's *Walden,* his voluminous and highly engaging *Journal* (which he kept assiduously over many years), and several key nature essays published posthumously in 1862 ("Walking," "Wild Apples," and "Autumnal Tints") expanded greatly on Emerson's descriptions of the spiritual importance of the natural world, making the study, celebration, and preservation of nature one of the characteristic themes and central legacies of transcendentalism. Thoreau's reputation rested largely on *Walden* throughout the twentieth century, but his *Journal* and later essays have come to gain more attention and respect. Those texts demonstrate his deep engagement with scientific thinking and botanical fieldwork, and they provide a greater sense of his deep commitment to environmental awareness and the protection and preservation of natural places. Considered now a founder of the modern American environmental movement, Thoreau offered a witness to his experience in nature that has had a shaping impact on American culture. As the severity of the threat to the environment has grown in the industrial age, Thoreau's writings have seemed more prophetic and more relevant to modern readers.

One of the most dramatic examples of the turn of transcendentalist thinking toward the political was the experience of Margaret Fuller in Italy. Fuller's work for the *Tribune* had substantially broadened her social awareness and deepened her commitment to progressive political change, perhaps preparing her for finding herself on the brink of a revolution in Italy. In the Risorgimento, as it came to be known, Giuseppe Mazzini led a revolutionary movement to unify Italy as a democratic state. While the 1848 uprisings that resulted in Mazzini's brief leadership in a Roman republic did not succeed, the struggle led the way for the eventual establishment of a unified and democratic Italian state later in the century. After her arrival in Italy, Fuller met and befriended Mazzini; she also met and married a young supporter of his cause, Giovanni Angelo Ossoli, and gave birth to a son, Angelo, in 1848.

Fuller saw the Italian Revolution as an important extension of democratic principles, part of the progressive movement of political history, and an essential aspect of human social development. In the movement for a democratic Italy, and in the resistance to it, she saw parallels to American history and to recent American political events. While in Italy, Fuller embraced more completely the doctrines of associationism and socialism that had been under intense discussion in the United States when she left, and she also accepted the necessity of militant struggle in the pursuit of significant progressive change and social justice. What she found in Italy, both personally and intellectually, was crucial to her, extending the path of self-cultivation and personal growth that she had begun years ago in her teaching experiences and in her work with *The Dial*. Her involvement with the Italian Revolution is a reminder that Fuller's feminism, the stance that she is best known for, was grounded in a wider commitment to democratic egalitarianism and universal justice.

Returning to the United States with her family in 1850, Fuller had begun to write a history of the Italian Revolution. But she and her family were killed in a shipwreck near the American coast. At age forty, with her public fame well-established and her skill as an essayist and commentator honed more finely through her *Tribune* work and Italian experiences, Fuller had been poised to make a significant public impact upon her return. It is tempting to speculate on how Fuller would have reacted to the American political scene in the 1850s, when the disputes over slavery were intensifying. It is a good probability that her new militancy would have found another outlet in the antislavery cause.

Emerson, who was a reluctant political activist, had grown increasingly outspoken on slavery and engaged in antislavery writing in the 1840s. The passage of the Fugitive Slave Law, part of the Compromise of 1850, ignited him as a piercing antislavery orator, in part because this new law brought the actual enforcement of enslavement into those parts of the country where slavery had long been outlawed. Emerson's gradual evolution from a spiritual poet of the inner life into an resolute advocate of political causes and influential public figure is one of the great transformations of American history, although it was not until the late twentieth century that his later career as a public intellectual truly came into focus. But his personal change, like Fuller's, was also the sign of the change in the transcendentalist movement itself, which responded to an era in which the claims of human rights, in the form of feminism and antislavery, became the dominant intellectual occupations.

LEGACIES OF TRANSCENDENTALISM

Transcendentalism had begun to lose cohesion as a "movement" by the mid-1840s. The termination of *The Dial* in 1844, Fuller's move to New York in that same year, the disbanding of Brook Farm in 1847, Thoreau's return from Walden Pond in 1847, Emerson's lecture tour in England in 1847 and 1848, and Fuller's death in 1850 are all markers of significant moments of change and adjustment in what was for six or seven years a somewhat synchronous intellectual insurgency. Although the

relatively brief duration of transcendentalism as a movement may appear to indicate finally a narrative of failure or collapse, a longer historical perspective suggests the pervasive and continuing influence of transcendentalist principles and goals in the shaping of American culture. As a literary figure Emerson has certainly played the role of a cultural founder, establishing a tradition of American poetry oriented to the exploration of transcendent vision and the corresponding linkages between the inner life and the world of nature. Walt Whitman (1819–1892), who was profoundly influenced by Emerson's ideas and also by aspects of his experimental and innovative commitment to an organic, free-flowing style, is a key transmitter of Emersonian vision in the American poetic tradition. Students of Emerson such as Richard Poirier in his 1987 study *The Renewal of Literature: Emersonian Reflections* have also taken note of Emerson's anticipation of the key themes of the American philosophical pragmatism, noting continuities between Emerson's work and that of William James (1842–1910) and John Dewey (1859–1952). Emerson's emphasis on process and multiple perspective, rather than his visionary idealism, is in this case taken to be his most lasting impact.

Thoreau, too, has become the originating voice in an important tradition of American nature and environmental writing, one that blossomed in the last three decades of the twentieth century as the environmental crisis of the modern industrial age became more acute and more alarming. Thoreau's advocacy for the value of wild places influenced John Muir (1838–1914) and other writers and activists on the environment and helped create the cultural understanding that made possible the preservation of the national parks and other wild areas. The renewed vogue for Thoreau's writings in the 1960s and 1970s reflected the strengthening of the environmental ethic during that era. Thoreau's *Walden* has also became representative of an American cultural yearning for the simpler life, embodying a growing collective longing for an escape from a society defined by hurry, meaningless work, and obsessive material consumption.

Although Fuller's early death in 1850, when she was expanding dramatically as a public intellectual and a cultural critic, curtailed her influence somewhat, she did have a formative influence on Elizabeth Cady Stanton (1815–1902) and other leaders the women's rights movement of the later nineteenth century. Fuller's feminist work, after a period of neglect in the early twentieth century, began to be rediscovered in the 1970s with the rise of the women's movement. The last three decades of the twentieth century saw an intensive rereading of Fuller's texts, especially *Woman in the Nineteenth Century*, and led to scholarly interest in the biographical reconstruction of her life and of her relationships with Emerson and other transcendentalists. The archival and editorial work of Robert N. Hudspeth resulted in a complete edition of her letters, one of her most revealing and absorbing modes of writing. Fuller stands in the twenty-first century as one of the most important and representative figures of her era, a woman who speaks directly to this later age.

During the late 1830s and early 1840s, the years of high transcendentalist activity, Emerson was prone to downplay the newness of transcendentalism, whose ideas were often referred to as the "new views" and which was identified with a novel and daring conception of spiritual experience and literary expression. The "*new views*," he wrote in an 1841 lecture, "The Transcendentalist," "are not new, but the very oldest of thoughts cast into the mould of these new times" (*CW* 1:201). While the origins of transcendentalist thinking may indeed have been ancient, its impact on American society was arousing, inspiriting, and finally progressive. The transcendentalists gave American culture its first distinctive literary voice, brought artistic endeavor and aesthetic appreciation into a more secure place in the culture, and advanced, on several fronts, the cause of human rights and social justice.

See also Concord, Massachusetts; *The Dial;* Lyceums; Nature; *Nature;* Reform; Romanticism; Unitarians; Utopian Communities; *Woman in the Nineteenth Century*

BIBLIOGRAPHY

Primary Works

Channing, William Ellery. *William Ellery Channing: Selected Writings.* Edited by David M. Robinson. Mahwah, N.J.: Paulist Press, 1985.

Emerson, Ralph Waldo. *The Collected Works of Ralph Waldo Emerson.* 6 vols. to date. Edited by Alfred R. Ferguson et al. Cambridge, Mass.: Belknap Press of Harvard University Press, 1971–. Cited parenthetically in the text as *CW.*

Emerson, Ralph Waldo. *The Complete Works of Ralph Waldo Emerson.* 12 vols. Edited by Edward Waldo Emerson. Boston: Houghton Mifflin, 1903–1904. Centenary edition. Cited parenthetically in the text as *W.*

Fuller, Margaret. *The Letters of Margaret Fuller.* Edited by Robert N. Hudspeth. Ithaca, N.Y.: Cornell University Press, 1983.

Fuller, Margaret. *Woman in the Nineteenth Century.* 1845. Facsimile ed., with introduction by Madeleine B. Stern and textual notes by Joel Myerson. Columbia: University of South Carolina Press, 1980.

Thoreau, Henry David. *Collected Essays and Poems.* Edited by Elizabeth Hall Witherell. New York: Library of America, 2001.

Thoreau, Henry David. *Faith in a Seed: The Dispersion of Seeds and Other Late Natural History Writings.* Edited by Bradley P. Dean. Washington, D.C.: Island Press, 1993.

Thoreau, Henry David. *Journal.* 7 vols. to date. Edited by John C. Broderick et al. Princeton, N.J.: Princeton University Press, 1981–.

Thoreau, Henry David. *Walden.* 1854. Edited by J. Lyndon Shanley. Princeton, N.J.: Princeton University Press, 1971.

Secondary Works

Belasco, Susan. "'The Animating Influences of Discord': Margaret Fuller in 1844." *Legacy* 20, nos. 1–2 (2003): 82–91.

Buell, Lawrence. *Literary Transcendentalism: Style and Vision in the American Renaissance.* Ithaca, N.Y.: Cornell University Press, 1973.

Capper, Charles. *Margaret Fuller: An American Romantic Life. The Private Years.* New York: Oxford University Press, 1992.

Cavell, Stanley. *The Senses of Walden.* Expanded ed. San Francisco: North Point Press, 1981.

Cole, Phyllis. "The Nineteenth-Century Women's Rights Movement and the Canonization of Margaret Fuller." *ESQ* 44, nos. 1–2 (1998): 1–35.

Delano, Sterling F. *Brook Farm: The Dark Side of Utopia.* Cambridge, Mass.: Harvard University Press, 2004.

Du Bois, Ellen. "Margaret Fuller in Italy." *Women's Writing* 10, no. 2 (2003): 287–305.

Francis, Richard. *Transcendental Utopias: Individual and Community at Brook Farm, Fruitlands, and Walden.* Ithaca, N.Y.: Cornell University Press, 1997.

Grodzins, Dean. *American Heretic: Theodore Parker and Transcendentalism.* Chapel Hill: University of North Carolina Press, 2002.

Guarneri, Carl J. *The Utopian Alternative: Fourierism in Nineteenth-Century America.* Ithaca, N.Y.: Cornell University Press, 1991.

Gura, Philip F. *The Wisdom of Words: Language, Theology, and Literature in the New England Renaissance.* Middletown, Conn.: Wesleyan University Press, 1981.

Harding, Walter. *The Days of Henry Thoreau: A Biography.* New York: Knopf, 1962. Reprint, Princeton, N.J.: Princeton University Press, 1992.

Hoag, Ronald Wesley. "Thoreau's Later Natural History Writings." In *Cambridge Companion to Henry David Thoreau,* edited by Joel Myerson, pp. 152–170. Cambridge, U.K.: Cambridge University Press, 1995.

Kelley, Mary. "'A More Glorious Revolution': Women's Antebellum Reading Circles and the Pursuit of Public Influence." *New England Quarterly* 76 (June 2003): 163–196.

Milder, Robert. *Reimagining Thoreau.* Cambridge, U.K.: Cambridge University Press, 1995.

Miller, Perry. *The Transcendentalists: An Anthology.* Cambridge, Mass.: Harvard University Press, 1950.

Myerson, Joel. "A Calendar of Transcendental Club Meetings." *American Literature* 44 (May 1972): 197–207.

Myerson, Joel. *The New England Transcendentalists and "The Dial": A History of the Magazine and Its Contributors.* Rutherford, N.J.: Fairleigh Dickinson University Press, 1980.

Myerson, Joel, ed. *Transcendentalism: A Reader.* New York: Oxford University Press, 2000.

Packer, Barbara. "The Transcendentalists." In *The Cambridge History of American Literature,* vol. 2, *Prose Writing 1820–1865,* edited by Sacvan Bercovitch, pp. 329–604. New York: Cambridge University Press, 1995.

Paul, Sherman. *The Shores of America: Thoreau's Inward Exploration.* Urbana: University of Illinois Press, 1958.

Peck, H. Daniel. *Thoreau's Morning Work: Memory and Perception in "A Week on the Concord and Merrimack Rivers," "The Journal," and "Walden."* New Haven, Conn.: Yale University Press, 1990.

Poirier, Richard. *The Renewal of Literature: Emersonian Reflections.* New York: Random House, 1987.

Richardson, Robert D., Jr. *Emerson: The Mind on Fire.* Berkeley: University of California Press, 1995.

Richardson, Robert D., Jr. *Henry Thoreau: A Life of the Mind.* Berkeley: University of California Press, 1986.

Robinson, David M. *Apostle of Culture: Emerson as Preacher and Lecturer.* Philadelphia: University of Pennsylvania Press, 1982.

Robinson, David M. *Emerson and "The Conduct of Life": Pragmatism and Ethical Purpose in the Later Work.* New York: Cambridge University Press, 1993.

Robinson, David M. "Margaret Fuller and the Transcendental Ethos: *Woman in the Nineteenth Century*." *PMLA* 97, no. 1 (1982): 83–98.

Robinson, David M. *Natural Life: Thoreau's Worldly Transcendentalism.* Ithaca, N.Y.: Cornell University Press, 2004.

Robinson, David M. *The Unitarians and the Universalists.* Westport, Conn.: Greenwood Press, 1985.

Sattelmeyer, Robert. "The Remaking of *Walden.*" In *Writing the American Classics,* edited by James Barbour and Tom Quirk, pp. 53–78. Chapel Hill: University of North Carolina Press, 1990.

Sattelmeyer, Robert. *Thoreau's Reading: A Study in Intellectual History with Bibliographical Catalogue.* Princeton, N.J.: Princeton University Press, 1988.

Von Frank, Albert J. *An Emerson Chronology.* New York: G. K. Hall, 1994.

Von Frank, Albert J. *The Trials of Anthony Burns: Freedom and Slavery in Emerson's Boston.* Cambridge, Mass.: Harvard University Press, 1998.

Walls, Laura Dassow. "Believing in Nature: Wilderness and Wildness in Thoreauvian Science." In *Thoreau's Sense of Place: Essays in American Environmental Writing,* edited by Richard J. Schneider, pp. 15–27. Iowa City: University of Iowa Press, 2000.

Walls, Laura Dassow. *Seeing New Worlds: Henry David Thoreau and Nineteenth-Century Natural Science.* Madison: University of Wisconsin Press, 1995.

Wright, Conrad. *The Beginnings of Unitarianism in America.* Boston: Starr King Press, 1955.

Wright, Conrad. *The Liberal Christians: Essays on American Unitarian History.* Boston: Beacon Press, 1970.

Zwarg, Christina. *Feminist Conversations: Fuller, Emerson, and the Play of Reading.* Ithaca, N.Y.: Cornell University Press, 1995.

David M. Robinson

TRAVEL WRITING

Travel writing is a difficult genre to classify as it shares in so many other genres. Histories, personal narratives, accounts of exploration, and tales of epic quests: travel writing derives from and adds to each of these forms. Travel writing has always been as much about the exploration of the writer's self as it has been about the places or peoples visited. Travel writers and critics of the genre have often argued that the destination is of relatively little consequence; it is the process of travel, the work or travail involved, that is the true subject of the travel writer.

If travel writing is as much about the traveler as it is about the destination, then American travel writing reveals as much about the American self as it does about other peoples. American travel writing during the period 1820–1870 reflected the nation's expansion of its territorial boundaries, its participation in the process of Manifest Destiny, and its developing sense of itself as a distinct nation with ties to its European past. That sense of nationhood and of a national self was to be severely tested during the American Civil War. Among the many political, historical, and social events that determined the scope and focus of American travel narratives during the period were the Lewis and Clark expedition (1803–1806), the voyages of the United States Exploring Expedition (1838–1842), the Mexican-American War (1846–1848), the California gold rush (1849), and the American Civil War (1861–1865).

TRAVEL WRITING AND WESTWARD EXPANSION

During the first half of the nineteenth century, the area of the United States markedly expanded. The lands added by the Louisiana Purchase (1803), the Florida Purchase (1819), and the territory ceded to the United States at the end of the Mexican-American War more than doubled the area governed by the United States at the start of the century. When France sold the territory of Louisiana to the United States, scarcely a third of America's population lived more than a two-day horseback ride from the eastern seaboard. The lands within the Louisiana Purchase were virtually terra incognita to most Americans. Except for fur trappers and traders, few white men had ever seen most of the new lands. In the East, the area was so unknown that Thomas Jefferson seriously believed that herds of mammoth might exist on the plains. Having read Alexander Mackenzie's (1803– 1848) *Voyages from Montreal, on the River St. Lawrence, through the Continent of North America to the Frozen and Pacific Oceans* (1801), Jefferson authorized Meriwether Lewis (1774–1809) and William Clark (1770–1838) and their Corps of Discovery not only to explore this vast territory but also to report on what they found.

Published in two volumes in 1814, the *History of the Expedition under the Command of Captains Lewis and Clark, to the Sources of the Missouri, thence across the Rocky Mountains and down the River Columbia to the Pacific Ocean* matched Mackenzie's work in the exhaustiveness of its title. Although it was not the first major American work on the trans-Mississippi West—that distinction belongs to Zebulon Pike's (1779–1813) *Account of Expeditions to the Sources of the Mississippi, and through the Western Parts of Louisiana* (1810)— Lewis and Clark's history constitutes one of the most significant contributions to American travel writing in the nineteenth century. The Lewis and Clark expedition spurred government interest in other expeditions and fueled the imaginations of later explorers, historians, and literary figures.

Although his travel writings recount his travels in Europe, James Fenimore Cooper's (1789–1851) fictional work was indirectly influenced by the writings of Lewis and Clark. In the Leatherstocking Tales—most particularly in *The Prairie* (1827)—Cooper celebrates a vanishing America and its vanquished and vanishing Indian peoples. Among writers more directly influenced by the journals of Lewis and Clark was Washington Irving (1783–1859). Although Irving is best known for accounts of his travels in Europe, many of which he put into *The Sketch Book* (1819–1820), he also traveled in and wrote about trans-Mississippi America. In 1832, after spending almost two decades in Europe, Irving

returned to America. In the fall of 1832 he set out on a trip to western New York State and northeastern Ohio. In Ashtabula, Ohio, Irving met Henry Ellsworth, newly appointed Indian Commissioner for the tribes in what are now Arkansas, Kansas, and Oklahoma. Irving and the two friends with whom he was traveling—Charles Latrobe and Count Albert-Alexandre de Pourtalés—decided to join Ellsworth on his journey to the Indian territories. Irving wrote about what he saw and experienced on this journey in *A Tour on the Prairies* (1835). At the start of his narrative, Irving, in an American form of nostalgia for a lost or vanishing innocence, states that among his reasons for making the journey was to see the prairies and the animals and peoples that inhabited them before they disappeared.

Irving, who had earlier shown his interest in exploration narratives in *A History of the Life and Voyages of Christopher Columbus* (1828), would continue to imaginatively explore the lands opened up by the Lewis and Clark expedition in *Astoria; or, Anecdotes of an Enterprise beyond the Rocky Mountains* (1836) and *The Rocky Mountains; or, Scenes, Incidents, and Adventures in the Far West* (1837).

TRAVEL WRITING AND MANIFEST DESTINY

The expedition of the Corps of Discovery and the account of its journey spurred interest in further discoveries on land and sea. The four-year voyage of the U.S. Exploring Expedition under the command of Charles Wilkes (1798–1877)—the last significant exploring voyage in wooden ships—not only established that Antarctica was a continent but also added immeasurably to America's knowledge of the Pacific, its islands, and inhabitants, and—most importantly for America's commercial interests at the time—the migration routes of whales. Wilkes wrote about this fantastic and arduous voyage in the *Narrative of the United States Exploring Expedition: During the Years 1838, 1839, 1840, 1841, 1842*. Published in five volumes in 1845, Wilkes's narrative detailed the voyages of his six-ship squadron from Norfolk, Virginia, down the east coast of South America, around Cape Horn, up the west coast of South America, west and south to Tahiti and Samoa, farther south to New South Wales (Australia) and Antarctica, back north again to Fiji, north and east to Hawaii, then farther east to the northwest coast of America and the mouth of the Columbia River. From the Columbia, the remaining ships in the squadron sailed to San Francisco, then to Honolulu and Singapore before turning east for the return voyage around Cape Horn and back north to New York. Wilkes was a stern disciplinarian and might have served as the model for Captain Ahab.

Among the reasons for Wilkes's exploration of the Antarctic coastline was a bizarre theory proposed in 1818 by a former infantry captain, John Cleves Symmes (1742–1814), who argued that the earth was hollow and open at the poles. In 1837 Edgar Allan Poe (1809–1849), a keen observer of popular scientific trends, published *The Narrative of Arthur Gordon Pym of Nantucket,* in which Pym, after a series of shipwrecks and other adventures, sails into a warm tropical world at the South Pole. A fascinating amalgam of racialist theories (Poe's work reveals his fear of a black slave revolt in his adopted South), pseudoscience, and narrative implausibility (how does Pym tell his tale if he is swept over a cataract of almost boiling water at the Pole?), *The Narrative of Arthur Gordon Pym* shows the degree to which imaginative fiction was shaped by travel narratives.

Other American writers who turned their own adventures at sea in the 1830s and 1840s into literature include Richard Henry Dana (1815–1882) and Herman Melville (1819–1891). Dana's *Two Years before the Mast: A Personal Narrative of Life at Sea* (1840) did much to dispel the Romantic image of life at sea. Melville, whose whaling voyages in the 1840s took him into the Pacific that Wilkes was exploring, converted his experiences into *Typee* (1846) and *Omoo* (1847). These works were well received by an American reading public who read them as rather straightforward travel narratives. Although Melville was honing his literary craft in these early works and disliked being categorized as a travel writer, his later work would never approach the commercial success of these two novels during his lifetime. In addition to using his own experiences at sea as a source for his fiction, Melville had an eye for the narrative possibilities in earlier travel narratives. Most memorably, he turned an incident from Amasa Delano's *Narrative of Voyages and Travels in the Northern and Southern Hemispheres* (1817) into one of his finest short stories, "Benito Cereno" (1856).

By the mid-nineteenth century American commercial interests in the Pacific and in Asia had propelled American sailors farther west. In 1852 Commodore Matthew Perry (1794–1858) sailed on a diplomatic mission to open up Japan to western commerce. He recounted his exploits in his *Narrative of the Expedition of an American Naval Squadron to the China Seas and Japan, Performed in the Years 1852, 1853, and 1854* (1856).

At the same time that Americans were plying the seas in pursuit of whales and trade, other Americans were pushing across the American prairies in the hopes of establishing overland trade routes. Of the travel narratives devoted to this aspect of American enterprise, Josiah Gregg's *Commerce of the Prairies; or, The Journal of a Santa Fé Trader* (1844) remains a classic account. Growing American interest in the Southwest and Central America led John Lloyd Stephens (1805–1852), who had already written *Incidents of Travel in Egypt, Arabia Petræa, and the Holy Land* (1838) and *Incidents of Travel in Greece, Turkey, Russia, and Poland* (1838), to explore Central America. Assisted in part by President Martin Van Buren's appointing him as a minister to the Central American Federation, Stephens traveled to Belize where he found enough time away from his diplomatic duties to purchase the ruins of the ancient Mayan city of Copán. Stephens wrote about his discoveries in adventures in Belize in *Incidents of Travel in Central America, Chiapas, and Yucatan* (1841) and about his later trip to Yucatán in *Incidents of Travel in Yucatan* (1843).

Not all American travel writing during the 1830s and 1840s was based on such exotic locales as Copán. Closer to home, Margaret Fuller (1810–1850), one of the leading figures in American transcendentalism, wrote about her excursion through the Great Lakes to the prairies of Illinois and Wisconsin in *Summer on the Lakes, in 1843* (1844). As Annette Kolodny notes in *The Land before Her: Fantasy and Experience of the American Frontiers, 1630–1860,* among the writers Fuller consulted "to prepare herself for her summer in Illinois and Wisconsin was Caroline Kirkland" (p. 131). Kirkland's *A New Home—Who'll Follow? or, Glimpses of Western Life* (1839) is important because it is one of the first accounts of pioneer life to point out that an experience that often proved liberating for men was confining for women.

No account of travels within America would be complete without mentioning the writings of Henry David Thoreau (1817–1862). Although only one of his "travel" narratives—*A Week on the Concord and Merrimack Rivers* (1849)—was published before his death in 1862, Thoreau possessed a remarkable eye for the pleasures and travails of travel. Few accounts of woodland travel can equal his description of the boggy, mosquito- and black fly–ridden, territory that is the subject of *The Maine Woods* (1864). Similarly, Thoreau's *Cape Cod* (1865) is a memorable journal of his observations of this special place.

TRAVEL WRITING AND THE CALIFORNIA GOLD RUSH

The writings and discoveries of Lewis and Clark and others were an important impetus in the development of travel writing about the American West but it was the discovery of gold in California in 1849 that fired the imagination of the American populace. Among those who would travel to and write about California was John Woodhouse Audubon (1812–1862), the son of the famous naturalist and illustrator, John James Audubon (1785–1851). In 1849, the younger Audubon joined an expedition to the goldfields of California with the expressed purpose of making a fortune that could be used to underwrite the costs of his father's projects. Although he did not achieve the wealth he had hoped for—partly due to the theft of some of his funds—Audubon did write a journal about his travels. The journal was published as *The Illustrated Notes of an Expedition through Mexico and California* (1852), and republished with extensive editing by his daughter, Maria Audubon, as *Audubon's Western Journal: 1849–1850* (1906).

Although Francis Parkman (1823–1893) went on his western journey to restore his health rather than to make his fortune in the California goldfields, his *The California and Oregon Trail* (1849) remained one of the most important books about the American West for the remainder of the nineteenth century. Another famous figure in California history who also explored the intermountain west was "The Pathfinder," John Charles Frémont (1813–1890). Although he was an astute observer of the plant and animal life and an excellent amateur scientist, Frémont was only modestly capable as a writer. It was his wife, Jessie Benton Frémont (1824–1902), the daughter of Senator Thomas Hart Benton (a champion of westward expansion), who provided Frémont's works with their literary verve.

TRAVEL WRITING AND THE EUROPEAN HOMELAND

The most popular forms of American travel writing during the five decades from 1820 to 1870 were those that reported on Americans' travels through Europe. Oftentimes these accounts were little more than "letters" home to the local newspapers in which the correspondent, a native son or daughter, recounted what she or he had seen in Europe. In the hands of a skilled writer like Washington Irving, these observations of Europe by an American abroad could and did achieve literary art. America's first professional man of letters, Irving virtually invented the genre of the American writing from abroad. In *The Sketch Book of Geoffrey Crayon, Gent.*, Irving intermingles descriptions of English life and culture with tales set in his native country such as "Rip Van Winkle," and "The Legend of Sleepy Hollow." The financial success of *The Sketch Book* led Irving to write *Bracebridge Hall* (1822) and *Tales of a Traveller* (1824). Although Irving, once again adopting the guise of Geoffrey Crayon, promises in his introduction to *Bracebridge Hall* to provide

In this passage, Washington Irving compares the grandeur of American scenery with the palpable sense of history that he finds in European places and scenes.

My native country was full of youthful promise: Europe was rich in the accumulated treasures of age. Her very ruins told the history of the times gone by, and every mouldering stone was a chronicle. I longed to wander over the scenes of renowned achievement—to tread, as it were, in the footsteps of antiquity—to loiter about the ruined castle—to meditate on the falling tower—to escape, in short, from the commonplace realities of the present, and lose myself among the shadowy grandeurs of the past.

Irving, "The Author's Account of Himself," in *The Sketch Book*, p. 9.

his readers with an intimate view of London, the work is mostly an uncritical celebration of life on English rural estates. *Tales of a Traveller* contains little actual travel writing; most of the work consists of generalized portraits of European types in stories with titles such as "The Italian Banditti."

James Fenimore Cooper, another important figure in the development of nineteenth-century American literature, also wrote about his travels in Europe. From 1826 until 1833, Cooper and his family traveled through France, England, Switzerland, Italy, and Germany. When he returned to America he used the material from his European journals to produce *Sketches of Switzerland* (1836), *Recollections of Europe* (1837), *England* (1837), and *Excursions in Italy* (1838).

England, which many Anglophile Americans viewed as their "old home," tops the list of those countries that American travelers in the 1820s through the 1840s most often visited and subsequently wrote about. As Allison Lockwood has shown in *Passionate Pilgrims: The American Traveler in Great Britain, 1800–1914*, England achieved the status of an almost-holy destination. In addition to Irving and Cooper, American writers such as Ralph Waldo Emerson, Lydia Sigourney, Catharine Maria Sedgwick, and Benjamin Silliman also visited and wrote about England.

If England represented a nostalgically imagined homeland, Italy represented a romantically conceived site of past glories and artistic possibilities. In *The*

Fortunate Pilgrims: Americans in Italy, 1800–1860, Paul Baker examines the allure that Italy held for American artists and writers. William Cullen Bryant, Margaret Fuller, Nathaniel Hawthorne, Joel Headley, William Dean Howells, Samuel Langhorne Clemens (Mark Twain), and Rembrandt Peale were among the prominent figures drawn to Italy in the 1830s through the 1860s.

Of the writers mentioned above, none is more closely associated with Italian history during the 1840s than Margaret Fuller (1810–1850). In 1846 Fuller traveled to a Europe on the brink of revolution. To pay some of the costs of her trip, she contracted with the *New-York Daily Tribune* to write "dispatches" from Europe, to which the *Tribune* gave front-page coverage. Fuller's European tour included the expected stops in England—visits to the Lake District, commentaries on picturesque castles, and conversations with poets. While in London, she met Giuseppe Mazzini, a leading Italian nationalist. When she traveled to Italy in 1847 she sensed it was a place in which she belonged and to which she could commit her energies. Her attachment to Italy was reinforced by her affair with Giovanni Ossoli, who was an ardent supporter of Mazzini. She and Ossoli were eyewitnesses to the revolutionary events in Italy in 1848 and 1849. Fuller, Ossoli, and their young son drowned in July 1850, when the ship on which they were traveling back to America went aground off of Fire Island, New York.

Nathaniel Hawthorne (1804–1864), who had modeled Zenobia in *The Blithedale Romance* (1852) on Fuller, was far from kind in his estimation of Fuller and her Italian family. He thought her attraction to Ossoli was purely sensual and accounted it an act of God that she, her lover, and her son had traveled on the ill-fated ship. Hawthorne and his family lived in Italy during 1858 and 1859. Despite his mistrust of Fuller's Italian politics, Hawthorne did find things to admire in Italy and in Rome in particular. His wife's edition of his Italian notebooks did not appear until after his death, but his last novel *The Marble Faun; or, the Romance of Monte Beni* (1860) owes a great deal to his Roman sojourn. The Roman scenes in the book were so well realized that versions of the work were sold in the late nineteenth century with the addition of picture postcards of Rome.

Although European travel during the period prior to the American Civil War was by and large the province of the well-to-do, literary figures with contacts in England or on the continent, and authors (Irving and Hawthorne among them) who had secured ambassadorial appointments, there were travelers and writers who represented otherwise disenfranchised or minority

voices. Chief among these were William Wells Brown (c. 1814–1884) and George Copway (1818–c. 1863).

Brown, who began life as a slave near Lexington, Kentucky, gained his freedom by escaping from a steamboat in Cincinnati in 1834 and making his way north through Ohio to Cleveland. He later moved to Michigan and then to Buffalo, New York. In 1849 Brown, by now once again being pursued by a former master, sailed to France as the representative of the American Peace Society to the Paris Peace Congress of 1849. Brown stayed in Europe for five years, eventually purchasing his freedom with the help of English friends. In 1852 he wrote about the first three years of his stay in *Three Years in Europe; or, Places I Have Seen and People I Have Met.*

Copway, whose parents were Ojibwa, was given the name Kah-ge-ga-gah-bowh at birth. A convert to Methodism, Copway was trained as a Methodist minister and served in that capacity in the upper Midwest during the 1840s. In August 1850 he was selected as one of forty American delegates (he was the only Native American among them) to the Fourth General Peace Conference at Frankfurt am Main. He turned his observations of this European trip into *Running Sketches of Men and Places, in England, France, Germany, Belgium, and Scotland* (1851). This work has the distinction of being the first book of travel writing by a Native American.

No overview of American travel writing from 1820 to 1870 would be complete without mentioning the travels and writings of Bayard Taylor (1825–1878). From the mid-1840s through mid-1870s, Taylor was the epitome of the indefatigable American traveler. Taylor's first introduction to Europe was as a poor young man who traveled on foot across much of Europe for two years (1844–1846). His account of that journey, *Views A-foot; or, Europe Seen with Knapsack and Staff* (1846) might appeal to young Americans walking and hitchhiking through Europe in the present day. In addition to writing about Europe, Taylor would later document his travels to California shortly after the gold rush (1850); to Central Africa (1854); to Palestine, Asia Minor, Sicily, and Spain (1854); to India, China, and Japan (1855); to Sweden, Denmark, and Lapland (1858); and to Greece and Russia (1859). From 1858 through much of the 1860s Taylor wrote fiction in addition to travel literature and was a fixture on the lecture circuit, presenting over five hundred lectures during these years.

As may have been the case with the peripatetic Taylor, the American Civil War interrupted American travel and tourism abroad during the early

Frontispiece engraving for *A Visit to India, China, and Japan, in the Year 1853* by Bayard Taylor, 1855. SPECIAL COLLECTIONS LIBRARY, UNIVERSITY OF MICHIGAN

1860s. The pace of American travel abroad resumed after the war and guidebook-toting Americans in Europe became so common that they would be gently satirized in Mark Twain's *Innocents Abroad* (1869) and become the subject of Henry James's *The American* (1877). In naming the central character of this work Christopher Newman, James was calling attention to the voyages of European discovery that Americans were making. Newman is just that—a new man in the Old World. Reversing the path taken by another famous Christopher (Columbus), Newman, having made his fortune in America, travels to Europe in search of what has eluded him at home.

See also Americans Abroad; Exploration and Discovery; Foreigners; Tourism; *Typee; Two Years before the Mast*

BIBLIOGRAPHY

Primary Works

Brown, William Wells. *Three Years in Europe; or, Places I Have Seen and People I Have Met*. London: C. Gilpin, 1852.

Cooper, James Fenimore. *England*. 2 vols. London: Richard Bentley, 1837.

Cooper, James Fenimore. *Excursions in Italy*. 2 vols. London: Richard Bentley, 1838.

Cooper, James Fenimore. *The Prairie*. 2 vols. Philadelphia: Carey, Lea & Carey, 1827.

Cooper, James Fenimore. *Recollections of Europe*. 2 vols. London: Richard Bentley, 1837.

Cooper, James Fenimore. *A Residence in France; with an Excursion up the Rhine, and a Second Visit to Switzerland*. London: Richard Bentley, 1836.

Cooper, James Fenimore. *Sketches of Switzerland*. Philadelphia: Carey, Lea & Blanchard, 1836.

Copway, George. *Running Sketches of Men and Places, in England, France, Germany, Belgium, and Scotland*. New York: J. C. Riker, 1851.

Dana, Richard Henry, Jr. *Two Years before the Mast: A Personal Narrative of Life at Sea*. New York: Harper, 1840.

Gregg, Josiah. *Commerce of the Prairies: or, The Journal of a Santa Fé Trader*. 2 vols. New York: H. G. Langley, 1844.

Fuller, Margaret. *Summer on the Lakes, in 1843*. Boston: C. C. Little and J. Brown, 1844.

Fuller, Margaret. *"These Sad But Glorious Days": Dispatches from Europe, 1846–1850*. Edited by Larry J. Reynolds and Susan Belasco Smith. New Haven, Conn.: Yale University Press, 1991.

Frémont, John Charles. *Report of the Exploring Expedition to the Rocky Mountains in the Year 1842, and to Oregon and North California in the Years 1843–44*. 28th

Congress, 2nd session, Serial 461. Washington, D.C.: Blair and Rives, 1845.

Frémont, John Charles. *A Report on an Exploration of the Country Lying between the Missouri River and the Rocky Mountains on the Line of the Kansas and Great Platte Rivers.* 27th Congress, 3rd session, Serial 416, Senate Document 243. Washington, D.C.: Printed by Order of the U.S. Senate, 1843.

Hawthorne, Nathaniel. *The Marble Faun; or, The Romance of Monte Beni.* 2 vols. Boston: Ticknor and Fields, 1860.

Hawthorne, Nathaniel. *Our Old Home: A Series of English Sketches.* Boston: Ticknor and Fields, 1863.

Hawthorne, Nathaniel. *Passages from the English Note-Books.* 2 vols. Edited by Sarah Peabody Hawthorne. Boston: Fields, Osgood, 1870.

Hawthorne, Nathaniel. *Passages from the French and Italian Note-Books.* 2 vols. Edited by Sarah Peabody Hawthorne. Boston: J. R. Osgood and Co., 1872.

Irving, Washington. *Astoria; or, Anecdotes of an Enterprise beyond the Rocky Mountains.* 3 vols. London: Richard Bentley, 1836.

Irving, Washington. *A History of the Life and Voyages of Christopher Columbus.* 4 vols. London: John Murray, 1828.

Irving, Washington. *The Rocky Mountains; or, Scenes, Incidents, and Adventures in the Far West.* 3 vols. London: Richard Bentley, 1837.

Irving, Washington. *The Sketch Book of Geoffrey Crayon, Gent.* 1819–1820. New York: Penguin Books, 1988.

Irving, Washington. *A Tour on the Prairies.* London: John Murray, 1835.

Kirkland, Caroline. *A New Home—Who'll Follow? or, Glimpses of Western Life.* 1839. Edited by William S. Osborne. Schenectady, N.Y.: New College and University Press, 1965.

Melville, Herman. *Omoo; A Narrative of Adventures in the South Seas.* London: Murray; New York: Harper, 1847.

Melville, Herman. *Typee: A Peep at Polynesian Life.* New York: Wiley and Putnam, 1846.

Taylor, Bayard. *Eldorado; or, Adventures in the Path of Empire.* New York: Putnam, 1850.

Taylor, Bayard. *A Journey to Central Africa; or, Life and Landscapes from Egypt to the Negro Kingdoms of the White Nile.* New York: Putnam, 1854.

Taylor, Bayard. *The Lands of the Saracen; or, Pictures of Palestine, Asia Minor, Sicily, and Spain.* New York: Putnam, 1854.

Taylor, Bayard. *Northern Travel: Summer and Winter Pictures of Sweden, Denmark, and Lapland.* New York: Putnam, 1858.

Taylor, Bayard. *Travels in Greece and Russia, with an Excursion to Crete.* New York: G. P. Putnam, 1859.

Taylor, Bayard. *Views A-foot; or, Europe Seen with Knapsack and Staff.* New York: Wiley and Putnam, 1846.

Taylor, Bayard. *A Visit to India, China, and Japan, in the Year 1853.* New York: G. P. Putnam and Co., 1855.

Secondary Works

Baker, Paul R. *The Fortunate Pilgrims: Americans in Italy, 1800–1860.* Cambridge, Mass: Harvard University Press, 1964.

Kolodny, Annette. *The Land before Her: Fantasy and Experience of the American Frontiers, 1630–1860.* Chapel Hill: University of North Carolina Press, 1984.

Lockwood, Allison. *Passionate Pilgrims: The American Traveler in Great Britain, 1800–1914.* Rutherford, N.J.: Farleigh Dickinson University Press, 1981.

Mulvey, Christopher. *Anglo-American Landscapes: A Study of Nineteenth-Century Anglo-American Travel* Literature. Cambridge, U.K., and New York: Cambridge University Press, 1983.

Ross, Donald, and James Schramer, eds. *American Travel Writers, 1850–1915.* Detroit: Gale Research, 1998.

Schramer, James and Donald Ross, eds. *American Travel Writers, 1776–1864.* Detroit: Gale Research, 1997.

James J. Schramer

"THE TWO OFFERS"

Frances Ellen Watkins Harper's (1825–1911) "The Two Offers" is believed to be the first short story published by an African American author. This accomplishment would be one of many firsts in the extraordinary career of the nineteenth century's most well-known black writer. By the time she published "The Two Offers" in 1859 Harper had already established herself as a popular and well-respected poet, lecturer, and activist. The story is especially unique in Harper's oeuvre for a number of reasons. During this period most of her published works centered around her abolitionist efforts. As such, she wrote as a black woman about the plight of black people. Although one of the protagonists of "The Two Offers" shares Harper's abolitionist sensibilities, neither are identified as black women, nor is the abolition of slavery the central concern of the text. Instead, the story is a meditation on marriage and education for women. As such, it actually foreshadows some of her more feminist writings of the postwar period when she specifically turned her attention to suffrage, temperance, and helping to organize the black women's club movement. Consequently, "The Two Offers" provides an early glimpse of Harper's feminist sensibilities that while evident in her own career had been less of a concern in her writing before and immediately following its publication. Finally, it is not insignificant that Harper would first broach gender issues in a form that she had not previously used. Both her speeches and her poetry were part of an effort to build and strengthen a social movement; in fact, she often recited her poetry in her public lectures. The short story is meant to be read rather than heard, and it offers the author the opportunity for an extended meditation on the topic at hand.

HARPER'S POLITICAL EDUCATION

The 1850s proved to be an exciting and turbulent decade for Watkins as well as the nation. The struggle over slavery took center stage and Watkins found herself in the middle of all of the major debates of her day. At the same time, the struggle for women's rights gained momentum as well. Watkins was greatly influenced by each of these separate but related social movements. The decade opened with the Compromise of 1850. The major issue facing the nation was over the expansion of slavery into the newly acquired Western territories. On 29 January 1850, Senator Henry Clay of Kentucky proposed a compromise that the Congress debated for the better part of the year. Under the Compromise of 1850 the inhabitants of the territories of New Mexico, Nevada, Arizona, and Utah would be allowed to decide if these areas were slave or free when they applied for statehood. The slave trade was to be abolished in Washington, D.C., although slavery would continue to be legal there. California was to be admitted to the union as a free state. In order to appease senators from the slave states, Congress passed the Fugitive Slave Act. Under this act, to be enforced by federal officials, citizens were required by law to assist in recovering fugitive slaves. This act immediately mobilized the abolitionist movement and it would also help to radicalize Harper.

Three years later, in 1853, Maryland passed a law forbidding free blacks from entering the state under the threat of slavery, thus making Harper an exile from the state of her birth. Shortly afterward a free black man entered the state and was immediately enslaved and sent to Georgia. He died while trying to escape. About his death, Harper wrote, "Upon this grave I pledged myself to the antislavery cause" (Still, p. 186).

In 1854 Harper moved to Philadelphia, which was by then a hotbed of abolitionist activity; she was soon part of a circle of activists and intellectuals committed to bringing an end to the dreaded institution. She lived in an Underground Railroad station and there she listened to stories of fugitives as they came to the city on the way to Canada. She also worked with a

Frances Ellen Watkins Harper. Illustration from William Still's *Underground Railroad*, 1872. THE LIBRARY OF CONGRESS

network of activists who helped to ensure their safe passage. She also continued to write, and she frequently published in the *Christian Recorder,* the journal of the African Methodist Episcopal Church. Her poems also appeared in national abolitionist publications such as *Frederick Douglass's Paper* and *The Liberator.* Not satisfied to only write, Harper sought to take a more public role in the movement. In 1854 she began her public speaking career in New Bedford, Massachusetts. Her articulate eloquence and charisma made her a very effective and popular speaker; soon the Maine Anti-Slavery Society hired her and sent her on a speaking tour. Throughout 1854 Harper lectured almost every night and she published her second volume, *Poems on Miscellaneous Subjects.* By 1857 the Supreme Court would issue the *Dred Scott* decision deeming that blacks were not citizens and therefore were privy to none of the rights and privileges of U.S. citizenship.

Although a number of her poems during this period centered on the plight of slave women, for the most part Harper's writings and speeches did not address issues of gender specifically. Only once did she even broach the subject of marriage; in a poem titled "Advice to Girls" Watkins writes:

Nay, do not blush! I only heard
You had a mind to marry;

I thought I'd speak a friendly word,
So just one moment tarry.
Wed not a man whose merit lies
In things of outward show,
In raven hair or flashing eyes,
That please your fancy so.
But marry one who's good and kind,
And free from all pretence;
Who, if without a gifted mind,
At least has common sense.

(Foster, A Brighter Coming Day, p. 68)

The poem is not so much a critique of marriage as it is a humorous admonition to women not to marry for superficial reasons. None of her other poetry of the period touches upon the issue of choice in marriage. However, of Harper's life as a single woman in the public sphere, Harper scholar Frances Smith Foster notes, "Her marital status was [a] barrier to be taken seriously. Being a single woman undermined her authority" (p. 12). Even though a number of black and white women had taken to the lectern prior to Harper, in mid-century a single woman in public life was deemed to be of questionable repute. Furthermore, her status as a single woman made it difficult to support herself as well. So it is not surprising that Harper might have been greatly concerned about the limitations marriage placed on women's development as well as the limitations that society placed on unmarried women.

She certainly would not have been the only prominent woman of her time to contemplate these issues. While the abolitionist movement dominated the activities of progressive social activists, male and female, black and white, white women were also beginning to organize for their own rights as well. The first women's rights convention was held in Seneca Falls, New York, in 1848. The convention produced the Declaration of Sentiments (drafted by Elizabeth Cady Stanton), an articulation of grievances and an agenda for the nascent women's rights movement. A number of the grievances address the issue of marriage and education:

He has made her morally, an irresponsible being, as she can commit many crimes with impunity, provided they be done in the presence of her husband. In the covenant of marriage, she is compelled to promise obedience to her husband, he becoming, to all intents and purposes, her master—the law giving him power to deprive her of her liberty and to administer chastisement.

After depriving her of all rights as a married woman, if single and the owner of property, he has taxed her to support a government which recognizes her only when her property can be made profitable to it.

He has monopolized nearly all the profitable employments, and from those she is permitted to follow, she receives but a scanty remuneration.

He closes against her all the avenues to wealth and distinction which he considers most honorable to himself. As a teacher of theology, medicine, or law, she is not known.

He has denied her the facilities for obtaining a thorough education, all colleges being closed against her.

The convention adopted twelve resolutions insisting upon the equal treatment of men and women and calling for voting rights for women. In 1850 the first National Woman's Rights Convention was held in Worcester, Massachusetts. The conventions would be held on an annual basis until 1860. At the convention of 1851, Sojourner Truth (c. 1797–1883) is believed to have delivered her "Ain't I a Woman?" speech. Truth's speech challenged the equation of "women" with white women only by offering her own experiences as a black slave woman as an alternative.

FEMINIST FICTIONS

With the publication of "The Two Offers" in 1859, Harper would enter into the debate about the role of marriage and education in women's lives. The story appeared in the *Anglo-African Magazine*, a black publication founded by Thomas Hamilton in 1859. The publication featured works by black authors, "designed to educate and to encourage, to speak for and to black Americans" (Foster, p. 105). Harper published a number of poems in the new journal and eventually she served on its editorial board. During the period that saw the publication of "The Two Offers," the magazine also serialized Martin Robinson Delany's militant novel, *Blake; or, The Huts of America*. (Also, 1859 was the year in which John Brown launched his failed raid on Harpers Ferry.)

It is not insignificant that during this time of heightened activism and awareness around the issue of slavery Harper chose to publish a story that focused neither on slavery nor race. Instead, "The Two Offers" centers on a critique of marriage and an argument for the full development of women's intellectual and spiritual capacities. Furthermore, the story does not advocate for women's education as future mothers but instead as intellectuals and political and social activists. Harper never names the race of her characters. That she was writing for a black audience, whom she might have assumed shared her abolitionist politics, might have freed her to write about gender. Perhaps she leaves the racial identity of her characters purposefully ambiguous so that she could write about gender issues in a way that would have been more difficult in a more racially specific context. In this way, she established a pattern that would be followed by twentieth-century writers, such as Paule Marshall, who first wrote stories that challenged conventional heterosexual marriage by focusing on white characters.

The story presents us with two protagonists, the beautiful young cousins Laura and Janette. Laura marries while Janette pursues a career as a writer and activist. While the title seems to refer to the heroines' two offers of marriage with which the story opens, it may also be about the two distinct choices made by each woman. Laura makes a bad marriage to an emotionally abusive, inattentive man who is also a drinker and gambler. She puts everything into mothering her only child, who dies prematurely. Lacking the love and affection of her husband, suffering the loss of her baby, and having failed to foster her own intellect and talent, Laura dies of a broken heart. Janette, who suffers heartbreak before marrying, instead chooses to devote herself to the pursuit of her craft and to working on behalf of the enslaved and the poor. The story closes with Janette as an elderly, fulfilled woman whose life has been an offering to humanity.

As with much of Harper's fiction "The Two Offers" has a pedagogical function as well as serving as entertainment, and much of it is written in direct address to the reader about the necessity of training women for callings other than marriage and motherhood. Janette is an accomplished writer and a respected activist *because* she is an "old maid." Because of the generosity with which she lives her life, she is not lonely and isolated in her old age nor does she look back at her earlier choices with regret. This is clearly a shift from fiction that insists that by story's end the heroine be either married or dead.

A year after the publication of "The Two Offers," Frances Ellen Watkins married Fenton Harper, a widower and father of three. The Harpers lived on a farm in Ohio and Frances eventually gave birth to a daughter, Mary. Upon Fenton Harper's death in 1864, Harper returned to the lectern and the written page. Following the Civil War she traveled south to lecture to and teach the freedmen and there she became even more convinced of the necessity of granting women access to education. She also became more fully associated with the women's rights movement. Consequently, "The Two Offers" provides evidence of her feminist sensibilities years before she would become publicly associated with the suffrage and temperance movements.

See also Female Authorship; Feminism; Marriage; Seneca Falls Convention; Short Story; Underground Railroad

BIBLIOGRAPHY
Primary Works
Declaration of Sentiments. http://www.fordham.edu/halsall/mod/Senecafalls.html.

Foster, Frances Smith, ed. *A Brighter Coming Day: A Frances Ellen Watkins Harper Reader.* New York: Feminist Press, 1990.

Still, William. *Underground Railroad.* 1872. New York: Arno Press, 1968.

Secondary Works
Boyd, Melba Joyce. *Discarded Legacy: Politics and Poetics in the Life of Frances E. W. Harper.* Detroit: Wayne State University Press, 1994.

Carby, Hazel, *Reconstructing Womanhood: The Emergence of the Afro-American Woman Novelist.* New York and Oxford: Oxford University Press, 1987.

Foster, Frances Smith. *Written by Herself: Literary Production by African American Women, 1746–1892.* Bloomington: Indiana University Press, 1993.

Griffin, Farah Jasmine. "Minnie's Sacrifice: Frances Ellen Watkins Harper's Narrative of Citizenship." In *The Cambridge Companion to Nineteenth Century American Women's Writing,* edited by Dale M. Bauer and Philip Gould, pp. 308–319. New York and Cambridge, U.K.: Cambridge University Press, 2001.

Peterson, Carla L. *"Doers of the Word": African-American Women Speakers and Writers in the North (1830–1880).* New York and Oxford: Oxford University Press, 1995.

Tate, Claudia. *Domestic Allegories of Political Desire: The Black Heroine's Text at the Turn of the Century.* New York: Oxford University Press, 1992.

Farah Jasmine Griffin

TWO YEARS BEFORE THE MAST

In 1834 Richard Henry Dana Jr. (1815–1882), concerned about his failing eyesight, abandoned his studies at Harvard and signed on as an ordinary seaman on the brig *Pilgrim* for a journey around Cape Horn to California. For a member of a prominent Boston family, this was an extreme move away from a life of privilege. *Two Years before the Mast* (1840) is Dana's record of his epic voyage, and its story falls into three stages: the journey to California, his time in and off of the coast of California, and finally the journey home.

TRAVEL NARRATIVES
Although purporting to be nothing more than an autobiographical memoir, *Two Years before the Mast,* as is true of any account of a journey, becomes a voyage of discovery and self-discovery. It takes its place in a

Painting of the *Pilgrim,* on which Richard Henry Dana Jr. sailed to California in 1834. COURTESY OF THE SAN DIEGO HISTORICAL SOCIETY

nineteenth-century flood of books about the opening up of America. At the same time, it also influenced the trajectory of the American novel, Herman Melville (1819–1891) owing more than a little to Dana in his understanding of what could be encapsulated in an account of a sea journey. The impetus behind *Two Years before the Mast* itself, however, is the fact that America in the first half of the nineteenth century was a country demanding to be explored. Travel narratives with which it can be compared include Washington Irving's *A Tour on the Prairies* (1835), which describes the author's adventures on the western frontier over a two-month period in 1832, Irving's *Astoria; or, Anecdotes of an Enterprise beyond the Rocky Mountains* (1836), and Henry David Thoreau's *A Week on the Concord and Merrimack Rivers* (1849). But there are also works by now largely forgotten authors, such as John Kirk Townsend's *Narrative of a Journey across the Rocky Mountains to the Columbia River* (1839) and Zenas Leonard's *Narrative of the Adventures of Zenas Leonard, Fur Trader* (1839). And the 1840s produced a wave of books about California, such as Thomas Jefferson Farnham's *Life and Adventures in*

California (1844) and Edwin Bryant's *What I Saw in California* (1848).

What separates *Two Years before the Mast* is that these are journeys across the landmass of America; Dana's is a sea journey. There are other accounts of sea journeys from this period, the most celebrated of which are fictional, such as Edgar Allan Poe's (1809–1849) *The Narrative of Arthur Gordon Pym of Nantucket* (1838) and Melville's *Typee* (1846), *White-Jacket* (1850), and *Moby-Dick* (1851). American sea stories, both fictional and nonfictional, tend to focus on heroes on the edge of a new frontier. This is underlined by their sense of space. British sea stories reflect a small island where people live in close proximity. The American sea story, by contrast, feels boundless: the distances are enormous, and the time spent away from land is lengthy. There is always a sense of an epic journey into the unknown. The purpose of this journey, however, is economic. America in the 1830s was a maritime trading nation; at the heart of *Two Years before the Mast* is the trade in animal hides, which are collected on the mainland by the crew and then brought back from California to Boston. But in 1834, although it would not have been apparent at the time, America's maritime-based economic order was about to go into decline. During the 1840s and 1850s the land frontier, the whole of mainland America, took over as the central feature of both the American economy and the American imagination. The change is reflected in Dana's "Twenty-Four Years After" postscript (1869), which replaced his original concluding chapter that had focused on sailors' rights; by this time, the sea no longer has the same significance in America's sense of its national identity.

Regardless of whether it is the land or sea frontier, however, similar assumptions inform all these travel narratives. In the words of Eric J. Sundquist: "The literal mapping of the United States was accompanied by a vast written record that established the psychological and political boundaries of the nation—a territory that existed as an act of prophetic vision even before poets and novelists expanded its horizons" (p. 129). American travel narratives describe a new territory but bring that place under control, absorbing it into America's narrative. When this pattern is acknowledged, it becomes apparent why the longest section of *Two Years before the Mast*, allegedly an account of a sea journey, is set in California. When the book was first published California was part of Mexico; following the Mexican-American War in 1846–1848, California became part of the United States. In 1849, the year of the gold rush, nearly 100,000 forty-niners entered the territory.

But every step of Dana's journey is rich in implications. The basic informing structure is that the values of Boston (values that are reasserted when Dana meets other cultivated people) are set against the different values and order of the ship and then set against the values encountered in California. On the journey home there is a feeling of captivity, with Dana longing for liberation, a liberation that can only be achieved through restoration to his own world. This secure sense of his own core values positions Dana in a certain way: he becomes an observer, and analyst, of the contradictions of America. The journey affects him profoundly—particularly the inhumane treatment of sailors that he witnesses—but in essence it reinforces his commitment to the values he held when he embarked.

THE REGIME OF THE SHIP

Problems emerge fairly slowly in the text. Initially the impression is positive. What is obvious as the work commences is the spirit and energy of America, people working together in a democratic, trading nation. Dana conveys the flavor of business and enterprise. There is a new challenge every day, the series of challenges reaching a climax with the rounding of Cape Horn on the journey home. One distinctive feature of the book is Dana's positive portrayal of his fellow seamen. The British naval writer Captain Marryat is always disparaging, leveling insults at his own characters. Dana, by contrast, is liberal and fair. This becomes clear if one compares Dana's stance with that of Poe in *The Narrative of Arthur Gordon Pym*. What appears to underlie Poe's strange allegorical work is a fear of blackness coupled with distrust of the working-class crew. Poe, a product of the antebellum South, seems driven by racial and class anxieties, his fear of anarchy leading to a desire for confrontation and destruction. Dana exemplifies a different position, that of the antebellum northern liberal conservative.

Dana's stance is evident in the way the fierce regime of the ship is at odds with his sense of justice. As always happens in sea stories, people are physically mistreated. The form it takes here is the ferocious, arbitrary punishments meted out by Captain Thompson. Dana was not opposed to corporal punishment, accepting that the conventions of polite society are not entirely applicable at sea. But a line can be crossed, and unreasonable corporal punishment is incompatible with everything America should stand for. As the captain flogs two crew members, they are robbed of their identities: "A man—a human being, made in God's likeness—fastened up and flogged like a beast! A man, too, whom I had

lived with and eaten with for months, and knew almost as well as a brother" (p. 153). Focusing on his own response to the punishment, Dana grasps some awkward truths about America. In a key sentence, he writes: "I thought of our own situation, living under a tyranny; of the character of the country we were in" (p. 157). This can be taken as a local reference, as the ship has now arrived in California, but if one accepts that Dana is writing about the country as a whole, what is striking is the juxtaposition of tyranny and America. The simplicity of the formulation is typical of the seemingly artless manner in which *Two Years before the Mast* offers a complex mediation on the state of the emergent nation; Dana has constructed a consideration of the gap between the democratic ideal and the complicated reality of America.

CALIFORNIA

The picture becomes even more complicated when the crew steps ashore in California. There is a sense, however, in which the interpretation of this unfamiliar territory has been determined in advance. In California, Dana meets "idle, thriftless people, [who] can make nothing for themselves. The country abounds in grapes, yet they buy bad wine made in Boston, and brought round by us" (p. 125). The Mexicans and Native Americans Dana encountered in California represent the opposite of everything America stands for, and his characterization of them is typical of many American travel narratives—true not only of the people's indolence but also evident in their domestic immorality and, at the political level, in the constant revolutions that characterize Mexican life. There is a natural abundance in California, but it is being squandered; it is crying out to be brought under American control. Indeed, the standard pattern in American travel narratives could also be said to be the pattern of all travel narratives: the traveler arrives on another shore, which is discovered to be a place of idleness, luxury, and excess. The new land is a place of Edenic possibility but is also a place of indulgence; it is, in particular, a land of sexual indulgence and as such a place of temptation. The traveler is in danger of being seduced by a way of life that is the opposite of everything that his (or, more rarely, her) culture represents.

The standard pattern of American travel narratives is also the pattern of all colonial and colonizing narratives. And California is not just successfully colonized but absorbed into the United States, a development considered in "Twenty-Four Years After," the postscript altering, and possibly concealing, some of the original implications of Dana's work. But even before the addition of the postscript, *Two Years before the*

Mast was probably being read in a different way after 1848 when, with the annexation of California, the book enjoyed a second burst of popularity. In a sense it became the authoritative guidebook, not only describing the nature of the territory but also by default suggesting what America would be able to do for California. All of this is confirmed in "Twenty-Four Years After," when the reader is presented with an impression of a vibrant economy—even if there is a hint of regret at how the world has moved on. Moreover, the annexation of California adds to the complexity and diversity of America. Dana depicts people drawn together, but not united, by the scramble for wealth. As always, there is a gap between the simple democratic ideal and the awkward economic reality of America.

DANA, DEMOCRACY, AND THE LAW

A travel narrative tells the reader about the country from which the traveler originates and about the country (or countries) encountered, yet it also tells about the traveler. In this context, it is helpful to call upon Jonathan Arac's description of the structure of a personal narrative, specifically how there is a "circular shape of descent and return—a touching of ground, even a humiliation before the return to the elevation of ordinary civilized life" (p. 661). If one looks for Dana's moment of humiliation, it could be argued that the moment occurs when he uses his social connections to avoid staying on in California. Summoned by Captain Thompson, he is told that he will not be permitted to return home for another twelve months. But Dana has "friends and interest enough at home to make them suffer for any injustice they might do me" (p. 350). Consequently, another sailor, "looking as though he had received his sentence to be hung" (p. 350), is ordered to take Dana's place, Dana having to provide him with $30 and a suit of clothes. A tense situation is resolved when a "harum-scarum lad" (p. 351) offers to stay on. It is a brief but telling episode. Once again it illustrates the disparity between the democratic ideal of America and the uncomfortable reality, that all men are not equal. But is also illustrates how Dana, as a privileged individual, is implicated in the larger issue. The problem is not a political abstraction; he is personally involved. Indeed, he has exploited the system to his own advantage. The reader can understand why, on the return leg of the voyage, Dana is keen to escape from the sea; it is as if he wishes to return to his insulated, slightly unreal life in Boston.

The journey, however, has made him aware of the contradictions at the heart of American life. In particular, as framed and developed in his narrative, Dana's experiences have enabled him to ponder, although never directly, questions about labor and individual rights. As such, *Two Years before the Mast* resembles a great many other nineteenth-century American works, texts generically labeled as romances. Traditionally, critical readings of such works focused on the idea of escape, but beginning in the late twentieth century more emphasis was placed on how these works engage with actual social and political conditions. Robert Clark notes that while American romance narratives may offer a picture of a society that believes it is "perfect" and "a spiritual example to the less enlightened peoples of the world," it is also a society "inflected by slavery, genocidal conquest and acute class tensions" (p. 586). In a word, what people are confronted with is a representation of nascent capitalism, with all of the ideals and ills attendant upon that formation.

If *Two Years before the Mast* evokes the nature of the problem, the rest of Dana's life demonstrates his commitment to the belief that the law can, and should, be used to restrain the worst excesses of a market economy. This is reflected in the original concluding chapter, focusing as it does on sailors' rights, where Dana puts his faith in "laws, with heavy penalties" (p. 469). His position is also made clear in the book he published in 1841, *The Seaman's Friend*—a handbook of sailors' rights—as well as in his work as a lawyer, where he acquired a reputation for taking on the cases or ordinary seamen. Of most interest, however, is his representation without charge of fugitive slaves captured in Boston under the Fugitive Slave Law. It was a form of legal work that inevitably antagonized his social peers in Boston, people who relied upon the southern plantations to maintain the prosperity of their cotton mills. This political stance was foreshadowed in *Two Years before the Mast,* a text that simultaneously exposes the unfairness, and inhumanity, of the market economy and Dana's commitment to the law as the best, possibly the only, means of correcting the balance.

See also Exploration and Discovery; Maritime Commerce; Nautical Literature; Reform; Travel Writing

BIBLIOGRAPHY
Primary Work
Dana, Richard Henry, Jr. *Two Years before the Mast.* 1840. New York and London: Penguin, 1986.

Secondary Works
Arac, Jonathan. "Narrative Forms." In *The Cambridge History of American Literature*, vol. 2, *1820–1865,* edited by Sacvan Bercovitch, pp. 607–777. Cambridge, U.K., and New York: Cambridge University Press, 1995.

Clark, Robert. "American Romance." In *Encyclopedia of Literature and Criticism,* edited by Martin Coyle, Peter

Garside, Malcolm Kelsall, and John Peck, pp. 576–588. London: Routledge, 1990.

Gale, Robert L. *Richard Henry Dana, Jr.* New York: Twayne, 1969.

Gilmore, Michael T. *American Romanticism and the Marketplace.* Chicago: Chicago University Press, 1985.

Labaree, Benjamin W., William W. Fowler, Edward W. Sloan, John B. Hattendorf, Jeffrey J. Safford, and Andrew W. German. *America and the Sea: A Maritime History.* Mystic, Conn.: Mystic Seaport, 1998.

Lawrence, D. H. *Studies in Classic American Literature.* 1923. Cambridge, U.K.: Cambridge University Press, 2002.

Porter, Carolyn. "Social Discourse and Nonfictional Prose." In *Columbia Literary History of the United States,* edited by Emory Elliott, pp. 345–363. New York: Columbia University Press, 1988.

Shapiro, Samuel. *Richard Henry Dana, Jr., 1815–1882.* East Lansing: Michigan State University Press, 1961.

Sundquist, Eric J. "The Literature of Expansion and Race." In *The Cambridge History of American Literature,* vol. 2, *1820–1865,* edited by Sacvan Bercovitch, pp. 127–328. Cambridge, U.K., and New York: Cambridge University Press, 1995.

John Peck

TYPEE

Modern readers typically know Herman Melville's (1819–1891) *Typee* (1846), if they know it at all, only as a modest first novel, certainly a lesser work compared to *Moby-Dick* (1851), *Pierre* (1852), or *Billy Budd* (written 1885–1891 and published posthumously in 1924). But *Typee* was not intended as a novel; Melville and his publishers represented it as a strictly factual narrative. And far from being a lesser work, it was the most popular of Melville's books in his lifetime; readers into the early twentieth century considered *Typee* to be among the author's best works. It was during the so-called Melville revival in the 1920s that *Typee* was nudged aside in favor of the later and more self-consciously fictional works.

Typee was, in fact, based on actual experience: Melville did ship aboard the whaler *Acushnet*, only to abandon her in the Marquesas Islands, where he sheltered in Nukuheva's Typee Valley for a few weeks among an indigenous tribe with a reputation for ferocity and cannibalism. In the book's preface, Melville speaks of his "anxious desire to speak the unvarnished truth," but some of the author's fictional "varnish" is rather obvious, such as his decision to name his first-person narrator "Tommo" rather than Herman. Even early reviews of *Typee* debated its credibility, and scholarship in the 1930s revealed more pronounced departures from fact, such as ships' logs showing that Melville's total time on Nukuheva was four weeks rather than the four month's residence the book claimed. Nonetheless, for about three-quarters of a century, *Typee* enjoyed a reputation among credulous readers as, among other things, a reliable source of firsthand anthropological knowledge. But informed modern readers must approach the work as a mix of experience and imagination and even as a synthesis of source works Melville used to "fill out" his manuscript. Though he would drop the pretense of direct autobiography in most later works, the blend of materials Melville employed for his first book would continue to inform his writing process throughout his career.

TYPEE'S MANY TEXTS

Further complicating how one reads *Typee* is the fact that it is not a single book. Owing to the circumstances of its publication, Melville's debut work was available in several distinct versions throughout his lifetime. When Melville's brother Gansevoort left for a diplomatic post in England in July 1845, he took a partial manuscript of Herman's book in hopes of finding a publisher. The brothers' plan was to try to bring out English and U.S. editions simultaneously. After some time, Gansevoort secured an agreement with the London publisher John Murray, who would include *Typee* in his nonfiction "Home and Colonial Library" series, and in January 1846, accompanied by an enthusiastic Washington Irving, Gansevoort shopped Murray's partial proof draft at the London offices of the American publishers Wiley and Putnam.

Wiley and Putnam soon brought out the book in New York, prepared from Murray's proofs but altered somewhat to align the text with their own house standards and with American spelling and usage. But Mr. Wiley was not comfortable with the work as published. It seems likely he had not read the book before publishing it, proceeding on the strength of Irving's recommendation alone. Wiley found parts of the narrative too racy for his taste, and he particularly objected to Melville's criticisms in the book of Protestant missionaries. Under Wiley's direction, Melville almost immediately began to revise and expurgate passages from the book for a revised American edition, which appeared in September 1846 and became the standard text for American readers in the author's lifetime.

The differences between the standard English and U.S. editions of *Typee* are not superficial, nor does

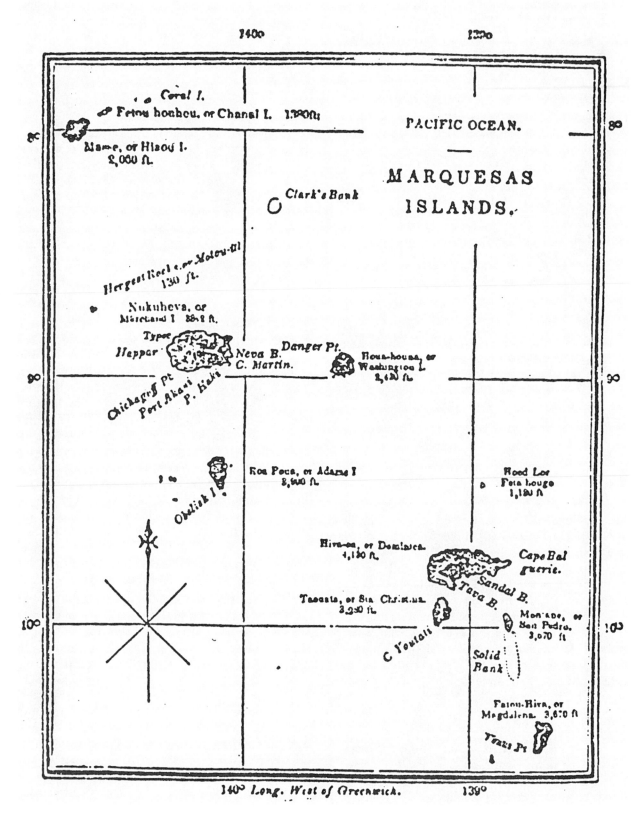

Map of the Marquesas Islands. Frontispiece from the first edition of *Typee*. THE GRANGER COLLECTION, NEW YORK

censorship alone account for them. As Melville revised the text in conformance with Wiley's demands, he took the opportunity to add to the text as well. Most notably, Melville added a "sequel" to the work. While the American publishers fretted over the book being read as irreligious and salacious, the English publishers worried about its authenticity. The latter concerns were largely pacified by the publication in the *Buffalo (New York) Commercial Advertiser* (on 1 July 1846) of the testimony of one Richard Tobias Greene, Melville's basis for the narrator's companion "Toby" in the book. Greene attested to the veracity of the author's account of their adventure, and a likely stunned Melville worked up Greene's account of his escape from the valley and included it as a postscript titled "The Story of Toby" in the American revised edition of *Typee.*

The story of the early editions of *Typee* does not end simply with the competing first English edition and revised U.S. edition. After Wiley and Putnam brought out the revised edition, Melville wrote to the English publishers recommending they bring out a second edition of their own based on the new American edition. Murray declined to adopt Melville's emendations and expurgations, but he did consent to reprint *Typee* with the "sequel." This brought to four the number of variant versions of *Typee* in print simultaneously.

After the publication of the English edition with "The Story of Toby," the text remained relatively stable throughout the rest of Melville's life. Subsequent printings in both the United States and England differed in ways attributable to plate damage, printer's style, and the like, but no substantive variants were introduced. At the end of Melville's life, however, Arthur Stedman sought permission from Melville to publish a new edition of *Typee.* Melville is known to have suggested two minor changes for the new edition, but as Stedman's edition came out in 1892, the year after Melville's death, later scholars would decline to consider it "authoritative." Along with reissues of the book from its English publishers around the same time, however, the 1892 edition sparked a revival of interest in *Typee* that carried its reputation into the twentieth century.

Since 1968 readers and scholars have had an excellent critical edition in the form of volume 1 of *The Writings of Herman Melville,* known as the Northwestern-Newberry edition. This version, titled *Typee: A Peep at Polynesian Life,* follows Sir Walter Greg's theory of copy text: the editors of the volume have tediously reconstructed the text they judge best represents Melville's final intention for the work (though discounting his final instructions to Stedman), and they have appropriately detailed the basis for each choice they have made among variants and listed all documentary evidence in appendices. Although the presence of a thorough, well-documented critical edition standardizes the work for modern readers, the critical text is not, technically speaking, Melville's text, but rather an informed synthesis of several texts. To discuss *Typee* as a book, then, one might legitimately ask the question, "which *Typee*?"

THE YOUNG AUTHOR AS SOCIAL CRITIC

Many of the issues that fueled *Typee*'s textual instability have remained central to its reputation. As noted earlier, Melville was pressured by his American publisher to revise and expurgate his book. Wiley chiefly objected, it seems, to the novice author's frank criticism of the Protestant missions in the South Sea Islands and his willingness to compare his own culture unfavorably to the "heathen" practices of the Typee people. The publisher's discomfort was not without justification: while *Typee* was greeted with delight by many early readers and reviewers, it was roundly savaged by the influential Protestant press in America. In addition to their umbrage at Melville's criticism of missionaries, religious critics blasted even the expurgated edition for depicting in a favorable light what a reviewer for the *Honolulu Friend* called "a tribe of filthy and debased savages" (1 June 1847).

Even as those offended by *Typee* railed against Melville's portrayal of the intersection of Western and Polynesian cultures, reform-minded readers praised the book along much the same lines. Writing in the *Harbinger* on 4 April 1846, the radical transcendentalist Charles A. Dana applauded Melville's veneration of Typee society, suggesting that here was a model Americans could apply in reforming their own industrial economy. On the same day, Margaret Fuller cautioned readers of the *New-York Daily Tribune* to consult Melville's descriptions of missionary activity in the islands before contributing money to such enterprises. Henry David Thoreau read *Typee* while in residence at Walden Pond, and he no doubt felt sympathy with Melville's perspective as a traveler who gains insight into his own society through his separation from it.

Melville's social critique in the book could be subtle and deftly nuanced, often injected after a seemingly innocuous humorous anecdote. An example of such layered criticism occurs at the end of chapter 14, following a scene Melville dubbed "Producing a Light à La Typee." In a slapstick depiction highly evocative of masturbation, the narrator describes the character Kory-Kory's labor to produce flame by straddling a stick and rubbing it vigorously with another. The action concluded, the narrator makes a characteristic comparison between Typee society and his own:

What a striking evidence does this operation furnish of the wide difference between the extreme of savage and civilized life. A gentleman of Typee can bring up a numerous family of children and give them all a highly respectable cannibal education, with infinitely less toil and anxiety than he expends in the simple process of striking a light; whilst a poor European artisan, who through the instrumentality of a lucifer [a match] performs the same operation in one second, is put to his wit's' end to provide for his starving offspring that food which the children of a Polynesian father, without troubling their parents, pluck from the branches of every tree around them. (P. 110)

On its surface, this is a simple and rather tame critique of Western industrial society. But the passage may also involve a subtle, broader criticism of Melville's culture. Through his hilarious description of Kory-Kory's efforts, Melville implies another "wide difference between the . . . savage and civilized life." After describing how Kory-Kory grasps a stick and "rubs its pointed end slowly up and down" (p. 109), the narrator seems to warm to the bawdy possibilities of his subject:

> At first Kory-Kory goes to work quite leisurely, but gradually quickens his pace, and waxing warm in the employment . . . the perspiration starting from every pore. As he approaches the climax of his effort, he pants and gasps for breath . . . with the violence of his exertions. (P. 109)

It seems unlikely that the strong hint of masturbation here is accidental. Throughout Melville's youth and adolescence, he would have read widely popular advice manuals such as the New England evangelist John Todd's 1835 volume, *The Student's Manual* (which Melville's older brother Gansevoort owned). Such books explicitly and repeatedly warned young men that masturbation was not only sinful but deeply corrosive of the very fabric of society. The general premise of these writers was that "self pollution" undermined a young man's willingness and fitness to be productive in an industrial economy. By setting up a playful equivalent between this most arduous and necessary task in Typee society and the most reviled and pernicious practice of masturbation, Melville coyly subverts the convictions of the arbiters of morality in his own society.

FROM SPINNING YARN TO THE ORIGIN OF A GENRE

In spite of its considerable impact as social critique, *Typee* was largely popular for the simple fact that it fed the public's appetite for dramatic accounts of adventure and exotic locales. Readers both in England and the United States were simply fascinated by Melville's tale: by the suspense, the remarkable characters, the relatively frank sexuality, and, perhaps above all, by Melville's considerable descriptive powers. Even critics who bitterly denounced the book often conceded that it was a spellbinding read.

It is likely Melville had some sense that the demand for such a book existed, as he appears to have written the book in the first place at the behest of friends and family. Certainly, Melville did not approach the experience from the outset as an author looking for material. Though he had published a couple of largely imitative short stories before shipping aboard the *Acushnet*, he did not keep a journal of his voyage or, as far as scholars can tell, keep any notes or other records of the trip. This fact has implications for how Melville composed *Typee*, including probably his reliance on materials from other published accounts of the Marquesas.

What Melville did have at his disposal was more than three years of rehearsing *Typee* as an oral text for various audiences. Of course, no direct records of Melville's oral text exist, but there is enough evidence to confirm that the author can be taken at his word when he writes in *Typee*'s preface, "the incidents recorded in the following pages have often served, when 'spun as a yarn,' not only to relieve the weariness of many a night-watch at sea, but to excite the warmest sympathies of the author's shipmates" (p. 1). No doubt the first draft of *Typee* was begun quite soon after the young castaway was picked up by the whaler that bore him away from Typee Valley, the *Lucy Ann*, and continued to develop

---

Quotations from those who knew him personally illustrate the extent to which Melville's reputation as a writer and a personality were shaped by his early autobiographical works, and they reveal how *Typee* was shaped by and persisted as oral text as Melville entertained friends and family with tales from the experiences he wrote about. Writing in the *New York Home Journal* in 1849, Nathaniel Parker Willis reported that "Herman Melville, with his cigar and his Spanish eyes, talks *Typee* and *Omoo*, just as you find the flow of his delightful mind on paper." Later, in *Hawthorne and His Circle* (1903), Julian Hawthorne recalled that Melville "normally . . . was not a man of noticeable appearance; but when the narrative inspiration was on him, he looked like all the things he was describing . . . savages, sea-captains, the lovely Fayaway in her canoe. . . ."

as Melville made his way home by way of his brief detention in Tahiti on mutiny charges; passage on another whaler, the *Charles and Henry;* a stint as a clerk in a dry-goods store in Honolulu; and, finally, a tour with the U.S. Navy on the man-of-war *United States.* This three-year succession of shifting audiences doubtless provided Melville ample opportunity to hone his story, experimenting with different strategies for inducing suspense, humor, and, of course, sexual arousal among his peers.

As his audiences became further removed from the facts, his opportunities for invention would have increased. The sailors aboard the *Lucy Ann* would certainly have demanded accounts of their new shipmate's escapades among the islanders, but they also would have known some facts, such as the relative brevity of his stay, that put limits on his creative freedom. On later ships, the storyteller may already have begun to exaggerate the time frame in order to increase suspense and lend greater credibility to his more "anthropological" observations. Clearly, though, of greatest interest to each of the all-male crews, cut off for long periods of time from female society, would have been sexual material, and, preferably, explicit sexual material.

Upon his return to New England, Melville's audience would change dramatically. Before returning to his family, the young adventurer visited the family who would become his in-laws: the home of Massachusetts Chief Justice Lemuel Shaw and Melville's future wife, the judge's daughter Elizabeth. In this new context, Melville would need to revise his stories to suit the taste of a more polite, mixed-gender audience. The racy sexual content, his shipboard mainstay, would have to be toned down. But rather than abandon it altogether, Melville found he could recast it as sly innuendo and excite "warm sympathies" in the parlor without crossing the line of good taste. At the same time, his role as an observer of social customs would take on greater importance as titillating details gave ground to cultural ones for the more literate audience.

As his stories shifted to meet the demands of new settings, Melville's "yarns" were evolving into a text that would come to define the "South Sea travel narrative" as a genre. Of course, accounts of the South Sea islands existed before Melville wrote *Typee.* In fact, Melville consulted several as he revised his manuscript. To put it simply, Melville did not have enough material from his four-week experience to sustain a book claiming a four-month time span, and his memory for details had to span a gap of three years. In order to fill the gaps, he turned to accounts of earlier visits to the Marquesas by explorers, missionaries, and military campaigns. More often than not, Melville incorporated information and descriptions from his sources without acknowledgment or attribution. When he does refer explicitly to his sources, it is typically to criticize the authors for their superficial encounters with and ill treatment of the indigenous people.

In some ways, Melville's use of sources points to what separated his narratives from the very works he borrowed from, and hence what set it apart as a new kind of travel narrative. The extant accounts of South Sea travels shared an implicit European colonial bias and a detached quasi-scientific focus. The opinions of Melville's most brutal critics, "that the islanders were simply filthy heathens," were opinions held by the writers Melville turned to in order to pad out his narrative. With his open criticism of these writers, Melville established a unique voice on the other side of a cultural divide. But perhaps more important, his perspective allowed him to portray the islanders as distinct, human characters—and these characters appealed to readers in a way the earlier superficial and judgmental accounts did not. Melville's uses of source material, both acknowledged and unacknowledged, signal his departure from their assumptions as well as a crucial and ultimately influential stylistic break. That is, Melville's blending of his own experience with the product of his imagination and details borrowed from other accounts of the islands results in an entirely new kind of book, something that flaunts a range of implicit rules of travel narratives, from their adherence to detached observation to their charge to be morally instructive along narrow, preconceived lines of Protestant orthodoxy. It was this novelty in approach that made the book so appealing to its readers and endured to inspire important later writers such as Jack London and Robert Louis Stevenson.

MELVILLE UNFOLDING

In 1851, while composing *Moby-Dick,* Melville wrote to his friend and colleague Nathaniel Hawthorne: "From my twenty-fifth year, I date my life. Three weeks have scarcely passed, at any time between then and now, that I have not unfolded within myself." His "twenty-fifth year" was the year Melville began writing *Typee.* And indeed, the habits and techniques he established at the beginning of his career remained part of his creative process as he continued to grow and unfold as a writer.

Not only did Melville continue to draw on firsthand observations and experiences throughout his writing career, but he also supplemented his own experience and imagination with extensive research and even occasional "borrowing" from other sources. In fact, after *Typee,* Melville would begin his writing projects by purchasing and borrowing vast numbers of books related to his subject. He would also turn time and again to the oral tradition of "spinning yarn" as a storytelling technique. Consider, for example, the "Town-Ho Story" in *Moby-Dick*. Melville sets up this famous encapsulated story as an entirely oral narrative, related in the book as told in a completely different time and context. The self-consciously constructed scene of storytelling hearkens back to the genesis of *Typee,* and given the author's enduring influence, it looks forward to such important later works as Joseph Conrad's *The Heart of Darkness* (1902). *Moby-Dick* also retains *Typee*'s careful blend of fact and fancy, appealing at once to the reader's wish to be informed about unfamiliar people and places and his desire to be carried away by adventure.

Melville later resented the popularity of his earlier books like *Typee* because they overshadowed what he considered his higher, more serious works. The public knew him as the "man who lived among the cannibals," but to Melville himself, that reputation competed with his desire to be known as serious writer. These competing views of Melville were reversed by twentieth-century scholars: long after his death, Melville achieved the reputation he sought in life, but then, paradoxically, the importance of his earliest books was largely overlooked. Since the late twentieth century, however, scholars have begun to recognize *Typee*'s crucial place in Melville's canon. We likely owe Melville's continued writing career to the popular success of his first book: if *Typee* had not sold, he would have had to look for a job. But more than that, writing and publishing *Typee* taught Melville how to write and publish books, and with its social criticism, cultural exploration, and probing psychology, Melville's first book launched the author's lifelong project of speaking Truth without obsessing over the facts.

See also "Bartleby, the Scrivener"; "Benito Cereno"; *The Confidence-Man;* Exploration and Discovery; *Moby-Dick;* Nautical Literature; Sexuality and the Body

BIBLIOGRAPHY

Primary Works
Melville, Herman. *Correspondence.* Edited by Lynn Horth. Vol. 14 of *The Writings of Herman Melville.* Evanston, Ill., and Chicago: Northwestern University Press and the Newberry Library, 1993.

Melville, Herman. *Typee: A Peep at Polynesian Life.* 1846. Vol. 1 of *The Writings of Herman Melville.* Edited by Harrison Hayford, Hershel Parker, and G. Thomas Tanselle. Evanston, Ill., and Chicago: Northwestern University Press and the Newberry Library, 1968.

Melville, Herman. *Typee: A Peep at Polynesian Life.* 1846. New York: Penguin, 1996. A paperback edition of the Northwestern-Newberry text. Page citations in article refer to this edition.

Secondary Works
Anderson, Charles Roberts. *Melville in the South Seas.* New York: Dover, 1966.

Bryant, John L. "The *Typee* Manuscript: A Reading Text." In Herman Melville, *Typee: A Peep At Polynesian Life,* edited by John L. Bryant, pp. 293–311. New York: Penguin, 1996.

Bryant, John L. "Versions of *Typee*: Typee, Chapter 14." In Herman Melville, *Tales, Poems, and Other Writings,* edited by John L. Bryant, pp. 14–25. New York: Modern Library, 2001. An experimental "fluid text" edition of chapter 14 of *Typee* with parallel passages transcribed and annotated from the extant fragment manuscript.

Herbert, T. Walter, Jr. *Marquesan Encounters: Melville and the Meaning of Civilization.* Cambridge, Mass.: Harvard University Press, 1980.

Higgins, Brian, and Hershel Parker, eds. *Herman Melville: The Contemporary Reviews.* Cambridge, U.K.: Cambridge University Press, 1995.

Leyda, Jay. *The Melville Log: A Documentary Life of Herman Melville, 1819–1891.* Vol. 1. New York: Harcourt, Brace, 1951.

Parker, Hershel. *Herman Melville: A Biography.* Vol. 1, *1819–1851.* Baltimore: Johns Hopkins University Press, 1996.

Samson, John. *White Lies: Melville's Narratives of Facts.* Ithaca, N.Y.: Cornell University Press, 1989.

Stern, Milton R., ed. *Critical Essays on Herman Melville's* Typee. Boston: G. K. Hall, 1982.

Patrick W. Bryant

UNCLE TOM'S CABIN

When *Uncle Tom's Cabin* burst on the American scene, first as a series of installments in the antislavery journal the *National Era* in 1851 and 1852 and then in 1852 as a two-volume edition published in Boston by John P. Jewett, many readers were overwhelmed by Harriet Beecher Stowe's powerful portrayal of the sufferings of slaves. Within the first eight weeks alone, sales of *Uncle Tom's Cabin* reached a whopping fifty thousand copies, and six months after that it had sold a quarter of a million volumes. On a scale hitherto unknown in America's publishing history, readers responded to Stowe's novel of sentiment, family, separation, and reunion.

UNCLE TOM'S STORY

In *Uncle Tom's Cabin* Harriet Beecher Stowe (1811–1896) was determined to make the case against slavery by using a series of tableaux that appealed to the emotions and to the Christian faith of her readers: "There is no arguing with *pictures,* and everybody is impressed by them, whether they mean to be or not," Stowe wrote in a March 1851 letter to Gamaliel Bailey, editor of the *National Era* (*Oxford Harriet Beecher Stowe Reader,* p. 66). The first of the pictures is of Uncle Tom and his family living as slaves on the Shelby plantation in Kentucky. Because of financial debts, Mr. Shelby decides to sell Uncle Tom along with the son of Mrs. Shelby's personal slave, Eliza, to a vulgar slave trader. Eliza learns of this plan, and in order to save her son Harry, she escapes with him, dramatically crosses the ice floes on the Ohio River, and finally makes her way to a Quaker settlement, where she meets up with her husband, George Harris, who has also run away from his master.

Uncle Tom, however, is put on a steamboat to be sold in New Orleans. On the boat he meets the five-year-old Evangeline, or "Little Eva," whom he saves from drowning. Evangeline convinces her father, Augustine St. Clare, to purchase Uncle Tom. At the New Orleanian St. Clare mansion, Uncle Tom is one of many slaves and serves as a coachman as well as a friend to Little Eva. Eva's aunt, Miss Ophelia, runs the household. In the course of the plot Evangeline becomes ill and eventually dies, but first she converts the recalcitrant slave girl Topsy through Christian love and, in doing so, converts Miss Ophelia to a more compassionate approach to racial difference. Also, in response to Evangeline's death, St. Clare decides to free Uncle Tom, but he is killed before he is able to do so. Eva's mother, an unsympathetic character throughout, cruelly sells Uncle Tom and the other slaves in a slave auction.

Uncle Tom and a beautiful and virtuous slave girl, Emmeline, are bought by the evil master Simon Legree. They travel down the Red River toward Legree's dilapidated Louisiana plantation, where the mulatto Cassy is Legree's mistress and slave. Uncle Tom tries to maintain his Christian beliefs, which waver under Legree's brutal treatment, but he ultimately triumphs. After Uncle Tom is severely beaten for helping another slave in the fields, Cassy comes to his aid. He tells her to escape with Emmeline. Cassy invents an elaborate ploy to trick Legree into thinking that his house is haunted, which so frightens Legree that she and Emmeline are

"Eliza Comes to Tell Uncle Tom that She is Sold, and that She is Running Away to Save Her Child." Illustration by Hammatt Billings for the first edition of *Uncle Tom's Cabin.* THE LIBRARY OF CONGRESS

able to escape. Legree demands that Uncle Tom disclose Cassy and Emmeline's whereabouts and forsake Christianity, but he refuses. He is beaten by Sambo and Quimbo, who eventually convert upon seeing the strength that Uncle Tom's Christian beliefs give him.

George Shelby, the son of the father who had sold Uncle Tom, searches for Uncle Tom, only to find out that he has died at the Legree plantation. On his way back to Kentucky, George Shelby runs into Cassy and Emmeline on a steamboat. The three then meet George Harris's long-lost sister, Madame de Thoux, and discover that Cassy is Eliza's mother. George Shelby returns to the Shelby plantation in Kentucky, where he frees the slaves. Cassy, Emmeline, and Madame de Thoux travel to Canada, where George Harris and Eliza live. Topsy becomes a missionary in Liberia. George Harris, Eliza, and Cassy eventually move to Liberia to found a colony for former slaves.

UNCLE TOM'S CABIN AND REFORM

The novel ends with slave families reunited, but Stowe's critique of "the peculiar institution" foregrounds the absolute vulnerability of the slave family. To be sure, the novel represents the unending labor of plantation slaves (with particular force as Tom journeys southward, eventually leading him to Legree's miserable plantation) and the physical punishments to which slaves were continually subjected, but the destruction of slave families was Stowe's special target. Chapter after chapter relentlessly repeats the charge that slavery's most baleful aspect was the separation of parents, especially mothers, and their children. This is Prue's story, Topsy's, Emmeline's, Eliza's, and Cassy's. The presence of light-skinned blacks in *Uncle Tom's Cabin* makes the point—though in a less-graphic way than in Lydia Maria Child's *Romance of the Republic* (1867) or Harriet Jacobs's *Incidents in the Life of a Slave Girl* (1861)—that slave women, who were raped by their white masters, were then forced to witness their children being sold from them. The devastation of the slave family is at once endless and economically advantageous to the master. The cycle begins with rape and ends with money, making black motherhood the site of avarice and pain, both of which could not have been more antithetical to the antebellum conceit of maternity as the apotheosis of female identity and the source of love and virtue.

That the biological family was one of the central institutions of antebellum American society, and the mother at its affective helm, make Stowe's polemic particularly effective. An indictment of slavery on the grounds of its pernicious domestic effects rather than a critique centered more on unfair labor practices (that might make northerners squirm by virtue of their own problems with labor) was one with which readers sympathized more easily. Indeed, Stowe's admonition to her readers to "see, then, to your sympathies in these matters" (p. 624), is based on her belief that *Uncle Tom's Cabin* had the potential to enable individuals to "see to it that *they feel right*" (p. 624) by activating their sympathies; by making equivalent the feelings that govern slaves as they face the annihilation of family ties and the feelings of those who are not slaves as they endure the pain of family wreckage.

Two events, one deeply personal and the other overtly political, converged to propel Stowe to write *Uncle Tom's Cabin*. The first was the death from cholera of her very young son Charley on 26 July 1849, and the second was the passage of the Compromise of 1850. The Fugitive Slave Law, which required that northerners cooperate in the capture of runaway slaves and suffer the legal consequences of noncompliance, was for many, including Stowe, the most outrageous part of the compromise in that it forced citizens of the North to become partners in slavery. That Stowe would even think to enter into this most divisive and important debate has much to do with the achievements and expectations of her family. Stowe was the daughter of Lyman Beecher (1775–1863), the wife of Calvin Stowe (1802–1886), and the sister of Henry Ward Beecher (1813–1887). Each of these three men was a New England minister, famous for religious activism (Lyman was one of the founders of Oberlin College; Calvin held professorships at Oberlin, Bowdoin, and Andover and also wrote religious treatises) and social activism (Henry was one of the most outspoken antislavery ministers in his Brooklyn church). The women in Beecher's family were similarly motivated. Catharine Beecher (1800–1878), Harriet's older sister, established Hartford Female Seminary and wrote several books, including *A Treatise on Domestic Economy* (1842), and Isabella Beecher Hooker (1822–1907), Stowe's half sister, was a women's rights advocate with close ties to Elizabeth Cady Stanton and Susan B. Anthony.

STOWE'S FICTIONAL FAMILIES

Uncle Tom's Cabin is, unsurprisingly, steeped in her family's commitment to the politically progressive possibilities of Christianity as well as what the historian Carroll Smith-Rosenberg has identified as "the female world of love and ritual" (p. 53). The chapter titled "The Quaker Settlement" brings together these two conceptual threads and offers a model of an ideal society as imaged by an ideal family. Rachel Halliday, whose "face and form . . . made 'mother' seem the most natural word in the world" (p. 216), is at the head of in an expansive domestic unit that gives shelter to fugitive slaves in the name of preserving and uniting their broken families. It is here that Eliza and Henry find comfort, and it is here that George, the husband and father, is reunited with them. Rachel's home represents a space of "motherly loving kindness" (p. 215), where Christian doctrine and Christian practice come together. Rachel's love extends the qualities of personhood to virtually every aspect of her world, whether it is the peaches that respond to her "gentle whispers" (p. 218) or the knives and forks with their "social clatter" (p. 223) or her rocking chair "whose wide arms breathed hospitable invitation" (p. 214). Most important, of course, are the fugitive slaves whose personhood she recognizes and works to protect. The Quaker settlement, in other words, serves as the antidote to and antithesis of families in bondage, where slavery presides and results in their nonrecognition as persons (legally speaking, they are things to be bought and sold) and the concomitant decimation of family ties. Over and again, whether it is in the opening scenes at the Shelby plantation or the middle passages that take place in Marie and Augustine St. Clare's household or the final scenes with Simon Legree, the reader witnesses how a slave owner's best intentions are no match for the economic incentives of slavery. Sympathy, or "feeling right," Stowe maintains, is simply impossible under a legalized regime that regards persons as things, that produces and profits from children like Topsy, who, when asked who her mother was, replies "never had none" (p. 355) and, when asked where she was born, answers "never was born!" (p. 355). For Stowe, slavery's greatest evil is the abrogation of consanguineous relations—that is, the bonds of blood.

UNCLE TOM'S CABIN AND RACE

How is it, one might wonder, that Stowe's antislavery novel generated anything other than, on the one hand, unanimous praise from antislavery readers who applauded its critique of the peculiar institution and, on the other hand, outrage from those on the proslavery side who accused the novel (and Stowe) of everything from a deliberate misrepresentation of the facts to an unfeminine entrance into the male world of politics? The fact is that from the moment of its publication up through the twenty-first century, some of the most powerful readings and critiques of *Uncle Tom's Cabin* have been conducted by African American writers, from Frederick Douglass and Martin Delany to James Baldwin and Richard Wright, who have been deeply troubled by several aspects of the novel that appear to undermine Stowe's progressive antislavery message. That one can find a thoroughgoing record of American racist thought by studying the afterlife of Stowe's novel—that is to say, the plays, minstrel shows, children's books, dolls, and household wares it inspired—suggests that *Uncle Tom's Cabin* perhaps not only invites these kinds of racist appropriations but that this antislavery novel is itself racist. For example, as appealing and idyllic as the Halliday home is, George, Harry, and Eliza can only be temporary residents of it. Stowe is unable to imagine a permanent domestic space in the United States where the relationships between black and white characters are not defined according to the logic of slavery. As a result, virtually every black character must emigrate from the United States. Unlike Tom, who goes to heaven, they travel first to Canada and then, like Topsy, to their final destination, Africa, and more specifically, Liberia.

Perhaps Douglass, despite being a staunch supporter of Stowe, put it best when he reminded her in a letter, "The truth is, dear madam, we are *here,* and here we are likely to remain" (Levine, p. 535). Indeed, Stowe's claim, tentative though it is, that Liberia might just be the answer to the "problem" of America's emancipated slave population is only one among several difficulties that readers have had with the novel. A more thorough list includes the use of racial stereotypes; the aesthetic, intellectual, and psychological distinctions made between full black characters as opposed to quadroons, mulattos, and octoroons; and the way Stowe's representation of "feeling right" does virtually nothing to bring about the end of the institution of slavery. Moreover, what is a reader to think of a moment such as the one when Tom finds himself purchased by Augustine St. Clare, heading farther away from his wife, Chloe, and their children, and responds to his new household with "an air of calm, still enjoyment" because "the negro, it must be remembered, is an exotic of the most gorgeous and superb countries of the world, and he has, deep in his heart, a passion for all that is splendid, rich, and fanciful" (p. 253)? Or how is one to make sense of the novel's "Concluding Remarks," in which Stowe both makes an argument for why freed blacks, once educated, ought to settle in Liberia and then goes on to record the success stories of some of Cincinnati's emancipated slaves, but not without also identifying them as "full black" or "three-fourths black"? What is the point of conveying the relative amounts of black and white blood unless it is evidence that Stowe's antislavery polemic is structured by racist foundations?

This last question can be convincingly answered by two very different, though valid, interpretations. The first is to argue that despite Stowe's objections to slavery, she nevertheless shares many of the racist assumptions of her culture, not least of which is the determining power of consanguinity. The relative proportions of black and white remain essential to her understanding of character, even in the case of the former slaves in Cincinnati, and therefore limit the progressive force of her antislavery polemic. The second is to read Stowe's insistence on the consanguineous makeup of blacks at the conclusion of the novel as evidence of her commitment to representing the biological origins of particular blacks. She is, quite simply, unwilling to erase the fact of black parentage because to do so would be to make her complicit in the very logic of the institution she is critiquing. After all, the slave economy functions by separating parents from children, by creating characters like Topsy, who think they have been "made," not born. That such consanguineous profiling so easily maps onto racist modes of identifying blacks is what makes Stowe's racial politics so difficult to assess.

UNCLE TOM'S CABIN AND ABOLITIONISM

In part, the interpretive difficulty this novel has encountered stems from a critical predisposition that wants to see Stowe as either completely progressive or utterly benighted rather than accepting her outlook as lying somewhere in between. Indeed, at the moment of its publication, Stowe's novel elicited a range of responses, which continue to get played out in contemporary critical analyses. The debate about Stowe and race has been polarized between those who insist that despite her essentialist view of African Americans, the case against slavery in *Uncle Tom's Cabin* was nevertheless influential, radical, and powerful: so influential that scenes from the novel were invoked in the U.S. Senate by no less a figure than the distinguished abolitionist Charles Sumner of Massachusetts; so radical that the novel was not permitted to enter southern states, and if it did, it was burned; so powerful that legend has it that when Stowe met President Abraham Lincoln, he greeted her with the words, "So you're the little woman that wrote the book that made this great war." On the other side of the political aisle, antebellum critics of Stowe's novel blasted her for her allegedly unladylike intervention into public discourse, for her unfair assault on southern life, and for her mendacious account of the peculiar institution. Some of the most scathing reviews of *Uncle Tom's Cabin* and *A Key to Uncle Tom's Cabin* (Stowe's fascinating 1853 defense of the novel's authenticity) appeared in the *Southern Literary Messenger* and the *Southern Quarterly Review* and made the rather paradoxical claim that Stowe's novel was "a miserable tissue of falsehoods and abominations" (Thompson, p. 58), but even if it were true, the novel helped make the case for slavery. So writes Nehemiah Adams, in his detestable proslavery allegory, *The Sable Cloud* (1861), when Mr. North asks, "What made Uncle Tom the paragon of perfection?" and the narrator replies, "SLAVERY MADE UNCLE TOM. Had it not been for slavery, he would have been a savage in Africa, a brutish slave to his fetishes" (p. 135). Here Adams subverts the novel's point that slavery and Christianity are mutually exclusive and appropriates the Christian qualities of Uncle Tom as evidence of Stowe's covert defense of slavery.

The notion that *Uncle Tom's Cabin* could be taken as a vindication of slavery might strike one as a strained counter-reading of the novel and certainly of its antislavery intentions, but the fact is that Stowe's text has produced some rather strange bedfellows. For very different reasons, of course, both apologists for slavery and abolitionist activists, particularly African American writers, found themselves deeply offended by the novel. Martin Delany, author of *Blake; or, The Huts of America* (1859–1862), not only criticized Stowe for her seeming endorsement of the colonizationist argument but then took Douglass to task for not being critical enough of Stowe. He also found fault with her unacknowledged use of the narratives of fugitive slaves, especially Josiah Henson's and Henry Bibb's (she would later cite Henson's 1849 autobiography, *The Life of Josiah Henson*, as one of the sources for Uncle Tom in *A Key to Uncle Tom's Cabin*), even going so far as to suggest that Stowe and her publisher share the profits of the novel with the fugitive slaves upon whose stories she had, in the words of Delany, "draughted largely" (p. 231).

IS UNCLE TOM AN UNCLE TOM?

Without a doubt, the character of Uncle Tom has been a special point of contention. He is a grown man who is consistently described as feminine and childlike, whether in the scene with Eva, where the narrator writes about their reading of the Bible, "she and her simple friend, the old child and the young one, felt just alike about it" (p. 380), or when "Tom's voice choked, and the tears ran down his cheeks" (p. 308) after talking with St. Clare about living a more Christian life. He loves the various masters who own him even when, in the case of Mr. Shelby, he is sold away from his family. Upon finding himself in the St. Clare mansion, his very soul seems to expand as he luxuriates in the Orientalism of their Louisiana household:

> The negro, it must be remembered, is an exotic of the most gorgeous and superb countries of the world, and he has, deep in his heart, a passion for all that is splendid, rich, and fanciful; a passion which, rudely indulged by an untrained taste,

draws on them the ridicule of the colder and more correct white (P. 253).

A passage like this, with its essentialist view of racial characteristics (both black and white), confirms the historian George Frederickson's description of Stowe as a romantic racialist influenced by the ethnological works of Alexander Kinmont and Francis Lieber, with which she was familiar: "Although romantic racialists acknowledged that blacks were different from whites and probably always would be, they projected an image of the Negro that could be construed as flattering or laudatory in the context of some currently accepted ideals of human behavior and sensibility" (p. 433). The context for Stowe's novel is a nineteenth-century sentimental sensibility—of the sort found in Phoebe Pyncheon in Nathaniel Hawthorne's *The House of the Seven Gables* (1851) or Ellen Montgomery in Susan Warner's *The Wide, Wide World* (1850)—in which the content of one's character is measured and validated by virtue of a childlike delight in and feminine sensitivity to one's environment. Add to these qualities Christian forbearance and, more literally, a Christlike ability to forgive one's tormentors (when Tom is being beaten by Simon Legree, Sambo, and Quimbo, he exclaims, "I loves every creatur', everywhar!" [p. 590]) and one has the ideal character that every nineteenth-century reader should strive to become.

Or not. Tom, after all, is not a youthful white sentimental heroine but a full black adult male slave who has been cruelly separated from his wife and children. Indeed, Tom's refusal to defend himself against his certain death at the hands of Legree and company has drawn critical fire. In a March 1852 piece that appeared in *The Liberator*, William Lloyd Garrison blasted Stowe for suggesting that slaves should suffer in Christian silence:

> Is there one law of submission and non-resistance for the black man, and another law of rebellion and conflict for the white man? When it is the whites who are trodden in the dust, does Christ justify them in taking up arms to vindicate their rights? And when it is the blacks who are thus treated, does Christ require them to be patient, harmless, long-suffering, and forgiving? And are there two Christs? (Nelson, pp. 239–240)

Garrison's pointed critique, as well as the arguments made by Douglass and Delany, has been taken up by twentieth-century authors, perhaps most famously by James Baldwin, whose collection of short stories, *Uncle Tom's Children* (1936), includes an epigraph with words that celebrate the end of Uncle Tom as an ideal of (black) nonresistance, "Uncle Tom is dead!" Ishmael Reed's *Flight to Canada* (1976) provides another example of an African American writer at once recognizing the powerful and, in his reading, invidious effects of Stowe's novel and the need to subvert authority. He uses the issue of Stowe's appropriation of Henson's narrative and turns the tables on her by asserting that the damage done by *Uncle Tom's Cabin* devolves not upon black readers and writers, trapped in Stowe's stereotypes, but upon its author: "When you take a man's story, a story that doesn't belong to you, that story will get you" (p. 9). The demise of the character of Uncle Tom (as well as the creator of the character) and the passivity for which he stands has often been viewed by African American writers as a key to their own literary and psychic liberation.

FEELING RIGHT (AND WRONG)

Yet Tom's death occurs in a chapter titled "The Victory." From another point of view, one that has been articulated most influentially by the feminist critic Jane Tompkins, the title character's reenactment of the crucifixion scene makes equivalent the sufferings of Tom and Jesus. Stowe, in this reading, is making the point that each time a slave is abused and killed, the death of Christ is being replayed. To end this pain, which is nothing less than the continued suffering of Christ, slavery must end. Tompkins urges readers to analyze *Uncle Tom's Cabin* from the perspective of a mid-nineteenth-century culture steeped in Christian ideology and knowledge of the Bible, in which to suffer as Tom does is to align oneself with God. To forgive is not to be weak; to submit is not to be docile. Such an argument also applies to the character of Eva, whose death scene, in the words of the literary critic Ann Douglas, is a distillation of how the novel's "political sense [is] obfuscated or gone rancid" (p. 307). According to Douglas, Eva's death releases tears, and lots of them, among the characters surrounding her as well as in some readers but does nothing to effect the end of slavery in the novel. In fact, Augustine never gets around to signing Tom's manumission papers, even though he intends to do so.

Is that not precisely the point, though? "Feeling right" only takes one so far. Doing right comes next. Readers who experience Stowe's novel cathartically only to do nothing with those feelings, or what she elsewhere refers to as that "atmosphere of sympathetic influence [that] encircles every human being" (p. 624), have not gotten the message. Indeed, their political sense has "gone rancid," and one can witness what that looks like by reading misappropriations of Stowe's call for sympathy. Many proslavery novels, such as Mary Eastman's *Aunt Phillis's Cabin; or, Southern Life as It Is* (1852) and Caroline Lee Hentz's *The Planter's Northern Bride* (1854)—to name just

two of the many "anti-Tom novels" (a term used by Thomas Gossett to describe the tremendous outpouring of novels specifically written as attacks on Stowe's) published in the 1850s—claimed that sympathy for slaves required their enslavement precisely because of their childlike and dependent nature. It was in response to such misreadings of her novel that Stowe, within just one year of its publication, wrote *A Key to Uncle Tom's Cabin*, in which she argued not only for the veracity of her representations of slavery but, more forcefully, linked sympathy with action. Because "to *mean* well is not enough" (p. 217), she urges Christians to become activists and break the law "not in form, but in fact . . . [and] to seek the ENTIRE ABOLITION OF SLAVERY" (p. 250). *A Key to Uncle Tom's Cabin* and, later, Stowe's novel *Dred: A Tale of the Great Dismal Swamp* (1856) represent Stowe's responses to proslavery critics who appropriated her call for sympathy and antislavery critics who chided her for her allegedly naive faith in "feeling right."

KEYS TO *UNCLE TOM'S CABIN*

An understanding of *Uncle Tom's Cabin* and, more precisely, Stowe's attitudes about race must take into account not only antebellum racial politics but also the many rewritings and critiques of the novel that appeared after its publication, ranging from the anti-Tom novels; to the ethnographic texts such as Adams's *A South-Side View of Slavery* (1854) and C. G. Parsons's *An Inside View of Slavery* (1855), which aimed to present readers with firsthand accounts of slavery that would either refute or confirm Stowe's fiction; to the twentieth-century responses such as James Baldwin's famous essay "Everybody's Protest Novel" (1949) and Robert Alexander's *"I Ain't Yo' Uncle": The New Jack Revisionist Uncle Tom's Cabin* (1992). It is impossible to read *Uncle Tom's Cabin* without having been exposed to scenes, characters, or interpretations of the novel before one even opens the first page. Just as most twentieth-first-century readers who have never read a word of Herman Melville come to *Moby-Dick* (1851) knowing that Captain Ahab is out to kill a white whale or have seen a film adaptation of the novel, those same readers have heard of Stowe's text, maybe even watched a Hollywood version of it, and are aware that it is a scathing indictment to call a black person an "Uncle Tom." And yet if one goes back to the novel, readers may find evidence of an Uncle Tom who is not docile, who does not play by the rules. One example can be found when a fellow slave, Lucy, is having difficulty picking enough cotton to satisfy Legree's minions, and Tom puts cotton from his sack into hers, knowing full well that this is a rebellious act that will lead to trouble. A subversive act with greater consequences is Tom's decision to assist in Cassy's escape from Legree's plantation. Although Tom is unwilling to effect his own escape, he instructs Cassy to take herself and Emmeline away: "If ye only could get away from here,—if the thing was possible,—I'd 'vise ye and Emmeline to do it" (p. 562). Clearly, this Uncle Tom is different from the Uncle Toms who have succeeded him, and yet he is the origin from which the others have developed. Like the many contexts (biographical, cultural, and literary) that were foundational to the production of *Uncle Tom's Cabin,* readers of the novel come to it from within a particular cultural context that is equally foundational to their consumption of her text, a consumption that shows no signs of abating.

See also Abolitionist Writing; *Blake;* Civil War; Domestic Fiction; Ethnology; Female Authorship; Proslavery Writing; Quakers; Reform; Sentimentalism; Slavery

BIBLIOGRAPHY

Primary Works

Adams, Nehemiah. *The Sable Cloud: A Southern Tale, with Northern Comments.* 1861. Westport, Conn.: Negro Universities Press, 1970.

Delany, Martin Robison. *Martin R. Delany: A Documentary Reader.* Edited by Robert S. Levine. Chapel Hill: University of North Carolina Press, 2003.

Nelson, Truman, ed. *Documents of Upheaval: Selections from William Lloyd Garrison's the "Liberator," 1831–1865.* New York: Hill and Wang, 1966.

Stowe, Harriet Beecher. *A Key to Uncle Tom's Cabin: Presenting the Original Facts and Documents upon Which the Story Is Founded. Together with Corroborative Statements Verifying the Truth of the Work.* Boston: John P. Jewett, 1853.

Stowe, Harriet Beecher. *The Oxford Harriet Beecher Stowe Reader.* Edited and with an introduction by Joan D. Hedrick. New York: Oxford University Press, 1999.

Stowe, Harriet Beecher. *Uncle Tom's Cabin; or, Life among the Lowly.* 1852. Edited with an introduction by Ann Douglas. New York: Penguin, 1981.

Thompson, John R. Editorial. *Southern Literary Messenger* (January 1853): 57–58.

Secondary Works

Alexander, Robert. *I Ain't Yo' Uncle: The New Jack Revisionist "Uncle Tom's Cabin."* 1992. In *Colored Contradictions: An Anthology of Contemporary African-American Plays,* edited by Harry J. Elam Jr. and Robert Alexander. New York: Plume, 1996.

Baldwin, James. "Everybody's Protest Novel." 1949. In *Uncle Tom's Cabin: Authoritative Text, Backgrounds and Contexts, Criticism,* edited by Elizabeth Ammons pp. 495–501. New York: Norton, 1994.

Brown, Gillian. *Domestic Individualism: Imagining Self in Nineteenth-Century America.* Berkeley: University of California Press, 1990.

Douglas, Ann. *The Feminization of American Culture.* New York: Avon, 1977.

Fisher, Philip. *Hard Facts: Setting and Form in the American Novel.* New York: Oxford University Press, 1985.

Frederickson, George M. "Uncle Tom and the Anglo-Saxons: Romantic Racialism in the North." In *Uncle Tom's Cabin: Authoritative Text, Backgrounds and Contexts, Criticism,* edited by Elizabeth Ammons, pp. 429–438. New York: Norton, 1994.

Gossett, Thomas F. *Uncle Tom's Cabin and American Culture.* Dallas, Tex.: Southern Methodist University Press, 1985.

Hedrick, Joan D. *Harriet Beecher Stowe: A Life.* New York: Oxford University Press, 1994.

Levine, Robert S. "*Uncle Tom's Cabin* in *Frederick Douglass' Paper:* An Analysis of Reception." In *Uncle Tom's Cabin: Authoritative Text, Backgrounds and Contexts, Criticism,* edited by Elizabeth Ammons, pp. 523–542. New York: Norton, 1994.

Railton, Stephen, director. *Uncle Tom's Cabin* and American Culture: A Multi-Media Archive. http://www.iath.virginia.edu/utc.

Reed, Ishmael. *Flight to Canada.* New York: Random House, 1976.

Smith-Rosenberg, Carroll. *Disorderly Conduct: Visions of Gender in Victorian America.* New York: Oxford University Press, 1985.

Stowe, Charles Edward. *Harriet Beecher Stowe: The Story of Her Life.* Boston: Houghton Mifflin, 1911.

Sundquist, Eric J., ed. *New Essays on "Uncle Tom's Cabin."* Cambridge, U.K.: Cambridge University Press, 1986.

Tompkins, Jane. *Sensational Designs: The Cultural Work of American Fiction, 1790–1860.* New York: Oxford University Press, 1985.

Weinstein, Cindy. *Family, Kinship, and Sympathy in Nineteenth-Century American Literature.* Cambridge, U.K.: Cambridge University Press, 2004.

Weinstein, Cindy, ed. *The Cambridge Companion to Harriet Beecher Stowe.* Cambridge, U.K.: Cambridge University Press, 2004.

Cindy Weinstein

UNDERGROUND RAILROAD

The Underground Railroad remains a central historical topic in both academic and popular knowledge. However, the idea of the Underground Railroad has become steeped in mythology, which obscures the historically accurate understanding of slavery, mainly in relation to escape as one form of rebellion against slavery. In part this is due to the necessary obscuration of the workings of the Underground Railroad during the antebellum period in published materials such as slave narratives. The disjunction between the facts of the Underground Railroad and the mythology built up around it deserve close study, as they are key to understanding slavery and freedom in America.

HISTORY OF THE UNDERGROUND RAILROAD

The Underground Railroad was comprised of a network of people and places that assisted fugitive slaves with their escape from slavery. While the Underground Railroad was not a formalized nationwide system, as sometimes represented, it was also not a haphazard set of paths that slaves would passively follow. Both descriptions defy the loosely constructed networks that allowed escaping slaves to connect with those who desired to assist the fugitives in their quest for freedom. The Underground Railroad provided numerous stations where runaways could receive shelter, food, money, clothes, advice, and transportation to the next safe haven. John Michael Vlach suggests

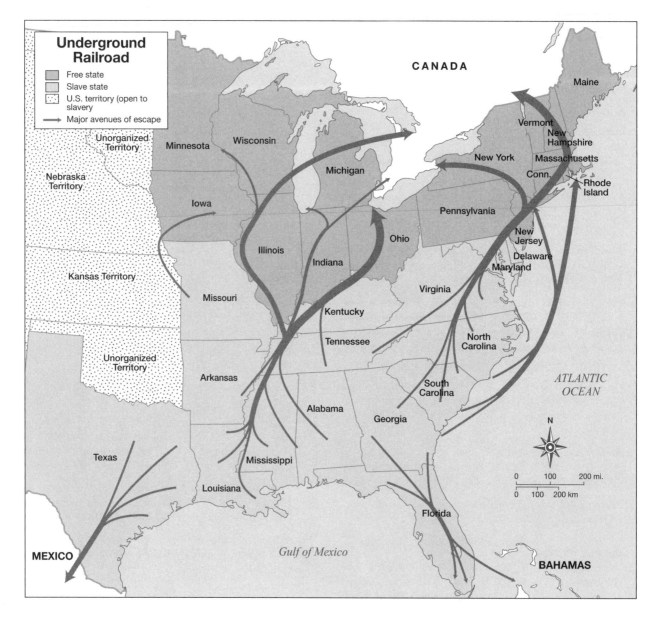

that slaves were not hidden in elaborate tunnels and secret hiding places as popular imagination suggests but were instead given places within the homes and barns of those who helped them progress along the escape route. Runaways were also often housed within the African American communities of cities and transported by black guides whom runaways tended to trust.

Runaways traveled the route to freedom by various means, including by boat, foot, rail, or horse. Escapees used the most available, convenient, safe, and expedient means of transportation during their journey. As James Horton points out, the actual number of slaves that escaped is very difficult to enumerate, although "some estimates climb to a hundred thousand or more in the decades before the Civil War" (p. 176). Slaves chose a number of destinations for their journey, including maroon colonies (a community of fugitive slaves, often hidden in swamps and forests), Canada, Mexico, Britain, and the free states. The final destination was often based on contemporary political situations, the initial location of the slave, and the familiarity of the slave with the area that he or she would have to journey through. In the earlier antebellum period, northern cities such as Boston or Cincinnati were havens to escaped blacks; in the later period, when the north was bound by the Fugitive Slave Law of 1850 to return runaways, escapees began to move to Canada for greater safety. In fact, the Fugitive Slave Law, which ordered all citizens to assist in the recapture of fugitive slaves, forced participants in the Underground Railroad to shift tactics, particularly as it destroyed the safety of fugitives in northern communities. The law's passage spurred large communities of northern African American fugitives to leave for Canada for fear of recapture. Gary Collison, in *Shadrach Minkins,* notes that, "In the first month after the law took effect an estimated 2,000 blacks left the North for Canada" (p. 76).

The term "Underground Railroad" is not one that can be historically validated. There are a number of possible sources for the coinage, but all situate the origins of the word in the 1830s. One story suggests that when fugitive slave Tice David escaped from Kentucky to Sandusky, Ohio, a slave catcher commented that he "must have gone off on an underground railroad" (Blight, p. 3). Another story attributes the term to a tortured fugitive slave who revealed he was heading to where "the railroad ran underground all the way to Boston" (Blight, p. 3). Certainly by 1852 when Harriet Beecher Stowe (1811–1896) writes that the "gals' been carried on the underground line," the term Underground Railroad was in play culturally (Stowe, p. 61).

The system took on the terminology of the railroad in the antebellum period, where those aiding the slaves were "conductors" and the escapees were "packages" or "passengers." It was this period, as well, that gave weight to the mythologized version of the Underground Railroad that depended on the heroic and moral white aiding the confused and passive escaping slave. However, new research rightly indicates that this mythologized version of the Underground Railroad incorrectly portrays the fugitive. In reality, African Americans were full and active participants. One such participant was the African American Lewis Hayden (1811–1889), who led two dramatic fights to shield escaped slaves traveling through Boston. In 1850 he protected escaping slaves William and Ellen Craft from slave catchers by putting gunpowder under his front porch and threatening to blow up the entire building should the slave catchers enter his home to retrieve the Crafts. He also led the armed group that attacked the Boston Courthouse in 1851 to successfully rescue and free fugitive slave Shadrach Minkins. Those who chose to run were generally young men traveling alone, and those involved with aiding the escapees were at times fellow African Americans, free and fugitive, as well as whites (Vlach, p. 99).

The runaways and conductors who participated in the Underground Railroad did so at a cost. For the runaways, recapture, abuse, and death were not unlikely. For conductors, arrest and fines were possible. For example, Thomas Garrett (1789–1871), a white abolitionist and Underground Railroad conductor, was fined a majority of his wealth in 1848 for assisting runaways. There are numerous additional examples of those who risked fines, imprisonment, abuse, and death working with the Underground Railroad.

Some of the other notable conductors of the railroad were Levi Coffin (in Newport, Indiana), Frederick Douglass (in Rochester, New York), William Still (in Philadelphia, Pennsylvania), and Reverend John Rankin (in Ripley, Ohio). The white men involved with the Underground Railroad, such as Garrett and Rankin, tended to be more outspoken about their activities than African Americans, such as Still, as they were assured a more secure social protection by virtue of race. Much of what is known about the Underground Railroad and its conductors is due to the meticulous records kept by William Still (1821–1902), an African American conductor in Philadelphia, published as *The Underground Railroad* (1872), and the white Indianan conductor Levi Coffin (1798–1877), who published his *Reminiscences* in 1876. Both books provide crucial information on the Underground Railroad, including details of runaways, conductors, passage routes, and safe houses. One may

Fugitive Slaves Escape from the Eastern Shore of Maryland. Wood engraving from William Still's *The Underground Railroad,* 1872. The son of a former slave, Still assisted fugitive slaves on their journey to Canada and collected their stories in what became an important contribution to antislavery literature. THE LIBRARY OF CONGRESS

argue that the most famous conductor is Harriet Tubman (c. 1820–1913). Her own 1849 escape from slavery in Maryland led her to Wilmington, Delaware. Working with Garrett, Still, and others, Tubman, often referred to as "Moses," made almost twenty trips to the South and rescued more than two hundred slaves.

LITERARY TREATMENTS OF THE UNDERGROUND RAILROAD

Various slave narratives and fictionalized accounts of slavery in the antebellum period reference the Underground Railroad in some manner. The representations tend to follow two separate approaches. Texts written by fugitives often obscured the details of escape to protect themselves, those who assisted their escape, and the escape mechanism in hopes that others might find the same path to freedom. White-authored texts, such as Stowe's *Uncle Tom's Cabin,* provided far more detail about the Underground Railroad and often focused extensively on white participation and responsibility. In part this is due to the autobiographical nature of narratives and the fictionalization of white-

authored novels. But other factors also contributed to the difference.

Fugitive slave narratives seem the likely place to look for references to the Underground Railroad, and a number of authors do indeed discuss the impact of the Underground Railroad on their journey from slavery to freedom. However, many escapees, such as Frederick Douglass (1818–1895) choose to obscure the details of their escape to protect those involved and to allow other runaways to use the same escape path and support. Those that provide a few more details about their escape reveal that the escapee formulated and implemented the great portion of the escape, with some support from the loosely configured Underground Railroad along the way. For example, William Wells Brown (c. 1814–1884) notes that his escape plot and the majority of his journey was made on his own, and although he did receive help from whites who might peripherally belong to the Underground Railroad, he reveals that he was not following a formalized Underground Railroad.

Harriet Jacobs's (1813–1897) *Incidents in the Life of a Slave Girl* (1861) follows a strategy of depicting the Underground Railroad typical of many slave narratives written in the antebellum period. Jacobs, writing pseudonymously as Linda Brent, notes, "I was to escape in a vessel; but I forbear to mention any further particulars" (p. 151). As Jean Fagan Yellin's biography *Harriet Jacobs: A Life* (2004) points out, Jacobs's obscuration "kept the details of Jacobs's escape a mystery—as she wished" (p.63). While Jacobs chose to protect those who aided her on her trip to the North, she does critique their participation, stating that some participants' assistance is made for financial motivations. Her initial boat trip

> accommodation had been purchased at a price that would pay for a voyage to England. But when one proposes to go to fine old England, they stop to calculate whether they can afford the cost of the pleasure; while in making a bargain to escape from slavery, the trembling victim is ready to say, 'take all I have, only don't betray me!' (P. 152)

Jacobs's comment serves to remind those who might view the conductors as heroes that there were other factors motivating some participants. It also leads the reader to focus on the heroism of the escaping slave, not the conductor.

The desire to mask the means of escape while still encouraging the activism of whites is made clear in a variety of texts written by Douglass. His treatment of the Underground Railroad pre- and post-abolition reveals much about the political conditions and the position of fugitives in America. Douglass published three versions of his autobiography during his life. The first two published versions of his life story, written before slavery is dissolved, reveal few details of his escape, while his 1881 *Life and Times of Frederick Douglass* gives the details of his escape.

Douglass emphasizes in the *Narrative of the Life of Frederick Douglass* (1845) that it is his "intention not to state all the facts connected with the transaction" He goes on to note that there are two reasons for his refusal:

> First, were I to give a minute statement of all the facts, it is not only possible, but quite probable, that others would thereby be involved in the most embarrassing difficulties. Secondly, such a statement would most undoubtedly induce greater vigilance on the part of slaveholders than has existed heretofore among them; which would, of course, be the means of guarding a door whereby some dear brother bondman might escape his galling chains. (P. 84)

He goes on to state that he has "never approved of the very public manner in which some of our western friends have conducted what they call the underground railroad, but which, I think, by their open declarations, has been made most emphatically the upperground railroad" (p. 85).

In *My Bondage and My Freedom* (1855) Douglass reiterates the problems of revealing the methods of escape:

> The practice of publishing every new invention by which a slave is known to have escaped from slavery, has neither wisdom nor necessity to sustain it. Had not Henry Box Brown and his friends attracted slaveholding attention to the manner of his escape, there might have had a thousand *Box Browns* per annum. The singularly original plan adopted by William and Ellen Crafts, perished with the first using, because every slaveholder in the land was apprised of it. The *salt water slave* who hung in the guards of a steamer, being washed three days and three nights—like another Jonah—by the waves of the sea, has, by the publicity given to the circumstance, set a spy on the guards of every steamer departing from southern ports. (P. 339)

Douglass's criticism is not reserved for whites who reported on the heroism of white abolitionists but is pointed at his fellow fugitives who published narratives relating the details of their escape.

Douglass chose to hide details of escape during the time when slaves were vulnerable to capture, but this does not mean that he discounted white participation in the rebellion against slavery. Douglass's fictional *The Heroic Slave* (1852) encourages whites to participate in the Underground Railroad due to his political agenda of spurring whites to participate in the rebellion against slavery. Furthermore, a fictionalized text offered no danger to fugitives or potential escapees. In *The Heroic Slave*, the white Mr. Listwell is moved by fugitive Madison Washington to offer help. He helps Madison run to Canada, regardless of the dire consequences of the decision, only to later find that Washington had returned to rescue his wife and become enslaved again. The detailed discussion of Listwell's aid to Washington serves to reinforce Douglass's message of aiding the escaping slave and seems to be the politically motivating factor behind the text.

A number of abolitionist authors highlighted and encouraged the participation of whites in the Underground Railroad through their writing. Certainly writers like Henry David Thoreau (1817–1862) were outspoken in their support of the Underground Railroad. Thoreau helped to move various fugitives, such as Henry Williams, through Concord on their way to Canada and was stridently in support of abolition. Thoreau's support of the Underground Railroad is clear in his "A Plea for Captain John Brown" (1859). Thoreau states,

> Suppose that there is a society in this State that out of its own purse and magnanimity saves all the fugitive slaves that run to us, and protects our colored fellow-citizens, and leaves the other work to the government, so-called. Is not that government fast losing its occupation, and becoming contemptible to mankind? . . . The only free road, the Underground Railroad, is owned and managed by the Vigilant Committee. They have tunneled under the whole breadth of the land.

Thoreau's statement, on the eve of the Civil War, indicates the importance of the idea of the Underground Railroad to the larger abolition project. The Underground Railroad comes to represent the right and moral organization, fast covering the land, working to end the scourge of slavery.

Harriet Beecher Stowe's *Uncle Tom's Cabin* (1852) grows out of the personal ties that Stowe had to the Underground Railroad. Stowe's abolitionist sentiment was formed early as her father, Lyman Beecher (1775–1863), spoke out against the Missouri Compromise, preaching fiery sermons against admitting the state as a slave state. When the Stowe family moved to Ohio, Stowe began to have contact with those who had experienced slavery. As Stowe indicates in a letter published by Douglass in his paper, "Time would fail to tell you all I have learned incidentally of the slave system, in the history of various slaves who came into my family, and of the workings of the underground railroad, which I may say ran through my barn" ("Letter," p. 1). Stowe gathered the stories of slavery from those whom she met, including numerous escaped slaves, such as Zillah, who worked as a servant for the Stowe family. During the time Stowe lived in Ohio, Stowe and a friend witnessed a slave auction in Kentucky a year before she met Reverend John Rankin, who told her the story of a young woman who escaped from slavery in 1838. The woman crossed a dangerous frozen river from the slave state of Kentucky to the free state of Ohio carrying a two-year-old child. These stories would resurface in *Uncle Tom's Cabin* in Stowe's depiction of the slave auction and Eliza's escape across the frozen river to freedom.

Uncle Tom's Cabin represents the Underground Railroad as central to the escape of slaves. The novel reveals the details of Eliza's escape, unlike slave narratives that conceal details. As soon as Eliza crosses the river, she is met by Mr. Symmes, a white man who starts her on her northern journey by guiding her to the Birds. The Birds provide Eliza and her child shelter and transport them to the next conductor. Both Symmes and the Birds, the novel implies, play a role in the Underground Railroad. The novel suggests that the Underground Railroad plays a part in the escape of most slaves. In trying to determine Eliza's route, Haley, the slave catcher, notes that like other escaped slaves, Eliza "makes tracks for the underground" (p. 50). The importance of the Underground Railroad to a fugitive's escape is echoed in the comments voiced by the slave traders and catchers at the tavern. Tom, a slave catcher, says, "Suppose you want to lie by a day or two, till the gal's been carried on the underground line up to Sandusky or so, before you start." (p. 61).

Unlike the slave narratives, Stowe's novel shifts attention from the fugitive to the conductor, which contributes to the mythologizing of the Underground Railroad in popular imagination. Stowe allows little agency for the slaves in the text, instead focusing on the Christian duty of the whites. Eliza's decision to flee is caused by her "maternal love, wrought into a paroxysm of frenzy by the near approach of a fearful danger" (p. 43), rather than a carefully wrought plan of escape. Without the desperate circumstances, Stowe suggests, Eliza would never have turned to escape. And, without the helpful whites, allied against slavery, her escape would have been unsuccessful. It is this underlying theme, and the popularity of the ideas that Stowe voiced, that has contributed to the skewed understanding of black agency in the Underground Railroad.

See also Abolitionist Writing; Blacks; Compromise of 1850 and Fugitive Slave Law; *Incidents in the Life of a Slave Girl; Narrative of the Life of Frederick Douglass;* Slave Narratives; Slavery; Transcendentalism; *Uncle Tom's Cabin*

BIBLIOGRAPHY
Primary Works
Brown, Henry Box. *Narrative of the Life of Henry Box Brown, Written by Himself.* 1851. New York: Oxford University Press, 2002.

Brown, William Wells. *Narrative of William W. Brown, a Fugitive Slave.* 1847. In *From Fugitive Slave to Free Man: The Autobiographies of William Wells Brown,* edited by William L. Andrews. New York: Mentor, 1993.

Coffin, Levi. *Reminiscences of Levi Coffin.* Cincinnati: Western Tract Society, 1876.

Craft, William, and Ellen Craft. *Running a Thousand Miles for Freedom; or, The Escape of William and Ellen Craft from Slavery.* London: William Tweedie, 1860.

Douglass, Frederick. *Autobiographies: Narrative of the Life of Frederick Douglass, an American Slave* [1845], *My Bondage and My Freedom* [1855], *Life and Times of Frederick Douglass* [1881]. Edited by Henry Louis Gates Jr. New York: Library of America, 1994.

Douglass, Frederick. *The Heroic Slave.* 1852. In *Three Classic African-American Novels,* edited and with an introduction by William L. Andrews. New York: Mentor, 1990.

Jacobs, Harriet A. *Incidents in the Life of a Slave Girl, Written by Herself.* 1861. Edited by Jean Fagan Yellin. Cambridge, Mass.: Harvard University Press, 1987.

Still, William. *The Underground Railroad.* 1872. New York: Arno Press, 1968.

Stowe, Harriet Beecher. "Letter in Frederick Douglass' Paper." 8 June 1855. In *Harriet Beecher Stowe: Electronic Edition,* http://www.iath.virginia.edu/utc/.

Stowe, Harriet Beecher. *Uncle Tom's Cabin.* 1852. Edited by Elizabeth Ammons. New York: W. W. Norton, 1994.

Thoreau, Henry David. "A Plea for Captain John Brown." 1859. American Transcendentalism Web, http://www.vcu.edu/engweb/transcendentalism/authors/thoreau/johnbrown.html.

Secondary Works

Blight, David W. "Introduction: The Underground Railroad in History and Memory." In *Passages to Freedom: The Underground Railroad in History and Memory,* edited by David W. Blight, pp. 1–12. Washington. D.C.: Smithsonian Books, 2004.

Collison, Gary. *Shadrach Minkins: From Fugitive Slave to Citizen.* Cambridge, Mass.: Harvard University Press, 1997.

Horton, James Oliver. "A Crusade for Freedom: William Still and the Real Underground Railroad." In *Passages to Freedom: The Underground Railroad in History and Memory,* edited by David W. Blight, pp. 175–194. Washington, D.C.: Smithsonian Books, 2004.

Vlach, John Michael. "Above Ground on the Underground Railroad: Places of Flight and Refuge." In *Passages to Freedom: The Underground Railroad in History and Memory,* edited by David W. Blight, pp. 95–115. Washington, D.C.: Smithsonian Books, 2004.

Yellin, Jean Fagan. *Harriet Jacobs: A Life.* New York: Basic Civitas Books, 2004.

Amy E. Earhart

UNITARIANS

Unitarianism was a theologically unorthodox liberal religious movement. In the early to mid-nineteenth century, most notable New England literary figures (especially those who lived and worked in eastern Massachusetts) identified themselves with Unitarianism, some throughout their lives, some as the faith they grew up in and left, some as the faith they joined. Unitarianism had few adherents when compared with the major forms of religion in America, evangelical Protestantism and Catholicism, yet it had a disproportionate influence on the New England "literary awakening."

Unitarian ideas had taken hold gradually in the late eighteenth century and early nineteenth century principally in the Puritan congregational churches of eastern Massachusetts. (The first Unitarian church in New England, however, was not Puritan congregational but Anglican: King's Chapel, Boston, became Unitarian in 1785.) In 1819 the Boston minister William Ellery Channing (1780–1842) laid out the original Unitarian platform in his best-selling sermon "Unitarian Christianity," and in 1825 the American Unitarian Association was founded, marking the effective creation of a new denomination.

Unitarians had no creed. They generally preferred to call themselves "liberal Christians" because they proclaimed the right of individual private judgment in matters of theology and held that theological differences should not prevent Christian fellowship, which they wished to be as broad as possible. Yet as a group, they rejected as unscriptural and irrational certain traditional Puritan articles of faith, in particular the Trinity (hence the name "Unitarian") and, most importantly, original sin. Unitarians believed that humans had at least some power to effect their own salvation through spiritual and moral self-culture, which they placed at the core of religious experience. Unitarians believed in the miraculous authority of the Bible, but they denied it was miraculously inspired word for word and insisted that it be read in a historical and critical, not literal, way.

Unitarianism appealed especially to highly educated and successful urbanites who had faith in their own abilities and in human reasonableness. It became the dominant religion of the eastern Massachusetts elite, made up of closely intermarried merchant, manufacturing, and professional families. This elite was decidedly conservative in its politics, favoring the Federalist and, later, Whig Parties. For most of the antebellum period, it strongly opposed the movement to abolish slavery. When the Unitarian novelist Lydia Maria Child published her influential antislavery tract, *An Appeal in Favor of That Class of Americans Called Africans* (1833), she was shut out of elite Unitarian society. Again, when the acclaimed Channing began to write moderate antislavery tracts starting in 1835, he alienated his own elite congregation. Although a

William Ellery Channing. THE LIBRARY OF CONGRESS

few prominent Unitarian writers with elite connections, notably the poets James Russell Lowell and Julia Ward Howe, showed strong antislavery sympathies as early as the 1840s, the Unitarian elite as a group turned to antislavery only just prior to, and during, the Civil War (1861–1865). The elite even produced a notable proslavery writer in the domestic novelist Caroline Howard Gilman, who grew up in New England as member of an elite Unitarian family but lived most of her life in Charleston, South Carolina, where her husband, another New England expatriate, was for decades the Unitarian minister.

Elite Unitarians were also generally conservative in their literary tastes. Well into the nineteenth century, they favored moralistic and Augustan literature over Romantic writers, although by 1820 many of them had come to admire, among British Romantic poets, William Wordsworth and Felicia Dorothea Hemans, and, among novelists, Sir Walter Scott. By the 1850s their taste had broadened enough to admire the psychologically complex novels and stories of Nathaniel Hawthorne, who had grown up a Unitarian in Salem, yet they still rejected the experimental novels of Hawthorne's friend Herman Melville, even though Melville, a Unitarian convert, had married into an elite Unitarian family.

A number of the writers who were either of the elite or championed by them have enduring reputations. Among them are the poets William Cullen Bryant and Henry Wadsworth Longfellow; the poet and essayist Oliver Wendell Holmes Sr.; the historians George Bancroft, William Hickling Prescott, Richard Hildreth, John Lothrop Motley, and Francis Parkman Jr.; and the literary historian George Ticknor. None of these writers, except Longfellow in his later career, made his living entirely or even principally in letters; they either were independently wealthy or pursued other vocations alongside literature (e.g., Bryant as a journalist, Holmes as a physician, and Longfellow, for decades, as a language teacher). Some of these writers even lost status with the Unitarian elite because of their notable political and reform commitments: Bryant and Bancroft were prominent Democrats, not Whigs, whereas Bryant and Hildreth were conspicuously involved in antislavery politics.

UNITARIANISM AND TRANSCENDENTALISM

The traditional Unitarianism of the elite received a transformative challenge in the 1830s and 1840s from transcendentalism. The transcendentalists were almost all Unitarians who came of age or who joined Unitarianism in the 1830s and 1840s. Ralph Waldo Emerson and Theodore Parker were both Unitarian ministers, although Emerson left the ministry for a literary career; George Ripley and Thomas Wentworth Higginson, meanwhile, left the Unitarian ministry for careers in reform and literature. Again, Henry David Thoreau grew up a Unitarian, although as an adult he ceased associating with any church; Margaret Fuller and Elizabeth Palmer Peabody were lifelong Unitarians; Amos Bronson Alcott joined Unitarianism in adulthood, married into a Unitarian family, and raised his children, among them Louisa May Alcott, as Unitarians.

Some of the transcendentalists had familial and other connections with the Unitarian elite, but they saw themselves as outsiders and in fact differed from the elite in theology, politics, and literary preferences. In theology, they dissented from the Unitarian claim that the Bible contained an authoritative, miraculous revelation. Instead, they held that divine inspiration was natural and universal and that anyone could potentially be the vehicle of a revelation as authoritative as that of scripture. Such views led more conservative, elite Unitarians, such as the biblical scholar Andrews Norton, to label the transcendentalists "infidels." The transcendentalists were far more sympathetic to social reform, especially antislavery and women's rights, than were elite Unitarians. They also were far more enthusiastic than the elite about European Romantic writers, especially Samuel Taylor Coleridge, Thomas Carlyle, and Johann Wolfgang von Goethe. Finally, many of the transcendentalists, unlike most of their Unitarian elite counterparts, did make their livings principally in literature, as writers, literary critics, and lyceum lecturers: Emerson, Thoreau, Fuller, Ripley, Higginson, Louisa May Alcott.

The conflict between transcendentalists and elite Unitarians, which was quite sharp and bitter in the 1830s and 1840s, grew somewhat less intense by the 1850s, although the slavery controversy continued to aggravate it until the elite, like the transcendentalists, adopted an antislavery position. During this period, transcendentalist theology gradually gained acceptance. By 1865 most Unitarians still identified themselves as Christian, but a significant minority, under transcendentalist influence, now called themselves "theists." Also, among the younger generation of the elite, transcendentalist writers, especially Emerson, ceased to be regarded as dangerous radicals and became instead literary icons.

THEOLOGY AND INFRASTRUCTURE

Unitarians developed such a rich literary culture in part because their theology, both in its traditional and transcendentalist forms, encouraged literary exploration and expression and in part because they developed a dense literary infrastructure. The effect of traditional Unitarian theology on literature can be seen in the Unitarian clergy, who played a leading role in founding "literary Boston" in the first two decades of the nineteenth century. Unitarian ministers, freed from having to preach traditional Calvinist doctrine from week to week, could express themselves in their sermons in creative new ways; they became known for their elegant yet affecting pulpit oratory. They also became notable for their belletristic productions. Literary criticism came naturally to them, as an extension of Unitarian views toward scripture. Strongly influenced by British examples, they began writing essays and poetry and helping establish literary journals, such as the *Monthly Anthology* (1803–1811).

This theological impulse toward literature received an even stronger push from transcendentalism. As the transcendentalists rejected the traditional distinction between natural and miraculous inspiration, regarding all inspiration as divine, they also blurred the line between the prophet and the poet. Poets, in their conception, became channels of divine information like prophets, who could be seen as poets of a specific sort. To the transcendentalist mind, literature became, at least potentially, an exalted, ecstatic calling, worthy of enormous sacrifice to pursue.

A significant Unitarian literary infrastructure, meanwhile, was in place by 1820. The most conspicuous piece of it was Harvard University. In 1805 Unitarians took control of this Puritan-founded school; soon afterward, they established a divinity school there. Unitarians also established, for the first time in any American university, professorial chairs in biblical criticism and modern languages. A large number of New England male writers went to college at Harvard (the school only admitted men), where they studied under Unitarian professors, including the influential professor of rhetoric, William Ellery Channing's younger brother Edward Tyrrell Channing (1790–1856).

Unitarians controlled all the large book collections in and around Boston and to some extent limited access to them. The Harvard library, with fifty-six thousand volumes in 1849, was the largest library in the Boston area, the largest college library in the United States, and the first American college library to collect literature. Yet use of the library was restricted principally to Harvard faculty, students, and alumni and some local ministers; all of these groups were made up almost entirely of Unitarians. The second largest library in the Boston area was the Boston Athenaeum, founded in 1807 by the same Unitarian-dominated group that established the *Monthly Anthology;* admission was by invitation only. Unitarians also owned the largest private book collections available, some with more than ten thousand volumes. Particularly notable were the personal libraries of George Ticknor; William Hickling Prescott; Theodore Parker; the Unitarian minister, classics scholar, and politician Edward Everett; and the lawyer and politician Rufus Choate.

Unitarians also controlled the leading literary periodicals of Boston. In the 1830s and 1840s, a distinction could be drawn between those affiliated with elite Unitarianism, notably the *North American Review* (founded 1821), and those affiliated with transcendentalism, such as *The Dial* (1840–1844), edited by Fuller and Emerson, and the *Massachusetts Quarterly Review* (1847–1850), edited by Parker. The distinction was blurred with the *Atlantic Monthly* (founded 1857), which had Lowell as its first editor and which was open to both elite and transcendentalist writers. Many of the leading Boston publishers were also Unitarians, the most well known being James T. Fields.

After 1865, the center of gravity of American literature shifted from Boston toward the new national center of publishing, New York, where Unitarians were less influential. Unitarian influence on American letters therefore began to diminish, at least proportionately. Many notable writers and critics, however, continued to be found in Unitarian pews through the twentieth century. Meanwhile, Unitarianism as a religion continued to evolve. Transcendentalist ideas became the norm by the early twentieth century, but by the mid-twentieth century, many Unitarians had rejected theism altogether. In 1961 the American Unitarian Association united with the Universalist Church of America, another theologically unorthodox liberal religious movement descended from New England Puritanism, to form the Unitarian Universalist Association.

See also Abolitionist Writing; *An Appeal in the Favor of That Class of Americans Called Africans;* The Bible; Boston; Calvinism; English Literature; Periodicals; Proslavery Writing; Protestantism; Transcendentalism

BIBLIOGRAPHY
Primary Works
Ahlstrom, Sydney E., with Jonathan Sinclair Carey, eds. *An American Reformation: A Documentary History of Unitarian Christianity.* 1985. San Francisco: International Scholars Publications, 1998.

Myerson, Joel, ed. *Transcendentalism: A Reader.* Oxford: Oxford University Press, 2000.

Secondary Works
Brooks, Van Wyck. *The Flowering of New England, 1815–1865.* New York: E. P. Dutton, 1936.

Buell, Lawrence. *New England Literary Culture: From Revolution through Renaissance.* Cambridge, U.K., and New York: Cambridge University Press, 1986.

Capper, Charles, and Conrad Edick Wright, eds. *Transient and Permanent: The Transcendentalist Movement and Its Contexts.* Boston: Massachusetts Historical Society, 1999.

Dictionary of Unitarian and Universalist Biography. http://www.uua.org/uuhs/duub.

Robinson, David. *The Unitarians and the Universalists.* Westport, Conn.: Greenwood Press, 1985.

Wright, Conrad Edick, ed. *American Unitarianism, 1805–1865.* Boston: Massachusetts Historical Society and Northeastern University Press, 1989.

Dean Grodzins

URBANIZATION

Perhaps no society in the history of the world has ever urbanized as rapidly as the United States did in the nineteenth century. In 1820 New York was a small port city on the margins of European culture. Although it was America's largest city, it had a population of only 123,706 in the U.S. census taken in that year. London,

by contrast, had 1.38 million inhabitants in the 1821 census. By 1870 New York and Brooklyn combined had a population of nearly 1.4 million. Within the living memory of many of its residents, the city had increased in size tenfold. The impact of urbanization in America was not confined to New York. Although New York was the only American city with more than 100,000 inhabitants in the 1820 census, the 1870 census listed fourteen American cities with more than 100,000 inhabitants. Between 1820 and 1870, the proportion of the American population living in areas designated as "urban" by the U.S. Census Bureau grew from 7.2 percent to 25.7 percent.

Rapid and extensive urbanization was often referred to as the most characteristic feature of the nineteenth century. In all of the countries of the industrializing West, urbanization had a significant impact on literature and culture, as is evident in the urban styles and subjects of the novels of Charles Dickens and Honoré de Balzac, the poetry of Charles Baudelaire, and the art of the impressionists. While American urbanization and its cultural responses need to be understood within this international context, several factors made the impact of urbanization in America unique. The sheer extent of American urbanization was especially dramatic because of the scale of immigration to America and the dynamism of the American economy. The social and cultural impact of urbanization was magnified in America by the fact that until the middle of the nineteenth century, there had simply not been any large American cities. London and Paris also grew by a considerable amount in the nineteenth century, but they had been large cities for centuries and they had well-established cultures for representing and interpreting urban life. In America the experience of great crowds and of massive, diverse, and dynamic urban environments was a novelty and it was a novelty that called into question some of the most common assumptions about the identity of the United States.

AMERICAN ANTIURBANISM

From the Age of Exploration onward the continents of America were often represented as offering Europeans a chance to make a fresh start in a new, green world: to establish a new Eden, or a version of the pastoral ideal of Arcadia. In the early history of the United States this ideal was influential in the form it had been given by writers such as Thomas Jefferson (1743–1826) and Hector St. John de Crèvecoeur (1735–1813), who believed that the United States had a mission to demonstrate to the world that it was possible to build a great civilization without large cities. Jefferson had written that honest and democratic government could only thrive in a nation of small towns and independent farmers. Democratic government, he believed, would be corrupted by the development of large cities like those he had seen in Europe. Such ideas remained influential in the United States long after it was obvious that the new nation could not and would not thrive without populous centers of industry and commerce. The influence of Jeffersonian antiurbanism is clearly evident in the writings of Ralph Waldo Emerson (1803–1882), Henry David Thoreau (1817–1862), and the other transcendentalists, who were also influenced by the antiurban ideas of European Romanticism, which stressed the importance of living as closely as possible to the influences of nature. In such works as Thoreau's *Walden* (1854) and the essays of Emerson, the urbanization of America was represented as an established fact that needed to be resisted by consciousness and culture.

For the transcendentalists the powerful standardizing effects of urban life and institutions threatened the independence and individualism that should ideally be characteristic of American life. The artificiality of urban environments and mores and the division of labor characteristic of urbanized societies threatened the personal authenticity and connection with the natural world that were also understood as essential American ideals. Following upon similar assertions by European Romantics including William Wordsworth, Samuel Taylor Coleridge, and Johann Wolfgang von Goethe, Emerson, Thoreau, and like-minded intellectuals represented urban life as a danger to the health and independence of the imagination. Overvaluing the sensational, rooted in abstractions, and divorced from nature, urban culture, in their view, would only produce diseased and corrupted works of literature and art.

In addition to the intellectual antiurban tradition, a popular moralistic antiurban tradition took root in early-nineteenth-century America. Temperance novels, crime narratives, sensationalist broadsheets, and "city-mysteries" novels like George Lippard's *Quaker City* (1844–1845), Maria Susanna Cummins's *The Lamplighter* (1854), and Edward Zane Carroll Judson's *The Mysteries and Miseries of New York* (1849) represented New York and Philadelphia as contemporary versions of Babylon or Sodom. Influenced by popular European works like Eugène Sue's *The Mysteries of Paris* (1842–1843) and G. M. W. Reynolds's *The Mysteries of London* (1844–1856), American authors understood that the appalling conditions of the urban poor and the dangerous yet fascinating labyrinth in which they lived offered a perfect backdrop for gothic and sentimental narratives. Although these urban gothic works often presented themselves as efforts to improve public health and morals, and although some were undoubtedly sincere in this intention, they did not fail to provide audiences with an entertaining atmosphere of fear and shock. Their considerable popularity suggests that their appeal may have had less to do with their moral content than with the prurient fascination American audiences had with urban squalor and the possibilities of losing or violating female chastity. Although the popular tradition of urban moralism or sensationalism produced little of lasting literary value, it was instrumental in strengthening the widespread American idea that the new and rapidly growing American cities were confusing and threatening environments, violations of the ideal purity of the American landscape and personality.

AMERICAN URBANISM

While many Americans were hostile to urbanization, others were fascinated by what they saw of the growth of the American cities and by what they read of London and Paris. A tradition of American urbanism began to develop in the 1820s as the number of

Population in select U.S. cities, 1820–1870

City	1820	1830	1840	1850	1860	1870
Baltimore	62,738	80,620	102,313	169,054	212,418	267,354
Boston	43,298	61,392	93,383	136,881	177,840	250,526
Charleston	24,780	30,289	29,261	42,985	40,522	48,956
Cincinnati	9,642	24,831	46,338	115,435	161,044	216,239
New Orleans	27,176	46,082	102,193	116,375	168,675	191,418
New York	123,706	202,589	312,710	515,547	813,669	942,292
Philadelphia	63,802	80,462	93,665	121,376	565,529	674,022
Washington, D.C.	12,247	18,826	23,364	40,001	61,122	109,199
Total U.S. population	9,638,453	12,866,020	17,069,453	23,191,876	31,443,321	39,818,449

SOURCE: U.S. Bureau of the Census.

American magazines grew as rapidly as the populations of American cities. Travelers' accounts of the great cities of Europe were an important staple of these magazines and in the best of these, by such authors as Washington Irving (1783–1859) and Nathaniel Parker Willis (1806–1867), Americans began to develop a tradition of representing cities favorably. The urbane appreciations of London and Paris written by Irving and Willis were modeled on a kind of writing that was familiar to Americans from the popular essays of Charles Lamb, Leigh Hunt, and other writers in the London periodical press, which was widely read in America. By the 1830s Willis and other New York writers, many of them associated with the most influential American magazine of its time, the *Knickerbocker*, would claim that New York had begun to rival London and Paris as a cosmopolitan center.

Writing in the popular English and French magazine tradition of the flaneur (or man-about-town), Irving, Willis, and the rest of the "Knickerbocker" authors offered sketches of New York from the perspective of a strolling or panoramic spectator who demonstrated the pleasures of random encounters and who offered the reassuring fantasy that the urban crowd consisted of amusing types who could be read in a single glance. The culture of the flaneur reached its peak in New York between 1835 and 1850 when it engaged the talents of many journalists, including Edgar Allan Poe (1809–1849) and the young Walt Whitman (1819–1892) of the *New York Aurora* and the *Brooklyn Daily Eagle*. In the 1840s and 1850s the urban spectatorial tradition produced a considerable number of highly popular panorama books, which represented cities in a style that owed a great deal not only to the magazine traditions but also to the popularity, at this time, of panoramas and dioramas of cities. In the best of these works, such as E. Porter Belden's *New York: Past, Present, and Future* (1849), George G. Foster's *New York by Gas-light* (1850), and Cornelius Mathews's *A Pen and Ink Panorama of New York* (1853), American authors followed the lead of European panoramists by offering vistas and slices of life in cities, with typologies of crowds and glimpses of what might be going on under the roofs of the metropolis. The encyclopedic ambitions of the panorama books allowed them to use a particularly broad array of tones and effects, offering readers a mixture of the amusing city of the flaneur and the sordid spectacle of the city-mysteries.

THE IMPACT OF URBANIZATION ON LITERATURE

Whether positive, negative, or ambivalent, most American writing about cities in the middle of the nineteenth century was highly derivative of European models. Most of it was predictable and uncomplicated as well, as authors in the marketplace represented cities according to well-established conventions and archetypes. There were, however, a few striking and important examples of originality and complexity in this period. Writers like Edgar Allan Poe, Herman Melville, Nathaniel Hawthorne, and Walt Whitman attempted in their writings to find a complex way of representing the ambivalent fascination they and other Americans had with the new reality of large cities.

Poe's most significant contribution to the literature of urbanization was his development of the urban detective story. In three stories written in the early 1840s, "The Man of the Crowd" (1840), "The Murders in the Rue Morgue" (1841), and "The Mystery of Marie Roget" (1842), Poe offered vivid images of the mysterious and illegible metropolis readers would have known from journalistic sketches and from crime and mystery narratives. Poe's most original contribution was to develop, out of the conventional image of the flaneur, a new detached observer of urban life who was able to see what no others could see, read what no others could read, and solve what no others could solve. Poe's detective, C. Auguste Dupin, had the implausible interpretive powers of the flaneur, but he read, not the amusingly benign city of the flaneur, but the terrifying city of the sensationalist mysteries and crime narratives. Inventing the detective, Poe offered an archetypal urban consciousness who was to have an enormous significance in the future as an urban literary type, largely because of the immense popularity of Sherlock Holmes, the creation of Poe's imitator, Sir Arthur Conan Doyle. The detective was a brilliant invention because he made possible an exciting exposure to the terrors of the urban abyss while providing a reassuring mechanism for reducing it to legibility.

Although Nathaniel Hawthorne (1804–1864) is not traditionally thought of as a writer concerned with urbanization, he offered compelling images of the opacity of urban life in several sketches and stories, the most important of which was "Wakefield" (1835). In *The Blithedale Romance* (1852), Hawthorne offered something more than this: a quintessentially American analysis of the impact of urban culture. In his study of the failure of a group of urbanites to establish a successful New Eden/Arcadia outside Boston Hawthorne tried to identify what it was about urban forms of consciousness, exemplified by the book's narrator, Miles Coverdale, and the main characters, that made it impossible for them to realize the Jeffersonian and Romantic ideals to which American antiurbanist intellectuals remained attached. Hawthorne offers an analysis of the way in which urban culture, with its spectatorial obsessions, theatricality, and narcissistic fads (such as mesmerism and utopianism), make it impossible for individuals to form the kinds of bonds and attachments that are necessary in a successful community.

Herman Melville (1819–1891) considered the impact of urbanization at several points in his work. His two most famous passages about the psychological dynamics of urban life are the opening chapter of *Moby-Dick* (1851), in which Melville creates a context for his epic by invoking the image of the sea-gazing inhabitants of Manhattan, dreaming of freedom from the constrictions of office-bound and apartment-bound urban life, and the long story "Bartleby, the Scrivener" (1853). Melville's representation, in "Bartleby," of the passive revolt of a Wall Street office clerk against the expectations of his employer has become one of the paradigmatic images of the impact of urban society on the effort to maintain a coherent and independent self. In its portrayal of the employer/narrator's moral confusion, "Bartleby" also raises the question of how it is possible to determine moral imperatives and responsibilities in a complex urban world. In several other novels, notably *White-Jacket* (1850), *Redburn* (1849), and *Pierre* (1852), Melville also engaged with urbanization. Adopting the premises and techniques of popular literature that represented the modern city as a labyrinth, Melville uses the city in these works as a metaphor for the impenetrable complexity of social and psychological experience. Although Melville never attempted to develop a consistent view or analysis of urban life, he was inventive and original in the way in which he uses the imagery of city life for purposes that vary from novel to novel or story to story.

The most significant, unique, and original American literary effort to respond to urbanization in the period from 1820 to 1870 is to be found in the poetry of Walt Whitman. In many of Whitman's poems, most notably sections of "Song of Myself" (1855), "Crossing Brooklyn Ferry" (1856), "Mannahatta" (1860), "A Broadway Pageant" (1860), and several poems in the *Calamus* series (1860), Whitman tried to develop a new kind of poetry, a poetry that was specifically and quintessentially urban, that would with its epic catalogs and moments of panoramic ecstasy be particularly suited to the representation of the urban crowd and the immensity and diversity of urban objects. In the best of his urban poems, "Crossing Brooklyn Ferry," Whitman expanded the spectatorial consciousness with which he was familiar from journalistic models, and by adding a fuller emotional and philosophical dimension, as well

---

Herman Melville's Moby-Dick *opens with a powerful image of the constraints of urban life.*

There now is your insular city of the Manhattoes, belted round by wharves as Indian isles by coral reefs—commerce surrounds it with her surf. Right and left, the streets take you waterward. Its extreme down-town is the battery, where that noble mole is washed by waves, and cooled by breezes, which a few hours previous were out of sight of land. Look at the crowds of water-gazers there.

Circumambulate the city of a dreamy Sabbath afternoon. Go from Corlears Hook to Coenties Slip, and from thence, by Whitehall northward. What do you see?—Posted like silent sentinels all around the town, stand thousands upon thousands of mortal men fixed in ocean reveries.

Herman Melville, *Moby-Dick; or, The Whale,* edited by Harrison Hayford, Herschel Parker, and G. Thomas Tanselle (Evanston, Ill., and Chicago: Northwestern University Press and the Newberry Library, 1988), p. 3.

---

as an awareness of human life in the context of time, he explored the way in which the urban crowd and urban objects could become as important to an urban poet as natural objects had been to Wordsworth and the Romantics. In "Crossing Brooklyn Ferry" and other urban poems Whitman offered fascinating suggestions about the possibility of a specifically urban form of spirituality and a specifically urban form of "adhesive" love that could be the emotional foundation of a democratic society. Whitman's celebration of the city is inseparable from his celebration of democracy. Writing against the Jeffersonian and Romantic traditions of antiurbanism, Whitman suggested that the true destiny of America was not to develop a civilization without cities. America, in his view, should fulfill its historical destiny by developing a culture that could celebrate the spirit of the masses and welcome the dynamism of urban modernity.

Although America did not produce significant contributions to the developing traditions of urban realism and naturalism until later in the century, Rebecca Harding Davis's novella *Life in the Iron Mills* (1861) deserves mention as an anticipation of this important future tradition in American literature.

Most poetry in the nineteenth century represented the city as a place that threatened the creative imagination. In poems such as "Crossing Brooklyn Ferry," Walt Whitman tried to invent a poetry that could celebrate and draw inspiration from cities.

Numberless crowded streets—high growths of
  iron, slender, strong, light, splendidly uprising toward clear skies;
Tide swift and ample, well-loved by me, toward
  sundown,
The flowing sea-currents, the little islands, larger
  adjoining islands, the heights, the villas,
The countless masts, the white shore-steamers,
  the lighters, the ferry-boats, the black sea-
  steamers well-model'd;
The down-town streets, the jobbers' houses of
  business—the houses of business of the
  ship-merchants, and money-brokers—the
  river-streets;
Immigrants arriving, fifteen or twenty thousand
  in a week; . . .
The mechanics of the city, the masters, well-
  form'd, beautiful-faced, looking you straight
  in the eyes;
Trottoirs throng'd—vehicles—Broadway—the
  women—the shops and shows,
The parades, processions, bugles playing, flags
  flying, drums beating;
A million people—manners free and superb—
  open voices—hospitality—the most courageous and friendly young men;
The free city! No slaves! No owners of slaves!
The beautiful city, the city of hurried and
  sparkling waters! the city of spires and
  masts!
The city nested in bays! my city! . . ."

Walt Whitman, *Leaves of Grass* (Philadelphia: David
McKay, c. 1900).

Influenced by recent European novels, like Dickens's *Hard Times* (1854), that had begun to treat the industrial city as a literary subject, *Life in the Iron Mills* deals with the aspirations and artistic expression of a millworker imprisoned for theft. It goes beyond the conventions of urban exposé moralism to try to represent the impact that the social conditions of nineteenth-century American industrialization might

have had upon the consciousness and the imagination of the urban working class. Set in a Virginia mill town, *Life in the Iron Mills* does not address urbanization itself, but it is an early and significant treatment of the impact of the industrialization that is central to the general issue of the urbanization of nineteenth-century America.

CONCLUSION

Rapid and extensive urbanization was one of the most significant features of life in mid-nineteenth-century America. American writers produced a diversity of responses to urbanization as they assimilated European influences and attempted to represent their own understanding of the cultural and psychological impact of cities on American life. Although city life would not become one of the most prominent themes in American literature until after 1870, the representation of urban life in American literature before 1870 illustrates the complexities and difficulties involved in reconciling the new American experience of urban life with the widespread belief that such a life was antithetical to American ideals of social existence. By the middle of the nineteenth century it had become clear that the Jeffersonian dream of America as a civilization without cities was no longer plausible. The rich and distinctive tradition of American writing about city life had been launched. At the same time, American traditions of antipathy toward urban life were still entrenched. The ambivalence toward the city that one finds in the literature of the mid-nineteenth century may still be found in American culture and the products of the earliest encounter of American writers with the city are still of considerable historical interest. The best of this work, notably the stories and novels of Poe, Hawthorne, and Melville and the poetry of Whitman, is an important part of the ongoing international discussion of the effect of urbanization upon the imagination.

See also Agrarianism; "Bartleby, the Scrivener"; *The Blithedale Romance;* Individualism and Community; Knickerbocker Writers; *Leaves of Grass; Life in the Iron Mills;* Sensational Fiction; Transcendentalism

BIBLIOGRAPHY

Secondary Works

Bender, Thomas. *Toward an Urban Vision: Ideas and Institutions in Nineteenth-Century America.* Baltimore: Johns Hopkins University Press, 1991.

Brand, Dana. *The Spectator and the City in Nineteenth-Century American Literature.* Cambridge, U.K., and New York: Cambridge University Press, 1991.

Kelley, Wyn. *Melville's City: Literary and Urban Form in Nineteenth-Century New York*. Cambridge, U.K., and New York: Cambridge University Press, 1996.

Machor, James L. *Pastoral Cities: Urban Ideals and the Symbolic Landscape of America*. Madison: University of Wisconsin Press, 1987.

Marx, Leo. *The Machine in the Garden: Technology and the Pastoral Ideal in America*. New York: Oxford University Press, 1964.

Miller, Perry. *The Raven and the Whale: The War of Words and Wits in the Era of Poe and Melville*. New York: Harcourt, Brace, and Company, 1956.

Reynolds, David S. *Beneath the American Renaissance: The Subversive Imagination in the Age of Emerson and Melville*. New York: Alfred A. Knopf, 1988.

White, Morton, and Lucia White. *The Intellectual versus the City*. Cambridge, Mass.: Harvard University Press, 1962.

Dana Brand

UTOPIAN COMMUNITIES

In her novel *Redwood* (1824), Catharine Maria Sedgwick (1789–1867) describes the Shaker villages of Lebanon and Hancock, Massachusetts, as a "religious republic" divided into communal "family" units "whose members are clothed from one store-house, fed at the same board, and perform their domestic worship together" (pp. 178–181) while also engaging in an enthusiastic bustle of industry around looms and the community dairy. She also praises the members for their "skillful cultivation" and "snow white linen" (p. 184). In the midst of this mostly flattering portrayal, however, she also observes that these communities "have been visited by foreigners and strangers from all parts of our union—all are shocked or disgusted by some of the absurdities of the shaker faith, but none have withheld their admiration from the results of their industry, ingenuity, order, frugality, and temperance" (p. 181). Sedgwick's conflicted assessment of Shaker culture is representative of the mixture of skepticism, abhorrence, and grudging respect extended by Americans to their brethren living in utopian communities during the same period. The first half of the nineteenth century ushered in a golden era of utopian experimentation. Owenists, Fourierists, Oneida Perfectionists, Mormons, Amana Inspirationalists, and New Icarians all founded utopian communities in America between 1820 and 1870. Each movement was greeted with a mix of revulsion and fascination from within the dominant culture, and their experiments were also registered by the nation's literary elite, who, like Sedgwick, could be simultaneously seduced and repulsed by the new utopianism.

THE ROOTS OF UTOPIANISM IN NORTH AMERICA

Thomas More coined the word "utopia"—a neologism from the Greek *ou*, "no or not," and *topos*, "place"—in his 1516 work "De optimo reipublicae statu deque nova insula Utopia" ("Concerning the highest state of the republic and the new island Utopia"; translated most often simply as *Utopia*). More's satirical fiction imagines an idyllic island republic ruled by reason where property is shared communally, the population of cities is controlled by resettlement, and wars are fought by mercenaries from among the islanders' warlike neighbors. *Utopia* inaugurated a genre of speculative fiction in the West that imagined the possibility of perfect societies existing outside the confines of Europe. More's novel also cemented the link between utopianism and communalism in the Western consciousness. The three texts that most profoundly shaped utopian thought in the Western world—Plato's *Republic*, Acts 2:42–47 in the New Testament, and *Utopia*—each describe an ideal society wherein property is shared by the entire community.

The cultural impact of More's novel on actual utopian experimentation is difficult to measure; more certain is the convergence of colonialist expansion, religious dissention, and millenarianism that opened North America to European utopian impulses during the seventeenth and eighteenth centuries. The continent provided a vast canvas upon which Anabaptists, radical Pietists, and millenarians painted their visions of Christian perfectionism. Most of these new utopians were refugees from religious persecution in Europe. Bohemia Manor (1683–1727), Woman in the Wilderness (1694–1720), Bethlehem (1741–1844), and the Ephrata Cloister (1732–1934) were founded by Labadists, German Pietists, Moravians, and Seventh Day Baptists respectively—all sects that had been branded as apostate or heretical by the mainline Calvinist and Lutheran Churches in Europe. All four settlements were founded in Pennsylvania around a migrant community within or near William Penn's "tolerant" Quaker territory. Some held millenarian beliefs. The theologian and mathematician Johann Kelpius—founder of the Woman in the Wilderness community—calculated that the millennium would arrive in 1694, and he led forty male settlers from Germany to present-day Germantown, Pennsylvania, to await the event. All of these communities experimented with communal ownership and control of property, and each experimented with alternative family arrangements. The New Bohemia community believed children belonged to God and raised them communally. The Ephrata Cloister demanded celibacy, even from married members. These Christian perfectionists created the template for subsequent utopian communities by demonstrating practical alternatives to the patterns of domesticity, radical individualism, and competitive capitalism that were cohering within the new American Republic.

THE SHAKER PHENOMENON

Of all the utopian communitarian movements established in America, the Shakers paved the widest path in nineteenth-century culture. Its principle founder, "Mother" Ann Lee, had been born into a poor family in Manchester, England, on 29 February 1736. Caught up in the evangelical fervor of the 1750s, the uneducated and extremely pietistic girl found a home among the "seekers," a Quaker-influenced sect based in Manchester. This "charismatic" group, known for its spirited demonstrations of shouting, turbulent movement, and speaking in tongues, was labeled "Shaking Quakers" by its detractors. Lee tried her hand at marriage and gave birth to four children who did not survive to adulthood. In the early 1770s she became more active in the movement that became known as the Shakers, and in 1774, driven by a series of visions about a new Eden in America, she and eight others crossed the Atlantic to found a community in Niskeyuna, New York, west of Albany. Within the next ten years before her death, her Shakers would create the infrastructure for what was arguably the most successful utopian movement in American history—one that survived for more than two hundred years and spawned eighteen communities from Maine to Kentucky. More than twenty thousand Americans have lived at least part of their lives in a Shaker community since Lee's time, and at the height of Shaker influence in 1850, nearly four thousand Americans were living as Shakers. With fewer than twelve Shakers living today in the sole remaining Shaker community at Sabbathday Lake, Maine, the Shakers may be technically on the verge of extinction, but the movement's place on the cultural landscape is secure.

Throughout the nineteenth century the Shakers served as a touchstone for other communal movements. The utopian leaders Robert Owen (New Harmony, in Indiana), John Humphrey Noyes (Oneida Perfectionists, in New York), Amos Bronson Alcott and Charles Lane (Fruitlands, in Massachusetts), and Cyrus Reed Teed (the Koreshan Unity, in Florida) all paid visits to Shaker villages and borrowed ideas from the sect. America's burgeoning literary class also weighed in on the Shaker phenomenon, but their assessment was somewhat less enthusiastic.

Ralph Waldo Emerson (1803–1882) visited the Canterbury, New Hampshire, Shakers in 1828 and again a year later with his fiancée, observing in a letter to Brother Charles on 7 August 1829 that the Shakers were "clean, well disposed, dull and incapable animals" led by "shrewd . . . male and female oligarchs" (1:276). Emerson renewed his interest in the Shakers and tempered his criticism in the 1840s, when, after visiting the Harvard community with Nathaniel Hawthorne (1804–1864) in 1842, he established lasting relationships with two Shaker elders. Emerson observed resonances between the homegrown Shaker communalism and the European waves of socialism sweeping the United States before the Civil War. He also admired the institutionalized equality among the Shakers.

Unlike Emerson, Hawthorne apparently never reconciled his disdain for the Shakers. Hawthorne penned two short stories set in a Shaker milieu, both representing the Shaker villages as sites for stagnation and death. "The Shaker Bridal" (1838) follows two young lovers into the Shaker community at Goshen, where young Martha succumbs to Shaker celibacy, dying in degrees "like a corpse in its burial clothes" (p. 476). An earlier story, "The Canterbury Pilgrims" (1833), whose title is a playful reference to both Chaucer's *Canterbury Tales* and the name of the New Hampshire Shaker village, chronicles the woes of three pilgrims en route to a Shaker village—a poet, a merchant, and a yeoman—all failures in "The World" seeking solace and a better life within the confines of a Shaker village. In this story the pilgrims meet a pair of young Shakers who have just fled the commune to marry, and they try, unsuccessfully, to convince the lovers to return to the village with stories of their own misfortunes on the outside.

Perhaps inspired by Hawthorne, Daniel Pierce Thompson (1795–1868)—the author the *Green Mountain Boys* (1839) and other adventure novels—published a story titled "The Shaker Lovers" in 1848 that chronicles the "escape" and impetuous wedding of two hot-blooded Shaker youths. The first chapter promises to "lift the curtain" on the "wonderfully honest exterior" (p. 7) of Shaker life, prefacing a story that will climax with the attempted murder of young Seth by an enraged Shaker elder wielding an oar.

Although she respectfully describes the structure and practices of the Shakers in an earlier section of her novel *Redwood*, Catharine Maria Sedgwick also finds "deceit lurking under many a broad brim" (p. 207) in the Shaker community. She devotes ten pages of the novel to the rescue of young Emily from the sect. Sedgwick also casts an elder, Reuban Harrington, in the role of villain. Crafty and unscrupulous, Reuban plots to spirit young Emily away from the Shakers and force her to marry him.

Herman Melville's (1819–1891) treatment of the Shakers in chapter 71 of *Moby-Dick* is also less than flattering. Melville describes an encounter between the *Pequod* and the plague-ridden *Jeroboam*, which has been taken over by a Shaker prophet named Gabriel. Hailing from the "crazy society of Neskyeuna Shakers," Gabriel is said to have ascended to heaven through a trapdoor during "their cracked, secret meetings" (p. 312). Melville's association of Shaker culture with religious fanaticism is consistent with the literary skepticism accorded these "Shaking Quakers" throughout the nineteenth century.

UTOPIAN COMMUNITIES: 1820–1870

Utopian communitarianism particularly flourished in the United States during the four decades before the Civil War. Yaakov Oved records thirty-two "American communes" founded in the United States between 1663 and 1820, most of them religious. Over the next five decades, however, 123 new communities would spring up. In 1800 sectarian religionists like the newly formed Shakers and the surviving remnants of the Ephrata Cloister and the Moravians dominated the "utopian" landscape—all faithful, pietistic Christians who framed their lifestyle choices as spiritual necessities. By 1900, however, the tableau of communitarian idealism had expanded greatly to include French Romanticism, Owenism, Darwinism, transcendentalism, Zionism, Fourierism, and the Koreshan tenet of "cellular cosmogony," among other philosophies and ideologies. Additionally, many of the new religious utopian communities were being founded by home-grown religious sects like the Mormons and the Oneida Perfectionists. In the nineteenth century, social, economic, and educational reform was replacing religious perfectionism as the primary impetus for founding new utopian communities. Enlightenment discourses on rationalism, utilitarianism, and social engineering edged out the Bible and Christian theology as source material for these new utopian experiments.

Two separate waves of European socialism arrived on American shores during the four decades preceding the Civil War, and each spawned utopian communities in the United States. The first was inspired by Robert Owen (1771–1858), a British textile baron, philanthropist, and self-proclaimed creator of a "new moral world," who had turned a factory town in New Lanark, Scotland, into a model community offering free housing and education to more than one thousand workers. Owen, an energetic but fickle reformer, became restless with his work in Britain and in 1825, he purchased New Harmony—an Indiana commune originally founded by George Rapp's Harmony Society of mostly German immigrants in 1814. With 180 buildings, housing for eight hundred people, four mills, a textile factory, two churches, and a brewery, New Harmony was an ideal launchpad for Owen's theories of educational and social reform. The Owenites never entirely abolished private property, but they did vigorously promote gender equality, communal experimentation, and widespread education. New Harmony was the first of seven Owenite communities founded in 1825 and 1826; by the end of the Civil War, there were nineteen. New Harmony would cease to be an Owenite community after just three years, but Owen's influence was profoundly felt by American intellectuals like Emerson, who affectionately quotes Owen in "Culture" (1860): "Give me a tiger, and I will educate him" (p. 1019). Catharine Beecher (1800–1878) in her *Essay on Slavery and Abolitionism* (1837) identifies Owen as a member of the "Atheist school" of reformers, encouraging her readers to expose the "absurdity of their doctrines" (p. 120).

In the same year New Harmony abandoned its Owenite charter, a pampered young man from upstate New York named Albert Brisbane (1809–1890) left for Europe for an extended student's tour of the continent. There he met Charles Fourier (1772–1837), a French socialist who believed competitive capitalism could be peacefully abolished through the establishment of large, single-dwelling communes called "phalanxes." Brisbane tried unsuccessfully to raise money to create a Fourieristic commune in the United States but instead settled for publishing the *Social Destiny of Man* in 1840—the first thorough explication of Fourier's theories in English. Brisbane successfully converted Horace Greeley to the ideas of Fourier, and with Greeley's help he convinced the residents of a fledgling experimental community in West Roxbury, Massachusetts, to adopt Fourierism.

Brook Farm had been founded by the Unitarian minister George Ripley (1802–1880) in 1841 with help from the music critic John Sullivan Dwight, along with Nathaniel Hawthorne and other writers and intellectuals from the Boston-Concord area. In 1845, after finally acceding to Greeley's and Brisbane's pressure to adopt a Fourieristic charter, Brook Farm officially became one of twenty-eight Fourierist phalanxes established in the United States before the outbreak of the Civil War. The commune was a rather modest experiment, never topping more than 120 members—often far fewer—with a shifting population of temporary

Birds-eye view of Robert Owen's plan for New Harmony, Indiana. THE LIBRARY OF CONGRESS

members, visitors, and unreliable hangers-on. Its experiments in agricultural self-sufficiency were mostly disappointing, but the community school was considered a success. Labor remained divided along traditional gender lines, with women completing domestic chores and men engaged in hard labor. The experiment lasted just five years, from 1841 to 1846, with the last two years under Fourierist governance; the community disbanded after it was razed by a fire.

The commune did become a vibrant center for intellectual discussion and debate. While it was functioning, Brook Farm became a locus for transcendentalist activity. Ripley and Dwight, both members of the original Transcendentalist Club, were founding members. Emerson declined Ripley's invitation to join but made frequent visits to lecture there, along with Margaret Fuller, William Ellery Channing, Theodore Parker, and Amos Bronson Alcott. The Catholic theologian Orestes Augustus Brownson sent his son to live there. The community became a pet project of the transcendentalists, which guaranteed that more than any other utopian community in U.S. history Brook Farm would become permanently enshrined in the nation's literary and cultural history.

UTOPIAN LITERATURE: 1820–1870

Ironically, utopian literature in early-nineteenth-century America was almost entirely disconnected from the reality of life in utopian communities. The success of More's *Utopia* may partially account for this gap between utopian experience and utopian literature. More's book had spawned a vibrant genre of speculative fiction that would later include such notable works as Johann Valentin Andreae's *Christianopolis* (1619), Tommaso Campanella's *Civitas Solis* (The city of the sun, 1623), and Francis Bacon's *The New Atlantis* (1627). By the nineteenth century this utopian format was already well established and easily appropriated by authors of that era. Twenty-nine utopian works were published in America between 1800 and 1860, but not one was written by a long-term resident of a utopian community. Hawthorne's eight-month sojourn at Brook Farm in 1841 distinguishes him as an expert on the subject of utopian communities among American writers who actually wrote utopian or dystopian fictions. Other canonical writers were experimenting with the utopian form, however. Herman Melville's autobiographical first novel *Typee* (1846) presents an idyllic Pacific Island community undercut by the fear of cannibalism. Edgar Allan Poe's short story

"Mellonta Tauta" (1850) imagines a future full of technological progress but devoid of democracy and individualism. James Fenimore Cooper's novel *The Monikins* (1835) satirizes humanity by presenting a society of monkeys, and his novel *The Crater; or, Vulcan's Peak: A Tale of the Pacific* (1847) presents still another Pacific Island utopia.

Among these utopian and dystopian visions, Hawthorne's *The Blithedale Romance* (1852) has emerged as the representative novel of *actual* utopian communalism in the antebellum period. Hawthorne was a founding member and investor in the Brook Farm commune and lived there on and off for eight months in 1841. His novelistic treatment of this sojourn into idealism, reformist politics, and communitarianism sounds a bitter, often bitingly satirical tone throughout. For many transcendentalists, Brook Farm was an opportunity to create what Ripley describes in a 1 October 1840 letter to his congregation as an "assembly of the first-born"—a community of "those who are united by no other tie than faith in divine things" (p. 406). Hawthorne's vision, however, is openly hostile to such high-minded intentions. His protagonist, Miles Coverdale, is a "bachelor" poet who joins the Blithedale community with lofty intentions but is quickly dissatisfied with the leadership of Hollingsworth, a charismatic, megalomaniacal reformer who ends up seducing the woman Coverdale loves. Coverdale is also dismayed by the rigors of farm life. (Hawthorne too complained about the physical labor, apologizing to his wife, Sophia, in a letter for his handwriting, blaming his poor penmanship on excessive manual labor.) At the start of the novel Coverdale reflects on the prospects of achieving the "better life": "Possibly, it would hardly look so now; it is enough if it looked so then" (p. 44). He joins his compatriots in decrying competition and selfishness for the "familiar love" of communal living, but by the final chapter he has thrown up his arms, proclaiming "as regards human progress . . . let them believe in it who can, and aid in it who choose" (p. 207). In between, he depicts the Blithedale reformers as well intentioned but ultimately self-deluded, overeducated, and woefully underskilled communitarians—a society of bunglers who must learn difficult lessons about the failure of their reformist zeal.

"Transcendental Wild Oats" (1873), Louisa May Alcott's (1832–1888) satire of her father's even shorter-lived commune, Fruitlands, sounds a more humorous note, but it is no less critical of transcendentalism's idealistic excesses. Her father, Amos Bronson Alcott (1799–1888), founded the commune along with the British reformers Henry Wright and Charles Lane in 1843, near the Shaker community at Harvard. The group, which never numbered more than eleven members, practiced vegetarianism and failed utterly to grow any crops for one planting season, finally disbanding after one winter. "Reform conventions of all sorts were haunted by these brethren, who said many wise things and did many foolish ones," observes Alcott in her satire. "Unfortunately, these wanderings interfered with their harvest at home; but the rule was to do what the spirit moved, so they left their crops to Providence and went a-reaping in wider and, let us hope, more fruitful fields than their own" (p. 166).

From the perspective of American literary history, Brook Farm and Fruitlands were fortunate to be associated with transcendentalism. Scholarly interest in canonical writers such as Hawthorne, Emerson, and Henry David Thoreau have guaranteed wide coverage of both experiments. The larger, more successful utopian communities did produce entire libraries of original texts, but they were not typically the kind of writing that would be valorized as "literary" later in American history. The Shaker writing now contained in several collections includes more than twelve thousand manuscripts and imprints of testimonies, doctrinal works, journals, letters, poetry, recipes, hymns, religious tracts, and scrapbooks, but Shakers did not even read novels until after 1850, and their sense of isolation from "The World" may have prevented them from writing in any of the forms (like the domestic novel) that were popular in the first half of the nineteenth century.

See also The Blithedale Romance; Concord, Massachusetts; Free Love; Individualism and Community; Reform; Transcendentalism; *Woman in the Nineteenth Century*

BIBLIOGRAPHY

Primary Works

Alcott, Louisa M., and Clara Endicott Sears. *Bronson Alcott's Fruitlands.* Cambridge, Mass.: Riverside Press, 1915.

Beecher, Catharine. *An Essay on Slavery and Abolitionism, with Reference to the Duty of American Females.* Boston: Perkins and Marvin, 1837.

Emerson, Ralph Waldo. "Culture." 1860. In *Essays & Lectures.* New York: Penguin, 1983.

Emerson, Ralph Waldo. *The Letters of Ralph Waldo Emerson.* 10 vols. Edited by Ralph L. Rusk and Eleanor M. Tilton. New York: Columbia University Press, 1939–.

Hawthorne, Nathaniel. *The Blithedale Romance.* 1852. Edited by William E. Cain. New York: Bedford/St. Martin's, 1996.

Hawthorne, Nathaniel. *Twice-Told Tales.* Boston: Houghton Mifflin, 1882.

Melville, Herman. *Moby Dick; or, The Whale.* 1851. Edited by Luther S. Mansfield. New York: Hendricks House, 1952.

Ripley, George. "Letter to the Church in Purchase Street." 1840. In Nathaniel Hawthorne, *The Blithedale Romance,* edited by William E. Cain, pp. 405–410. Boston and New York: Bedford/St. Martin's, 1996.

Sedgwick, Catharine Maria. *Redwood: A Tale.* New York: E. Bliss and E. White, 1824.

Thompson, Daniel Pierce. *The Shaker Lovers, and Other Stories.* Burlington, Vt.: C. Goodrich & S. B. Nichols, 1848.

Secondary Works

Brewer, Priscilla J. "Emerson, Lane, and the Shakers: A Case of Converging Ideologies." *New England Quarterly* 55, no. 2 (June 1982): 254–275.

Brewer, Priscilla J. "The Shakers of Mother Ann Lee." In *America's Communal Utopias,* edited by Donald E. Pitzer, pp. 37–56. Chapel Hill: University of North Carolina Press, 1997.

Durnbaugh, Donald F. "Communitarian Societies in Colonial America." In *America's Communal Utopias,* edited by Donald E. Pitzer, pp. 14–36. Chapel Hill: University of North Carolina Press, 1997.

Foster, Lawrence. "Free Love and Community: John Humphrey Noyes and the Oneida Perfectionists." In *America's Communal Utopias,* edited by Donald E. Pitzer, pp. 253–279. Chapel Hill: University of North Carolina Press, 1997.

Francis, Richard. *Transcendental Utopias: Individual and Community at Brook Farm, Fruitlands, and Walden.* Ithaca, N.Y.: Cornell University Press, 1997.

Holloway, Mark. *Heavens on Earth: Utopian Communities in America 1680–1880.* 2nd ed., rev. New York: Dover, 1966.

Lauber, John. "Hawthorne's Shaker Tales." *Nineteenth-Century Fiction* 18, no. 1 (1963): 82–86.

Madden, Etta M. *Bodies of Life: Shaker Literature and Literacies.* Westport, Conn.: Greenwood, 1998.

Oved, Yaacov. *Two Hundred Years of American Communes.* New Brunswick, N.J.: Transaction, 1988.

Pitzer, Donald E. "The New Moral World of Robert Owen and New Harmony." In *America's Communal Utopias,* edited by Donald E. Pitzer, pp. 88–134. Chapel Hill: University of North Carolina Press, 1997.

Sargent, Lyman Tower. *British and American Utopian Literature 1516–1985.* New York: Garland, 1988.

Stockwell, Foster. *Encyclopedia of American Communes 1663–1963.* Jefferson, N.C.: McFarland, 1998.

Daniel R. Vollaro

WALDEN

Although Henry David Thoreau's (1817–1862) *Walden* ranks securely among the handful of best-known American books in the early twenty-first century, this lofty status was not achieved until nearly a century after its publication in 1854. Like many other famous nineteenth-century works—Herman Melville's *Moby-Dick* (1851) and the poems of Walt Whitman and Emily Dickinson, for example—*Walden* was not particularly successful in its own day. Its reputation as a classic of American literature is a product not only of changing literary tastes but also of many decades of work by scholars and teachers to bring to the attention of students and other readers books whose language and thoughts challenge familiar assumptions about American culture and the purposes of reading.

Many readers encountering *Walden* for the first time are initially put off. Expecting, on the basis of Thoreau's popular reputation, a pleasant sort of back-to-nature treatise, they find instead a linguistically and intellectually complex book, dense with allusions to Greek and Roman and early English literature and full of puns and wordplays. Even the quintessential story of *Walden*, how Thoreau built his cabin with his own hands on the shores of Walden Pond and lived alone for two years, is sandwiched into a long first chapter called "Economy," which contains a lengthy and satirical critique of American values, society, business, philanthropy, and even clothing and dietary practices. Because the narrative voice of Walden is both intensely personal and directly challenging to a reader, it tends to provoke strong reactions, both positive and negative.

And it has been taken by readers as everything from a mystic's treatise to a how-to book for simplifying one's life to the rantings of a misguided crank. Sorting through its often conflicting claims and facets requires exploring both its formal characteristics—its language and structure, primarily—and the cultural forces and movements to which Thoreau was responding in his experiment and his critique.

WRITING AND READING *WALDEN*

Thoreau lived at Walden Pond, a mile or so outside his hometown of Concord, Massachusetts, for just over two years, from the summer of 1845 until early fall 1847. He began writing *Walden* while he was at the pond, and many of its passages come directly from the journal he kept while he lived there. By the time he left he had a draft nearly finished, and he hoped to publish it shortly after his first book, *A Week on the Concord and Merrimack Rivers,* which he also worked on at the pond. But he had trouble finding a publisher for *A Week,* and when it finally came out in 1849, it sold so poorly that no publisher would take a chance on *Walden.*

In many ways this was a fortunate setback, though it was deeply disappointing to Thoreau at the time. He spent the next several years, until just before *Walden* was finally published in the summer of 1854, carefully reworking, revising, and adding to his manuscript until, compared with the first draft, it had more than doubled in size and developed into a much different book. Over the years he had produced at least eight major drafts, and each of these manuscript versions (now housed at the Huntington Library in California)

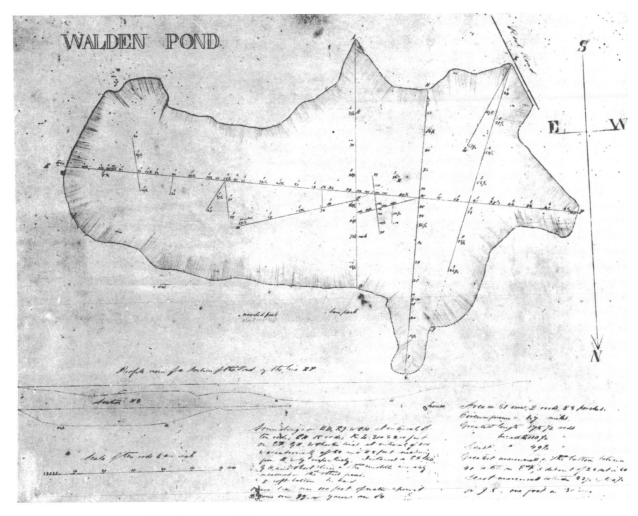

Survey of Walden Pond by Thoreau, 1846. COURTESY OF THE CONCORD FREE PUBLIC LIBRARY

shows evidence of much revision as well. The density and complexity of Thoreau's prose owes much to this long gestation period and to the careful revision virtually every sentence in the book underwent. This quality puts demands on the reader, demands that Thoreau himself frankly acknowledges in the chapter "Reading." Though he is speaking of the classics here, he obviously has his own book in mind as well when he says: "To read well, that is to read true books in a true spirit, is a noble exercise, and one that will task the reader more than any exercise which the customs of the day esteem. It requires a training such as the athletes underwent, the steady intention almost of the whole life to this object. Books must be read as deliberately and reservedly as they were written" (p. 69).

The specific forms this complexity tends to take are discussed below, but one other ramification of *Walden*'s long period of development needs to be

mentioned. The fact that Thoreau wrote many passages in the book as they happened while he was living at the pond, and then revised and added to these passages over the next eight years, means that the final version is at once both dramatic and retrospective. That is, it combines the immediacy of the experiences themselves with later and more measured reflections on their significance. In some cases the later reflections are not entirely harmonious with Thoreau's first thoughts, and the implicit contradictions are allowed to remain. In the problematic chapter "Higher Laws," for example, the narrator begins by praising the wild: "I love the wild not less than the good" (pp. 140–141). But the revisions he added over the years took the chapter in a somewhat different direction, and eventually he concludes by associating this same wild with sensuality and sexual energy, which he feels compelled to repress: "Nature is hard to be overcome, but she must be overcome" (p. 148). Such ambivalence finally provides a true record of thoughts and moods and emphases changing over time and constitutes part of both the difficulty and the richness of the text.

For a reader today, understanding the language of *Walden,* even at the atomic level of the individual word, requires entertaining a different view of the relation between language and the external world than we normally hold. As a thoroughgoing transcendentalist, Thoreau was committed to a search for meaning and truth through (not in—the difference is important) nature. It is a truism that *Walden* records the narrator's search to understand and to know himself through nature, but how that process works and what that truth consists of are much less obvious.

The basic premises of a transcendentalist theory of language can be expressed most economically by citing the pseudo-syllogism that Ralph Waldo Emerson (1803–1882) employs in the "Language" chapter of the basic scripture of transcendentalism, *Nature* (1836): (1) words are signs of natural facts; (2) particular natural facts are symbols of particular spiritual facts; and (3) nature is the symbol of spirit.

Briefly (and simplistically) put, this means that because nature (and all the objects that make it up) are potentially radiant with meaning that can lead one to the divine, and because individual words can stand for the objects of nature, words themselves are potentially carriers of divine significance. Words are inherently dual in that they point simultaneously to the thing they represent and to what lies behind that thing. Furthermore, the more primitive and original a word is, the closer it is likely to be to its potential spiritual meaning. And, whereas one tends to think of reality as those things in nature themselves, for the transcendentalist the ultimate reality is the spiritual meaning that lies behind them. Thoreau himself was fond of distinguishing between the "actual," by which he meant ordinary material reality, and the "real," by which he meant spiritual reality.

A specific passage that illustrates this theory and teaches how, in effect, to read the descriptions of nature in *Walden* comes from the conclusion to the second chapter, "Where I Lived, and What I Lived For." After speaking of the need to penetrate through the accumulated layers of "mud and slush of opinion" that have gathered over everything in order to find "a hard bottom and rocks in place, which we can call *reality,*" the narrator says:

If you stand right fronting and face to face to a fact, you will see the sun glimmer on both of its surfaces, as if it were a cimeter [a curved Oriental sword], and feel its sweet edge dividing you through the heart and marrow, and so you will happily conclude your mortal career. Be it life or death, we crave only reality. (P. 66)

The two surfaces of a fact, rightly perceived, are its physical and spiritual dimensions simultaneously grasped. The reality we crave, according to the narrator, the hard bottom and rocks in place, is not physical reality but spiritual reality, or a fusing of the two perhaps. Throughout the text of *Walden* this double perception is suggested by a wide variety of literary and rhetorical devices (both playful and serious) that attempt to make the reader aware of the shallowness of ordinary perception and to point toward a deeper underlying reality.

Perhaps the most obvious and potentially off-putting rhetorical strategy employed by the narrator to startle his audience into going beyond ordinary perception is invective—a verbal attack on the reader's presumed values. This sort of direct challenge may or may not have its intended effect on a reader, but one should keep in mind that *Walden*, like most of Thoreau's other works, began life as a lecture or series of lectures, which he delivered at lyceums in Concord and elsewhere in New England. The voice that begins *Walden,* especially in the first chapter, "Economy," is a voice that delivered its critique to a live audience. "It is very evident to me what mean and sneaking lives many of you live" (p. 4), the narrator says near the beginning of the book, and one can only wonder how Thoreau's neighbors reacted when he delivered it as the opening of a lecture.

In a similarly unsettling way, the narrator often seems perversely to assert the opposite of what everyone knows to be true. "I see young men, my townsmen," he says, "whose misfortune it is to have inherited farms, houses, barns, cattle, and farming tools; for these are more easily acquired than got rid of" (p. 3). Is it a misfortune to inherit wealth? Is it more difficult to acquire things than get rid of them? By such assertions, of course, the narrator hopes to startle the reader into questioning received wisdom and to ponder the way in which material goods may constrain as well as enrich one's life.

On a subtler level, the language of *Walden* always points toward the deeper meanings accessible one looks at things from an original and not merely an inherited perspective. Language, according to transcendental theory, is a kind of accumulation of dead metaphors, and one has lost the original power and significance of words. So the narrator frequently invokes figurative expressions and treats them as though they were literal—"I felt the spur of the moment go deep in

WALDEN;

OR,

LIFE IN THE WOODS.

By HENRY D. THOREAU,

AUTHOR OF "A WEEK ON THE CONCORD AND MERRIMACK RIVERS."

I do not propose to write an ode to dejection, but to brag as lustily as chanticleer in the morning, standing on his roost, if only to wake my neighbors up. — Page 92.

BOSTON:

TICKNOR AND FIELDS.

M DCCC LIV.

Title page of the 1854 edition of *Walden.* Thoreau lived at Walden Pond for two years in the small cabin that he built. THE LIBRARY OF CONGRESS

my side," for example, or "as if you could kill time without injuring eternity" (p. 4)—in order to renew their original metaphoric force.

In a similar vein, and especially in "Economy," he uses the language of business to suggest that he (and others) might have a destiny that transcends the mere making and spending of money. He frames his decision to go live at Walden Pond in this way, as though he were a kind of venture capitalist of the imagination:

> I determined to go into business at once, and not wait to acquire the usual capital, using such slender means as I had already got. My purpose in going to Walden Pond was not to leave cheaply nor to live dearly there, but to transact rivate business with the fewest possible obstacles. (P. 13)

As this passage continues, the narrator invokes the most important New England trade as an analog to his private "business": "I have always endeavored to acquire strict business habits; they are indispensable to every man. If your trade is with the Celestial Empire, then some small counting house on the coast, in some Salem harbor, will be fixture enough" (p. 13). The Celestial Empire, in the nineteenth century, meant China, and New England merchants made great fortunes through trading voyages to China, even from small ports like Salem, Massachusetts. But clearly the narrator puns on "Celestial Empire," suggesting a higher kind of spiritual trade that can be engaged in from one's own locality, however obscure.

Similarly (examples might be multiplied almost indefinitely), in the opening paragraph of "Where I Lived, and What I Lived For," he describes in some detail the experience of looking at, and then buying in his imagination, farms in his vicinity. At the end of the passage he says that "this experience entitled me to be regarded as a kind of real-estate broker by my friends" (p. 55). Because he is "entitled" (that is, takes a title to) the land only in his imagination, the kind of "real estate" he deals with is not the conventional one of buildings and land but rather the domain of thought and imagination, which constitutes one's real estate.

In this way language serves not only to convey information but also to reattach one to meanings that have been lost in conventional usage. Even etymology (the origin and historical development of words) helps in this process. In the climactic section of the "Spring" chapter, in which the narrator experiences a sense of rebirth and renewal upon seeing the thawing sand and mud "vegetation" that flows out of the railroad cut near his house, he describes the appearance of this apparent foliage as "a truly *grotesque* vegetation" (p. 203). Why, if he admires this display of nature's vital force, does he describe the vegetation as "grotesque"—a word that normally has a negative valence—and further emphasize it with italics? If one looks up "grotesque," the answer is apparent: it derives from the same Latin word as "grotto," meaning an underground chamber. So this vegetation is not grotesque like a Poe story but truly grotesque in that it comes from below the ground.

Presumably an educated reader in Thoreau's day would not need to look up "grotesque" because the curriculum in most colleges emphasized the study of Latin and Greek. But the sort of recovery process a modern reader needs to undertake to understand the nuances of the text and something like the full range of its references is in itself a kind of creative reading that involves participating in the act of creating meaning itself. It is the sort of reading that Thoreau himself advocates when he promotes the study of the classics written in the "dead" languages: "we must laboriously seek the meaning of each word and line, conjecturing a larger sense than common use permits out of what wisdom and valor and generosity we have" (p. 68).

STRUCTURE AND VOICE

The major structural feature of *Walden* is the collapsing of Thoreau's two years and two months' residence into a single year from one spring through to the following spring. Given the narrator's desire to know himself through his immersion in the natural world, the utility of this scheme is obvious: it accords with a yearning for spiritual fulfillment to coincide with the rebirth of nature. But this compression of time and the selectivity of details it implies should also alert the reader to the fact that this book is not conventional autobiography but a carefully constructed version of Thoreau's actual life, or in early-twenty-first-century terms, a kind of virtual reality. Neither is the narrative voice of the book to be equated with the historical Thoreau. It is, rather, a kind of projection of the ideal Thoreau and a rhetorical device designed to reinforce his various themes. It is primarily a self-confident and optimistic voice (despite its criticisms) that promotes the perennial possibility of waking to a higher life: "I do not propose to write an ode to dejection, but to brag as lustily as chanticleer in the morning, standing on his roost, if only to wake my neighbors up" (p. 1). Although the actual Thoreau confided afterward in his journal that he was not sure why he left the woods, the narrator of *Walden* confidently sidesteps the issue by saying, "I left the woods for as good a reason as I went there" (p. 215). Thus it is perhaps most productive to read *Walden* as a kind of fiction, not in the sense that it is untrue but rather in the sense that it is a carefully constructed and highly selective re-creation of the experience on which it is based.

Neither the genre nor the structure of *Walden*, however, follows a strict or conventional pattern. Writers associated with the Romantic movement in literature, especially in America, tended to resist conventional forms, which they regarded as promoting a kind of mechanical operation of the spirit. Instead they privileged imagination and the creative impulse and favored literary structures that were original and that grew out of the material itself rather than some preexisting form or genre. In Emerson's famous formulation of this organic theory in his essay "The Poet" (1844), "It is not metres, but a meter-making argument, that makes a poem,—a thought so passionate and alive, that, like the spirit of a plant or an animal, it has an architecture of its own, and adorns nature with a new thing" (pp. 9–10).

The structure of *Walden* is almost literally organic in this sense, as it is based upon the natural life cycle of the year. At the same time, it is capacious enough to include essays and seeming digressions on other subjects, like "Economy" and "Reading," that seem to have little or nothing to do with the book's original subtitle, "Life in the Woods." Also, within the movement provided by the progress of the seasons, there is another internal pattern of alteration, in which the subject of one chapter will frequently invoke a kind of opposite in the following chapter. Thus, "Reading" is followed by "Sounds," "Solitude" by "Visitors," "Higher Laws" by "Brute Neighbors," and so on. But this pattern is only loose and not strictly followed, again in keeping with Romantic distrust of system and hierarchical forms.

At its extreme, this distrust of artificial forms and structures extends even to a sense of the limits of written expression itself. Another famous dictum from Emerson's "The Poet" is "Art is the path of the creator to his work" (p. 38), which strongly favors the artist's inspiration and conception over his execution in the finished product. In *Walden* this principle expresses itself in a tension between the book's rhetoric of clarity ("Simplify! Simplify!") and highly polished style on the one hand, and its almost equally strong (though easy to overlook) impulses toward mystification and an undercutting of the most apparently certain formulations on the other. In its ideal incarnation, a work of art will be a sort of self-effacing artifact, as the narrator hints in the book's concluding chapter: "The volatile truth of our words should continually betray the inadequacy of the residual statement" (p. 217). (The alert reader, noting the somewhat unusual word choice "volatile" in this construction, will have looked it up and found that it not only means "explosive" and potentially dangerous in ordinary usage but also "easily transforming from one state into another," as in evaporation. Truth, in other words, is fleeting and unstable.)

Throughout the book, then, the narrator tends to undermine his own formulations and most self-confident pronouncements. Usually this move tends to take the form of setting up his own practice as an implicit model and then warning the reader not to follow his example. In the second paragraph of the book, already, the narrator advises the reader not to "stretch the seams in putting on the coat" (pp. 1–2). The long first chapter, "Economy," takes great pains to describe the narrator's simplification of his life at Walden as an antidote to the heedless pursuit of wealth and material goods by his countrymen, frequently listing to the penny in his pseudo-accounts how much his house cost him to build and how much he spent on food. But the majority of items on the list of foods are also labeled "All experiments which failed" (p. 40). And it is evident that the narrator did not really follow his own regimen, slyly admitting, "The reader will perceive that I am treating the subject rather from an economic than a dietetic point of view, and he will not venture to put my abstemiousness to the test unless he has a well-stocked larder" (p. 42). "Economy" itself is followed by a poem by Thomas Carew, "The Pretensions of Poverty," that satirizes just the sort of claims of virtue in a simple rural life that the narrator makes throughout the chapter.

The fact that *Walden* almost always undercuts its own pronouncements should illustrate the dangers of taking it literally as a how-to book. While the would-be disciple is boiling his acorns in the woods, Thoreau himself would be likely to be dropping in at his family's house in the village, having a second helping of pie. The point is that no guidebook is trustworthy, and none may lead another to enlightenment.

THEMES AND CONTEXTS

Somewhat ironically, the critical movement that helped *Walden* to achieve its canonical status in the middle of the twentieth century also had the effect of emptying the book, as it were, of many of its most important concerns. Books such as F. O. Matthiessen's *American Renaissance: Art and Expression in the Age of Emerson and Whitman* (1941), Sherman Paul's *The Shores of America: Thoreau's Inward Exploration* (1958), and Charles Anderson's *The Magic Circle of "Walden"* (1968) taught generations of students to appreciate the artistry of *Walden* and to explore its style, symbolism, and what might be called self-referentiality. This approach, broadly consistent with what was called the New Criticism at the time, focused on the book as a self-contained work of art, understandable without reference to the biography of its author or its historical context. As the subtitle of Paul's work— "Thoreau's Inward Exploration"—suggests, the focus of this criticism was also on the work as a reflection of the problems and possibilities of the self.

The narrator's self-exploration is, to be sure, an important theme in *Walden* and even becomes increasingly the focus of the book as the seasons progress toward the second spring. As shown, the transcendentalists believed that the self was capable of achieving moments of direct insight into divinity through an immersion in the natural world, and *Walden* certainly embodies Emerson's observation in "The American Scholar" (1837) that "the ancient precept, 'Know thyself,' and the modern precept, 'study nature,' become at last one maxim" (p. 87). There are many memorable moments of such spiritual confirmation and fulfillment in *Walden* where nature's veil drops and the narrator sees through it to a higher reality. One such moment, which may serve as a model for this kind of experience, occurs in "The Ponds" chapter, when the narrator gazes down on the surface of the water as a breeze ripples it:

> A field of water betrays the spirit that is in the air. It is continually receiving new life and motion from above. It is intermediate in its nature between land and sky. On land only the grass and trees wave, but the water itself is rippled by the wind. I see where the breeze dashes across it by the streaks or flakes of light. It is remarkable that we can look down on its surface. We shall, perhaps, look down thus on the surface of the air at length, and mark where a still subtler spirit sweeps over it. (P. 127)

Here the phenomenon of a puff of wind blowing across the water provides a perfect illustration of the transcendental principle that, as Walt Whitman put it, the seen proves the unseen—in this case the spirit that animates nature itself. The pond itself is *Walden*'s ultimate "fact," whose physical and spiritual surfaces are grasped simultaneously.

Such perceptions are not only ahistorical but also timeless, and they lie at the heart of the narrator's quest to experience heightened spiritual understanding through nature. And yet *Walden* is at the same time a book that grows out of and seeks to address its immediate historical moment and the many crosscurrents of American culture in the 1840s and 1850s. Thoreau was so successful in creating the persona of the solitary seeker after truth that readers may overlook the fact that *Walden* is also a product of the ferment of reform movements and writing that characterized these decades. To withdraw temporarily from and to critique one's culture is still to be part of it, still to write from within the circle. Even the most familiar narrative element of *Walden,* the narrator building his house in the woods and practicing subsistence farming, is not so much an act of withdrawal as it is an ironic inversion of the dominant heroic myth of this era, the self-sufficient frontiersman exploring, clearing land, building a cabin, and planting his crops on the frontier.

Reform movements of various kinds swept the country, and more than a hundred experimental communities sprang up between 1825 and the Civil War. Emerson wrote to his English friend Thomas Carlyle in 1840: "We are all a little wild here with numberless projects of social reform. Not a reading man but has a draft of a new community in his pocket" (p. 283). Many of the reformers and communitarians were religious (e.g., the Shakers), while others were concerned with social and governmental organization, abolition, women's rights, and even sexual mores and diet. Transcendentalism itself grew out of the zeal for religious reform, as a group of loosely affiliated Unitarian ministers in New England rebelled against what they considered the "corpse-cold" (Emerson's phrase) formalism and tradition-bound character of Unitarianism and sought a more direct and intuitive experience of divinity.

Obviously *Walden* is in many ways a dramatization of transcendentalism's fundamental urge for spiritual enlightenment, but it also reflects and addresses many of the other cultural transformations and reform topics of the time, including but not limited to slavery and abolition, western expansion and the Mexican-American War, Irish immigration, technological change (the railroad and telegraph), education, urbanization and the development of mass markets, agricultural practices, alcohol abuse, and the ways in which diet and sexual practices influenced the development of disease. The vantage point from which it addresses these issues, however, also constitutes a critique of transcendentalism itself as a reform movement.

Transcendentalism was never an organized or coherent movement, but those who allied themselves with its ideals tended to favor either a communitarian or associationist approach toward reform on the one hand or an individualistic approach on the other. The former worked to reform society as a whole, either through direct social action or the creation of communities that would ideally serve as models for society at large. A number of such believers in organized reform participated in the transcendentalist-related communities at Fruitlands (1843–1844) or the more successful and longer-lived Brook Farm (1841–1847). The individualists believed in reform, too, but thought that it could only be achieved in a meaningful way by the individual person. They distrusted organized reform movements as liable to the same weakness as other flawed organizations like the church or the government. This perspective is the one Thoreau expresses in his most famous political essay, "Resistance to Civil Government" or "Civil Disobedience" (1849).

Both Thoreau and Emerson were invited to join Brook Farm, and much as they valued some of the ideals and goals of its founders, both refused, preferring the individual path. Thoreau's Walden experiment of 1845–1847 came at the high point of communitarian reform, and *Walden* itself is in large measure a response to this activity, appropriately though also paradoxically a manual of individualistic reform and the record of an experimental community of one.

The rhetorical stance that enables the narrator to cast a critical eye at the practices of his countrymen (both those in need of reform and the reformers themselves) is that of the traveler. Hypothesizing a removal from society by virtue of his retreat to Walden Pond, the narrator presumes to be able to describe the foibles and weaknesses of that society as though he were a traveler describing the oddities of some exotic culture. "I have travelled a good deal in Concord" (p. 2), goes one of the most familiar of *Walden*'s witty paradoxes, referencing both this traveler-at-home perspective and the fact that he himself rarely traveled and yet was a great reader of travel literature. In fact he was also a great writer of travel narrative himself because most of what he published in his lifetime was travel narrative based upon his infrequent excursions in and around New England: *A Week on the Concord and Merrimack Rivers* (1849), *The Maine Woods* (1864), *Cape Cod* (1865), and *A Yankee in Canada* (1866). In these works, too, Thoreau was less the iconoclast than the public intellectual, engaging not only the landscape but also the society and culture of his times.

The reformist edge to this traveler's perspective is announced early in the text of *Walden:*

> I would fain say something, not so much concerning the Chinese and Sandwich Islanders [Hawaiians] as you who read these pages, who are said to live in New England; something about your condition, especially your outward condition or circumstances in this world, in this town, what it is, whether it is necessary that it be as bad as it is, whether it cannot be improved as well as not. (P. 2)

The local focus of this anticipated critique ("this town") betrays once again *Walden*'s origins as a lecture manuscript first delivered in Concord, as does the harshness of its tone. But the individualist reformer is more or less confined to this tack of negative commentary (balanced only by the accounts of his own individual practices) because he distrusts direct social action and organized reform. In fact some of his harshest words are directed against reformers themselves:

> There are a thousand hacking at the branches of evil to one who is striking at the root, and it may be that he who bestows the largest amount of time and money on the needy is doing the most by his

mode of life to produce that misery which he strives in vain to relieve. (P. 51)

Only if the individual—the root of the problem—can be startled into change by seeing things differently can meaningful reform take place. This position leads the narrator into some rhetorical excesses that were actually at odds with Thoreau's own beliefs and practices, especially as he got older. At one point, for example, he says:

> I sometimes wonder that we can be so frivolous, I may almost say, as to attend to the gross but somewhat foreign [because not practiced in New England] form of servitude called Negro Slavery, there are so many keen and subtle masters that enslave both north and south. It is hard to have a southern overseer; it is worse to have a northern one; but worst of all when you are the slave-driver of yourself. (P. 4)

Elsewhere he despairs of improving the lot of the poor Irish immigrants who are seduced, as it were, by the dream of American prosperity but are apparently incapable of thinking for themselves or escaping their "inherited Irish poverty" (p. 140). This sort of discourse belongs to the early versions of *Walden*, when Thoreau was eager to criticize organized reform from an individualist platform. By the time the book was published in 1854, he was lending his hand to abolitionist causes both through his writing and through personal action supporting escaped slaves through the Underground Railroad. And he was also active in attempting to improve the lot of Irish immigrants in Concord.

The book remains a testament to the individualist position, however, and this fact probably contributes to the rise in Thoreau's (and *Walden*'s) reputation in the twentieth century. Individualism has been the hallmark of American culture at least since the French writer Alexis de Tocqueville coined the term to describe the distinctive feature of American life in the 1830s, and along with it goes a distrust of anything that hints of communitarian or socialistic ideology. This distrust reached its peak in the red scares and the cold war in the 1950s and 1960s, at the very time when *Walden* was solidifying its canonical status.

The narrator's other satiric targets in *Walden* are self-evident, of course, and may be generally grouped around the question that dominates "Economy"—what is the true cost of the material advances, the so-called improvements in our standard of living that we constantly strive for? And although his examples, such as the telegraph and the railroad, are now outdated, analogues in contemporary culture are obvious. If the rush to construct a telegraph from Maine to Texas overlooked the possibility that Maine and Texas might not have anything to say to one another, the same sort of possibility might be raised about the myriad of advances in communication technology that mark the early twenty-first century.

Less obvious are the cultural issues that underlie his own practices at Walden Pond, but nearly all of the narrator's activities interrogate and comment upon contemporary concerns. The range of issues raised in his description of his house building and daily life, for example, question assumptions about domestic life, agricultural practices, and even food production. In one sense *Walden* may be viewed as an alternative model of domestic life that comments upon his contemporaries' concern for bracketing off housekeeping and household work as an exclusively female province. The narrator's presumed local audience, including those "uneasy housekeepers who pried into my cupboard and bed when I was out" (p. 103), would have recognized his descriptions of cleaning, furniture, and food preparation as a sly commentary on such popular guidebooks for women as Catharine Beecher's *Treatise on Domestic Economy* (1841). Even his extended description of baking his own bread alludes to the loss of that skill in contemporary New England, where cheaper processed wheat from the West and commercial baking were replacing the tradition of household bread making and raising questions about the healthiness of the commercial product.

On the largest scale, the extended descriptions of nature not only depict the narrator's search for self-knowledge and enlightenment but also convey a sense of contemporary practices and theories of natural science. Both of these issues converge in the climactic "Spring" chapter, where the narrator describes in great detail a sort of "pre-Spring" in which the earth itself exudes vegetative forms of leaves, vines, and tendrils from a thawing bank along the railroad. The length and exuberance of these passages derive from many years of careful observation of this phenomenon, as Thoreau returned each spring to this site to add more data, as it were, to his representation of the principle of life renewing itself.

His conclusion, which we would tend to read as metaphoric or symbolic, chiefly, is meant as an accurate scientific as well as spiritual truth. "There is nothing inorganic," for:

> The earth is not a mere fragment of dead history, stratum upon stratum like the leaves of a book, to be studied by geologists and antiquaries chiefly, but living poetry like the leaves of a tree, which precede flowers and fruit,—not a fossil earth, but a living earth; compared with whose great central life all animal and vegetable life is merely parasitic. (P. 206)

Employing a characteristic play on words (contrasting the leaves of a book to the leaves of a tree), this passage references contemporary discourse about the age of the earth and the origins of life just before Charles Darwin's *On the Origin of Species* (1859) would forever change the debate. A few pages earlier in this description the narrator says that in viewing this phenomenon he felt as though he "stood in the *laboratory of the Artist* who made the world and me" (p. 204, emphasis added), deliberately fusing what most would consider two opposed modes of perception—the artistic and the scientific.

Walden is a text, then, with a rich and varied set of purposes and modes of discourse, ranging from the caustic and critical commentary on American preoccupations to the intensely personal and even mystical search for individual enlightenment. Because it addresses directly persistent American assumptions about society, nature, individual fulfillment, business, material wealth, and technological change, it remains a work that invites readers to examine and critique their own attitudes toward these issues. At the same time, it grows out of and reflects a vibrant period of rapid social and intellectual change in America and thus sheds light on many of the controversies and anxieties that marked the turbulent antebellum era. Perhaps it remains most persistently American in its portrayal of the perennial possibility of renewal and reawakening and of a life as an experiment yet untried. The experience and the mode of life re-created in the text were not a destination or a solution so much as a confirmation that, as the narrator concludes, "Only that day dawns to which we are awake."

See also "Resistance to Civil Government"; Nature; Reform; Transcendentalism

BIBLIOGRAPHY

Primary Works

Emerson, Ralph Waldo. "The American Scholar." 1837. In *The Complete Works of Ralph Waldo Emerson*, vol. 1, *Nature, Addresses, and Lectures*, edited by Edward W. Emerson, pp. 81–115. Boston: Houghton Mifflin, 1903.

Emerson, Ralph Waldo. "The Poet." 1844. In *The Complete Works of Ralph Waldo Emerson*, vol. 3, *Essays: Second Series*, edited by Edward W. Emerson, pp. 5–42. Boston: Houghton Mifflin, 1903.

Slater, Joseph, ed. *The Correspondence of Emerson and Carlye.* New York: Columbia University Press, 1964.

Thoreau, Henry David. *Walden and Resistance to Civil Government.* Edited by William Rossi. Norton critical edition. New York: Norton, 1992.

Secondary Works

Buell, Lawrence. *The Environmental Imagination: Thoreau, Nature Writing, and the Formation of American Culture.* Cambridge, Mass.: Harvard University Press, 1995.

Cavell, Stanley. *The Senses of Walden: An Expanded Edition.* Chicago: University of Chicago Press, 2002.

Harding, Walter. *The Days of Henry Thoreau.* Princeton, N.J.: Princeton University Press, 1992.

Michaels, Walter Benn. "*Walden*'s False Bottoms." *Glyph* 1 (1977): 132–149.

Myerson, Joel, ed. *The Cambridge Companion to Henry David Thoreau.* Cambridge, U.K., and New York: Cambridge University Press, 1995.

Richardson, Robert D., Jr. *Henry Thoreau: A Life of the Mind.* Berkeley: University of California Press, 1986.

Sattelmeyer, Robert. "The Remaking of *Walden.*" In *Writing the American Classics,* edited by James Barbour and Tom Quirk, pp. 53–78. Chapel Hill: University of North Carolina Press, 1990.

Shanley, J. Lyndon. *The Making of Walden.* Chicago: University of Chicago Press, 1957.

Walls, Laura Dassow. *Seeing New Worlds: Henry David Thoreau and Nineteenth-Century Natural Science.* Madison: University of Wisconsin Press, 1995.

Robert Sattelmeyer

Frontispiece from the 1848 edition of the *Appeal*.
THE LIBRARY OF CONGRESS

WALKER'S APPEAL

Walker's Appeal, in Four Articles, Together with a Preamble, to the Coloured Citizens of the World, but in Particular, and Very Expressly, to Those of the United States of America had a huge impact. First published in 1829, it urged "coloured citizens of the world" to do everything necessary to abolish slavery and oppose white racism. Whites—even the antislavery Quaker Benjamin Lundy (1789–1839)—responded with "condemnation"; African Americans read the pamphlet "until [Walker's] words were stamped in letters of fire upon our soul" (Lundy, p. 107; Amos Beman, quoted in Hinks, "Introduction," p. 109).

DAVID WALKER'S LIFE

Walker's date of birth is uncertain. In 1848 the black abolitionist Henry Highland Garnet's "Brief Sketch of the Life and Character of David Walker" proposed 1785, but tax records, Walker's absence from the 1810 census, and his probable age at his death in 1830 indicate 1796 or 1797 as more likely. He was born free in Wilmington, North Carolina, because his mother was also free (black southern children took their mother's status). His father, however, was probably not free, but a slave. As Peter Hinks points out in *To Awaken My Afflicted Brethren,* although two-thirds of Wilmington's population was African American, only nineteen of these were free.

Meaningful black freedom at this time scarcely existed in Wilmington. Walker's mother or "The Associates of Dr. Bray" (founded in 1723) may have educated him rudimentarily, but his erudition would have been largely self-acquired (perhaps explaining why the *Appeal* emphasizes education's importance so heavily). Walker witnessed slavery's excesses in Wilmington and again in Charleston, South Carolina, where he moved between 1815 and 1820. Charleston offered employment opportunities and possessed a large free black community that governed its own churches. Although Walker probably belonged to a black congregation in Wilmington, he would have been attracted by free blacks' long commitment to emancipation in Charleston. In particular, Charleston's African Methodist Episcopal (AME) Church was militantly antislavery. It had been founded in 1817, following the AME's establishment in Philadelphia by Richard Allen (1760–1831) in 1816. Walker deeply respected Allen, as his *Appeal* makes plain (pp. 60–62), and he probably quickly joined the AME Church.

Charleston's AME Church also figures in history. Denmark Vesey's (c. 1767–1822) 1822 conspiracy against slavery centered upon this church; possibly as many as forty members were involved. After a black informant betrayed Vesey (perhaps accounting for Walker's contempt for black collaborators) and the AME Church was destroyed, Walker left Charleston. He departed just after Vesey's trial in 1822, perhaps because he was a coconspirator. The tenor of his explanation for his departure suggests this: "If I remain in this bloody land, I will not live long. As true as God reigns, I will be avenged for the sorrow which my people have suffered" (quoted in Garnet, p. 7).

Possibly following some southern and western traveling, Walker settled in Boston. Although appalled by Boston's racism (pp. 36, 42, 56), he opened a clothing shop there in 1824 and married Eliza Butler, daughter of a well-established black Boston family, in 1826. The Walkers probably had three children—two sons and one daughter. Walker's used-clothing business did well, despite an unsuccessful prosecution over a false charge of selling stolen goods, and he became Boston agent for John Russwurm and Samuel Cornish's *Freedom's Journal,* the first black journal, launched in 1827. Walker contributed to *Freedom's Journal* until it folded in 1829 (and supported Cornish's short-lived anti-colonizationist journal, *The Rights of All,* 1829–c. 1830). When the Massachusetts General Colored Association (MGCA) was founded in 1828, Walker became a leading member (alongside his involvement with Boston's Prince Hall African Masonic Lodge, from 1826 onward, and May Street Black Methodist Church). The MGCA offered a unique platform for open public commitment to the immediate abolition of slavery. An address by Walker to the MGCA in 1828 (reproduced in *Freedom's Journal*) urged that "it is indispensably our duty . . . to hasten our emancipation," thereby foreshadowing his *Appeal's* radicalism (Hinks, "Introduction," p. 87). Possibly the *Appeal* also took inspiration from Robert Alexander Young's *Ethiopian Manifesto,* published in early 1829, an allusive apocalyptic call for international black unity foreseeing the abolition of slavery and racial oppression. Publication of the incendiary *Appeal,* in three editions between September 1829 and June 1830, was quickly followed by Walker's death, on 6 August 1830.

The cause of Walker's death remains mysterious. He possibly died from tuberculosis, as his death certificate records "consumption"; his daughter had died

from this only one week before and it was a common cause of death at the time. But Walker may have been the victim of a conspiracy, with the (white) coroner falsifying the document. A contemporary allegation was that $3,000 had been offered for his death (*The Liberator,* 22 January 1831). Garnet's "Sketch" also mentions, if skeptically, a death plot by southerners. Southern alarm concerning black militancy was widespread: Vesey's 1822 conspiracy and the inspiration it drew from the successful revolt in Saint-Domingue (1791–1804) was a recent memory; Gabriel Prosser's 1800 rebellion in Richmond, Virginia, was not forgotten; and shortly after Walker's death, in 1831, Nat Turner (1800–1831) led his uprising in Southampton, Virginia. Such alarm could have led proslavery whites to plot Walker's death; it certainly explains the scale of attempts to stifle his *Appeal.*

Walker endeavored to circulate his pamphlet widely during his life, but Walker's bold attempts to increase his *Appeal's* circulation were systematically blocked. The mayor of Savannah and the governors of Virginia and Georgia in 1830 even wrote to the mayor of Boston asking him to curtail Walker's activities. Yet, seemingly, the *Appeal* was read extensively—being linked, for example, to an uprising in New Bern, North Carolina, in December 1830, during which sixty slaves were killed. White southerners became so alarmed after sighting Walker's *Appeal* that laws were passed in Georgia, Louisiana, Mississippi, and North Carolina to prevent African Americans from becoming literate or obtaining antislavery literature. In this climate, Walker's forecast seems reasonable: "I do not only expect to be held up to the public as . . . disturber of the public peace . . . [but also to be] put in prison or to death" (p. 4). Since the *Appeal* was viewed as seditious by white southerners, and they knew fully about Walker's attempts to circulate it in the U.S. mail and by hand (mostly using Atlantic coast sailors, some of whom were black), assassination cannot be ruled out as a cause of death.

WALKER'S APPEAL

David Walker's *Appeal* stands as an innovative fusion of counter-history, prophetic history, advocacy of human rights, and theological arguments. Its central call is for whites, as well as blacks, to observe key ethical and political values: justice, righteousness, freedom, and dignity. But in Walker's view, continuing abysmal failure by whites to observe these human values legitimized action by blacks to take control of their lives and enforce these values' preeminence as a God-sanctioned mission. Sometimes Walker seems to advocate awaiting the rise of a leader, or for God to take vengeance upon whites for their willful failings. But predominantly he calls for direct action. He clearly argues that if whites were not prepared

On 8 December 1829 David Walker wrote to Thomas Lewis, a free black man, urging him to circulate the Appeal widely "among the Coloured people." Walker aggressively sought ways to distribute his work in the South to those who would be receptive to its message.

Having written an Appeal to the Coloured Citizens of the World it is now ready to be submited for inspection, of which, I here send you 30c which Sir, your Hon, will be please to sell, among the Coloured people. The price of these Books is Twelve cents pr Book,—to those who can pay for them,—and if there are any who, cannot pay for a Book give them Books for nothing—If your Hon. should want any more of these Books, please to direct any communication to me at No. 42 Brattle St. where all letters or advices eminating from your Hon. will mee[t] with a hearty and greatful Reception—I assume the Liberty Esteemed Sir, to subscribe myself

Letter from David Walker to Thomas Lewis of Richmond, Slave and Free Negro Letterbook Executive Papers of Governor John Floyd, Virgina State Library, Richmond.

to emancipate blacks, then blacks should seek their own release, renouncing "death-like apathy" (pp. 54, 65, 79). Walker is scathing about black collaboration with whites, defining any such acts as "servile deceit" (p. 29). Prophetic calls for black unity as a means of opposing white oppression are his constant burden.

Walker's Appeal is always prophetic. It stresses God's call for justice and righteousness and his care and concern for enslaved blacks. Such sentiments are shaped by the discourses and rhetoric of Old Testament prophets such as Malachi ("ye have not kept my ways, but been partial in the law. . . . hath not one God created us? why do we deal treacherously every man against his brother?" 2:9–10). Such rhetoric infuses the *Appeal,* as slavery is represented as an abomination before the Lord. *Walker's Appeal* is thoroughly millenarian in tone—linking the pamphlet not only to Isaiah and Jeremiah but also to New England millenarian revivals of the late 1820s and early 1830s (mentioned in Walker's third edition).

Yet the *Appeal* interweaves such religious prophecy with a passionate engagement with contemporary cultural politics. Following a "Preamble" the pamphlet is divided into four "Articles" detailing African American

sufferings at the hands of "Slavery," "Ignorance," "the Preachers of the Religion of Jesus Christ," and "the Colonizing Plan." Excoriating attacks are launched in turn upon slavery's barbaric cruelty, blacks' educational deprivations, white Christian theological hypocrisy, and the way that African colonization, by reducing free blacks' population levels, undermined their ability to promote effective resistance ("you must go to work and prepare the way of the Lord . . . by teaching . . . [slaves] they are MEN . . . and *must* be FREE," pp. 32, 49). Although the predominant invocation is to God, in ways laying the foundations of a black liberation theology, the *Appeal* also consistently invokes the natural-rights discourse of the Enlightenment. Thus, whites are represented in the *Appeal* not only as "backsliders" from the ways of mankind's common creator but also as "natural" enemies.

Such discursive hybridity means that the *Appeal,* read in one sitting, does not always develop a settled logic. This has been seen as a limitation (see Wilentz, p. xix). But it is necessary to read such crosscutting in Walker's argument as tactical. Shifts of emphasis in the *Appeal's* argument, as successive editions were published, support this idea. For example, the *Appeal* comes to reassess whites' largely undifferentiated identification as "enemies" in the first edition. Instead, the last two editions give implicit recognition to the growing strength of white abolitionism in Britain, about to bear fruit in Thomas Buxton's Emancipation Bill, passed by the British Parliament in 1833, abolishing slavery throughout the British colonies. Walker in 1830 would have been aware of this trend, promoted by the Anti-Slavery Society, founded in 1823 by Thomas Clarkson, William Wilberforce, and others. Although carefully noting Britain's nefarious colonial practices, the *Appeal's* later editions nevertheless increasingly seek to make common cause with such transatlantic allies: "the English [are] our real friends and benefactors," Walker claims in 1830 (p. 51). Such a repositioning is strategic. It not only highlights the geopolitical dimensions of slavery and racism, their evil and unnatural consequences, and the rise of worldwide resistance, but also embarrasses white America by highlighting how Britons could be held to support liberty in 1830 much better than did unregenerate proslavery Americans.

Such tactical astuteness is a recurrent modus operandi. Definitively, it is used to counter U.S. whites' incoherent allegations about black entitlements and intellectual capacities. White proslavery arguments proposed that blacks were intellectually weak, indolent, and primitive yet also somehow—even in the selfsame accounts—cunning, dissembling, and violently predatory (especially sexually). Such racist arguments characteristically incorporated the paradoxical proposals that blacks were enslaved because of the benevolence of white slaveholders who were paternalistically concerned to watch over their welfare and that slaves were somehow also held in bondage at the direction of the Lord. Walker's goal was to counter such incoherent arguments, part theological, part "natural," and based in placing distorted biblical readings of Genesis alongside "scientific racism"—racism drawing on scientific discourse to support its bigoted allegation that blacks were "different species of the same genius [read "genus"]" (Jefferson, [mis]quoted in Walker, p. 29; Jefferson, p. 243). Walker had to discover a means of advancing beyond simple outrage, as when confronted by Thomas Jefferson's suggestion that female Africans mate with *"Orang-Outangs"*: "O! My God! I appeal to every man of feeling—is not this insupportable?" (p. 12).

Walker achieves this by first identifying Jefferson as a hugely influential opponent, one whose support legitimated contemporary white attacks on African American's capacities by endorsing the idea that "nature" is a root cause of blacks' enslavement: "nature has been less bountiful to them in the endowments of the head" (Jefferson, p. 242). Walker then stresses the importance of countering such a prominent voice: "unless we try to refute Mr. Jefferson's arguments respecting us, we will only establish them" (pp. 17–18). So Walker's 1830 *Appeal* adds a commentary on the Declaration of Independence, aimed at exposing the hypocritical way in which whites read the United States's founding document only partially. Walker seeks to suborn Jefferson's Lockean philosophy to his side: "Compare your own language . . . from your Declaration of Independence, with your cruelties and murders . . . 'But when a long train of abuses and usurpation . . . evinces a design to reduce them under absolute despotism, it is their *right,* it is their *duty,* to throw off such government'" (pp. 78–79). In adopting this counterstrategy, Walker anticipates later black abolitionists including Frederick Douglass (1818–1895) and William Wells Brown (c. 1814–1884).

Walker's Appeal confronts racists' discursive resources and rebuts or transforms them. As such, his *Appeal* is part of a long tradition of African American intellectual challenges to white epistemic authority. His multiply stranded tactical argumentation can also accommodate a range of African American political positions and even allow through the backdoor sympathetic whites: "Treat us like men, and there is no danger but we will all live in peace and happiness together" (p. 73). Even though Walker expected his primary audience to be black, he was well aware that whites would take an interest: "I am awfully afraid that pride, prejudice, avarice and blood, will, before long prove the final ruin

of this . . . land of *liberty!!!!* . . . Oh [white] Americans! Americans!! I warn you in the name of the Lord . . . to repent and reform, or you are ruined!!!" (p. 42).

Such outbursts fire up Walker's arguments. At one high point, Walker records how he must break off: "Here I pause to get breath" (p. 54). An emotively charged reasonableness results, aimed primarily at African Americans and taking as its burden, "we are MEN" (p. 8). The whole pamphlet stands as a self-reflexive demonstration of blacks' essential humanity by offering an admixture of emotions (anger, hate, love), argument, and reason. Walker's implicit point is that African Americans both experience human emotions and exercise reason perfectly well. By making an "appeal" to these capacities, Walker demonstrates that African Americans *self-evidently* possess them, despite the rise of scientific racism's propaganda.

The pamphlet makes plain the consequences that flow from his analysis. Blacks must fight ideologically, politically, and even physically to oppose racism and secure freedom. To do this is mere self-defense. Such self-defense must depend upon unity and be accompanied by systematic education to counter ignorance and repair psychological trauma. These steps must be accompanied by a profound skepticism concerning the motives of American whites—a theme that intensifies as the *Appeal* evolves through its second and third editions, which increasingly often level at whites the charge of hypocrisy, particularly Christian hypocrisy.

The *Appeal* thus stands as an early manifestation of radical black Christianity, even down to its incorporation of the rhetorical tropes of the African American sermon (rhetorical questions, anaphoras, and calls for response). Its rhetorical brilliance contributes to its effectiveness. Its arguments were taken up by such writers as Maria W. Stewart (1803–1879), who, in "Religion and the Pure Principles of Morality" (1831), regarded Walker as "noble, fearless, and undaunted" (p. 30) and Henry Highland Garnet (1815–1882), who reprinted *Walker's Appeal* in 1848. Walker may only develop black nationalist thought rather than found it (Hinks, *To Awaken My Afflicted Brethren,* pp. 171–195, 249), but his *Appeal's* publication marks a decisive advance in militant African American abolitionist and antiracist campaigning.

See also Abolitionist Writing; Blacks; Slave Narratives; Slave Rebellions

BIBLIOGRAPHY

Primary Works

Garnet, Henry Highland. "A Brief Sketch of the Life and Character of David Walker." In *Walker's Appeal, in Four Articles [by] David Walker [and] An Address to* the Slaves of the United States of America. 1848. New York: Arno Press, 1969.

Jefferson, Thomas. Notes on the State of Virginia; Written in the Year 1781. In The Life and Selected Writings of Thomas Jefferson, edited by Adrienne Koch and William Peden, pp. 173–267. New York: Modern Library, 1998.

Lundy, Benjamin. "Walker's Boston Pamphlet." In The Genius of Universal Emancipation, April 1830. In Walker, pp. 107–108.

Stewart, Maria W. "Religion and the Pure Principles of Morality [on Which We Must Build]." 1831. In Maria Stewart, America's First Black Woman Political Writer: Essays and Speeches, edited by Marilyn Richardson, pp. 30–40. Bloomington: Indiana University Press, 1987.

Walker, David. David Walker's Appeal to the Coloured Citizens of the World. 1829–1830. Edited by Peter P. Hinks. University Park: Pennsylvania State University Press, 2000.

Young, Robert Alexander. The Ethiopian Manifesto. New York: Robert Alexander Young, 1829.

Secondary Works

Burrow, Rufus, Jr. God and Human Responsibility: David Walker and Ethical Prophecy. Macon, Ga.: Mercer University Press, 2003.

Ernest, John. Liberation Historiography: African American Writers and the Challenge of History, 1794–1861. Chapel Hill: University of North Carolina Press, 2004.

Hinks, Peter P. "Introduction." In David Walker's Appeal to the Coloured Citizens of the World. University Park: Pennsylvania State University Press, 2000.

Hinks, Peter P. To Awaken My Afflicted Brethren: David Walker and the Problem of Antebellum Slave Resistance. University Park: Pennsylvania State University Press, 1997.

Wilentz, Sean. "Introduction." In David Walker's Appeal to the Coloured Citizens of the World, but in Particular, and Very Expressly, to Those of the United States of America. New York: Hill and Wang, 1995.

R. J. Ellis

WASHINGTON, D.C.

As a city that was planned from scratch to be a great capital, "a city of magnificent distances," Washington was considered to be quite a story and something to see. The city itself was a monument to George Washington, the man most responsible for the city's site and design. On their American tours, the British authors Frances Trollope (in 1832), Charles Dickens (in 1842),

and Anthony Trollope (in 1861) made sure to visit the capital and the grave at nearby Mount Vernon of the "great man" behind it. In her Domestic Manners of the Americans (1832), Frances Trollope (1780–1863) praised the capital above everything else in America while her son Anthony (1815–1882), in North America (1862), deemed it a "failure." The Atlantic Monthly of January 1861 called the capital a "paradise of paradoxes": "the city of magnificent distances but of still more magnificent discrepancies"; a city whose great avenues were unpaved fields of mud, and whose ideal statesmen traded political favors as avidly as they traded bets at the gaming tables. "Blessed with the name of the purest of men, [the city] has the reputation of Sodom" ("Washington City," pp. 1–8). Most embarrassing and obnoxious to many was the fact that slavery was legal in the District of Columbia until 1850 (the cheap labor of slaves had in fact made it possible to build such expensive monumental buildings as the Capitol). William Wells Brown (c. 1814–1884), a leading abolitionist lecturer and writer, dramatized the shameful juxtaposition of slavery in the capital of political freedom in his novel Clotel (1853), the first African American novel. By 1861 the city's exposé of the nation's troubles gained a new dimension as it became the central hospital for the Union army during the Civil War.

Washington was understood as an emblem of the nation, offering proof of the viability or fragility of the American political experiment. Joseph P. Varnum, in an essay that first appeared in Hunts Merchants' Magazine in 1848, argued that as the nation expanded westward so too the capital city's neighborhoods would expand, giving hope that George Washington's ambitious plan would eventually be filled in. As the nation thrived, so did its capital; as it struggled, its capital struggled too. Anthony Trollope arrived in time to see a nation "splitting into pieces" and a capital overrun by carts filled with wounded men. If George Washington could look down upon his capital, filled by soldiers now that the North and the South were "concentrated on the art of killing," how, Trollope asked, would the view "address the city of his hopes?" (pp. 322, 316).

AN IDEAL CITY?

Much Washington, D.C., literature describes Washington as an exceptional and even ideal space. The author Margaret Bayard Smith (1778–1844) was one of the first Washingtonians, moving to the city when it officially became the capital in 1800. Her letters, published in a posthumous collection, The First Forty Years of Washington Society (1906), describe the capital in glowing terms. Smith was the close friend of many of the nation's political elite. During the hotly contested presidential election of 1824, one of the four

The west front of the Capitol Building, Washington, D.C., 1826. Painting by John Rubens Smith. Executed soon after completion of the building, this painting illustrates the relatively pastoral nature of the city during much of the nineteenth century. GETTY IMAGES

candidates, William Crawford, played chess with Mrs. Smith while waiting to hear the results of the vote. Smith describes busy days from 10 A.M. to 10 P.M., living the drama of the national scene and exercising not insignificant power through the capital's already established custom of doing political business over private suppers. If someone noteworthy was speaking in Congress she made a point to attend, Congress being open, unlike England's Parliament, to ladies. As Smith writes, "Washington possesses a peculiar interest and to an active, reflective, and ambitious mind, has more attractions than any other place in America" (p. 94).

After being shocked by the lack of manners she found in America, Frances Trollope viewed Washington with relief. Here was a city both cosmopolitan and refined; it was the best American city and destined to be an elegant success. Trollope particularly approved of the freedom from commercial life in a city whose main business was conversation: "instead of the busy bustling hustle of men . . . you see very well-dressed personages lounging leisurely up and down Pennsylvania Avenue"; congressmen were paid handsomely to simply sit around and "talk a little" (p. 169). Trollope's and Smith's appreciation of Washington's uniqueness would

later be echoed by Henry James, who dubbed the capital the "city of conversation" (*The American Scene,* p. 341).

Yet idealized Washington images of lofty debate among eloquent, heroic statesmen were often contrasted by the actual congressmen on display. Noting some impressive political performances, Frances Trollope and Charles Dickens spend even more time being shocked by the rough and vulgar behavior of many congressman, their obsessive tobacco chewing most of all. Dickens starts his Washington portrait with withering descriptions of men spitting, expensive carpets soaked, spittoons everywhere and everywhere missed. This view contributed to the popular view of Washington as largely a man's town. Congressional sessions were so short (lasting only two months) that many wives did not accompany their husbands, and this made for the sort of freedom from decorum that might be enjoyed in a frontier town. Frances Trollope was appalled by the general lack of manners, men sprawling, "legs above their heads," swearing, gambling, and of course, spitting (p. 175). Later scholarship has revised this image of antebellum Washington to show that women had a very marked presence in the capital from its beginnings and were a real political force.

CAPITAL OF FREEDOM, CAPITAL OF SLAVERY

Washington had many promoters, but perhaps the most idealistic view of the city was voiced by freedmen. In her memoir *Behind the Scenes* (1868), Elizabeth Keckley (c. 1818–1907), dressmaker to Mary Todd Lincoln, reports the magnet Washington had become for freedmen. Washington was the mid-century city on a hill, Lincoln's city, the city of Emancipation. Many blacks shared the belief of one woman that "Mr. and Mrs. Lincoln" were "Mister and Missus government" and would take care of them. But as Keckley reports, they received no organized assistance but instead a harsh introduction to "northern" manners and disdain. Forced to live in makeshift camps with no amenities, some complained that slavery was no worse.

That slavery and slave auctions had existed in the nation's capital up until 1850 was perhaps the paradox that received the most comment and complaint. William Wells Brown dramatized the irony of slavery at the center of political freedom in *Clotel*. The irony begins with the novel's heroine, Clotel, who is the daughter Thomas Jefferson had by one of his slaves. At the novel's climax Clotel makes a mad dash toward freedom from a slave prison in Washington. Brown uses the ironies of the capital's actual landscape to dramatic effect. The prison is the one that existed on Pennsylvania Avenue between the Capitol and the White House. Clotel runs to the Potomac River and starts across Long Bridge (which was just below today's Memorial Bridge) toward the Virginia shore and a deep wood where she hopes to hide from her pursuers. The wood Clotel seeks is part of the estate of George Washington's descendant George Washington Custis, whose mansion, Arlington House, still overlooks the capital. For Brown the house also oversees the city's faithfulness to its founder's vision. Just as Clotel believes she will succeed, she sees men on the Virginia side. "True to their Virginian instincts," they respond to her jailers' cry for aid and wait to catch her at the end of the bridge. As Thomas Jefferson loved liberty, so does his slave daughter. She jumps into the river to her death. Brown's factual setting exposes the weakness of George Washington's legacy (Washington freed most of his slaves upon his death) and the shortsightedness of his vision. Clotel's "appalling tragedy" takes place "within plain sight of the President's house and the capital of the Union" (pp. 205–207).

Brown's account revises an earlier version of this tale published as a poem in 1851 by the Washington author Grace Greenwood (Sarah Jane Clarke, 1823–1904), who claimed it was based on an actual event. Brown's scene still more notably revises the famous successful escape of the slave Eliza in Harriet Beecher Stowe's (1811–1896) *Uncle Tom's Cabin,* serialized in 1851–1852 in the Washington antislavery newspaper the *National Era*. Clotel runs not from Kentucky to the free state of Ohio, as Eliza does, but from the nation's capital to the slave state of Virginia. Instead of the friendly man who lends Eliza a helping hand on the Ohio shore, Clotel meets only more slave catchers. Eliza's Ohio River becomes the River Jordan, but the Potomac River offers no such passage to freedom. The Long Bridge, which joins the Maryland side of the Potomac to the Virginia side, rather gives physical proof that the nation's union is held together by its support of slavery.

Washington emerges from such accounts as a promise betrayed. Contemplating the capital's paltry fulfillment of its grand design, Anthony Trollope argued that "nothing but disappointment is felt" (p. 305). Many authors treated the city with Dickens's disdain: "To the admirer of cities, [Washington] is a monument raised to a deceased project" (p. 154). Henry Adams (1838–1918) offered his version: "As in 1800 and 1850, so in 1860, the same rude colony camped in the same forest, with the same unfinished Greek temples for workrooms, and sloughs for roads" (p. 810). At the heart of such accounts lay Congress, soulless and corrupt, in Dickens's words, "The meanest perversion of virtuous Political Machinery that the worst tools ever wrought" (p. 159).

WAR AND REDEMPTION

The Civil War brought the capital's rocky career to a head. Once again the city's physical situation provided all the irony a critic might seek and made the capital an accurate emblem of its beleaguered nation. Due to its proximity to the front, Washington became the hospital headquarters for the Union. As Walt Whitman (1819–1892) wrote to Ralph Waldo Emerson, here was "America already brought to Hospital in her fair youth—brought and deposited here in this great whited sepulcher of Washington itself" (*Correspondence,* p. 69). Whitman served as a nurse in the capital's hospitals and gathered material that he turned into newspaper pieces, poems, and sketches, later published in his collection *Specimen Days* (1882). For Whitman, Washington provided a revealing, behind-the-scenes view of the war, one that featured the quiet heroism of men not on the battlefield but in the sad and moving hospitals. The capital in crisis became the ultimate test of Whitman's vision of the Union as the fraternal affection possible among the widest range of rugged men. Whitman's romanticized Washington generates an irresistible poetry in the unimaginable scenes that are part of its everyday life—the moonlit stillness of the White House guarded by sentries, the drowsy perseverance of congressmen up all hours in the gaslit chambers of the Capitol, and the "curious" scene at the Patent Office, where, for lack of anyplace else to put them, stricken soldiers were housed in its museum of inventions, the men's sad "cases" wedged between the glass "cases" holding the objects on display. The Patent Office Hospital documents the cold wastefulness of the national leadership—young men sacrificed and displayed in the cold marble halls that Congress built. "Strange" too is the fact that in those very halls, when the men have finally been moved to newly built hospitals, Lincoln would hold his second inaugural ball. Yet Whitman's use of words such as "curious" and "strange" shows the restraint in many of his descriptions of Washington during the war. He does not accuse Lincoln and his party of dancing on the graves of the dead but simply gives the scene its jaw-dropping sense of weird coincidence. Ultimately the ironies of Washington that others found so much fault with served to deepen Whitman's ever-ready faith in the Union, and the loss it required to sustain and redeem itself made it only more profound.

As the nation's internal struggle was registered so fully on the face of its capital, so too the nation's reconstruction was marked in what came to be called the "new Washington." Washington's infamous muddy streets were paved. As the Union now became an established permanent fact, its capital began the long road toward looking less like a precarious settlement. Many of its improvements were achieved, however, through the corrupt practices of its new mayor, "Boss Shepherd." In a few years, Mark Twain and Charles Dudley Warner would publish *The Gilded Age* (1873), their scathing satire of the capital's sublime mixture of idealism and corruption, and argue thus that the new Washington was not very different from the old.

See also Civil War; *Clotel;* Democracy; English Literature; Female Authorship; Slavery; Tourism

BIBLIOGRAPHY
Primary Works
Adams, Henry. *The Education of Henry Adams.* 1907. In *Novels, Mont Saint Michel, The Education,* edited by Ernest Samuels and Jayne N. Samuels. New York: Library of America, 1983.

Brown, William Wells. *Clotel.* 1853. Edited by Robert S. Levine. Boston: Bedford/St. Martin's, 2000.

Dickens, Charles. *American Notes.* 1842. New York: Modern Library, 1996.

James, Henry. *The American Scene.* 1907. New York: Scribners, 1946.

Keckley, Elizabeth, *Behind the Scenes.* 1868. Edited by Frances Smith Foster. Chicago: Donnelley and Sons, 1998.

Smith, Margaret Bayard. *The First Forty Years of Washington Society.* 1906. Edited by Gailard Hunt. New York: Frederick Ungar, 1965.

Trollope, Anthony. *North America.* New York: Harper & Brothers, 1862.

Trollope, Frances. *Domestic Manners of the Americans.* 1832. Barre, Mass. Imprint Society, 1969.

Twain, Mark, and Charles Dudley Warner. *The Gilded Age.* 1873. New York: Meridian, 1994.

Varnum, Joseph B., Jr. *The Seat of Government of the United States of America.* New York: Press of Hunt's Merchants' Magazine, 1848.

"Washington City." *Atlantic Monthly* (January 1861): 1–8.

Whitman, Walt. *The Correspondence of Walt Whitman.* Vol. 1. Edited by Edwin Haviland Miller. New York: New York University Press, 1961.

Whitman, Walt. *Memoranda during the War [&] Death of Abraham Lincoln.* 1875. Facsimile edition with an introduction by Roy P. Basler. Bloomington: Indiana University Press, 1962.

Whitman, Walt. *Specimen Days.* 1882. In *Complete Poetry and Collected Prose.* Edited by Justin Kaplan. New York: Library of America, 1982.

Secondary Works
Allgor, Catherine. *Parlor Politics: In Which the Ladies of Washington Help Build a City and a Government.* Charlottesville: University of Virginia Press, 2000.

Carson, Barbara. *Ambitious Appetites: Dining, Behavior, and Patterns of Consumption in Federal Washington.* Washington, D.C.: American Institute of Architects, 1990.

Earman, Cynthia D. "Remembering the Ladies: Women, Etiquette, and Diversions in Washington City, 1800–1814." *Washington History* (spring–summer 2000): 102–117.

Kinney, Katherine. "Making Capital: War, Labor, and Whitman in Washington, D.C." In *Breaking Bounds: Whitman and American Cultural Studies,* edited by Betsy Erkkila and Jay Grossman, pp. 174–189. New York: Oxford University Press, 1996.

Reynolds, David S. *Walt Whitman's America.* New York: Knopf, 1995.

Sarah Luria

"WHEN LILACS LAST IN THE DOORYARD BLOOM'D"

Between the publication of the third edition of *Leaves of Grass* in 1860 and the fourth in 1867, Walt Whitman's (1819–1892) life and the life of the country underwent major changes revolving around the outbreak of the Civil War. In December 1862 Whitman traveled from New York City to Fredericksburg, Virginia, to find his brother George, who had been wounded in the battle there. Whitman stayed for nearly two weeks, searching for his brother in the hospitals of the capital and eventually finding him in Fredericksburg. In January 1863 he moved to Washington, D.C., in order to visit the wounded, sick, and dying soldiers in the military hospitals. In three years Whitman visited thousands of young men, dispensing small gifts and writing letters for the badly wounded and illiterate. Meanwhile the poet managed to find a part-time position as a copyist in the Army Paymaster's Office; eventually he would become a clerk in the Interior Department and in the Attorney General's Office, remaining in government service until he suffered a paralytic stroke in 1873. In the little free time he had left, Whitman walked along Rock Creek with a new friend, the naturalist John Burroughs (1837–1921), who would become his first biographer and lifelong defender. Whitman's aesthetic revolution, both in subject matter and in technique, led to censorship, dismissal from government service, and moral outrage, but Burroughs was a steadfast critical voice from 1865 to his own death in 1921.

Many of the changes brought about by the Civil War pertain to the scale of economic and social life, for in the years following the war America moved toward an urban, industrial model of society and culture. But these developments made the Civil War a vast field of maiming and death. In a dramatic fashion, the scale of technological change is figured in the torn bodies of the wounded soldiers. The technology of weaponry, for example, far outran the military training in field tactics, so that breech-loading repeating rifles combined with frontal assaults to produce astronomical numbers of casualties. The dead piled high, as did the wounded, but perhaps most horrific were the piles of mutilated, amputated limbs, such as the scene Whitman recorded at a field hospital in Falmouth, Virginia:

> Out doors, at the foot of a tree, within ten yards of the front of the house, I notice a heap of amputated feet, legs, arms, hands, &c., a full load for a one-horse cart. Several dead bodies lie near, each cover'd with its brown woolen blanket. In the door-yard, towards the river, are fresh graves, mostly of officers, their names on pieces of barrelstaves or broken boards, stuck in the dirt. (*Prose Works 1892* 1:32)

The transportation of troops by railroad was another technological development, but again the result was the massing of troops against one another in spectacular slaughters. Battles like Antietam, Wilderness, and Petersburg inflicted deep wounds on an entire generation. When President Abraham Lincoln said of General Ulysses S. Grant that he had at last found a commander who could "face the arithmetic" (Neely, p. 74), he clearly discerned the new scale of death.

The assassination of President Lincoln took place on the evening of 14 April 1865, and the president died on the morning of 15 April. In May 1865 Whitman published the volume *Drum-Taps*, a collection of fifty-three poems that he had been writing from early in the war years. But after only a few copies had been bound, Whitman printed an eighteen-poem *Sequel to Drum-Taps* and bound it in with the first volume. The *Sequel* contained his most popular poem—"O Captain! My Captain!"—and his most important elegy—"When Lilacs Last in the Dooryard Bloom'd." Soon after the publication of the two volumes, Whitman was abruptly dismissed from his clerkship in the Bureau of Indian Affairs by the new secretary of the interior, James Harlan, who discovered Whitman's copy of the 1861 *Leaves of Grass* in the clerk's desk and declared it obscene. Whitman's friend William D. O'Connor visited Attorney General J. Hubley Ashton, who reinstated Whitman and transferred him to his own department. O'Connor then published his biographical vindication of Whitman in January 1866, *The Good Gray Poet*. Meanwhile John Burroughs's essay "Walt Whitman and His 'Drum-Taps'" appeared in *Galaxy* magazine in December 1866, and in 1867 Burroughs published the book *Notes on Walt Whitman, as Poet and Person*, the first critical book on Whitman's poetry.

THE ROLE OF NATURE

As was the case with O'Connor's hagiography, Whitman exercised great control over Burroughs's critical study, even drafting the important chapter "Standard of the Natural Universal." The chapter gives a highly developed version of Whitman's thinking about nature in the 1860s, and for that reason it deserves special mention in relation to "When Lilacs Last in the Dooryard Bloom'd." The argument of the chapter centers on the role of nature as a standard for all of culture, beginning with the first rhetorical question: "What is the reason that the inexorable and perhaps deciding standard by which poems, and other productions of art, must be tried, after the application of all minor tests, is the standard of absolute Nature?" (Burroughs, *Notes on Walt Whitman,* p. 37). The thirteen pages of the chapter argue that the most important poetic quality is the writer's "passionate affiliation and identity with Nature" and that "the most vaunted beauties of the best artificial productions" should be subordinated "to the daily and hourly beauty of the shows and objects of outward Nature. I mean inclusively, the objects of Nature in their human relations" (p. 38). Moreover, the "objects of Nature" provide the human spirit "its only inlet to clear views of the highest Philosophy and Religion. Only in their spirit can he himself have health, sweetness, and proportion" (p. 38).

Despite the centrality of nature to Burroughs's account of Whitman, relatively few poems in the 1865 *Drum-Taps* volume focus on it. Instead, the war and the suffering of soldiers take center stage, and nature functions more as choral commentary upon the main actions and actors than as a full-fledged participant in the drama. Nature plays a limited role in *Drum-Taps* because it plays a decidedly minor role in the poet's vision of the Civil War. That is far from the case in "When Lilacs Last in the Dooryard Bloom'd." The poem is a pastoral elegy for Abraham Lincoln, but like all great elegies it transcends the particular loss of a beloved to become a deep, sustained meditation on death. In "Lilacs," moreover, Whitman meditates on the Civil War and the fate of America.

Nature provides the three most important images in the elegiac drama. The lilacs and "great star" are associated with the season during which Lincoln died, and as such they function as metonymic images for his loss. Whitman follows the conventions of pastoral elegy quite closely, especially in the ways nature joins in the mourning of the beloved's death. In particular, the "drooping star in the west" (l. 5) evokes both Lincoln and the poet's sense of powerlessness. In section 2 of the poem, the "powerful western fallen star" disappears in a "black murk" or "harsh surrounding cloud" (ll. 7, 9, 11). Whitman recurs to this image in section 8, in a more developed situation; here, the poet recalls the star "sailing the heaven" a month before and imagines that the star had "something to tell" and was "full . . . of woe" (ll. 55, 59, 62). But as in section 2, the star sinks and is lost, and the poet's soul sinks as well.

In the retrospective vision of the prose work *Specimen Days* (1882), Whitman evokes the western star in a more general and hopeful way. The chapter called "The Weather.—Does It Sympathize with These Times?" ponders the analogies between the weather and the upheaval of the Civil War, and then Whitman notes, "As the President came out on the capitol portico, a curious little white cloud, the only one in that part of the sky, appear'd like a hovering bird, right over him" (*Prose Works 1892* 1:94). This natural augury becomes more pronounced in the second half of the chapter, in which Whitman focuses on "the western star, Venus" and notes that it "has never been so large, so clear; it seems as if it told something, as if it held rapport indulgent with humanity, with us Americans. . . . Then I heard, slow and clear, the deliberate notes of a bugle come up out of the silence, sounding so good through the night's mystery, no hurry, but firm and faithful, floating along, rising, falling leisurely, with here and there a long-drawn note" (1:94–95). The unspoken message and portentous imagery foretell the death of President Lincoln, but they also foretell the survival of the Union. That is exactly how Whitman treats the "tragic splendor" of Lincoln's assassination in the chapter "Death of President Lincoln," for he figures the death as "purging, illuminating all" and "throw[ing] round his form, his head, an aureole that will remain and will grow brighter through time, while history lives, and love of country lasts" (1:98).

As the title of the poem suggests, the lilacs occupy an even more important place in the symbolism of the elegy. Whitman first figures the blossom as "blooming perennial" (l. 5), and in section 3 he describes a ceremonial moment. The poet approaches a pastoral "dooryard fronting an old farm-house near the white-wash'd palings" (l. 12), describes the lilac bush growing there, and then breaks "a sprig with its flower" (l. 17). Only in section 6 does one learn that the sprig of lilac is the poet's public offering to the president's coffin. Sections 5 and 6 give the most realistic description of the poem, recounting the journey of the presidential train through the American landscape, "with the great cloud darkening the land" (l. 34) and "with all the mournful voices of the dirges pour'd around the coffin" (l. 41). Even as the poet offers the coffin his sprig of lilac, however, ending section 6, he begins section 7 with an expansion of his gesture of mourning. The single sprig becomes armloads of lilacs, roses, and lilies, and they are offered to the plural "coffins" and ultimately to death itself.

In the beginning of the poem the poet praises the "trinity sure" (l. 4) that spring always brings to him, but in section 1 the third part of the trinity seems to be "thought of him I love" (l. 6). The personal designation of a beloved is appropriate to pastoral elegy, which traditionally is the lament of a shepherd for a deceased comrade. As Whitman's elegy progresses, however, the "thought of him I love" becomes the figure of the hermit thrush, a bird that Whitman had learned about from Burroughs.

In the essay "The Return of the Birds," first published in the May 1865 issue of *Galaxy* magazine, Burroughs notes that the hermit thrush is "quite a rare bird, of very shy and secluded habits" and is found "only in the deepest and most remote forests, usually in damp and swampy localities" (pp. 22–23). He describes the song of the hermit thrush as "wild and ethereal," a kind of "silver horn which he winds in the most solitary places" (pp. 23). According to Burroughs's old-age reminiscences, when Whitman told him his plans for the elegy he asked the naturalist for an appropriate bird for the poem, and Burroughs described the hermit thrush and its "pure, serene, hymn-like" (p. 23) song. The poet exclaimed, "That's my bird!"

The hermit thrush is introduced in section 4, solitary in a way that recalls the mockingbird of "Out of the Cradle Endlessly Rocking" and, like the earlier bird, elegiacally singing a "song of the bleeding throat, / Death's outlet song of life" (ll. 23–24). In sections 9 and 13 the poet addresses the thrush, commanding it to continue singing and apologizing for delaying his visit to it, for the star and lilac detain him. In the intervening sections 10–12, Whitman develops three gorgeous images of the American landscape. In the first section he imagines the "sea-winds" meeting in the central prairies (ll. 74–75), and they provide the perfume for Lincoln's grave. In the second, he paints pictures of country and city at sundown, and these will adorn the "burial-house" (l. 81). Finally, in the third section he clears away any trace of the black cloud, giving a bright panorama of the "varied and ample land" (l. 92).

THE ROLE OF THE BIRDSONG

The poem does not develop as a linear narrative, but in section 14 the poet begins with "the large unconscious scenery of my land with its lakes and forests" (l. 111), lovingly retracing the panoramic vision of section 12. Suddenly, however, the cloud reappears, and the poet announces a new dimension to the poem: "Appear'd the cloud, appear'd the long black trail, / And I knew death, its thought, and the sacred knowledge of death" (ll. 118–119). The narrative is not wholly realistic, for in section 14 the poet walks with the two companions, the knowledge of death and the thought of death. This second trinity approaches "the solemn shadowy cedars and ghostly pines so still" (l. 126), and the poet at last hears the song of the hermit thrush. In seven free-verse quatrains, with varying line lengths, Whitman renders the song of the bird as the voice of his own spirit. The song welcomes death as a personified "dark mother" and "strong deliveress," and it brings together the "sights of the open landscape" and the "husky whispering wave" (ll. 144, 148,

154, 157). Unlike the birdsong in "Out of the Cradle Endlessly Rocking," however, the thrush's song ends in joy, not grief.

The birdsong is a distinct opening in Whitman's pastoral elegy, moving the tone from grief toward consolation. In addition, the song leads to the opening of the poet's vision: "While my sight that was bound in my eyes unclosed, / As to long panoramas of visions" (ll. 169–170). In this visionary opening Whitman first sees a nightmare vision of battle, in which fragments and shreds splinter and break into silence and "battle-corpses" become "white skeletons of young men" (ll. 178, 179). The bodies become body parts, and as the vision widens the parts become "the debris and debris of all the slain soldiers of the war" (l. 180). Then, in a magical turn, the debris gives way to a further vision of consolation, for the poet sees "they were not as was thought" (l. 181). The poet's knowledge of death encompasses both the peace of the dead, who no longer suffer, and the suffering of the survivors, who must continue to mourn their losses. The wisdom of that knowledge is large and copious, and it leads Whitman to his final affirmations in section 16 of the poem. As he "resumes" the principal images of the poem—lilac and star and bird—he portrays himself as passing beyond the visionary experience of elegy, beyond the need for nature's meanings. And yet he finally knows there is no such passage beyond, but rather a perennial experience of retrievement. That is the final, perennial wisdom Whitman gains from the experience: "Lilac and star and bird twined with the chant of my soul, / There in the fragrant pines and the cedars dusk and dim" (ll. 207–208).

ELEGY IN WHITMAN'S CAREER

"When Lilacs Last in the Dooryard Bloom'd" is properly recognized as Whitman's finest elegy, combining the powerful sense of tragic loss with the persuasive movement toward consolation and acceptance. Whitman himself must have recognized the success of the poem, for he revised it very little after its initial publication. Moreover, he kept the poem in a separate cluster devoted to President Lincoln through the last three editions of *Leaves of Grass* (1867, 1871, and 1881), though many of the other poems migrated widely from one cluster to another before coming to rest in the final arrangements of the 1881 edition.

The Civil War and the death of Lincoln continued to exercise a profound influence on Whitman during the last quarter century of his life. He wrote extensively on both the common soldiers and the president in his prose works *Memoranda during the War* (1875) and *Specimen Days*. In addition, from 1879 on he delivered a memorial lecture on Lincoln whenever his health permitted. The ritual of memory is itself elegiac, as if the mourner is never able to be completely consoled but must relive the loss and grief caused by the million deaths of the war. Indeed, the last two Civil War chapters of *Specimen Days,* "The Million Dead, Too, Summ'd Up" and "The Real War Will Never Get in the Books," dwell upon the unknown, mysterious violence and death of the four years. The "eternal darkness" and "interior history" of the unknown soldiers are buried with them, but for Whitman that was the spur to return, "with ever-returning spring" (l. 3), to the central importance of the war to his work and to the country.

Late poems are part of the pattern of recurrence or return. The beautiful lyric "Warble for Lilac-Time," for instance, creates a tone of tranquil joy, but it also evokes the restlessness of the soul, "the restlessness after I know not what" (l. 16). The two-line "Abraham Lincoln, Born Feb. 12, 1809," published in 1888, deifies the dead president by commanding readers to send their thoughts and prayers "to memory of Him—to birth of Him" (l. 2). In one of his last poems, "A Twilight Song," Whitman revisits the "long-pass'd war scenes" and "countless buried unknown soldiers" (l. 2), musing on the "million unwrit names" as the "dark bequest from all the war" (l. 10). Although the poet claims that he recognizes now "a flash of duty long neglected" (l. 11), in fact he had already recorded the "mystic roll entire of unknown names" deep within his heart (ll. 13–14).

Such is the nature of elegy, and such the nature of Whitman's elegies for the Civil War dead. Perhaps that is why Whitman could rightly look to the war as the most important impetus to his poetry. Writing in "A Backward Glance o'er Travel'd Roads" (1888), therefore, the poet once again connects the war and his poetic career:

> Only from the occurrence of the Secession War, and what it show'd me as by flashes of lightning, with the emotional depths it sounded and arous'd (of course, I don't mean in my own heart only, I saw it just as plainly in others, in millions)—that only from the strong flare and provocation of that war's sights and scenes the final reasons-for-being of an autochthonic and passionate song definitely came forth. (*Prose Works 1892,* p. 724)

Although Whitman is often criticized for his outsized ego, the retrospective vision suggests that he was fully capable of imagining the suffering of millions.

See also Civil War; Death; *Leaves of Grass;* Lyric Poetry; Mourning; Nature; Technology

BIBLIOGRAPHY

Primary Works

O'Connor, William Douglas. *The Good Gray Poet: A Vindication.* New York: Bunce and Huntington, 1866.

Whitman, Walt. *The Collected Writings of Walt Whitman.* 22 vols. Edited by Gay Wilson Allen and Sculley Bradley. New York: New York University Press, 1961– .

Whitman, Walt. *Leaves of Grass: Comprehensive Reader's Edition.* Edited by Harold W. Blodgett and Sculley Bradley. New York: New York University Press, 1965. Reprint, edited by Michael Moon, New York: Norton, 2002.

Whitman, Walt. *Prose Works 1892.* 2 vols. Edited by Floyd Stovall. New York: New York University Press, 1963–1964.

Secondary Works

Basler, Roy P., ed. *Walt Whitman's Memoranda during the War and Death of Abraham Lincoln.* Bloomington: Indiana University Press, 1962.

Burroughs, John. *Notes on Walt Whitman, as Poet and Person.* 1867. New York: J. S. Redfield, 1871.

Burroughs, John. "Return of the Birds." In *The Writings of John Burroughs,* vol. 1, *Wake-Robin.* Boston: Houghton Mifflin, 1895.

Burroughs, John. *Whitman: A Study.* Boston: Houghton Mifflin, 1896.

Erkkila, Betsy. *Whitman: The Political Poet.* New York: Oxford University Press, 1989.

Greenspan, Ezra, ed. *The Cambridge Companion to Walt Whitman.* Cambridge, U.K., and New York: Cambridge University Press, 1995.

LeMaster, J. R., and Donald D. Kummings, eds. *Walt Whitman: An Encyclopedia.* New York: Garland, 1998.

Lowenfels, Walter, ed. *Walt Whitman's Civil War.* New York: Knopf, 1960.

Miller, James E., Jr. *Walt Whitman.* New York: Twayne, 1962. Rev. ed., Boston: G. K. Hall, 1990.

Myerson, Joel. *Walt Whitman: A Descriptive Bibliography.* Pittsburgh, Pa.: University of Pittsburgh Press, 1993.

Myerson, Joel. *Whitman in His Own Time: A Biographical Chronicle of His Life, Drawn from Recollections, Memoirs, and Interviews by Friends and Associates.* Expanded ed. Iowa City: University of Iowa Press, 2000.

Neely, Mark E., Jr. *The Last Best Hope of Earth: Abraham Lincoln and the Promise of America.* Cambridge, Mass.: Harvard University Press, 1993.

Thomas, M. Wynn. *The Lunar Light of Whitman's Poetry.* Cambridge, Mass.: Harvard University Press, 1987.

James Perrin Warren

THE WIDE, WIDE WORLD

In December 1850, just in time to seduce the eyes and pocketbooks of holiday shoppers, New York publisher George Palmer Putnam (1814–1872) brought out a handsome red-edged, two-volume edition of a novel titled *The Wide, Wide World:* the first from an author, Susan Warner (1819–1885), who veiled herself, for a while, behind the pen name Elizabeth Wetherell. Despite his own doubts, on the firm advice of his mother Catherine—who reportedly declared, after vetting the submission for him, "If you never publish another book, publish this" (Anna Warner, p. 283)—Putnam had accepted a very long manuscript from Henry Warner, father of the author, about a young girl's arduous journey to Christian womanhood. No other publishing house in New York wanted it: before approaching Putnam, the father, a once-prosperous attorney ruined by the financial panic of 1837 and his own ill-judged speculations, had carried a dispiriting handful of dismissals back to his semi-impoverished family on a Hudson River island near West Point.

Catherine Putnam's instinct, however, proved right: within three years, demand for the book carried it

Susan Warner. BURTON HISTORICAL COLLECTION, DETROIT PUBLIC LIBRARY

into 22 editions (a number that now tops 130), and the concept of the "best-seller," according to many scholars, thus entered the lexicon of America's commercial life. This giddy story of unlooked-for success is not unlike many in the modern literary marketplace, and in fact *The Wide, Wide World* quickly won enough cultural currency to invite exploitation by advertisers in familiar ways familiar—"In the 'Wide, Wide World' cannot be found better undergarments and hosiery than at James E. Ray's, 108 Bowery" (Anna Warner, p. 345)—but at the time such success was virtually unprecedented.

Catherine Putnam (1792–1869), a maternal figure possessed of private influence; Henry Warner (1787–1875), a father with public presence and apparent enterprise; and Susan Warner, a daughter who courts invisibility despite her central role as author: these leading characters in the drama of the novel's publication stand in strong and complicated kinship with the novel's leading characters. Family relations and home scenes not only occupy center stage in *The Wide, Wide World,* rather curiously for a novel so titled, but also have much to do with the extraordinary power over readers that gave it wide national (and eventually international) reach in Susan Warner's day.

THE WORLD OF HOME

The Wide, Wide World begins and ends in the privacy of domestic space. As the story opens, Ellen Montgomery, a ten-year-old protagonist with a passionate nature, hovers close to her frail mother in the firelight of a genteel New York parlor. In the conclusion Warner originally wrote, a grown, newly married, and seemingly chastened Ellen is handed by her masterful older husband into his fine house, then upstairs into a room of her own—one richly furnished at his direction and accessible only through his private study. And the conclusion Putnam published (omitting Warner's final chapter) likewise turns to home: a brief paragraph projects, teasingly, the now-adolescent Ellen's future entry into marriage and her duty to act as "the light of the eyes" to her husband's family (p. 569). Between these points of domestic departure and arrival, Warner unfolds a tale of orphanhood and female maturation—a variant of bildungsroman (broadly, a novel of character development) that Nina Baym, one of several scholars responsible for bringing this novel to the attention of late-twentieth-century readers, describes as typical of the "overplot" common to the nineteenth-century genre she names "woman's fiction." Like such sister novels as Maria Susanna Cummins's (1827–1866) *The Lamplighter* (1854), Marion Harland's (1830–1922) *Alone* (1854), and E. D. E. N. Southworth's (1819–1899) *The Hidden Hand* (1859), it chronicles the fortunes of a young woman deprived of parents and left, in

In Warner's original conclusion to The Wide, Wide World, *John Humphreys shows Ellen, his new bride, over the private room he has prepared for her.*

Up a low staircase and along a wide, pleasant hall John led her into his study, and through it into the room he called hers.

There was a strong contrast here to all the other parts of the house. They indeed bespoke easy circumstances and refined habits, but also an utter carelessness of display; the appliances of comfort and ease and literary and studious wants,—no luxury or parade. But here apparently nothing had been spared which wealth could provide or taste delight in, or curious affection contrive for its object. There was no more formality than appeared in the sitting-room; elegance reigned in all the seemingly careless arrangements; but *here* there was no mixture of incongruous things; all was in keeping though nothing was like anything else. Splendour was not here certainly for the wealth of the room must be found by degrees; and though luxuriously comfortable, luxury was not its characteristic; or if, it was the luxury of the mind. *That* had been catered for. For that nothing had been spared. A few very fine old paintings hung on the walls in lights that showed them well; in the glow of that warm afternoon they showed marvellously. A number of engravings by the best hands were disposed to the best advantage. Beautiful bits of statuary, in various kinds . . . all disposed with such perfection that though full the room hardly seemed so.

Warner, *The Wide, Wide World,* pp. 574–575.

large part, to find her own difficult path to adulthood and the reward of marriage.

Early on, in Warner's rendering of this plot, the protagonist loses both home and beloved mother, thanks to Mr. Montgomery (a fictional stand-in for Henry Warner), who fails as businessman, provider, and father to Ellen. Thereafter, the abandoned and eventually orphaned child finds herself shifted from household to household—from the remote farm of a brusque, un-motherly aunt; to the country parsonage, more happily, of Alice Humphreys and her brother John, who call Ellen sister but treat her as a daughter

and protégée in piety; then, unwillingly, to the aristocratic homes of relations in Scotland, who wall her round with affectionate but (Ellen feels) ungodly dominion. When at plot's end the "brotherly" minister John Humphreys offers rescue (offers, that is, himself as lifetime spiritual guide and husband), he comes into his own as earthly representative of the divine Father—who overarches all the novel's complex figurations of family. To John and his patriarchal counterpart in heaven, Warner overtly insists, the heroine owes her all.

The lifespan of woman's fiction—a literary type also termed "exploratory," or "sentimental" and "domestic" (often with a critical shrug of disdain)—stretched across much of the nineteenth century, first taking distinct shape in Catharine Maria Sedgwick's (1789–1867) novels of the 1820s and 1830s and extending in varied form through Augusta Evans's (1835–1909) *St. Elmo* (1866). But it held particular sway in the American literary marketplace (to the private dismay of more self-consciously cultured and less commercially successful writers like Herman Melville and Nathaniel Hawthorne) during the 1850s and 1860s, and *The Wide, Wide World* commonly wins pride of place, in modern critical assessments, as its peak expression. What Warner's novel and others like it tendered for public view were, paradoxically, the inward dramas of heart and home, centered on the virtues of domesticity, submission, sympathetic community, moral purity and—potently, in Warner's strain of woman's fiction—evangelical piety. This was the proper territory of "true womanhood." At least, so said the gendered ideology of "separate spheres" then promoted by such white, middle-class cultural authorities as New England religious leaders; *Godey's Lady's Book,* among other women's periodicals; and Catharine Beecher (1800–1878), sister of Harriet Beecher Stowe (1811–1896), in her popular manuals on household science (*A Treatise on Domestic Economy,* 1841, to name one important example).

Presiding tenderly over this private domain and providing moral ballast for the "masculine" sphere of commerce and politics was—as the parts played by Mrs. Montgomery (as well as Alice Humphreys) in Warner's narrative and by Catherine Putnam in its publication history suggest—the figure of the mother, as influential after death as in life. "Though we *must* sorrow, we must not rebel," the doomed Mrs. Montgomery lovingly admonishes her hot-hearted daughter (p. 12), thus setting up the didactic thrust of the novel's surface plot: Ellen's experiences will steadily teach her to furl her desires and let them be folded into the will of the Father. And Ellen's author-creator, absenting herself at first under a pen name and professing in journal entries and letters her struggle to let God's voice cover her own in the project of writing, tries to perform and preach an authorial version of the selfless submission required by her Protestant faith—the "New School" form of Presbyterianism that valued the conversion of a prostrated heart over the careful adherence to doctrine taught by the "Old School."

THE WORLD OF REFORM

Outside the walls of home that confined and precariously sheltered both Warner and her heroine, mid-nineteenth-century American society churned—not only with the spirit of evangelical Protestant revival broadcast through such magnetic pulpiteers as Charles Grandison Finney (1792–1875), members of the prominent Beecher family, and Warner's own pastor, Thomas Harvey Skinner, but also with more secular movements for social reform. In 1850, the year *The Wide, Wide World* appeared, Paulina Kellogg Wright Davis (1813–1876) organized the first national woman's rights convention in Worcester, Massachusetts, following on the Seneca Falls, New York, gathering of 1848; Congress passed the omnibus "compromise" bill in 1850 that included strict new fugitive slave laws, requiring northern citizens to return slaves escaping by way of the Underground Railroad to their so-called owners in the South and thereby stoking the fires of abolitionism; experiments in communal living abounded; and debate over the doctrine of Manifest Destiny flared from podium, editorial desk, and pen. Such women as Davis and Margaret Fuller (1810–1850), among New Englanders, as well as the southern sisters Angelina Emily Grimké (1805–1879) and Sarah Moore Grimké (1792–1873), spoke and acted with public energy to forward progressive causes, but Warner's novel, like others of its genre, bears few conspicuous marks of such concerns: what little overt attention the manuscript paid to race dropped out almost entirely with the disappearance, from the print version, of an episode about Ellen's encounter with a lower-class black child; and the Christian ethos of femininity Warner purports to champion seems sharply at odds with the woman's rights movement in particular. The world of her best-seller is really a "narrow, narrow" one, according to derisive critical voices of the late nineteenth century and early twentieth century.

But modern recuperators of *The Wide, Wide World* find otherwise. For Warner as for her sister writers, Baym and Jane Tompkins argue, home encompassed the only world of reform that truly counted—the reaches of the human soul, its capacity for moral growth, which women were manifestly destined to influence in quietly familial and domestic, yet deeply world-changing, ways. This is what Tompkins has resonantly termed the "cultural work" of best-selling

sentimental fiction of the nineteenth century. The critical recovery of woman's fiction, unexpectedly, thus supports a partial analogy to a robust branch of current scholarship on transcendentalism, which contends that the mid-century mind work of such writers as Ralph Waldo Emerson and Henry David Thoreau, despite its abstracted, inward turn to contemplation and self-culture, made its force felt in socially vital ways. Amy Kaplan and John Carlos Rowe have pushed and troubled the idea of sentimentality's global reach by mapping the "domestic" territory centered in woman and home onto the "domestic" territory marked off by U.S. borders and defined against all that was "foreign." In texts like Warner's, whose heroine reveres General George Washington almost as much as she reveres God, this opposition becomes the ground for religious imperialism—a nationalist vision of Manifest Destiny and world conquest in Christian guise.

The Wide, Wide World, then, claimed uneasy title to the public sphere by serving as a kind of pulpit for its female author, even while it imaged home as her rightful place and self-suppression as her rightful state: writers of woman's fiction, a number of scholars observe, styled themselves with varying degrees of consciousness as "preachers of the printed page," thus finding a way around the prevailing conviction that women should not seek to be heard in public (Kelley, pp. 285–315). In Warner's fictional world, Alice Humphreys figures an unobtrusive version of the female pulpiteer—gently eloquent, preferring to "preach" in private "without taking orders" (p. 217), she takes the place of her minister father with homebound church members—but Ellen herself identifies, powerfully if obliquely, with the more "masculine" and publicly charismatic master of the Word embodied in John; in this, she represents Warner, an unquiet spirit who wrestled throughout life with a strong will, a muscular desire for broad fields of both spiritual and literary influence, that her faith taught her had to be subdued.

In letters that Anna Warner (1824–1915) selected for inclusion in a lengthy biography of her sister, Susan pays less-than-wholehearted allegiance to a conventionally self-effacing style of "feminine" self-presentation akin to Alice's, though not in specifically religious terms. Here, the author records her impressions of two public women, Catharine Beecher (whom she heard speak about female educators several years before beginning *The Wide, Wide World*) and the singing sensation Jenny Lind (1820–1887) (whose concert she attended just after arriving at Putnam's home on Staten Island to correct proofs of the novel): "Whatever anticipations might have been formed of somewhat bold, unbecoming, unwomanly in the exhibition," she tells Anna after Beecher's talk, "they were not fulfilled. . . . Her address was well written and very interesting, and most part read by her brother; and her own deportment was very modest, delicate, and proper." In apparent contrast, the "compass and power" of Lind's voice seem to Warner, "so to speak, unlimited," reducing her duet partner, who acts the part of her singing teacher, to an inarticulate "grunted 'OH!' of wonder"—a reaction mirrored by the enraptured audience. Yet to the new novelist just beginning to forge her own public identity, "the most *moving* part of the whole exhibition" is purportedly Lind's "manner of courtesying." "It seemed as if she could not get low enough," Warner recalls; "it seemed to my fancy as if a certain feeling of humility, the sense of gratitude and the desire of acknowledgement, were *labouring* to express themselves. They did express themselves to me" (Anna Warner, pp. 232, 290–291). Complimenting such manifest female modesty while responding to the expressive power with which it is joined, Warner, who was hardly retiring or humble by nature, intimates her own competing and competitive desires, her anxieties about public "exhibition" in lecture hall and marketplace—about "feminine" versus "masculine" voice.

THE WORLD OF LITERARY COMMERCE AND CULTURE

Like most categories half-derived, half-devised to assist in comprehending social and literary experience, these three—the worlds of home, reform, and finally literary commerce—are useful but less tidy and comprehensive than the subheads above may suggest. The influential notion of separate spheres for women and men, for instance (circumscribing home and religion in one sphere and secular reform and commerce, among other dimensions of outward social life, in the other), carried at least a fair degree of cultural force in nineteenth-century America and a good deal of explanatory force for late-twentieth-century scholars of the period. It has since come under question for its limited ability to describe not only the varied experience of a broad spectrum of geographical, racial, and social groups but even the lives of the northeastern white middle class it especially purports to consider. The fluidity of such interpretive categories—their lively refusal to keep a predictable shape—becomes more apparent upon a return to this essay's place of departure: *The Wide, Wide World* as a market phenomenon. At the point where Warner uneasily and perhaps most flagrantly crosses the conventional divide between the "feminine" private and the "masculine" public, other borderlines show their instability.

The career of *The Wide, Wide World* as an object of literary commerce was not a simple one, despite the over-simple story of both its author and its audience

told by literary history from the late nineteenth century through much of the twentieth century. This novel was the first commercial offering of a young woman who strenuously disavowed any personal creative or professional stake in the enterprise of writing but who would go on to pen thirty-seven more book-length works of fiction, some independently and some in collaboration with her sister Anna. Along the way, in private and public texts alike, Warner would register the stubborn tug of her contradictory desires: not just to make a modest living as God allowed but, more, to reclaim financial ease and not only to channel God's word but also, contradictorily, to take deep, individual, even seductive pleasure in the act of writing itself and in the literary as well as evangelical power that followed from publication.

Necessity was certainly a motivating factor, and as Mary Kelley observes, the economic straits that brought Warner and other "literary domestics" to write for a living testify to the breakdown of masculine responsibility, the failure of fathers and husbands to fulfill the roles assigned them in the sphere of money making. Warner, however, also thirsted for a return to the prosperous gentility of the upper middle class (which was gaining an unsteady footing in mid-nineteenth-century society), as evidenced in the sumptuously tasteful fantasy of her original ending to *The Wide, Wide World*. Canniness about the marketplace wraps itself up in sincere religious feeling here: as Susan Williams's study of Warner's manuscript revisions suggests, the author likely fine-tuned her text to a sense of what was selling best, editing out worldly tales of riverboat peril along with, perhaps, the fantasy conclusion (though Warner's part in this decision is unclear) and bringing forward the passages of sentimental godliness her projected audience seemed to want most.

This apparently sexless, self-effacing piety did sell—very, very well—seducing legions of readers in an irresistible way that it is hard to imagine Warner, with her self-confessed love of sway, not relishing. A veiled, surprisingly eroticized ambition for power over her audience makes its presence felt textually in Ellen's near-obsession for winning and withholding kisses from one and all, a gesture that vies for prominence with persistent scenes of crying—which critics have sometimes parodied and at other times recognized as outbursts of Ellen and Warner's subversive anger at the stifling of womanly passion and at their exclusion from patriarchal power. In some modern readings, sexuality slips into Warner's narrative in the form of masochism: the thrill that trembles through Ellen, for example, at the thought of John relentlessly breaking a spirited horse. *The Wide, Wide World* is all about power, many have observed, and though the exquisite pain of powerlessness certainly runs through the text, it is countered by a strong undertow of feminine agency that issues from Warner's covert writerly ambitions and her discovery of narrative's potent effect.

In terms of personal material gain, Warner's enthralling first novel was not as brilliant a success as its sales figures imply, largely because the deficiency of international copyright laws meant publishers outside the United States could pirate the text without sharing a cent of profit with its author; in a representative instance, Warner's second novel, *Queechy* (1852), would reportedly sell ten thousand copies at one English train station, with no return to the woman who labored to create it. Yet because Warner remained single and attached to an increasingly feeble father, she escaped subjection to the persistent influence of "coverture": a feature of common law transplanted to the colonies from England, according to which women vanished in a legal sense at the point of marriage, ceding most rights to their property and, until as late as 1860 in New York State, their earnings. Such liberation into self-sufficiency would likely have seemed a dappled blessing at best to Warner, who grieved for the marital prospects that ended with her family's fall from social grace and whose inclination toward energetic mastery was shot through with a love of toil-free, aristocratic languor: "Her particular delight was to have a low seat at the corner of the hearth and read by firelight," sister Anna recalls, "but all her life long she liked to have some one else keep up the fire" (p. 88). So the fantasy ending of sexual and material fulfillment was left unrealized in life as it was in fiction.

The reception of *The Wide, Wide World* in a newly developing mass market for books further complicates this picture. Detractors of the novel in Warner's era—and through much of the twentieth century—attributed its huge popularity to a kind of mass simple-mindedness: the appeal of an author steeped in banal sentimentalities and weepy piety for a mostly female reading public, neither author nor audience bold or searching enough to question the common wisdom of the age. Contemporary scholars, however, see wrinkles in this easy explanation of success. Beyond the unexpected complexity of Warner's motives, there is evidence that more than a few men came under her narrative spell: acquaintances recorded the effect of her storytelling on male auditors not accustomed to bookish indoor pleasures; some studies—by Glenn Hendler, notably—show that men both responded to sentimental discourse and produced it themselves; and Warner received fan mail and favorable reviews from male as well as female readers (authors Henry James [1843–1916] and Caroline Matilda Kirkland [1801–1864] among them). Admirers paid tribute not only to her potent evangelical voice but also to her skillful way with prose, her vivid rendering of rural customs and dialects—putting her in company with other female local colorists now acknowledged as foremothers of postbellum realism—and, in Kirkland's case, her characteristic "Americanness," her unsung part in the campaign for a national literature advanced, for example, by the Young America movement. Such kudos—not least those of an aesthetic bent—pleased Warner, who harbored half-guilty ambitions for high-cultural as well as preacherly greatness. As for the undeniably large audience of antebellum women that embraced *The Wide, Wide World* and wept in sympathy with Ellen: the scholar Joanne Dobson and others persuasively contend that the discontent roiling beneath the submissive surface of Warner's narrative would have spoken in secret to those whose lives were similarly constrained.

See also Book Publishing; Domestic Fiction; Evangelicals; Female Authorship; Literary Marketplace; Manifest Destiny; Reform; Religion

BIBLIOGRAPHY

Primary Works
Stokes, Olivia Eggleston Phelps. *Letters and Memories of Susan and Anna Bartlett Warner.* New York: G. P. Putnam's Sons, 1925.

Warner, Anna B. *Susan Warner ("Elizabeth Wetherell").* New York: G. P. Putnam's Sons, 1909.

Warner, Susan. *The Wide, Wide World.* 1850. New York: Feminist Press, 1987. Includes the original conclusion, which had not previously been published with the full text.

Secondary Works
Argersinger, Jana L. "Family Embraces: The Unholy Kiss and Authorial Relations in *The Wide, Wide World.*" *American Literature* 74 (2002): 251–285.

Barnes, Elizabeth. "Literate and Literary Daughters: *The Wide, Wide World.*" In her *States of Sympathy: Seduction and Democracy in the American Novel*, pp. 104–110. New York: Columbia University Press, 1997.

Baym, Nina. "Susan Warner, Anna Warner, and Maria Cummins." In her *Woman's Fiction: A Guide to Novels by and about Women in America, 1820–1870*, 2nd ed., pp. 140–157, 160–163. Urbana: University of Illinois Press, 1993.

Cowie, Alexander. "The Vogue of the Domestic Novel, 1850–1870." *South Atlantic Quarterly* 41 (1942): 416–424.

Dobson, Joanne. "The Hidden Hand: Subversion of Cultural Ideology in Three Mid-Nineteenth-Century American Women's Novels." *American Quarterly* 38 (1986): 223–242.

Foster, Edward Halsey. *Susan and Anna Warner*. Boston: Twayne, 1978.

Goshgarian, G. M. "His Sister's Keeper: Susan Warner's *The Wide, Wide World*." In *To Kiss the Chastening Rod: Domestic Fiction and Sexual Ideology in the American Renaissance*, pp. 76–120. Ithaca, N.Y.: Cornell University Press, 1992.

Hendler, Glenn. *Public Sentiments: Structures of Feeling in Nineteenth-Century American Literature*. Chapel Hill: University of North Carolina Press, 2001.

Hovet, Grace Ann, and Theodore Hovet. "Tableaux Vivants: Masculine Vision and Feminine Reflections in Novels by Warner, Alcott, Stowe, and Wharton." *American Transcendental Quarterly*, n.s., no. 7 (1993): 335–356.

Kaplan, Amy. "Manifest Domesticity." *American Literature* 70 (1998): 581–606.

Kelley, Mary. *Private Woman, Public Stage: Literary Domesticity in Nineteenth-Century America*. New York: Oxford University Press, 1984.

Noble, Marianne. "'An Ecstasy of Apprehension': The Erotics of Domination in *The Wide, Wide World*." In *The Masochistic Pleasures of Sentimental Literature*, pp. 94–125. Princeton, N.J.: Princeton University Press, 2000.

Roberson, Susan L. "Ellen Montgomery's Other Friend: Race Relations in an Expunged Episode of Warner's *Wide, Wide World*." *ESQ: A Journal of the American Renaissance* 45 (1999): 1–31.

Rowe, John Carlos. "Religious Transnationalism in the American Renaissance: Susan Warner's *Wide, Wide World*." *ESQ: A Journal of the American Renaissance* 49 (2003): 45–57.

Schnog, Nancy. "Inside the Sentimental: The Psychological Work of *The Wide, Wide World*." *Genders* 4 (1989): 11–25.

Stewart, Veronica. "The Wild Side of *The Wide, Wide World*." *Legacy* 11 (1994): 1–16.

Tompkins, Jane. "The Other American Renaissance." In her *Sensational Designs: The Cultural Work of American Fiction, 1790–1860*, pp. 147–185. New York: Oxford University Press, 1985.

Williams, Susan. "Widening the World: Susan Warner, Her Readers, and the Assumption of Authorship." *American Quarterly* 42 (1990): 565–586.

Jana Lea Argersinger

WILDERNESS

"A wilderness, in contrast with those areas where man and his own works dominate the landscape, is hereby recognized as an area where the earth and its community of life are untrammeled by man, where man himself is a visitor who does not remain." This famous definition of wilderness became official in August 1964, when President Lyndon B. Johnson signed United States Public Law 88-577, creating a National Wilderness Preservation System charged with permanently maintaining the "primeval character and influence" of a portion of federally controlled land so that it "appears to have been primarily affected by the forces of nature." The Wilderness Act was the culmination of multiple congressional hearings, innumerable legislative drafts, thousands of pages of public testimony, and seven years of intensive lobbying both by established timber, pulp, oil, mining, and grazing interests as well as by the newly powerful preservation movement spearheaded by the Wilderness Society's Howard Zahniser and the Sierra Club's David Brower. On the longer view, it also represented the crystallization of a centuries-long American trend toward the appreciation and protection of uninhabited and scenic public lands into a tangible and comprehensive national policy. As of 2005, the 9 million acres originally set aside by the act had grown to more than 100 million acres spread over 667 areas in 44 states, with Alaskan preserves accounting for about half of the total—meaning that, in all, slightly less than 5 percent of the land within the borders of the United States was officially protected as wilderness.

As might be expected in a country completely resettled by waves of immigrants over more than four hundred years, the idea of wilderness—along with related notions of nature and the frontier—plays a large part in the traditional telling of American history. And although wilderness protection is not unique to American culture—the Soviet Union and its successor states, to take a notable example, extended much stricter protections for much different reasons to similarly large tracts of wilderness *(zapovedniki)* beginning in 1916—Americans played a relatively large role until the late twentieth century in the definition and deployment of the idea of wilderness worldwide. This mutually defining relationship between American culture and the idea of wilderness has long been the subject of intense debate among historians, philosophers, literary critics, scientists, and land managers. Among the major questions they continue to ask are: Does true wilderness really exist? Where do the values associated with wilderness come from? Whose values are they? What interests does the protection of wilderness serve? And what effects does it have on other modes of environmental concern? The answers to these questions are complex and unsettled, but their dimensions can be illuminated by the specific history of the idea of wilderness in North America.

PRE-CONTACT WILDERNESS

Of more than semantic concern is the question of whether wilderness, defined as large tracts of land in a state unaltered by mankind, could be said to exist in North America at the time of its discovery by Europeans. Various groups of natives had, after all, started crossing the Bering land bridge into the Americas more than twenty thousand years before and were well established from the Arctic Sea to Tierra del Fuego long before Columbus sighted land. Though it is impossible to generalize about so enormous a temporal and geographic slice of human history, such a long tenure implies that native peoples had likely altered their environments in ways that favored their survival. Indeed, archaeological work suggests that even nonagricultural tribes used the means available to them—most notably fire—to shape the landscape in significant ways. The mass extinction of large mammals like the wooly mammoth at the end of the Pleistocene has been speculatively linked to increased pressure by native Amerindian hunters, and highly wasteful practices have been documented among the bison-hunting tribes of the Great Plains. Environmental devastation, however, depends on a combination of shortsightedness and technological power, and though the natives were far from the ecological saints that western myth has made of them, their long-term experience with their environments coupled with the absence of extensive agriculture and mechanized industry meant that the ecosystems the first Europeans encountered, though hardly empty of human inhabitants, were more stable than they would be in subsequent years.

RELIGIOUS ORIGINS

While some of those first European explorers and settlers on the North American coast made passing reference to the relative wildness of the territory they encountered, "wilderness" as a touchstone concept first entered the American lexicon with the Puritans who settled around the Massachusetts Bay starting in the 1620s. This fact has large significance for the current connotations of wilderness in American culture, where it has always retained a religious ring even as it moved far beyond recognizably Christian dogma. For the Puritans, whose foremost frame of reference was the Christian scriptures, "wilderness" initially had more to do with the spiritual state in which they found themselves than with the physical environments they confronted. Frequently identifying themselves with the Israelites in the book of Exodus, the chosen people who were tested and formed through their wanderings in the desert, the Puritans came to understand wilderness as a name for their condition as Christian saints sojourning in the fallen world. Wilderness in this sense was another name for the totality of the adversities that beset them as a Christian community and as such could include even the highly urbanized European milieu from which they came. The Puritan leader John Winthrop (1588–1649), quite counterintuitively to modern understandings, described the Protestant emigration to the Massachusetts Bay Colony as a movement *out* of the wilderness.

Against such an abstract conception, the concrete wilderness that confronted the Puritans in North America quickly came to have a double-edged significance. As an alternative to the materially overabundant but spiritually deadening urban "wilderness" in which reformed Calvinists had wandered in Europe, the North American environment represented an austere and uncorrupted landscape where a saintlier community might flower. To be sure, the immigrants' new home presented substantial material challenges to the establishment of that community. William Bradford (1590–1657), the leader and historian of the Plymouth Plantation, seemed to be drawing on the Old English roots of the word "wilderness"—from *wild(d)éornes,* a compound of *wild-* (undomesticated), *-deor-* (animal), and *-ness* (place), meaning "a place of wild animals"—when he described the appearance of the forests that surrounded his starving settlement as "a hideous and desolate wilderness, full of wild beasts and wild men" (p. 62). Marking their untamed surroundings as the antithesis of the tight-knit "city upon a hill" they were laboring so mightily to establish (as urged by Winthrop in his sermon "A Modell of Christian Charity," p. 199), the Puritans quickly set about an ambitious plan to reform or simply clear away the material wilderness to bring God's plans for the "New-English Israel" to fruition. This antipathy for wilderness and the need for environmental remaking is an important strain of Puritan thought, advocated most vociferously by Edward Johnson (c. 1594–1672) in *Wonder-Working Providence of Sion's Saviour in New England* (1654). But the Puritan attitude was more complex than Johnson's text suggests, and Bradford goes on to recast his pessimistic assessment of the New England environment in redemptive language drawn from the book of Isaiah: "Our fathers were Englishmen which came over this great ocean, and were ready to perish in this wilderness; but they cried unto the Lord, and He heard their voice and looked on their adversity" (p. 63).

In this subtler conception of New England as a temperate version of the Sinai of the Israelites, the wilderness condition is a sign of both God's displeasure with his chosen people and his particular concern with their eventual fate. Unable either to surrender to wilderness completely or to disregard its chastening message, the earliest religious immigrants to New England were caught in a double bind. In recognition of this, Bradford and others came to take on the unsettled land surrounding Plymouth, in which wilderness was a negative presence not because it threatened to extinguish settlers' worldly hopes or because it symbolized the fallenness of the world but because paradoxically it offered to gratify them with an agricultural wealth that might fracture the sense of community enforced by deprivation and fear. All three of these partial definitions of wilderness—as a place of renewal, of testing, and of dissolution—continue in modern debates about the value of the wild.

THE CONTENTS OF THE WILD

At this early stage the question of wilderness was related in complex ways to scriptural precedents and community dynamics, but the actual content of wilderness (the geological formations, flora, fauna, and so on) was infrequently considered. And when these specificities were considered in the pragmatic agricultural writings of the colonial period, they were usually discussed in a context other than "wilderness" as we know it today. To non-Puritan settlers in New England, especially those who enjoyed good relations with local natives, understanding the populated and abundant region as wilderness, with its connotations of barrenness and solitude, was irrational. As Thomas Morton (1575–1646) saw it, in the midst of his cheeky *New English Canaan* (1637), the American environment was "Natures Masterpeece; Her chiefest Magazine of all, where lives her store" (p. 180). Elsewhere in the colonies the mood was seldom so sunny, but there was a shared assumption that the primary question about the land was not whether it was to be the site of a religious drama but whether and how it could be made to yield its riches to human labor. As a result, most of the accounts that do survive from the southern colonies, such as Robert Beverley's *History of Virginia* (1705), William Byrd's twin histories of a surveying expedition along the border between Virginia and North Carolina (1709, 1729), James Grainger's *The Sugar-Cane* (1764), and George Ogilvie's *Carolina; or, The Planter* (1776, 1791), downplay the issue of wilderness, focusing rather on the more concrete and specific questions of settling the territory.

Two aspects of this settlement process deserve special consideration. The first is the widespread presence, beginning in the seventeenth century and growing by fits and starts into the nineteenth century, of slavery. Most of the experience of contact with wilderness—the diking of rice paddies in Carolina, the carving out of tobacco plantations in Virginia, and the draining of swamps in Georgia—was performed by slave or indentured laborers. Very few of these were literate, and as a result a large body of wilderness witness by those who had direct contact with it has been mostly lost to history. The second aspect of settlement that interferes with a continuous history of wilderness is the relationship between settlement patterns and native tribes. In the eighteenth century the American landscape was in a sense both too full and too empty to support the notion of wilderness. Too empty in the sense that English settlers were confined to a narrow strip of land along the Atlantic seaboard (the French and Spanish had penetrated the continent more deeply), engaged mostly in seaborne trade with other colonies and European nations and thus imaginatively disconnected from the interior. Too full in the sense that, when white settlers like Daniel Boone did press into "wild" regions like the Appalachian frontier during the middle portion of the century, the native tribes were still a strong, well-organized presence. As a result, the wilderness concept's requirement of emptiness was not met by the conditions of the contact zone between European settlers and native tribes. For a significant portion of American history and through a large swath of American geography, the idea of wilderness did not exist.

The disconnect between the abstract religious notion of the wilderness and the chaotic facticity of the American frontier began to lose some of its starkness as the eighteenth century wore on. Jonathan Edwards (1703–1758), a New England evangelical theologian and philosopher, laid the intellectual foundation for this synthesis in his writings of the middle third of the century. Possessed with a keen interest in and knowledge of natural science, Edwards came to regard the natural world as a second site, after the scriptures, of the revelation of divine truth. For him it was thus a matter of fundamental importance to pay close attention to the specific workings of the unmodified natural world, be it the web weaving of a common spider, the course of an undammed river, or the dietary habits of the raven, as these provided windows onto the goodness and beauty of God that could instruct humans in their devotion. As a result, he approached such phenomena with a sense of wonder related to religious awe. Such thoughts never led Edwards to propose preservation of wild areas, he never went deliberately far from human settlement to experience wilderness, and the direct cultural impact of Edwards's thoughts on spiritual uses of wilderness were for all practical purposes nonexistent in his own time. The notion that the natural world reflects the divinity of its creator and that the wilderness is therefore a spiritual sanctuary is one that would, however, be resurrected a century later by another New England theologian-philosopher, Ralph Waldo Emerson.

The same delay in recognition did not befall William Bartram (1739–1823), a bona fide natural historian and ethnographer whose record of exploration in the southeastern tropics had a direct and powerful impact on at least two major figures in British Romanticism. His descriptions of the subtropical forests of the American Southwest, recorded in *Travels through North and South Carolina, Georgia, East & West Florida, the Cherokee Country, the Extensive Territories of the Muscogulges, or Creek Confederacy, and the Country of the Chactaws* (1791) matched minutely detailed description with a mysterious mood and reverent tone that influenced the writing of Samuel Taylor Coleridge's "This Lime-Tree Bower My Prison," "The Rime of the Ancient Mariner," "Christabel," "Frost at Midnight," and "Kubla Khan" as well as William Wordsworth's "Ruth," *The Prelude*, and "The Excursion." Despite its appropriation in Romantic meditations on the irrational, the immediate context of Bartram's work was as part of a much larger scientific enterprise sweeping the present and former colonies of Europe. Botanists, ornithologists, fossil hunters, ethnographers, and natural historians of all persuasions combed the continental interiors for specimens that could be sent back to European academic centers to be described and systematized according to one or another system of classification. The rationale for wilderness as a biodiversity preserve derives in large part from the detailed work of these early natural historians.

NATIONALIZING WILDERNESS

If this scientifically inflected exploration of the wilderness began as a colonial venture, it quickly became an object of national pride in the years following the American Revolution. Foremost among the powerful supporters of natural history was Thomas Jefferson (1743–1826), whose *Notes on the State of Virginia* (1787) tabulates a great deal of the scientific knowledge produced by these early forays into the wilderness in the course of refuting an argument about the degeneracy of American fauna promulgated by the French naturalist Georges-Louis Leclerc, comte de Buffon. At about the same time that Bartram and Jefferson were consolidating the geopolitical and scientific significance of the American wilderness, Hector St. John de Crèvecoeur (1735–1813), a French-born settler in Revolutionary America, was proposing a national identity based upon the experience of wilderness. His *Letters from an American Farmer* (1782), which mix vignettes about the wondrous qualities of American nature with others evincing a deep terror at the threat true wilderness posed to civilized white identity, tell of the birth of a new kind of man created at the frontier between civilization and wilderness. St. John de Crèvecoeur's understanding of American distinctiveness as arising from the unique conditions of the frontier bound American identity to the wilderness for more than a century to come; after his writings, to be American meant to have a privileged knowledge of and relation to the wild.

As scientific knowledge and the frontier mythos developed, political events gave Americans an increasing share of the lightly settled lands in the interior of North America. As president, Jefferson was also responsible for the purchase of the Louisiana Territory in 1803, which doubled the size of the United States and led to the most famous of the many American exploratory expeditions of the nineteenth century, the voyage of Meriwether Lewis and William Clark up the Missouri and down the Snake and Columbia to the Pacific. The political and imaginative connection between wilderness and the American identity was furthered by the reception of these two explorers into national myth and by a series of nationalistic displays of American wilderness wealth in the form of comprehensive catalogs of animals and plants. The most famous of these are John James Audubon's (1785–1851) massive *Birds of America* (1827–1838) and the equally ambitious study of mammals, *Viviparous Quadrupeds* (1845–1854), left unfinished at his death.

From the beginning of the nineteenth century, writers such as William Cullen Bryant, Washington Irving, James Fenimore Cooper, and William Gilmore Simms produced, respectively, poems, short stories, and novels that explored and developed this notion of the wilderness American in the context of the United States's growing dominion over western lands. Establishing that dominion often involved double-dealing and violence against the native tribes whose claims to lands in the South, Midwest, and Far West interfered with the plans of land speculators and white politicians. In the literary works of the time, natives are depicted as irredeemably premodern; they are a people that progress will inevitably pass by, leaving behind a vacuum to be filled by white settlers. Even the most sympathetic chroniclers of native life, such as the painter and exhibitor George Catlin (1796–1872), often represented native peoples as a vanishing breed. Such sentiments obscure the fact that the emptiness that has become so definitive of wilderness is less a natural characteristic of the land than the by-product of specific historical conflicts between native inhabitants of the land and white settlers. The problematic masculinization of wilderness can also be traced to this period, as romances like Cooper's five Leatherstocking Tales (1823–1841) tended to draw a strong and influential contrast between the domestic sphere, overseen by women, and the masculine space of violence and adventure in the wilderness, itself often depicted as a female object of male brutality. Though these distinctions can be seen in an unbroken chain throughout subsequent American cultural history, they did not go uncontested in their own time. Writers like Catharine Maria Sedgwick (*Hope Leslie,* 1827) and Lydia Maria Child (*Hobomok,* 1824) countered the emphasis on wildness and racial animosity with narratives of intercultural cooperation on the borderlands, and Caroline Kirkland (*A New Home—Who'll Follow?* 1839) contributed a romance-withering assessment of domestic settlement on the Michigan frontier. Susan Fenimore Cooper, the romancer's daughter, wrote one of the best records of naturalistically aware settlement in the form of *Rural Hours* (1850). By mid-century, the conventions of the wilderness romance had become the target of burlesques like Thomas Bangs Thorpe's story "The Big Bear of Arkansas" (1841).

BACKWOODS TRANSCENDENTALISM

The three strands of wilderness explored above—the rapprochement between religion and nature, the intensive and well-publicized scientific investigation of the continental hinterlands, and the imaginative connection between Americanness and wildness—receive their most articulate and influential synthesis beginning in the middle third of the nineteenth century with Ralph Waldo Emerson's (1803–1882) *Nature* (1836). Emerson urged his readers to turn away from the old ideas of Europe and to rejuvenate their minds through contact with and consideration of the natural world they possessed in abundance. Emerson, a lapsed Unitarian minister, moved beyond Jonathan Edwards's intimation of the natural world as a secondary revelation to claim that nature was the primary source of spiritual truths. Gesturing toward the burgeoning field of natural history and the steadily enlarging continental reach of American empire, Emerson and, later, Walt Whitman identified the American future with an imaginative appropriation of its wilderness materials.

Though Emerson's vision of nature owed more to natural history museums like the Jardin des Plantes in Paris than to the American backwoods, his essay provided the framework for subsequent writers and thinkers who delved much more deeply into the problems of wilderness. The most notable of Emerson's

followers in this regard is Henry David Thoreau (1817–1862), who took Emerson's injunction to look for wisdom in nature to an extreme. Interested in natural science throughout his life (from an early essay, "Natural History of Massachusetts," through later ruminations, including "Autumnal Tints," "Wild Apples," "The Succession of Forest Trees," and "Huckleberries"), Thoreau addressed the paradoxes of living in contact with wild nature most forcefully in *Walden* (1854). Although Thoreau stands as one of the deepest thinkers on the question of environmental ethics that form so large a part of our contemporary concern about wilderness, it is worth noting that Thoreau's forays into wilder territory than his Concord home (trips to Minnesota, Canada, and Maine) did not inspire him as did his life on the margins of the settled lands. A trip to Mount Katahdin, documented in *The Maine Woods* (1864), famously left him in terror of "vast, Titanic, inhuman nature" (p. 640).

Alongside this explosion of literary treatments, the mid-nineteenth century witnessed the development of a visual language of wilderness. The Hudson River School, a name given to a loose assemblage of more than one hundred landscape painters in the latter two-thirds of the century, created and popularized paintings of large-scale landscapes bathed in luminous light in upstate New York, the Ohio frontier, the Far West, and South America. The dean of this group, Thomas Cole (1801–1848), is renowned for his panoramic depictions of atmospheric disturbance over landscapes along the Hudson and Ohio Rivers. Asher Durand (1796–1886) focused on somewhat more intimate, vertical pastoral landscapes. Frederick Church (1826–1900), perhaps the most accomplished American landscapist of the nineteenth century, focused like Cole on sublime landscapes from Niagara Falls to the Andes. Together their work provides a grandiose and ravishing vision of American wilderness as a unique aesthetic resource, and the familiar emphasis of modern-day wilderness preservation campaigns on the scenic properties of wilderness draws heavily on the tradition inaugurated by the Hudson River School. Two of the later artists in the tradition started by Cole became closely associated with the first two national park preserves. Thomas Moran (1837–1926) made his name with spectacular paintings of Yellowstone, set aside as the first official national park in 1872. Albert Bierstadt (1830–1902), a German immigrant, became famous with his portraits of California's Sierra Nevada, called by John Muir in appreciation of its aesthetic distinctiveness "The Range of Light," with a particular focus on Yosemite, which was designated a national park in 1890 though it had enjoyed state protection since 1864.

***Kindred Spirits,* 1849.** Painting by Asher B. Durand. Durand depicts William Cullen Bryant, a renowned nature poet, and Thomas Cole, the dean of the Hudson River school of landscape painters, together in a wilderness setting. © FRANCIS G. MAYER/CORBIS

THE BEGINNINGS OF PRESERVATION

These early preserves were termed parks because their major function was to serve as recreation for human visitors, most of them wealthy industrialists. The plans for the building of trails, bridges, and camps in Yosemite were first drawn up by the landscape architect Frederick Law Olmsted (1822–1903), better known as the designer of New York's Central Park and Boston's Emerald Necklace. Often these parks brought a wave of development (roads, accommodations, sewers, and so on) that threatened to destroy the wilderness values they made accessible, a major paradox of national parks to this day.

Despite these class-bound and environmentally destructive effects, the emerging park system was symptomatic of a sea change in attitudes toward the wilderness. If an earlier embrace of wilderness understood its natural beauty and sublimity as a symbol of present and future national greatness, by mid-century the optimistic conjunction of progress and wilderness had begun to break down. The industrialization of the eastern cities, with its correspondent increase in pollution, poverty, crowding, and disease, coupled with the disruptive extension of the railways into every corner of the nation, produced a backlash of preservation sentiment that would extend far into the twentieth century. Although when Thoreau famously wrote that "in Wildness is the preservation of the world" ("Walking," p. 665) he was speaking of a state of mind rather than a concrete place, he had recognized early on that actual wilderness was something under threat from the forces of industrialization. At several points in his life Thoreau mused about the value of maintaining woodlots as a philosophical resort for town dwellers ("Walking"), of managing human affairs for the value of nonhuman life ("The Bean-Field"), and even of setting aside virgin forest as a permanent preserve. Even before Thoreau, James Fenimore Cooper had displayed a sensitivity to the problem of wilderness destruction in his major novel of settlement, *The Pioneers* (1823). These early stirrings aside, the Vermont polymath George Perkins Marsh (1801–1882) was the first to consider systematically the sensitivity of natural systems to "disturbing agents." His *Man and Nature; or, Physical Geography as Modified by Human Action* (1864) drew out the disastrous consequences of the ongoing exploitation of the wilderness as a resource and placed it in historical context stretching back to ancient Rome. The broad-based justifications for wilderness preservation that would enter into the wilderness management philosophies of the twentieth-century land manager and environmentalist Aldo Leopold are anticipated in Marsh's work.

Henry David Thoreau's "Walking" was published posthumously in the Atlantic Monthly *in 1862.*

The West of which I speak is but another name for the Wild; and what I have been preparing to say is, that in Wildness is the preservation of the world. Every tree sends its fibres forth in search of the Wild. The cities import it at any price. Men plough and sail for it. From the forest and wilderness come the tonics and barks which brace mankind. Our ancestors were savages. The story of Romulus and Remus being suckled by a wolf is not a meaningless fable. The founders of every State which has risen to eminence have drawn their nourishment and vigor from a similar wild source. It was because the children of the Empire were not suckled by the wolf that they were conquered and displaced by the children of the Northern forests who were.

I believe in the forest, and in the meadow, and in the night in which the corn grows. We require an infusion of hemlock-spruce or arbor-vitae in our tea. There is a difference between eating and drinking for strength and from mere gluttony. The Hottentots eagerly devour the marrow of the koodoo and other antelopes raw, as a matter of course. Some of our Northern Indians eat raw the marrow of the Arctic reindeer, as well as various other parts, including the summits of the antlers, as long as they are soft. And herein, perchance, they have stolen a march on the cooks of Paris. They get what usually goes to feed the fire. This is probably better than stall-fed beef and slaughter-house pork to make a man of. Give me a wildness whose glance no civilization can endure,—as if we lived on the marrow of koodoos devoured raw.

Thoreau, "Walking," p. 665.

It was only at the very end of this period that the change in attitude began to have definitive effects in the way of policy. Scientists with varying levels of preservationist spirit began to flock to the Sierra Nevada in the 1860s and 1870s: John Muir came to Yosemite in 1868; Clarence King wrote his account of *Mountaineering in the Sierra Nevada* in 1871; Joseph Le Conte performed geological surveys of the mountains in the 1870s. In the desert southwest, John Wesley Powell was blazing the trail into the Colorado drainage in 1869, and Charles Dutton drew attention to the Grand Canyon from the 1870s. In the East, the movement for the preservation of New York's watershed in the Adirondacks began to gain steam under the direction of the surveyor Verplanck Colvin during the 1870s. The great era of preservation beginning with John Muir and extending through the Wilderness Act, with all that it owed to the foregoing cultural and material history of America, was yet to come.

See also Borders; Exploration and Discovery; Nature; *Nature;* Romanticism; *Walden*

BIBLIOGRAPHY

Primary Works

Bartram, William. *Travels through North and South Carolina, Georgia, East & West Florida, the Cherokee Country, the Extensive Territories of the Muscogulges, or Creek Confederacy, and the Country of the Chactaws.* Philadelphia: James and Johnson, 1791.

Bradford, William. *Of Plimoth Plantation.* 1651. Reprinted as *Of Plymouth Plantation, 1620–1647.* Edited by Samuel Eliot Morison. New ed. New York: Knopf, 1952.

Emerson, Ralph Waldo's *Nature.* Boston, J. Munroe, 1836.

Johnson, Edward. *Wonder-Working Providence of Sion's Saviour in New England.* 1654. Reprinted as *Johnson's Wonder-Working Providence, 1628–1651.* Edited by J. Franklin Jameson. New York: Scribners, 1910.

Marsh George Perkins. *Man and Nature; or, Physical Geography as Modified by Human Action.* New York: Scribner, 1864.

Morton, Thomas. *New English Canaan.* 1637. With introduction and notes by Charles Francis Adams Jr. Boston: Prince Society, 1883.

St. John de Crèvecoeur, Hector. *Letters from an American Farmer.* London: T. Davies, 1782.

Thoreau, Henry David. "Walking." *Atlantic Monthly* 9, no. 56 (1862): 657–674. Reprinted as *Walking.* San Francisco: HarperSanFrancisco, 1994.

Thoreau, Henry David. *A Week on the Concord and Merrimack Rivers, Walden, The Maine Woods,* and *Cape Cod.* New York: Library of America, 1989.

U.S. Congress. *Congressional Record,* 88th Cong., 2nd sess., 1964. The Wilderness Act of 1964, Public Law 88–577.

Winthrop, John. "A Modell of Christian Charity." In *The Puritans: A Sourcebook of Their Writings.* 1938. Edited by Perry Miller and Thomas H. Johnson. Reprint, Mineola, N.Y.: Dover, 2001.

Secondary Works

Branch, Michael P., ed. *Reading the Roots: American Nature Writing before Walden.* Athens: University of Georgia Press, 2004.

Buell, Lawrence. *The Environmental Imagination: Thoreau, Nature Writing, and the Formation of American Culture.* Cambridge, Mass.: Harvard University Press, 1995.

Callicott, J. Baird, and Michael P. Nelson, eds. *The Great New Wilderness Debate.* Athens: University of Georgia Press, 1998.

Cronon, William, ed. *Uncommon Ground: Rethinking the Human Place in Nature.* New York: Norton, 1996.

Edwards, Thomas S., and Elizabeth A. De Wolfe, eds. *Such News of the Land: U.S. Women Nature Writers.* Hanover, N.H.: University Press of New England, 2001.

Evernden, Neil. *The Social Creation of Nature.* Baltimore: Johns Hopkins University Press, 1992.

Gatta, John. *Making Nature Sacred: Literature, Religion, and Environment in America from the Puritans to the Present.* New York: Oxford University Press, 2004.

Hallock, Thomas. *From the Fallen Tree: Frontier Narratives, Environmental Politics, and the Roots of a National Pastoral, 1749–1826.* Chapel Hill: University of North Carolina Press, 2003.

Knott, John R. *Imagining Wild America.* Ann Arbor: University of Michigan Press, 2002.

Krech, Shepard. *The Ecological Indian: Myth and History.* New York: Norton, 2001.

Merchant, Carolyn. *Reinventing Eden: The Fate of Nature in Western Culture.* London: Routledge, 2003.

Nash, Roderick. *Wilderness and the American Mind.* 4th ed. New Haven, Conn.: Yale University Press, 2001.

Oelschlaeger, Max. *The Idea of Wilderness: From Prehistory to the Age of Ecology.* New Haven, Conn.: Yale University Press, 1991.

Steinberg, Ted. *Down to Earth: Nature's Role in American History.* New York: Oxford University Press, 2002.

Warren, Louis S., ed. *American Environmental History.* Malden, Mass.: Blackwell, 2003.

Michael G. Ziser

WOMAN IN THE NINETEENTH CENTURY

In 1855 the British novelist George Eliot favorably compared Margaret Fuller's *Woman in the Nineteenth Century* (1845) to Mary Wollstonecraft's *A Vindication of the Rights of Woman* (1792). Eliot's comparison is an apt one since both works link the emancipatory rhetoric

Margaret Fuller. Undated portrait engraving. GETTY IMAGES

of their day to a consideration of woman's social role, making each an important document for the history of feminism in Britain and the United States.

Recognizing her indebtedness to Wollstonecraft, Margaret Fuller (1810–1850) subtly alludes to *Vindication* in *Woman,* though she is careful to distance herself from the political implications of Wollstonecraft's work in order to establish a less controversial argument for the social and cultural equality of women. While Fuller drew her authority from a wide range of writings and practices concerning women around the world, she was only partially successful in muting criticism of *Woman.* For just as the end of slavery did not purge prejudices restricting and sometimes imperiling the lives of many people in this country, so too support for full equality between men and women would take another century to gather effective momentum and force. Certainly people who resisted change in the normal view of women, like the New England editor and clergyman Orestes Brownson, went on to dismiss Fuller's work as misguided. Even so, *Woman* received sympathetic reviews from writers like Edgar Allan Poe and Lydia Maria Child, and the book sold briskly enough to have a pirated edition printed in England.

A revision of an earlier 1843 article, *Woman in the Nineteenth Century* is best understood as a work in progress, one of many provisional texts needed to widen the Enlightenment concept of emancipation in the aftermath of the American and French Revolutions. The Constitution of the United States is perhaps the primary political document of this sort, emerging as it did from a narrow understanding of the "universal" citizen (conceived as white and male) and slowly amended over time in an effort to align this abstract political subject with social justice. With its broad cultural focus, Fuller's *Woman* is closer in kind to works that were being written and revised by people like Frederick Douglass (1818–1895) and William Wells Brown (c. 1814–1884), two fugitive slaves eager to show how they were living at a still greater distance from the freedom so vital to the young nation's myth of equality. Though working in different genres (the essay, the slave narrative, and the novel) all three authors shared a belief that real change would emerge by enlarging perceptions of the social and cultural discriminations working daily against them. Early-twenty-first-century critics debate the effectiveness of this approach to reform, particularly as they review the complex legacy of Harriet Beecher Stowe's (1811–1896) novel *Uncle Tom's Cabin* (1851–1852), the most famous, if sentimental, work of this kind. Yet it is important to remember that Fuller and others took seriously Thomas Jefferson's assertion that all men are created equal and labored throughout their careers to give palpable meaning to his famous rhetoric.

Douglass produced at least three versions of his autobiographical slave *Narrative* during his life, altering the tale over time (1845, 1855, 1881) as amendments to the Constitution gradually awarded black men political status. William Wells Brown revised and republished his novel *Clotel; or, The President's Daughter* (the fictional account of Thomas Jefferson's unacknowledged slave "family") many times (1853, 1860, 1864, 1867) as the conflicted meanings of the Civil War for African Americans became more evident. Because Fuller died in a tragic shipwreck in 1850, she never revised *Woman* again, though it is likely that the political and social climate in the second half of the nineteenth century would have inspired her to do so.

The publication of *Woman* is often viewed as a significant event from the early days of the woman's movement both here and in England. Indeed, during the 1870s the spirit of Fuller was sometimes conjured in spiritualist séances to give virtual guidance to the cause. Fuller encouraged this practice through both her early focus on the therapeutic efficacy of mesmerism and what in *Woman* she identifies as woman's "electrical" nature. There Fuller also makes productive use of one of the earliest case histories in the prehistory of psychoanalysis, Justinus Kerner's analysis of a German clairvoyant. Yet the people gathering at those later séances might have been surprised by the revised analysis of the woman's movement Fuller would have offered had she actually been among them, for she likely would have observed the gap between its political ideal and social reality by noting the movement's failure to include subaltern women who were not white and middle class.

TRANSLATING EDUCATION AND GENDER

Born in Massachusetts in 1810 to Timothy and Margaret Crane Fuller, Sarah Margaret received strong support from her parents: her mother's subtle influence, while typical of the day, served as an important counterbalance to her father's determination to educate his daughter as if she were a boy. The success of this parental dynamic early made Fuller aware of both the arbitrary nature and the potential authority of gender roles. Trained in ancient and modern languages, Fuller became one of this nation's first successful comparativists, learning as easily from Latin writers as from contemporary European authors, often translating a work to share her assessment of it with friends. Though aware of the excesses of her father's ambition, Fuller continued to value the motive behind his cultivation of her unorthodox training, as one of her vignettes in *Woman* (the conversation with Miranda) makes clear. Certainly Fuller realized that her unusual training enabled her to be taken seriously as a thinker by many prominent writers of the nineteenth century, Ralph Waldo Emerson and George Eliot among them.

Emerson (1803–1882) was a particularly close friend at the time of the writing of *Woman*. He met Fuller as he was finishing his famous essay *Nature* (1836). Fuller's obvious ability as an interlocutor, particularly her interest in German writers like Johann Wolfgang von Goethe and Novalis, whom Emerson previously had neglected, provided the basis for the strong intellectual bond that quickly developed between them. Fuller became an accomplished teacher soon after meeting Emerson, first working at Amos Bronson Alcott's progressive though controversial Temple School in Boston and then moving on to the Green Street School in Providence, where she experimented with a mix of pedagogical styles, tempering her father's harsher techniques with the student-focused approach of the Temple School. Although Fuller assumed these jobs out of necessity (her father died suddenly in 1835, leaving the family in financial need), her desire to write, coupled with her growing success as a translator, made a move into more independent projects a happier experience for her. Fuller continued throughout her career to sustain an interest in women's education, however, and her "Conversations," held in Elizabeth Peabody's famous Boston bookstore during the early 1840s, were seminars designed to enrich the substance and method of intellectual exchange both among women and between women and men. Elizabeth Cady Stanton, a prominent leader of the 1848 Seneca Falls Convention and later women's movement, was among the seminars' participants.

Emerson provided support and encouragement for Fuller's move beyond a limited teaching career, helping her to find publishers for her translations of Johann Eckermann's *Conversations with Goethe, in the Last Years of His Life* (1839) and Bettine Arnim's *Günderode* (1842). He also strongly supported her years as editor of *The Dial* (1840–1842), the periodical that published poetry and criticism of transcendentalists like Henry David Thoreau, Amos Bronson Alcott, Elizabeth Peabody, Theodore Parker, and George Ripley. After two years Emerson replaced Fuller as editor, and under his watch Fuller published the earlier draft of *Woman* as "The Great Lawsuit: Man versus Men; Woman versus Women." Emerson reported to Fuller that even Thoreau, "who will never like anything," found praise for the essay, calling it "rich extempore writing, talking with pen in hand." Emerson added his own support by noting that it will "teach us to revise our habits of thinking on this head" (Stern, pp. xii–xiii).

Emerson's journals are filled with comments about the work and influence of Margaret Fuller. First written after Fuller's untimely death in 1850, this notebook entry is later used by Emerson to describe significant attributes of the "hero" in his essay "Fate." In moving from private journal to public essay, the name "Margaret" is dropped from the passage.

A personal influence towers up in memory the only worthy force when we would gladly forget numbers or money or climate, gravitation & the rest of Fate. Margaret, wherever she came, fused people into society, & a glowing company was the result. When I think how few persons can do that feat for the intellectual class, I feel our squalid poverty.

Emerson, *The Journals and Miscellaneous Notebooks of Ralph Waldo Emerson* 11:449.

THE VALUE OF CONFLICTING CULTURES

When she revised her 1843 *Dial* essay for its independent publication as *Woman*, Fuller added a preface and lengthy appendix and extended large sections of her argument. Many of these changes were the product of her intervening visit to the Midwest and Great Lakes region, an account of which Fuller published in her travel narrative *Summer on the Lakes, in 1843* (1844). There Fuller brought a unique range of concerns to bear on her encounter with both pioneer women and Native Americans. In adapting to the exigencies of both, Fuller's thinking about the rhetoric of equality assumed a still more sophisticated character. If Fuller took with her to the Midwest a naive sense of the progressive myth of democracy, the misfires of Manifest Destiny gave her pause, helping her to revise some of her basic assumptions about feminism. At the time that she composed *Summer,* the prevailing sense of the majority culture was that Native Americans would "vanish" from the family of humans. Seeing the great damage to their world as she moved across the landscape, Fuller understood the apparent sense of this view. Yet her own frustration with another "fatal" discourse—particularly the argument that prostitution is an inevitable product of civilization—made her consider the subtle contradictions at work in the narrative of the "vanishing American," allowing her to mark its uncanny parallel to restrictive narratives about women throughout history.

In her preface to *Woman in the Nineteenth Century,* Fuller comments on the change in her title from her first draft, noting her preference for "The Great Lawsuit" even as she acknowledges the efficacy of the new title. Fuller's revision reflects her growing realization that her first essay depended on a flawed progressive discourse. Still, the lawsuit imagined in her earlier title was conceived not as an adversarial encounter between men and women but as a struggle between the ideal and realized understandings of both "man" and "woman." Such subtle rhetorical moves are typical of Fuller's approach, for she is determined to show that "no age was left entirely without a witness of the equality of the sexes in function, duty and hope" (p. 157). That is, she seeks to show that there are historic precedents for the ideal of equality between men and women, making such claims appear more deeply conservative than radical. But in another sense Fuller means to draw her reader into a consideration of the "passions and prejudices" that continue to keep larger democratic ideals from unfolding in practice.

Concern for those same prejudices were at the heart of much reforming effort during this period, and the push for a better realization of democratic principles assumed a variety of forms throughout the volatile decade of the 1840s. Until this moment Fuller had restricted her reformist ambitions to feminist concerns, but the growing ranks of the abolitionist movement and the fervor among many of her New England friends for experimental or utopian communities began to push Fuller into bolder theoretical territory. It is often said that her relationship with Emerson kept her from experimenting with the communal living project at Brook Farm, and there is strong evidence to support this idea. At the same time, Emerson's support of her intellectual ambition helped Fuller to become more proficient than her transcendentalist friends in the critiques of value being produced by thinkers from both Europe and the United States. Thus, for example, when the doctrines of the French utopian Charles Fourier became central to the Brook Farm experiment, Fuller began reading his work in French and discovering within his elaborate plan for social harmony a strong emphasis on the limited role of women in society. This association cannot be emphasized enough, since Fourier is credited with coining the word "feminism" (*feminisme*), and his criticism of the isolated household and traditional marriage challenged Fuller to revise the way that she talked about this vital social bond. With Fourier's help, Fuller found a more effective way to critique the prevailing middle-class idea that there should be separate spheres of activity for both men and women.

Fuller revised "The Great Lawsuit" into *Woman* at an important time in her career and during an exciting moment in the decade. Horace Greeley, the newspaper editor of the *New-York Daily Tribune,* was impressed by the argument in *Summer on the Lakes* and hired Fuller to begin in 1845 to write regularly for his newspaper. The same year that *Woman* was published with Greeley's help, Fuller reviewed the *Narrative of the Life of Frederick Douglass* in the *Tribune* and translated there news about Friedrich Engels and Karl Marx from a piece in the German immigrant newspaper *Deutsche Schnellpost.* Fuller's association with the *Tribune* continued until her death in 1850 and included a wide range of articles, among them book and theater reviews, translations from French and German newspapers, and social commentary on issues such as health, prison reform, and treatment of the insane as well as an important correspondence from Europe, particularly reports relating her experience and observation of the Italian Revolution of 1848.

Fuller's writing after *Woman* displays her range across a spectrum of social and cultural concerns, for in her reviews she became nearly as comfortable with the plastic forms of popular culture as with the highbrow aesthetic of Goethe and Beethoven. Indeed, a review of Fuller's *Tribune* writing aptly reveals the myriad issues occupying both liberal and more radical reformers during the years leading to the fractious decade of the 1850s. Her interest in the revolutionary and socialist movements of Europe took sharper focus while she was writing for Greeley, and many have argued that this tendency could only flourish beyond the influence of self-reliant writers like Emerson. But Emerson's continuing support remained important to Fuller, who remembered how he had earlier helped her to break many traditional restraints. And it was Emerson who described Fuller as "our citizen of the world by quite special diploma" in his letter of introduction for her successful trip to England, France, and Italy (Stern, p. xxxvi). Emerson's description could not have been more apt, as people befriending Fuller (the French novelist George Sand, the Italian social critic Giuseppe Mazzini, and the Polish poet Adam Mickiewicz) went on to agree.

RETHINKING SOCIAL RELATIONS: WOMAN'S TIME

A compendium of ideas about women gathered from a wide range of texts, Fuller's *Woman* gives equal attention to events and people both humble and famous. For some readers the organization of *Woman* appears an indiscriminate assembly of facts where an account of Greek mythology can hold equal status with a passage from John Quincy Adams, Maria Edgeworth, or a foreign newspaper extolling the obscure political party "Las Exaltados" (which Fuller cannot resist changing to "Las Exaltadas"). And while nothing can prepare the modern reader for the unique nature of Fuller's presentation of her material, the early-twenty-first-century student familiar with the Internet can be impressed by the fact that Fuller's quick associative mind was her only "search" engine. Fuller herself complained that the work required "too much culture in the reader to be quickly or extensively diffused" (*Letters* 3:352). Yet her audacious decision to use the idea of woman as an index for thinking through social relations over time is one now recognized as central to sophisticated trends in modern criticism. And of course such a method is fundamental to the discipline of women's studies. Fuller's writing depends upon a fluid movement between fable and history, poetry and fact, for she feels compelled to draw from, and elaborate upon, realms of experience not yet properly legitimized for the women of her day.

Perhaps most provocative is Fuller's sense of time's complexity in *Woman*, for she refuses there to assume a progressive narrative form. Like the historian Mary Beard, who a hundred years later would write *Woman as Force in History* (1946), Fuller makes the counterintuitive suggestion that equality between men and women may have been more fully conceptualized both at particular moments in the past and in the history of other cultures around the world. In understanding how a narrow or prejudiced view of the past can be as limiting as prejudice against unfamiliar habits and cultures of the present, Fuller initiates a series of questions that continue to vex the discipline of history itself. If history is, as Thomas Carlyle then insisted, the biography of great men, what is the place of women in that record? If by history one means merely biography, the fate of women is not much improved, for as Fuller observes, great women rarely had biographers. Fuller's innovation lies in moving beyond the call for a series of biographical recoveries to her experiment with a heterogeneous narrative structure. That structure depends upon a gender shift in temporality, moving history itself to the threshold of a more synchronous, or anthropological, understanding of culture.

For this reason, Fuller interrupts the flow of her critical narrative in *Woman* with a variety of fictional vignettes and staged conversations. In so doing she recognizes the performative nature not only of gender roles but also of the critical enterprise itself. Those readers unfamiliar with Goethe or Fourier, for example, are given an opportunity to see, through the dramatic renderings framing her discussion of both authors, how "vaguely" yet unfairly the equality of women with men is "proposed and discussed" among contemporaries (p. 19). Fuller's sense of her unevenly educated audience fosters this method; as in her famous Boston seminars, such appeals to common experience allow men and women to think again about their behavior in the company of others. This technique is one that Harriet Beecher Stowe went on to adapt in *Uncle Tom's Cabin*, where she interrupts the flow of her narrative to provoke a personal response in her reader. Like Stowe, Fuller assumes that frustration over the scene will goad her audience to action. Unlike Stowe, however, Fuller hopes that her reader will also go on to explore the literature and criticism about women that she alternately supplies, enlisting them more deeply in the work of critical thought.

Critics have noted how both racial and class considerations are insufficiently explored in Fuller's early writing, and one must acknowledge that Fuller began her career working with a "liberal" but limited understanding of women in society. For example, she never wrote directly about the factory workers made famous by the *Lowell Offering* (though one can detect the influence of *Woman* in the 1845 work that Sarah Bagley published in the *Voice of Industry*, the paper supporting the earliest labor union among women). Yet in revising her *Dial* essay Fuller began to recover from these lapses when she added stories about women like the Indian translator "Malinche" and when she shames politicians claiming to spare women the "hardship" of political life by reminding them of the women enslaved and working in the fields. And it is typical of Fuller's shifting critical sense that in her revisions she inquires if the founding national myth of equality is "the bloom of healthy blood or a false pigment artfully laid on?" (p. 17). Fuller's figurative language provokes her reader to associate the performance of gender roles with twinning dramas of the day: the politics of equality and the counterfeit of blackface minstrelsy. Fuller's latter analogy is merely suggestive, however, because in 1844 she has been exposed only indirectly to this increasingly popular and problematic dramatic form. Indeed, even the more explicit abolitionist sentiments that appear through her revisions of "The Great Lawsuit" reveal Fuller's relatively late commitment to the antislavery cause. At the same time, such fleeting but acute references show her vigilant receptivity to the broader social implications of her feminism. It is not surprising to discover her reviewing the *Narrative of the Life of Frederick Douglass* within months of her move to New York.

FREEDOM'S WORKING PAPERS

Perhaps it is best to view all of Fuller's work as a series of revisions on the theme of emancipation. Such an approach allows one to see a continuity of reception and change throughout her career. It also allows one to consider how a provisional work like *Woman* provides insight into a mind actively engaged with the shifting complexities of social reform. Thus a reader noting how Fuller establishes sex and gender as categories deserving separate consideration in her *Tribune* work can also discover this turn of mind taking root in *Woman*. There, in her discussion of marriage, for example, Fuller makes an impassioned plea for the "despised auxiliaries" of men and women who choose not to live normal domestic lives. That Fuller refers not only to the category of "bachelor" and "old maid" in her comments about "mental and moral Ismaelites" (p. 85) is not lost on a writer as adept as Herman Melville, whose fiction and poetry often broaches the possibility of queer social relations.

One could argue that it is the process of revision itself that Fuller best models for others, though few are as adept as Fuller in distinguishing between mere repetition of a thought or feeling and its successful reformulation. Fuller's easy transition from the writing of ancient authors to contemporary Indian rituals suggests the fugue of temporalities that are contained for her within the present. Such an approach opens an exciting set of possibilities for rethinking the procedural nature of social reform. Her title *Woman in the Nineteenth Century* itself inscribes something of this temporal compression, for it simultaneously marks the present and projects the future by summoning a latency of meaning across temporal and cultural boundaries.

A cosmopolitan critic and translator, Fuller was well prepared to explore the concept of freedom being transformed by the cultural and commercial traffic of the Atlantic Ocean. *Woman* both contributes to and analyzes this transformation, challenging many in the process to rethink the "ways" of the world. The poet Walt Whitman is said to have pasted a page from one of Fuller's essays on his wall for inspiration. When writing about the woman's movement, Fuller's voice seems to flow through the words of Frederick Douglass. However perversely, heroines from the novels of Nathaniel Hawthorne act out some of the themes of Fuller's work. What Henry James calls the "Fuller Ghost" (he was only seven when she died in 1850) haunts his fictional depiction of women crossing the same Atlantic Ocean so fatal to Fuller's life and his own. In their work, as in their lives, Edith Wharton, Emily Dickinson, Louisa May Alcott, and Julia Ward Howe are each indebted to this woman from the nineteenth century. And it was a devastated Emerson who tried three different ways to deal with Fuller's untimely death: he contributed to the 1852 *Memoirs of Margaret Fuller Ossoli,* he agreed to lecture before the Boston Woman's Rights Convention in 1855, and he made Fuller the spectral heroine of his famous essay "Fate" (1852, 1860). None of these efforts satisfied him, however, as one sees when he observes in his journal that a book about Fuller would have to trace an "essential line of American history" (*The Journals and Miscellaneous Notebooks of Ralph Waldo Emerson* 11:258). That freedom is not inevitable proves too traumatic a realization for Emerson. But like many another, Emerson learned from Fuller how labor-intensive freedom's "fate" can be, constituting, as it forever does, a work in progress.

See also Education; Female Authorship; Feminism; Philosophy; Reform; Rhetoric; Seneca Falls Convention; Suffrage; Transcendentalism; Utopian Communities

BIBLIOGRAPHY

Primary Works

Emerson, Ralph Waldo. *The Journals and Miscellaneous Notebooks of Ralph Waldo Emerson.* 16 vols. Edited by William H. Gilman et al. Cambridge, Mass.: Harvard University Press, 1960–1982.

Fuller, Margaret. *The Letters of Margaret Fuller.* 6 vols. Edited by Robert N. Hudspeth. Ithaca, N.Y.: Cornell University Press, 1983–1995.

Fuller, Margaret. *Margaret Fuller: Essays on American Life and Letters*. Edited by Joel Myerson. New Haven, Conn.: College and University Press, 1978.

Fuller, Margaret. *Summer on the Lakes in 1843*. 1844. Edited by Susan Belasco Smith. Urbana: University of Illinois Press, 1991.

Fuller, Margaret. *Woman in the Nineteenth Century*. 1845. Edited by Larry J. Reynolds. Norton critical edition. New York: Norton, 1998.

Secondary Works

Berlant, Lauren. "The Queen of America Goes to Washington City: Notes on Diva Citizenship." In her *The Queen of America Goes to Washington City: Essays on Sex and Citizenship*. Durham, N.C., and London: Duke University Press, 1997.

Butler, Judith, and Joan W. Scott. *Feminists Theorize the Political*. New York and London: Routledge, 1992.

Capper, Charles. *Margaret Fuller: An American Romantic Life*. Vol. 1, *The Private Years*. New York: Oxford University Press, 1992.

Chevigny, Bell Gale, ed. *The Woman and the Myth: Margaret Fuller's Life and Writings*. Rev. and expanded ed. Boston: Northeastern University Press, 1994.

Douglas, Ann. *The Feminization of American Culture*. New York: Knopf, 1977.

Ellison, Julie. *Delicate Subjects: Romanticism, Gender, and the Ethics of Understanding*. Ithaca, N.Y., and London: Cornell University Press, 1990.

Kolodny, Annette. "Inventing a Feminist Discourse: Rhetoric and Resistance in Margaret Fuller's *Woman in the Nineteenth Century*." *New Literary History* 25 (1994): 355–382.

Machor, James L. *Readers in History: Nineteenth-Century American Literature and the Contexts of Response*. Baltimore and London: Johns Hopkins University Press, 1993.

Showalter, Elaine. "Miranda and Cassandra: The Discourse of the Feminist Intellectual." In *Tradition and the Talents of Women*, edited by Florence Howe. Urbana: University of Illinois Press, 1991.

Spivak, Gayatri Chakravorty. "Can the Subaltern Speak?" In her *Other Worlds: Essays in Cultural Politics*. New York: Methuen, 1987.

Stern, Madeleine B. "Introduction." In *Woman in the Nineteenth Century*, edited by Joel Myerson. Columbia: University of South Carolina Press, 1980.

Wiegman, Robyn. "The Alchemy of Disloyalty." In her *American Anatomies: Theorizing Race and Gender*. Durham, N.C., and London: Duke University Press, 1995.

Wood, Mary E. "'With Ready Eye': Margaret Fuller and Lesbianism in Nineteenth-Century Literature." *American Literature* 65 (March 1993): 1–18.

Zwarg, Christina. *Feminist Conversations: Fuller, Emerson, and the Play of Reading*. Ithaca, N.Y., and London: Cornell University Press, 1995.

Christina Zwarg

YOUNG AMERICA

An energetic fusion of art and politics, the Young America movement (1840–1850) called for an American culture dissociated from European tradition. The movement united dissimilar personalities such as the colorful John O'Sullivan and the patrician Evert A. Duyckinck, while promoting such favored writers as Nathaniel Hawthorne, Herman Melville, Margaret Fuller, and Edgar Allan Poe. Stung by Sydney Smith's question "Who reads an American book?" in the *Edinburgh Review* (1820), writers and critics promoted an American art consistent with democratic principles. Essential to the movement was New York City's network of book, magazine, and newspaper publishers and contributors and the city's primacy as a distribution center.

A prominent Bostonian, the transcendentalist spokesman Ralph Waldo Emerson, issued a call for American independence from the European literary and philosophical past in his 1837 Phi Beta Kappa address at Harvard, "The American Scholar." His address linked physical expansionism to cultural nationalism, a cry articulated the same year in the inaugural issue of John O'Sullivan and Samuel Langtree's *United States Magazine and Democratic Review* (October 1837), published in Washington, D.C. The first issue called for writers to promote the democratic principles of a new, participatory political system while scorning the past and lauding the "expansive," "boundless" future before the nation.

NEW YORK CITY

Calls for a national culture coalesced in New York City, the nation's commerce capital. The October 1825 inauguration of the Erie Canal, linking Albany and Buffalo, signaled the city's eminence in merchandizing. The 363-mile Erie Canal, built by Irish immigrants at a cost of $8 million, allowed New York City merchants control over half of the nation's imports and one-third of the exports. Within just a few years the canal annually saw $15 million worth of freight. The year the canal opened, five hundred new merchants, twelve new banks, and thirteen new marine insurance firms opened for business in the city. Between 1840 and 1860 publishing became one of the city's fastest-growing commercial activities. The prolific magazine contributor Edgar Allan Poe (1809–1849) was convinced of New York's dominance in 1846 when he noted that one-quarter of all U.S. authors lived there. Because of technological advances such as the steam press and the Hoe rotary press, which could print eight thousand papers an hour, the production of books, magazines, and newspapers became more profitable. Between 1820 and 1852 New York City marketed 345 newspapers. The expansive publishing network facilitated John O'Sullivan and Evert Duyckinck's efforts to market a literary nationalism influenced by Jacksonian democracy's egalitarian ideals.

O'SULLIVAN, DUYCKINCK, AND THEIR NATIONALISTIC QUEST

John O'Sullivan (1813–1895), whose longtime family friend was Martin Van Buren (U.S. president, 1837–1841), graduated from Columbia College with a master's degree in 1834. The following year he passed the bar. At age twenty-five O'Sullivan cofounded the *United States Magazine and Democratic Review* with his brother-in-law Samuel Langtree, who had been

Old and Young America. Illustration from *Godey's Lady's Book,* February 1857. The Young America movement is personified as a young boy accepting the homage of a Revolutionary War soldier. CLEMENTS LIBRARY, UNIVERSITY OF MICHIGAN

one of the founders of the *Knickerbocker* magazine in 1833. O'Sullivan, a "Locofoco," the sobriquet for radical Democratic Party members, shrewdly combined literature and politics to ensure a catholic readership. The voice of the Democratic liberal wing, which advocated states' rights, abolition of capital punishment, and westward expansion, the *Democratic Review* boasted six thousand subscriptions by 1839.

One of the intellectual leaders of the Locofoco movement was the periodical press writer William Leggett (1801–1839), a Georgia native who had moved to New York City in the 1820s. Writing for the *Plaindealer,* the *Examiner,* and the *New York Evening Post,* Leggett espoused equal rights to liberty and property (citing Thomas Jefferson) and antimonopoly reform (resulting in the Free Banking Act of 1838) and inspired the Independent Treasury Act, which removed federal deposits from state banks. Opposed to the

entrenched Whig and Wall Street interests, Leggett argued that the periodical press had a role in promoting democratic values to the masses. The poet William Cullen Bryant gave the eulogy at Leggett's 1839 funeral, while O'Sullivan and Walt Whitman admitted their admiration for the fiery editorialist.

President Andrew Jackson (1829–1837), the Locofoco idol, is reported to have been the first subscriber to the *Democratic Review,* while President Van Buren was rumored to have provided some funding. In addition to promoting young authors such as Hawthorne and Walt Whitman, the periodical engendered two slogans: "The best government is that which governs least" and "Manifest Destiny," the justification for acquisition of new land for a steadily increasing population. While geographic expansionism had been advocated by others, John O'Sullivan coined the phrase "Manifest Destiny," which cast the policy of procuring territories as "providential." In addition, aided by Jacksonian democracy's philosophy of states' rights, universal suffrage, and easy land acquisition, Manifest Destiny argued for the U.S. role in saving the unenlightened "heathen" of the continent, a philosophy that led to the expulsion of Native Americans from lands east of the Mississippi (the Indian Removal Act of 1830) and the annexation of Mexican territories in 1846.

In the magazine's infancy O'Sullivan shrewdly made the acquaintance of Nathaniel Hawthorne (1804–1864), soliciting his work for the magazine. O'Sullivan's April 1837 letter to the struggling author promised him a new public for his work. Hawthorne was flattered enough to send "The Toll Gatherer's Day" for the inaugural issue, which would also include poems by John Greenleaf Whittier and William Cullen Bryant. The magazine published twenty-five of Hawthorne's short stories.

After an April 1840 fire destroyed the magazine's office and bindery, O'Sullivan moved the *Democratic Review* to New York City. Despite recurrent financial crises (1837, 1839, 1841), New York, next to London, was the world's busiest port; in 1840 the city's population was close to 400,000. While New York suffered a dearth of laboring jobs, immigrants, especially Irish, flocked to the city—100,000 in 1842 alone. Suspicion of Catholicism reigned: New York City elected the Whig mayor Aaron Clark in 1837; he had campaigned on an anti-Irish, anti-Catholic platform. The era was also violent: riots of the 1830s, 1840s, and 1850s pitted nativists against Irish, Irish against Irish, and whites against blacks. Against this backdrop of social and economic uncertainty, O'Sullivan and others espousing Young America hoped to remind the nation of its

The following passage, from Young America's primary organ Democratic Review, captures the movement's ringing endorsement of democracy as an amalgamation of politics and aesthetics. Freedom is alliance with literature in an emergent democratic nation, created in opposition to an oppressive European hierarchical society.

The spirit of Literature and the spirit of Democracy are one. . . . Literature is not only the natural ally of freedom, political or religious; but it also affords the firmest bulwark the wit of man has yet devised, to protect the interests of freedom. . . . Of all men the author and scholar should come nearest to the ideal of the Patriot. . . . Every discovery he makes is for the benefit of his countrymen: every truth vigorously enunciated should instruct them. . . . The novelist, the historian, and the poet . . . are essentially democratic.

O'Sullivan, "Democracy and Literature," pp. 196, 197.

inherent promise to all citizens: freedom from feudalism and tyranny. Named by the author and playwright Cornelius Mathews, Young America promoted universal enfranchisement and free trade, along with a national literature written by the people and for the people. O'Sullivan argued that "The spirit of Literature and the spirit of Democracy are one" (pp. 196–197).

Along with O'Sullivan, the New Yorker Evert Duyckinck (1816–1878) was arguably the most influential advocate of the Young America movement. Duyckinck too had attended Columbia College, earning a master's degree, and had been accepted to the bar upon graduation in 1836. That year, in the hope of creating the definitive American novel, he and Cornelius Mathews formed the Tetractys Club; its goals included literary criticism and advocacy of an original native literary culture. In December 1840 Duyckinck and Mathews's first commercial venture appeared: *Arcturus,* a periodical with essays, notices of the city's cultural events, and short stories. Like O'Sullivan, Duyckinck recognized Hawthorne as a seminal American author: as early as 1838 he had traveled to Salem with a letter of introduction from Henry Wadsworth Longfellow. Four of Hawthorne's short stories appeared in *Arcturus:* "The Old Maid in the Winding Sheet," "The Man of Adamant," "The

Canterbury Pilgrims," and "Sir William Pepperell." (Hawthorne had offered *Arcturus* "Young Goodman Brown" and "Monsieur du Miroir," but for some reason they did not appear in its pages.) O'Sullivan, a tireless Hawthorne advocate, was gratified by Duyckinck's six-page essay simply called "Nathaniel Hawthorne," which appeared in May 1841. The essay called the author one of the most original American writers, the "one least indebted to foreign models or literary precedents of any kind." *Arcturus,* along with the *Democratic Review,* provided Hawthorne little financial recompense; however, it did provide him access to a combined public of fiction and political readers.

In 1844 O'Sullivan, in addition to publishing the *Democratic Review,* began publishing a daily newspaper, the *New York Morning News,* which reprinted some of the *Review*'s articles and stories. For example, Hawthorne's "A Select Party," a story written expressly for the Young America audience, appeared in both periodicals. The *Democratic Review* also gave the young Walt Whitman (1819–1892) his first national audience for his early fiction. Arguing against the Whig elitist view that literature could not be appreciated, much less written, by the masses, the *Democratic Review* contained O'Sullivan's essay "Democracy and Literature" in its August 1842 issue. Native authors like Hawthorne and Whitman, O'Sullivan believed, demonstrated the innate superiority of American letters, unsullied by European influence. However, despite its early success, the *Democratic Review* claimed only two thousand subscribers in 1845, so O'Sullivan withdrew as editor. The same year, Duyckinck became its literary editor. An important vehicle for an emergent aesthetic, the *Review* published instrumental essays such as "Poetry for the People," "Nationality in Literature," Duyckinck's "On Writing for the Magazines," his review of Fuller's *Papers on Literature and Art* ("Modern English Poets"), and Whitman's own review of *Leaves of Grass.* Read today, the *Democratic Review* illustrates the dynamism of a society struggling to define itself in opposition to European cultural and political traditions.

LIBRARY OF AMERICAN BOOKS

After the demise of *Arcturus* in 1842, Duyckinck had sought a publisher for a series of inexpensive American books. After shopping at the Wiley and Putnam bookstore on Broadway and investing in its publishing house, Duyckinck and the firm made a deal in February 1845. Duyckinck would edit two series: Library of Choice Reading, which featured reprints of European titles; and Library of American Books. The Library of American Books, which marketed known and little-known authors, served as an early attempt at native canon formation and, even more important to authors, a venue for providing equitable payment for work. In an arrangement Poe applauded, Library of American Books authors received a 10 percent profit and copyright to their titles once editions met costs.

The latter series saw its first title, *Journal of an African Cruiser,* hit the streets in May 1845. Duyckinck had approached Hawthorne for a history of witchcraft for the series; Hawthorne had declined but agreed to edit his friend Horatio Bridge's travel narrative, a popular genre of the era. Hawthorne would later contribute twenty-two previously published tales and the new "The Old Manse" for the two-volume *Mosses from an Old Manse* (1846), volumes 17 and 18 of the series. Appearing two months into his tenure at the Salem Custom House (a position O'Sullivan helped him obtain), Hawthorne, the "Loco-foco Surveyor," vowed never to write magazine articles again. *Mosses* is a testimony to Duyckinck's business acumen: the book underwent six printings in six years. Whitman, editor of the *Brooklyn Eagle,* lauded the goals of the series while he hoped that native geniuses could earn the monies awarded to foreign authors. O'Sullivan's *Democratic Review* and *Morning News* both promoted the series in reviews and notices of new titles.

Although many of the titles have not survived canon formation, several of the works and their authors have. The Library of American Books published Melville's *Typee* (1846); Fuller's *Papers on Literature and Art* (1846), a collection of *Dial* and *Tribune* essays, along with the original "American Literature"; Poe's *The Raven, and Other Poems* (1845) and his *Tales* (1845); Caroline Kirkland's *Western Clearings* (1845); and William Gilmore Simms's *Views and Reviews in American Literature* (1845). With Hawthorne's assistance Duyckinck approached Emerson and Thoreau about contributing to the series: Emerson decided to publish *Representative Men* (1850) elsewhere, as did Thoreau for *A Week on the Concord and Merrimack Rivers* (1849). The series should be recognized for its promotion of new writers, especially women writers, and its shrewd recognition that literary art is both culture and a commodity.

THE *LITERARY WORLD*

The first issue of the *Literary World,* a weekly magazine melding politics, art, gossip, and advertising, appeared in February 1847. Hired initially as its editor, Evert Duyckinck joined with his brother George to buy the weekly outright in October 1848, and they published it until its demise in 1854.

The Duyckincks argued for a public receptive to American culture; hence various issues would call for a funded system of public education. Good magazines, Evert argued, served as "companions" to the cultivated. Generous in attention to Poe, Fuller, Melville, and Hawthorne, the *Literary World* published excerpts, reviews, and notices of their work, usually soliciting Library of American Books authors to review the books of other writers in the series. Hawthorne contributed reviews of *Typee* and *Views and Reviews in American History;* Fuller reviewed *Typee* and *Mosses from an Old Manse.* The *Literary World,* like the *Democratic Review,* promoted Hawthorne as an original American voice; it lauded *The Scarlet Letter* as a "psychological romance" and termed *The House of the Seven Gables* as original and creative.

Gratified by the success of Melville's *Typee,* Duyckinck had become a literary mentor to the former sailor; as he opened his copious library to Melville, the *Literary World* published excerpts of *Omoo* (1847) and *Mardi* (1849) while soliciting from Melville reviews of other works, including J. Ross Browne's *Etchings of a Whaling Cruise* (1850). Bewildered by *Mardi,* which had been intended as a travel narrative, the *Literary World* loyally promoted the novel as "Rabelaisian." (Duyckinck knew Melville had borrowed Rabelais from his 15,000-volume library.) *Mardi* was not a commercial success, so Melville authored two more traditional nautical books: *Redburn* (1849) and *White-Jacket* (1850). Moving to Pittsfield, Massachusetts, to work on his latest book, Melville was introduced to Hawthorne: Duyckinck had brought a copy of *Mosses from an Old Manse,* which he wanted Melville to review for *Literary World.* The result was the two-part essay "Hawthorne and His Mosses," a review in which Melville posited Hawthorne as Melville's own literary precursor. Melville then recast his whaling novel as an allegorical, metaphysical epic. Duyckinck, so desirous of a friendship between his two heavily promoted authors, would later be displeased with the creative result of that meeting. *Literary World*'s anonymous two-part review of *Moby-Dick,* which may have been authored by brother George Duyckinck, praised the novel's striking narration and style while curiously condemning its originality and irreverence toward Christianity. Melville retaliated with his parody of Young America in the 1852 *Pierre,* ridiculing the fickleness of the marketplace. Neither *Moby-Dick* nor *Pierre* was a financial success. The two men would eventually reconcile: visiting Evert Duyckinck on a monthly basis for the last three years of the editor's life, Melville would be his final visitor before the editor's death in 1878.

THE END OF AN ERA

By 1850 Young America was nearly spent. The May 1849 Astor Place theater riot sounded a symbolic death knell: New York's Seventh Regiment fired upon a mob protesting the British classical actor William Macready's portrayal of Macbeth; 29 people died and 150 were injured. The *Literary World* published two columns condemning New York's hostility to Macready and applauded the use of force against the unruly crowd. Duyckinck and Melville had previously signed a published letter pleading with the British actor to continue his American tour after a disruption during an earlier performance. Cornelius Mathews too, while advocating power to the people, condemned their unruly behavior in a cultural arena. Duyckinck, Mathews, and Melville were horrified when participatory democracy ran amok.

After 1850 Hawthorne became a popular writer, obtaining a Boston publisher for *The Scarlet Letter* in 1850; Melville returned to the periodical press, with his finest short stories appearing in *Putnam's Monthly Magazine*. In 1856 Duyckinck and his brother George published the two-volume *Cyclopaedia of American Literature*, an exhaustive catalog of some two thousand men and women of American thought and letters. Upon his death Duyckinck left his library of books, pamphlets, and papers to the Lenox Library, where the materials became an invaluable source on the formation of nineteenth-century literary art. O'Sullivan, fictionalized as the political daguerreotypist in Hawthorne's *The House of the Seven Gables*, was arrested in 1851 for arming a vessel to attack Cuba; his trial ended with a hung jury. In endorsing the southern states' rights, he sympathized with the Confederacy, remaining in England during the Civil War. Returning to New York City in 1879, he died in obscurity in 1895.

LEGACIES: WALT WHITMAN AND YOUNG AMERICA

While such authors as Hawthorne, Melville, Fuller, Poe, and Simms received much attention during Young America's heyday, the writer who best articulated O'Sullivan's and Duyckinck's vision of a distinctive native literature was Walt Whitman. Whitman revered the Locofoco hero Andrew Jackson after seeing him at an 1833 rally in Brooklyn. The *Democratic Review* published his early fiction, written as Whitman also contributed to several daily newspapers, including O'Sullivan's *Morning News*. Whitman's revolutionary *Leaves of Grass* (1855), printed in Brooklyn, even then a working-class neighborhood, celebrated a singular American sensibility with a diverse range of characters and idioms Duyckinck would not have approved. Whitman, who clipped articles from *Democratic*

Review, internalized Young America's call while ignoring Mathews's and Duyckinck's insistence that this new style be formal and sublime. Emerson applauded *Leaves of Grass*, foretelling an illustrious career for Whitman; however, the collection received mixed critical reviews. After the second edition (1856), Whitman assumed editorship of the *Brooklyn Daily Times* (1857), where he wrote editorials and reviewed books and magazines. He continued revising *Leaves of Grass* up to his death, so no definitive edition exists. Now recognized for his singular genius, Whitman commemorated the democratic masses: his poetry answered Young America's call for a people's literature.

See also Democracy; Knickerbocker Writers; Manifest Destiny

BIBLIOGRAPHY

Primary Works

Duyckinck, Evert A., and George L. Duyckinck, eds. *Cyclopaedia of American Literature*. 1856. Detroit: Gale, 1965.

Emerson, Ralph Waldo. *The Complete Essays and Other Writings*. Edited by Brooks Atkinson. New York: Modern Library, 1950.

"The Great Nation of Futurity." *Democratic Review*, November 1839, pp. 426–430.

O'Sullivan, John. "Democracy and Literature." *Democratic Review* (August 1842): 196–200.

Whitman, Walt. *Leaves of Grass*. 1855. Edited by Sculley Bradley and Harold W. Blodgett. New York: Norton, 1973.

Secondary Works

Bender, Thomas. *New York Intellect: A History of Intellectual Life in New York City from 1750 to the Beginnings of Our Own Time*. Baltimore: John Hopkins University Press, 1987.

Miller, Perry. *The Raven and the Whale: The War of Words and Wits in the Era of Poe and Melville*. New York: Harcourt, Brace, 1956.

Spencer, Benjamin T. *The Quest for Nationality: An American Literary Campaign*. Syracuse, N.Y.: Syracuse University Press, 1957.

Stafford, John. *The Literary Criticism of "Young America": A Study in the Relationship of Politics and Literature 1837–1850*. New York: Russell and Russell, 1957.

Weinberg, Albert K. *Manifest Destiny: A Study of Nationalist Expansionism in American History*. Gloucester, Mass.: Peter Smith, 1958.

Widmer, Edward L. *Young America: The Flowering of Democracy in New York City*. Oxford: University Press, 1999.

Cheryl D. Bohde

"YOUNG GOODMAN BROWN"

Among the earliest works of the short story genre, "Young Goodman Brown" (1835) by Nathaniel Hawthorne (1804–1864) is also among the most brilliant. Few can match it in its dramatic appeal, linguistic precision and economy, irony, philosophical depth, or controlled ambiguity. It has lent itself to widely and wildly different interpretations, ranging from being regarded as a Puritan parable to an attack on Puritanism, and from affirming the presence of incarnate evil in the world in the form of the devil and witches, to treating evil merely as a matter of perception. Drawn to the story by its complexity and the demands it places on careful reading, scholarship has made considerable headway in reconstructing its intellectual background and the relationship of the author's biography to it, and in identifying and charting its subtle patterns of structure and effects. As a result, although like any other literary classic it may never be definitively explicated, its area of productive literary interpretation has been considerably narrowed but deepened. Generations of scholars have approached a consensus that in addition to being attracted to, and knowledgeable about, the history of Puritan New England, Hawthorne was a serious student of the psychology of not just the Puritan but also the religious mind. In the final analysis, "Young Goodman Brown" is not only about the Puritans, nor is it only an analysis of what a member of a seventeenth-century American Protestant sect believed and how he acted; it also transcends the particulars of time and place and is a universally valid study of how belief, and especially certitude of belief, can affect the human mind.

Because of the story's ambiguity, even a summary of its plot is not a simple matter, and for that reason plot summary is likely to reveal as little about the true power of the story as a plot summary of *Hamlet* would of the play. At all levels, the story is highly dramatic and gripping, but readers who take the story line literally find its gloom upsetting and may be moved by it to see Hawthorne as a critic of the evils of society and to conclude that the world that they know is more sinister than they thought. This view, however, would invert the story and mistake the vehicle for the contents it carries. The power and appeal of the story are enhanced by scholarship that demonstrates that the plot is deceptive and the underlying conflicts much more complex and even more compelling than the surface narrative.

TECHNIQUES AND THEMES

Although written relatively early in Hawthorne's career, the story nevertheless contains some of his most characteristic themes and techniques. Had it not appeared six years before Ralph Waldo Emerson's "Self-Reliance" (1841), it might have been regarded as a counter or antidote to the radical individualism that essay preaches. Whereas Emerson tends to see things in black and white and as either/or issues, Hawthorne's tale eloquently depicts how inaccurate perception can be and how often ambiguity attends reality or illusion cloaks it and, therefore, how recognition of these complications should discourage simplistic judgments. In the forest with his companion, for instance, Brown is shaken by the revelation that the Puritan community and his own family are not as perfectly virtuous as they seem, and he precipitously leaps to the extravagant conclusion that they are totally wicked.

Technically, the tale is highly sophisticated. The story is told, for example, by an omniscient but unobtrusive—almost to the point of effacement—narrator who, with few but important exceptions, is restricted to the limited functions of narrating the plot and channeling the protagonist's thoughts. The protagonist seems to be a good young man with whom it is easy to identify. Readers are therefore inclined to sympathize with him and to overlook the considerable amount of evidence subtly introduced throughout the tale that indicates that most of what he believes he experiences on his night journey into the forest is a dream and that, because he never suspects this, his impressions are not to be accepted as prima facie truths but are to be interpreted. In large measure, therefore, "Young Goodman Brown" is a tale about what goes on in Brown's mind. But the narrator never identifies with Brown, whose perceptions are erroneous, or endorses the conclusions Brown reaches that unfairly malign not just his own community but the world at large. Readers who sympathize with Goodman Brown are led by almost imperceptible degrees to the slippery position that he alone is good and everyone else is evil.

When Hawthorne wrote the story, he was already a master of symbolism, allegory, ambiguity, and irony, four of the story's outstanding features. As with John Bunyan's *Pilgrim's Progress,* a literary progenitor, each character in Hawthorne's tale has symbolic in addition to dramatic value, and while the narrative succeeds at a literal level, the interplay of the symbols effectively constitutes an artful and absorbing allegory. The central personage of young Goodman Brown, who symbolizes youth (although he is no longer young at the end) and goodness (although that value is qualified), focuses the story into an allegory of the plight of every human being who seeks to achieve and maintain mature integrity in a murky world.

A wide spectrum of irony colors the story, from the obvious, such as the comment that the devil

"Young Goodman Brown, his Wife Faith, and All the Other Prospective Converts are Brought Before the Devil Figure." Illustration from the autograph edition of the *Complete Writings of Hawthorne,* 1900. GRADUATE LIBRARY, UNIVERSITY OF MICHIGAN

It is easier to describe an impression of the tale than to articulate what it supports. This was done most famously by Herman Melville, Hawthorne's contemporary and friend, in his 1850 review essay "Hawthorne and His Mosses." Melville stated that a "great power of blackness in him derives its force from its appeals to that Calvinistic sense of Innate Depravity and Original Sin, from whose visitations, in some shape or other, no deeply thinking mind is always and wholly free" (p. 51). Melville's genius and eloquence have endowed this view with long life, but while it is true that Hawthorne had Calvinist roots and was a student of Puritanism, it is far from a foregone conclusion that there is a "power of blackness" in him. In "Young Goodman Brown," in fact, Hawthorne illuminates what is dark rather than projects darkness. Insofar as he addresses the issue of innate depravity derived from a Calvinistic view of original sin (i.e., the corruption of human nature), he rejects it.

BIOGRAPHICAL AND HISTORICAL BACKGROUND

When approaching the story from a biographical perspective, one learns that Hawthorne was reticent about explaining his personal beliefs; he preferred to express them indirectly in his fiction. It is certain, however, that he was neither a Puritan nor a latter-day Calvinist. This understanding is important because years of studying the Puritans enabled him to penetrate so deeply into the Puritan mind and psyche that he was able to represent with authority unmatched until the mid-twentieth century the historical framework of belief and mind-set of Young Goodman Brown. This is done so convincingly that many readers assume that Hawthorne essentially agrees with his main character. For the same reason, the poet William Blake considered Satan to be the real hero of Milton's *Paradise Lost.* The reasoning in both cases is understandable but wrong. Great authors, including Chaucer and Shakespeare as well as Hawthorne and Melville, have always been able to represent believably the humanity of characters of whom they did not approve.

Hawthorne was thirty years old and unemployed when he published "Young Goodman Brown" in the April 1835 issue of the *New-England Magazine.* It was collected and reprinted in *Mosses from an Old Manse* (1846), which received favorable general reviews, including Melville's and one by Edgar Allan Poe. At the beginning of his writing career, however, there was little reason to suspect that he would be a literary success. After he graduated Bowdoin College in Maine in 1825, he returned to Salem to live somewhat reclusively in his mother's house for approximately thirteen years. Most biographers agree that Hawthorne spent those years

"would not have felt abashed at the governor's dinner table, or in King William's court" (p. 76), to subtle revelations that emerge gradually, such as the fact that Brown is faithless to both Faith and faith, his wife and his religion. Controlled ambiguity, together with irony, thoroughly but deftly permeates the narrative. Indeed, the majority of sentences have ironic capabilities, and certainty is the victim of the invitation of many passages to be read in more than one way, a consequence of Hawthorne's use of the device of multiple choice, one of his favorites. He clearly wanted readers to ponder the text carefully. The least effect of so much alternate possibility is to render literal readings of the story line unlikely. However, not all alternate possibilities lead to full interpretations. The tale has main themes that supply purposeful direction through the ambiguities and ironies.

reading and acquiring what the poet Dylan Thomas called the "craft or sullen art" of writing. The details of what he read are important to know; he furthered the education begun at Bowdoin. All students enrolling at Bowdoin knew from the moment of registration which courses and books they would study for the next four years and which professors they would have. There were no "majors" or different tracks; the course of study was the same for all students.

A major component of a Bowdoin education was training in classical rhetoric, Aristotelian logic, and the elements of religion. It does not follow, of course, that all students would have fully agreed with everything they studied, but at least they would have demonstrated competence in the subjects. From what little we know of Hawthorne at Bowdoin, he was uncommunicative about his true interests, but when he returned to Salem, approximately 10 percent of the books he checked out from the library of the Salem Atheneum related to religion and philosophy.

Hawthorne's training in logic and philosophy is applied to the following passage from "Young Goodman Brown":

> "My Faith is gone!" cried he, after one stupefied moment. "There is no good on earth; and sin is but a name. Come, devil! for to thee is this world given."
>
> And maddened with despair, so that he laughed loud and long, did Goodman Brown grasp his staff and set forth again, at such a rate, that he seemed to fly along the forest path, rather than to walk or run. (P. 83)

This passage is rife with faulty logic and moral danger signals, too ingeniously concocted to have been accidental on Hawthorne's part. It shows Brown to be both confused and in a state of despair, a major sin for Christians, and it is strong evidence that Hawthorne has distanced himself from Brown by exposing the unreliability of his point of view.

A substantial part of the rest of Hawthorne's reading dealt with New England history. It was this reading that gave him the familiarity with the details of Puritan history and religious culture that he drew upon for *The Scarlet Letter* and many of his short stories, especially "Young Goodman Brown." David Levin and Michael J. Colacurcio have demonstrated persuasively that an essential element in the story's historical background is the seventeenth-century controversy over the validity of "specter evidence," testimony based on the perhaps sincere but unverifiable beliefs of individuals that they witnessed others (or their likenesses) in the community engaging in such forbidden activities as witchcraft or devil worship. Specter evidence played a crucial role in the Salem witch trials; lives were lost and great personal damage was suffered before such testimony was banned. It is known that Hawthorne familiarized himself with the details of specter evidence and the ultimately telling objections to it, and one of his towering achievements is the creation of the character of Young Goodman Brown, who was ruled by it without knowing it.

COMPLEXITY DISGUISED AS SIMPLICITY

Indeed, Brown is rendered so matter-of-factly that readers are likely not to ask crucial questions of the narrative. The first sentence of the story, for example, is by itself a tour de force of how a heavily loaded statement can be presented with disarming casualness: "Young Goodman Brown came forth, at sunset, into the street of Salem village, but put his head back, after crossing the threshold, to exchange a parting kiss with his young wife" (p. 74). Brown sets out on his journey at sunset, an ominous time in a village surrounded by wilderness and enemies. He crosses a threshold and exchanges a "parting" kiss with his Faith. Each of these three elements will have major repercussions. Inasmuch as we soon learn that Brown has an "evil purpose" (p. 75) we must ask what it is and when he encounters evil. Brown simply wishes to know what evil is. As soon as he encounters the devil figure in the forest, Brown tells him that having kept "covenant" (p. 76) by meeting him, he now intends to return home. His journey had been motivated only by intellectual curiosity. It was a brilliant stroke of Hawthorne's genius to realize that a young seventeenth-century Puritan was likely to conceive of evil in the tangible figure of the devil. He also understood that a naive young man raised in a holy community of "visible saints" (which was the standard to which Puritans aspired) might actually believe that in order to find out what evil is he has to leave the community, and that to be evil one must dedicate himself formally to the devil. Ironically, therefore, the story really begins before the first sentence; it begins when Brown decides to find out what evil is. But the mere interest in evil is evil, so it is inside of Brown all the time, concealed by his naive misconception that when found it will be external to himself in the shape of the devil and can be easily left behind at will.

Hawthorne handles the details of the meeting with exquisite irony. Brown, we are told, "passed a crook of the road" and looking forward "beheld the figure of a man, in grave and decent attire" (p. 75). The subtle pun "crook of the road" can refer both to a bend in the road and to the devil, who is believed to bend minds and steal souls. It is important to note that the narrator never refers to the devil by that name: he is always a "figure," or "elder person," "traveller," "the other," or some such term. Hawthorne uses these circumlocutions purposefully; he deliberately distinguishes between the omniscient narrator as channeler of Brown's fantasies and the narrator's own views, which are usually presented inobviously. The narrator never says the devil is present; Brown convinces himself that he literally meets the devil incarnate. If Brown expected to find the devil in red, with horns, tail, and pitchfork, he is surprised to find only the "figure" of a man, possibly ominous only in that his attire is "grave" (p. 75). The figure not only looks like a Puritan, he even resembles Brown. By such adroit touches, Hawthorne suggests that evil is not "out there" but inside of us.

By the same token, Brown's conviction that he apprehends fellow villagers in the forest prevents him—and sympathetic readers—from recognizing them as projections of his mind, extensions of his original delusion. Goody Cloyse, his catechism teacher and spiritual adviser, is introduced only as a "female figure" (p. 78). This figure identifies Brown's companion as the devil, but in counterpoint to the figure's admissions of witchery are the narrator's understated but factual descriptions of Cloyse as "a very pious and exemplary dame" and "pious old lady" (p. 78). Brown is made to choose between his lifetime knowledge of the real Cloyse and this aberrant apparition. He instantly loses faith in the real Goody Cloyse. Next, Brown does not even think he sees the town minister and Deacon Gookin, he only believes he recognizes their voices in the "empty air" (p. 82). Again he trusts his impressions and abandons his experiential knowledge. He discards everything in which he believes except for Faith. She (and what she symbolizes: love, trust, and support) is all that stands between him and despair. And so when Faith's pink ribbon seems to float down from a "black mass" (p. 82) of cloud overhead, Brown surrenders to despair.

PROBLEMS IN DISTINGUISHING ILLUSION FROM REALITY

The critic F. O. Matthiessen errs in analyzing the story when he claims "the literal insistence on that damaging pink ribbon obtrudes the labels of a confining allegory, and short circuits the range of associations" (p. 284). In other words, within the context of a hallucinatory vision, the appearance of something concrete breaks the otherwise seamlessly consistent narrative. But the ribbon is as much an illusion as everything else Brown thinks he sees or hears. From the moment, early in the story, when the devil figure urges Brown to accompany him farther into the forest, and Brown "unconsciously" (p. 76) resumes his walk, all that happens is part of a dream: the apparitions, the voices, the ribbon, and the devil's conclave in the forest. Intensely wrought up by

his purpose to meet the devil, Brown is so overcome by his imagination that first he convinces himself that he is with the devil and then he becomes unconscious. In the story's last two paragraphs, the possibility of a dream is mentioned twice. When Brown awakens in the morning, he is not where the devil supposedly held court, the remote glade in the forest to which Brown "flew" (p. 84), but near enough to the village to walk to it.

When he arrives, all is as he left it, including Faith "with the pink ribbons" (p. 89). All is as he left it, but he is changed, perceiving not what is there but what his dream causes him to see. He is perturbed by the congregation's singing of a holy hymn that sounds to him like an "anthem of sin" (p. 89) and by the "blasphemer" (p. 89) minister's preaching from the Bible. If readers have completely identified with Brown, then they share his unrealistic insistence on associating only with pure people, and they forget that the Bible and religion are there for humans who are not perfect but aspire to become better. If readers are troubled by hypocrites preaching and singing, they might reflect that if the Bible is true, the fact that a hypocrite reads from it or sings hymns based on it does not detract at all from its truth. And if it discomfits readers to think that their ministers and fellow congregants are sinners, then readers should recall that religion teaches that no one, themselves included, is without sin. In recognizing no middle ground between depravity and his notion of saintliness, Brown's "goodness" is evilly narrow.

The story's ending is all the more tragic because the persisting consequences on Brown of his dream are baseless and unnecessary. He lives out his life in the immature either/or fallacy, unable to cope with humans who though not saints are yet more good than bad. He continues to live with Faith, despising her, and yet begets children with her. It is a horrifying picture of how delusion can poison even the most beautiful gifts that life has to offer and pervert legitimate and innocent happiness into gloom. The story's final irony is in its last sentence: "And when he had lived long, and was borne to his grave, a hoary corpse, followed by Faith, an aged woman, and children and grandchildren, a goodly procession, besides neighbors, not a few, they carved no hopeful verse upon his tomb-stone; for his dying hour was gloom" (pp. 89–90). Brown is followed to his grave by a "goodly" procession. This is the narrator's judgment. The procession is goodly not just by being numerous but by being virtuous. Troubled by fellow humans whom he feared did not tell the truth, Brown at the last is not lied about by them.

"Young Goodman Brown," then, is a tale that does not explicitly advance an agenda of its own so much as criticize a fallacious one. But its own moral import is inferable when it is closely and thoughtfully examined for the grounds of its criticism. While undercutting belief in the literal existence of the devil and witches by exposing the dangerously subjective nature of specter evidence, it proposes that the mere knowledge of evil can be sufficiently destructive by itself if indulged and acted upon. Furthermore, the attendant belief that one is the only virtuous and infallible person is itself a form of evil because it bases action on a fallacy and blinds one to seeing good in the world. Young Goodman Brown is most vulnerable when he rejects the wholesome influences of other human beings—especially those who earned and deserved his trust: his minister, Deacon Gookin, Goody Cloyse, and his wife, Faith—and the faith of his religion, which warned him against the presumptuous beliefs he adopted, and thus makes possible their aid in moderating his obsession.

In "Young Goodman Brown," paralleled in Hawthorne's oeuvre by such other tales as "The Minister's Black Veil" (1835), "The Birth-mark" (1843), "Egotism, or the Bosom Serpent" (1843), "Ethan Brand" (1850), and also *The Scarlet Letter* (1850), readers are warned against extreme self-reliance before Emerson advocated it. No single work of Hawthorne, this story included, can be regarded by itself as a representative microcosm of his personal philosophy, but "Young Goodman Brown" reflects his classical conservatism in its emphatic acknowledgment of human limitations. In the tradition of that standard primer of American principles, *The Federalist* (1787–1788), and in its distrust of infallibility, extremism, and other simplistic responses to life's complexities, the story is one of literature's most rationally and psychologically convincing arguments for humanity's need of a balance of powers, to protect ourselves against ourselves.

See also The Bible; "The Birth-mark"; *The Blithedale Romance;* Calvinism; "The Custom-House"; Gothic Fiction, "Hawthorne and His Mosses"; *The House of the Seven Gables;* Individualism and Community; Puritanism; The Romance; *The Scarlet Letter;* Short Story; Transcendentalism; Utopian Communities; Wilderness

BIBLIOGRAPHY

Primary Work

Hawthorne, Nathaniel. "Young Goodman Brown." 1835. In *Mosses from an Old Manse*, pp. 74–90. Centenary Edition of the Works of Nathaniel Hawthorne, vol. 10. Columbus: Ohio State University Press, 1974.

Secondary Works

Bell, Michael Davitt. *Hawthorne and the Historical Romance of New England*. Princeton, N.J.: Princeton University Press, 1971.

Berkove, Lawrence I. "'Reasoning as We Go': The Flawed Logic of Young Goodman Brown." *Nathaniel Hawthorne Review* 24, no. 1 (1998): 46–52.

Colacurcio, Michael J. *The Province of Piety: Moral History in Hawthorne's Early Tales*. Cambridge, Mass.: Harvard University Press, 1984.

Crews, Frederick C. *The Sins of the Fathers: Hawthorne's Psychological Themes*. New York: Oxford University Press, 1965.

Doubleday, Neil Frank. *Hawthorne's Early Tales: A Critical Study*. Durham, N.C.: Duke University Press, 1972.

Fogle, Richard H. "Ambiguity and Clarity in Hawthorne's 'Young Goodman Brown.'" *New England Quarterly* 18 (1943): 446–465.

Gollin, Rita. *Nathaniel Hawthorne and the Truth of Dreams*. Baton Rouge: Louisiana State University Press, 1979.

Hoffman, Daniel G. *Form and Fable in American Fiction*. New York: Oxford University Press, 1961.

Levin, David. "Shadows of Doubt: Specter Evidence in Hawthorne's 'Young Goodman Brown.'" *American Literature* 34 (1962): 344–352.

McWilliams, John P., Jr. *Hawthorne, Melville, and the American Character: A Looking-Glass Business*. Cambridge, U.K.: Cambridge University Press, 1984.

Male, Roy R. *Hawthorne's Tragic Vision*. Austin: University of Texas Press, 1957.

Matthiessen, F. O. *American Renaissance*. New York: Oxford University Press, 1941.

Mellow, James R. *Nathaniel Hawthorne in His Times*. Boston: Houghton Mifflin, 1980.

Melville, Herman. "Hawthorne and His Mosses." 1850. In *Tales, Poems, and Other Writings,* edited by John Bryant. New York: Modern Library, 2002.

Turner, Arlin. *Nathaniel Hawthorne: An Introduction and Interpretation*. New York: Barnes and Noble, 1961.

Lawrence I. Berkove

Contributor Biographies

Terrie Dopp Aamodt is Professor of History and English, Walla Walla College, and the author of *Righteous Armies, Holy Cause: Apocalyptic Imagery and the Civil War* (2002). Religion

Robert E. Abrams is Associate Professor, University of Washington. He has been awarded a Walter Chapin Simpson Research Fellowship for 2005–2006. His major publications include *Landscape and Ideology in American Renaissance Literature: Topographies of Skepticism* (2004); "Critiquing Colonial American Geography: Hawthorne's Landscape of Bewilderment," *Texas Studies in Literature and Language* (1994); and "Image, Object, and Perception in Thoreau's Landscapes: The Development of Anti-Geography," *Nineteenth-Century Literature* (1991). Borders

Alan Ackerman is Associate Professor in the Department of English at the University of Toronto. He is author of *The Portable Theater: American Literature and the Nineteenth-Century Stage* (1999) and coeditor, with Martin Puchner, of *Against Theatre: Creative Destructions on the Modernist Stage* (forthcoming). Theater

Joseph Alkana is Associate Professor in the Department of English at the University of Miami. His is author of *The Social Self* (1997) as well as articles on American and Jewish American literature. He is also coeditor of *Cohesion and Dissent in America* (1994). Jews; Psychology

William L. Andrews, E. Maynard Adams Professor of English at the University of North Carolina at Chapel Hill, is the author of *The Literary Career of Charles W. Chesnutt* (1980) and *To Tell a Free Story: The First Century of Afro-American Autobiography, 1760–1865* (1986). He is the editor or coeditor of more than thirty books on African American literature, including *The Oxford Companion to African American Literature* (1997); *The Norton Anthology of African American Literature* (2003); and *North Carolina Slave Narratives* (2003). *Narrative of the Life of Frederick Douglass*

David Anthony is Associate Professor in the Department of English at Southern Illinois University, Carbondale. A specialist in nineteenth-century literature and culture, he has published essays on the role of "lowbrow" urban sensationalism in reflecting and helping shape standards of class and taste in journals such as *American Literature* (September 1997 and December 2004), the *Yale Journal of Criticism* (1999), and *Early American Literature* (2005). He has completed a book-length study of the relations between the unstable form of masculine sensibility offered in early-nineteenth-century gothic sensationalism and the precarious nature of the period's credit-based boom-and-bust economy. Taste

Jana Lea Argersinger is coeditor of *ESQ: A Journal of the American Renaissance* and *Poe Studies/Dark Romanticism,* both published at Washington State University, and an executive officer of the Council of Editors of Learned Journals. She has published articles in *American Literature* and the *Edgar Allan Poe Review* as well as in *Writers of the American Renaissance: An A-to-Z Guide,* edited by Denise D. Knight. Argersinger's scholarly interest in American women writers encompasses Elizabeth Stoddard, the northwest regionalist Carol Ryrie Brink, and the nineteenth-century sentimental tradition generally. *The Wide, Wide World*

Charlene Avallone, an independent scholar based in Lanikai, Hawai'i, is working on a study of nineteenth-century U.S. women's literary conversation. Her publications include "What American Renaissance? The Gendered Genealogy of a Critical Discourse," *PMLA* (1997); "The 'Red Roots' of White Feminism in Margaret Fuller's Writings," in *Doing Feminism: Teaching and Research in the Academy,* edited by Mary Anderson, Lisa Fine, Kathleen Geissler, and Joyce R. Ladenson (1997); and "Catharine Sedgwick and the Art of Conversation," in *Catharine Maria Sedgwick: Critical Perspectives,* edited by Lucinda L. Damon-Bach and Victoria Clements (2003). Oral Tradition

Eric Baker is a senior English major at Calvin College, widely traveled and academically distinguished. He followed work on this essay with a hike up Mt. Kilimanjaro and research in Nairobi. **Religious Periodicals**

Louise Barnett is Professor of English and American Studies at Rutgers University, New Brunswick, New Jersey. She has written a number of books, among them, *The Ignoble Savage: American Literary Racism* (1976); *Touched by Fire: The Life, Death, and Mythic Afterlife of George Armstrong Custer* (1996); and *Ungentlemanly Acts: The Army's Notorious Incest Trial* (2000). She is coeditor of *The Art of Leslie Marmon Silko: A Collection of Critical Essays* (1999). **Indians**

Dale M. Bauer is Professor of English at the University of Illinois, Urbana-Champaign. She has published *Feminist Dialogics* (1988), *Edith Wharton's Brave New Politics* (1994), and is completing a book titled "Sex Expression and American Women, 1860–1940." **Marriage**

Mark Bauerlein is Professor of English at Emory University. He is the author of several books and articles on American literature, history, and philosophy, and he contributes frequently to national magazines and newspapers. **"Out of the Cradle Endlessly Rocking"**

Nina Baym is Swanlund Endowed Chair and Center for Advanced Study Professor of English Emerita, and Jubilee Professor of Liberal Arts and Sciences, at the University of Illinois, Urbana. Among books not cited in her article, she is author of *The Shape of Hawthorne's Career* (1976); *American Women Writers and the Work of History, 1790–1860* (1995); and *American Women of Letters and the Nineteenth-Century Sciences: Styles of Affiliation* (2002). In 2000 she was awarded the Jay B. Hubbell medal for lifetime achievement in furthering American literary study. **Feminism**

Damien-Claude Bélanger is a course lecturer at the McGill Institute for the Study of Canada. He is a founding coeditor of *Mens,* Quebec's journal of intellectual history and historical commentary, and is currently completing a doctoral dissertation at McGill University entitled "Pride and Prejudice: Canadian Intellectuals Confront the United States, 1891–1945." **Canada**

Klaus Benesch is Professor of English and Director of the American Studies Program at the University of Bayreuth (Germany). He is the author of *Romantic Cyborgs: Authorship and Technology in the American Renaissance* (2002); editor of *African Diasporas in the Old and the New World* (2004) and *Space in America: Theory, History, Culture* (2005); and general editor (with David Nye, Miles Orvell, and Joseph Tabbi) of "Architecture—Technology—Culture" (ATC), A Rodopi International Book series. **Technology**

James M. Bergquist is Emeritus Professor at Villanova University, where he taught from 1963 to 2001. He has written numerous articles and essays on the immigrant experience, including "The German-American Press," in *The Ethnic Press in the United States,* edited by Sally M. Miller (1987); "Germans and German-Speaking Peoples," in *Our Multicultural Heritage: A Guide to American Ethnic Groups,* edited by Elliott Barkan (1999); and "The Forty-Eighters: Catalysts of German-American Politics," in *Being Present in the Other Culture: The Dynamic of German-American Interactions,* edited by Frank Trommler and Elliott Shore (2001). **Immigration**

Lawrence I. Berkove is Professor Emeritus in English at the University of Michigan-Dearborn, where he was Chair of the Humanities Department and Director of the American Studies Program. He is a specialist in nineteenth- and early twentieth-century American literature, and has published extensively in his field, including two previous articles on Hawthorne. Most of his work centers on the literature of the American West, especially that of Ambrose Bierce, Mark Twain, Jack London, and the authors of Nevada's Sagebrush School. He is the author or editor of ten books and monographs, including *The Fighting Horse of the Stanislaus: Stories & Essays by Dan De Quille* (1990), *Ethical Records of Twain and His Circle of Sagebrush Journalists* (1994), and *A Prescription for Adversity: The Moral Art of Ambrose Bierce* (2002). He is currently completing a collection of Sagebrush literature. **"Young Goodman Brown"**

Rebecca Berne is a doctoral candidate in the Department of English Language and Literature at Yale University. **Short Story**

Dennis Berthold is Professor of English at Texas A&M University, the coeditor of *Dear Brother Walt: The Letters of Thomas Jefferson Whitman* (1984) and *Hawthorne's American Travel Sketches* (1989), and the author of articles on American literature and cultural politics in such journals as *American Literary History, American Literature,* and *Nineteenth-Century Literature.* **Political Parties**

Michael Berthold is an Associate Professor of English at Villanova University and has published a variety of essays on Melville, American slave narratives, and other aspects of American literature and culture. *Battle-Pieces*

Michael L. Birkel teaches at Earlham College in Richmond, Indiana. His works include *A Near Sympathy: The Timeless Quaker Wisdom of John Woolman* (2004) and *Silence and Witness: Quaker Spirituality* (2005). **Quakers**

Steven Blakemore, Associate Professor of English, Florida Atlantic University, has published on a variety of topics in English and American literature. His publications include *Intertextual War: Edmund Burke and the French Revolution in the Writings of Mary Wollstonecraft, Thomas Paine, and James Mackintosh* (1997) and *Crisis in Representation: Thomas Paine, Mary Wollstonecraft, Helen Maria Williams, and the Rewriting of the French Revolution* (1997). **"Rip Van Winkle"**

Shelley R. Block is a doctoral candidate in American literature at the University of Missouri–Columbia. She has articles published in *American Periodicals* (2002) and *Legacy* (2003) and is working on her dissertation, which examines the cultural work of American temperance literature of the nineteenth century. *Blake*

Cheryl D. Bohde is a Professor at McLennan Community College, where she teaches American literature. Her most recent publications are "Anne Moody" and "Harlem," forthcoming in Greenwood Publishing's *Encyclopedia of African American Literature.* **Young America**

Michael Borgstrom is Assistant Professor of English at San Diego State University. He is the author of "Passing Over: Setting the Record Straight in *Uncle Tom's Cabin*," *PMLA* (2003). Same-Sex Love

Kristin Boudreau is Associate Professor of English at the University of Georgia. She is the author of *Sympathy in American Literature: American Sentiments from Jefferson to the Jameses* (2002). Friendship

Dana Brand is Professor of English and American Literature at Hofstra University. He is the author of *The Spectator and the City in Nineteenth-Century American Literature* (1991) and numerous articles on nineteenth- and twentieth-century American literature and film. Urbanization

James R. Britton is a Lecturer at the University of Miami, where he teaches writing and literature. He has published on antebellum social reform in the journal *Nineteenth-Century Prose* and is working on an essay on Edgar Allan Poe soon to be published in the MLA Approaches to Teaching series. Suffrage

Nick Bromell is Professor of American Literature at the University of Massachusetts, Amherst. He is the author of *By the Sweat of the Brow: Labor and Literature in Antebellum America* (1993) and *Tomorrow Never Knows: Rock and Psychedelics in the 1960s* (2000), both published by the University of Chicago Press. Labor

Candy Gunther Brown is an Assistant Professor of American Studies at Saint Louis University. She is the author of *The Word in the World: Evangelical Writing, Publishing, and Reading in America, 1789–1880* (2004). Evangelicals

Stephen Howard Browne is Professor of Rhetorical Studies at Pennsylvania State University. He is the author of *Edmund Burke and the Discourse of Virtue* (1993); *Angelina Grimké: Rhetoric, Identity, and the Radical Imagination* (1999); and *Jefferson's Call for Nationhood* (2003). "Letters on the Equality of the Sexes"; "Plymouth Rock Oration"

Dickson D. Bruce Jr. is Professor of History, University of California, Irvine. His books include *Violence and Culture in the Antebellum South* (1979); *Black American Writing from the Nadir: The Evolution of a Literary Tradition, 1877–1915* (1989); and *The Origins of African American Literature, 1680–1865* (2001). The Bondwoman's Narrative

A fulltime software developer, **Patrick W. Bryant's** doctoral thesis (in progress at Georgia State University) is an "online, fluid text" edition of Herman Melville's *Typee*. Using custom software Bryant is writing for the project, the edition comprises a website that will allow readers to collate all extant materials that contribute to "*Typee's* many texts" along with "revision narratives" explicative annotations describing differences among textual variants. Typee

Louis J. Budd, James B. Duke Professor of English (Emeritus), Duke University, has written *Mark Twain: Social Philosopher* (1962, new ed. 2001) and *Our Mark Twain* (1983) and has edited *Mark Twain: The Contemporary Reviews* (1999). The Innocents Abroad

Martin T. Buinicki is an Assistant Professor of English at Valparaiso University, specializing in nineteenth-century American literature and the history of the book and authorship. He has published articles in *American Literary History* and *American Literary Realism*. His book *Negotiating Copyright: Authorship and the Discourse of Literary Property Rights in Nineteenth-Century America* is forthcoming from Routledge Press. Periodicals

Bruce Burgett is Professor of American Studies in the Interdisciplinary Arts and Sciences Program at the University of Washington–Bothell and graduate faculty in the English Department at the University of Washington–Seattle. He is the author of *Sentimental Bodies: Sex, Gender, and Citizenship in the Early Republic* (1998) and has published widely on American cultural studies. Sexuality and the Body

Robert E. Burkholder is Associate Professor of English at Penn State University, University Park. He is coauthor of *Ralph Waldo Emerson: An Annotated Bibliography of Criticism* (1994), a member of the Editorial Board of the Collected Works of Ralph Waldo Emerson, and a past president of the Ralph Waldo Emerson Society. Concord, Massachusetts

John A. Burrison is Regents Professor of English and Director of the Folklore Curriculum at Georgia State University. His publications include "'The Golden Arm': The Folk Tale and Its Literary Use by Mark Twain and Joel C. Harris," Arts and Sciences Research Paper no. 19 (1968) and *Storytellers: Folktales and Legends from the South* (1989). Folklore

William E. Cain is the Mary Jewett Gaiser Professor of English at Wellesley College. His publications include (as coeditor) *The Norton Anthology of Literary Theory and Criticism* (2001), and the section on "Literary Criticism" for *The Cambridge History of American Literature*, vol. 5 (2003). *The Blithedale Romance*

Barbara Cantalupo is Associate Professor of English at the Pennsylvania State University and founding editor of *The Edgar Allan Poe Review*. She has published essays on Poe, Hawthorne, and Emma Wolf, among others. She edited and wrote an introduction for the reissue of Emma Wolf's 1892 novel, *Other Things Being Equal*, and is coeditor of *Prospects for the Study of American Literature, Volume II* (forthcoming). "The Philosophy of Composition"

Lorrayne Carroll is Associate Professor of English at the University of Southern Maine. Her book "Rhetorical Drag: Gender, Captivity and the Writing of History" is forthcoming from Kent State University Press. Captivity Narratives

Scott E. Casper is Associate Professor of History at the University of Nevada, Reno. He is the author of *Constructing American Lives: Biography and Culture in Nineteenth-Century America* (1999) and the coeditor, with Joanne D. Chaison and Jeffrey D. Groves, of *Perspectives on American Book History: Artifacts and Commentary* (2002). Biography

Russ Castronovo is Jean Wall Bennett Professor of English and American Studies at the University of Wisconsin–Madison. He is the author of *Fathering the Nation: American Genealogies of Slavery and Freedom* (1995) and

Necro Citizenship: Death, Eroticism, and the Public Sphere in the Nineteenth-Century United States (2001). He coedited, with Dana Nelson, *Materializing Democracy: Toward a Revitalized Cultural Politics* (2002). **Death**

Nancy D. Chase is Associate Professor in the Department of English at Georgia State University in Atlanta, Georgia. She teaches American literature and has published about family alcoholism and parentified children. She edited and contributed to the first volume of collected essays on parentification, *Burdened Children: Theory, Research, and Treatment of Parentification* (1999), and has coedited a monograph, *High-Performing Families: Causes, Consequences, and Clinical Solutions* (Family Psychology and Counseling series, 2001). **Childhood**

Eileen Ka-May Cheng teaches history at Sarah Lawrence College. She is editor of *Women in American History: Civil War, Reconstruction, and Industrialization, 1820–1900*, vol. 2 (2002), and author of "American Historical Writers and the Loyalists, 1788–1856: Dissent, Consensus, and American Nationality," *Journal of the Early Republic* (winter 2003). **History**

Amanda Claybaugh is Assistant Professor of English and Comparative Literature at Columbia University. She is the author of a forthcoming book about the nineteenth-century novel and Anglo-American social reform. **Temperance**

Samuel Chase Coale teaches American literature at Wheaton College in Massachusetts. He has taught in several countries, such as India, Pakistan, Brazil, Greece, and Belarus, and his most recent books include *Mesmerism and Hawthorne: Mediums of American Romance* (1998); *The Mystery of Mysteries: Cultural Differences and Designs* (2000); and *Paradigms of Paranoia: The Culture of Conspiracy in Contemporary American Fiction* (2005). **Popular Science**

Lorinda B. Cohoon is an Assistant Professor in the English Department at the University of Memphis, where she teaches undergraduate and graduate courses in children's literature and culture. Her current research focuses on children's periodicals of the nineteenth century and constructions of childhood citizenship. **Gift Books and Annuals; Pictorial Weeklies**

Carol Colatrella is Professor of Literature and Cultural Studies and Codirector of the Center for the Study of Women, Science, and Technology at the Georgia Institute of Technology. She is the author of *Evolution, Sacrifice, and Narrative: Balzac, Zola, and Faulkner* (1990) and *Literature and Moral Reform: Melville and the Discipline of Reading* (2002) and coeditor, with Joseph Alkana, of *Cohesion and Dissent in America* (1994). **Crime and Punishment**

William Conlogue is Associate Professor of English at Marywood University. In addition to articles in several journals, he has published a book, *Working the Garden: American Writers and the Industrialization of Agriculture* (2001). **Agrarianism**

Susan Coultrap-McQuin earned her Ph.D. from the University of Iowa in American Studies. She is the author of articles on nineteenth-century women writers and publishing as well as on women's studies and teaching topics. Her book

Doing Literary Business (1990) won a Choice Award and other recognition. She edited the book *Gail Hamilton: Selected Writings* (1992) and coedited *Explorations in Feminist Ethics: Theory and Practice* (1992). She currently serves as Provost and Vice President for Academic Affairs at the State University of New York College (SUNY) at Oswego. **Female Authorship**

Amy Cummins, Assistant Professor of English at Fort Hays State University, specializes in American literature and women's history. **Seneca Falls Convention**

John Patrick Daly is Associate Professor of History at the State University of New York College at Brockport. He is the author of *When Slavery Was Called Freedom: Evangelicalism, Proslavery, and the Causes of the Civil War, 1830–1865* (2003), which won honorable mention for the 2002 Seaborg Prize for Civil War Scholarship. **Proslavery Writing**

Michael J. Davey is Assistant Professor of early and nineteenth-century American literature at Valdosta State University in Valdosta, Georgia. He has published on Henry James, Susan Fenimore Cooper, and Herman Melville. **The Romance**

Cynthia J. Davis is an Associate Professor of English at the University of South Carolina in Columbia. She is the author of *Bodily and Narrative Forms: The Influence of Medicine on American Literature, 1845–1915* (2000); coeditor of *Approaches to Teaching Gilman's "The Yellow Wall-Paper" and Herland* (2003); and coauthor of *Women Writers in the United States: A Timeline of Social, Cultural, and Literary History* (1996). She is working on a biography of Charlotte Perkins Gilman for Stanford University Press. **Health and Medicine**

David A. Davis is Georgia Carroll Kyser Fellow in American Literature at the University of North Carolina at Chapel Hill. He is managing editor of *Southern Literary Journal* and associate editor of *North Carolina Slave Narratives*. **The Confessions of Nat Turner**

Marcy J. Dinius is a visiting Assistant Professor at Northwestern University. She has published articles on antebellum American literature and publishing, including "Slavery in Black and White: Daguerreotypy and *Uncle Tom's Cabin*," *ESQ: A Journal of the American Renaissance* (2005); and "Poe's Moon Shot: 'Hans Phaall' and the Art and Science of Antebellum Print Culture," *Poe Studies/Dark Romanticism* (2005). **Publishers**

Stacey Lee Donohue is the Chair of the Fine Arts Department and Professor of English at Central Oregon Community College in Bend, Oregon, where she teaches American, Native American, African American, and immigrant literatures as well as composition. **Irish**

Amy E. Earhart is Coordinator of Instructional Technology and Lecturer in the English Department at Texas A&M University. She is the developer of the 19th Century Concord: A Historical and Literary Place digital database website. Her publications include "Representative Men, Slave Revolt, and Emerson's 'Conversion' to Abolitionism" in *ATQ: American Transcendental Quarterly* (1999), and "Elizabeth Peabody on 'the Temperament of the Colored

Classes': African-Americans, Progressive History, and Education in a Democratic System" in the forthcoming *Reinventing the Peabody Sisters.* Underground Railroad

Gregory Eiselein is Professor and Director of Graduate Studies in the Department of English at Kansas State University, where he teaches American literature and cultural studies. He is the author of *Literature and Humanitarian Reform in the Civil War Era* (1996) and editor, with Anne K. Phillips, of *The Louisa May Alcott Encyclopedia* (2001) and the Norton critical edition of *Little Women* (2003). Reform

Monika Elbert, Professor of English at Montclair State University, has published widely on Hawthorne and is associate editor of the *Nathaniel Hawthorne Review.* The House of the Seven Gables

R. J. Ellis teaches at the University of Birmingham, U.K., and edits *Comparative American Studies.* His publications include *"Liar! Liar!": Jack Kerouac, Novelist* (1999); *Harriet Wilson's Our Nig: A Cultural Biography of a "Two-Story" African American Novel* (2003); and "African American Fiction and Poetry," in *A Companion to the Literature and Culture of the American South,* edited by Richard Gray and Owen Robinson (2004). *Walker's Appeal*

Allan Moore Emery is an Associate Professor in the Department of English at Bowling Green State University in Bowling Green, Ohio. He has published articles on Melville's tales in *American Literature, Nineteenth-Century Fiction, New England Quarterly,* and *ESQ: A Journal of the American Renaissance.* He is completing a book on Melville's short fiction of the 1850s as well as an article on Edgar Allan Poe's "The Pit and the Pendulum." "Benito Cereno"

Paul J. Erickson earned his Ph.D. in American Studies from the University of Texas at Austin. He is the author of "Judging Books by Their Covers: Format, the Implied Reader, and the 'Degeneration' of the Dime Novel," *ATQ* (1998); "Help or Hindrance? The History of the Book and Electronic Media," in *Rethinking Media Change: The Aesthetics of Transition* (2003); and "New Books, New Men: City-Mysteries Fiction, Authorship, and the Literary Market," *Early American Studies: An Interdisciplinary Journal* (2003). Dime Novels

John Evelev is an Assistant Professor of English at the University of Missouri–Columbia. He is the author of *Tolerable Entertainment: Herman Melville and Professionalism in Antebellum New York City* (2006). New York

Ann Fabian teaches American Studies and History at Rutgers University, New Brunswick, New Jersey. She is the author of *Card Sharps, Dream Books, and Bucket Shops: Gambling in Nineteenth-Century America* (1990) and *The Unvarnished Truth: Personal Narratives in Nineteenth-Century America* (2000). Amateurism and Self-Publishing

Mark Fackler is Professor of Communications at Calvin College, Grand Rapids, Michigan. He is coauthor of *Media Ethics: Cases and Moral Reasoning* (1983, 1987); *Good News: Social Ethics and the Press* (1993); and *Popular Religious Magazines of the United States* (1995). He teaches and conducts research in East Africa. Religious Periodicals

Steven Fink is Associate Professor of English, the Ohio State University. He is the author of *Prophet in the Marketplace: Thoreau's Development as a Professional Writer* (1992, 1999) and coeditor of *Reciprocal Influences: Literary Production, Distribution, and Consumption in America* (1999). Book Publishing

Paul Finkelman is the Chapman Distinguished Professor of Law at the University of Tulsa College of Law. His recent books include *Defending Slavery: Proslavery Thought in the Old South* and *Landmark Decisions of the United States Supreme Court,* both published in 2003. He coedited *The Library of Congress Civil War Desk Reference* (2002). *Dred Scott v. Sandford*

Elżbieta Foeller-Pituch, Associate Director of the Alice Berline Kaplan Center for the Humanities at Northwestern University, has published articles on contemporary authors such as John Barth and John Gardner, on Henry James, and on aspects of the classical tradition in nineteenth-century American fiction. She has also contributed chapters to *As Others Read Us: International Perspectives on American Literature* (1991) and *The Classical Tradition and the Americas* (forthcoming). Her research interest in the classical tradition in American culture stems from an American Council of Learned Societies postdoctoral fellowship at Harvard University. She is working on a book-length study of nineteenth-century American writers' use of Greek and Roman myths. Classical Literature

Ed Folsom is the Carver Professor of English at the University of Iowa, where he edits the *Walt Whitman Quarterly Review,* the Whitman Series for the University of Iowa Press, and coedits the online Walt Whitman Archive (www.whitmanarchive.org). He is the author or editor of numerous books and essays on Whitman and American poetry, including *Walt Whitman's Native Representations* (1994) and *Re-Scripting Walt Whitman: An Introduction to His Life and Work* (2005). "Song of Myself"

Janet Gabler-Hover is a Professor of nineteenth-century American literature in the Department of English at Georgia State University in Atlanta, Georgia. She is the author of *Truth in American Fiction: The Legacy of Rhetorical Idealism* (1990) and *Dreaming Black/Writing White: The Hagar Myth in American Cultural History* (2000). She has also published numerous essays in book collections and journals. *Clotel;* Spiritualism

Lynée Lewis Gaillet is Associate Professor of Rhetoric and Composition at Georgia State University and Executive Director of the South Atlantic Modern Language Association. She is the editor of *Scottish Rhetoric and Its Influences* (1998) and author of numerous articles and book chapters examining the history of rhetorical practices. Her work has appeared in journals such as *Rhetoric Society Quarterly, Rhetoric Review, Journal of Advanced Composition, Writing Program Administrator, Issues in Writing,* and *Composition Studies.* Curricula

Christopher Gair is Senior Lecturer in American Studies at the University of Birmingham, United Kingdom. He is the author of *Complicity and Resistance in Jack London's Novels: From Naturalism to Nature* (1997) and *The American*

Counterculture (forthcoming). He is managing editor of *Symbiosis: A Journal of Anglo-American Literary Relations.* Literary Nationalism

Granville Ganter is Associate Professor of English at St. John's University, Queens, New York. He writes on nineteenth-century oratory and is presently completing an edition of the collected speeches of the Seneca orator Red Jacket. Rhetoric

Eric Gardner is Associate Professor of English at Saginaw Valley State University and the editor of *Major Voices: The Drama of Slavery* (2005). His *"The Complete Fortune Teller and Dream Book: An Antebellum Text 'By Chloe Russel, A Woman of Colour,'"* was published in the *New England Quarterly* (2005). Our Nig

LeAnne Garner, an English instructor at Shorter College and Georgia State University, is a doctoral candidate at Georgia State University. Cincinnati

Roger L. Geiger is Distinguished Professor of Higher Education at Pennsylvania State University and head of the higher education program. His study *Knowledge and Money: Research Universities and the Paradox of the Marketplace* was published in 2004. His volumes on American research universities in the twentieth century, *To Advance Knowledge: The Development of American Research Universities, 1900–1940* and *Research and Relevant Knowledge: American Research Universities since World War II,* were published in 2004. In 2000 he published *The American College in the Nineteenth Century.* He has edited the *History of Higher Education Annual* since 1993 and is senior associate editor of the *American Journal of Education.* Colleges

Gregory Scott George is a doctoral candidate at Georgia State University. He is a scholar of nineteenth-century American Romantics and is interested in textual criticism of Walt Whitman's *Leaves of Grass.* Baltimore

Peter Gibian teaches in the English Department at McGill University. His publications include *Mass Culture and Everyday Life* (editor and contributor; 1997) and *Oliver Wendell Holmes and the Culture of Conversation* (2001). *The Autocrat at the Breakfast-Table*

Paul Giles is Reader in American Literature at the University of Oxford, U.K., and the author of *American Catholic Arts and Fictions* (1992), *Transatlantic Insurrections* (2001), and *Virtual Americas* (2002). English Literature

Terryl Givens is the author of *The Viper on the Hearth: Mormons, Myths, and the Construction of Heresy* (1997) and *By the Hand of Mormon: The American Scripture That Launched a New World Religion* (2002) as well as other books and articles in religious and literary studies. He teaches at the University of Richmond, where he is Professor of Literature and Religion and holds the James A. Bostwick Chair of English. Mormonism

William Gleason is Director of Graduate Studies and Associate Professor of English at Princeton University. He is the author of *The Leisure Ethic: Work and Play in American Literature, 1840–1940* (1999). Leisure

Everett C. Goodwin is the Senior Minister of the Scarsdale Community Baptist Church, Scarsdale, New York, and from 1981 to 1994 was the Senior Minister of the First Baptist Church of the City of Washington, D.C., a church unique for its historic affiliation with Baptists of divergent expression or identity. He is a third-generation Baptist minister and a noted authority on Baptist history and life. He is the author or editor of three books about Baptists, *The New Hiscox Guide for Baptist Churches* (1995); *Baptists in the Balance: The Tension between Freedom and Responsibility* (editor, 1997); and *Down by the Riverside: A Brief History of Baptist Faith* (2002), all published by Judson Press. Baptists

Philip Gould is Professor of English at Brown University. He is the author of *Barbaric Traffic: Commerce and Antislavery in the 18th Century Atlantic World* (2003). Hope Leslie

John M. Grammer is Professor of English and Director of the Sewanee School of Letters at the University of the South and the author of *Pastoral and Politics in the Old South* (1996). His essays and reviews have appeared in *The Sewanee Review, American Literary History,* and other publications. *Sociology for the South*

Bruce Greenfield, Associate Professor of English, Dalhousie University, is the author of *Narrating Discovery: The Romantic Explorer in American Literature, 1790–1855* (1992). His articles on travel and discovery writing include "The Mi'kmaq Hieroglyphic Prayer Book: Writing and Christianity in Maritime Canada, 1675–1921," in *The Language Encounter in the Americas, 1492 to 1800,* edited by Edward Gray and Norman Fiering (2000); "The West/California: The Site of the Future," in *The Cambridge Companion to Travel Writing* (2002); "Creating the Distance of Print: The Memoir of Peter Pond, Fur Trader," *Early American Literature* (2002). Exploration and Discovery

Farah Jasmine Griffin is Professor of English and Director of the Institute for Research in African American Studies at Columbia University. Author of *Who Set You Flowin': The African American Migration Narrative* (1995) and *If You Can't be Free, Be a Mystery: In Search of Billie Holiday* (2001), she is also the editor of *Beloved Sisters and Loving Friends: Letters from Addie Brown and Rebecca Primus* (1999); coeditor, with Cheryl Fish, of *Stranger in the Village: Two Centuries of African American Travel Writing* (1998); and coeditor, with Robert O'Meally and Brent Hayes Edwards, of *Uptown Conversation: The New Jazz Studies* (2004). "The Two Offers"

Dean Grodzins is Associate Professor of History at Meadville Lombard Theological School. Unitarians

Paul C. Gutjahr is Associate Professor of English, American Studies, and Religious Studies at Indiana University. He is the author of *An American Bible: A History of the Good Book in the United States, 1777–1880* (1999); the editor of *Popular American Literature of the 19th Century* (2001); and the coeditor of *Illuminating Letters: Typography and Literary Interpretation* (2001). The Bible

Bruce A. Harvey teaches a variety of American literature and American studies courses at Florida International University.

He has published *American Geographics: U.S. National Narratives and the Representation of the Non-European World, 1830–1865* (2001), and his current project, "After Elvis after Cook: From Anthropology to Pop Culture," focuses on representations of Polynesia. **Foreigners**

Susan Carol Hauser is Professor of English at Bemidji State University. She received an M.F.A. from Bowling Green State University. She is the author of *Wild Rice Cooking: History, Natural History, Harvesting and Lore* (2000); *You Can Write a Memoir* (2001); and *Outside after Dark: New & Selected Poems* (2002). **Lyric Poetry**

Kevin J. Hayes, Professor of English at the University of Central Oklahoma, is the author of *Folklore and Book Culture* (1997), *Melville's Folk Roots* (1999), and *Poe and the Printed Word* (2000) and editor of *The Cambridge Companion to Edgar Allan Poe* (2000). His essays on Poe have appeared in *Biography, Nineteenth-Century Literature,* and *Prospects.* **"The Big Bear of Arkansas"; "Fall of the House of Usher"; Swallow Barn**

April Rose Haynes is a doctoral candidate in history and women's studies at the University of California, Santa Barbara. She is currently a Social Science Research Council Sexuality Dissertation Fellow. See also her article "The Trials of Frederick Hollick: Obscenity, Sex Education, and Medical Democracy in the Early American Republic," in *Journal of the History of Sexuality* (2003). **Sex Education**

David K. Heckerl is Assistant Professor of English at Saint Mary's University in Halifax, Nova Scotia. His most recent publications include articles on Emerson and historicism in the *Canadian Review of American Studies* and on Edmund Burke and modern liberalism in the *Dalhousie Review.* He is currently preparing research for a book on Lionel Trilling's conception of the "liberal imagination" in relation to questions raised in the political thought of Hannah Arendt, Isaiah Berlin, and Leo Strauss. *Democracy in America*

Desirée Henderson is Assistant Professor of English at the University of Texas at Arlington. Her articles have appeared in *Early American Literature, American Drama,* and *Walt Whitman Quarterly Review.* **Compromise of 1850 and Fugitive Slave Law; Gettysburg Address; Native American Literature**

T. Walter Herbert is Brown Professor of English and University Scholar at Southwestern University in Georgetown, Texas. He has been awarded an NEH Junior Humanist Fellowship, a Guggenheim Fellowship, and a Residency at the Rockefeller Foundation Study Center at Bellagio, Italy. His publications include *Marquesan Encounters: Melville and the Meaning of Civilization* (1980); *Dearest Beloved: The Hawthornes and the Making of the Middle-Class Family* (1993); and *Sexual Violence and American Manhood* (2002). **Manhood**

Kay Seymour House was Professor of English and American Literature at San Francisco State University and is the retired editor in chief of the ongoing edition of James Fenimore Cooper's works. She also edited the texts of Cooper's *The Pilot* and *Satanstoe.* She is the author of *Cooper's*

Americans (1966); "Francesco Caracciolo, Fenimore Cooper, and 'Billy Budd,'" in *Studi Americani* (1973–1974); and "James Fenimore Cooper: Cultural Prophet and Literary Pathfinder," in *American Literature to 1900* (1986, 1993). **Leatherstocking Tales**

Michael Householder is an Assistant Professor of English at Southern Methodist University. He is currently revising a book-length study on European discourses of intercultural encounter during the early modern period. **Miscegenation**

Nikolas Huot is a doctoral candidate at Georgia State University in Atlanta, Georgia. His research interests and recent publications include analyses of Asian American, Asian Canadian, and multicultural literatures. **Chinese**

Christoph Irmscher is Professor of English and Chair of the English Department at the University of Maryland Baltimore County. The recipient of two fellowships from the National Endowment for the Humanities and book awards from the Association of American Publishers and the American Studies Network, he is the author of *Masken der Moderne* (1992), *The Poetics of Natural History* (1999), and has edited John James Audubon's *Writings and Drawings* for the Library of America. His new book, *Longfellow Redux,* will be published by the University of Illinois Press. Several of his recent articles are about Longfellow, notably "Longfellow Redux," *Raritan* (2002); and "Mediterranean Metamorphoses: Enrico Longfellow's Contribution to Multilingual American Literature," in *America and the Mediterranean* (2003). He is currently writing a biography of Louis Agassiz. **Fireside Poets; The Song of Hiawatha**

Gavin Jones is Associate Professor of English at Stanford University. He is the author of *Strange Talk: The Politics of Dialect Literature in Gilded Age America* (1999) as well as a range of articles on nineteenth- and twentieth-century American literature. **Dialect**

Daniel Heath Justice, an enrolled citizen of the Cherokee Nation, is Assistant Professor of Aboriginal literatures at the University of Toronto. Among his publications are "We're Not There Yet, Kemo Sabe: Positing a Future for American Indian Literary Studies," *American Indian Quarterly* (2001); "Seeing (and Reading) Red: Intellectual Sovereignty and the Study of Native Literatures," in *Indigenizing the Academy: Transforming Scholarship and Empowering Communities,* edited by Devon A. Mihesuah and Angela Cavender Wilson (2004); and *Our Fire Survives the Storm: A Cherokee Literary History* (forthcoming). **Cherokee Memorials**

Carolyn L. Karcher, currently visiting Professor at the University of Maryland, is the author of *Shadow over the Promised Land: Slavery, Race, and Violence in Melville's America* (1980); "The Riddle of the Sphinx: Melville's 'Benito Cereno' and the *Amistad* Case," in *Critical Essays on Herman Melville's "Benito Cereno,"* edited by Robert E. Burkholder (1992); and *The First Woman in the Republic: A Cultural Biography of Lydia Maria Child* (1994). She is also the editor of Child's *Hobomok and Other Writings on Indians, An Appeal in Favor of That Class of Americans Called Africans* (1986, 1995); *A Lydia Maria Child Reader*

(1997); and the Melville selections in the *Heath Anthology of American Literature. An Appeal in Favor of That Class of Americans Called Africans; Moby-Dick*

Merit Kaschig is a doctoral student in American Studies at the College of William and Mary. Her paper "'Vice Breeds Crime': The Germs of Mark Twain's *Puddn'head Wilson*" appeared in *American Periodicals*. Calvinism; Methodists

Louis J. Kern teaches in the History Department of Hofstra University. He is the author of *An Ordered Love: Sex Roles and Sexuality in Victorian Utopias: The Shakers, the Mormons and the Oneida Community* (1981). Free Love

Carol Farley Kessler is Professor Emerita of English, American Studies, and Women's Studies at the Delaware County Campus of the Pennsylvania State University. She is also author of *Elizabeth Stuart Phelps* (1982) and *Charlotte Perkins Gilman: Her Progress toward Utopia* (1995) and editor of the anthology *Daring to Dream: Utopian Fiction by United States Women before 1950* (2nd ed., 1995), including Phelps's "A Dream within a Dream." The Gates Ajar

Daniel Kilbride is Associate Professor of History at John Carroll University. He is writing a book on American travelers in Europe, 1700–1870. His book *An American Aristocracy: Culture and Community in Antebellum Philadelphia* is forthcoming from the University of South Carolina Press. Americans Abroad; Revolutions of 1848

M. Jimmie Killingsworth, Professor of English at Texas A&M University, is the author of many articles, chapters, and books on American literature and rhetoric, including *Whitman's Poetry of the Body* (1989), *The Growth of Leaves of Grass* (1993), and the forthcoming *Walt Whitman and the Earth: A Study in Ecopoetics. Leaves of Grass*

Lovalerie King is Assistant Professor of English and Affiliate Faculty in Women's Studies at the Pennsylvania State University–University Park. Her special foci include intertextual and extratextual relationships among African American writers, African American women writers, and African American feminist and womanist thought. Her publications include *A Students' Guide to African American Literature* (2003); "African American Womanism from Zora Neale Hurston to Alice Walker," in *The Cambridge Companion to the African American Novel* (2004); and "Counterdiscourses on the Racialization of Theft and Morality in Douglass's 1845 *Narrative* and Jacobs's *Incidents*," *MELUS* (2003). Projects in progress include a monograph, "Expropriations and Reparations: A Study of Property, Race, and Ethics in African American Literature" (under review); a coedited essay collection, "James Baldwin and Toni Morrison: Comparative Critical and Theoretical Essays"; and "Zora Neale Hurston: An Introduction." *Incidents in the Life of a Slave Girl*

Denise D. Knight is Professor of English at the State University of New York at Cortland, where she specializes in nineteenth-century American literature. She is the author of *Charlotte Perkins Gilman: A Study of the Short Fiction* (1997) and editor of the two-volume edition of *The Diaries of Charlotte Perkins Gilman* (1994) as well as volumes of Gilman's poems and fiction. Declaration of Sentiments

Michael Kowalewski is Professor of English at Carleton College. From 2001 to 2004 he was Director of the Program in American Studies at Carleton. He is a former president of the Western Literature Association. He is the author of *Deadly Musings: Violence and Verbal Form in American Fiction* (1993) and the editor of *Reading the West: New Essays on the Literature of the American West* (1996) and *Gold Rush: A Literary Exploration* (1997). California Gold Rush

Arnold Krupat teaches in the Global Studies Faculty Group at Sarah Lawrence College. Among his many books, the most recent are *The Turn to the Native: Studies in Criticism and Culture* (1996); *Red Matters: Native American Studies* (2002); and the forthcoming "All that Remains: Studies in Native American Literatures." "An Indian's Looking-Glass for the White Man"; Indian Wars and Dispossession

An Associate Professor of English at George Mason University, **David Kuebrich** is the author of *Minor Prophecy: Walt Whitman's New American Religion* (1989) and various articles on American literature. "Bartleby, the Scrivener"

Ross Labrie, who teaches in the Arts One interdisciplinary program at the University of British Columbia, is the author of several books on American literature. These include a general study of Catholic American literature and specific studies of the American Catholic authors Thomas Merton and Daniel Berrigan. Catholics

Emma J. Lapsansky-Werner is Professor of History, Haverford College. Her publications include *Quaker Aesthetics* (with Anne Verplanck, 2003) and *Back to Africa* (with Margaret Hope Bacon, 2005). Philadelphia

William E. Lenz is Professor of English and Chair of the Division of Writing, Literary and Cultural Studies, at Chatham College. He is the author of articles on American literature, American humor, and American exploration and of *Fast Talk and Flush Times: The Confidence Man as a Literary Convention* (1985) and *The Poetics of the Antarctic: A Study in Nineteenth-Century American Cultural Perceptions* (1995). His current research is tentatively called "The Narrative Construction of Central America." Confidence Men

Philip W. Leon is a Professor of American literature at The Citadel, Charleston, South Carolina. He is the author of *Walt Whitman and Sir William Osler: A Poet and His Physician* (1995); *Mark Twain and West Point* (1996); *Bullies and Cowards: The West Point Hazing Scandal, 1898–1901* (2000); and *Nanny Wood: From Washington Belle to Portland's Grande Dame* (2003). Mental Health; Presbyterians

James S. Leonard is Professor and Head of the Department of English at The Citadel. He is coauthor of *The Fluent Mundo: Wallace Stevens and the Structure of Reality* (1988); coeditor of *Satire or Evasion? Black Perspectives on Huckleberry Finn* (1992); editor of *Making Mark Twain Work in the Classroom* (1999); and coeditor of Prentice Hall's two-volume *Anthology of American Literature* (8th ed., 2004). "The Celebrated Jumping Frog of Calaveras County"

Lázaro Lima teaches Spanish and Latino Studies at Bryn Mawr College were he codirects the Program in Hispanic Studies. His articles have appeared in various national and international journals and collections including *The Wallace Stevens Journal, Dactylys, Voz latina,* and *Cuba Transnational.* He is completing a book on Latino literature, tentatively titled "The Latino Body in American Literary and Cultural Memory." Spanish Speakers and Early "Latino" Expression

Kent P. Ljungquist, Professor of English at Worcester Polytechnic Institute, is the author of *The Grand and the Fair: Poe's Landscape Aesthetics and Pictorial Techniques,* editor of *Nineteenth-Century American Fiction Writers,* and coeditor of James Fenimore Cooper's *The Deerslayer.* Knickerbocker Writers; Lyceums

Helen Lock is Professor of English at the University of Louisiana at Monroe and author of *A Case of Mis-Taken Identity: Detective Undercurrents in Recent African American Fiction* (1994) and of numerous articles on African American, American, and multicultural fiction. Slave Rebellions

Lisa M. Logan is Associate Professor of English and Director of the Women's Studies Program at the University of Central Florida. She has published several articles on American women writers that have appeared in journals such as *Legacy* and *Early American Literature* and several edited collections. Domestic Fiction

Mason I. Lowance Jr. is a Professor of English at the University of Massachusetts at Amherst. His publications include *The Language of Canaan: Metaphor and Symbol in New England from the Puritans to the Trancendentalists* (1980); *The Stowe Debate: Rhetorical Strategies in Uncle Tom's Cabin* (1994); *Against Slavery: An Abolitionist Reader* (2000); and *A House Divided: The Antebellum Slavery Debates in America, 1776–1865* (2003). Puritanism

Dana Luciano teaches sexuality and gender studies and nineteenth-century U.S. literature in the English Department at Georgetown University. She is the author of a forthcoming study entitled "Styling Grief: Loss and Time in Nineteenth-Century America." Recent publications include "Passing Shadows: Melancholy Nationality and Black Publicity in Pauline Hopkins's *Of One Blood,*" in *Loss: The Psychic and Social Contexts of Melancholia,* edited by David Eng and David Kazanjian (2003); and "Melville's Untimely History: 'Benito Cereno' as Counter-Monumental Narrative," *Arizona Quarterly* (2004). Mourning

Roger Lundin is the Blanchard Professor of English at Wheaton College. His publications include *The Culture of Interpretation: Christian Faith and the Postmodern World* (1993); *Emily Dickinson and the Art of Belief* (1998; 2nd rev. ed., 2004); and *From Nature to Experience: The American Search for Cultural Authority* (2005). Protestantism

Sarah Luria teaches in the English Department of Holy Cross College and is the author of "The Architecture of Manners: Henry James, Edith Wharton, and The Mount," in *American Quarterly* (1997); "National Domesticity in Early Washington, D.C.," *Common-Place: Special Issue on* *Early Cities of the Americas* (2003); and *Capital Speculations: Writing and Building Washington, D.C.* (2005). Washington, D.C.

Anne Scott MacLeod is Professor Emerita, University of Maryland, College Park. She is author of *A Moral Tale: Children's Fiction and American Culture, 1820–1860* (1975) and *American Childhood: Essays on Children's Literature of the Nineteenth and Twentieth Centuries* (1994) as well as numerous articles on children's literature and American culture. Children's and Adolescent Literature

R. D. Madison is Professor of English at the U.S. Naval Academy. He has edited many volumes of literature and history, including Jack London's *The Cruise of the Snark* (2004) for Penguin Classics. He is an editorial associate of the Northwestern-Newberry edition of *The Writings of Herman Melville* and is on the editorial board of *The Writings of James Fenimore Cooper.* Maritime Commerce

W. Barksdale Maynard teaches art and architectural history at Johns Hopkins University and the University of Delaware. He is the author of three books: *Architecture in the United States, 1800–1850* (2002); *Walden Pond: A History* (2004); and "Buildings of Delaware" for the Buildings of the United States series (forthcoming). Architecture

Jeffrey Alan Melton is Associate Professor of English at Auburn University Montgomery. He is the author of "Keeping the Faith in Mark Twain's *The Innocents Abroad,*" *South Atlantic Review* (1999); "Touring Decay: Nineteenth-Century American Travel Writers in Europe," in *Papers on Language and Literature* (1999); and *Mark Twain, Travel Books, and Tourism: The Tide of a Great Popular Movement* (2002). Tourism

Robert Milder, Professor of English at Washington University in St. Louis, has written widely on American Renaissance subjects, including essays in *The Cambridge Companion to Herman Melville* (1998) and *The Cambridge Companion to Ralph Waldo Emerson* (1999). He is the author of *Reimagining Thoreau* (1995) and of "Exiled Royalties: Melville and the Life We Imagine" (forthcoming). "Experience"

David C. Miller is Professor of English at Allegheny College. He is currently completing a book on the interaction of words and images in nineteenth-century New England titled "Beyond the Sister Arts Idea." Art

Domhnall Mitchell is Professor of Nineteenth-Century American Literature at the Norwegian University of Science and Technology in Trondheim. He has written articles on Dickinson for *American Literature, Legacy, Nineteenth-Century Literature,* and *The Emily Dickinson Journal* and has a chapter on poetry and class in *The Cambridge Companion to Emily Dickinson* (2002). He is the author of *Emily Dickinson: Monarch of Perception* (2000) and *Emily Dickinson: Measures of Possibility* (2005). Poems of Emily Dickinson

William M. Morgan is a Lecturer in the Expository Writing Program at New York University. He is the author of *Questionable Charity: Gender, Humanitarianism, and Complicity in U.S. Literary Realism* (2004). Philosophy

Wesley T. Mott is Professor of English at Worcester Polytechnic Institute. In 1989 he organized the Ralph Waldo Emerson Society, which he has served as secretary/treasurer, president, and managing editor of *Emerson Society Papers*. He has written *"The Strains of Eloquence": Emerson and His Sermons* (1989) and edited volume 4 of *The Complete Sermons of Ralph Waldo Emerson* (1992) as well as five reference books on New England transcendentalism and antebellum literature. "Self-Reliance"

Elsa Nettels is a Professor Emeritus at the College of William and Mary in Williamsburg, Virginia, where she taught in the Department of English from 1967 to 1997. She is the author of *James and Conrad* (1977); *Language, Race, and Social Class in Howells's America* (1988); and *Language and Gender in American Fiction: Howells, James, Wharton, and Cather* (1997). American English

Frederick Newberry is Professor of English at Duquesne University and author of *Hawthorne's Divided Loyalties: England and America in His Works* (1987). He is also editor of *Nathaniel Hawthorne Review*. "The Custom-House"

Michael Newbury is an Associate Professor of American Literature and Civilization at Middlebury College and the author of *Figuring Authorship in Antebellum America* (1997). *Lowell Offering*

Lance Newman, Associate Professor of Literature and Writing Studies, California State University, San Marcos, is the author of *Our Common Dwelling: Henry Thoreau, Transcendentalism, and the Class Politics of Nature* (2005). Nature

Kevin E. O'Donnell is Professor of English at East Tennessee State University and editor of *Seekers of Scenery: Travel Writing from Southern Appalachia, 1840–1900* (2004). Book and Periodical Illustration

Patricia Okker is Professor of English at the University of Missouri–Columbia, and is the author of *Our Sister Editors: Sarah J. Hale and the Tradition of Nineteenth-Century Women Editors* (1995) and *Social Stories: The Magazine Novel in Nineteenth-Century America* (2003). Editors; Fashion; *Godey's Lady's Book*

Kelli M. Olson teaches college composition and American literature at Piedmont Virginia Community College in Charlottesville, Virginia. Her literary interests and publications concentrate on the works of Henry David Thoreau and other nineteenth-century American writers. Ethnology

Frank Palmeri is Professor of English at the University of Miami and author of *Satire in Narrative: Petronius, Swift, Gibbon, Melville, Pynchon* (1990); *Satire, History, Novel: Narrative Forms 1665–1815* (2003); and several articles on Thomas Pynchon. Satire, Burlesque, and Parody

William Pannapacker is Assistant Professor of English and Towsley Research Scholar at Hope College in Holland, Michigan. He is the author of *Revised Lives: Walt Whitman and Nineteenth-Century Authorship* (2004) and numerous articles on American literature and culture. Autobiography

Donald H. Parkerson is Distinguished Professor of Teaching and Professor of History at East Carolina University, Greenville, North Carolina. He has a doctorate from the University of Illinois–Chicago (1983). His publications include *The Agricultural Transition in New York State* (1995); *The Emergence of the Common School in the U.S. Countryside* (1998); and *Transitions in American Education* (2001). Education

Jo Ann Parkerson is Professor Emeritus of Education at Methodist College in Fayetteville, North Carolina. She completed her doctorate from the University of South Carolina (1989). She has published in the *Journal of Educational Psychology* and is coauthor of *The Emergence of the Common School in the U.S. Countryside and Transitions in American Education* (2001). Education

Donald E. Pease is the Avalon Foundation Chair of the Humanities at Dartmouth College. He is the author of *Visionary Compacts: American Renaissance Writing in Cultural Context* (1987), which won the Mark Ingraham Prize for the best book in the humanities in 1987. Pease is also the editor of eight volumes, including *The American Renaissance Reconsidered, Cultures of U.S. Imperialism* (with Walter Benn Michaels, 1985); *Cultures of American Imperialism* (with Amy Kaplan, 1993); *Revisionist Interventions into the American Canon, Postnational Narratives* (1994); and *The Futures of American Studies* (with Robyn Wiegman, 2002). The recipient of Guggenheim, Mellon, NEH, Dickey, Hewlett and Rockefeller Foundation Fellowships, Pease is the General Editor for the book series New Americanists at Duke University Press, the Founding Director of a Summer Institute for American Studies at Dartmouth, and the Head of Dartmouth's Liberal Studies Program. Mexican-American War

John Peck is Reader in Victorian Literature at Cardiff University. He is the author of *War, the Army and Victorian Literature* (1998) and *Maritime Fiction: Sailors and the Sea in British and American Novels, 1719–1917* (2001). He is also the coauthor of *A Brief History of English Literature* (2002). Nautical Literature; *Two Years before the Mast*

Scott Peeples, Associate Professor of English at the College of Charleston, is the author of *Edgar Allan Poe Revisited* (1998) and *The Afterlife of Edgar Allan Poe* (2004). "The Raven"

Melissa McFarland Pennell is Professor of English at the University of Massachusetts Lowell. She is the author of the *Student Companion to Nathaniel Hawthorne* (1999), the *Student Companion to Edith Wharton* (2003), and numerous essays on American literature. *The Scarlet Letter*

Mark A. Peterson teaches history at the University of Iowa. He is the author of *The Price of Redemption: The Spiritual Economy of Puritan New England* (1997) and is currently at work on a history of Boston in the Atlantic World, 1630–1865. *History of the Conquest of Mexico*

Joseph M. Petrulionis is a graduate student of history at Indiana University of Pennsylvania. Harpers Ferry

Sandra Harbert Petrulionis is Associate Professor of English at Penn State Altoona. She is the editor of *Journal 8: 1854*

(2002) in The Writings of Henry D. Thoreau series and has published articles on Henry David Thoreau, Herman Melville, and other nineteenth-century figures. *The Liberator*

Anne K. Phillips is Associate Professor in English at Kansas State University where she specializes in American children's literature. With Gregory Eiselein, she coedited *The Louisa May Alcott Encyclopedia* (2001) and *Little Women* (2003); with Chris Doyle, she is coediting a forthcoming special issue of the annual *Children's Literature* on Louisa May Alcott's literature for young readers. *Little Women*

Ed Piacentino, Professor of English at High Point University in North Carolina, has published widely in American and southern literature and culture. He is coeditor, with M. Thomas Inge, of *The Humor of the Old South* (2001) and author of "The Enduring Legacy of Old Southwest Humor," to be published by Louisiana State University Press. Humor; Tall Tales

Yolanda Pierce is Associate Professor of English and African American Studies, University of Kentucky, and teaches and publishes in the fields of cultural studies, African American literature, and American religious studies. Her most recent book is *Hell without Fires: Slavery, Christianity, and the Antebellum Spiritual Narrative* (2005). Slave Narratives

An Assistant Professor at Texas Christian University, **Ronald L. Pitcock** researches the history of U.S. literacy and publishes work on nineteenth-century Native American literacy and schooling. *Life and Adventures of Joaquín Murieta*

Carole Policy teaches literature and composition at Palm Beach Community College. She earned her B.A. at the University of Virginia, her M.A. at Florida Atlantic University, and her Ph.D. at Florida State. *The Hidden Hand*

Julie Prebel teaches literature at Occidental College in Los Angeles. Her articles include "Engineering Womanhood: The Politics of Rejuvenation in Gertrude Atherton's *Black Oxen*," *American Literature* (2004), and essays on Anzia Yezierska, Theodore Dreiser, and Fanny Fern. She is currently completing a book examining the interaction between science and nineteenth- and twentieth-century women's fiction. Democracy

Tom Quirk is a Professor of English at the University of Missouri–Columbia. He is the author of five scholarly books on American literature and editor or coeditor of a dozen other volumes. His most recent publications include *The Portable Mark Twain* (2004) and *Nothing Abstract: Investigations in the American Literary Imagination* (2001). *The Confidence-Man*

Harriet Rafter teaches California literature at San Francisco State University. San Francisco

Judith A. Ranta is an independent scholar who has taught at Queens College and York College of the City University of New York (CUNY). In 1999 she received a doctorate in American literature from the CUNY Graduate Center. Her publications include *Women and Children of the Mills: An Annotated Guide to Nineteenth-Century American Textile Factory Literature* (1999); *The Life and Writings of Betsey*

Chamberlain: Native American Mill Worker (2003); and "'A True Woman's Courage and Hopefulness': Martha W. Tyler's *A Book without a Title; or, Thrilling Events in the Life of Mira Dana (1855–56)*," *Legacy: A Journal of American Women Writers* (2004). She continues to research the lives and writings of nineteenth-century U.S. female factory workers, including Harriot F. Curtis, Charlotte Hilbourne, and Jennie Collins. Factories

Gregory J. Renoff is Assistant Professor of History at Drury University in Springfield, Missouri. His primary field of specialization is the nineteenth-century American South, with an interest in the history of race relations, popular culture, consumerism, and labor. His publications include "Circuses in Georgia," in the *New Georgia Encyclopedia* and "'Wait for the Big Show!': The Circus in Georgia, 1865–1930," in *Atlanta History* (2004). Circuses and Spectacles

David S. Reynolds is a Distinguished Professor at Baruch College and the Graduate Center of the City University of New York. His books include *Faith in Fiction: The Emergence of Religious Literature in America* (1981); *George Lippard* (1982); *Beneath the American Renaissance: The Subversive Imagination in the Age of Emerson and Melville* (1988; winner of the Christian Gauss Award); *Walt Whitman's America: A Cultural Biography* (1995; winner of the Bancroft Prize); and *John Brown, Abolitionist: The Man Who Killed Slavery, Sparked the Civil War, and Seeded Civil Rights* (2005). Sensational Fiction

Judith Richardson, author of *Possessions: The History and Uses of Haunting in the Hudson Valley* (2003), is an Assistant Professor in the Department of English at Stanford University. "The Legend of Sleepy Hollow"

LaVern J. Rippley is a Professor in the German Department at St. Olaf College and the editor/publisher of the Newsletter of the Society for German-American Studies. He is the author of numerous articles and books on German Romanticism and the influence of German culture in the United States, including *The German-Americans* (1976) and *German-Bohemians: The Quiet Immigrants* (1995). German Scholarship

David M. Robinson is Oregon Professor of English and Director of the Center for the Humanities, Oregon State University. He is author of *Emerson and the Conduct of Life* (1993) and *Natural Life: Thoreau's Worldly Transcendentalism* (2004), and since 1988 he has been the author of the annual chapter "Emerson, Thoreau, Fuller, and Transcendentalism" for *American Literary Scholarship*. Romanticism; Transcendentalism

Angelic Rodgers holds a Ph.D. in American literature (1865–1914). She has taught at a variety of schools, including the University of Central Arkansas, the University of Southern Mississippi, and Auburn University. She is an independent scholar and managing editor of the online journal *Virtually Employed*. Her publications include "Diving for Pearls: Using the Tarot as Subtext in *The Waste Land*," *Yeats Eliot Review* (1999), and "Jim Crow and Veiled Ladies: Mesmerism and the Rise of the Middle-Class in Hawthorne's *House of the Seven Gables*," *Victorian*

Literary Mesmerism (forthcoming). She is working on a critical biography of Alice French. **Bachelors and Spinsters**

Deane L. Root is Professor of Music and Chair of the Department of Music, Director and Fletcher Hodges, Jr., Curator of the Center for American Music in the University Library System, and Professor of History at the University of Pittsburgh. The Center for American Music is the world repository for materials concerning Stephen Foster. **Music**

Jane E. Rose is Associate Professor of English at Purdue University North Central in Westville, Indiana, where she teaches courses in American literature, including African American and women's literature. Her publications include "Expanding Woman's Sphere, Dismantling Class, and Building Community: The Feminism of Elizabeth Oakes Smith," *College Language Association Journal* (2001); and "Conduct Books for Women, 1830–1860: A Rationale for Women's Conduct and Domestic Role in America," in *Nineteenth-Century Women Learn to Write*, edited by Catherine Hobbs (1995). *Life in the Iron Mills*

Patricia Spence Rudden is Associate Professor of English, New York City College of Technology, City University of New York. She has published on Melville and Whitman, nineteenth-century American literature, and American popular music of the twentieth century. **"Crossing Brooklyn Ferry"**

James Emmett Ryan is Associate Professor of English at Auburn University. His essays on nineteenth-century American literature and culture have appeared in *American Quarterly, American Literary History,* and *Studies in American Fiction*. His current book project examines representations of the Religious Society of Friends (Quakers) in early American literature. **Literary Criticism**

Ingrid Satelmajer is a Lecturer in the English Department at the University of Maryland, College Park. Her publications on nineteenth-century American poetry and periodicals include "Dickinson as Child's Fare: The Author Served up in *St. Nicholas*," *Book History* (2002) and "Unbinding the Book: Bryant's 'The Fountain' in the *Democratic Review*," *American Periodicals* (2003). **Popular Poetry**

Robert Sattelmeyer is Regents Professor of English at Georgia State University and the author and editor of numerous studies of such nineteenth-century American writers as Ralph Waldo Emerson, Henry David Thoreau, Herman Melville, and Mark Twain, including *Thoreau's Reading: A Study in Intellectual History with Bibliographical Catalogue* (1988). **"The American Scholar"; Fur Trade;** *Walden*

Gary Scharnhorst is Professor of English at the University of New Mexico, author or editor of over thirty books, editor of *American Literary Realism*, and editor in alternating years of the research annual *American Literary Scholarship*. *Miss Ravenel's Conversion from Secession to Loyalty*

Richard J. Schneider is Professor of English at Wartburg College. He is the author o f *Henry David Thoreau* (1987) and editor of *Approaches to Teaching Thoreau's* Walden *and Other Works* (1996) and *Thoreau's Sense of Place: Essays in American Environmental Writing* (2000). **"Resistance to Civil Government"**

Robert J. Scholnick is Professor of English and American Studies at the College of William and Mary and author of *Edmund Clarence Stedman* (1977), editor of *American Literature and Science* (1992), and editor of the forthcoming *Jamaica in 1850*. He has published numerous articles on nineteenth-century American literature and culture and is at work on a study of theories of evolution in America in the years before Darwin. **Manifest Destiny**

James J. Schramer is a Professor of English and Professional Writing at Youngstown State University, Youngstown, Ohio. Among his publications, he has coedited, with Donald Ross, two collections of essays on American travel writers as part of the Dictionary of Literary Biography series. He has also written articles for this series on Charles Wilkes and Richard Harding Davis. For the Dictionary of Literary Biography series on British Travel Writers, he has written essays on Bruce Chatwin, Jonathan Raban, and Colin Thubron. In addition to his work on travel writing, he has published essays on the Vietnam War fiction of Tim O'Brien. **Landscape Architecture; Travel Writing**

Malini Johar Schueller is Professor of English at the University of Florida. She is the author of *The Politics of Voice: Liberalism and Social Criticism from Franklin to Kingston* (1992) and *U.S. Orientalisms: Race, Nation, and Gender in Literature, 1790–1890* (1998); with Edward Watts she is coeditor of *Messy Beginnings: Postcoloniality and Early American Studies* (2003). She has published essays in journals such as *American Literature, SIGNS,* and *Cultural Critique*. **Orientalism**

Nancy Lusignan Schultz is Professor and Coordinator of Graduate Programs in English and American Studies at Salem State College in Salem, Massachusetts. She is the editor of *Fear Itself: Enemies Real and Imagined in American Culture* (1999) and coeditor of *Salem: Place, Myth, and Memory* (2004). She is the author of *Fire and Roses: The Burning of the Charlestown Convent, 1834* (2002). Her current project, "A Capital Miracle," a social history of a miraculous cure that took place in Washington, D.C., in 1824, will be published by Yale University Press. *Foreign Conspiracy against the Liberties of the United States*

Larry Schweikart is Professor of History at the University of Dayton and is the coauthor of *A Patriot's History of the United States* (2005). **Banking, Finance, Panics, and Depressions**

Thomas E. Scruggs is the Director of the Ph.D. in Education Program, College of Education and Human Development, George Mason University, Fairfax, Virginia. His recent articles on David Crockett include "The Physical Stature of David Crockett: A Re-Analysis of the Historical Record," *Journal of South Texas* (1996); and "Davy Crockett and the Thieves of Jericho: An Analysis of the Shackford-Parrington Conspiracy Theory," *Journal of the Early Republic* (1999). *Narrative of the Life of David Crockett of the State of Tennessee*

Ellery Sedgwick is Professor Emeritus of English at Longwood University in Farmville, Virginia, and the author of *A History of the Atlantic Monthly, 1857–1909* (1994). *The Atlantic Monthly*

Mary Lamb Shelden is Assistant Editor for *The Writings of Henry D. Thoreau* and Visiting Assistant Professor of English at Northern Illinois University. She contributed the gender entry for *The Louisa May Alcott Encyclopedia* (2001) and the cross-dressing entry for *An Encyclopedia of African-American Literature* (2005). Her dissertation, "Novel Habits for a New World" (2003), which she is currently revising for a book, surveys cross-dressing used in American novels throughout the nineteenth century, tracing the tradition back to European American, Native American, and African American literary and folkloric origins. Shelden also serves as inaugural secretary for the recently established Louisa May Alcott Society. Cross-Dressing

Johanna Nicol Shields is Professor Emerita of History at the University of Alabama in Huntsville. Her publications include *The Line of Duty: Maverick Congressmen and the Development of American Political Culture, 1836–1860* (1985); "White Honor, Black Humor, and the Making of a Southern Style," *Southern Cultures* (1995); and "A Sadder Simon Suggs: Freedom and Slavery in the Humor of Johnson Hooper," in *The Humor of the Old South*, edited by M. Thomas Inge and Edward J. Piacentino (2001). *Some Adventures of Captain Simon Suggs*

Robert Shulman is Professor of English at the University of Washington, interested in the intersection of American literature, politics, and history. He is the author of *Social Criticism and Nineteenth-Century American Fictions* (1987); the chapter "Realism" in *The Columbia History of the American Novel*, edited by Emory Elliott et al. (1991); and *The Power of Political Art: The 1930s Literary Left Reconsidered* (2000). Individualism and Community

Joseph W. Slade III is Professor of Telecommunications and Codirector of the Central Region Humanities Center at Ohio University in Athens. He is the coeditor of *Beyond the Two Cultures: Essays on Science, Technology and Literature* (1990) and *The Midwest* (2004), a volume in the Greenwood Encyclopedia of American Regional Cultures series, and author of *Thomas Pynchon* (1974; 1990), *Pornography in America* (2000), and *Pornography and Sexual Representation*, 3 vols. (2001), as well as several dozen articles on literature, technology, film, and culture. Pornography

John Stauffer is Professor of English and the History of American Civilization at Harvard. He is the author of *The Black Hearts of Men: Radical Abolitionists and the Transformation of Race* (2002), which received the Frederick Douglass Book Prize, the Avery O. Craven Award, and the Lincoln Prize runner-up. He edited Frederick Douglass's *My Bondage and My Freedom* (2003) for the Modern Library and has published numerous essays on the Civil War and race relations. Civil War; Photography

Richard F. Teichgraeber III is Director of the Murphy Institute and Professor of History at Tulane University. He is the author of *Sublime Thoughts/Penny Wisdom: Situating Emerson and Thoreau in the American Market* (1995) and coeditor, with Thomas L. Haskell, of *The Culture of the Market: Historical Essays* (1993). Literary Marketplace

Joseph M. Thomas, Associate Dean at Caldwell College and advisory editor of the Harriet Jacobs Papers Project, is author of "Late Emerson: *Selected Poems* and the 'Emerson Factory,'" *ELH* (1998), and "'The Property of My Own Book': Emerson and the Literary Marketplace," *New England Quarterly* (1996). "The Poet"

Shirley E. Thompson works in the Department of American Studies at the University of Texas at Austin. She has published articles in *American Quarterly* and the *Journal of Ecology, Culture, and Community*. She is finishing a manuscript on the racial, cultural, and political identities of Creoles of color in mid-nineteenth-century New Orleans. New Orleans

Karen Tracey is an Associate Professor of English at the University of Northern Iowa. She is the author of *Plots and Proposals: American Women's Fiction, 1850–1890* (2000) and coauthor of *The Craft of Argument with Readings* (2003). Courtship

Natalie Collins Trice is a doctoral student at Georgia State University. Specializing in twentieth-century American literature, she has presented on various authors including William Faulkner and Thomas Pynchon. Charleston

Gustaaf Van Cromphout is Professor of English at Northern Illinois University. He is the author of *Emerson's Modernity and the Example of Goethe* (1990) and *Emerson's Ethics* (1999). Nature

Emily E. VanDette is a doctoral candidate at the Pennsylvania State University. Abolitionist Writing

Wil Verhoeven is Professor of American Culture at the University of Groningen, The Netherlands. His publications include two edited collections: *Revolutionary Histories: Transatlantic Cultural Nationalism, 1775–1815* (2002) and *Epistolary Histories: Letters, Fiction, Culture* (with Amanda Gilroy, 1999). He is general editor of a series of anti-Jacobin novels (10 vols., 2005); he has also edited George Walker's *The Vagabond* (2004) and coedited Gilbert Imlay's *The Emigrants* (with Amanda Gilroy, 1998). He is the general editor of a forthcoming volume of novels and selected plays of Thomas Holcroft. The Oregon Trail

Daniel R. Vollaro is a writer and teacher who lives in Atlanta, Georgia. He teaches American literature and writing at Georgia State University. The Dial; Utopian Communities

Laura Dassow Walls is the Bennett Chair of Southern Letters at the University of South Carolina. She has published widely on literature and science in the nineteenth century, including *Seeing New Worlds: Henry David Thoreau and Nineteenth-Century Natural Science* (1995); *Emerson's Life in Science: The Culture of Truth* (2003); and "Romancing the Real: Thoreau's Technology of Inscription," in *A Historical Guide to Henry David Thoreau*, edited by William E. Cain (2000). Science

Ronald G. Walters is Professor of History at Johns Hopkins University. He is a U.S. social and cultural historian who works in two different areas, nineteenth-century radical and reform movements and twentieth-century popular culture.

His major publications include *The Antislavery Appeal: American Abolitionism after 1830* (1976) and *American Reformers: 1815–1860* (rev. ed, 1996). More recently he contributed "Harriet Beecher Stowe and the American Reform Tradition" to *The Cambridge Companion to Harriet Beecher Stowe,* edited by Cindy Weinstein (2004). *The Impending Crisis of the South*

James Perrin Warren is S. Blount Mason Jr. Professor of English at Washington and Lee University. He earned his Ph.D. at Yale University in 1982. He has published *Walt Whitman's Language Experiment* (1990); *Culture of Eloquence* (1999); and *John Burroughs and the Place of Nature* (2006), and is the author of several articles on nineteenth-century American literature and environmental writing. Oratory; "When Lilacs Last in the Dooryard Bloom'd"

Joyce W. Warren is a Professor of English and Director of Women's Studies at Queens College, CUNY. She is the author of *The American Narcissus: Individualism and Women in Nineteenth-Century American Fiction* (1984); *Fanny Fern: An Independent Woman* (1992); and *Women, Money, and the Law: Nineteenth-Century Fiction, Gender, and the Courts* (2005). She is editor of *Ruth Hall and Other Writings* (1986) and *The (Other) American Traditions* (1993) and coeditor of *Challenging Boundaries* (2000). *Ruth Hall;* Sentimentalism

Margaret Washington is Professor of History at Cornell University. She is the editor of the *Narrative of Sojourner Truth* (originally published 1850; 1993) and author of *A Peculiar People: Slave Religion and Community-Culture among the Gullahs* (1988) and the forthcoming "Sojourner Truth's America: Slavery, Race, and Reform in the Nineteeth Century." "Ain't I a Woman?"

Ellen Weinauer is the coeditor, with Robert McClure Smith, of *American Culture, Canons, and the Case of Elizabeth Stoddard* (2003) and the author of articles on Hawthorne, Melville, Stoddard, and others. She is Associate Professor of English at the University of Southern Mississippi. Gothic Fiction

Cindy Weinstein is Associate Professor of English at the California Institute of Technology. She is the author of *The Literature of Labor and the Labors of Literature: Allegory in Nineteenth-Century American Fiction* (1995) and *Family, Kinship, and Sympathy in Nineteenth-Century American Literature* (2004). She is also the editor of *The Cambridge Companion to Harriet Beecher Stowe* (2004). "The Birthmark"; *Uncle Tom's Cabin*

An Assistant Professor of English at Georgia State University, **Elizabeth J. West** conducts research and teaches with particular interest in intersections of gender, race, class, and the spiritual in literary works. She has published essays and reviews in the *Journal of Colonialism and Colonial History, MELUS, South Atlantic Review, South Central Review, Womanist,* and *CLA Journal.* Blacks; Slavery

Brenda Wineapple is the author of *Sister Brother: Gertrude and Leo Stein* (1997); *Hawthorne: A Life* (2003); and an edition of the poems of John Greenleaf Whittier for the American Poets Project of the Library of America (2004).

She teaches at Union College and Columbia University. "Hawthorne and His Mosses"

Jennifer M. Wing is a doctoral candidate in early-nineteenth-century American literature at Georgia State University. She is also an instructor of English composition and American literature and the author of "Defining Women in *Moby Dick,*" in *Misogynism in Literature: Any Place, Any Time,* edited by Britta Zangen (2004). Trail of Tears

Bertram Wyatt-Brown is Richard J. Milbauer Professor Emeritus, University of Florida. His publications include *Yankee Saints and Southern Sinners* (1985); *The Shaping of Southern Culture: Honor, Grace and War, 1770s–1890s* (2001); and *Hearts of Darkness: Wellsprings of a Southern Literary Tradition* (2003). Honor

Longman Professor of English at Oberlin College, **Sandra A. Zagarell** is a senior editor of the *Heath Anthology of American Literature;* editor of collections of writing by Caroline M. Kirkland, Elizabeth Stoddard, and Mary E. Wilkins Freeman; and author of essays on Herman Melville, Sarah Orne Jewett, Elizabeth Stoddard, and other nineteenth-century writers. *The Morgesons; A New Home—Who'll Follow?*

Mary Saracino Zboray, a Research Associate in the Department of Communication at the University of Pittsburgh, is coauthor with Ronald J. Zboray of over a dozen scholarly articles and essays on the sociocultural history of mid-nineteenth-century New England, as well as *A Handbook for the Study of Book History in the United States* (2000), *Literary Dollars and Social Sense: A People's History of the Mass Market Book* (2005), and *Everyday Ideas: Socio-Literary Experience among Antebellum New Englanders* (forthcoming). Boston; *Harper's New Monthly Magazine;* Journals and Diaries; Letters; Literacy

Ronald J. Zboray, Associate Professor of Communication and History at the University of Pittsburgh, is author of *A Fictive People: Antebellum Economic Development and the American Reading Public* (1993) and coauthor, with Mary Saracino Zboray, of *A Handbook for the Study of Book History in the United States* (2000), *Literary Dollars and Social Sense: A People's History of the Mass Market Book* (2005), and *Everyday Ideas: Socio-Literary Experience among Antebellum New Englanders* (forthcoming). Boston; *Harper's New Monthly Magazine;* Journals and Diaries; Letters; Literacy

Michael G. Ziser is Assistant Professor of English at the University of California, Davis. He is the author of " Walden and the Georgic Mode," *Nineteenth Century Prose* (2004). Wilderness

Christina Zwarg, Associate Professor of English, teaches at Haverford College in Pennsylvania. Author of *Feminist Conversations: Fuller, Emerson, and the Play of Reading* (1995) and articles on Frederick Douglass, Harriet Beecher Stowe, Mark Twain, Edith Wharton, and W. E. B. Du Bois, she is writing a book on trauma and Reconstruction in the writing of Douglass, Henry James, Du Bois, and Pauline Hopkins. *Woman in the Nineteenth Century*

Thematic Outline of Contents

The thematic outline provides a general overview of the conceptual scheme of the encyclopedia, listing the titles of each entry. Published works, no matter how rich or expansive, appear in a single category.

The outline is divided into twelve parts: *Genres; Historical Events; Language, Learning, and the Arts; Places; Politics, Economy, and Society; Publishing; Race and Ethnicity; Religious Beliefs and Groups; Science and Technology; Sexuality and Gender; Slavery; and Social and Philosophical Values/Concepts.*

GENRES

Abolitionist Writing
   An Appeal on Behalf of That Class of Americans Called Africans
   The Liberator
   Walker's Appeal
Autobiography
   Narrative of the Life of David Crockett of the State of Tennessee
   "Song of Myself"
Biography
Captivity Narratives
Children's Literature
   Little Women
Dime Novels
Domestic Fiction
   The Hidden Hand
   Ruth Hall
   The Wide, Wide World
Folklore
Gothic Fiction
   "The Fall of the House of Usher"
History
   History of the Conquest of Mexico

Humor
   Some Adventures of Captain Simon Suggs
Journals and Diaries
Knickerbocker Writers
Letters
Lyric Poetry
   Leaves of Grass
   "Out of the Cradle Endlessly Rocking"
   Poems of Emily Dickinson
Nautical Literature
   Moby-Dick
   Two Years before the Mast
Popular Poetry
Fireside Poets
   The Song of Hiawatha
Proslavery Writing
   Sociology for the South
   Swallow Barn
The Romance
   "The Custom-House"
   The House of the Seven Gables
   Leatherstocking Tales
Satire, Burlesque, and Parody
   The Autocrat of the Breakfast-Table
Sensational Fiction

List of Entries to Companion Set

In addition to American History through Literature, 1820–1870, *Charles Scribner's Sons and Thomson Gale are pleased to offer a companion set,* American History through Literature, 1870–1920 *(edited by Tom Quirk and Gary Scharnhorst). A list of entries included in the companion set follows.*

Addiction
Adolescence
Adventures of Huckleberry Finn
Aestheticism
Aging and Death
Agnosticism and Atheism
The Ambassadors
American Indian Stories
The American Language
American Literature
Americans Abroad
The American Scene
Anarchism
Anglo-Saxonism
Annexation and Expansion
Anti-Intellectualism
Appeal to Reason
Art and Architecture
Arts and Crafts
Assimilation
The Atlantic Monthly
Autobiography
The Autobiography of an Ex-Colored Man
The Awakening
Banking and Finance
Battle of the Little Bighorn
Best-Sellers
The Bible
Billy Budd

Biography
The Birth of a Nation
Blacks
Bohemians and Vagabondia
Book Publishing
Boston and Concord
Boxing
Business and Industry Novels
Capital Punishment
Catholics
Centennial
Century Magazine
Chicago
Children's Literature
Chinese
Christianity
Christianity and the Social Crisis
Christian Science
Circuses
City Dwellers
Civil Rights
Civil War Memoirs
Civil War Memorials and Monuments
Clubs and Salons
The Conjure Woman
A Connecticut Yankee in King Arthur's Court
Copyright
The Country of the Pointed Firs
Courtship, Marriage, and Divorce

Primary Sources for Further Reading

The following is a list of related primary sources available through Primary Source Microfilm, the leading provider of archival research materials.

GENERAL

African-American Religious Serials, 1850–1950. This collection includes the *AME Zion Quarterly,* a publicaton of the AME Zion church, as well as other religious periodicals that are vital to fully understanding the growth of African American churches within various religious traditions. Also included are church annuals and reports and reports for social service agencies.

American Fiction, 1774–1910. Based on Lyle H. Wright's *American Fiction: A Contribution Towards a Bibliography* and the "Library of Congress Shelf List of American Adult Fiction" and includes 10,800 novels, romances, tales, short stories, fictitious biographies, travels and sketches, allegories and tract-like tales typifying the development of American literature in a changing culture. Volume 1: 1774–1850; volume 2: 1851–1875; volume 3: 1876–1900; volume 4: 1901–1905; volume 5: 1906–1910.

American Literary Annuals and Gift Books, 1825–1865. Based on Ralph Thompson's definitive bibliography of the same name, *American Literary Annuals and Gift Books, 1825–1865,* contains some of the best literature and art from the pre–Civil War period. This collection contains 469 titles, focusing on *The Atlantic Souvenir: A Christmas and New Year's Offering*—a lavishly decorated, fully illustrated anthology of prose and poetry.

American Literary Manuscripts, 1650–1850. A varied collection including verse, short stories, prose fiction, satirical plays, and humorous writings by native or naturalized American authors from the period 1650 to 1850. Also included are a number of sermons, speeches, belles lettres, and journals deemed to be of considerable literary interest (e.g., the sermons of Cotton Mather, the *Autobiography of Benjamin Franklin,* etc.).

American Poetry, 1609–1870. Based on the Harris Collection of American Poetry and Plays, Brown University. Nearly 300 years of American verse is incorporated in this collection to bring your library a complete history of America's finest poetry. *American Poetry, 1609–1870* includes works by all the major American poets, and many minor writers, as they appear in individual and collected works.

The Anti-Slavery Collection. Consisting of approximately 2,252 items, the *Anti-Slavery Collection* from Oberlin College Library comprises the contents of the *Catalogue of the Collection of Anti-Slavery Propaganda* compiled in 1931–1932 by Geraldine Hopkins Hubbard, plus materials acquired since 1932. The entire collection is now available on microfiche cards with U.S. MARC records.

The Baldwin Library Collection of Historical Children's Literature. This vast and comprehensive collection contains historic children's titles that were published in Great Britain and the United States from 1850 to 1869. The result of Ruth Baldwin's efforts, this collection provides a window into mid-nineteenth-century society and culture with works such as *Aesop's Fables, Pilgrim's Progress, Robinson Crusoe,* and *Gulliver's Travels.*

Nineteenth-Century American Literature and History. A comprehensive study of the geographic area known as the Trans-Mississippi West, including the "Old Southwest" and Texas. It includes selected titles from Dr. J. Christian Bay's bibliography *Three Handfuls of Western Books* and other material with an emphasis on late-nineteenth-century imprints. It is an invaluable resource for the study of nineteenth-century Americana.

The Sabin Collection: Selected Americana from Sabin's Dictionary of Books Relating to America. From Joseph Sabin's *Bibliotheca Americana: A Dictionary of Books Relating to America from Its Discovery to the Present Time,* which has been heralded as a cornerstone in the study of the history of the western hemisphere. *The Sabin Collection* aims to locate and film as many of the most significant works in the bibliography as possible, as well as a variety of others that provide the greater depth of research material necessary for intensive studies of the history of the New World. To support targeted collection needs, *The Sabin Collection* is also offered in ten special subject collections: American Women; Campaign Literature; Cities and States; The Civil War; Constitution; Discovery and Exploration of the Americas; Immigration; Indians of North America; Reconstruction; and Slavery.

PERIODICALS

Southern Literary Messenger. Southern Literary Messenger was the leading belletristic journal of the Old South for three decades (1834–1864). Under the editorship of Edgar Allan Poe from 1835 to 1837, circulation increased from 500 to 3,500. Poe also contributed many of his works, including eighty-three reviews, six poems, four essays, and three stories. Other editors included J. R. Thompson (1847–1860), G. W. Bagby (1860–1864), and Frank H. Alfriend (1864).

MANUSCRIPT COLLECTIONS

Earl Conrad/Harriet Tubman Collection. Reproduced here are the letters, clippings, manuscripts, and other materials accumulated by the historian and journalist Earl Conrad while preparing various writings on Harriet Tubman, especially his 1943 biography of the famous abolitionist. This collection will be a valuable tool for anyone studying Tubman, slavery, the Underground Railroad, the Civil War, and the black experience in nineteenth-century America.

Horace Greeley Papers, 1831–1873. As editor of the *New York Tribune* and presidential candidate in 1872, Horace Greeley was an important nineteenth-century political and literary figure. Greeley launched the *New York Tribune* in 1841 and expressed his political views freely in the newspaper. In addition, he cofounded *The New*

Yorker, a literary and news weekly in 1834, and he wrote for several influential Whig newspapers. An egalitarian, Greeley opposed monopoly and supported Fourerism, the agrarian movement, cooperative shops and labor unions. He was a staunch supporter of the antislavery movement and the Union in the Civil War years.

The John Pendleton Kennedy Papers. John Pendleton Kennedy (1795–1870) figured significantly in nineteenth-century literary, intellectual, and political life. His writings included novels, political treatises, and pamphlets. These papers, including manuscripts, journals, letters, and notebooks, are a valuable source of information on nineteenth-century America.

The Papers of Elizabeth Cady Stanton and Susan B. Anthony. These papers of suffrage proponents Elizabeth Cady Stanton and Susan B. Anthony span the years 1831 through 1906 and consist of more than 14,000 documents. Included are such items as legislative testimony, correspondence, diaries, speeches, accounts of meetings, and financial papers.

The Slavery and Abolition Collections. This publication reproduces an assortment of letters, bills of sale, manumission papers, and other documents relating to slavery and its abolition, primarily in the Anglo-American colonies and the United States.

Slavery Miscellaneous Manuscripts, 1780–[1860]. This collection contains seven scrapbooks, "Tracts on Slavery in the United States"; a book of punishments administered to slaves in a South American mining camp, 1836–1847; slave deeds; newspaper clippings; and a book containing a census of slaves in Chester Country, Pennsylvania, 1780–1815.

The Washington Irving Papers, 1759–1898. From the Rare Books and Manuscripts Division, Center for the Humanities, The New York Public Library, Astor, Lenox and Tilden Foundations. This collection of Washington Irving's papers covers the years 1759–1898 and includes private and official correspondence; manuscripts and notes for many of Irving's works; journals, 1804–1842, on his travels; personal and literary notebooks, 1807–1844; Irving family papers.

In addition, Primary Source Microfilm is the authorized distributor of the following manuscript collections at the Library of Congress: Papers of Frederick Douglass, Papers of Daniel Webster, Papers of William Tecumseh Sherman, Papers of Walt Whitman, Scrapbooks of Susan B. Anthony, Papers of Elizabeth Cady Stanton, and the Collection of Anna Elizabeth Dickinson.

For more information and how to order these and other related primary source materials, contact your Thomson Gale representative at 1-800-699-4253 or your Primary Source Microfilm Representative at 1-800-444-0799 or browse the online catalog at www.gale.com.

Numbers followed by a colon indicate volume number. Page numbers in boldface refer to major entries about the subject. Page numbers in italics refer to illustrations, maps, and tables.

"Self-Reliance" and, **3:**1048
transcendentalists and, **3:**1222,
1264
Brook Farm (Wolcott), **1:***136*
Brook Farm Association for Industry
and Education, **1:**137; **3:**958
Brook Farm Phalanx, **1:**442
Brooklyn, **1:**296–297; **3:**1214, 1269
Brooklyn Bridge, **1:**297
Brooklyn Daily Eagle (newspaper),
1:296, 323; **2:**713, 733, 767;
3:1055, 1159, 1216, 1268
Brooklyn Daily Times (newspaper),
3:1269
Brooks, Charles T., **1:**461
Brooks, Peter, **3:**1163
Brooks, Preston, **2:**832
Brooks, Shirley, **3:**1110
Brooks, Van Wyck, **1:**304; **2:**715
Brotherhood of the New Life, **2:**916
Brother Jonathan (periodical), **1:**151;
2:677
Brothers in Unity (Yale literary
society), **2:**826
Brougham, John, **2:**770; **3:**1162
Brower, David, **3:**1251
Brown, Annie, **2:**483
Brown, Charles Brockden, **1:**477;
2:601, 638, 647, 723, 931, 935
as romance writer, **3:**996, 998
Brown, Charles Farrar. *See* Ward,
Artemus
Brown, George Loring, **1:**467
Brown, Gillian, **1:**344
Brown, Goold, **1:**26
Brown, Henry Box, **2:**653, 862;
3:1085, *1086*
Brown, Herbert Ross, **1:**345; **3:**1060
Brown, James, **2:**939
Brown, John, **1:**6, 60, 98, 235; **2:**654,
699, 832; **3:**1188
"Bleeding Kansas" and, **1:**261;
3:1130
Calvinism and, **1:***178;* **2:**944
Concord visits of, **1:**266
Harpers Ferry raid and, **2:**483–486,
553–554
Henry David Thoreau's defense of,
3:977, 978, 1210
martyrdom of, **1:**235
Ralph Waldo Emerson address on,
3:958
slave rebellions and, **1:**271; **3:**1089
violent tactics and, **3:**1130–1131
Brown, Martha, **2:**483
Brown, Richard D., **2:**665, 677
Brown, Sterling, **1:**7
Brown, Thomas, **2:**934
Brown, Wells, **1:**4

Brown, William Henry, **3:**1160
Brown, William Hill, **1:**448; **2:**647;
3:1060
Brown, William Wells, **1:**314–315;
2:653, 782, 862; **3:**1090
abolitionist speaking and, **2:**831
abolitionist writing and, **1:**4, 6, 39,
142; **3:**963, 1130, 1237
background of, **3:**1184
as best-selling author, **3:**1083
black political rights and, **3:**1259
borrowings from Lydia Maria Child
by, **1:**249–250, 252, 253
cross-dressing and, **1:**294
escape journey of, **3:**1208
expatriate writing and, **1:**30;
3:1184
Margaret Fuller's feminism and,
3:1259
on Nat Turner's slave rebellion,
1:271
theatrical productions and, **1:**4;
3:1160
tragic mulatto theme and, **1:**130,
249–250, *249,* 479
Washington, D.C., and, **2:**252;
3:1238, 1240
See also Clotel
Browne, Charles Farrar. *See* Ward,
Artemus
Browne, John Ross, **1:**438; **3:**1268
Browne, William Hand, **2:**731
Brownell, Henry Howard, **3:**969
Browning, Elizabeth Barrett, **1:**470;
2:652, 870, 905
"The Raven" and, **3:**954, 955–956
Brownson, Orestes Augustus, **1:**265,
358, 460; **2:**583, 584–585, 613,
671; **3:**1259
Brook Farm and, **3:**1222
Catholicism and, **1:**192, *192,* 193,
194–195; **3:**958, 1126
on labor exploitation, **3:**958
spiritualism and, **3:**1126
Brownson's Quarterly Review, **1:**192,
194
Brown University, **1:**89, 301, 321;
2:913
Bruce, Georgiana, **1:**289
"Brutus" (S. Morse pen name), **1:**433
Bryant, Edwin, **2:**604; **3:**1019, 1190
Bryant, William Cullen, **1:**158; **2:**629,
640, 696, 933, 941; **3:***1256,*
1260
abolitionist writing and, **2:**652
Caroline Kirkland and, **2:**809
Democratic Review and, **3:**1266
as Fireside Poet, **1:**420; **2:**695, 790
Frederick Law Olmsted and, **2:**620

gift book poetry and, **1:**470
Italian travel of, **3:**1184
as Knickerbocker writer, **2:**608, 609,
816
as literary pictorialist, **1:**46, 47
as popular poet, **2:**903, 904, 905,
906
religious belief of, **3:**965
as Schoolroom Poet, **1:**165
science and, **3:**1043
spiritualism and, **3:**1124
travel writing and, **1:**159–160
Unitarianism and, **3:**966, 1212
wilderness notion and, **3:**1254
Bryant, and His Friends (H. Wilson),
2:610
Buade, Louis de, **2:**837
Buchan, William, **2:**496
Buchanan, James, **1:**58, 351, 353;
2:900, 901, 918
Buckingham, Edwin, **1:**56
Buckminster, Joseph Stevens, **3:**1171
Bucknell University, **1:**89
Budick, Emily Miller, **3:**997, 1033
"Buds and Bird-Voices" (Hawthorne),
2:491
Buell, Lawrence, **1:**477; **2:**827, 865,
866; **3:**1077
Buena Vista, battle of (1847), **2:**733
*Buffalo (New York) Commercial
Advertiser* (newspaper), **3:**1195
Buffalo Hunt, The (A. Fisher), **1:**467
Buffon, comte de (Georges-Louis
Leclerc), **3:**1254
Buffum, Edward Gould, **1:**173
Bulfinch, Charles, **1:**246
Bulkeley, Elizabeth, **1:**264
Bulkeley, Peter, **1:**262–263, 264
Bullard, Laura Curtis, **2:**825; **3:**1053
Bull Run, first battle of (1861), **1:**463;
3:1027
Bulwer-Lytton, Edward, **1:**26; **2:**609
Bunker Hill Monument address (D.
Webster), **1:**163
Buntline, Ned, **1:**193, 341; **2:**735,
902; **3:**1057, 1058, 1215
New York and, **2:**814, 817–818
Bunyan, John, **1:**383, *383;* **2:**589,
685, 779, 943; **3:**1126, 1149,
1270
Bureau of Indian Affairs, **2:**902;
3:1108, 1242
Burke, Edmund, **1:**26
burlesque. *See* satire, burlesque, and
parody
burned-over district, New York, **3:**967
Burnham, George Pickering, **3:**1054
"Burning Drift-Wood" (Whittier),
1:424

Dick, Archibald L., **1**:473

Dickens, Charles, **1**:24, 26, 143, 166, 274, 339; **2**:487, 547, 681, 686, 869, 939; **3**:1162

on American prisons, **1**:289

caricature of, **1**:*369*

negative view of America of, **1**:368–370

plays based on works of, **3**:1160

urbanization theme and, **3**:1214, 1218

on Washington, D.C., **3**:1238, 1240

"Dick Harlan's Tennessee Frolic" (Harris), **2**:538

Dickinson, Anna, **1**:*415;* **2**:694

Dickinson, Austin, **2**:885

Dickinson, Emily, **1**:257–258, 397, 429; **2**:643, 659, 755, 823, *886;* **3**:1061

Atlantic Monthly and, **1**:59

Civil War and, **1**:235; **2**:884

cross-border references of, **1**:160

death and, **2**:887–888

drunkenness metaphor of, **3**:1158

editing of works of, **2**:889–891

Elizabeth Stuart Phelps's view of heaven and, **1**:456

Fireside Poets contrasted with, **1**:421

fusion of letters and poems of, **1**:448

introspective verse of, **1**:66

letter writing and, **2**:646

literary nationalism and, **2**:682

lyric poets' popularity vs., **2**:695, 697

on marriage, **2**:718

nature themes and, **2**:793

political views of, **2**:888–889

prejudices of, **2**:888–889

reclusiveness of, **1**:448

religious influences on, **2**:885–886, 926, 927, 928; **3**:965, 966

same-sex love and, **3**:107, 1014–1015, 1017

science and, **2**:886–888, 911, 912; **3**:1043

twentieth-century status of, **3**:1225

Walt Whitman contrasted with, **2**:682

See also poems of Emily Dickinson

Dickinson, Lavinia, **2**:889

Dickinson, Susan Gilbert ("Sue"), **2**:883, 885, 887; **3**:1014–1015, 1017

dictionaries, **1**:21, 22, 25

classical, **1**:244

woodcut relief engraving and, **1**:146

Dictionary (N. Webster), **2**:941

Dictionary of American Authors, **2**:938

Dictionary of Americanisms (J. R. Bartlett), **1**:22, 337

didacticism

children's literature and, **1**:213

feminist fiction and, **1**:416–418; **3**:1189

gift books and, **1**:469, 470, 471

religious periodicals and, **3**:971, 974

temperance literature and, **3**:1156, 1157

women authors and, **3**:968

"Diddling Considered as One of the Exact Sciences" (Poe), **1**:277–278

Diégarias (Séjour), **3**:1159

diet reform, **3**:961

Dillard, J. L., **1**:339

Dillistin's Bank Note Reporter (publication), **1**:85

Dillon, Elizabeth Maddock, **3**:1064

dime biographies, **1**:120

Dime Novel Companion (J. R. Cox), **1**:399

dime novels, **1**:**340–343;** **2**:787, 878, 916

bad-boy genre and, **1**:211

cheap postal rates and, **1**:85–86, 151, 341

crime sensation stories and, **1**:290

factory writing and, **1**:399

frontiersmen as heroes of, **2**:776, 818

literary marketplace and, **1**:238

Mexican-American War and, **2**:735

mountain men as heroes of, **1**:450, 451, 453

New York and, **2**:817

taste and, **3**:1144–1146

youth readership of, **1**:218–219

Directory to the Seraglios in New York, Philadelphia, Boston, and All the Principal Cities of the Union (roué's guidebook), **1**:441

"disappearing Indian" theme, **2**:561, 783, 787; **3**:1109, 1181, 1254, 1261

Disarming the Nation (E. Young), **1**:295

Disciples of Christ (Campbellites), **1**:91, 112; **3**:963, 967

Disclosures from the Interior and Superior Care for Mortals (periodical), **3**:1125

"Discourse of the Latest Form of Infidelity, A" (A. Norton), **3**:1174

"Discourse on the Transient and Permanent in Christianity, A" (T. Parker), **1**:335

discovery. *See* exploration and discovery

Dissertations on the English Language (N. Webster), **1**:21–22, 25

District of Columbia. *See* Washington, D.C.

"Diversity of Origin of Human Races, The" (Agassiz), **1**:377

dividing lines. *See* borders

Divine and Supernatural Light, Immediately Imparted to the Soul by the Spirit of God, Shown to Be Both a Scriptural and Rational Doctrine, A (J. Edwards), **1**:177

divine grace. *See* grace

"Divine Presence in Nature and in the Soul, The" (T. Parker), **1**:335

"Divinity School Address, The" (Emerson), **1**:32, 332; **2**:946; **3**:1046, 1048

controversy and, **3**:1174–1175

division of labor

farmwork and, **2**:612

industrialism and, **2**:611, 612, 614

Irish immigrants and, **2**:593

marriage and, **2**:722

separate spheres doctrine and, **2**:614, 652–653, 755

divorce, **1**:60, 442, 443, 444; **2**:722

women's rights and, **3**:1130

Dix, Dorothea, **1**:166, 289

Dix and Edwards (publisher), **1**:92; **2**:853

"Dixie" (Emmett), **2**:906

Dixon, George Washington, **2**:769

Dixon, Thomas, **1**:250; **2**:554

Dixon, William Hepworth, **1**:441

Dobson, Joanne, **3**:1063, 1250

Doc Hollywood (film), **2**:847

doctors. *See* health and medicine

"Doctrine and Discipline of Human Culture, The" (A. B. Alcott), **3**:1173

Doctrine and Discipline of the African Methodist Episcopal Church, **2**:730

Documentos para la Historia de Mexico (Palóu), **3**:1018

Dodd, Mead, and Company, **1**:150

Dodge, Augusta, **1**:410

Dodge, Mary Abigail, **1**:60, 166, 410, 457

on inequality of female authors, **1**:411, 412

Emerson, Ralph Waldo (*continued*)
  reform movements and, **3**:958–959,
    1231
  Representative Man concept and,
    2:511
  Revolutions of 1848 and, **3**:980,
    981, 983
  Robert Owen's influence on,
    3:1221
  Romanticism and, **1**:35, 386;
    2:617, 672, 802, 891, 893–894;
    3:996, 1000, 1001, 1002, 1003,
    1047, 1048
  same-sex romantic friendship of,
    3:1015, 1017
  as school teacher, **1**:299
  science and, **3**:1043–1044
  self-knowledge and, **3**:1231
  on sensationalist press, **3**:1055
  sermon rejecting sacraments of,
    2:928
  on *The Song of Hiawatha,* **3**:1106
  Spirit concept and, **2**:801–802
  style of, **1**:387–388
  technology and, **3**:1146, 1147
  temperance reform and, **3**:1157
  Transcendental Club and, **1**:135;
    3:1175
  as transparent eyeball (caricature),
    2:*797*
  on underachievers, **1**:387
  Unitarianism and, **2**:928; **3**:966,
    1047, 1048, 1172, 1212
  utopian communities and, **3**:959,
    1220, 1222, 1223, 1232
  Walt Whitman and, **1**:64, 298–299;
    2:631, 634, 671–672, 709, 895,
    911; **3**:1178, 1240, 1269
  wilderness and, **3**:1254, 1255
  on woman's proper function,
    3:1008
  See also "American Scholar, The'";
    "Divinity School Address, The";
    Essays; "Experience"; *Nature;*
    "Poet, The"; *Representative Men;*
    "Self-Reliance"; transcendentalism
Emerson, Waldo, **1**:210, 386*;*
  2:897
Emerson, William, **1**:263–264, 265,
  333; **3**:1171
Emersonian vision, **3**:1059, 1178
Emile (Rousseau), **1**:208
Emilia Galotti (Lessing), **1**:459
Emmett, Daniel Decatur, **2**:906
Emory, William H., **1**:392, *393;*
  3:1039
Emory College, **2**:923
Empire City, The (Lippard), **3**:1056
Empire of the Eye, The (Miller), **1**:156

Empirical Psychology (Hickock), **2**:933
empiricism, 865, **1**:332; **2**:863–864
  John Locke and, **3**:1070
  liberal theology and, **3**:172
  transcendentalism vs., **1**:303
employees. *See* labor
"Encantadas, or Enchanted Isles, The"
  (Melville), **1**:52
Enclosure Acts (Britain), **1**:9
Encyclopaedia Americana (Lieber),
  1:460
*Encyclopedia of Cottage, Farm, and
  Villa Architecture* (Loudon), **1**:41
"Endicott and the Red Cross"
  (Hawthorne), **1**:291; **2**:943
Enfan's d'Adam (Whitman poem
  cluster), **2**:632
Engels, Friedrich, **3**:1261
engineering, architectural, **1**:43
England. *See* English literature; Great
  Britain
England (Cooper), **3**:1183
English, Thomas Dunn, **2**:868
English and Scottish Popular Ballads
  (F. J. Child), **3**:987
English Bible. *See* Bible, the
English-Chinese Phrase Book, An
  (Wong), **1**:222
English Civil War, **3**:1030
English Composition (Wendell), **3**:988
English Composition and Rhetoric
  (Bain), **1**:302; **3**:988
English Grammar (Murray), **1**:25–26;
  2:860
English language. *See* American
  English
"English Language in America, The"
  (Bristed), **1**:26, 336
English Language in America, The
  (Krapp), **1**:23
English literature, **1**:367–374
  American book publishers and,
    1:149–150
  American English and, **1**:26
  as American literary influence,
    2:536, 604, 607, 608, 609, 610,
    806
  American periodicals and, **1**:57
  American travelers and, **1**:29
  architectural description and, **1**:43,
    46
  biography and, **1**:119–120
  as *The Bondwoman's Narrative*
    influence, **1**:142–143
  classical tradition and, **1**:243, 303
  college curricula and, **1**:255–257,
    303–304
  epistolary fiction and, **2**:647
  gentlemen-authors of, **2**:816

gothic fiction and, **1**:475, 476
Harper's New Monthly Magazine
  and, **2**:487, 853
in high school curriculum, **1**:304
influence on philosophy of, **2**:865,
  928
New York writers and, **2**:815
pictorialists and, **1**:46–47, 49, 53
popularity of in United States,
  2:905, 906, 937
rhetoric and, **3**:987
Romanticism and, **3**:995, 1048,
  1212, 1254
satire and, **3**:1023
sea stories and, **3**:1190
short story and, **3**:1076
transatlantic perspective and, **1**:160
See also gothic fiction; Great Britain;
  literary nationalism
English Men of Letters series,
  1:138–139
English Notebooks (Hawthorne), **1**:379
"English Reformers, The" (Emerson),
  1:335
English Traits (Emerson), **1**:370, 372,
  437; **2**:940
engravers
  gift books and, **1**:467, 470
  Godey's Lady's Book and, **1**:473–474
Enlightenment, **1**:65, 92, 177;
  2:665–666; **3**:1100, 1259
  as feminist influence, **1**:414
  gothic fiction and, **1**:475
  liberal theology and, **3**:1172
  progress belief of, **3**:1147
  Romanticism vs., **3**:1000
  utopian communities and, **3**:1221
  See also Scottish Enlightenment
Enquirer (Richmond newspaper),
  1:353
*Enquiry concerning the Intellectual
  and Moral Faculties, and
  Literature of Negroes* (Grégoire),
  1:36
entertainment. *See* circuses and
  spectacles; lyceums; theater
entrepreneurs. *See* capitalism
environmentalism, **1**:49; **3**:978
  beginnings of, **3**:1044
  Francis Parkman and, **2**:834, 837
  George Perkins Marsh and, **2**:621
  Henry David Thoreau and, **2**:793;
    3:1177, 1178, 1255
  James Fenimore Cooper and,
    2:837
  Walt Whitman's "This Compost"
    and, **2**:632
  wilderness preservation and,
    3:1251, 1256–1257

Graham, George Rex, **2:**854, 871
Graham, Isabella, **1:**117
Graham, Sylvester, **2:**827, 910, 916; **3:**961, 1065, 1067, 1068, 1069
Graham's Magazine, **1:**145, 360; **2:**529, 669, 674, 854, 857; **3:**1024, 1076–1077, 1078
    Edgar Allan Poe and, **3:**1076–1077, 1078
grain
    alcohol conversion from, **3:**1154
    prices, **1:**86
Grainger, James, **3:**1253
Grammar of Rhetoric and Polite Literature, A (Jamieson), **1:**301
Grammatical Institute of the English Language, A (N. Webster), **1:**300
Gramsci, Antonio, **1:**96
Grand Canyon, **1:**393; **3:**1258
Grandfather's Chair (Hawthorne), **1:**216
Grandissimes, The (Cable), **2:**810
grand opera. *See* opera
grand tour, **1:**29
Grangerford, Emmeline, **1:**469
Grant, Ulysses S., **2:**587, 728; **3:**1025, 1242
    Memoirs of, **1:**120
Gratz, Rebecca, **2:**600
graves. *See* cemeteries
Graves, James R., **1:**91
Graves, Mrs. A. J., **2:**614
Gray, Asa, **1:**58, 68; **3:**1037, 1039, 1040, *1040*
    evolution theory and, **3:**1042, 1043
Gray, Francis, **1:**289
Gray, Thomas Ruffin, **1:**268–269, *270,* 272; **3:**1082
Grayson, William John, **1:**13, 439; **2:**924
"greasers" (Mexican stereotype), **3:**1119, *1120*
Great Awakening (1730s–1740s), **1:**381; **2:**944; **3:**957, 966, 971. *See also* Second Great Awakening
Great Basin, **1:**393
Great Britain
    actors in America from, **3:**1160
    African American intellectuals' flight to, **1:**261
    American Anglophobia and, **1:**182–183; **3:**993
    American attitudes toward, **1:**363–364, 367–373, 437; **2:**513
    American book publishing and, **1:**149–150, 151
    American borders and, **1:**158, 161, 182; **2:**712

    American Civil War and, **1:**182, 371–372
    American publishing agents in, **2:**678
    American travelers in, **1:**28, 29, 30; **3:**1181, 1183, 1184, 1262
    antislavery movement and, **1:**36; **3:**1236
    architecture and, **1:**40, 41
    border disputes with, **2:**710, 712
    Bret Harte in, **3:**1021
    British English vs. American English and, **1:**23, 26; **3:**114
    Canada and, **1:**181–183
    Clotel first published in, **1:**248
    Egypt and, **2:**838
    exploration and, **1:**390, 392, 394
    female-authored factory writing in, **1:**397
    feminism in, **3:**1259
    folklore and, **1:**427, 428, 429
    Francis Parkman on, **2:**510, 837
    as fugitive slave haven, **3:**1207
    fur trade and, **1:**450
    The Gates Ajar sales in, **1:**455
    Herman Melville published in, **3:**1193
    immigration from, **2:**546, 547–548
    industrial economy and, **2:**688
    influence of, **2:**517, 518
    international copyright and, **1:**153–154
    James Fenimore Cooper's response to, **1:**372–373
    landscape architecture in, **2:**616
    lecture series movement in, **2:**691–692
    literary criticism and, **2:**669
    literature of. *See* English literature
    manhood and, **2:**704
    maritime commerce and, **2:**714
    medieval romances and, **3:**994
    Nathaniel Hawthorne on, **2:**372
    Native American land claims and, **1:**204
    Oregon Territory and, **1:**158, 161, 182; **2:**712
    Puritans in, **3:**1030
    Ralph Waldo Emerson's lectures in, **3:**981, 1178
    Revolutions of 1848 and, **3:**979, 980
    rhetoric texts and, **1:**301–302; **3:**985–986
    scientific institutions in, **3:**1037
    sentimentalism and, **3:**1059–1060
    slave narrative sales in, **2:**778; **3:**1083
    slavery's abolishment by, **1:**184; **2:**557; **3:**1236

    slavery supporters in, **1:**371–372
    slave trade abolishment by, **3:**1090
    theatrical burlesque and, **3:**1027
    as theatrical source, **3:**1159, 1160
    travel writing about, **3:**1183
    Washington Irving's literary prominence in, **2:**610; **3:**989, 1075
    women's marital loss of identity in, **3:**1010–1011
    woodcut relief engraving in, **1:**145, 148
    See also French and Indian War; London; Scotland; War of 1812
"Great Chain of Being," **3:**1082
Great Christian Doctrine of Original Sin Defended, The (J. Edwards), **1:**177
Great Comet of 1843, **3:**1040
Great Disappointment of 1844, **3:**967
Great Dismal Swamp (Virginia), **3:**1087
Great Exhibition of 1851 (London), **1:**28
Great Lakes region, **1:**391; **2:**577; **3:**1182, 1261
    immigration and, **2:**548
"Great Lawsuit, The" (Fuller), **1:**334; **2:**719; **3:**959, 1129, 1176, 1260, 1261, 1263
Great Man theory of history, **2:**837
"Great Nation of Futurity, The" (O'Sullivan), **1:**177; **2:**712
Great Peace Jubilee (1869), **1:**162–163, 167
Great Plains Indians, **1:**430; **3:**1252
Great Potato Famine (Ireland), **1:**191; **2:**546
Great Revival, **2:**922
Great Salt Lake, **1:**391; **3:**967
Great Short Works (Poe), **3:**1078
Great West (journal), **1:**227
Great Western Revival, **1:**15
Greece, **2:**514, 574, 576; **3:**1184
    deforestation's effects in, **3:**1040
Greek culture. *See* classical literature
Greek language, **1:**244–245, 253, 254, 255, 303; **3:**987
Greek revival style, **1:**40, 243
Greeley, Horace, **1:**137, 235; **2:**613, 659, 916
    biography of, **1:**119–120
    The Confidence-Man and, **1:**276
    crime sensation stories and, **1:**290
    divorce debate and, **1:**444
    Dred Scott opinion published by, **1:**349
    Fourierism and, **1:**442; **3:**1221
    hiring of Margaret Fuller by, **2:**817; **3:**1261, 1262

Hicks, Elias, **2:**947–948, 951; **3:**1158
Hidden Hand, The (Southworth),
  1:75, 283, 284; **2:500–504,** 878
  cross-dressing and, **1:**294, 417;
    3:1053
  as domestic fiction, **1:**347–348
  influence on fashion of, **1:**408
  self-reliant female heroine of, **1:**417;
    3:1053, 1246–1247
  sentimentalism and, **3:**1062
Higginson, Thomas Wentworth, **1:**39;
  2:604, 643, 654, 945
  abolitionism and, **1:**2
  African American spirituals and,
    1:429
  Atlantic Monthly and, **1:**59, 60
  as Emily Dickinson mentor, **2:**884,
    885, 890–891; **3:**1014
  Harvard and, **3:**986
  as lecturer, **2:**693, 694–695
  on slave rebellions, **3:**1088, 1089,
    1091
  transcendentalism and, **3:**1213
  Unitarianism and, **3:**1212
highbrow taste, **1:**238; **3:**1141
high culture, **2:**676, 677; **3:**1141
Higher Criticism. *See* biblical criticism
higher education. *See* colleges
higher law, **1:**233; **3:**976
Highland Garden (Downing house),
  1:41, 44
*High Life in New York by Jonathan
  Slick, Esq.* (A. S. Stephens), **2:**535
Hildreth, Richard, **1:**37, 142; **2:**508,
  741; **3:**1212
Hill, Adams Sherman, **3:**984, 987
Hill, William, **1:***201*
Hillside (Alcott Concord home), **1:**267
Hillside Chapel (Concord), **1:**267
Hine, L. A., **2:**856
Hinks, Peter, **3:**1234
Hinton, Richard, **2:**485
Hinton, Sarah, **2:**728–729
Hints to My Countrymen (Sedgwick),
  2:647
"Hints to Young Wives" (Fern), **2:**539
Hireling and the Slave, The (Grayson),
  1:13, 439; **2:**924
Hirt, Hermann, **1:**459
Hiscox, Edward T., **1:**91
Hiscox Guide for Baptist Churches, The,
  1:91
Hispanics. *See* Spanish speakers and
  early "Latino" expression
*Historical and Statistical Information
  Respecting the History, Condition
  and Prospects of the Indian Tribes
  of the United States* (Schoolcraft),
  1:375

"Historical Discourse, Delivered to
  the Citizens of Concord, A"
  (Emerson), **1:**264–265
historical novel
  Hope Leslie as, **2:**521–525
  Mexican American, **3:**1119, 1120
  Nathaniel Hawthorne and,
    3:996–997, 1028, 1029–1030,
    1078
Historical Society of Pennsylvania,
  2:859
"Historic Notes on Life and Letters in
  New England" (Emerson),
  3:1102
Historic Tales of Olden Time
  (J. F. Watson), **2:**823
history, **2:504–511**
  American romance parallels with,
    3:996
  biography and, **1:**118–120
  captivity narratives and, **1:**186
  frontier thesis and, **2:**823
  gothic fiction and, **1:**477–478
  Great Man theory of, **2:**837
  G. W. F. Hegel as "Father of
    American History" and,
    1:459–460
  "The Legend of Sleepy Hollow"
    and use of, **2:**637
  Nathaniel Hawthorne and, **2:**527,
    529, 531; **3:**1029–1030
  Puritan New England and,
    3:1029–1030
  slave narratives as, **3:**1084, 1086
  women's place in, **3:**1262
  women writers of, **2:**508
  See also specific works
"History" (Emerson), **3:**1048
History of American Socialisms
  (J. H. Noyes), **1:**441
*History of Architecture from the
  Earliest Times* (Tuthill), **1:**44
History of California (H. H.
  Bancroft), **3:**1020
History of Columbus, A (Irving),
  2:770
History of Haverhill, Massachusetts, A
  (Mirick), **1:**186
History of Louisiana (Gayarré), **2:**812
History of Maria Kittle, The
  (Bleecker), **1:**186
History of New York (Irving), **2:**608,
  635, 816; **3:**990, 993, 994
  satire and, **3:**1022–1023, 1027
History of Sexuality, The (Foucault),
  3:1070
*History of the Condition of Women, in
  Various Ages and Nations*
  (L. M. Child), **2:**650

History of the Conquest of Mexico
  (Prescott), **1:**159, 438; **2:**507,
  511–516, 733
History of the Conquest of Peru
  (Prescott), **2:**507
History of the Conspiracy of Pontiac
  (Parkman), **2:**837
History of the Dividing Line, The
  (Byrd), **3:**1135
*History of the Expedition under the
  Command of Captains Lewis and
  Clark, to the Sources of the
  Missouri, thence across the Rocky
  Mountains and down the River
  Columbia to the Pacific Ocean*
  (Lewis and Clark), **3:**1181
History of the Hen Fever (Burnham),
  3:1054
*History of the Life and Voyages of
  Christopher Columbus, A* (Irving),
  3:1181
History of the Quakers (Sewell), **2:**490
*History of the Reign of Ferdinand and
  Isabella the Catholic* (Prescott),
  2:507, 511
*History of the Rise, Progress, and
  Accomplishment of the Abolition of
  the African Slave Trade by the
  British Parliament* (Clarkson),
  2:717
History of the United Netherlands, The
  (Motley), **2:**507
History of the United States (G.
  Bancroft), **2:**506, 514, 939
History of the United States (Hildreth),
  2:508
History of the Work of Redemption, A
  (J. Edwards), **2:**944
History of Virginia (Beverley), **3:**1253
History of Woman's Suffrage, **1:**18
history painting, **1:**53–55
Hitchcock, Edward, **2:**886–887, 912,
  913; **3:**1041
Hive of "The Bee-Hunter", The
  (Thorpe), **1:**114
Hoar, Elizabeth, **1:**332
Hoar, Samuel, **3:**977
Hobomok (L. M. Child), **1:**35, 233;
  2:523, 557, 564, 577–578, 653,
  718, 739, 790; **3:**958, 1255
Hoe, Richard M., **3:**1054
Hoe, Robert, **1:**150
Hoe rotary press, **1:***149*
Hoffman, Charles Fenno, **2:**608, 807
Hoffman, Daniel, **2:**824, 870–871
Hoffmann, E. T. A., **1:**459
"Ho! For California!" (song), **1:**172
Hogarth, George, **1:**357
Holberg, Ludvig, **1:**403

mountain men and, **1**:452–453

nature and, **2**:789–790

oral tradition and, **2**:824

portrayals of women and, **1**:418

single man theme and, **1**:73–74

vanishing wilderness theme and, **2**:836–837

wilderness and, **3**:1255

See also Deerslayer, The; Last of the Mohicans, The; Pathfinder, The; Pioneers, The; Prairie, The

Leaves from Margaret Smith's Journal (Whittier), **2**:604

Leaves of Grass (Whitman), **2**:629–635, 669, 777, 818, 847–848, 866, 875, 895, 902, 909, 916

on American diversity, **3**:1098, 1269

autobiographical elements in, **1**:61, 64

Civil War and, **2**:498; **3**:1242

democracy and, **1**:323, 325

dignity of work and, **1**:12

editions of, **3**:1072, 1112, 1114

final edition of (1881), **3**:1115

first edition of (1855), **3**:1112, 1114

form and structure of, **2**:680

front cover of, **2**:*630*

frontispiece of, **3**:1115, *1115*

gift-book conventions and, **1**:468

leisure activity and, **2**:643

on literary theory, **2**:671–672

Louisa May Alcott on, **1**:468–469

"manly attachments" and, **1**:447; **3**:962, 1016

mountain men and, **1**:452–453

nature themes and, **2**:633, 634, 635, 794

New York depiction and, **2**:819

obscenity charges against, **3**:1242

phrenology references in, **2**:725–726

poems to Lincoln and, **3**:1244

print-run of, **3**:1107

Ralph Waldo Emerson's praise for, **1**:299

reception of, **3**:1269

Tocqueville's anticipation of, **1**:329, 330

Walt Whitman's own review of, **3**:1267

See also "Crossing Brooklyn Ferry"; "Song of Myself"

Le Beau, Bryan F., **1**:159

Le Claire, Antoine, **2**:785

Leclerc, Georges-Louis, comte de Buffon, **3**:1254

Le Conte, Joseph, **3**:1257–1258

"Lecture, Read before the Worcester Lyceum" (Washburn), **2**:693

lectures. *See* lyceums; oratory

Lectures (E. T. Channing), **3**:986

Lectures (J. Q. Adams), **3**:986

Lectures for Ladies on Anatomy and Physiology (M. G. Nichols), **1**:444

Lectures on American Literature (S. Knapp), **2**:822

Lectures on Phrenology (Combe), **2**:725

"Lectures on Poetry" (W. C. Bryant), **2**:933

Lectures on Rhetoric and Belles-Lettres (H. Blair), **1**:301–302; **2**:826, 933; **3**:985

Lectures on Rhetoric and Oratory (Adams), **2**:826

Lectures on Slavery and Its Remedy (Phelps), **1**:37

Lectures on the English Language (Marsh), **1**:337

Lectures on the Philosophy of the Human Mind (T. Brown), **2**:934

Lectures on the Revival of Religion (Finney), **3**:1001

Lectures on the Science of Human Life (Graham), **3**:961

Lectures Read to the Seniors in Harvard College (Channing), **1**:302

"Lecture to Young Men, on Chastity, A" (Graham), **3**:961

Ledger (weekly), **1**:85

Lee, George L., **2**:519

Lee, Jarena, **2**:558, 728, 730

Lee, "Mother" Ann, **3**:1220

Lee, Robert E., **1**:463; **2**:484, 518; **3**:970

Lee, Samuel, **2**:652

Lee, Yan Phou, **1**:223

"Lee in the Capitol" (Melville), **1**:99

Leeser, Isaac, **1**:113–114; **2**:600

Legaré, Hugh Swinton, **1**:202

"Legend of Sleepy Hollow, The" (Irving), **1**:278; **2**:533, 536, 608, 635–639, *636*, 815; **3**:989–990, 1183

black racial identity and, **1**:128

critical acclaim for, **3**:1075

German folklore and, **1**:426

legacy of, **2**:638

legends. *See* folklore; oral tradition

Legends of Mexico (Lippard), **1**:439; **2**:735

Legends of New-England in Prose and Verse (Whittier), **1**:186, 427

Leggett, William, **1**:83; **2**:608, 701; **3**:1266

Lehman, George, **2**:859

leisure, **2**:639–644

Leland, Charles G., **1**:89, 257, 337

Lemay, J. A. Leo, **1**:115, 116

Lemire, Elise, **2**:740

Lenderman's Adventures among the Spiritualists and Free-Lovers (A. J. Davis), **1**:442

Lenni Lenape Indians, **2**:739, 764

Lenox Library (Massachusetts), **3**:1269

Lenz, William E., **1**:279

Leonard, Zenas, **1**:391; **3**:1190

Leonidas, **1**:244

Leonora (opera), **2**:770, 859

Leopold, Aldo, **3**:1257

Leopold Association, **1**:434

lesbianism, **3**:1067

nineteenth-century culture and, **1**:417; **3**:1013, 1014, 1015, 1016

See also gay and lesbian studies

Leslie, Frank (pseud. of Henry Carter), **1**:148; **2**:879, 880

Lessing, Gotthold Ephraim, **1**:459, 461

Lessing: His Life and His Works (Stahr), **1**:461

letters, **2**:644–648

Americans abroad and, **1**:28

of California gold rush, **1**:172

content and form of, **2**:644–645

of Emily Dickinson to sister-in-law, **3**:1015

epistolary novel and, **1**:448–449; **2**:647

as literature, **2**:646–647

private friendships and, **1**:448–449

as readership profile source, **2**:666–667

on same-sex physical friendships, **3**:1070

satire and, **3**:1026

by slaves, **2**:644–645, 647, 652

transmission of, **2**:645–646

Letters Found in the Ruins of Fort Braddock (Brainard), **2**:647

Letters from an American Farmer (Crèvecoeur), **1**:9–10

"Letters from a Travelling Bachelor" (Whitman), **1**:296, 297

Letters from Lucius M. Piso [pseud.] from Palmyra (W. Ware), **2**:647

Letters from New York (L. M. Child), **1**:166; **2**:557, 817

Letters from the South (Paulding), **2**:536; **3**:1132

Letters of J. Downing, Major, Downingville Militia, Second Brigade, to His Old Friend, Mr. Dwight, of the "New York Daily Advertiser" (C. A. Davis), **2**:534

Mackenzie, Henry, **3:**1059
McKissack, Frederick L., **3:**1091
McKissack, Patricia C., **3:**1091
McLaren, John, **3:**1021
McLean, John, **1:**227, 352
McLenan, John, **3:**1111
McLeod, General, **3:**1119, 1120
McNally, Andrew, **2:**942
Maconochie, Alexander, **1:**288
McPhee, John, **1:**394
McPherson, James, **2:**520
Macready, William Charles, **2:**817,
    818; **3:**1141, 1160, 1161, 1269
McWilliams, John, **2:**711
Madame Bovary (Flaubert), **2:**720
Madge Bufford (anon.), **2:**915
Madison, James, **1:**232; **2:**898
Madsen, Deborah L., **2:**943
Madsen, William G., **1:**177
Maeder, James Gaspard, **2:**770
magazines. *See* periodicals
Magic Circle of "Walden," The
    (C. Anderson), **3:**1230
Magnalia Christi Americana
    (C. Mather), **1:**278; **2:**490;
    3:1029, 1126
Magnolia (periodical), **2:**538
Maher, Margaret, **2:**889
Mailer, Norman, **2:**746
"Mail Has Come, The" (Lambert),
    2:646
mailing rates. *See* postal service
Main Currents in American Thought
    (Parrington), **1:**139; **2:**776
Maine, **3:**1024
    admission as free state of, **1:**259
    Down East humor and, **2:**533–535
    free blacks' status in, **3:**1128
    Henry David Thoreau's trip to,
        1:266; **3:**1182, 1255
    teetotalism in, **3:**1156
Maine Anti-Slavery Society, **3:**1187
Maine Laws, **3:**1156
Maine Woods, The (Thoreau), **1:**58,
    379; **3:**1132, 1182, 1255
"Maine Woods, The" (Thoreau),
    2:832
Main Street (S. Lewis), **1:**462
Major Jones's Courtship (W. T.
    Thompson), **2:**537
Makemie, Francis, **2:**918
*Malaeska, the Indian Wife of the White
    Hunter* (A. Stephens), **1:**340,
    342, 451; **2:**878
male friendship, **1:**445–446
    romantic and physical, **3:**1013,
        1014, 1015–1016
male sexuality, **1:**443, 444
Malinche, **3:**1262

"mammy" figure, **1:**8
Man, Thomas, **1:**398
Manabozho (trickster hero),
    1:430–431; **2:**577; **3:**1107,
    1108–1109
Man and Nature (G. P. Marsh),
    2:621; **3:**1257
Manchester Operative (periodical),
    1:399
Manhattan *See* New York
"Manhattan from the Bay"
    (Whitman), **1:**297
manhood, **2:703–710**
    fashion and, **1:**405, 408
    as Frederick Douglass theme,
        2:583, 708, 709, 778, 781, 782,
        866
    free-love doctrines and, **1:**443,
        444
    friendship and, **1:**445–446; **2:**628,
        708; **3:**1013, 1014, 1015–1016
    honor and, **2:**516–520
    humor and, **2:**538
    leisure activities and, **2:**640, 643
    literary labor and, **2:**614
    Margaret Fuller on, **3:**1176
    marriage and, **2:**706–707
    mourning and, **2:**765
    pornography and, **2:**915
    postbellum concepts of, **1:**240–241
    same-sex love and, **3:**1015–1016,
        1017
    sentimentalism vs., **3:**1060, 1061
    sentimental writing and, **3:**1063
    sexual anxieties and, **2:**707, 708
    sexuality and, **1:**443, 444
    suffrage and, **3:**1128, 1131
    transcendentalism and, **2:**705–706
    urbanization and, **2:**704–705
    wilderness and, **3:**1255
    See also gender; separate spheres
"Maniac Wife, The" (F. Gage),
    2:718
Manifest Destiny, **1:**49; **2:**562, 700,
    710–714, 789; **3:**1060, 1248,
    1261
    American exceptionalism and, **1:**435
    American expansionism as, **1:**155,
        259; **2:**710, 712; **3:**1122, 1180,
        1266
    "Benito Cereno" and, **1:**102,
        103–106
    California and, **3:**1018–1019
    Canada seen as threat to, **1:**182
    coining of phrase, **1:**155; **3:**1266
    Cuba annexation movement and,
        1:132–133
    dime novels and, **1:**342
    ideology of, **1:**259

Jacksonian democracy and,
    1:323–324
John O'Sullivan's coining of phrase,
    1:437; **2:**710, 943; **3:**1266
literary nationalism and, **2:**680
manhood and, **2:**704
Mexican-American War and,
    2:712–713, 732
Puritan Calvinism and, **1:**177, 178;
    2:943–944
technology and, **3:**1147–1150
travel writing and, **3:**1180,
    1181–1182
women's views on, **2:**682
Young America and, **2:**670; **3:**1266
"manly attachments" (Whitman
    concept), **1:**447; **3:**962, 1016
Mann, Horace, **1:**166, 209, 210;
    2:666
    as lecturer, **2:**692, 693
    lyceum movement and, **3:**1039
    Prussian school system model and,
        1:460
    as public education influence, **3:**960
Mann, Mary Tyler Peabody, **1:**209,
    210; **3:**961
"Mannahatta" (Whitman), **3:**1217
*Manners and Customs of Several
    Indian Tribes* (Hunter), **1:**189
*Manners and Customs of the Principal
    Nations of the Globe* (Goodrich),
    1:435–436
Manning, Susan, **1:**373
Manning family, **1:**135
"Man of Adamant, The"
    (Hawthorne), **1:**122; **3:**1267
Man of Feeling, The (Mackenzie),
    3:1059–1060
"Man of the Crowd, The" (Poe),
    1:115, 290; **3:**1216
"Man That Was Used Up, The" (Poe),
    3:956, 1149
"Man the Reformer" (Emerson),
    1:389; **3:**958–959
"Man Thinking" (Emerson), **1:**322
Manual of Composition and Rhetoric
    (Hart), **3:**985
Manual of Political Ethics (Lieber),
    1:460
manufacturing. *See* industrialism
Mapes, James Jay, **2:**694
Marble Faun, The (Hawthorne),
    1:138, 178, 193, 245, 379–380;
    2:601, 604, 943; **3:**1028
    gender relations in, **1:**419
    portrayal of Catholicism and, **1:**437,
        440
    as romance, **3:**996
    Roman scenes in, **3:**1184

N

"Song for Occupations, A"
(Whitman), **2**:631
Song of Drop o' Wather, The (parody),
3:1110
Song of Hakawatha, The (parody),
3:1111
Song of Hiawatha, The (Longfellow),
1:379; **2**:564, 577, 769, 783,
790–791, 904, 905; **3**:**1106–1112**
Indian folklore and, **1**:430–431
parodies of, **3**:1110–1111
popularity and financial success of,
3:1107
sources for, **3**:1107–1109
symphonic adaptation of, **2**:772
Song of Higher-Water, The (Hiawatha
parody), **3**:1110
"Song of Myself" (Whitman), **1**:64,
69, 330; **2**:501, 585–586, 630,
631, 633, 634, 680, 719, 819,
847; **3**:1073, **1112–1117**
American romantic symbols in,
3:996
changed reading of, **3**:1117
on child's insight, **1**:211
"Crossing Brooklyn Ferry" and,
1:296, 297
evolutionary process and, **3**:1042
first publication of, **3**:1114–1115
form and structure of, **2**:680;
3:1116–1117
friendship and, **1**:446
fur trapper image in, **1**:451–452;
2:719
intermarriage representation in,
2:719
New York depiction in, **2**:819
origins of, **3**:1112–1114
"Over-Soul" concept and, **1**:180
poetic narrator of, **3**:1002, 1116
same-sex love and, **3**:1016, 1114
self-exploration in, **1**:299
sexuality and the body and, **3**:1072,
1073, 1114
slavery and, **3**:1098, 1113
as urban poetry, **3**:1217
versions of, **3**:1117
"Song of the Broad Ax" (Hawthorne),
2:911
"Song of the Exposition" (Whitman),
1:243, 297; **2**:612
"Song of the Open Road"
(Hawthorne), **2**:911
"Song of the Prairie, The" (J. K.
Mitchell), **2**:701
"Song of the Redwood-Tree"
(Whitman), **2**:634
"Song of the Rolling Earth, A"
(Whitman), **2**:631

"Song of the Spinners" (*Lowell
Offering*), **2**:613
"Song of the Universal" (Hawthorne),
2:911
songs, **2**:767–768
black spirituals, **1**:429
California gold rush, **1**:172
oral tradition and, **2**:821, 822, 823,
825
rural life and, **1**:10
Ruth Hall–inspired, **3**:1008–1009
sheet music cover, **1**:*282*; **3**:*1009*
Songs in Many Keys (Holmes), **1**:424
Sonnambula, La (Bellini), **3**:1020
"Sonnet to Science" (Poe), **2**:911
Sonntag-Schule Glocke (Cincinnati
juvenile paper), **1**:228
Son of the Forest, A (Apess), **2**:565,
565–566, *565*, 667, 728, 730,
783
Sons of Temperance, **3**:692
"Sophie May" (pseud.), **1**:219
Sophocles, **1**:246
sorrow. *See* mourning
Sorrows of Young Werther, The
(Goethe), **1**:459
soul mate, **1**:441
South, the
agrarian ideal in, **1**:13, 14, 235,
243
banking system in, **1**:86, 87
Baptists in, **1**:89, 92
biographers of, **1**:119
book publishing in, **1**:150
borders and, **1**:157
Calvinism in, **1**:175
Catholic population of, **3**:968
classical interest in, **1**:243–244, 245
Compromise of 1850 and,
1:259–260
courtship in, **1**:282–283
Democratic Party and, **2**:899
dialect and, **1**:338
Dred Scott decision and, **1**:86
exceptionalist argument for, **3**:1101
feudal system and, **3**:1101
folklore of, **1**:427–428
frontier humor and, **3**:1002–1006,
1080
Fugitive Slave Law and, **1**:260–262
German literature readers in,
1:461
honor and, **2**:516–520
humor of the Old Southwest of,
1:114–115, 427, 431;
2:535–539, 541; **3**:1024, 1138
leisure activities in, **2**:640
Lost Cause religion of, **3**:970
manhood concept in, **1**:241

Married Women's Property Acts
and, **3**:1011
Missouri Compromise of 1820 and,
1:233, 292
Northern travel writer critiques of,
1:157
panic of 1837 and, **1**:86
periodicals in, **2**:854–855, 941
polygenesis theory and, **3**:1043
postbellum religion in, **3**:970
Presbyterians in, **2**:917, 918
proslavery writing and,
3:1100–1102
publishers in, **1**:80
publishing and, **2**:941
regional values and vision of, **1**:157,
158, 235–236
religion and, **2**:921
Revolutions of 1848 reaction in,
3:981
slave economy of, **3**:1094
slave rebellion fears in, **2**:484;
3:1088–1089
tall tales in, **3**:1138–1139
travel writing about, **3**:1132
Uncle Tom's Cabin's reception in,
3:969
wilderness and, **3**:1253
See also Civil War; plantation system;
slavery; *specific cities and states*
South America, **1**:394–395; **2**:514
American expansionism and,
1:438–439; **3**:1122
American travel writing on,
1:438–439
exploratory voyages around,
3:1184
immigrants from, **1**:158; **3**:1118
independence from Spain of,
3:1118, 1122
slave rebellions in, **3**:1087, 1091
as theatrical subject, **3**:1159–1160,
1162
wilderness landscape painting and,
3:1255
South Carolina, **1**:129; **2**:517;
3:1167, 1235. *See also* Charleston
*Southern and Western Monthly
Magazine and Review*, **1**:201
Southern Baptists, **3**:973
Southern Baptist Theological
Seminary, **1**:89
Southern Christian Advocate (journal),
2:731
Southern Commercial Conventions,
1:132
"Southern Cross, The" (song), **2**:946
Southern Homestead Act of 1866,
1:13–14

conclusions of, **3:**1233

disdain for fashion in, **1:**408

drafts of, **3:**1225–1226

as environmental classic, **2:**793;
3:1177

haunted table incident and, **3:**1126

as industrialism critique, **2:**612,
613, 661, 793

legacy of, **3:**1178

on Native American primitivism,
3:1170

nature celebrated in, **2:**793;
3:1002–1003

on night spent in jail, **3:**975

origins of, **2:**694, 832

on philanthropy, **3:**958

psychological theory and, **2:**935

reform and, **3:**958, 1231–1232

on same-sex intimate friendship,
3:1015

secular jeremiad in, **1:**178

structure of, **3:**1229–1230

symbols of progress in, **3:**1046

textual complexity and density of,
3:1225, 1226, 1229

title page of, **3:***1228*

transcendentalism and, **3:**974, 1231

twentieth-century canonical status
of, **3:**1225, 1230

wilderness-civilization balance and,
1:155–156

Walden Pond, **1:**233, 265–266;
2:929; **3:**975, 1132, 1177, 1178,
1195

cabin on, **3:**1225, *1227*

contemporary status of, **1:**267

decision to live at, **3:**1229

meaning to Henry David Thoreau
of, **3:**1002–1003

survey of, **3:***1226*

Walden Pond (Maynard), **1:**267

Waldo, John, **1:**22

Walker, Alice, **2:**844

Walker, David, **1:**36, 127, 166; **2:**652

abolitionist writing and, **1:**6; **3:**963

cause of death of, **3:**1235

higher-law thesis and, **1:**233

letter of, **3:**1236

life of, **3:**1234–1235

Puritan typology and, **1:**180

slave rebellion and, **1:**271; **3:**1089,
1090, 1128

See also Walker's Appeal

Walker, Eliza Butler, **3:**1235

Walker, Franklin, **1:**171

Walker, Jeffrey, **2:**625

Walker, Jonathan, **1:**2, *3*

Walker, Joseph, **1:**356, 391

Walker, Timothy, **2:**913

Walker's Appeal (Walker), **1:**6, 36,
166, 233; **2:**652; **3:**1128,
1234–1238

frontispiece of, **3:***1234*

influence and legacy of, **1:**39

militancy of, **1:**279; **3:**1089, 1096,
1234–1235

Puritan typology and, **1:**189

slave rebellion and, **3:**1089

Walker's Pass, **1:**391

"Walking" (Thoreau), **1:**161; **2:**713,
793, 832; **3:**1177, 1257

Walking toward Walden (Hanson),
1:267

*Walks and Talks of an American
Farmer in England* (Olmsted),
2:620

Wallace, Henry A., **2:**918

Wallace, Lewis, **2:**647

Wallace, Paul A. W., **1:**379

Wallack's Theatre (New York), **2:**769

Wall Street, **1:***94*

"Bartleby, the Scrivener" and,
1:93–94

*Wall Street, Half Past Two O'Clock,
October 13, 1857* (Cafferty and
Rosenberg), **1:***84*

Walpole, Horace, **1:**401, 475, 476;
2:528

Walpole, Robert, **1:**26

"Walt Whitman" (Whitman). *See*
"Song of Myself"

"Walt Whitman and His 'Drum Taps'"
(J. Burroughs), **3:**1242

Walt Whitman Archive, **2:**630

Walvin, James, **1:**224

Wampanoag and Operatives's Journal
(periodical), **1:**399

Wampanoag Indians, **2:**578

Wandering Boy, Careless Sailor, The
(H. Lane), **1:**288

"Wan Lee, the Pagan" (Harte), **1:**223

War and Peace (Tolstoy), **2:**746

"Warble for Lilac-Time" (Whitman),
3:1245

war correspondents, **2:**732

Ward, Anna Barker, **2:**929

Ward, Artemus, **1:**197, 198; **2:**590;
3:1126

humor and, **2:**539, 540, 541

satire and, **3:**1026

Ward, Maria, **2:**721, 761

Ward, Samuel, **1:**56, 336; **2:**929

War Department, U.S., **1:**394

Wardrop, Daneen, **1:**208

Ware, Charles Pickard, **1:**429; **2:**823

Ware, Henry, Jr., **3:**1001, 1172, 1175

Ware, Henry, Sr., **3:**1171, 1172

Ware, William, **2:**647, 840

Warner, Ann, **3:**1248, 1250

Warner, Anna Bartlett, **2:**919

Warner, Charles Dudley, **2:**621;
3:1028, 1241

Warner, Henry, **3:**1246, 1247

Warner, Susan, **1:**109, 178, 210,
250, 383, 384, *384;* **2:**614, 685,
686, 744, 756, 762, 764; **3:**964,
1246

as best-selling author, **1:**409; **2:**940;
3:968, 1062, 1246, 1249

on Catharine Beecher and Jenny
Lind, **3:**1248–1249

critical views of, **2:**682

domestic fiction and, **1:**344, 345,
346–347

exclusion from twentieth-century
canon of, **3:**1061

fashion critique by, **1:**408

female heroines' realistic problems
and, **3:**1005, 1010

lack of international copyright and,
3:1250

moral reform and, **3:**968, 1248

mourning portrayal and, **2:**762,
764

Presbyterianism and, **2:**919

pseudonym of, **3:**1246

publisher of, **2:**940

sentimentalism and, **1:**468; **3:**1062,
1203

singlehood of, **3:**1250

See also Wide, Wide World, The

war novels, **2:**743–746

War of 1812, **1:**367, 373; **2:**565, 569,
715, 788

American nationalism following,
1:214

Baltimore and, **1:**78

banking and, **1:**82

Canada and, **1:**182

economic depression and, **3:**1155

professional writing and, **1:**20

western expansionism following,
1:450

War of Independence. *See* American
Revolution

Warren, E. W., **2:**924

Warren, Josiah, **1:**444

Washburn, Emory, **2:**693

washing machine, **1:**416

Washington, Booker T., **1:**244;
2:782

Washington, D.C., **3:1238–1241**

Lincoln Memorial and, **1:**466

population by decades of, **3:***1215*

slavery in, **3:**1187, 1238, 1240

Walt Whitman and, **3:**1240–1241,
1242